Douglas Reed

The Controversy of Zion

Douglas Reed

Douglas Reed

Published by Omnia Veritas Ltd

www.omnia-veritas.com

Contents

A Preface

By Ivor Benson

The Author: In Europe during the years immediately before and after World War II the name of Douglas Reed was on everyone's lips; his books were being sold by scores of thousand, and he was known with intimate familiarity throughout the English-speaking world by a vast army of readers and admirers. Former London Times correspondent in Central Europe, he had won great fame with books like Insanity Fair, Disgrace Abounding, Lest We Regret, Somewhere South of Suez, Far and Wide and several others, each amplifying a hundredfold the scope available to him as one of the world's leading foreign correspondents.

The disappearance into almost total oblivion of Douglas Reed and all his works was a change that could not have been wrought by time alone; indeed, the correctness of his interpretation of the unfolding history of the times found some confirmation in what happened to him when at the height of his powers.

After 1951, with the publication of Far and Wide, in which he set the history of the United States of America into the context of all he had learned in Europe of the politics of the world, Reed found himself banished from the bookstands, all publishers' doors closed to him, and those books already published liable to be withdrawn from library shelves and "lost", never to be replaced.

His public career as a writer now apparently at an end, Reed was at last free to undertake a great task for which all that had gone before was but a kind of preparation and education that no university could provide and which only the fortunate and gifted few could fully use - his years as a foreign correspondent, his travels in Europe and America, his conversations and contacts with the great political leaders of his day, plus his eager absorption through reading and observation of all that was best in European culture.

Experiences which other men might have accepted as defeat, served only to focus Douglas Reed's powers on what was to be his most important undertaking - that of researching and retelling the story of the last 2000 years and more in such a way as to render intelligible much of modern history which for the masses remains in our time steeped in darkness and closely guarded by the terrors of an invisible system of censorship.

The Book: Commencing in 1951, Douglas Reed spent more than three years - much of this time separated from his wife and young family - working in the New York Central Library, or tapping away at his typewriter in spartan lodgings in New York or Montreal. With workmanlike zeal, the book was rewritten, all 300,000 words of it, and the Epilogue only added in 1956.

The story of the book itself - the unusual circumstances in which it was written, and how the manuscript, after having remained hidden for more than 20 years, came to light and was at last made available for publication - is part of the history of our century, throwing some light on a struggle of which the multitudes know nothing: that conducted relentlessly and unceasingly on the battleground of the human mind.

It needed some unusual source of spiritual power and motivation to bring to completion so big a book involving so much laborious research and cross-checking, a book, moreover, which seemed to have little or no chance of being published in the author's lifetime.

Although there is correspondence to show that the title was briefly discussed with one publisher, the manuscript was never submitted but remained for 22 years stowed away in three zippered files on top of a wardrobe in Reed's home in Durban, South Africa.

Relaxed and at peace with himself in the knowledge that he had carried his great enterprise as far as was possible in the circumstances of the times, Douglas Reed patiently accepted his forced retirement as journalist and writer, put behind him all that belonged to the past and adjusted himself cheerfully to a different mode of existence, in which most of his new-found friends and acquaintances, charmed by his lively mind and rich sense of humour, remained for years wholly unaware that this was indeed the Douglas Reed of literary fame.

Of this he was sure, whether or not it would happen in his lifetime, there would come a time when circumstances would permit, and the means be found, to communicate to the world his message of history rewritten, and the central message of Christianity restated.

Interpretation: For the rest, The Controversy of Zion can be left to speak for itself; indeed, it is a work of revisionist history and religious exposition the central message of which is revealed in almost every page, understanding and compassionate of people but severely critical of the inordinate and dangerous ambitions of their leaders.

In the final chapter, under the heading the Climacteric, Douglas Reed remarks that if he could have planned it all when he began writing his book in 1949, he could not have chosen a better moment than the last months of 1956 to review the long history of Talmudic Zionism and re-examine it against the background of what was still happening on the stage of world politics.

For 1956 was the year of another American presidential election in which, once again, the Zionists demonstrated their decisive power to influence Western politics; it was the year in which the nations of the West stood by as helpless spectators as Soviet forces were used to crush a spontaneous revolt and re-install a Jewish-Communist regime in Hungary; and it was the year in which Britain and France, under Zionist pressure, were drawn into the disastrous fiasco of an attempt to capture the Suez Canal, an adventure from which, once again, Israel alone gained any advantage.

Everything that has happened since Reed wrote those last sentences in 1956 has continued to endorse the correctness of his interpretation of more than 2000 years of troubled history.

The Middle East has remained an area of intense political activity and of the maximum falsification of news and suppression of genuine debate, and it was only the few with some knowledge of the role of Talmudic Zionism and Communism who could have had any chance of solving the problem of successive events of major importance, like the so-called Six Day War in 1967 and the massive Israeli invasion of Lebanon in 1982.

Those who have read The Controversy of Zion will not be surprised to learn that there were clear signs of collusion between the Soviet Union and Israel in precipitating the Israeli attack on Egypt, for it was only because Colonel Nasser had been warned by the Kremlin bosses that Israel was about to attack Egypt's ally Syria that he moved nearly all his armed forces to his country's northern border, where they fell an easy prey to Israel's vastly superior army.

It seemed as if nothing had changed when in 1982 Israel launched a massive and most ruthless attack on Southern Lebanon, ostensibly for the purpose of rooting out the Palestine Liberation Organisation, but actually in furtherance of an expansionist policy about which Jewish leaders have always been remarkably frank.

By this time, however, the pro-Zionist mythology generated by Western politicians and media in which Israel was always represented as a tiny and virtuous nation in constant need of help and protection, was obviously beginning to lose much of its plausibility, so that few were surprised when the British Institute of Strategic Studies announced that Israel could now be regarded as fourth in the world as a military power, after the USA, the Soviet Union and the People's Republic of China - well ahead of nations like Britain and France.

More deeply significant was the reaction of the Jewish people, both in Israel and abroad, to an apparent triumph of Zionist arms in Lebanon. While Western politicians and media remained timorously restrained in their comment, even after news of the massacre of an estimated 1500 men, women and children in two Beirut refugee camps, 350,000 of the residents of Tel Aviv staged a public demonstration against their government and there were reports in the Jewish press that controversy over the Lebanese war had rocked the Israel army and affected all ranks.

Of this, too, Douglas Reed seems to have had some presentiment, for among the last words in his book are these: "I believe the Jews of the world are equally beginning to see the error of revolutionary Zionism, the twin of the other destructive movement, and, as this century ends, will at last decide to seek involvement in common mankind."

IVOR BENSON.

"For it is the day of the Lord's vengeance and the year of recompences for the controversy of Zion"

Isaiah 34:8.

"An event has happened, upon which it is difficult to speak and impossible to be silent"

Edmund Burke, 1789.

Douglas Reed

Chapter 1

THE START OF THE AFFAIR

The true start of this affair occurred on a day in 458 BC which this narrative will reach in its sixth chapter. On that day the petty Palestinian tribe of Judah (earlier disowned by the Israelites) produced a racial creed, the disruptive effect of which on subsequent human affairs may have exceeded that of explosives or epidemics. This was the day on which the theory of the master-race was set up as "the Law."

At the time Judah was a small tribe among the subject-peoples of the Persian king, and what today is known as "the West" could not even be imagined. Now the Christian era is nearly two thousand years old and "Western civilization," which grew out of it, is threatened with disintegration.

The creed born in Judah 2,500 years ago, in the author's opinion, has chiefly brought this about. The process, from original cause to present effect, can be fairly clearly traced because the period is, in the main, one of verifiable history.

The creed which a fanatical sect produced that day has shown a great power over the minds of men throughout these twenty-five centuries; hence its destructive achievement. *Why* it was born at that particular moment, or ever, is something that none can explain. This is among the greatest mysteries of our world, unless the theory that every action produces an equal and opposite reaction is valid in the area of religious thought; so that the impulse which at that remote time set many men searching for a universal, loving God produced this fierce counter-idea of an exclusive, vengeful deity.

Judah-ism was retrogressive even in 458 BC, when men in the known world were beginning to turn their eyes away from idols and tribal gods and to look for a God of all men, of justice and of neighbourliness. Confucius and Buddha had already pointed in that direction and the idea of one-God was known among the neighbouring peoples of Judah. Today the claim is often made that the religious man, Christian, Muslim or other, must pay respect to Judaism, whatever its errors, on one incontestable ground: it was the first *universal* religion, so that in a sense all universal religions descend from it. Every Jewish child is taught this. In truth, the idea of the one-God of all men was known long before the tribe of Judah even took shape, and Judaism was above all else the denial of that idea. The Egyptian Book of the Dead (manuscripts of which were found in the tombs of kings of 2,600 BC, over two thousand years before the Judaist "Law" was completed) contains the passage: "Thou art the one, the God from the very beginnings of time, the heir of immortality, self-produced and self-born; thou didst create the earth and make man." Conversely, the Scripture produced in Judah of the Levites asked, "Who is like unto thee, O Lord, *among* the Gods?" (*Exodus*).

The sect which attached itself to and mastered the tribe of Judah took this rising concept of one-God of all-peoples and embodied it in its Scripture only to destroy it, and to set up the creed based on its denial. It is denied subtly, but with scorn, and as the creed is based on the theory of the master-race this denial is necessary and inevitable. A master-race, if there be one, must *itself* be God.

The creed which was given force of daily law in Judah in 458 BC was then and still is unique in the world. It rested on the assertion, attributed to the tribal deity (Jehovah), that "the Israelites" (in fact, the Judahites) were his "chosen people" who, if they did all his "statutes and judgments," would be set over all other peoples and be established in a "promised land." Out of this theory, whether by forethought or unforeseen necessity, grew the pendent theories of "captivity" and "destruction." If Jehovah were to be worshipped, as he demanded, at a certain place in a specified land, all his worshippers had to live there.

Obviously all of them could not live there, but if they lived elsewhere, whether by constraint or their own choice, they automatically became "captives" of "the stranger," whom they had to "root out," "pull down" and "destroy." Given this basic tenet of the creed, it made no difference whether the "captors" were conquerors or friendly hosts; their ordained lot was to be destruction or enslavement.

Before they were destroyed or enslaved, they were, for a time, to be "captors" of the Judahites, not in their own right, but because the Judahites, having failed in "observance," deserved punishment. In *this* way, Jehovah revealed himself as the one-God of all-peoples: though he "knew" only the "chosen people," he would employ the heathen to punish them for their "transgressions," before meting out the foreordained destruction to these heathen.

The Judahites had this inheritance thrust on them. It was not even theirs, for the "covenant," according to these Scriptures, had been made between Jehovah and "the children of Israel," and by 458 BC the Israelites, spurning the non-Israelitish Judahites, had long since been absorbed by other mankind, taking with them the vision of a universal, loving God of all men. The Israelites, from all the evidence, never knew this racial creed which was to come down through the centuries as the Jewish religion, or Judaism. It stands, for all time, as the product of Judah of the Levites.

What happened before 458 BC is largely lore, legend and mythology, as distinct from the period following, the main events of which are known. Before 458 BC, for instance, there were in the main only "oral traditions"; the documentary period begins in the two centuries leading up to 458 BC, when Judah had been disavowed by the Israelites. At this stage, when the word-of-mouth tradition became written Scripture, the perversion occurred. The surviving words of the earlier Israelites show that their tradition was a widening one of neighbourliness under a universal God. This was changed into its opposite by the itinerant priests who segregated the Judahites and established the worship of Jehovah as the god of racialism, hatred and revenge.

In the earlier tradition Moses was a great tribal leader who heard the voice of one-God speak from a burning bush and came down from a mountain bearing this one-God's moral commandments to the people. The time when this tradition took shape was one when the idea of religion was first moving in the minds of men and when all the peoples were borrowing from each other's traditions and thought.

Whence the idea of one-God may have come has already been shown, although the earlier Egyptians themselves may have received it from others. The figure of Moses himself, and his Law, both were taken from material already existing. The story of Moses's discovery in the bulrushes was plainly borrowed from the much earlier legend (with which it is identical) of a king of Babylonia, Sargon the Elder, who lived between one and two thousand years before him; the Commandments much resemble earlier law codes of the Egyptians, Babylonians and Assyrians. The ancient Israelites built on current ideas, and by this means apparently were well on the way to a universal religion when they were swallowed up by mankind.

Then Judah put the process into reverse, so that the effect is that of a film run backward. The masters of Judah, the Levites, as they drew up their Law also took what they could use from the inheritance of other peoples and worked it into the stuff they were moulding. They began with the one just God of all men, whose voice had been briefly heard from the burning bush (in the oral tradition) and in the course of five books of their written Law turned him into the racial, bargaining Jehovah who promised territory, treasure, blood and power over others in return for a ritual of sacrifice, to be performed at a precise place in a specified land.

Thus they founded the permanent counter-movement to all universal religions and identified the name Judah with the doctrine of self-segregation from mankind, racial hatred, murder in the name of religion, and revenge.

The perversion thus accomplished may be traced in the Old Testament, where Moses first appears as the bearer of the moral commandments and good neighbour, and ends as a racial mass-murderer, the moral commandments having been converted into their opposites between *Exodus* and *Numbers*. In the course of this same transmutation the God who begins by commanding the people not to kill or to covet their neighbours' goods or wives, finishes by ordering a tribal massacre of a neighbouring people, only the virgins to be saved alive!

Thus the achievement of the itinerant priests who mastered the tribe of Judah, so long ago, was to turn one small, captive people away from the rising idea of a God of all men, to reinstate a bloodthirsty tribal deity and racial law, and to send the followers of this creed on their way through the centuries with a destructive mission.

The creed, or revelation of God as thus presented, was based on a version of history, every event of which had to conform with, and to confirm the teaching.

This version of history went back to the Creation, the exact moment of which was known; as the priests also claimed to possess the future, this was a complete story and theory of the universe from start to finish. The end was to be the triumphant consummation in Jerusalem, when world dominion was to be established on the ruins of the heathen and their kingdoms.

The theme of mass-captivity, ending in a Jehovan vengeance ("all the firstborn of Egypt"), appears when this version of history reaches the Egyptian phase, leading up to the mass-exodus and mass-conquest of the Promised Land. This episode was necessary if the Judahites were to be organized as a permanent disruptive force among nations and for that reason, evidently, was invented; the Judaist scholars agree that nothing resembling the narrative in *Exodus* actually occurred.

Whether Moses even lived is in dispute. "They tell you," said the late Rabbi Emil Hirsch, "that Moses never lived. I acquiesce. If they tell me that the story that came from Egypt is mythology, I shall not protest; it is mythology. They tell me that the book of Isaiah, as we have it today, is composed of writings of at least three and perhaps four different periods; I knew it before they ever told me; before they knew it, it was my conviction."

Whether Moses lived or not, he cannot have led any mass-exodus from Egypt into Canaan (Palestine). No sharply-defined Israelitish tribes existed (says Rabbi Elmer Berger) at any time when anyone called Moses may have led some small groups out of Egyptian slavery. The Habiru (Hebrews) then were *already* established in Canaan, having reached it long before from Babylonia on the far side: Their name, Habiru, denoted no racial or tribal identity; it meant "nomads." Long before any small band led by Moses can have arrived they had overrun large Canaanite areas, and the governor of Jerusalem reported to Pharaoh in Egypt, "The King no longer has any territory, the Habiru have devastated all the King's territory."

A most zealous Zionist historian, Dr. Josef Kastein, is equally specific about this. He will often be quoted during this narrative because his book, like this one, covers the entire span of the controversy of Zion (save for the last twenty-two years; it was published in 1933). He says, "Countless other Semitic and Hebrew tribes *were already settled in the Promised Land* which, Moses told his followers, was *theirs by ancient right of inheritance;* what matter that *actual conditions in Canaan had long since effaced this right* and rendered it illusory."

Dr. Kastein, a fervent Zionist, holds that the Law laid down in the Old Testament must be fulfilled to the letter, but does not pretend to take the version of history seriously, on which this Law is based. In this he differs from Christian polemicists of the "every word is true" school. He holds that the Old Testament was in fact a political programme, drafted to meet the conditions of a time, and frequently revised to meet changing conditions.

Historically, therefore, the Egyptian captivity, the slaying of "all the firstborn of Egypt," the exodus toward and conquest of the Promised Land are myths. The story was invented, but the lesson, of vengeance on the heathen, was implanted in men's minds and the deep effect continues into our time.

It was evidently invented to turn the Judahites away from the earlier tradition of the God who, from the burning bush, laid down a simple law of moral behaviour and neighbourliness; by the insertion of imaginary, allegorical incident, presented as historical truth, this tradition was converted into its opposite and the "Law" of exclusion, hatred and vengeance established. With this as their religion and inheritance, attested by the historical narrative appended to it, a little band of human beings were sent on their way into the future. By the time of that achievement of 458 BC, many centuries after any possible period when Moses may have lived, much had happened in Canaan. The nomadic Habiru, supplanting the native Canaanites by penetration, intermarriage, settlement or conquest, had thrown off a tribe called the Ben Yisrael, or Children of Israel, which had split into a number of tribes, very loosely confederated and often at war with each other. The main body of these tribes, the Israelites, held the north of Canaan. In the south, isolated and surrounded by native Canaanitish peoples, a tribe called Judah took shape. This was the tribe from which the racial creed and such words as "Judaism," "Jewish" and "Jew" in the course of centuries emerged.

From the moment when it first appears as an entity this tribe of Judah has a strange look. It was always cut off, and never got on well with its neighbours. Its origins are mysterious. It seems from the beginning, with its ominous name, somehow to have been set apart, rather than to have been "chosen." The Levitical Scriptures include it among the tribes of Israel, and as the others mingled themselves with mankind this would leave it the last claimant to the rewards promised by Jehovah to "the chosen people." However, even this claim seems to be false, for the *Jewish Encyclopaedia* impartially says that Judah was "in all likelihood *a non-Israelitish tribe*."

This tribe with the curious air was the one which set out into the future saddled with the doctrine drawn up by the Levites, namely, that it was Jehovah's "chosen people" and, when it had done "all my statutes and judgments," would inherit a promised land and dominion over all peoples.

Among these "statutes and judgments" as the Levites finally edited them appeared, repeatedly, the commands, "utterly destroy," "pull down," "root out." Judah was destined to produce a nation dedicated to destruction.

Chapter 2

THE END OF ISRAEL

About five hundred years before the event of 458 BC, or nearly three thousand years ago today, the brief and troubled association between Judah and the Israelites ("the children of Israel") came to an end. Israel rejected the chosen people creed which was beginning to take shape in Judah and went its own way. (The adoption of the name "Israel" by the Zionist state which was set up in Palestine in 1948 was transparent false pretence).

The events which led to the short-lived, unhappy union covered earlier centuries. The mythological or legendary period of Moses was followed by one in Canaan during which "Israel" was the strong, cohesive and recognizable entity, the northern confederation of the ten tribes. Judah (to which the very small tribe of Benjamin attached itself) was a petty chiefdom in the south.

Judah, from which today's Zionism comes down, was a tribe of ill repute. Judah sold his brother Joseph, the most beloved son of Jacob-called-Israel, to the Ishmaelites for twenty pieces of silver (as Judas, the only Judean among the disciples, much later betrayed Jesus for thirty pieces of silver), and then founded the tribe in incest, *(Genesis* 37-38). The priestly scribes who wrote this Scriptural account centuries afterwards had made themselves the masters of Judah and as they altered the oral tradition, whenever it suited them, the question prompts itself: why were they at pains to preserve, or possibly even to insert, this attribution of incestuous beginnings and a treacherous nature to the very people who, they said, were the chosen of God? The thing is mysterious, like much else in the Levitical Scriptures, and only the inner sect could supply an answer.

Anyway, those Scriptures and today's authorities agree about the separateness of "Israel" and "Judah." In the Old Testament Israel is often called "the house of Joseph," in pointed distinction from "the house of Judah." The *Jewish Encyclopaedia* says, "Joseph and Judah typify *two distinct lines of descent*" and adds (as already cited) that Judah was "in all likelihood a non-Israelitish tribe." The *Encyclopaedia Britannica* says that Judaism developed *long after the Israelites had merged themselves with mankind,* and that the true relationship of the two peoples is best expressed in the phrase, *"The Israelites were not Jews."* Historically, Judah was to survive for a little while and to bring forth Judaism, which begat Zionism. Israel was to disappear as an entity, and it all came about in this way:

The little tribe in the south, Judah, became identified with the landless tribe, that of the Levites. These hereditary priests, who claimed that their office had been bestowed on them by Jehovah on Mount Sinai, were the true fathers of Judaism. They wandered among the tribes, preaching that the war of one was the war of all, and Jehovah's war. Their aim was power and they strove for a theocracy, a state in which God is the sovereign and religion the law. During the period of the Judges they achieved their aim to some extent, for they naturally *were* the Judges. What they, and isolated Judah, most needed was union with Israel. Israel, which distrusted this lawgiving priesthood, would not hear of unification unless it were under a king; all the surrounding peoples had kings.

The Levites grasped this opportunity. They saw that if a king were appointed the ruling class would supply the nominee, and they were the ruling class. Samuel, at their head, set up a puppet monarchy, behind which the priesthood wielded true power; this was achieved through the stipulation that the king should reign only for life, which meant that he would not be able to found a dynasty. Samuel chose a young Benjaminite peasant, Saul, who had made some name in tribal warfare and, presumably, was thought likely to be tractable (the choice of a Benjaminite suggests that Israel would not consider any man of Judah for the kingship). The unified kingdom of Israel then began; in truth it survived but this one reign, Saul's.

In Saul's fate (or in the account given of it in the later Scriptures) the ominous nature of Judaism, as it was to be given shape, may be discerned. He was commanded to begin the holy war by attacking the Amalekites "and *utterly destroy* all that they have, and spare them not; but slay both man and woman, infant and suckling, ox and sheep, camel and ass." He destroyed "man and woman, infant and suckling," but spared King-Agag and the best of the sheep, oxen, yearlings and lambs. For this he was excommunicated by Samuel, who secretly chose one David, of *Judah,* to be Saul's successor. Thereafter Saul vainly strove by zeal in "utter destruction" to appease the Levites, and then by attempting David's life to save his throne. At last he killed himself.

Possibly none of this happened; it is the account given in the Book of Samuel, which the Levites produced centuries later. Whether it is true or allegorical, the importance lies in the plain implication: Jehovah demanded literal obedience when he commanded "utter destruction," and mercy or pity were capital offences. This lesson is driven home in many other depictments of events which were possibly historical and possibly imaginary.

This was really the end, three thousand years ago, of the United Kingdom, for Israel would not accept the man of Judah, David, as king. Dr. Kastein says that "the rest of Israel ignored him" and proclaimed Saul's son, Ishbosheth, king, whereon the re-division into Israel and Judah "really took place." According to *Samuel,* Ishbosheth was killed and his head was sent to David, who thereon restored a nominal union and made Jerusalem his capital.

He never again truly united the kingdom or the tribes; he founded a dynasty which survived one more reign.

Formal Judaism holds to this day that the Messianic consummation will come about under a worldly king of "the house of David"; and racial exclusion is the first tenet of formal Judaism (and the law of the land in the Zionist state). The origins of the dynasty founded by David are thus of direct relevance to this narrative.

Racial discrimination and segregation were clearly unknown to the tribes people in those days of the association between Israel and Judah, for the Old Testament says that David, the Judahite, from his roof, saw "a very beautiful woman" bathing, commanded her to him and made her with child, and then had her husband, a Hittite, sent into the front battle-line with orders that he be killed. When he was dead David added the woman, Bathsheba, to his wives, and her second son by him became the next king, Solomon (this story of David and Bathsheba, as related in the Old Testament, was bowdlerized in a Hollywood-made moving picture of our day).

Such was the racial descent of Solomon, the last king of the riven confederacy, according to the Levitical scribes. He began his reign with three murders, including that of his brother, and vainly sought to save his dynasty by the Habsburg method, marriage, though on grander scale. He married princesses from Egypt and many neighbouring tribes and had hundreds of lesser wives, so that in his day, too, racial segregation must have been unknown. He built the temple and established a hereditary high priesthood.

That was the story, concluded in 937 BC, of the short association between Israel and Judah. When Solomon died the incompatible associates finally split, and in the north Israel resumed its independent life. Dr Kastein says:

"The two states had *no more in common*, for good or evil, than any other two countries with a common frontier. From time to time they waged war against each other or made treaties, *but they were entirely separate. The Israelites ceased to believe that they had a destiny apart from their neighbours and King Jeroboam made separation from Judah as complete in the religious as in the political sense.*" Then, of the Judahites, Dr. Kastein adds, "they decided that they were destined to develop as *a race apart* … they demanded an order of existence *fundamentally different from that of the people about them*. These were *differences which allowed of no process of assimilation to others*. They demanded *separation, absolute differentiation.* "

Thus the cause of the breach and separation is made clear. Israel believed that its destiny lay with involvement in mankind, and rejected Judah on the very grounds which recurrently, in the ensuing three thousand years, caused other peoples to turn in alarm, resentment and repudiation from Judaism. Judah "demanded separation, absolute differentiation." (However, Dr. Kastein, though he says "Judah," means "the Levites." How could even the tribes people of Judah, at that stage, have demanded "separation, absolute differentiation," when Solomon had had a thousand wives?)

It was the Levites, with their racial creed, that Israel rejected. The next two hundred years, during which Israel and Judah existed separately, and often in enmity, but side by side, are filled with the voices of the Hebrew "prophets," arraigning the Levites and the creed which they were constructing. These voices still call to mankind out of the tribal darkness which beclouds much of the Old Testament, for they scarified the creed which was in the making just as Jesus scarified it seven or eight hundred years later, when it was long established, at the Temple in Jerusalem.

These men were nearly all Israelites; most of them were Josephites. They were on the road to the one-God of all-peoples and to participation in mankind. They were not unique among men in this: soon the Buddha, in India, was to oppose his Sermon at Benares and his Five Commands of Uprightness to the creed of Brahma, the creator of caste-segregation, and to the worship of idols. They were in truth Israelite remonstrants against the Levitical teaching which was to become identified with the name of Judah. The name "Hebrew prophets" is inapt because they made no pretence to power of divination and were angered by the description ("I was no prophet, neither was I a prophet's son," *Amos*). They were protestants in their time and gave simple warning of the calculable consequences of the racial creed; their warning remains valid today.

The claims of the Levite priesthood moved them to these protests, particularly the priestly claim to the firstborn ("That which openeth the womb is mine," *Exodus)*, and the priestly insistence on sacrificial rites. The Israelite expostulants (to whom this "so-called law of Moses" was unknown, according to Mr. Montefiore) saw no virtue in the bloodying of priests, the endless sacrifice of animals and the "burnt offerings," the "sweet savour" of which was supposed to please Jehovah. They rebuked the priestly doctrine of slaying and enslaving "the heathen." God, they cried, desired moral behaviour, neighbourly conduct and justice towards the poor, the fatherless, the widow and the oppressed, not blood sacrifices and hatred of the heathen.

These protests provide the first forelight of the dawn which came some eight hundred years later. They find themselves in strange company among the injunctions to massacre in which the Old Testament abounds. The strange thing is that these remonstrances survived the compilation, when Israel was gone and the Levites, supreme in Judah, wrote down the Scriptures.

Today's student cannot explain, for instance, why King David suffers Nathan publicly to rebuke him for taking Uriah's wife and having Uriah murdered. Possibly among the later scribes who compiled the historical narrative, long after Israel and the Israelite expostulants were gone, were some of their mind, who contrived in this way to continue their protest.

Conversely, these benevolent and enlightened passages are often followed by fanatical ones, attributed to the same man, which cancel them, or put the opposite in their place. The only reasonable explanation is that these are interpolations later made, to bring the heretics into line with Levitical dogma.

Whatever the explanation, these Israelite protests against the heresy of Judah have an ageless appeal and form the monument to vanished Israel. They force their way, like little blades of truth, between the dark stones of tribal saga. They pointed the way to the rising and widening road of common involvement in mankind and away from the tribal abyss.

Elijah and Elisha both worked in Israel, and Amos spoke solely to the Josephites. He in particular attacked the blood sacrifices and priestly rites: "I hate, I despise your feasts and I take no delight in your solemn assemblies. Yea, though ye offer me burnt offerings and your meal offerings, I will not accept them. Neither will I regard the peace offerings of your fat beasts. Take thou away from me the noise of thy songs" (the Levites' chanted liturgies) "and let me not hear the melody of thy viols. But let judgment run as water and righteousness as a mighty stream." And then the immortal rebuke to the "peculiar people" doctrine: "Are ye not as the children of the Ethiopians unto me, O children of Israel, saith the Lord."

Hosea, another Israelite, says, "I desired mercy and not sacrifice, and the knowledge of God more than burnt offerings." Hosea exhorts to the practice of "justice and righteousness," "loving kindness and compassion and faithfulness," not discrimination and contempt.

In Micah's time the Levites apparently still demanded the sacrifice of all the firstborn to Jehovah:

"Wherewith shall I come before the Lord and bow myself before God on high? Shall I come before him with burnt offerings, with calves of a year old? Will the Lord be pleased with thousands of rams or with ten thousands of rivers of oil. *Shall I give my firstborn for my transgressions, the fruit of my body for the sin of my soul?* It hath been told to thee, O man, what is good and what the Lord doth require of thee: only to do justly and to love mercy and to walk humbly with thy God."

These men contended for the soul of the tribes people during the two centuries when Israel and Judah existed side by side, and sometimes at daggers drawn. During this period the Levites, earlier distributed among the twelve tribes, were driven more and more to congregate in tiny Judah and in Jerusalem, and to concentrate their energies on the Judahites.

Then, in 721 BC, Israel was attacked and conquered by Assyria and the Israelites were carried into captivity. Judah was spared for that moment and for another century remained an insignificant vassal, first of Assyria and then of Egypt, and the stronghold of the Levitical sect.

At that point "the children of Israel" disappear from history and if promises made to them are to be redeemed, this redemption must evidently be from among the ranks of mankind, in which they became involved and merged. Given the prevalent westward trend among the movements of peoples during the last twenty-seven hundred years, it is probable that much of their blood has gone into the European and American peoples.

The Judaist claim, on the other hand, is that Israel was totally and deservedly "lost," because it rejected the Levitical creed and chose "rapprochement with neighbouring peoples." Dr. Kastein, whose words these are, nearly twenty-seven centuries later ardently rejoiced, on that very account, in their downfall: "The ten northern tribes, with their separate development, had drifted so far from their kindred in the south that the chronicle of their fall takes the form of a brief bald statement of fact unrelieved by any expression of grief. No epic poem, no dirge, no sympathy marked the hour of their downfall."

The student of the controversy of Zion has to plod far before he begins to unveil its mysteries, but very soon discovers that in all things it speaks with two tongues, one for "the heathen" and one for the initiates.

The Levites of that ancient time did not, and today's Zionists do not believe that the Israelites "vanished without leaving a trace" (as Dr. Kastein says). They were *pronounced* "dead," in the way that a Jew marrying out of the fold today is pronounced dead (for instance, Dr. John Goldstein); they were excommunicated and only in that sense "vanished."

Peoples do not become extinct; the North American Indians, the Australian Blackfellows, the New Zealand Maoris, the South African Bantu and others are the proofs of that. For that matter, the Israelites could not have been "taken away captive," had they been physically exterminated. Their blood and thought survive in mankind, somewhere, today.

Israel remained separate from Judah of its own will, and for the very reasons which ever since have aroused the mistrust and misgiving of other peoples. The Israelites "were not Jews"; the Judahites were "in all likelihood non-Israelitish."

The true meaning of the assertion that Israel "disappeared" is to be found in the later Talmud, which says: "The ten tribes have no share in the world to come." Thus, "the children of Israel" are banned from heaven by the ruling sect of Judah because they refused to exclude themselves from mankind on earth.

The Chief Rabbi of the British Empire in 1918, the Very Rev. J.H. Hertz, in answer to an enquiry on this point said explicitly, "The people known at present as Jews are descendants *of the tribes of Judah and Benjamin* with a certain number of descendants of the tribe of Levi." This statement makes perfectly clear that "Israel" had no part in what has become Judaism (no authority, Judaist or other, would support the claim made to blood-descent from Judah, for the Jews of today, but this is of little account).

Therefore the use of the name "Israel" by the Zionist state which was created in Palestine in this century is in the nature of a forgery. Some strong reason must have dictated the use of the name of a people who were not Jews and would have none of the creed which has become Judaism. One tenable theory suggests itself. The Zionist state was set up with the connivance of the great nations of the West, which is also the area of Christendom. The calculation may have been that these peoples would be comforted in their consciences if they could be led to believe that they were fulfilling Biblical prophecy and God's promise to "Israel," at whatever cost in the "destruction" of innocent peoples.

If that was the motive for the misuse of the name "Israel," the expedient may for the time being have been successful; the multitude was ever easily "persuaded." However, truth will out in the long run, as the surviving remonstrances of the Israelite prophets show.

If the Zionist state of 1948 could lay claim to any name whatever taken from far antiquity, this could only be "Judah," as this chapter has shown.

Douglas Reed

Chapter 3

THE LEVITES AND THE LAW

During the hundred years that followed the Assyrian conquest of Israel, the Levites in Judah began to compile the written Law. In 621 BC they produced *Deuteronomy* and read it to the people in the temple at Jerusalem.

This was the birth of "the Mosaic law," which Moses, if he ever lived, never knew. It is called the Mosaic law because it is attributed to him, but the authorities agree that it was the product of the Levites, who then and later repeatedly made Moses (and for that matter, Jehovah) say what suited them. Its correct description would be "the Levitical law" or "the Judaic law."

Deuteronomy is to formal Judaism and Zionism what the Communist Manifesto was to the destructive revolution of our century. It is the basis of the Torah ("the Law") contained in the Pentateuch, which itself forms the raw material of the Talmud, which again gave birth to those "commentaries" and commentaries-on-commentaries which together constitute the Judaic "law."

Therefore *Deuteronomy* is also the basis of the political programme, of worldly dominion over nations despoiled and enslaved, which has been largely realized in the West during this Twentieth Century. *Deuteronomy* is of direct relevancy to the events of our day, and much of the confusion surrounding them disperses if they are studied in its light.

It was read, in 621 BC, to so small an audience in so small a place that its great effects for the whole world, through the following centuries into our time, are by contrast the more striking.

Before *Deuteronomy* was compiled only the "oral tradition" of what God said to Moses existed. The Levites claimed to be the consecrated guardians of this tradition and the tribespeople had to take their word for it (their pretensions in this respect chiefly caused the anger of the Israelite "prophets"). If anything had been written down before *Deuteronomy* was read, such manuscripts were fragmentary and in priestly keeping, and as little known to the primitive tribesmen as the Greek poets to Kentucky hillsfolk today.

That *Deuteronomy* was *different* from anything that had been known or understood before is implicit in its name, which means "Second Law." *Deuteronomy*, in fact, was Levitical *Judaism*, first revealed; the Israelites (as already shown) "were not Jews" and had never known *this* "Law."

Significantly, *Deuteronomy* which appears as the fifth book of today's Bible, with an air of growing naturally out of the previous ones, was the first book to be completed as a whole. Though *Genesis* and *Exodus* provide the historical background and mount for it, they were later produced by the Levites, and *Leviticus* and *Numbers*, the other books of the Torah, were compiled even later.

Deuteronomy stood the earlier tradition on its head, if it was in harmony with the moral commandments. However, the Levites were within their self-granted right in making any changes they chose, for they held that they were divinely authorized to amend the Law, as orally revealed by God to Moses, in order to meet "the constantly changing conditions of existence in the spirit of traditional teaching" (Dr. Kastein).

For that matter, they also claimed that Moses had received at Sinai a *secret* oral Torah, which must *never* be committed to writing. In view of the later inclusion of the Old Testament in one volume with the Christian New Testament, and the average Gentile's assumption that he thus has before his eyes the whole of "the Mosaic Law," this qualification is of permanent interest.

The Talmud, as quoted by Dr. Funk, says, "God foresaw that one day a time would come when the Heathen would possess themselves of the Torah and would say to Israel, 'We, too, are sons of God.' Then will the Lord say: 'Only he who knows my secrets is my son.' And what are the secrets of God? The oral teachings."

The few people who heard *Deuteronomy* read in 621 BC, and then first learned what "the Mosaic Law" was to be, were told that the manuscripts had been "discovered." Today's Judaist authorities dismiss this and agree that *Deuteronomy* was the independent work of the Levites in isolated Judah after Judah's rejection by the Israelites and the conquest of Israel. Dr. Kastein puts the matter like this:

"In 621 BC, a manuscript hoary with the dust of ages was discovered among the archives. It contained *a curious version of the laws* which had been codified up to that time, a sort of repetition *and variation* of them, giving a host of instructions regarding man's duty to God and to his neighbour. It was couched in the form of speeches *supposed* to have been delivered by Moses just before his death on the farther side of Jordan. *Who the author was it is impossible to say.*"

Thus Dr. Kastein, a zealot who awaits the literal fulfillment of "the Mosaic Law" in every detail, does not believe that its author was either Jehovah or Moses. It is enough for him that it was produced by the lawgiving priesthood, which for him *is* divine authority.

None can now tell how closely *Deuteronomy*, as we know it, resembles *Deuteronomy* as it was read in 621 BC, for the books of the Old Testament were repeatedly revised up to the time of the first translation, when various other modifications were made, presumably to avoid excessive perturbation among the Gentiles. No doubt something was then excised, so that

Deuteronomy in its original form may have been ferocious indeed, for what remains is savage enough.

Religious intolerance is the basis of this "Second Law" (racial intolerance was to follow later, in another "New Law") and murder in the name of religion is its distinctive tenet. This necessitates the destruction of the moral Commandments, which in fact are set up to be knocked down. Only those of them which relate to the exclusive worship of the "jealous" Jehovah are left intact. The others are buried beneath a great mound of "statutes and judgments" (regulations issued under a governing Law, as it were) which in effect cancel them.

Thus the moral commandments against murder, stealing, adultery, coveting, bad neighbourliness, and the like are vitiated by a mass of "statutes" expressly enjoining the massacre of other peoples, the murder of apostates individually or in communities, the taking of concubines from among women captives, "utter destruction" that leaves "nothing alive," the exclusion of "the stranger" from debt- remission and the like.

By the time the end of *Deuteronomy* is reached the moral commandments have been nullified in this way, for the purpose of setting up, in the guise of a religion, the grandiose political idea of a people especially sent into the world to destroy and "possess" other peoples and to rule the earth. The idea of *destruction* is essential to *Deuteronomy*. If it be taken away no *Deuteronomy*, or Mosaic Law, remains.

This concept of destruction as an article of faith is unique, and where it occurs in political thought (for instance, in the Communist philosophy) may also derive originally from the teaching of *Deuteronomy*, for there is no other discoverable source.

Deuteronomy is above all a complete *political* programme: the story of the planet, created by Jehovah for this "special people," is to be completed by their triumph and the ruination of all others. The *rewards* offered to the faithful are exclusively material: slaughter, slaves, women, booty, territory, empire. The only *condition* laid down for these rewards is *observance* of "the statutes and judgments," which primarily command the destruction of others. The only *guilt* defined lies is non-observance of these laws. *In*tolerance is specified as *observance;* tolerance as *non-observance,* and therefore as guilt. The punishments prescribed are of this world and of the flesh, not of the spirit. Moral behaviour, if ever demanded, is required only towards co-religionists and "strangers" are excluded from it.

This unique form of nationalism was first presented to the Judahites in *Deuteronomy* as "the Law" of Jehovah and as his literal word, spoken to Moses. The notion of world domination through destruction is introduced at the start (chapter 2) of these "speeches supposed to have been delivered" by the dying Moses:

"The Lord spake unto me, saying ... This day will I begin to put the dread of thee and the fear of thee upon the nations that are under the whole heaven, who shall hear report of thee, and shall tremble, and be in anguish because of thee." In token of this, the fate of two nations is at once shown. The King of Sihon and the King of Bashan "came out against us, he and all his people," whereon they were "utterly *destroyed,* the men, and the women, and the little ones," only the cattle being spared and "the spoil" being taken "for a prey unto ourselves." (The insistence on *utter* destruction is a recurrent and significant feature of these illustrative anecdotes).

These first examples of the power of Jehovah to destroy the heathen are followed by the first of many warnings that unless "the statutes and judgments" are observed Jehovah will punish his special people by dispersing them among these heathen. The enumeration of these "statutes and judgments" follows the Commandments, the moral validity of which is at once destroyed by a promise of tribal massacre:

"Seven nations greater and mightier than thou" are to be delivered into the Judahites' hands, and: "Thou shalt *utterly destroy* them; thou shalt make no covenant with them, nor show mercy unto them ... ye shall *destroy* their alters ... for thou art an holy people unto the Lord thy God; the Lord thy God hath chosen thee to be a special people unto himself, above all people that are on the face of the earth ... Thou shalt be blessed above all people ... And thou shalt *consume* all the people which the Lord thy God shall deliver thee; thine eye shall have *no pity* upon them ... the Lord thy God will send the hornet among them, until they that are left, and hide themselves from thee, be *destroyed* ... And the Lord thy God will put out these nations before thee by little and little ... But the Lord thy God shall deliver them unto thee, and shall *destroy* them with a mighty *destruction* until they be *destroyed.* And he shall deliver their kings into thine hand, and thou shalt *destroy* their name from under heaven; there shall no man be able to stand before thee, until thou have *destroyed* them ..."

By the Twentieth Century AD the peoples of the West, as a whole, had ceased to attach any present meaning to these incitements, but the peoples directly concerned thought differently. For instance, the Arab population of Palestine fled en masse from its native land after the massacre at Deir Yasin in 1948 because this event meant for them (as its perpetrators intended it to mean) that if they stayed they would be "utterly destroyed."

They knew that the Zionist leaders, in the palavers with British and American politicians of the distant West, repeatedly had stated that "the Bible is our Mandate" (Dr. Chaim Weizmann), and they knew (if the Western peoples did not realize) that the allusion was to such passages as that commanding the "utter destruction" of the Arab peoples. They knew that the leaders of the West had supported and would continue to support the invaders and thus they had no hope of even bare survival, save by flight. This massacre of 1948 AD relates directly to the "statute and judgment" laid down in chapter 7 of the book of The Law which the Levites completed and read in 621 BC.

The incitements and allurements of *Deuteronomy* continue: "… Go in to *possess* nations greater and mightier than thyself … the Lord thy God is he which goeth over before thee; as a consuming fire he shall *destroy* them, and he shall bring them down before thy face; so shalt thou drive them out, and *destroy* them quickly, as the Lord hath said unto thee … For if ye shall diligently keep all these commandments which I command you … then will the Lord *drive out* all these nations from before you, and ye shall *possess* greater nations and mightier than yourselves … even unto the uttermost sea shall your coast be. There shall no man be able to stand before you: for the Lord your God shall lay the fear of you and the dread of you upon all the land that ye shall tread upon …"

Then Moses, in this account, enumerates the "statutes and judgments" which must be "observed" if all these rewards are to be gained, and again "the Law" is to destroy:

"These are the statutes and judgments, which ye shall observe to do … Ye shall *utterly destroy* all the places, wherein the nations which ye shall *possess* served their gods … When the Lord thy God shall *cut off* the nations from before thee, whither thou goest to *possess* them, and thou succeedest them, and dwellest in their land: Take heed to thyself that thou be not snared by following them … and that thou inquire not after their gods."

This tenet of "the Law" requires the faithful to destroy other religions. It was impartial when enacted but gained a specific application in later centuries from the fact that the Christian faith grew up in, and the mass of Jews then moved into, the same geographical area: the West. (This made Christianity the primary object of the command to "utterly destroy the places …," and the dynamiting of Russian cathedrals, the opening of "anti-God museums," the canonization of Judas and other acts of early Bolshevist governments, which were to nine-tenths comprized of Eastern Jews, were evidently deeds of "observance" under this "statute" of *Deuteronomy*).

The ideas of the inquisition of heretics and of the informer, which the West has used in its retrogressive periods and repudiated in its enlightened ones, also find their original source (unless any can locate an earlier one) in *Deuteronomy*. Lest any such heretic should call in question the Law of destruction, summarized in the preceding paragraphs, *Deuteronomy* next provides that "if there arise among you a prophet or a dreamer of dreams … (he) shall be put to death"; the crucifixion of Jesus (and the deaths of numerous expostulants against literal Judaism) fall under this "statute."

The denunciation of kinsfolk who incur suspicion of heresy is required. This is the terrorist device introduced in Russia by the Bolshevists in 1917 and copied in Germany by the National Socialists in 1933. The Christian world at the time professed horror at these barbarbous innovations, but the method is plainly laid down in *Deuteronomy*, which requires that any who say, "Let us go and serve other gods," be denounced by their brothers, sisters, sons, daughters, wives and so on, and be stoned to death.

Characteristically, *Deuteronomy* prescribes that the hand of the bloodkinsman or spouse shall be "first upon" the victim of denunciation at the killing, and only afterwards "the hand of all the people." This "statute of the Law" is still observed today, in a measure dictated by local conditions and other circumstances. Apostates cannot be publicly stoned to death in the environment of foreign communities, where the law of "the stranger" might hold this to be murder, so that a formal pronunciation of "death" and ceremony of mourning symbolically takes the place of the legal penalty; see Dr. John Goldstein's account both of the symbolic rite and of a recent attempt to exact the literal penalty, which during the centuries was often inflicted in closed Jewish communities where the law of "the stranger" could not reach.

The Law also demands that entire communities shall be massacred on the charge of apostasy: "Thou shalt surely smite the inhabitants of that city with the edge of the sword, *destroying it utterly,* and all that is therein."

In this matter of destroying cities, *Deuteronomy* distinguishes between near (that is, Palestinian) and far cities. When a "far off city" has been captured, "thou shalt smite every male thereof with the edge of the sword, but the women, and the little ones, and the cattle, and all that is in the city, even all the spoil thereof, shalt thou take unto thyself ..." This incitement in respect of captured women is a recurrent theme and *Deuteronomy* lays down the law that a Judahite captor who sees among captives "a beautiful woman" may take her home, but if he had "no delight in her" may turn her out again.

The case of a near city is different; the law of *utter* destruction (against which Saul transgressed) then rules. "But of the cities of these people which the Lord thy God doth give thee for an inheritance, thou shalt *save alive nothing that breatheth; But thou shalt utterly destroy them* ... as the Lord thy God hath commanded thee." (This verse 16 of chapter 20, again, explains the mass flight of the Palestinian Arabs after Deir Yasin, where nothing that breathed was saved alive. They saw that literal fulfillment of the Law of 621 BC was the order of the day in 1948 AD, and that the might of the West was behind this fulfillment of the Law of "utter destruction.")

The Second Law continues: "Thou art an holy people unto the Lord thy God, and the Lord hath chosen thee to be a peculiar people unto himself, above all the nations that are upon the earth." Further "statutes and judgments" then provide that "anything that dieth of itself," being unclean, may not be eaten, but "thou shalt give it to the stranger ... or thou mayest sell it to the alien; for thou art an holy people unto the Lord thy God."

Every seven years a creditor shall remit his "neighbour's" debt, but "of a foreigner thou mayest exact it again." Chapter 10 (surprisingly in this context) says, "Love ye therefore the stranger; for ye were strangers in the land of Egypt," but chapter 23 brings the familiar cancellation: "Thou shalt not lend upon usury to thy brother ... unto a stranger thou mayest lend upon usury" (and graver examples of this legal discrimination between the "neighbour" and "the "stranger" appear in later books, as will be seen).

Deuteronomy ends with the long-drawn-out, rolling, thunderous curse-or-blessing theme. Moses, about to die, once more exhorts "the people" to choose between blessings and cursings, and these are enumerated.

The blessings are exclusively material: prosperity through the increase of kith, crop and kine; the defeat of enemies; and world dominion. "The Lord thy God will set thee on high above all nations of the earth ... The Lord shall establish thee an holy people unto himself ... And all people of the earth shall see that thou art called by the name of the Lord; and they shall be afraid of thee ... *thou shalt lend unto many nations, and thou shalt not borrow.* And the Lord shall make thee the head, and not the tail; and thou shalt be above only, and thou shalt not be beneath ..."

These blessings occupy thirteen verses; the cursings some fifty or sixty. The deity in whose name the curses are uttered clearly was held capable of doing evil (indeed, this is explicitly stated in a later book, *Ezekiel*, as will be shown).

Literal Judaism is ultimately based on terror and fear and the list of curses set out in chapter 28 of The Second Law shows the importance which the priesthood attached to this practice of cursing (which literal Judaists to this day hold to be effective in use). These curses, be it remembered, are the penalties for *non-observance*, not for moral transgressions! "If thou will not hearken unto the voice of the Lord thy God, to observe to do all his commandments and statutes ... all these curses shall come upon thee ..."

The city and the dwelling, the children, crops and cattle, are to be cursed "until thou be *destroyed* and until thou *perish* utterly." Plague, wasting, inflammation, mildew, botch, emerods, scab, itch, madness, blindness, famine, cannibalism and drought are specified. Men's wives are to lie with other men; their children are to be lost into slavery; any that remain at home are to be eaten by their parents, the father and mother contesting for the flesh and denying any to the children still alive. (These curses were included in the Great Ban when it was pronounced on apostates down to relatively recent times, and in the fastnesses of Talmudic Jewry are probably in use today).

The diseases and disasters were to be visited on the people "if thou wilt not observe to do all the words of this law that are written in this book, that thou mayest fear this glorious and fearful name, the Lord Thy God. I call heaven and earth to record this day against you, that I have set before you life and death, blessing and cursing; therefore choose life, that both thou and thy seed may live for ever."

Such was the life and the blessing which the Judahites, gathered in the Temple in 621 BC, were exhorted in the name of Jehovah and Moses to choose by their tribal chieftain Josiah, the mouthpiece of the priesthood. The purpose and meaning of existence, under this "Mosaic Law," was the destruction and enslavement of others for the sake of plunder and power. Israel might from that moment have counted itself happy to have been pronounced dead and to have been excluded from such a world to come. The Israelites had mingled in the living bloodstream of mankind; on its banks the Judahites were left stranded in the power of a fanatical priesthood which commanded them, on pain of "all these curses," to *destroy*.

To the terror inspired by "all these curses" the Levites added also an allurement. If "the people" should "return and obey the voice of the Lord, and do all his commandments ...," then "all these curses" would be *transferred to their "enemies"* (not because these had sinned, but simply to swell the measure of the blessing conferred on the rehabilitated Judahites!)

In this tenet *Deuteronomy* most clearly revealed the status allotted to the heathen by The Second Law. In the last analysis, "the heathen" have no legal existence under this Law; how could they have, when Jehovah only "knows" his "holy people"? Insofar as their actual existence is admitted, it is only for such purposes as those stated in verse 65, chapter 28 and verse 7, chapter 30: namely, to receive the Judahites when they are dispersed for their transgressions and then, when their guests repent and are forgiven, to inherit curses lifted from the regenerate Judahites. True, the second verse quoted gives the pretext that "all these curses" will be transferred to the heathen because they "hated" and "persecuted" the judahites, but how could they be held culpable of this when the very presence of the Judahites among them was merely the result of punitive "curses" inflicted by Jehovah? For Jehovah himself, according to another verse (64, chapter 28) took credit for putting the curse of exile on the Judahites:

"And the Lord shall scatter thee among all people, from the one end of the earth even unto the other ... and among these nations shalt thou find no ease, neither shall the sole of thy foot have rest..."

Deuteronomy employs this Doublespeak (to use the modem idiom) throughout: the Lord makes the special people homeless among the heathen for their transgressions; the heathen, who have no blame either for their exile or for those transgressions, are their "persecutors "; ergo, the heathen will be destroyed.

The Judaist attitude towards other mankind, creation, and the universe in general, is better understood when these and related passages have been pondered, and especially the constant plaint that Jews are "persecuted" everywhere, which in one tone or another runs through nearly all Jewish literature. To any who accept this book as The Law, the mere existence of others is in fact persecution; *Deuteronomy* plainly implies that.

The most nationalist Jew and the most enlightened Jew often agree in one thing: they cannot truly consider the world and its affairs from any but a Jewish angle, and from that angle "the stranger" seems insignificant. Thinking makes it so, and this is the legacy of twenty-five centuries of Jewish thinking; even those Jews who see the heresy or fallacy cannot always divest themselves entirely of the incubus on their minds and spirits.

The passage from *Deuteronomy* last quoted shows that the ruling sect depicted homelessness at one and the same time as the act of the special people's god and as persecution by the special people's enemies, deserving of "all these curses." To minds of such extreme egotism a political outrage in which 95 Gentiles and 5 Jews lose their lives or property is simply an anti-Jewish disaster, and they are not consciously hypocritical in this. In the Twentieth Century this standard of judgment has been projected into the lives of other peoples and applied to all major events in the ordeal of the West. Thus we live in the century of the Levitical fallacy.

Having undertaken to put "all these curses" on innocent parties, if the Judahites would return to observance of "all these statutes and judgments," the resurrected Moses of *Deuteronomy* promised one more blessing ("The Lord thy God, he will go over before thee, and he will *destroy* these nations from before thee, and thou shalt *possess* them ... ") and then was allowed to die in the land of Moab.

In "the Mosaic Law" the destructive idea took shape, which was to threaten Christian civilization and the West, both then undreamed of. During the Christian era a council of theologians made the decision that the Old Testament and the New should be bound in one book, without any differentiation, as if they were stem and blossom, instead of immovable object and irresistible force. The encyclopaedia before me as I write states laconically that the Christian churches accept the Old Testament as being of "equal divine authority" with the New.

This unqualified acceptance covers the entire content of the Old Testament and may be the original source of much confusion in the Christian churches and much distraction among the masses that seek Christianity, for the dogma requires belief in opposite things at the same time. How can the same God, by commandment to Moses, have enjoined men to love their neighbours and "utterly to destroy" their neighbours? What relationship can there be between the universal, loving God of the Christian revelation and the cursing deity of *Deuteronomy*?

But if in fact all the Old Testament, including these and other commands, is of "equal divine authority" with the New, then the latterday Westerner is entitled to invoke it in justification of those deeds by which Christendom most denied itself: the British settlers' importation of African slaves to America, the American and Canadian settlers' treatment of the North American Indian, and the Afrikaners' harsh rule over the South African Bantu. He may justly put the responsibility for all these things directly on his Christian priest or bishop, if that man teaches that the Old Testament, with its repeated injunction to slay, enslave, and despoil is of "equal divine authority." No Christian divine can hold himself blameless if he so teaches. The theological decision which set up this dogma cast over Christendom and the centuries to come the shadow of *Deuteronomy*, just as it fell on the Judahites themselves when it was read to them in 621 BC.

Only one other piece of writing has had any comparable effect on the minds of men and on future generations; if any simplification is permissible, the most tempting one is to see the whole story of the West, and particularly of this decisive Twentieth Century, as a struggle between the Mosaic Law and the New Testament and between the two bodies of mankind which rank themselves behind one or other of those two messages of hatred and love respectively.

In *Deuteronomy* Judaism was born, yet this would have been a stillbirth, and *Deuteronomy* might never again have been heard of, if that question had rested only with the Levites and their captive Judahites. They were not numerous, and a nation a hundred times as many could never have hoped to enforce this barbarous creed on the world by force of its own muscle. There was only one way in which "the Mosaic Law" could gain life and potency and become a disturbing influence in the life of other peoples during the centuries to follow. This was if some powerful "stranger" (among all those strangers yet to be accursed), some mighty king of those "heathen" yet to be destroyed, should support it with arms and treasure.

Precisely that was about to happen when Josiah read The Second Law to the people in 621 BC, and it was to repeat itself continually down the centuries to our day: the gigantic improbability of the thing confronts the equally large, demonstrable fact that it is so! The rulers of those "other nations" which were to be dispossessed and destroyed repeatedly espoused the destructive creed, did the bidding of the dominant sect, and at the expense of their own peoples helped to further its strange ambition.

Some twenty years after the reading of *Deuteronomy* in Jerusalem, Judah was conquered by the Babylonian king, in about 596 BC. At the time, this looked like the end of the affair, which was a petty one in itself, among the great events of that period. Judah never again existed as an independent state, and but for the Levites, their Second Law and the foreign helper the Judahites, like the Israelites, would have become involved in mankind.

Instead, the Babylonian victory was the start of the affair, or of its great consequences for the world. The Law, instead of dying, grew stronger in Babylon, where for the first time a foreign king gave it his protection. The permanent state-within-states, nation-within- nations was projected, a first time, into the life of peoples; initial experience in usurping power over them was gained. Much tribulation for other peoples was brewed then.

As for the Judahites, or the Judaists and Jews who sprang from them, they seem to have acquired the unhappiest future of all. Anyway, it was not a happy man (though it was a Jewish writer of our day, 2,500 years later, Mr. Maurice Samuel) who wrote: "... we Jews, the destroyers, will remain the destroyer forever ... nothing that the Gentiles will do will meet our needs and demands."

At first sight this seems mocking, venomous, shameless. The diligent student of the controversy of Zionism discovers that it is more in the nature of a cry of hopelessness, such as the "Mosaic Law" must wring from any man who feels he cannot escape its remorseless doctrine of destruction.

Chapter 4

THE FORGING OF THE CHAINS

The Babylonian episode was decisive in its consequences, both for the petty tribe of Judah at the time and for the Western world today. During this period the Levites achieved things which were permanently to affect the life of peoples. They added four Books to *Deuteronomy* and thus set up a Law of racio-religious intolerance which, if it could be enforced, would for all time cut off the Judahites from mankind. By experiment in Babylon, they found ways of enforcing it, that is to say, of keeping their followers segregated from those among whom they dwelt. They acquired authority among their captors, and at last they "pulled down" and "utterly destroyed" their captors' house; or if this did not truly happen, they handed on this version of history to a posterity which accepted it and in time began to see in these people an irresistibly destructive force.

The first "captivity" (the Egyptian) seems to have been completely legendary; at any rate, what is known confutes it and as *Exodus* was completed after the Babylonian incident the Levitical scribes may have devised the story of the earlier "captivity," and of Jehovah's punishment of the Egyptians, to support the version of the Babylonian period which they were then preparing.

In any case, what truly happened in Babylon seems to have been greatly different from the picture of a mass-captivity, later followed by a mass-return, which has been handed down by the Levitical scriptures.

No mass-exodus of captives from Jerusalem to Babylon can have occurred, because the mass of the Judahite people, from which a Jewish nation later emerged, was already self-distributed far and wide about the known world (that is, around the Mediterranean, in lands west and east of Judah), having gone wherever conditions for commerce were most favourable.

In that respect the picture was in its proportions very much like that of today. In Jerusalem was only a nucleus, comprizing chiefly the most zealous devotees of the Temple cult and folk whose pursuits bound them to the land. The authorities agree that merely a few tens of thousands of people were taken to Babylon, and that these represented a small fraction of the whole.

Nor were the Judahites unique in this dispersion, although the literature of lamentation implies that. The Parsees of India offer a case nearly identical and of the same period; they, too, survived the loss of state and country as a religious community in dispersion. The later centuries offer many examples of the survival of racial or religious groups far from their original clime. With the passing of generations such racial groups come to think of their ancestors' homeland simply as "the old country"; the religious ones turn their eyes towards a holy city (say, Rome or Mecca) merely from a different spot on earth.

The difference in the case of the Judahites was that old country and holy city were the same; that Jehovaism demanded a triumphant return and restoration of temple-worship, over the bodies of the heathen destroyed; and that this religion was also their law of daily life, so that a worldly political ambition, of the ancient tribal or nationalist kind, was also a primary article of faith. Other such creeds of primitive times became fossilized; this one survived to derange the life of peoples throughout the ages to our day, when it achieved its most disruptive effect.

This was the direct result of the experiments made and the experience gained by the Levites in Babylon, where they were first able to test the creed in an alien environment.

The benevolent behaviour of the Babylonian conquerors towards their Judahite prisoners was the exact opposite of that enjoined on the Judahites, in the reverse circumstances, by the Second Law which had been read to them just before their defeat: "Save nothing alive that breatheth ..." Dr. Kastein says the captives "enjoyed complete freedom" of residence, worship, occupation and self- administration.

This liberality allowed the Levites to make captives of people who thus were largely free; under priestly insistence they were constrained to settle in closed communities, and in this way the ghetto and Levite power were born. The Talmudic ruling of the Christian era, which decreed the excommunication of Jews if without permission they sold "neighbour-property" to "strangers," comes down from that first experiment in self-segregation, in Babylon.

The support of the foreign ruler was necessary for this corralling of expatriates by their own priests, and it was given on this first occasion, as on innumerable other occasions ever since.

With their people firmly under their thumbs, the Levites then set about to complete the compilation of "The Law." The four books which they added to *Deuteronomy* make up the Torah, and this word, which originally meant doctrine, is now recognized to mean "the Law." However, "completion" is a most misleading word in this connection.

Only *the Torah* (in the sense of the five books) was completed. The *Law* was not then and never can be completed, given the existence of the "secret Torah" recorded by the Talmud (which itself was but the later continuation of the Torah), and the priestly claim to divine right of interpretation. In fact, "the Law" was constantly changed, often to close some loophole which might have allowed "the stranger" to enjoy a right devolving only on "a neighbour." Some examples of this continuing process of amendment have already been given, and others follow in this chapter. The effect was usually to make hatred of or contempt for "the stranger" an integral part of "the Law" through the provision of discriminatory penalties or immunities.

When the Torah was complete a great stockade, unique in its nature but still incomplete, had been built between any human beings who at any time accepted this "Law" and the rest of mankind. The Torah allowed no distinction between this Law of Jehovah and that of man, between religious and civil law. The law of "the stranger," theologically and juridically, had no existence, and any pretension to enforce one was "persecution," as Jehovah's was the *only* law.

The priesthood claimed that the Torah governed every act of daily life, down to the most trivial. Any objection that Moses could not have received from Jehovah on the mountain detailed instructions covering every conceivable action performed by man, was met with the dogma that the priesthood, like relay runners, handed on from generation to generation "the oral tradition" of Jehovah's revelation to Moses, and infinite power of reinterpretation. However, such objections were rare, as the Law prescribed the death penalty for doubters.

Mr. Montefiore remarks, accurately, that the Old Testament is "revealed legislation, not revealed truth," and says the Israelite prophets cannot have known anything of the Torah as the Levites completed it in Babylon. Jeremiah's words, "the pen of the Scribes is in vain" evidently refer to this process of Levitical revision and to the attribution of innumerable new "statutes and judgments" to Jehovah and Moses.

"Sin" was not a concept in the Torah as it took shape. That is logical, for in law there cannot be "sin," only crime or misdemeanour. The only offence known to this Law was *non-observance*, which meant crime or misdemeanour. What is commonly understood by "sin," namely, moral transgression, was sometimes expressly enjoined by it or made absolvable by the sacrifice of an animal.

The idea of "the return" (together with the related ideas of destruction and dominion) was basic to the dogma, which stood or fell by it. No strong impulse to return from Babylon to Jerusalem existed among the people (any more than today, when the instinct of the vast majority of Jews is completely against "return," so that the Zionist state is much more easily able to find money abroad than immigrants).

Literal fulfillment was the supreme tenet and that meant that possession of Palestine, the "centre" of the dominant empire to come, was essential (as it still is); its importance in the pattern was political, not residential.

Thus the Levites in Babylon added *Exodus, Genesis, Leviticus* and *Numbers* to *Deuteronomy*. *Genesis* and *Exodus* provide a version of history moulded to fit the "Law" which the Levites by then had already promulgated, in *Deuteronomy*. This goes right back to the Creation, of which the Scribes knew the exact date (however the first two chapters of *Genesis* give somewhat different accounts of the Creation and the Levitical hand, as scholars believe, is more to be seen in the second chapter than the first).

Whatever has survived of the former Israelite tradition is in *Genesis* and *Exodus,* and in the enlightened passages of the Israelite prophets. These more benevolent parts are invariably cancelled out by later, fanatical ones, which are presumably Levitical interpolations.

The puzzle is to guess why the Levites allowed these glimpses of a loving God of all men to remain; as they invalidated the New Law and could have been removed. A tenable theory might be that the earlier tradition was too well known to the tribespeople to be merely expunged, so that it had to be retained and cancelled out by allegorical incident and amendment.

Although *Genesis* and *Exodus* were produced after *Deuteronomy* the theme of fanatical tribalism is faint in them. The swell and crescendo come in *Deuteronomy, Leviticus* and *Numbers,* which bear the plain imprint of the Levite in isolated Judah and Babylon.

Thus in *Genesis* the only fore-echo of the later sound and fury is, "And I will make of thee a great nation and I will bless thee, and make thy name great; and thou shalt be a blessing; and I will bless them that bless thee, and curse him that curseth thee; and in thee shall all families of the earth be blessed ... and the Lord appeared unto Abram, and said, Unto thy seed will I give this land ..."

Exodus is not much different: for instance, "If thou shalt indeed ... do all that I speak, then I will be an enemy unto thine enemies ... and I will cut them off"; and even these passages may be Levitical interpolations.

But in *Exodus* something of the first importance appears: this promise is *sealed in blood,* and from this point on blood runs like a river through the books of The Law. Moses is depicted as "taking the blood and sprinkling it on the people" and saying, "Behold the blood of the covenant, which the Lord hath made with you concerning all these words." The hereditary and perpetual office of the Aaronite priesthood is founded in this blood-ritual: Jehovah says unto Moses, "And take unto thee Aaron thy brother and his sons with him that he may minister unto me in the priest's office."

The manner of a priest's consecration is then laid down in detail by Jehovah himself, according to the Levitical scribes:

He must take a bullock and two rams "without blemish," have them butchered "before the Lord," and on the altar burn one ram and the innards of the bullock. The blood of the second ram is to be put "upon the tip of the right ear of Aaron and upon the tip of the right ear of his sons and upon the thumb of their right hands and upon the great toe of their right foot" and sprinkled "upon the altar round about

... and upon Aaron, and upon his garments, and upon his sons and the garments of his sons."

The picture of blood-bespattered priests, thus given, is worth contemplation. Even at this distance of time the question prompts itself: why was this insistent emphasis laid on *blood*-sacrifice in the books of the Law which the Levites produced. The answer seems to lie in the sect's uncanny genius for instilling fear by terror; for the very mention of "blood," in such contexts, made the faithful or superstitious Judahite tremble for his own son!

It is all spelt out in *Exodus*, this claim of the fanatical priests to the firstborn of their followers:

"And the Lord spake unto Moses, saying, Sanctify unto me all the firstborn, whatsoever openeth the womb among the children of Israel, both of man and of beast: it is mine."

According to the passage earlier quoted from *Micah*, this practice of sacrificing the human firstborn long continued, and the sight of the bloodied Levite must have had a terrible significance for the humble tribesman, for in the words attributed to God, quoted above, the firstborn "of man and of beast" are coupled. This significance remained long after the priesthood (in a most ingenious way which will later be described) contrived to discontinue human sacrifice while retaining the prerogative. Even then the blood which was sprinkled on the priest, though it was an animal's, was to the congregation still symbolically that of their own offspring!

Moreover, in the Talmudic strongholds of Jewry this ritual bloodying of priests has continued into our time; this is not a reminiscence from antiquity. Twenty-four centuries after *Exodus* was compiled the Reform Rabbis of America (at Pittsburgh in 1885) declared: "We expect neither a return to Palestine, *nor a sacrificial worship under the administration of the sons of Aaron;* nor the restoration of any of the laws concerning the Jewish State." The importance of this statement lay in the need, thus felt in 1885, to make it publicly; it shows that the opposite school of Jewry still practiced literal observance, including the ritual of "sacrificial worship." (By the 1950's the Reform Rabbis of America had lost much ground and were in retreat before the force of Zionist chauvinism).

The Levitical authorship of the Torah is indicated, again, by the fact that more than half of the five books are given to minutely detailed instructions, attributed directly to the Lord, about the construction and furnishings of altars and tabernacles, the cloth and design of vestments, mitres, girdles, the kind of golden chains and precious stones in which the blood-baptized priest is to be arrayed, as well as the number and kind of beasts to be sacrificed for various transgressions, the uses to be made of their blood, the payment of tithes and shekels, and in general the privileges and perquisites of the priesthood. Scores of chapters are devoted to blood sacrifice, in particular.

God probably does not so highly rate the blood of animals or the fine raiment of priests. This was the very thing, against which the Israelite "prophets" had protested. It was the mummifying of a primeval tribal religion; yet this is still The Law of the ruling sect and it is of great potency in our present-day world.

When they compiled these Books of the Law, the Levitical scribes included many allegorical or illustrative incidents of the awful results of "non-observance." These are the parables of the Old Testament, and their moral is always the same: death to the "transgressor." *Exodus* includes the best known of these, the parable of the golden calf. While Moses was in the mountain Aaron made a golden calf; when Moses came down and saw it he commanded "the sons of Levi" to go through the camp "and slay every man *his brother,* and every man *his companion,* and every man *his neighbour,*" which these dutiful Levites did, so that "there fell of the people that day about three thousand men."

Christendom also has inherited this parable of the golden calf (having inherited the Old Testament) and holds it to be a warning against the worship of idols. However, a quite different motive may have produced whatever trend among the people caused the Levites to invent it. Many Judahites, and possibly some priests, at that time may have thought that God would be better pleased with the symbolic offering of a *golden* calf than with the eternal bleating of butchered animals, the "sprinkling" of their blood, and the "sweet savour" of their burning carcasses. The Levites at all times fought fiercely against any such weakening of their ritual, so that these parables are always directed against any who seek to change it in any detail.

A similar case is the "rebellion of Korah" *(Numbers),* when "two and fifty hundred princes of the assembly, famous in the congregation, men of renown, gathered themselves together against Moses and against Aaron and said unto them, Ye take too much upon you, seeing all the congregation are holy, every one of them, and the Lord is among them; wherefore then lift ye yourselves above the congregation of the Lord."

The Israelite "prophets" had made this very complaint, that the Levites took much on themselves, and the parable in *Numbers* is plainly intended to discourage any other objectors: "So the earth opened and swallowed Korah and his two hundred and fifty men of renown" (however, the congregation "continued to murmur," whereon the Lord smote it with the plague, and by the time Aaron interceded, "fourteen thousand and seven hundred" lay dead.)

The lesson of these parables, respect for the priesthood, is driven home immediately after this anecdote by the enumeration, in words attributed to the Lord, of the Levite's perquisites: "All the best of the oil, and all the best of the wine, and of the wheat, the first fruits of them which they shall offer unto the Lord, them have I given thee."

Presumably because the older tradition imposed some restraint in the writing of history, *Genesis* and *Exodus* are relatively restrained. The fanatical note, first loudly sounded in *Deuteronomy,* then becomes ever louder in *Leviticus* and *Numbers*, until at the end a concluding parable depicts a racio-religious massacre as an act of the highest piety in "observance," singled out for reward by God! These last two books, like *Deuteronomy*, are supposed to have been left by Moses and to relate his communions with Jehovah. In their cases, no claim was made that "a manuscript hoary with the dust of ages" had been discovered; they were just produced.

They show the growth of the sect's fanaticism at this period, and the increasing heat of their exhortations to racial and religious hatred. *Deuteronomy* had first decreed, "Love ye therefore the stranger," and then cancelled this "judgment" (which probably came down from the earlier Israelite tradition) by the later one which excluded the stranger from the ban on usury.

Leviticus went much further. It, too, began with the admonition to love: "The stranger that dwelleth with you shall be unto you as one born among you, and thou shalt love him as thyself" (chapter 19). The reversal came in chapter 25: "Of the children of the stranger that do sojourn among you, of them shall ye buy, and of their families that are with you, which they begat in your land, and they shall be your possession. And ye shall take them as an inheritance for your children after you, to inherit them for a possession; they shall be your bondmen for ever: but over your brethren, the children of Israel, ye shall not rule over one another with rigour."

This made hereditary bondage and chattel-slavery of "strangers" a tenet of the Law (which is still valid). If the Old Testament is of "equal divine authority" with the New, professing Christians of the pioneer, frontiersman or Voortrekker kind were entitled in their day to invoke such passages as these in respect of slavery in America or South Africa.

Leviticus introduced (at all events by clear implication) what is perhaps the most significant of all the discriminations made by the Law between "thy neighbour" and "the stranger." *Deuteronomy*, earlier, had provided (chapter 22) that "if a man find a betrothed damsel in the field, and the man force her, and lie with her: then the man only that lay with her shall die; but unto the damsel thou shalt do nothing; there is in the damsel no sin worthy of death; for as when a man riseth against his neighbour, and slayeth him, even so is this matter." This is the kind of provision, in respect of rape, which probably would have been found in any of the legal codes which were then taking shape, and for that matter it would fit into almost any legal code today, save for the extreme nature of the penalty. This passage, again, may very well represent the earlier Israelite attitude towards this particular transgression; it was impartial and did not vary according to the person of the victim.

Leviticus (chapter 19) then provided that a man who "lieth carnally" with a betrothed woman *slave* might acquit himself of fault by bringing a ram to the priest "as a trespass offering," when "the sin which he hath done shall be forgiven him," but the woman "shall be scourged." Under this Law the word of a woman *slave* clearly would not count against that of her owner, on a charge of rape, so that this passage appears to be an amendment, of the discriminatory kind, to the provision in *Deuteronomy*. Certain allusions in the Talmud support this interpretation, as will be shown.

Leviticus also contains its parable depicting the awful consequences of non-observance, and this particular example shows the extreme lengths to which the Levites went. The transgression committed by the two allegorical characters in this case (who were themselves two Levites, Hadab and Abihu) was merely that they burned the wrong kind of fire in their censers. This was a capital offence under "the Law" and they were immediately devoured by the Lord!

Numbers, the last of the five Books to be produced, is the most extreme. In it the Levites found a way to rid themselves of their chief prerogative (the claim to the firstborn) while perpetuating "the Law" in this, its supreme tenet. This was a political move of genius. The claim to the firstborn evidently had become a source of grave embarrassment to them, but they could not possibly surrender the first article of a literal Law which knew no latitude whatever in "observance"; to do so would have been itself a capital transgression. By one more reinterpretation of the Law they made themselves proxies for the firstborn, and thus staked a permanent claim on the gratitude of the people without any risk to themselves:

"And the Lord spake unto Moses, saying, And I, behold. I have taken the Levites from among the children of Israel *instead of all the firstborn* that openeth the matrix among the children of Israel: therefore the Levites shall be mine; because all the firstborn are mine..." (As the firstborn to be so redeemed outnumbered their Levite redeemers by 273, payment of five shekels each for these 273 was required, the money to be given "to Aaron and his sons.")

Proceeding from this new status of redeemers, the Levites laid down many more "statutes and judgments" in *Numbers.* They ruled by terror and were ingenious in devising new ways of instilling it; an example is their "trial of jealousy." If "the spirit of jealousy" came on a man, he was legally obliged (by "the Lord speaking unto Moses, saying") to hale his wife before the Levite, who, at the altar, presented her with a concoction of "bitter water" made by him, saying, "If no man have lain with thee and if thou hast not gone aside to uncleanness with another instead of thy husband, be thou free from this bitter water that causeth the curse. But if thou hast gone aside to another instead of thy husband, and if thou be defiled, and some man have lain with thee beside thine husband ... the Lord make thee a curse and an oath among thy people, when the Lord doth make thy thigh to rot, and thy belly to swell."

The woman then had to drink the bitter water and if her belly swelled the priests "executed the law" of death on her. The power which such a rite put in the hands of the priesthood is apparent; ascribed to the direct command of God, it resembles the practices of witch doctors in Africa.

The final touch is given to "the Law" in the last chapters of this, the last book to be compiled. It is provided by the parable of Moses and the Midianites. The reader will have remarked that the life and deeds of Moses, as related in *Exodus*, made him a capital transgressor, several times over, under the "Second Law" of *Deuteronomy* and the numerous other amendments of *Leviticus* and *Numbers*. By taking refuge with the Midianites, by marrying the Midianite highpriest's daughter and by receiving instruction in priestly rites from him, and in other ways, Moses had "gone a-whoring after other gods," had "taken of their daughters," and so on. As the whole structure of the law rested on Moses, in whose name the commands against these things were laid down in the later books, something evidently had to be done about him before the Books of the Law were completed, or the whole structure would fall to the ground.

The last small section of *Numbers* shows how the difficulty was overcome by the scribes. In these final chapters of "the Law" Moses is made to conform with "all the statutes and judgments" and to redeem his transgressions by massacring the entire Midianite tribe, save for the virgins! By what in today's idiom would be called a fantastic "twist," Moses was resurrected so that he might dishonour his saviours, his wife, two sons and father-in-law. Posthumously he was made to "turn from his wickedness," to validate the racio- religious dogma which the Levites had invented, and by complete transfiguration from the benevolent patriarch of earlier legend to become the founding father of their Law of hatred and murder!

In Chapter 25 Moses is made to relate that "the anger of the Lord was kindled" because the people were turning to other gods. He is commanded by the Lord, "Take all the heads of the people and hang them up before the Lord against the sun," whereon Moses instructs the judges, "Slay ye everyone his men that were joined unto Baalpeor" (Baal-worship was extensively practiced throughout Canaan, and the competition of this cult with Jehovah-worship was a particular grievance of the Levites).

The theme of *religious* hatred is thus introduced into the narrative. That of *racial* hatred is joined to it when, in the direct sequence, a man brings "a *Midianitish* woman in the sight of Moses." Phinehas (the grandson of Moses's brother Aaron) goes after them "and thrust both of them through, the man of Israel, and the women through her belly." Because of this deed, "the plague was stayed," and "the Lord spake unto Moses, saying, Phinehas hath turned away my wrath from the children of Israel, *while he was zealous for my sake* ... Wherefore say, Behold, I give unto him my covenant of peace!"

Thus the covenant between Jehovah and the hereditary Aaronite priesthood was again sealed (by the Levitical scribes) in blood, this time the blood of a racio-religious murder, which "the Lord" then describes as "an atonement for the children of Israel." Moses, the witness of the murder, is then ordered by the Lord, "Vex the Midianites and smite them." The symbolism is plain. He is required, in resurrection, to strike equally at "other gods" (the god of the high priest Jethro, from whom he had received instruction) and at "strangers" (his wife's and father-in-law's race).

The Levites even made the ensuing massacre Moses's last act on earth; he was rehabilitated on the brink of eternity! "And the Lord spake unto Moses, saying, Avenge the children of Israel of the Midianites; afterwards thou shalt be gathered to thy people." Thus ordered, Moses's men "warred against the Midianites as the Lord commanded Moses; and they slew all the males ... and took all the women of Midian captives, and their little ones, and took the spoil of their cities, and all their flocks, and all their gods, and burnt their cities."

This was not enough. Moses, the husband of a loving Midianite wife and the father of her two sons, was "wroth" with his officers because they had "saved all the Midianite women alive. Behold these caused the children of Israel ... to commit trespass against the Lord in the matter of Peor, and there was a plague among the congregations of the Lord. Now therefore *kill every male among the little ones and kill every woman that hath known man by lying with him.* But all the women children, that have not known a man by lying with him, *keep alive for yourselves.*" (The booty is then listed; *after* the enumeration of sheep, beeves and asses follow "thirty and two thousand persons in all, of women that had not known man by lying with him." These were shared among the Levites, the soldiers and the congregation; "the gold" was brought to the Levites "for the Lord.")

With that, Moses was allowed at last to rest and the Books of the Law were concluded. Incitement could hardly be given a more demoniac shape. Chapters 25 and 31 of *Numbers* need to be compared with chapters 2, 3 and 18 of *Exodus* for the full significance of the deed foisted on Jehovah and Moses by the Levites to become apparent. It was a plain warning to the special people of what Jehovaism was to mean to them; it remains today a warning to others.

On that note The Law ended. Its authors were a small sect in Babylon, with a few thousand followers there. However, the power of their perverse idea was to prove very great. By giving material ambition the largest shape it can have on earth, they identified themselves forever with the baser of the two forces which eternally contend for the soul of man: that downward pull of the fleshly instincts which wars with the uplifting impulse of the spirit.

The theologians of Christendom claim more for this Law than the scholars of Jewry. I have before me a Christian Bible, recently published, with an explanatory note which says the five books of the Torah are "accepted as true," and for that matter also the historical, prophetic and poetic books. This logically flows from the dogma, earlier quoted, that the Old Testament is of "equal divine authority" with the New.

The Judaist scholars say differently. Dr. Kastein, for instance, says that the Torah was "the work of an *anonymous compiler*" who "produced a *pragmatic* historical work." The description is exact; the scribe or scribes provided a *version* of history, subjectively written to support the compendium of laws which was built on it; and both history and laws were devised to serve a "*political* purpose. "A unifying idea underlay it all," says Dr. Kastein, and this unifying idea was tribal nationalism, in a more fanatical form than the world has otherwise known. The Torah was not revealed religion but, as Mr. Montefiore remarked, "revealed legislation," enacted to an end.

While the Law was being compiled (it was not completed until the Babylonian "captivity" had ended) the last two remonstrants made their voices heard, Isaiah and Jeremiah. The hand of the Levite may be traced in the interpolations which were made in their books, to bring them into line with "the Law" and its supporting "version of history." The falsification is clearest in the book of Isaiah, "which is the best known case because it is the most easily demonstrable. Fifteen chapters of the book were written by someone who knew the Babylonian captivity, whereas Isaiah lived some two hundred years earlier. The Christian scholars circumvent this by calling the unknown man "Deutero-Isaiah," or the second Isaiah.

"This man left the famous words (often quoted out of their context), "The Lord hath said ... I will also give thee for a light unto the Gentiles, that thou mayest be my salvation unto the end of the earth." This was heresy under the Law which was in preparation and the Levite apparently added (as the same man presumably would not have written) the passages foretelling that "the kings and queens" of the Gentiles "shall bow down to thee with their face towards the earth and lick up the dust of thy feet ... I will feed them that oppress thee with their own flesh and they shall be drunken with their own blood, as with sweet wine; and all flesh shall know that I am the Lord thy Saviour and thy Redeemer" (This sounds like the voice of Ezekiel, who was the true father of the Levitical Law, as will be seen.)

Jeremiah's book seems to have received Levitical amendment at the start, because the familiar opening passage sharply discords with other of Jeremiah's thoughts: "See, I have this day set thee over the nations and over the kingdoms, to *root out*, and to *pull down,* and *to destroy* ..."

That does not sound like the man who wrote, in the next chapter: "The word of the Lord came to me saying, Go and cry in the ears of Jerusalem, saying, Thus saith the Lord: I remember thee, the kindness of thy youth, the love of thine espousals, when thou wentest after me in the wilderness, in a land that was not sown ... What iniquity have your fathers found in me, that they are gone far from me

... my people have forsaken me, the fountain of living waters ..."

Jeremiah then identified the culprit, Judah (and for this offence well may have come by his death): "The backsliding Israel hath justified herself more than *treacherous Judah*." Israel had fallen from grace, but Judah had *betrayed;* the allusion is plainly to the Levites' new Law. Then comes the impassioned protest, common to all the expostulants, against the priestly rites and sacrifices:

"Trust ye not in lying words, saying, The Temple of the Lord, the Temple of the Lord, the Temple of the Lord ..." (the formal, repetitious incantations) "... but thoroughly amend your ways and your doings, oppress not the stranger, the fatherless and the widow, and shed not innocent blood in this place ..." (the ritual of blood-sacrifice and the ordained murder of apostates) "Will ye steal, murder and commit adultery, and swear falsely ... and come and stand before me in this house, which is called by my name, and say, We are delivered to do all these abominations" (the ceremonial absolution after animal-sacrifice). "Is this house, which is called by my name, become a den of robbers in your eyes? ... I spake not unto your fathers, nor commanded them in the day that I brought them out of the land of Egypt, concerning burnt offerings or sacrifices..."

In such words Jeremiah, like Jesus later, protested against the "destruction" of the Law in the name of its fulfillment. It seems possible that even in Jeremiah's time the Levites still exacted the sacrifice of firstborn children, because he adds, "And they have built the high place ... to burn their sons and daughters in the fire; which I commanded not, neither came it into my heart."

Because of these very "abominations," Jeremiah continued, the Lord would "cause to cease from the cities of Judah, and from the streets of Jerusalem, the voice of mirth, and the voice of gladness, the voice of the bridegroom, and the voice of the bride; for the land shall be desolate."

This is the famous political forecast which was borne out; the Levites, with their genius for perversion, later invoked it to support their claim that Judah fell because their Law was not observed, whereas Jeremiah's warning was that their Law would destroy "treacherous Judah." Were he to rise from the earth today he might use the word without change in respect of Zionism, for the state of affairs is similar and the ultimate consequence seems equally foreseeable.

When Judah fell Jeremiah gave his most famous message of all, the one to which the Jewish masses today often instinctively turn, and the one which the ruling sect ever and again forbids them to heed: "*Seek the peace of the city* whither I have caused you to be carried away captives, and pray unto the Lord for it; *for in the peace thereof shall ye have peace.*" The Levites gave their angry answer in the 137th Psalm:

"By the waters of Babylon we sat down and wept ... Our *tormentors* asked of us mirth: Sing us one of the songs of Zion. How shall we sing the Lord's song in a strange land? If I forget thee, O Jerusalem, let my right hand forget her cunning, let my tongue cleave to the roof of my mouth ... O daughter of Babylon, *who art to be destroyed,* happy shall he be, that rewardeth thee as thou hast served us. *Happy shall he be, that taketh and dasheth thy little ones against the stones."*

In Jeremiah's admonition and the Levites' reply lies the whole story of the controversy of Zion, and of its effects for others, down to our day.

Jeremiah, who was apparently put to death, would today be attacked as a "crackpot," "paranoiac," "antisemite" and the like; the phrase then used was "prophet and dreamer of dreams." He describes the methods of defamation, used against such men, in words exactly applicable to our time and to many men whose public lives and reputations have been destroyed by them (as this narrative will show when it reaches the present century): "For I heard the defaming of many, fear on every side. Report, they say, and we will report it. All my familiars watched for my halting, saying, Peradventure he will be enticed, and we shall prevail against him, and we shall take our revenge on him."

While Jeremiah was a refugee in Egypt, the second Isaiah, in Babylon, wrote those benevolent words which glow like the last light of day against the dark background of the teaching which was about to triumph: "Thus saith the Lord, Keep ye judgment, and do justice...... let not the son of *the stranger,* that hath joined himself to the Lord, speak, saying The Lord hath utterly separated me from his people ... The sons of the stranger, that join themselves to the Lord, to serve him, and to love the name of the Lord, to be his servants ... even them will I bring to my holy mountain, and make them joyful in my house of prayer ... *for mine house shall be called an house of prayer for all people."*

With this glimpse of a loving God of all mankind the protests ended. The Levites and their Law were left paramount, and therewith the true captivity of "the Jews" began, for their enslavement to the law of racial and religious hatred is the only genuine captivity they have suffered.

Jeremiah and the Second Isaiah, like the earlier Israelite remonstrants, spoke for mankind, which was slowly groping its way towards the light when the Levites reverted to darkness. Before the Law was even completed Prince Siddhartha Gautama, the Buddha, had lived and died and founded the first religion of all mankind, founded on his First Law of Life: "From good must come good, and from evil must come evil." This was the answer to the Levites' Second Law, though they probably never heard of it. It was also time's and the human spirit's inevitable answer to Brahminism, Hindu racialism and the cult of the perpetual master-caste (which strongly resembles literal Judaism).

Five hundred years ahead lay a second universal religion, and five hundred years after that a third. The little nation of Judah was held back in the Law's chains from this movement of mankind; it was arrested in the fossil stage of spiritual development, and yet its primitive tribal creed retained life and vigour. The Levitical Law, still potent in the Twentieth Century, is in its nature a survival from sunken times.

Such a Law was bound to cause curiosity, first, and alarm next among peoples with whom the Judahites dwelt, or to their neighbours, if they dwelt alone. When the Judahites returned from Babylon to Jerusalem, about 538 BC, this impact on other peoples began. At that moment in time it was felt only by little clans and tribes, the immediate neighbours of the repatriated Judahites in Jerusalem. It has continued ever since in widening circles, being felt by ever greater numbers of peoples, and in our century has produced its greatest disturbances among them.

Chapter 5

THE FALL OF BABYLON

B efore this first impact of "the Mosaic Law" could be felt by other peoples came the event of 536 BC which set the pattern of the Twentieth Century AD: the fall of Babylon.

The resemblance between the pattern of events today (that is to say, the shape taken by the outcome of the two World Wars) and that of the fall of Babylon is too great to be accidental, and in fact can now be shown to have been deliberately produced. The peoples of the West in the present century, had they realized it, were governed under "the Judaic Law," not under any law of their own, by the forces that controlled governments.

The grouping of characters and the final denouement are alike in all three cases. On one side of the stage is the foreign potentate who has oppressed and affronted the Judahites (or, today, the Jews). In Babylon this was "King Belshazzar"; in the first World War it was the Russian Czar; in the second war, it was Hitler. Confronting this "persecutor," is the other foreign potentate, the liberator. In Babylon, this was King Cyrus of Persia; in the second case, it was a Mr. Balfour; in the third, it was a President Truman.

Between these adversaries stands the Jehovan prophet triumphant, the great man at the foreign ruler's court who foretells, and survives, the disaster which is about to befall the "persecutor." In Babylon, this was Daniel. In the first and second world wars of this century it was a Dr. Chaim Weizmann, the Zionist prophet at foreign courts.

These are the characters. Then comes the denouement, a Jehovan vengeance on "the heathen" and a Jewish triumph in the form of a symbolic "restoration." "King Belshazzar," when Daniel has foretold his doom, is killed "in the same night" and his kingdom falls to the enemy. The Jewish captors who killed the Russian Czar and his family, at the end of the First Twentieth Century war, quoted this precedent in a couplet "written on the wall" of the room where the massacre occurred; the Nazi leaders, at the end of the Second Twentieth Century war, were hanged on the Jewish Day of Atonement.

Thus the two World Wars of this century have conformed, in their outcomes, to the pattern of the Babylonian-Persian war of antiquity as depicted in the Old Testament.

Presumably the peoples who fought that ancient war thought that something more than the cause of the Judahites was at stake, and that they strove for some purpose or interest of their own. But in the narrative that has come down through the centuries all else has been expunged. The only significant results, in the picture which has been imprinted on the minds of peoples, are the Jehovan vengeance and Judahite triumph, and the two world wars of this century followed that same pattern.

King Belshazzar survives only as the symbolic foreign "persecutor" of the Judahites (although Jehovah made them his captives, as a punishment, he is nevertheless their "persecutor" and hence must be barbarously destroyed). King Cyrus, similarly, is but the fulfilling instrument of Jehovah's promise to visit "all these curses" on "thine enemies" when they have served their turn as captors (and thus deserves no credit in his own right, either as conqueror or liberator; he is not truly any better than King Belshazzar, and his house will in turn be destroyed).

King Cyrus, from what true history tells of him, seems to have been an enlightened man, as well as the founder of an empire which spread over all Western Asia. According to the encyclopaedias, "he left the nations he subjected free in the observance of their religions and the maintenance of their institutions." Thus the Judahites may have benefited by a policy which he impartially applied to all, and possibly King Cyrus, could he return to earth today, would be surprised to find that his portrait in history is that of a man whose only notable and enduring achievement was to restore a few thousand Judahites to Jerusalem.

However, if by any chance he thought this particular question to be of paramount importance among his undertakings (as the Twentieth Century politicians demonstrably think), he would at his return to earth today be much gratified, for he would find that through this act he exerted a greater influence on human events in the 2,500 years to come, probably than any other temporal ruler of any age. No other deed of antiquity has had consequences in the present time so great or so plain to trace.

In the Twentieth Century AD two generations of Western politicians, in the quest for Jewish favour, competed with each other to play the part of King Cyrus. The result was that the two World Wars produced only two enduring and significant results: the Jehovan vengeance on the symbolic "persecutor" and the Jewish triumph in the form of a new "restoration." Thus the symbolic legend of what happened at Babylon had by the Twentieth Century gained the force of the supreme "Law," overriding all other laws, and of truth and history.

The legend itself seems to have been two-thirds untruth, or what today would be called propaganda. King Belshazzar himself was apparently invented by the Levites. The historical book which records the fall of Babylon was compiled several centuries later and was attributed to one "Daniel." It states that he was a Judahite captive in Babylon who rose to the highest place at court there and "sat in the gate of the king" (Nebuchadnezzar) through his skill in interpreting dreams. Upon him devolved the task of interpreting the "writing on the wall" *(Daniel,* 5).

King "Belshazzar, the son of Nebuchadnezzar," is then depicted as offering an insult to the Judahites by using "the golden and silver vessels" taken by his father from the temple in Jerusalem for a banquet with his princes, wives and concubines. Thereon the fingers of a man's hand write on the wall the words, "Mene, Mene, Tekel, Upharsin." Daniel, being called to interpret, tells the king that they mean, "God hath numbered thy kingdom, and finished it; thou art weighed in the balance and found wanting; thy kingdom is divided and given to the Medes and Persians." Thereon King Belshazzar *"in the same night"* is slain, and the Persian conqueror enters, who is to "restore" the Judahites.

Thus the end of a king and a kingdom is related directly to an affront offered to Judah and given the guise of a Jehovan retribution and Jewish vengeance. What matter if Daniel and King Belshazzar never existed: by its inclusion in the Levitical scriptures this anecdote gained the status of a legal precedent! When the murder of the Russian Czar, his wife, daughters and son in 1918, again, was related directly to this legend by words quoted from it and scrawled on a blood-bespattered wall this was at once an avowal of authorship of the deed, and a citation of the legal authority for it.

When an ancient legend can produce such effects, twenty-five centuries afterwards, there is little gain in demonstrating its untruth, for politicians and the masses they manipulate alike love their legends more than truth. However, of the three protagonists in this version of the fall of Babylon, only King Cyrus certainly existed; King Belshazzar and Daniel seem to be figures of Levitical phantasy!

The *Jewish Encyclopaedia,* which points out that King Nebuchadnezzar had no son called Belshazzar and that no king called Belshazzar reigned in Babylon when King Cyrus conquered it, says impartially that "the *author* of *Daniel* simply did not have correct data at hand," and thus does not believe that Daniel wrote *Daniel.* Obviously, if an important Judahite favourite at court, called Daniel, had written the book he would at least have known the name of the king whose end he foretold, and thus have had "correct data." Evidently the book of Daniel, like the books of the Law attributed to Moses, was the product of Levitical scribes who in it patiently continued to make history conform with their Law, already laid down. If a King Belshazzar could be invented for the purpose of illustration and precedent, so could a prophet Daniel. This, apparently mythical Daniel is the most popular prophet of all with the fervent Zionists of today, who rejoice in the anecdote of the Judahite vengeance and triumph foretold on the wall, and see in it the legal precedent for all later time. The story of our present century has done more than that of any earlier one to strengthen them in this belief and for them Daniel, with his "interpretation" fulfilled "in the same night," gives the conclusive, crushing answer to the earlier Israelite prophets who had envisioned a loving God of all men. The fall of Babylon (as depicted by the Levites) gave practical proof of the truth and force of the "Mosaic" Law.

However, it would all have come to nothing without King Cyrus, who alone of the three protagonists *did* exist and *did* either allow, or compel, a few thousand Judahites to return to Jerusalem. At that point in history the Levitical theory of politics, which aimed at the exercise of power through the acquirement of mastery over foreign rulers, was put to its first practical test and was successful.

The Persian king was the first of a long line of Gentile oracles worked by the ruling sect, which through him demonstrated that it had found the secret of infesting, first, and then directing the actions of foreign governments.

By the present century this mastery of governments had been brought to such a degree of power that they were all, in large measure, under one supreme control, so that their actions, in the end, always served the ambition of this supreme party. Towards the end of this book the reader will see how the Gentile oracles were worked, so that the antagonisms of peoples might be incited and brought into collision for this super-national purpose.

However, the reader will need to look into his own soul to find, if he can, the reason *why* these oracles, his own leaders, submitted. King Cyrus was the first of them. Without his support the sect could not have set itself up again in Jerusalem and have convinced the incredulous Judahite masses, watching from all parts of the known world, that the racial Law *was* potent and *would* be literally fulfilled. The line of cause-and-effect runs straight and clear from the fall of Babylon to this century's great events; the West today owes its successive disappointments and its decline even more to King Cyrus, the first of the Gentile puppets, than to the ingenious, stealthy priesthood itself.

"Judaism originated in the name of the Persian king and by the authority of his Empire, and thus the effect of the Empire of the Alchemenides extends with great power, as almost nothing else, directly into our present age," says Professor Eduard Meyer, and this authority's conclusion is demonstrably true. Five hundred years before the West even began, the Levites laid down the Law, and then through King Cyrus set the precedent and pattern for the downfall of the West itself.

The five books of the Law were still not complete when King Cyrus came to Babylon and conquered. The sect in Babylon was still busy on them and on the supporting version of history which, by such examples as that of "King Belshazzar," was to give plausibility to the unbelievable and supply the precedent for barbaric deeds twenty-five centuries later. The mass of Judahites still knew nothing of the Law of *racial* intolerance which was being prepared for them, though *religious* intolerance was by this time familiar to them:

The sect had yet to complete the Law and then to apply it to its own people. When that happened in 458 BC, under another Persian king, the controversy of Zion at last took the shape in which it still implacably confronts its own people and the rest of mankind. The umbilical cord between the Judahites and other men was then finally severed.

These segregated people, before whom the priesthood flaunted its version of the fall of Babylon like a banner, then were set on the road to a future which would find them a compact force among other peoples, to whose undoing they were by their Law dedicated.

Chapter 6

THE PEOPLE WEPT

The first people to feel the impact of this "Mosaic Law" which the Levites were developing in Babylon were the Samaritans, who in 538 BC warmly welcomed the Judahites returning to Jerusalem and in token of friendship offered to help rebuild the temple, destroyed by the Babylonians in 596 BC. At the Levites' order the Samaritans were brusquely repulsed and at this affront became hostile, so that the restoration of the temple was delayed until 520 BC. (The feud against the Samaritans continued throughout the centuries to the present time, when they have been reduced to a few score or dozen souls).

The friendly approach shows that the new "Law" of the Judeans was unknown to their neighbours, who were taken by surprise by this rebuff. It seems to have been just as little known to, or understood by the Judeans themselves, at that period. The books of the Law were still being compiled in Babylon and, despite anything the priests may have told them, they clearly did not at that time realize that they were to be racially, as well as religiously, debarred from their fellow men.

The repulse of the Samaritans gave the first hint of what was to follow. The Samaritans were Israelites, probably infused with other blood. They practiced Jehovah-worship but did not recognize the supremacy of Jerusalem and on that account alone would have incurred the hatred of the Levites, who probably saw in them the danger of an Israelite revival and absorption of Judah. Thus the Samaritans were put under the major ban; even by taking a piece of bread from a Samaritan a Judahite broke all the statutes and judgments of the Levites and abominably defiled himself.

After this first clash with their neighbours, the Judeans looked around them at ruined and depopulated Jerusalem. None of them, unless they were ancients, can have known it before. They were few in number: those who "returned" numbered about forty thousand, which was perhaps a tenth or twentieth of the total, for centuries self-dispersed in other lands.

It was not a happy or triumphant return for these people, though it was a major political success for the priesthood. The Levites met the same difficulty as the Zionists in 1903, 1929 and 1953: the chosen people did not want to go to the promised land. Moreover, the leaders did not intend to head "the return"; they wished to stay in Babylon (as the Zionist leaders today wish to stay in New York).

The solution found in 538 BC was similar to the one found in 1946: the zealots were ready to go, and a hapless few, who were too poor to choose, were rounded up to accompany them. Those who desired the privilege of remaining in Babylon (under their own prince, the Exilarch, in his own capital!) were mulcted in fines (just as the wealthy Jews of America are pressed today to provide funds for the Zionist state).

The Jewish *nation* was already and finally dispersed; obviously it could never again be reassembled in Canaan. That was a fact, unalterable and permanent; "from the exile the nation did not return, but a religious sect only," says Professor Wellhausen. But this symbolic "return" was of the utmost importance to the priesthood in establishing its mystic power over the scattered mass. It could be held up as the proof that "the Law" was true and valid, and that the destiny of the "special people" *was* to destroy and dominate.

The "return" meant quite different things to the few who returned and to the many who watched from the dispersion. To the few it meant the possibility to practice Jehovah-worship in the way and on the spot prescribed by "the Law." To the many it was a triumph of Judahite nationalism and the portent of the final triumph foreseen by the Law.

This watching mass had seen the means by which the success had been achieved, the conqueror undone and overthrown, and the "captivity" transformed into the "return." Segregation had proved effective, and the chief methods of enforcing this segregation were the ghetto and the synagogue. The ghetto (essentially a Levitical concept) had been tried out in Babylon, in the form of the closed- community in which the Judahites lived.

The collective reading of the law had also proved to be an effective substitute for the ritual of worship which, under the Law, could be performed only at the temple in Jerusalem (this was the beginning of the synagogue). The institutions of the ghetto and the synagogue were adopted by the communities of the dispersion, and gave them a feeling of union with the exiled Judahites and the returned Judeans.

Thus the "religious sect" which "returned" to an unknown Jerusalem was also the core of the nation-within-nations, state-within-states. The priesthood had shown itself able to maintain its theocracy without a territory of its own and under a foreign king. It had ruled its followers under its own Law; and of this Law as it was first imposed in exile on the Judahites in Babylon Dr. Kastein says: "Instead of the constitution of the defunct state, communal autonomy was established, and, instead of the power of the state, there came into being another power, more reliable and more enduring: *the stern and inexorable regime enforced by the obligation to render unquestioning obedience to the regulations of the ritual.*"

The words deserve careful study; many of "the regulations of the ritual" have been quoted in this book. The Levites had succeeded, in "captivity" and on foreign soil, in "enforcing" a "stern and inexorable regime." The achievement is unique, and it has been a continuing one, from that time to our day.

"Strangers" are usually puzzled to imagine any means by which the ruling sect could keep so firm a hold over a community scattered about the world. This power is based, ultimately, on terror and fear. Its mysteries are kept hidden from the stranger, but by diligent study he may gain some idea of them.

The weapon of excommunication is a dreaded one, and the fear which it inspires rests to some extent on the literal Judaist's belief in the physical efficacy of the curses enumerated in *Deuteronomy* and other books; the *Jewish Encyclopaedia* testifies to this continuing belief. In this matter there is a strong resemblance to the African Native's belief that he will die if he is "tagati'd," and to the American Negro's fear of voodooist spells. Casting out of the fold is a much-feared penalty (and in the past was often a lethal one), of which examples may be found in the literature of our day.

Also, for pious (or for that matter superstitious) Judaists the Torah-Talmud is the *only* Law, and if they submit formally to the laws of countries where they dwell, it is with this inner reservation. Under that only-Law the priesthood wields all judicial and magisterial powers (and often has had these formally delegated to it by governments), and literally the Law includes capital punishment on numerous counts; in practice the priesthood in closed-communities of the dispersion has often exacted that penalty.

The Jerusalem to which a few returned was far from Babylon, in those times, and after their first coup (the repulse of the Samaritans' offer of friendship) the Levites apparently found themselves unable, from a distance, to restrain the normal impulses of human kind. The Judahites, in their impoverished fragment of land, began to settle down and intermarry with their neighbours for all that. They broke no law comprehended by them. The books of the Law were still being compiled in Babylon; they knew about Solomon's hundreds of wives and Moses's Midianite father-in-law, but did not yet know that Moses had been resurrected in order to exterminate all the Midianites save the virgins. Thus they married their neighbours' sons and daughters and this natural intermingling continued for about eighty years after the return.

During that period the Levites in Babylon completed the Law, the impact of which all nations have felt ever since. Ezekiel of the High Priest's family was its chief architect and probably all five books of the Law, as they have come down, bear his mark. He was the founding-father of intolerance, of racialism and vengeance as a religion, and of murder in the name of God.

The book of Ezekiel is the most significant of all the Old Testament books. It is more significant than even *Deuteronomy*, *Leviticus* and *Numbers* because it seems to be the fountainhead from which the dark ideas of those books of the Law first sprang. For instance, the student of the curses enumerated in *Deuteronomy* is bound to suspect that the deity in whose name they were uttered was of diabolic nature, not divine; the name, "God," in the sense which has been given to it, cannot be coupled with such menaces. In Ezekiel's book the student finds this suspicion expressly confirmed. Ezekiel puts into the very mouth of God the statement that he had made *evil* laws in order to inspire misery and fear! This appears in chapter 20 and gives the key to the whole mystery of "the Mosaic Law."

In this passage Ezekiel appears to be answering Jeremiah's attack on the Levites in the matter of sacrificing the firstborn: "And they have built the high places to burn their sons and daughters in the fire; *which I commanded not, neither came it into my heart.*" Ezekiel is not much concerned about the lot of the sons and daughters but is clearly enraged by the charge that the Lord had *not* commanded the sacrifice of the firstborn, when the scribes had repeatedly ascribed this command to him. His retort is concerned only to show that God *had* so commanded and thus to justify the priesthood; the admission that the commandment was evil is casual and nonchalant, as if this were of no importance:

"I am the Lord your God; walk in my statutes and keep my judgments, and do them....Notwithstanding the children rebelled against me; they walked not in my statutes, neither kept my judgments to do them.... then I said, I would pour out my fury upon them, to accomplish my anger against them in the wilderness....*Wherefore I gave them also statutes that were not good and judgments whereby they should not live; And I polluted them in their own gifts, in that they caused to pass through the fire all that openeth the womb, that I might make them desolate, to the end that they might know that I am the Lord.*"

The ruling of Christian theologians, that the Old Testament is of "equal divine authority" with the New, presumably includes this passage! Ezekiel, in his day, forbade any protest by quickly adding, "And shall I be enquired of by you, O house of Israel? As I live, saith the Lord, I will not be enquired of by you."

Ezekiel experienced the Fall of Judah and the removal of the sect to Babylon, so that his book is in parts an eye-witness account of events. Its other, "prophetic" parts show this founding-father of literal Judaism to have been a man of dark, even demoniac obsessions; indeed, parts of the book of Ezekiel probably could not be publicly printed as anything but Scripture.

Early in it he portrays (in words which he also attributes to the Lord God) a siege of Jerusalem in which he, Ezekiel, to atone "for the iniquity of the people," is commanded to eat human excrement baked before his eyes. At his plea, that he has always scrupulously observed the dietary laws and never taken anything abominable in his mouth, this is mitigated to cow's dung. Then he threatens transgressors with cannibalism, a curse on which the Levites laid marked stress: "... the fathers shall eat the sons in the midst of thee and the sons shall eat their fathers ... a third part shall fall by the sword ... and I will scatter a third part unto all the winds ... famine and evil beasts ... pestilence and blood."

All this is to be the retribution for non-observance, not for evil deeds. Pages of cursings follow and Jehovah promises to use the Gentiles as the rod of chastisement: "Wherefore I will bring the worst of the heathen ... and they shall possess your houses." Portraying what will happen to those who worship "other gods," Ezekiel in a characteristic vision sees "them that have charge over the city" (Jerusalem) "draw near, every man with his destroying weapon in his hand," One, with a writer's inkhorn by his side, is commanded by the Lord, "go through the midst of Jerusalem and set a mark upon the foreheads of the men that sigh and that cry for all the abominations that be done in the midst thereof" (these are the zealots in "observance"). The foreheads having been marked, Ezekiel quotes the Lord, "in my hearing," as saying to the men, "Go ye through the city and smite; let not your eye spare, neither have ye pity; slay utterly old and young, both maids, and little children and women; but come not near any man upon whom is the mark ... and they went forth and slew in the city."

After Ezekiel's time men may have thought it wise to be seen sighing and crying in Jerusalem; hence, perhaps, the Wailing Wall. Chapter on chapter of menaces follow, always with the alluring proviso that if the transgressors turn from their wickedness towards observance, even worse things will then be visited on the heathen:

"I will take you from among the heathen, and gather you out of all countries, and will bring you into your own land.... And ye shall dwell in the land that I gave to your fathers, and ye shall be my people, and I will be your God.... Assemble yourselves, and come; gather yourselves on every side to my sacrifice that I do sacrifice for you, even a great sacrifice for you, even a great sacrifice upon the mountains of Israel, that ye may eat flesh and drink *blood.* Ye shall eat the flesh of the mighty, and drink the *blood* of the princes of the earth.... And ye shall eat fat till ye be full, and drink *blood* till ye be drunken.... and I will set my glory among the heathen, and all the heathen shall see my judgment that I have executed, and my hand that I have laid upon them."

While the school of scribes founded by Ezekiel continued for eighty years, in Babylon, to compile their Law, the repatriated Judahites in Jerusalem gradually developed normal relationships with their neighbours. They had never known the regime of bigotry and exclusion which was being prepared for them in Babylon. Many of the people still prayed to "other gods" for rain, crops, sun and herds, and to Jehovah in tribal feuds.

Then, in 458 BC, the Levites struck.

Their Law was ready, which was not by itself of much importance. *The Persian King was ready to enforce it for them,* and that was of the greatest importance, then and up to the present moment. For the first time the ruling sect accomplished the wonder which they have since repeatedly achieved: by some means they induced a foreign ruler, who was their ostensible master and to all outer appearances a mighty potentate in his own right, to put his soldiers and money at their disposal.

On this day in 458 BC the Judahites in Jerusalem were finally cut off from mankind and enslaved in a way they never knew in Babylon. This was the true "start of the affair." The story is told in the books of Ezra and Nehemiah, the Levitical emissaries from Babylon who were sent to Jerusalem to enforce Ezekiel's law.

Ezra of the high priesthood came from Babylon to Jerusalem with some 1500 followers. He came in the name of the Persian King Artaxerxes the Longhanded, with Persian soldiers and Persian gold. He arrived just as Dr. Chaim Weizmann arrived in Palestine in 1917, supported by British arms and British gold, and in 1947, supported by American money and power. Ezra was in legal form a Persian emissary (Dr. Weizmann, a Russian-born Jew, was in legal form a British emissary in 1917).

What means the sect found to bend King Artaxerxes to its will, none can now discover; after King Cyrus, he was the second potentate to play a puppet's part and in our century this readiness has become a strict qualification for public life.

Ezra brought the new *racial* Law with him. He enforced it first among his own travelling companions, allowing only those to accompany him who could prove that they were Judahites by descent, or Levites. When he reached Jerusalem he was "filled with horror and dismay" (Dr. Kastein) by the prevalence of mixed marriages. The Judahites were finding happiness in their fashion; "by tolerating *miscegenation* with neighbouring tribes they had established *peaceful relations based on family ties.*"

Dr. Kastein (who was equally horrified by this picture many centuries afterwards) has to admit that the Judahites by this intermingling "observed their tradition as it was understood at the time" and broke no law known to them. Ezra brought Ezekiel's *new Law,* which once more supplanted the old "tradition." In his status as emissary of the Persian king he had the Jerusalemites assembled and told them that all mixed marriages were to be dissolved; thenceforth "strangers" and everything foreign were to be rigorously excluded. A commission of elders was set up to undo all the wedlocks forged and thus to destroy the "peaceful relations based on family ties."

Dr. Kastein says that "Ezra's measure was undoubtedly *reactionary;* it raised to the *dignity of a law* an enactment which at that time *was not included in the Torah*" (which the Levites, in Babylon, were still writing down). Dr. Kastein's use of the word "dignity" is of interest in this connection; his book was published, in Berlin, in the year, twenty-four centuries later, when Hitler enacted exactly the same kind of law; it was then called "infamous" by the Zionists, and the armies of the West, reversing the role of the Persian soldiers of 458 BC, were mobilized to destroy it!

The effect of this deed was the natural one, in 458 BC as in 1917 AD: the neighbouring peoples were affronted and alarmed by the unheard-of innovation. They saw the threat to themselves and they attacked Jerusalem, tearing down the symbols of the inferiority imputed to them: its walls. By that time Ezra, like any Twentieth Century Zionist, had evidently returned to his home abroad, for once more the artificial structure began to crumble and natural tendencies were resumed: intermarriage began again and led anew to "peaceful relations based on family ties." Only force can prevent this from happening.

After thirteen years, in 445 BC, the elders in Babylon struck again. Nehemiah was another figure, as typical of our century as of that time in Babylon. He was of Judahite descent and stood high in the Persian king's favour (as Zionist "advisers" today habitually stand at the right hand of British Prime Ministers and American Presidents; the parallel could not be much closer). He was cupbearer to Artaxerxes himself. He arrived from Babylon in Jerusalem with dictatorial power and enough men and money to re-wall the city (at *Persian* expense; the parallel with today continues), and it thus became the first true ghetto. It was an empty one, and when the walls were ready Nehemiah ordered that one in ten of the Judahites be chosen by lot to reside in it.

Race thus became the supreme, though still unwritten tenet of the Law. Jehovah-worshippers who could not satisfy Persian officials and the Levite elders of their descent from Judah, Benjamin or Levi were rejected "with horror" (Dr. Kastein). Every man had to establish "the undisputed purity of his stock" from the registers of births (Hitler's Twentieth Century edict about the Aryan grandmothers was less extreme).

Then, in 444 BC, Nehemiah had Ezra embody the ban on mixed marriages in the Torah, so that at last what had been done became part of the much-amended "Law" (and David and Solomon presumably were posthumously cast out of the fold). The heads of clans and families were assembled and required to sign a pledge that they and their peoples would keep all the statutes and judgments of the Torah, with special emphasis on this new one.

In *Leviticus* the necessary insertion was made: "I have *severed* you from other people that ye should be mine." Thenceforth no Judahite might marry outside the clan, under penalty of death; every man who married a foreign woman committed a sin against God *(Nehemiah*, 13.27; this is the law in the Zionist state today). "Strangers" were forbidden to enter the city, so that the Judahites "might be *purified* from everything foreign."

Nehemiah and Ezra were both eye-witnesses. Nehemiah is the ideal, unchallengeable narrator: he was there, he was the dictator, his was the deed. He says that when Ezra for the first time read this new Law to the Jerusalemites:

"All the people wept when they heard the words of the Law."

These twelve words of contemporary journalism bring the scene as clearly before today's reader as if it had occurred twenty-four hours, not twenty-four centuries ago. He sees the weeping, ghettoized throng of 444 BC through the eyes of the man who, with Persian warriors at his side, forced them into their first true captivity, the spiritual one which thereafter was to enclose any man who called himself "Jew."

Nehemiah remained twelve years in Jerusalem and then returned to the Babylonian court. At once the artificial structure he had set up in Jerusalem began to disintegrate, so that some years later he descended again on the city, where once more mixed marriages had occurred. He "forcibly dissolved" these, also setting "the severest penalties" on further transgressions of the kind. Next, "with a view to applying rigorously the selective principle, he again carefully studied the register of births" and ejected all, including even Aaronite families, in whose descent the slightest flaw could be detected. Last, he "ruthlessly purged" the community of all who had failed in "unquestioning and unhesitating allegiance to the established order and the law" and made the entire people renew their pledge.

This is known as "the *New* Covenant" (as *Deuteronomy* was the *Second* Law; these qualifying words are the milestones of the supplanting heresy). It had to be signed, at Levite order and under Persian duress, by every man in Jerusalem singly, as if it were a business contract. Then Nehemiah finally departed for Babylon, his home, having "completed the task of isolation" and "left behind him a community which, *agreed as it now was* on all fundamental questions, was able to fend for itself. He had organized their everyday life for them and built up their spiritual foundations." These words are Dr. Kastein's; the reader has seen, also in his words, by what means these Jerusalemites were brought to "agree on all fundamental questions."

By this time about four hundred years had passed since the repudiation of Judah by Israel, and three hundred since the Assyrian conquest of Israel. This period of time the Levites had used to complete the perversion of the older tradition, to put their racio-religious Law in writing, and at last to clamp it, like shackles, on the Judahites in the little Persian province of Judea. They *had* succeeded in setting up their fantastic, tribal creed and in establishing their little theocracy. They had started the catalytic agent on its journey through the centuries.

For more than a hundred generations, since that day when the New Covenant was enforced by Persian arms, and the people who had wept were compelled to sign it anew, a mass of human beings, changing in blood but closely or loosely held in the bonds of this Law, have carried its burden and inheritance, in spiritual isolation from the rest of mankind. The singular paradox remains: though their enchainment was devised by the Levites the chains were Persian. On that day as ever since, though the fanatical sect has dictated their continuing captivity, foreign arms and foreign money have kept them in it.

Where does responsibility lie between those who incite to a deed and those who commit it? If the answer is that the greater and final responsibility lies with the perpetrator, then the verdict of history is incontestably, though strangely, that responsibility for the heresy of Judaism lies with the Gentiles, who from the time of the Persian kings to this century have done the bidding of the sect that devised it.

It *was* a heresy: On the day when King Artaxerxes's soldiers forced the Jerusalemites to sign Ezekiel's New Covenant, *the perversion of the earlier Israelite tradition* was made complete *and the affirmation of God was supplanted by the denial of God.*

No resemblance remained between the God of the moral commandments and Ezekiel's malevolent deity who boasted that he commanded men to kill their firstborn in order to keep them in awe of himself! This was not revealed God, but a man-made deity, the incarnation of primitive tribalism. What those ancient people signed under duress, in the New Covenant, was either the formal denial of God or the formal claim that God was Judah, and this in fact is the claim expressly made in many Zionist utterances of our time, so that the heresy is openly avowed:

"God is absorbed in the nationalism of Israel. He becomes the national ethos … He creates the world in the Hebrew language. He is the National God" (Rabbi Solomon Goldman).

"We and God grew up together … We have a national God … We believe that God is a Jew, that there is no English or American God" (Mr. Maurice Samuel).

"It was not God who willed these people and their meaning. It was this people who willed this God and this meaning" (Dr. Kastein). These statements are explicit, and such phrases are easy to pen in this century, in New York or Chicago, London or Berlin. But at the start of this affair, as Nehemiah recorded:

"All the people wept when they heard the words of the Law" and since that day it has given very many cause to weep.

Douglas Reed

Chapter 7

THE TRANSLATION OF THE LAW

The most important event (as it proved) of the next four hundred years was the first translation of the Judaic scriptures (later to become known as the Old Testament) into a foreign tongue, Greek. This enabled, and still enables, "the heathen" to become partially acquainted with the Law that ordained their own enslavement and destruction and the supremacy of Judah. Save for this translation the nature of literal Judaism must have remained a matter of surmise, whereas the translation made it appear to be one of evidence and proof.

For that reason it is at first sight surprising that the translation was ever made (as tradition says, by seventy-two Jewish scholars at Alexandria between 275 and 150 BC.) Dr. Kastein explains that it was undertaken "with a definite object in view, that of making it comprehensible to the Greeks; this led to the *distortion and twisting of words, changes of meaning, and the frequent substitution of general terms and ideas for those that were purely local and national."*

Dr. Kastein's words in this instance are carelessly chosen if they were intended to disguise what occurred: a matter is not made "comprehensible" to others by distorting and twisting it, changing its meaning, and substituting ambiguous terms for precise ones. Moreover, so learned a Judaic scholar must have known what the *Jewish Encyclopaedia* records, that the later Talmud even "prohibited the teaching to a Gentile of the Torah, anyone so teaching 'deserving death.'" Indeed, the Talmud saw such danger in the acquirement by the heathen of knowledge of the Law that it set up the *oral* Torah as the last repository of Jehovah's secrets, safe from any Gentile eye.

If the Judaic scriptures were translated into Greek, then, this was not for the benefit of the Greeks (Dr. Kastein wrote for a largely Gentile audience). The reason, almost certainly, was that the Jews themselves needed the translation. The Judahites had lost their Hebrew tongue in Babylon (thereafter it became a priestly mystery, "one of the *secret* spiritual bonds which held the Judaists of the Diaspora together," as Dr. Kastein says), and spoke Aramaic. However, the largest single body of Jews was in Alexandria, where Greek became their everyday language; many of them could no longer understand Hebrew and a Greek version of their Law was needed as a basis for the rabbinical interpretations of it.

Above all, the elders could not foresee that centuries later a new religion would arise in the world which would take over their scriptures as part of its own Bible, and thus bring "the Mosaic Law" before the eyes of all mankind. Had that been anticipated, the Greek translation might never have been made.

Nevertheless, the translators were evidently reminded by the priests that their work would bring "the Law," for the first time, under Gentile scrutiny; hence the distortions, twistings, changes and substitutions mentioned by Dr. Kastein. An instance of these is apparently given by *Deuteronomy* 32.21; the translation which has come down to the heathen alludes vaguely to "a foolish nation," whereas the reference in the Hebrew original, according to the *Jewish Encyclopaedia,* is to "vile and vicious Gentiles."

What was translated? First, the five books of the Law, the Torah. After the "New Covenant" had been forcibly imposed on the Jerusalemites by Ezra and Nehemiah, the priesthood in Babylon had given the Torah yet another revision: "once again *anonymous editors lent their past history, their traditions, laws and customs a meaning* entirely in keeping with theocracy and applicable to that system of government.... The form which the Torah then received was the final and conclusive form which was not to be altered by one iota; no single thought, word or letter of it was to be changed."

When mortal men repeatedly "lend meaning" to something supposed already to be immutable, and force all spiritual tradition into the framework of their worldly political ambition, what remains cannot be an original revelation of God. What had happened was that the earlier, Israelite tradition had been expunged or cancelled, and in its place the Judaic racial law had assumed "final and conclusive form."

The same method was followed in the compilation of the other books, historical, prophetic or lyrical. The book of *Daniel,* for instance, was completed at about this time, that is to say, some four hundred years after the events related in it; small wonder that the anonymous author got all his historical facts wrong. Dr. Kastein is candid about the manner in which these books were produced:

"The editors who put the books of *Joshua, Judges, Samuel* and *Kings* into their final form gathered *every fragment*" (of the old teachings and traditions) and "creatively *interpreted* them ... It was impossible always definitely to assign particular words to particular persons, for they had so frequently worked *anonymously,* and, *as the editors were more concerned with the subject matter than with philological exactitude,* they were content with stringing the sayings of the prophets together as best they could." (This method might account for the attribution of the identical "Messianic" prophecy to two prophets, *Isaiah* 2, 2-4, and *Micah* 4, 1-4, and for the numerous repetitions to be found in other books).

The *subject matter,* then, was the important thing, not historical truth, or "philological exactitude," or the word of God. The subject matter was political nationalism in the most extreme form ever known to man, and conformity with this dogma was the only rule that had to be observed. The way in which these books were compiled, after Judah was cast off by Israel, and the reasons, are clear to any who study their origin.

The resultant product, the growth of five or six hundred years and the work of generations of political priests, was the book which was translated into Greek around 150 BC. After the lifetime of Jesus it, and the New Testament, was translated into Latin by Saint Jerome, when both "came to be regarded by the Church as of equal divine authority and as sections of one book" (from a typical modern encyclopaedia), a theological dictum which was formally confirmed by the Council of Trent in the sixteenth century of our era and has been adopted by nearly all Protestant churches, although in this matter they might have found valid reason to protest.

In view of the changes which were made, at the translation, (see Dr. Kastein's words, above), none but Judaist scholars could tell today how closely the Old Testament in the Hebrew-Aramaic original compares with the version which has come down, from the first translation into Greek, as one of the two sections of Christendom's Bible. Clearly substantial changes were made, and quite apart from that there is the "oral Torah," and the Talmudic continuation of the Torah, so that the Gentile world has never known the whole truth of the Judaic Law.

Nevertheless, the essence of it is all in the Old Testament as it has come down to Christendom, and that is a surprising thing. Whatever may have been expunged or modified, the vengeful, tribal deity, the savage creed and the law of destruction and enslavement remain plain for all to ponder. The fact is that no amount of twisting, distortion, changing or other subterfuge could conceal the nature of the Judaic Law, once it was translated; although glosses were made, the writing beneath remains clear, and this is the best evidence that, when the first translation was authorized, the universal audience it would ultimately reach was not foreseen.

With that translation the Old Testament, as we now call and know it, entered the West, its teaching of racial hatred and destruction only a little muted by the emendations. That was before the story of the West even had truly begun.

By the time the West, and Christianity, were nineteen and a half centuries old, the political leaders there, being much in awe of the central sect of Judaism, had begun to speak with pious awe of the Old Testament, as if it were the better half of the Book by which they professed to live. Nevertheless it was, as it always had been, the Law of their peoples' destruction and enslavement, and all their deeds, under *the servitude which they accepted,* led towards that end.

Chapter 8

THE LAW AND THE IDUMEANS

While the Judaic scriptures, thus compiled, were on their way, thus translated, from the Alexandrine Jews to the Greeks and thereafter to the other heathen, Persian, Greek and Roman overlords followed each other in little Judea.

These chaotic centuries brought in their course the second significant event of the period: the enforced conversion of the Idumeans to Jehovaism ("Judaism" is a word apparently first used by the Judean historian Josephus to denote the culture and way of life of Judea, as "Hellenism" described those of Greece, and originally had no religious connotation. For want of a better word it will now be used in this book to identify the racial religion set up by the Levites on their perversion of the "Mosaic Law.")

Only one other mass-conversion to Judaism is known to recorded history, and that one, which came about eight or nine centuries later, was of immediate importance to our present generation, as will be shown. Individual conversion, on the other hand, was at this period frequent, and apparently was encouraged even by the rabbis, for Jesus himself, according to Saint Matthew, told the scribes and Pharisees, rebukingly, that they "compass sea and land to make one proselyte."

Thus, for some reason, the racial ban introduced by the Second Law and the New Covenant was not, at this time, being enforced. Presumably the explanation is the numerical one; if the racial law had been strictly enforced the small tribe of Judah would have died out and the priesthood, with its creed, would have been left like generals with a plan of battle, but no army.

Evidently there was much intermingling, for whatever reason. The *Jewish Encyclopaedia* says that "early and late Judah derived strength from the absorption of outsiders" and other authorities agree, so that anything like a purebred tribe of Judah must have disappeared some centuries before Christ, at the latest.

Nevertheless, the racial *Law* remained in full vigour, not weakened by these exceptions, so that in the Christian era proselytizing virtually ceased and the Judaists of the world, although obviously they were not descended from Judah, became again a community separated from mankind by a rigid racial ban. Racial exclusion remained, or again became, the supreme tenet of formal Zionism, and the Talmudic ruling was that "proselytes are as injurious to Judaism as ulcers to a sound body."

Fervent Zionists still beat their heads on a wall of lamentation when they consider the case of the Idumeans, which, they hold, proves the dictum just quoted. The problem of what to do with them apparently arose out of the priests' own sleight-of-hand feats with history and The Law. In the first historical book, *Genesis*, the Idumeans are shown as the tribe descended from Esau ("Esau the father of the Edomites"), who was own brother to Jacob-called-Israel. This kinsmanship between Judah and Edom was apparently the original tradition, so that the Idumeans' special status was still recognized when *Deuteronomy* was produced in 621 BC, the Lord then "saying unto Moses":

"And command thou the people, saying, Ye are to pass through the coast of your brethren the children of Edom ... Meddle not with them; for I will not give you of their land, no, not so much as a foot breadth ... And when we *passed by* from our brethren the children of Esau ..."

When *Numbers* came to be written, say two hundred years later, this situation had changed. By then Ezra and Nehemiah, escorted by Persian soldiery, had enforced their racial law on the Judahites, and the Idumeans, like other neighbouring peoples, became hostile (for exactly the same reasons that cause Arab hostility today).

They learned, from *Numbers,* that, far from being "not meddled" with, they were now marked down for "utter destruction." Thus in *Numbers* Moses and his followers no longer "pass by our brethren the children of Esau"; they demand to pass *through* the Idumean land. The King of Idumea refuses permission, whereon Moses takes another route and the Lord promises him that "Edom shall be a *possession.*"

From other passages in The Law the Idumeans were able to learn the fate of cities so taken in possession; in them, nothing was to be left alive that breathed. (The scribes dealt similarly with the Moabites; in *Deuteronomy* Moses is commanded "Distress not the Moabites, neither contend with them in battle; for I will not give thee of their land for a possession"; in *Numbers,* the divine command is that the Moabites be destroyed).

From about 400 BC on, therefore, the Judeans were distrusted and feared by neighbouring tribes, including the Idumeans. They were proved right in this, for during the brief revival of Judah under the Hasmoneans, John Hyreanus, who was king and high priest in Judea, fell on them and at the swordpoint forced them to submit to circumcision and the Mosaic Law. Of the two versions of The Law ("not to meddle" and "take possession") he obeyed the second, which might have been a satisfactory solution if the matter had ended there, for any good rabbi could have told him that either, neither or both of these decrees was right ("If the Rabbis call left right and right left, you must believe it"; Dr. William Rubens).

But the matter did not end there. A law set up in this way throws up a new problem for each one that is solved. Having "taken possession," was John Hyreanus to "utterly destroy" and "save nothing alive that breatheth" of "our brethren, the children of Esau"? He disobeyed *that* law, and contented himself with the forcible conversion. But by so doing he made himself a capital transgressor, like Saul, the first king of the united kingdom of Israel and Judah, long before. For this very thing, stopping short of utter destruction (by sparing King Agag and some beasts), Saul had been repudiated, dethroned and destroyed (according to the Levitical version of history).

John Hyrcanus had to deal with two political parties. Of these, the more moderate Sadducees, who supported the monarchy, presumably tendered the counsel to spare the Idumeans, and merely by force to make them Jews. The other party was that of the Pharisees, who represented the old despotic priesthood of the Levites and wished to restore it in full sovereignty.

Presumably these fanatical Pharisees, as heirs of the Levites, would have had him exact the full rigour of the Law and "utterly destroy" the Idumeans. They continued fiercely to oppose him (as Samuel opposed Saul) and to work for the overthrow of the monarchy. What is of particular interest today, they later claimed that from his clemency towards the Idumeans the entire ensuing catastrophe of Judea came! They saw in the second destruction of the temple and the extinction of Judea in AD 70 the prescribed penalty for John Hyrcanus's failure in observance; like Saul, he had "transgressed."

The Pharisees had to wait about 150 years for the proof of this argument, if proof it was to any but themselves. Out of the converted Idumeans came one Antipater who rose to high favour in the little court at Jerusalem (as the legendary Daniel had risen at the much greater courts of Babylon and Persia). The Pharisees themselves appealed to the Roman truimvir, Pompey, to intervene in Judea and restore the old priesthood, while abolishing the little monarchy. Their plan went agley; though the Hasmonean dynasty was in fact exterminated in the chaotic decades of little wars and insurrections that followed, Antipater the Idumean rose until Caesar made him procurator of Judea, and his son, Herod, was by Antony made king of Judea!

In the sequel, utter confusion reigned in the little province so that even the shadow of independence vanished and Rome, left no other choice, began directly to rule the land.

For this denouement the Pharisees, as the authors of Roman intervention, were apparently to blame. They laid the fault on "the half caste" and "Idumean slave," Herod. Had John Hyrcanus but "observed the Law" and "utterly destroyed" the Idumeans, 150 years before, all this would not have come about, they said. It is illuminating to see with what bitter anger Dr. Josef Kastein, two thousand years later, took up this reproach, as if it were an event of the day before. A Twentieth Century Zionist, who wrote in the time of Hitler's advent to power in Germany, he was convinced that this offence against the racial law had brought the second calamity on Judea.

However, the calamity of Judea was also the victory of the Pharisees, as will be seen, and this is typical of the paradoxes in which the story of Zion abounds from its start.

Chapter 9

THE RISE OF THE PHARISEES

These Pharisees, who formed the most numerous political party in the little Roman province of Judea, contained the dominant inner sect, earlier represented by the Levite priesthood. They made themselves the carriers of the Levitical idea in its most fanatical form, as it had found expression in Ezekiel, Ezra and Nehemiah; they were sworn to "the strict observance of Levitical purity," says the *Jewish Encyclopaedia*.

As the Levites had triumphed over the Israelite remonstrants, and had succeeded in severing Judah from its neighbours, so did the Pharisees, their successors, stand ready to crush any attempt to reintegrate the Judeans in mankind. They were the guardians of the destructive idea, and the next chapter in the story of Zion was to be that of their victory; as in the case of the Levites, the background to it was to be that of Jerusalem destroyed.

Among the priests themselves, the passing generations had produced something of a revolt against the process of constant amendment of The Law, begun by the scribes of the school of Ezekiel and Ezra. These priests held that The Law was now immutable and must not be further "reinterpreted."

To this challenge (which strikes at the very root of Judaist nationalism) the Pharisees in deadly enmity opposed their reply: that *they* were the keepers of "the traditions" and o that *oral* Law, directly imparted by God to Moses, which must never be put in writing but which governed all the rest of The Law. This claim to possess the secrets of God (or, in truth, to *be* God) is at the heart of the mystic awe in which so many generations of Jews hold "the elders"; it has a power to affright which even enlightened beings on the far fringes of Jewry cannot quite escape.

Nevertheless, the instinctive impulse to break free from this thrall has at all times thrown up a moderate party in Judaism, and at this period it was that of the Sadducees, which represented the bulk of the priesthood and stood for "keeping the peace of the city" and avoiding violent conflict with the Roman overlords. The Pharisees and the Sadducees were bitter foes. This internal dissension among Jews has continued for twenty-five hundred years into our time.

It is chiefly of academic interest to the rest of mankind (though it has to be recorded) because history shows that whenever the dispute for and against "seeking the peace of the city" has reached a climax, the party of segregation and destruction has always prevailed, and the Judaist ranks have closed behind it. The present century has given the latest example to this. At its start the established Jewish communities of Germany, England and

America (who may be compared with the Sadducees) were implacably hostile to the Zionists from Russia (the Pharisees), but within fifty years the extreme party had made itself the exclusive spokesman of "the Jews" with the Western governments, and had succeeded in beating down nearly all opposition among the Jewish communities of the world.

The Pharisees occupy the second place in the pedigree of the sect which has brought about such large events in our time. The line of descent is from the Levites in Babylon, through the Pharisees in Jerusalem, through the Talmudists of Spain and the rabbis of Russia, to the Zionists of today.

The name "Pharisee," according to the Judaist authorities, means "one who separates himself," or keeps away from persons or things impure in order to attain the degree of holiness and righteousness required in those who would commune with God. The Pharisees formed a league or brotherhood of their own, admitting to their inmost councils only those who, in the presence of three members, pledged themselves to the strict observance of Levitical purity. They were the earliest specialists in secret conspiracy, as a political science.

The experience and knowledge gained by the Pharisees may be plainly traced in the methods used by the conspiratorial parties which have emerged in Europe during the last two centuries, and particularly in those of the destructive revolution in Europe, which has been Jewish-organized and Jewish-led.

For instance, the Pharisees originally devised the basic method, resting on mutual fear and suspicion, by which in our day conspirators are held together and conspiratorial bodies made strong. This is the system of spies-on-spies and informers-among-informers on which the Communist Party is built (and its Red Army; the official regulations of which show the "political commissar" and "informer" to be a recognized part of the military structure, from the high-command level to the platoon one).

The Pharisees first employed this device, basing it on a passage in Leviticus: "Ye shall place a guard around my guard" (quoted by the *Jewish Encyclopaedia* from the Hebrew original, in use among Jews). The nature of the revolutionary machine which was set up in Europe in the Nineteenth Century cannot be understood at all unless the Talmudic knowledge and training be taken into account, which most of its organizers and leaders inherited; and the Pharisees were the first Talmudists. They claimed divine authority for any decision of their Scribes, *even in case of error,* and this is a ruling concept of the Talmud.

Under the domination of the Pharisees the Messianic idea first emerged, which was to have great consequences through the centuries. It was unknown to the earlier Israelite prophets; they never admitted the notion of an exclusive, master-race, and therefore they could not be aware of the later, consequential concept of a visitant who would come in person to set up the supreme kingdom of this exclusive master-race on earth.

The nature of this Messianic event is clear, in the Judaist authorities. The *Jewish Encyclopaedia* says the Pharisees' conception of it was that "God's kingship shall be *universally recognized* in the future ... God's kingship *excluded* any other." As Jehovah, according to the earlier Torah, "knew" only the Jews, this meant that the world would belong to the Jews. The later Talmud confirmed this, if any doubt remained, by ruling that "the non-Jews are as such precluded from admission to a future world" (the former Rabbi Laible).

The mass of the Judeans undoubtedly expected that "the Anointed one," when he came, would restore their national glory; in the perfect theocratic state he would be their spiritual leader, but also their temporal one who would reunite the scattered people in a supreme kingdom of this world. The Messianic idea, as it took shape under the Pharisees, was not an expectation of any kingdom of heaven unrelated to material triumph on earth, or at any rate it was not this among the mass of the people.

The Messianic expectation, indeed, must in a sense have been the logical and natural result of the sect's own teaching. The Pharisees, like the Levites whose message they carried on, claimed to know all things, from the date of the world's creation, and its purpose, to the manner of the special people's triumph.

Only one thing they never stated: the moment of that glorious consummation. The burden of observance which they laid on the people was harsh, however, and it was but natural that, like prison inmates serving a term, the people should clamour to know *when* they would be free.

That seems to be the origin of Messianism. The people who once had "wept" to hear the words of the New Law, now had borne its rigour for four hundred years. Spontaneously the question burst from them: When? When would the glorious consummation come, the miraculous end? They were "doing all the statutes and judgments," and the performance of them meant a heavy daily task and burden. They were doing all this under "a covenant," which promised a specific reward. When would this reward be theirs? Their rulers were in direct communion with God, and knew God's mysteries; they must be able to answer this question, *When?*

This was the one question which the Pharisees could not answer. They seem to have given the most ingenious answer they could devise: though they would not say *when*, they would say that one day "the Messiah the Prince" would appear *(Daniel)*, and *then* there would be given to him "dominion, and glory, and a kingdom, that all people, nations, and languages, should serve him."

Thus the compressed, ghettoized Judean spirit was anaesthetized with the promise of a visitant; Messianism appeared and produced the recurrent outbreaks of frenzied anticipation, the latest of which our Twentieth Century is experiencing.

Such was the setting of the scene when, nearly two thousand years ago, the man from Galilee appeared. At that time those Judeans who remained in Judea had spent the six hundred years since their casting-off by Israel in what Dr. John Goldstein, in our day, calls "Jewish darkness," and at the end of this period had come to wait and hope for the liberating Messiah.

The visitant who then appeared claimed to point them the way to "the kingdom of heaven." He was the very opposite road from that, leading over ruined nations to a temple filled with gold, towards which the Pharisees beckoned them, crying "Observe!"

The Pharisees were strong and the foreign "governor" quailed before their menaces (the picture was very much like that of our day) and those of the people who saw in the newcomer the Messiah they awaited, despite his contempt for worldly rewards, put themselves in danger of death by saying so. They were "transgressing," and the Roman ruler, like the Persian king five hundred years earlier, was ready to enforce "the Law."

Evidently many of these people were only too ready to listen, if they were allowed, to any who could show them the way out of their darkness into the light and the community of mankind. However, victory lay with the Pharisees (as with the Levites of yore), so that, once more, many of these people had cause to weep, and the catalytic force was preserved intact.

Chapter 10

THE MAN FROM GALILEE

When Jesus was born the vibrant expectation that a marvelous being was about to appear was general among the Judeans. They longed for such proof that Jehovah intended to keep the Covenant with his chosen people, and the scribes, reacting to the pressure of this popular longing, gradually had introduced into the scriptures the idea of the anointed one, the Messiah, who would come to fulfill his bargain.

The *Targums*, the rabbinical commentaries on the Law, said: "How beautiful he is, the Messiah king who shall arise from the house of Judah. He will gird up his loins and advance to do battle with his enemies and *many kings shall be slain.*"

This passage shows what the Judeans had been led to expect. They awaited a militant, avenging Messiah (in the tradition of "all the firstborn of Egypt" and the destruction of Babylon) who would break Judah's enemies "with a rod of iron" and "dash them in pieces like a potter's vase"; who would bring them empire of this world and the literal fulfillment of the tribal Law; for this was what generations of Pharisees and Levites had foretold.

The idea of a lowly Messiah who would say "*love* your enemies" and be "despised and rejected of men, a man of sorrows" was not present in the public mind at all and would have been "despised and rejected," had any called attention to these words of Isaiah (which only gained significance after Jesus had lived and died).

Yet the being who appeared, though he was lowly and taught love, apparently claimed to be this Messiah and was by many so acclaimed!

In few words he swept aside the entire mass of racial politics, which the ruling sect had heaped on the earlier, moral law, and like an excavator revealed again what had been buried. The Pharisees at once recognized a most dangerous "prophet and dreamer of dreams." The fact that he found so large a following among the Judeans shows that, even if the mass of the people wanted a militant, nationalist Messiah who would liberate them from the Romans, many among them must subconsciously have realised that their true captivity was of the spirit and of the Pharisees, more than of the Romans. Nevertheless, the mass responded mechanically to the Pharisaic politicians' charge that the man was a blasphemer and bogus Messiah.

By this response they bequeathed to all future generations of Jews a tormenting doubt, no less insistent because it must not be uttered (for the name Jesus may not even be mentioned in a pious Jewish home): Did the Messiah appear, only to be rejected by the Jews, and if so, what is their future, under The Law?

What manner of man was this? Another paradox in the story of Zion is that in our generation Christian divines and theologians often insist that "Jesus was a Jew," whereas the Judaist elders refuse to allow this (those Zionist rabbis who occasionally tell political or "interfaith" audiences that Jesus was a Jew are not true exceptions to this rule; they would not make the statement among Jews and seek to produce an effect among their non-Jewish listeners, for political reasons).[1]

This public assertion, "Jesus was a Jew," is always used in our century for political purposes. It is often employed to quell objections to the Zionist influence in international politics or to the Zionist invasion of Palestine, the suggestion being that, as Jesus was a Jew, none ought to object to anything purporting to be done in the name of Jews. The irrelevance is obvious, but mobs are moved by such phrases, and the paradoxical result, once again, is that a statement, most offensive to literal Jews, is most frequently made by non- Jewish politicians and ecclesiastics who seek Jewish favour.

The English abbreviation, "Jew," is recent and does not correspond to anything denoted by the Aramaic, Greek or Roman terms for "Judahite" or "Judean," which were in use during the lifetime of Jesus. In fact, the English noun "Jew" cannot be defined (so that dictionaries, which are scrupulously careful about all other words, are reduced to such obvious absurdities as "A person of *Hebrew race*"); and the Zionist state has no legal definition of the term (which is natural, because the Torah, which is *the* Law, exacts pure Judahite descent, and a person of this lineage is hardly to be found in the entire world).

If the statement, "Jesus was a Jew," has meaning therefore, it must apply to the conditions prevailing in his time. In that case it would mean one of three things, or all of them: that Jesus was of the tribe of Judah (therefore Judahite); that he was of Judean domicile (and therefore Judean); that he was religiously "a Jew," if any religion denoted by that term existed in his time.

Race, residence, religion, then. This book is not the place to argue the question of Jesus's racial descent, and the surprising thing is that Christian divines allow themselves some of the statements which they make. The reader should form his own opinion, if he desires to have one in this question.

The genealogy of Mary is not given in the New Testament, but three passages might imply that she was of Davidic descent; St. Matthew and St. Luke trace the descent of Joseph from David and Judah, but Joseph was not

---

[1] Rabbi Stephen Wise, the leading Zionist organizer in the United States during the 1910-1950 period, used this phrase for the obvious political motive, of confusing non-Jewish hearers. Speaking to such an "inter-faith" meeting at the Carnegie Hall at Christmastide 1925, he stated "Jesus was a Jew, not a Christian" (Christianity was born with the *death* of Jesus).
For this he was excommunicated by the Orthodox Rabbis Society of the United States, but a Christian Ministers Association "hailed me as a brother." Rabbi Wise adds the characteristic comment: "I know not which was more hurtful, the acceptance of me as a brother and welcoming me into the Christian fold, or the violent diatribe of the rabbis."

the blood father of Jesus. The *Judaist* authorities discredit all these references to descent, holding that they were inserted to bring the narrative into line with prophecy.

As to residence, St. John states that Jesus was born at Bethlehem in Judea through the chance that his mother had to go there from Galilee to register; the *Judaist* authorities, again, hold that this was inserted to make the account agree with Micah's prophecy that "a ruler" would "come out of Bethlehem."

The *Jewish Encyclopaedia* insists that Nazareth was Jesus's *native* town, and indeed, general agreement exists that he was a Galilean, whatever the chance of his actual birthplace. Galilee, where nearly all his life was spent, was politically entirely separate from Judea, under its own Roman tetrarch, and stood to Judea in the relationship of "a foreign country" (Graetz). Marriage between a Judean and a Galilean was forbidden and even before Jesus's birth all Judeans living in Galilee had been forced by Simon Tharsi, one of the Maccabean princes, to migrate to Judah.

Thus, the Galileans were racially and politically distinct from the Judeans.

Was this Galilean, religiously, what might today be called "a Jew"? The Judaist authorities, of course, deny that most strenuously of all; the statement, often heard from the platform and pulpit, might cause a riot in the synagogue.

It is difficult to see what responsible public men can mean when they use the phrase. There was in the time of Jesus no "Jewish" (or even Judahite or Judaist or Judean) religion. There was Jehovahism, and there were the various sects, Pharisees, Sadducees and Essenes, which disputed violently between themselves and contended, around the temple, for power over the people. They were not only sects, but also political parties, and the most powerful of them were the Pharisees with their "oral traditions" of what God had said to Moses.

If today the Zionists are "the Jews" (and this is the claim accepted by all great Western nations), then the party which in Judea in the time of Jesus corresponded to the Zionists was that of the Pharisees. Jesus brought the whole weight of his attack to bear on these Pharisees. He also rebuked the Sadducees and the scribes, but the Gospels show that he held the Pharisees to be the foe of God and man and that he used an especial scarifying scorn towards them. The things which he singled out for attack, in them and in their creed, are the very things which today's Zionists claim to be the identifying features of Jews, Jewishness and Judaism.

Religiously, Jesus seems beyond doubt to have been the opposite and adversary of all that which would make a literal Jew today or would have made a literal Pharisee then.

None can say with certainty who or what he was, and these suggestive statements by non-Jewish politicians ring as false as the derisive and mocking lampoons about "the bastard" which circulated in the Jewish ghettoes.

What he did and said is of such transcendental importance that nothing else counts. On a much lesser scale Shakespeare's case is somewhat comparable. The quality of inspiration in his works is clear, so that it is of little account whether he wrote them, or who wrote them if he did not, yet the vain argument goes on.

The carpenter's son from Galilee evidently had no formal schooling: "The Jews marvelled, saying, How knoweth this man letters, having never learned?"

What is much more significant, he had known no rabbinical schools or priestly training. His enemies, the Pharisees, testify to that; had he been of their clan or kind they would not have asked, "Whence hath this man this wisdom, and these mighty works."

What gives the teaching of this unlettered young man its effect of blinding revelation, the quality of light first discovered, is the black background, of the Levitical Law and the Pharisaic tradition, against which he moved when he went to Judea. Even today the sudden fullness of enlightenment, in the Sermon on the Mount, dazzles the student who has emerged from a critical perusal of the Old Testament; it is as if high noon came at midnight.

The Law, when Jesus came to "fulfil" it, had grown into a huge mass of legislation, stifling and lethal in its immense complexity. The Torah was but the start; heaped on it were all the interpretations and commentaries and rabbinical rulings; the elders, like pious silkworms, span the thread ever further in the effort to catch up in it every conceivable act of man; generations of lawyers had laboured to reach the conclusion that an egg must not be eaten on the Sabbath day if the greater part of it had been laid before a second star was visible in the sky.

Already the Law and all the commentaries needed a library to themselves, and a committee of international jurists, called to give an opinion on it, would have required years to sift the accumulated layers.

The unschooled youth from Galilee reached out a finger and thrust aside the entire mass, revealing at once the truth and the heresy. He reduced "all the Law and the Prophets" to the two commandments, Love God with all thy heart and thy neighbour as thyself.

This was the exposure and condemnation of the basic heresy which the Levites and Pharisees, in the course of centuries, had woven into the Law.

Leviticus contained the injunction, "Love thy neighbour as thyself," but it was governed by the limitation of "neighbour" to fellow- Judeans. Jesus now reinstated the forgotten, earlier tradition, of neighbourly love irrespective of race or creed; this was clearly what he meant by the words, "I am not come to destroy the law, but to fulfil." He made his meaning plain when he added, "Ye have heard that it hath been said ... hate thine enemy. But I say unto you, Love your enemy." (The artful objection is sometimes made that the specific commandment, "Hate thine enemy," nowhere appears in the Old Testament. Jesus's meaning was clear; the innumerable injunctions to the murder and massacre of neighbours who were not "neighbours," in which the Old Testament abounds, certainly required hatred and enmity).

This was a direct challenge to The Law as the Pharisees represented it, and Jesus carried the challenge further by deliberately refusing to play the part of the nationalist liberator and conqueror of territory for which the prophecies had cast the Messiah. Probably he could have had a much larger following, and possibly the support of the Pharisees, if he had accepted that role.

His rebuke, again, was terse and clear: "My kingdom is *not of this world* ... The kingdom of Heaven is *within you* ... Lay not up for yourselves treasures upon earth ... but lay up for yourselves treasures in heaven, where neither moth nor rust doth corrupt, and where thieves do not break through nor steal."

Everything he said, in such simple words as these, was a quiet, but direct challenge to the most powerful men of his time and place, and a blow at the foundations of the creed which the sect had built up in the course of centuries.

What the entire Old Testament taught in hundreds of pages, the Sermon on the Mount confuted in a few words. It opposed love to hatred, mercy to vengeance, charity to malice, neighbourliness to segregation, justice to discrimination, affirmation (or reaffirmation) to denial, and life to death. It began (like the "blessings-or-cursings" chapters of *Deuteronomy)* with blessings, but there the resemblance ended.

Deuteronomy offered material blessings, in the form of territory, loot and slaughter, in return for strict performance of thousands of "statutes and judgments," some of them enjoining murder. The Sermon on the Mount offered no material rewards, but simply taught that moral behaviour, humility, the effort to do right, mercy, purity, peaceableness and fortitude would be blessed for their own sake and receive spiritual reward.

Deuteronomy followed its "blessings" with "cursings." The Sermon on the Mount made no threats; it did not require that the transgressor be "stoned to death" or "hanged on a tree," or offer absolution for non-observance at the price of washing the hands in the blood of a heifer. The worst that was to befall the sinner was that he was to be "the least in the kingdom of heaven"; and most that the obedient might expect was to be "called great in the kingdom of heaven."

The young Galilean never taught subservience, only an *inner* humility, and in one direction he was consistently and constantly scornful: in his attack on the Pharisees.

The name, Pharisees, denoted that they "kept away from persons or things impure." The *Jewish Encyclopaedia* says, "Only in regard to intercourse with the unclean and the unwashed multitude did Jesus differ widely from the Pharisees." Echo may answer, "Only!" This was of course the great cleavage, between the idea of the tribal deity and the idea of the universal god; between the creed of hatred and the teaching of love. The challenge was clear and the Pharisees accepted it at once. They began to bait their traps, in the very manner described by Jeremiah long before: "All my familiars watched for my halting, saying, Peradventure he will be enticed, and we shall prevail against him, and we shall take our revenge on him."

The Pharisees watched him and asked, "Why eateth your Master with publicans and sinners" (a penal offence under their Law). He was equally their master in debate and in eluding their baited traps, and answered, swiftly but quietly, "They that be whole need not a physician, but they that are sick … I am not come to call the righteous, but sinners to repentance."

They followed him further and saw his disciples plucking ears of corn to eat on the Sabbath (another offence under the Law), "Behold, thy disciples do that which is not lawful to do upon the Sabbath day." They pursued him with such interrogations, always related to the rite, and never to faith or behaviour; "why do thy disciples transgress the tradition of the elders, for they wash not their hands when they eat bread?" "Ye hypocrites, well did Esaias prophecy of you, saying, this people draweth nigh unto me with their mouth and honoureth me with their lips; but their heart is far from me. But in vain do they worship me, teaching for doctrines *the commandments of men*."

This was the lie direct: The Law, he charged, was not *God's* law, but the law of the Levites and Pharisees: "the commandments of men"!

From this moment there could be no compromise, for Jesus turned away from the Pharisees and "called the multitude, and said unto them, Hear, and understand: Not that which goeth into the mouth defileth a man, but that which cometh out of the mouth, this defileth a man."

With these words Jesus cast public scorn on one of the most jealously-guarded of the priestly prerogatives, involving the great mass of dietary laws with the whole ritual of slaughter, draining of blood, rejection of "that which dieth of itself," and so on. All this was undoubtedly a "commandment of man," although attributed to Moses, and strict observance of this dietary ritual was held to be of the highest importance by the Pharisees, Ezekiel (the reader will recall) on being commanded by the Lord to eat excrement "to atone for the iniquities of the people," had pleaded his unfailing observance of the dietary laws and had had his ordeal somewhat mitigated on that account. Even the disciples were apparently so much under the influence of this dietary tradition that they could not understand how "that which cometh out of the mouth" could defile a man, rather than that which went in, and asked for an explanation, remarking that the Pharisees "were offended, after they heard this saying."

The simple truth which Jesus then gave them was abominable heresy to the Pharisees: "Do not ye understand, that what whatsoever entereth in at the mouth goeth into the belly, and is cast out into the draught? But those things which proceed out of the mouth come forth from the heart; and they defile the man. For out of the heart proceed evil thoughts, murders, adulteries, fornications, thefts, false witness, blasphemies: these are the things which defile a man; *but to eat with unwashen hands defileth not a man.*"

This last remark was another penal offence under the Law and the Pharisees began to gather for the kill. They prepared the famous trick questions: "Then went the Pharisees and took counsel how they might entangle him in his talk." The two chief questions were, "To whom shall we render tribute?" and "Who then is my neighbour?" A wrong answer to the first would deliver him to punishment by the foreign ruler, Rome. A wrong answer to the second would enable the Pharisees to denounce him to the foreign ruler as an offender against their own Law, and to demand his punishment.

This is the method earlier pictured by Jeremiah and still in use today, in the Twentieth Century. All who have had to do with public debate in our time, know the trick question, carefully prepared beforehand, and the difficulty of answering it on the spur of the moment. Various methods of eluding the trap are known to professional debaters (for instance, to say "No comment," or to reply with another question). To give a complete *answer*, instead of resorting to such evasions, and in so doing to avoid the trap of incrimination and yet maintain the principle at stake is one of the most difficult things known to man. It demands the highest qualities of quick-wittedness, presence of mind and clarity of thought. The answers given by Jesus to these two questions remain for all time the models, which mortal man can only hope to emulate.

"Tell us therefore, What thinkest thou? Is it lawful to give tribute unto Caesar, or not?" (the affable tone of honest enquiry can be heard). "But Jesus perceived their wickedness and said, Why tempt ye me, ye hypocrites? ... Render unto Caesar the things which are Caesar's; and unto God the things that are God's. When they heard these words, they marvelled, and left him and went their way."

On the second occasion, "a certain lawyer stood up and tempted him, saying, what shall I do to inherit eternal life?" In his answer Jesus again swept aside the great mass of Levitical Law and restated the two essentials: "Thou shalt love the Lord thy God with all thy heart ... and thy neighbour as thyself." Then came the baited trap: "And who *is* my neighbour?"

What mortal man would have given the answer that Jesus gave? No doubt some mortal men, knowing like Jesus that their lives were at stake, would have said what they believed, for martyrs are by no means rare. But Jesus did much more than that; he disarmed his questioner like an expert swordsman who effortlessly sends his opponent's rapier spinning into the air. He was being enticed to declare himself openly; to say that "the heathen" were also "neighbours," and thus to convict himself of transgressing The Law. In fact he replied in this sense, but in such a way that the interrogator was undone; seldom was a lawyer so confounded.

The Levitical-Pharisaic teaching was that only Judeans were "neighbours," and of all the outcast heathen they especially abominated the Samaritans (for reasons earlier indicated). The mere touch of a Samaritan was defilement and a major "transgression" (this continues true to the present day). The purpose of the question put to him was to lure Jesus into some statement that would qualify him for the major ban; by choosing the Samaritans, of all peoples, for the purpose of his reply, he displayed an audacity, or genius, that was more than human:

He said that a certain man fell among thieves and was left for dead. Then came "a priest" and "likewise a Levite" (the usual stinging rebuke to those who sought the chance to put him to death), who "passed by on the other side." Last came "a certain Samaritan," who bound the man's injuries, took him to an inn, and paid for his care: "which now of these three, thinkest thou, was neighbour unto him that fell among the thieves?"

The lawyer, cornered, could not bring himself to pronounce the defiling name "Samaritan"; he said, "He that showed mercy on him" and thereby joined himself (as he probably realized too late) with the condemnation of those for whom he spoke, such as "the priest" and "the Levite." "Then said Jesus unto him, Go, and do thou likewise." In these few words, and without any direct allusion, he made his interrogator destroy, out of his own mouth, the entire racial heresy on which the Law had been raised.

One moderate Judaist critic, Mr Montefiore, has made the complaint that Jesus made one exception to his rule of "love thine enemies"; he never said a good word for the Pharisees.

Scholars may debate the point. Jesus knew that they would kill him or any man who exposed them. It is true that he especially arraigned the Pharisees, together with the scribes, and plainly saw in them the sect responsible for the perversion of the Law, so that the entire literature of denunciation contains nothing to equal this:

"Woe unto you, scribes and Pharisees, hypocrites! for ye shut up the kingdom of heaven against men; for ye neither go in yourselves neither suffer ye them that are entering to go in … ye compass sea and land to make one proselyte, and when he is made, ye make him twofold more the child of hell than yourselves … ye pay tithe of mint and anise and cummin, and have omitted the *weightier matters of the law, judgment, mercy and faith* ... ye make clean the outside of the cup and of the platter, but within they are full of extortion and excess ... ye are like unto whited sepulchres, which indeed appear beautiful outward, but are within full of dead men's bones, and of all uncleanness ... ye build the tombs of the prophets, and garnish the sepulchres of the righteous, and say, if we had been in the days of our fathers, *we would not have partaken with them in the blood of the prophets. Wherefore ye be witnesses unto yourselves that ye are the children of them which killed the prophets. Fill ye up then the measure of your fathers.* Ye serpents, ye generation of vipers ..."

Some critics profess to find the last six words surprisingly harsh. However, if they are read in the context of the three sentences which precede them they are seen to be an explicit allusion to his approaching end, made by a man about to die to those who were about to put him to death, and at such a moment hardly any words could be hard enough. (However, even the deadly reproach, "Fill ye up then the measure of your fathers," had a later sequel: "Father, forgive them; for they know not what they do.")

The end approached. The "chief priests, and the scribes, and the elders" (the Sanhedrin) met under the high priest Caiaphas to concert measures against the man who disputed their authority and their Law. The only Judean among the Galilean disciples, Judas Iscariot, led the "great multitude with swords and staves," sent by the "chief priests and elders of the people," to the garden of Gethsemane and identified the man they sought by the kiss of death.

This Judas deserves a passing glance. He was twice canonized in the Twentieth Century, once in Russia after the Bolshevist Revolution, and again in Germany after the defeat of Hitler, and these two episodes indicated that the sect which was more powerful than Rome, in Jerusalem at the start of our era, was once more supremely powerful in the West in the Twentieth Century.

According to St. Matthew, Judas later hanged himself and if he thus chose the form of death "accursed of God," his deed presumably brought him no happiness. To Zionist historians of Dr. Kastein's school Judas is a sympathetic figure; Dr. Kastein explains that he was a good man who became disappointed with Jesus and therefore "secretly broke" with him (the words "secretly broke" could only occur in Zionist literature).

The Pharisees, who controlled the Sanhedrin, tried Jesus first, before what would today be called "a Jewish court." Possibly "a people's court" would be a more accurate description in today's idiom, for he was "fingered" by an informer, seized by a mob, hailed before a tribunal without legitimate authority, and condemned to death after false witnesses had spoken to trumped-up charges.

However, the "elders," who from this point on took charge of events in exactly the same way as the "advisers" of our century control events, devised the charge which deserved death equally under their "Law" and under the law of the Roman ruler. Under "the Mosaic Law," Jesus had committed blasphemy by claiming to be the Messiah; under the Roman law, he had committed treason by claiming to be the king of the Jews.

The Roman governor, Pilate, tried one device after another, to avoid complying with the demand of these imperious "elders," that the man be put to death.

This Pilate was the prototype of the Twentieth Century British and American politician. He feared the power of the sect in the last resort, more than anything else. His wife urged him to have no truck with the business. He tried, in the politician's way, to pass the responsibility to another, Herod Antipas, whose tetrarchy included Galilee; Herod sent it back to him. Pilate next tried to let Jesus off with a scourging, but the Pharisees insisted on death and threatened to denounce Pilate in Rome: "Thou art not Caesar's friend."

This was the threat to which Pilate yielded, just as one British Governor after another, one United Nations representative after another, yielded in the Twentieth Century to the threat that they would be defamed in London or New York. Evidently Pilate, like these men nineteen centuries later, knew that his home government would disavow or displace him if he refused to do as he was bid.

The resemblance between Pilate and some British governors of the period between the First and Second World Wars is strong, (and at least one of these men knew it, for when he telephoned to a powerful Zionist rabbi in New York he jocularly asked, as he relates, that the High Priest Caiaphas be informed that Pontius Pilate was on the line).

Pilate made one other attempt to have the actual deed done by other hands: "Take ye him, and judge him according to *your* law." With the ease of long experience it was foiled: "it is not lawful for *us* to put any man to death."

After that he even tried to save Jesus by giving "the people" the choice between pardoning Jesus or Barabbas, the robber and murderer. Presumably Pilate had small hope from this quarter, for "the people" and "the mob" are synonyms and justice and mercy never yet came from a mob, as Pilate would have known; the function of the mob is always to do the will of powerful sects. Thus, "the chief priests and elders *persuaded the multitude* that they should ask Barabbas, and destroy Jesus."

In this persuasion of the multitude the sect is equally powerful today.

The longer the time that passes, the more brightly glow the colours of that unique final scene. The scarlet robe, mock sceptre, crown of thorns and derisive pantomime of homage; only Pharisaic minds could have devised that ritual of mockery which today so greatly strengthens the effect of the victim's victory. The road to Calvary, the crucifixion between two thieves: Rome, on that day, did the bidding of the Pharisees, as Persia, five hundred years before, had done that of the Levites.

These Pharisees had taught the people of Judea to expect a Messiah, and now had crucified the first claimant. That meant that the Messiah was still to come. According to the Pharisees the Davidic king had yet to appear and claim his empire of the world, and that is still the situation today.

Dr. Kastein, in his survey of Judaism from its start, devotes a chapter to the life of Jesus. After explaining that Jesus was a failure, he dismissed the episode with the characteristic words, "His life and death are *our* affair."

Douglas Reed

Chapter 11

THE PHARISAIC PHOENIX

Then comes the familiar, recurrent paradox; the catastrophe of Judea, which followed within a few decades of the death of Jesus, was the triumph of the Pharisees, for it left them supreme in Jewry. By the crucifixion of Jesus they rid themselves of a "prophet and dreamer" who would have cast down their Law. The brief remaining years of Judea rid them of all other parties that contended with them for power *under* that Law.

After the death of Jesus the Pharisees, according to the *Jewish Encyclopaedia,* found "a supporter and friend" in the last Herodian king of Judea, Agrippa I. Agrippa helped dispose of the Sadducees, who disappeared from the Judean scene, leaving all affairs there in the hands of the Pharisees (whose complaint about the Idumean line, therefore, seems to have little ground). They were thus left all-powerful in Jerusalem, like the Levites after the severance of Judah from Israel, and as on that earlier occasion disaster at once followed. In rising, phoenix-like, from the ashes of this, the Pharisees also repeated the history of the Levites.

During the few remaining years of the tiny and riven province the Pharisees once more revised "the Law," those "commandments of *men*" which Jesus had most scathingly attacked. Dr. Kastein says, *"Jewish life was regulated by the teachings of the Pharisees; the whole history of Judaism was reconstructed from the Pharisaic point of view ... Pharisaism shaped the character of Judaism and the life and the thought of the Jew for all the future.... It makes 'separatism' its chief characteristic."*

Thus, in the immediate sequel to Jesus's life and arraignment of the "commandments of men," the Pharisees, like the Levites earlier, intensified the racial and tribal nature and rigour of the Law; the creed of destruction, enslavement and dominion was sharpened on the eve of the people's final dispersion.

Dr. Kastein's words are of especial interest. He had earlier stated (as quoted) that after the infliction of the "New Covenant" on the Judahites by Nehemiah, the Torah received a "final" editing, and that "no word" of it was thereafter to be changed. Moreover, at the time of this Pharisaic "reconstruction" the Old Testament had already been translated into Greek, so that further changes made by the Pharisees could only have been in the original.

It seems more probable that Dr. Kastein's statement refers to the Talmud, the immense continuation of the Torah which was apparently begun during the last years of Judea, although it was not reduced to writing until much later. Whatever happened, "the life and the thought of the Jew" were once again settled "for all the future," and "separatism" was reaffirmed as the supreme tenet of the Law.

In AD 70, perhaps thirty-five years after the death of Jesus, all fell to pieces. The confusion and disorder in Judea were incurable and Rome stepped in. The Pharisees, who had originally invited Roman intervention and were supreme in Judea under the Romans, remained passive.

Other peoples of Palestine, and most especially the Galileans, would not submit to Rome and after many risings and campaigns the Romans entered and razed Jerusalem. Judea was declared conquered territory and the name vanished from the map. For long periods during the next nineteen hundred years no Jews at all lived in Jerusalem (the Samaritans, a tiny remnant of whom have survived all the persecutions, are the only people who have lived continuously in Palestine since Old Testamentary times).

Dr. Kastein calls the seventy years which ended with the Roman destruction of Jerusalem "The Heroic Age," presumably because of the Pharisaic triumph over all others in the contest for the soul of Judaism. He can hardly intend to apply the adjective to the fighting against the Romans, as this was so largely done by the alien Galileans, of whom he is no admirer.

Chapter 12

THE LIGHT AND THE SHADOW

Before Jerusalem fell in 70 AD two bands of travellers passed through its gates. The disciples bore a new message to mankind, for Christianity had been born. The Pharisees, foreseeing the fate which they had brought on Jerusalem, removed to a new headquarters from which (as from Babylon of yore) the ruling sect might exercise command over "the Jews," wherever in the world they lived.

These two small groups of travellers were the vanguard of parties of light and of darkness which, like a man and his shadow, have gone ever since through the centuries, and ever westward.

The crisis of "the West" today traces directly back to that departure from doomed Jerusalem nineteen centuries ago, for the two groups bore into the West ideas that could never be reconciled. One had to prevail over the other, sooner or later, and the great bid for victory of the destructive idea is being witnessed in our generation.

In the centuries between the story of the West was always, in essentials, that of the struggle between the two ideas. When "the Law" according to the Levites and Pharisees was in the ascendant, the West made slaves of men, brought heretics before an inquisition, put apostates to death, and yielded to primitive visions of master-racehood; thus the Twentieth Century was the time of the worst backsliding in the West. When the West made men and nations free, established justice between them, set up the right of fair and open trial, repudiated master-racehood and acknowledged the universal fatherhood of God, it followed the teaching of him who had come to "*fulfil* the Law.*"

The Romans, when they took Jerusalem, struck medals with the inscription, "Judaea devicta, Judaea capta." This was a premature paean; Jerusalem might be ruined and Judea be empty of Jews, but the ruling sect was free and victorious. Its opponents around the temple had been swept away by the conqueror and it was already established in its new "centre," to which it had withdrawn before the fall of the city.

The Pharisees were as supreme in this new citadel as the Levites once in Babylon, but in the outer world they espied a new enemy. The sect which believed that the Messiah had appeared, and called itself Christian, did not acknowledge this enmity; on the contrary, its ruling tenet was "love your enemies." But as the first tenet of the Pharisaic law was "hate your enemies," this was in itself a deliberate affront and challenge to the elders in their retreat.

They saw from the start that the new religion would have to be destroyed if their "Law" were to prevail, and they were not deterred by the warning voices which (at this juncture as on all earlier and later occasions) were heard within their own ranks; for instance, Gamaliel's words when the high priest and council were about to have Peter and John scourged for preaching in the temple: "Consider well what you are about to do. If this be the work of men, it will soon fall to nothing; but if it be the work of God you cannot destroy it." The majority of the Pharisees felt strong enough, in their own manmade Law, to "destroy it," and if necessary to work for centuries at that task.

Thus the Pharisees, when they left the surviving Judeans to their fate and set up their new headquarters at Jamnia (still in Palestine), took their dark secrets of power over men into a world different from any before it.

Previously their tribal creed had been one among many tribal creeds. Blood vengeance had been the rule among all men and clans. The neighbouring "heathen" might have been alarmed by the especial fierceness and vindictiveness of the Judaic creed, but had not offered anything much more enlightened. From this time on, however, the ruling sect was confronted by a creed which directly controverted every tenet of their own "Law," as white controverts black. Moreover, this new idea in the world, by the manner and place of its birth, was forever a rebuke to themselves.

The Pharisees in their stronghold prepared to vanquish this new force that had risen in the world. Their task was larger than that of the Levites in Babylon. The temple was destroyed and Jerusalem was depopulated. The tribe of Judah had long since been broken up; now the race of Judeans was dissolving. There remained a "Jewish nation," composed of people of many admixtures of blood, who were spread all over the known world, and had to be kept united by the power of the tribal idea and of the "return" to a land "promised" to a "special people"; this dispersed nation had also to be kept convinced of its destructive mission among the nations where it dwelt.

"The Law," in the form that was already becoming known to the outer world, could not again be amended, or new historical chapters be added to it. Moreover, Jesus had addressed his rebukes specifically to the falsification of these "commandments of men" by the scribes. He had been killed but not controverted or even (as the growth of the Christian sect showed) given his quietus. Thus his arraignment of the Law stood and was so conclusive that not even the Pharisees could expect to convince anybody simply by calling him a transgressor of it.

Nevertheless, the Law needed constant reinterpretation and application to the events of changing times, so that the "special people" could always be shown that each and every event, however paradoxical at first sight, was in fact one of Jehovan fulfilment. The Pharisees at Jamnia invoked once more their claim to possess the oral secrets of God and began, under it, to reinterpret the "statutes and commandments" so that these could be shown to apply to Christianity. This was the origin of the Talmud, which in effect is the anti-Christian extension of the Torah.

The Talmud became, in the course of centuries, "the fence around the Law"; the outer tribal stockade around the inner tribal stockade. The significance lies in the period at which it was begun: when Judea was gone, when "the people" were scattered among all nations, and when a new religion was taking shape which taught that God was the father of all men, not merely the patron of a selected tribe.

Looking back from this distance of time, the task which the Pharisees undertook looks hopeless, for the wish to become part of mankind must surely have had strong appeal to a scattered people.

The Pharisees, as the event has proved, were successful in their huge undertaking. The Talmud was effective in interposing a fence between the Jews and the forces of integration released by Christianity.

Two examples from our present time illustrate the effect of the Talmud, many centuries after its compilation. The brothers Thoreau in their books give the diligent student some rare glimpses behind the Talmudic walls; in one book they depict the little Jewish boy in Poland who had been taught to spit, quite mechanically, as he passed the wayside Calvary and to say, "Cursed be thou who created another religion." In 1953, in New York, a young missionary of the Moravian Church in Jerusalem described the seizure by the Zionists of the Moravian leper home there, called "The Jesus Mission"; their first act was to putty over the name "Jesus" which for more than a hundred years had been inscribed above its door.

Such incidents as these (and the ban on the mention of the name Jesus) derive directly from the teaching of the Talmud, which in effect was another "New Law" with a specifically anti-Christian application. For this reason the next period in the story of Zion is best described as that of the Talmudists, the former ones being those of the Pharisees and of the Levites.

While the Pharisaic Talmudists, in their new academy at Jamnia, worked on the new Law, the tidings of Jesus's life and lesson spread through the territories of Rome.

A Pharisee greatly helped to spread them; Saul of Tarsus set out from Jerusalem (before its fall) to exterminate heretics in Damascus and before he arrived there became a follower of Christ. He preached to Jew and Gentile alike, until he was prevented, and he told the Jews, "It was necessary that the word of God should first have been spoken to you; but seeing that ye put it from you and judge yourselves worthy of everlasting life, we turn to the Gentiles."

Dr. Kastein says of Saul, named Paul, that "he made all those whom he persuaded to believe in his prophecy renegades in the widest sense, whether they were Jew or Gentile."

However, what Paul (and others) said was in fact inevitable at that point in time, because men everywhere were groping towards the universal God and turned to the teaching of Jesus as growing things to the light. Possibly this impulse in men was also the reason why Jesus had to appear *among* the Judeans; the Judaic creed was tribalism in its most fanatical form, even at that time, and, as every action produces its reaction, the counter-idea was bound to appear where the pressure was greatest.

This was a fateful moment for that great area, then little known or populated, which today is called The West. Had not the disciples turned their faces westward, the term, "the West," and that which it denotes, might never have come about.

What is called "Western civilization" cannot be conceived without Christianity. During the nineteen hundred years which followed the death of Jesus the West improved so greatly that it left the rest of the world behind. In material things its advance was so great that at the time when this book was written it was on the brink of the conquest of space; it was about to open the universe to exploration by man. But that was much the lesser part of its achievement.

Its greatest improvement was in the field of the spirit and of man's behaviour towards man. The West established men's right to public charge and open trial, or release, (a right which was again in jeopardy in the Twentieth Century) and this was the greatest advance in the entire history of man; on the survival or destruction of this achievement depends his future.

The shadow that followed the disciples out of the gates of Jerusalem, before the Romans entered, also followed Christianity into the West and the Talmudic sect dogged it during all those centuries. The West, in the Twentieth Century, became the scene of the struggle between the nations which had risen with Christianity and the sect dedicated to the destructive idea.

Not only the West is involved in its issue. About five hundred years after the life of Jesus the instinctive impulse of men to seek one God produced another challenge to Talmudic racialism, and this time it came from among the Semitic masses. The Arabs, too, attained to the concept of one God of all men.

Muhammad (dismissed by Dr. Kastein as "a half-educated Bedouin"), like Saul on the road to Damascus, had a vision of God. His teaching in many ways resembled that of Jesus. He held Jesus to have been, like Abraham and Moses, a prophet of God (not the Messiah). He regarded himself as the successor of Moses and Jesus and as the prophet of God, whom he called Allah. There was but *one* God, Allah, the creator of mankind, and Allah was *not* the tribal god of the Arabs, but *the God of all men.*

This religion, like Christianity, taught no hatred of other religions. Muhammad showed only reverence for Jesus and his mother (who are both the subjects of profane derision in Talmudic literature).

However, Muhammad held the Jews to be a destructive force, self-dedicated. The Koran says of them, "*Oft as they kindle a beacon fire for war, shall God quench it. And their aim will be to abet disorder on the earth; but God loveth not the abettors of disorder.*" All down the centuries the wisest men spoke thus of the tribal creed and the sect, until the Twentieth Century of our era, when public discussion of this question was virtually suppressed.

Thus was Islam born, and it spread over the meridianal parts of the known world as Christianity spread over the West and Buddhism, earlier, over the East. Great streams began to move, as if towards a confluence at some distant day, for these universal religions are in no major tenet as oil and water, and in the repudiation of master-racehood and the destructive idea they agree.

Christianity and Islam spread out and embraced great masses of mankind; the impulse that moved in men became clear. Far behind these universal religions lay Judaism, in its tribal enclosure, jealously guarded by the inner sect.

In the Twentieth Century this powerful sect was able to bring the masses of Christendom and Islam to the verge of destructive battle with each other. If the present generation sees that clash, the spectacle will be that of one great universal religion contending with another for the purpose of setting up the creed of the "master-race."

Towards this strange denouement, nineteen centuries ahead, the two parties of men set out from Jerusalem long ago.

Chapter 13

THE FENCE AROUND THE LAW

The story of Zion, from its start, falls into five distinct phases: those of the Levites, the Pharisees, the Talmudists, the "emancipation" interlude and the Zionists. This narrative has now reached the third phase.

The Levitical phase was that of isolated Judah, the Babylonian "captivity" and "return," and the production and enforcement of "the Mosaic Law." The Pharisaic phase, which followed and roughly coincided with the Roman overlordship of the province of Judea, ended with the second destruction of Jerusalem, the dispersion of the last Judeans, the Pharisaic supremacy and the withdrawal of the "government" to its new "centre" at Jamnia.

The third, Talmudic phase was much the longest for it lasted seventeen centuries, from 70 AD to about 1800 AD. During this period the Jews entered the West and the "government," from a succession of "centres," worked tirelessly to keep the dispersed nation under its control, subject to "the Law," and separate from other peoples.

As this was also the period of Western civilization and of the rise of Christianity, it was inevitable that Christendom specifically (and not merely the generic "heathen," or "strangers," or "other gods") should become the chief target of the Law's destructive commands. In the eyes of the dominant sect and its devotees, this period, which seems so long and important to Western minds, was essentially as insignificant as the Babylonian period. The fact that the one lasted seventeen centuries and the other fifty years made no real difference: both were merely periods of "exile" for the special people; and under the Law the long Western episode, like the short Babylonian one, was ordained to terminate in disaster for the "captors," a Jewish triumph and a new "return," all of which some new Daniel would interpret in those terms.

The seventeen centuries represented a new "captivity," under the Law, which laid down that wherever the chosen people dwelt outside Jerusalem they were in captivity, and that this captivity was in itself "persecution."

To a literal Zionist like Dr. Kastein, therefore, the seventeen centuries which saw the rise of Christendom form a page of history which is blank save for the record of "Jewish persecution" inscribed on it. The rest was all sound and fury, signifying nothing; it was a period of time during which Jehovah used the heathen to plague the Jews while he prepared the triumph of his special people; and for what they did the heathen have yet to pay (he cries). The one positive result of the seventeen Christian centuries, for him, is that the Jews emerged from them still segregated from mankind, thanks to their Talmudic governors.

Certainly this was an astounding feat; in the entire history of negative achievement, nothing can approach the results obtained by the elders of Zion. In the Talmud they built that "fence around the Law" which successfully withstood, during seventeen hundred years, all the centrifugal forces which attracted the Jews towards mankind.

While they reinforced their stockade, European men, having accepted Christianity, toiled through the centuries to apply its moral law to daily life, by abolishing serfdom and slavery, reducing privilege and inequality and generally raising the dignity of man. This process was known as "emancipation" and by the year 1800 it was about to prevail over the system of absolute rulers and privileged castes.

The Jews, directed by their Talmudic rulers, took a leading part in the struggle for emancipation. That in itself was fair enough. The masses of Christendom held from the start that the liberties to be won should ultimately accrue to all men, without distinction of race, class or creed; that was the very meaning of the struggle itself, and anything else or less would have made it meaningless.

Nevertheless, in the case of the Jews there was an obvious paradox which repeatedly baffled and alarmed the peoples among whom they dwelt: The Jewish Law expressed the theory of the master-race in the most arrogant and vindictive form conceivable to the human imagination; how then could the Jews attack nationhood in others? Why did the Jews demand the levelling of barriers between men when they built an ever stronger barrier between the Jews and other men? How could people, who claimed that God had made the very world itself for them to rule, and forbade them to mix with lesser breeds, complain of discrimination?

Now that another hundred and fifty years have passed, the answer to such questions has been given by events.

It was true that the Jewish clamour for emancipation was not truly concerned with the great idea or principle at issue: human liberty. The Judaic Law denied that idea and principle. The Talmudic governors of Jewry saw that the quickest way to remove the barriers between themselves and power over nations was to destroy legitimate government in these nations; and the quickest way to that end was to cry "emancipation!."

Thus the door opened by emancipation could be used to introduce the permanent revolutionary force into the life of nations; with the destruction of all legitimate government, the revolutionaries would succeed to power, and these revolutionaries would be Talmud- trained and Talmud-controlled. They would act always under the Mosaic Law, and in this way the end of Babylon could be reproduced in the West.

The evidence of events in the Twentieth Century now shows that this was the plan to which the Talmudic elders worked during the third phase of the story of Zion, from 70 AD to about 1800 AD. Thus there was the widest possible difference in the understanding of "emancipation" by the Christianized European peoples among whom the Jews dwelt and among the Talmudic rulers of the Jews. For the great mass of peoples emancipation represented an end: the end of servitude. For the powerful, secret sect it represented a means to the opposite end; the imposition of a new and harsher servitude.

One great danger attended this undertaking. It was, that the destruction of barriers between men might also destroy the barrier between the Jews and other men; this would have destroyed the plan itself, for that force would have been dispersed which was to be used, emancipation once gained, to "pull down and destroy" the nations.

This very nearly happened in the fourth phase of the story of Zion; the century of emancipation (say, from 1800 to 1900 AD) brought the peril of "assimilation." In the century of "freedom" a great number of Jews, in Western Europe and in the new "West" oversea, did evince the desire to cast off the chains of the Judaic Law and to mingle themselves with the life of peoples. For that reason our Zionist historian, Dr. Kastein, considers the Nineteenth Century to be the darkest age in all Jewish history, fraught with the deadly peril of involvement in mankind, which happily was averted. He cannot contemplate without horror the destruction, through assimilation, of the Judaic barriers of race and creed. Thus he calls the Nineteenth Century movement towards emancipation "retrograde" and thanks God that "the Zionist ideology" preserved the Jews from the fate of assimilation.

That led to the fifth phase, the one which began in about 1900 and in which we live. The Talmudic stockade held fast and at the end of the fourth phase the Jews, fully "emancipated" in the Western understanding, were still segregated under their own Law. Those who tended to escape, towards "assimilation," were then drawn back into the tribal enclosure by the mystic power of nationalism.

Using the power over governments which it had gained through emancipation, the ruling sect achieved a second "return" to the chosen land, and thus re-established the Law of 458 BC, with its destructive and imperial mission. A chauvinist fever, which yet must run its course, was injected into the veins of world Jewry; the great power wielded over Western governments was used to a co-ordinated end; and the whole destructive ordeal of the West in the Twentieth Century was related to and dominated by the ancient ambition of Zion, revived from antiquity to become the dogma of Western politics.

This fifth phase is about fifty-five years old as the present book is written, and its first results are formidable. The "Mosaic Law" has been superimposed on the life of Western peoples, which in fact is governed by that law, not by any law of their own. The political and military operations of two world wars have been diverted to promote the Zionist ambition and the life and treasure of the West have been poured out in support of it.

Forty years of continuous bloodshed in Palestine have obviously been but the prelude to what is yet to come there. Any third world war may begin and spread outward from Palestine, and if one were to start elsewhere it would in its course foreseeably revolve around and turn on the ambition of Zion, which will not be fulfilled until a much greater area in the Middle East has been conquered, "other Gods" have been thrown down, and "all nations" have been enslaved.

Dr. Kastein sees in this fifth phase the golden age when "history may be resumed" (after the meaningless interregnum known as the Christian era) and Zionism, as "the possessor of a world mission," will re-enter into a destined inheritance, culminating in world dominion, of which it was criminally dispossessed in AD 70 (when "history" was interrupted).

This narrative has now reached the third of these five phases, the long one when the Talmudic scribes in the Academy at Jamnia began with infinite industry to spin The Law into a much greater web, of endless ramifications, from which a Jew could hardly escape without dire penalty. By means of it the seemingly impossible was achieved: a breed of people dispersed throughout the world was for seventeen hundred years kept apart from mankind and was trained for a destructive task in the Twentieth Century of the Christian era. Some account of that remarkable period of preparation and organization, when a fence was built around the Judaic Law, so that "liberty" should not absorb the special people or weaken their destructive force, is here appropriate.

Chapter 14

THE MOVABLE GOVERNMENT

The Pharisaic elders who moved to Jamnia from Jerusalem before its destruction in 70 AD intended, like the Levites in Babylon earlier, to set up a centre of power and remote-control, from which they might keep in subjection a tribal organization, by that time distributed over the earth. They took with them to Jamnia the accumulated experience of Jerusalem and Babylon and the stored secrets of ages and they succeeded in establishing a mobile government which has continued to exercise authority over the Jews until the present day.

Before the last battles with Rome (says Dr. Kastein) "a group of teachers, scholars and educators repaired to Jamnia, taking the fate of their people on their shoulders so as to be responsible for it through the ages ... At Jamnia the central body for the administration of the Jewish people was established ... As a rule, when a nation has been utterly routed as the Jews were on this occasion, they perish altogether. But the Jewish people did not perish ... They had already learnt how to change their attitude during the Babylonian captivity ... And they followed a similar course now."

At Jamnia the Old Sanhedrin, the source of all legislative, administrative and judicial authority, was established under a new name. In addition, an academy was created for the further development of The Law. In it, the scribes continued the revelation of Jehovah's mind and the interpretation of The Law, so often said to have been put in its final form. In fact, as the dogma is that the Law governs every act of human life in circumstances which continually change, it never could or can be finally codified and must ever be expanded.

Apart from that permanent reason for revision, the new factor, Christianity, had arisen and the Law's application to it had to be defined. Thus the Torah (the Law) began to receive its huge supplement, the Talmud, which was of equal or greater authority.

From Jamnia the Law was administered which "raised an insuperable barrier against the outside world," enforced a discipline "*rigid to the point of deadliness*," and "kept proselytes at arm's length." The aim was to "make the life of the Jew utterly different from that of the Gentiles." Any law that received a majority of votes of the Sanhedrin became enforceable throughout the dispersed Judaist communities everywhere; "opponents were threatened with the ban, which meant being excluded from the community."

In this way, "the centre of the circle was finally fixed, and the circle itself fully described in the form of the law and the hedge that was set about the people." During this period (before Christianity became the religion of

Rome) the secret edict went out from "the centre" at Jamnia, authorizing Jews to pretend denial of their creed and profess conversion to "pagan religions," if circumstances made this expedient.

The period of government from Jamnia lasted for about a century, and then it was transferred to Usha in Galilee, where the Sanhedrin was re-established. "Judaism set limitations about itself and *grew ever more exclusive*"; at this time the special curse on Jewish Christians was pronounced. In 320 AD the Roman Emperor Constantine was converted to Christianity, and enacted laws which forbade marriages between Christians and Jews and forbade Jews to keep Christian slaves. These were the natural response to the Law of exclusion and "stranger"-slavery administered by the Talmudic government at Usha, but they were held to be "persecution" and to escape their reach "the centre" was moved back to Babylonia, where the Judean colony, which eight centuries earlier had preferred to stay there rather than "return" to Jerusalem, "was still intact." The Talmudic government was set up at Sura, and academies were established there at Pumbedita.

The Talmud, begun at Jamnia and Usha, was completed at Sura and Pumbedita. "A ring of vast proportions and colossal elasticity" was built around the Jews everywhere; the mystic circle of fear and superstition was drawn tighter. From Sura an Exilarch (prince of the captivity of the house of David), ruled, but in time he became a figurehead. Thereafter "the president of the academy" (in effect, the high priest and prime minister) "laid down the rules and regulations not only for the Babylonian Jews but for the whole of Judaism... The Jews *throughout the world* recognized the academies in Babylonia as the authoritative centre of Judaism, and regarded any laws they passed as binding."

Thus the nation-within-nations, the state-within-states, was enfettered and ruled by the Talmudic government in Babylonia.

The core of dogma remained as Ezekiel, Ezra and Nehemiah had shaped and enforced it; but the Talmud, in effect, had taken the place of the Torah, as the Torah earlier had supplanted the "oral traditions." The heads of the academies of Sura and Pumbedita were called Gaonim and began to exercise autocratic power over the scattered Jews. The shadowy Exilarchs (later Nasim, or princes) were dependent on their approval and the Sanhedrin surrendered its functions to them, or was deprived of these. When doubt arose among Jews, anywhere in the world, about the interpretation or application of the Law in any matter of the day, the question was referred to the Gaonate. The verdicts and judgments returned (in the name of Jehovah) from the distant government were the Gaonic Reponses, or laws enacted from Babylonia, to which Jews everywhere submitted, or incurred danger of excommunication.

In this manner the Talmudic thrall spread round the dispersed Jews, wherever they dwelt, "like a closely woven net ... over ordinary days and holidays, over their actions and over their prayers, over their whole lives and every step they took … Nothing in their external lives was any longer allowed to be the sport of arbitrary settlement or of chance." This is the picture of an absolute despotism, different from other despotisms only in the element of distance between the despots and their subjects. Given a benevolent mission, a community of people so closely controlled might immensely fructify the life of peoples; given a destructive one, their presence among others is like that of a blasting charge in rock, operated by a distant hand on a plunger.

For six hundred years the Talmudic government, at Jamnia, Usha, and Sura, remained in or near to its native, oriental climate, where its nature was comprehended by other peoples; they knew how to cope with and counter the savage tribal creed and, as long as they were not hampered or constrained by foreign powers in their dealings with it, they were always able to find a workaday compromise, which enabled all to live in practical amity side by side.

Then came the event which has produced such violent results in our time: the Talmudic government *moved into Christianized Europe* and established itself among peoples to whom the nature of its dogma and its methods were strange and even incomprehensible. This led, in the course of many centuries, to the recurrent clash of the alien ambition and creed against native interest, which our century is again experiencing.

The nature of Westerners (more especially in the northern latitudes) is to be candid, to declare purposes, and to use words to express intention, and Christianity developed these native traits. The force which appeared among them was of the opposite character, oriental, infinitely subtle, secretive, conspiratorial, and practised in the use of language to disguise real purposes. Therein lay its greatest strength in the encounter with the West.

The removal to Europe came about through the Islamic conquests. The Arabs, under the Prophet's banner, drove the Romans from Palestine. By this means the native inhabitants of Palestine, who had inhabited it some two thousand years before the first Hebrew tribes entered, became the rulers of their own country, and remained so for nine hundred years (until 1517, when the Turks conquered it). An instructive comparison may be made between the Islamic and the Judaic treatment of captives:

The Caliph's order to the Arab conquerors in 637 AD was, "You shall not act treacherously, dishonestly, commit any excess or mutilation, kill any child or old man; cut or burn down palms or fruit trees, kill any sheep, cow or camel, and shall leave alone those whom you find devoting themselves to worship in their cells." Jehovah's order, according to *Deuteronomy* 20.16, is, "Of the cities of these people, which the Lord thy God doth give thee for an inheritance, thou shall save alive nothing that breatheth."

From Palestine, Islam then spread its frontiers right across North Africa, so that the great mass of Jews came within the boundaries of the same external authority. Next, Islam turned towards Europe and invaded Spain. Therewith the shadow of Talmudic Zionism fell across the West. The Moorish conquest was "supported with both men and money" by the Jews, who as camp-followers were treated with remarkable favour by the conquerors, city after city being handed to their control! The Koran itself said, "Their aim will be to abet disorder on the earth"; the Islamic armies certainly facilitated this aim.

Christianity thus became submerged in Spain. In these propitious circumstances the Talmudic government was transferred from Babylonia to Spain, and the process began, the results of which have become apparent in our generation. Dr. Kastein says:

"Judaism, dispersed as it was over the face of the globe, was always inclined to set up a fictitious state in the place of the one that had been lost, and always aimed, therefore, at looking to a common centre for guidance ... This centre was now held to be situated in Spain, whither the national hegemony was transferred from the East. Just as Babylonia had providentially taken the place of Palestine, so now Spain opportunely replaced Babylonia, which, *as a centre of Judaism,* had ceased to be capable of functioning. All that could be done there had already been accomplished; it had forged the chains with which the individual could bind himself, to avoid being swallowed up by his environment: the Talmud."

The reader will observe the description of events: "individuals" do not commonly bind themselves, of choice, with chains forged for them. Anyway, the Jewish captivity was as close as ever, or perhaps had been made closer. That was for the Jews to ponder.

What was to become of vital importance to the West was that the Jewish government was now *in Europe.* The directing centre and the destructive idea had both entered the West.

The Talmudic government of the nation-within-nations was continued from Spanish soil. The Gaonate issued its directives; the Talmudic academy was established at Cordova; and sometimes, at least, a shadowy Exilarch reigned over Jewry.

This was done under the protection of Islam; the Moors, like Babylon and Persia before, showed remarkable benevolence towards this force in their midst. To the Spaniards the invader came to bear more and more a Jewish countenance and less and less a Moorish one; the Moors had conquered, but the conqueror's power passed into Jewish hands. The story which the world had earlier seen enacted in Babylon, repeated itself in Spain, and in later centuries was to be re-enacted in every great country of the West.

The Moors remained in Spain for nearly eight hundred years. When the Spanish reconquest, after this long ordeal, was completed in 1492 the Jews, as well as the Moors, were expelled. They had become identified with the invaders' rule and were cast out when it ended, as they had followed it in.

The "centre" of Talmudic government was then transferred to Poland.

At that point, less than four centuries before our own generation, a significant mystery enters the story of Zion: *why* was the government set up *in Poland?* Up to that stage the annals reveal no trace of any large migration of Jews to Poland. The Jews who entered Spain with the Moors came from North Africa and when they left most of them returned thither or went to Egypt, Palestine, Italy, the Greek islands and Turkey. Other colonies had appeared in France, Germany, Holland and England and these were enlarged by the arrival among them of Jews from the Spanish Peninsula. *There is no record that any substantial number of Spanish Jews went to Poland, or that any Jewish mass-migration to Poland had occurred at any earlier time.*

Yet in the 1500's, when the "centre" was set up in Poland, "a Jewish population of millions *came into being there*," according to Dr. Kastein. But populations of millions do not suddenly "come into being." Dr. Kastein shows himself to be aware that something needs explanation here, and to be reluctant to go into it, for he dismisses the strange thing with the casual remark that the size of this community, of which nothing has previously been heard, "was more due to immigration, *apparently* from France, Germany and Bohemia, *than to any other cause.*" He does not explain what other cause he might have in mind and, for a diligent scholar, is on this one occasion strangely content with a random surmise.

But when a Zionist historian thus slurs over something the seeker after knowledge may be fairly sure that the root of the matter may by perseverance be found.

So it is in this case; behind Dr. Kastein's artless conjecture the most important fact in the later story of Zion is concealed. The "centre" of Jewish government was at this time planted among a large community of people who were unknown to the world as Jews and in fact were not Jews in any literal sense. They had no Judahite blood at all (for that matter; Judahite blood must by this time have been almost extinct even among the Jews of Western Europe) and their forefathers had never known Judea, or any soil but that of Tartary.

These people were the Khazars, a Turco-Mongolian race which had been converted to Judaism in about the 7th century of our era. This is the only case of the conversion of a large body of people of quite distinct blood to Judaism (the Idumeans were "brothers"). The reason why the Talmudic elders permitted or encouraged it can only be guessed; without it, however, the "Jewish question" would by now have joined the problems that time has solved.

This development (which will be further discussed in a later chapter) was of vital, and perhaps even mortal importance to the West. The natural instinct of Europe was always to expect the greatest danger to its survival from Asia. From the moment when "the centre" was transferred to Poland these Asiatics began to move towards, and later to enter the West in the guise of "Jews" and they brought Europe to its greatest crisis. Though their conversion had occurred so long before they were so remote that the world might never have known of them, had not the Talmudic centre been set up among them, so that they came to group themselves around it.

When they became known, as "Eastern Jews," they profited by the confusing effect of the contraction of the word Judahite, or Judean, to "Jew"; none would ever have believed that they were *Judahites* or *Judeans*. From the time when they took over the leadership of Jewry the dogma of "the return" to Palestine was preached in the name of people who had no Semitic blood or ancestral link with Palestine whatever!

From this period the Talmudic government operated with a *masse de manoeuvre* of a different Asiatic order.

Once again, a virtually independent state was formed within the Polish state, which like so many states before and after showed the greatest benevolence to the nation-within-nations that took shape within its gates. As in the earlier and later cases this in no wise mitigated the hostility of the Talmudic Jews towards it, which was proverbial.

Dr. Kastein gives the picture of this independent Jewish government during the Polish phase. The Talmudists were allowed to draw up "a constitution," and through the 1500's and 1600's the Jews in Poland lived under "an autonomous government." This administered "an *iron* system of autonomy and an *iron* religious discipline, which inevitably resulted in the formation of an oligarchic body of administrators and the development of an extreme form of mysticism" (this gives the picture of the training, under rigid discipline in close confinement, which produced the Communist and Zionist revolutionaries of our century).

This autonomous Talmudic government was called the Kahal. In its own territory the Kahal was a fully-empowered government, under Polish suzerainty. It had independent authority of taxation in the ghettoes and communities, being responsible for payment of a global sum to the Polish government. It passed laws regulating every action and transaction between man and man and had power to try, judge, convict or acquit.

This power *only nominally* stopped short of capital punishment: Professor Salo Baron says, "In Poland, where the Jewish court had no right to inflict capital punishment, *lynching, as an extra-legal preventive, was encouraged by rabbinical authorities such as Solomon Luria.*" (This quotation reveals the inner meaning of Dr. Kastein's frequent, but cautious, allusions to "iron discipline," "inexorable discipline," "discipline rigid to the point of deadliness," and the like).

In effect, a Jewish state, Talmud-ruled, was recreated on the soil of Poland.

As Dr. Kastein says, "Such was *the constitution of the Jewish state*, planted on foreign soil, hemmed in by a wall of foreign laws, with a structure partly self-chosen and partly forced upon it ... It had *its own Jewish law*, its own priesthood, its own schools, and its own social institutions, and its own representatives in the Polish government ... in fact, it possessed all the elements which go to form a state." The achievement of this status was due "in no small measure to the co-operation of the Polish Government."

Then, in 1772, Poland was partitioned and this great community of "Eastern Jews," organized as a state-within-the-state, was divided by national boundaries, most of it coming under Russian rule. At that point, for the first time in more than 2500 years and less than two hundred years before our own day, the "centre" of Jewish government disappears from sight. Up to 1772 there had always been one: in Poland, Spain, Babylonia, Galilee, Judea, Babylon and Judah.

Dr. Kastein says that "the centre ceased to exist." The suggestion is that the centralized control of Jewry at that moment ended, but the length and strength of its earlier survival, and the significant events of the ensuing century, confute that. In a later passage Dr. Kastein himself reveals the truth, when he jubilantly records that in the Nineteenth Century "a Jewish international took shape."

Clearly "the centre" continued, but from 1772 in secret. The reason for the withdrawal into concealment may be deduced from the shape of later events.

The century which followed was that of the revolutionary conspiracy, Communist and Zionist, culminating in the open appearance of these two movements, which have dominated the present century. The Talmudic "centre" was also the centre of this conspiracy. Had it remained in the open the source of conspiracy would have been visible, and the identification of the Talmudic, Eastern Jews with it obvious.

In the event this only became clear when the revolution of 1917 produced an almost all-Jewish government in Russia; and by that time power over governments in the West was so great that the nature of this new regime was little discussed, a virtual law of heresy having come into force there. Had the visible institution continued, the masses of the West would in time have become aware that the Talmudic government of Jewry, though it led the clamour for "emancipation," was also organizing a revolution to destroy all that the peoples might gain from this emancipation.

The Russians, among whom this largest single community of Jews at that time dwelt, knew what had happened. Dr. Kastein says, "The Russians wondered what could possibly be the reason why the Jews did not amalgamate with the rest of the population, and came to the conclusion that *in their secret Kahals* they possessed a strong reserve, and that *a 'World Kahal'* existed." Dr. Kastein later confirms what the Russians believed, by his own allusion to the "Jewish international" of the Nineteenth Century.

In other words, the "government" continued, but in concealment, and probably in the different form suggested by Dr. Kastein's word "international." The strong presumption is that the "centre" today is not located in any one country and that, although its main seat of power is evidently in the United States, it now takes the form of a directorate distributed among the nations and working in unison, over the heads of governments and peoples.

The Russians, who at the time of the disappearance of "the centre" from public view were better informed than any others about this matter, have been proved right.

The manner in which this international directorate gains and wields its power over Gentile governments is no longer quite mysterious; enough authentic, published information has come out of these last fifty years to explain that, as this book will later show.

The mystery of its age-long hold over "Jews" is more difficult to penetrate. How has a sect been able to keep people, distributed around the globe, in the clutch of a primitive tribalism during twenty-five centuries?

The next chapter seeks to give some insight into the methods used during the third and longest phase of the story of Zion, the Talmudic period which lasted from AD 70 to about 1800. These methods have so much of the Orient and of Asia in them that they are puzzling to Western minds and are best comprehended by those whose own experience took them much among the communities of "Eastern Jews" before the Second World War, and into secret-police states, where rule is also by fear and terror.

Chapter 15

THE TALMUD AND THE GHETTOES

Whatever else is in dispute, one thing is incontestable: that great force must repose in a Law which for nineteen centuries obtains obedience from people scattered over the earth, when by an effort of will they could escape its thrall. The Talmud was (and is) such a law, and the only one of its kind.

"The Talmud was regarded almost as the supreme authority by the majority of Jews ... *Even the Bible was relegated to a secondary place"* (the *Jewish Encyclopaedia*). "The *absolute superiority of the Talmud over the Bible of Moses* must be recognized by all" (the *Archives Israelites,* quoted by Mgr. Landrieux). "The words of the elders *are more important than the words of the Prophets"* (the *Talmud,* Treatise Berachoth, i.4.).

The compilation of the Talmud began at Jamnia, the part played in Babylon by Ezekiel and Ezra being played in this new revision of the Law, by the rabbi known as Judah the Holy or the Prince.

It was in effect a massive addition to the "statutes and judgments" of *Deuteronomy, Leviticus* and *Numbers.* All the laws which "the centre" enacted were appended to the Torah as the "Oral Torah," having equal divine origin. Then they were written down in the *Mishna.* Later again (under the oft-used pretext of "completing" the work) immense records of rabbinical discussions and rulings were added in the *Gemara,* but as the *Gemara* was the product of two distinct Jewish communities, those of Jerusalem in the fifth and of Babylon in the seventh century, there are two Talmuds, known as the Palestinian and the Babylonian.

The Talmud, which thus was produced during the Christian era, is anti-Christian. It is supposed to derive from the same original source as the Torah; the priestly scribes who compiled it once more claimed to revise or expand under powers "orally" bestowed on Mount Sinai.

The copy of the Christian Bible which I have states that "the churches of all denominations receive and accept" the Old Testament "as given by inspiration of God, therefore being for them a Divine rule or guide of faith and practice," a ruling which comes down from the Council of Trent. A question therefore arises: in what way was the inspiration of the Talmud different from that of the Torah? If it was *not* different, then why should not the anti-Christian Talmud be added to the Christian Bible?

If that were done the entire work would extend along several shelves of a library, and the New Testament would be a tiny pamphlet, lost among and excommunicated by the Talmudic mass, the teaching of which is thus summarized by the Talmudic scholar Drach: "The precepts of justice, of equity, of charity towards one's neighbours, are not only not applicable with regard to the Christian, but constitute a crime in anyone who would act differently … The Talmud expressly forbids one to save a non-Jew from death … to restore lost goods, etc., to him, to have pity on him."

The theological decision about the "equal divine authority" of the Torah seems to have introduced an element of confusion into the Christian lesson from which Christianity itself in the end might not recover.

The Talmudic precepts just quoted are not essentially different in nature from those included in *Deuteronomy* when *that* "second Law" was made public a thousand years before the Palestinian Talmud was completed; they are merely given a specifically anti-Christian application.

Why was the Talmud necessary at all? The reasons seem clear. The Judeans had been finally dispersed about the world, or at any rate until such time as these "exiles" should be "in-gathered" and congregate again around the temple. The world where they were scattered contained a new "enemy" in the form of a religion which had been born in the very declaration that Phariseeism was heresy: "Woe unto you, scribes and Pharisees, hypocrites!" Moreover, the Judaic Law had become known through translation to the heathen world, which had even found some things in it that it could use. Thus the special people, if they were to be kept apart, needed a new Law of their own, which could be kept from the eyes of the Gentiles. The Torah needed "a hedge" about it, strong enough to preserve the exiles both from absorption by other peoples and from "a-whoring after other gods."

The Talmud was essentially the hostile answer to Christianity, the order-of-battle revised in the light of "the enemy's" new dispositions. The lay encyclopaedias (which in our generation have been made untrustworthy on subjects related to Judaism) disguise this fact from Gentile readers. The one now before me, for instance, says, "The Talmud has been attacked by Christians at times - quite unfairly - as anti-Christian." The insertion of two suggestive words by some partisan Scribe causes this volume to purvey demonstrable untruth and to convert a factual statement into a propagandist one. The attack on Christianity gave the Talmud its distinctive tone and is indeed the only new thing in the Talmud. Its other teaching remains that of Ezekiel and the Pharisees.

The *Jewish Encyclopaedia* says, "It is the tendency of Jewish legends in the Talmud, the Midrash" (the sermons in the synagogues) "and in the Life of Jesus Christ (*Toledoth Jeshua*) that originated in the Middle Ages to belittle the person of Jesus by ascribing to him illegitimate birth, magic and a shameful death." He is generally alluded to as "that anonymous one," "liar," "impostor" or "bastard" (the attribution of bastardy is intended to bring him under The Law as stated in *Deuteronomy* 23.2: "A bastard shall not enter into the congregation of the Lord"). Mention of the name, Jesus, is prohibited in Jewish households.

The work cited by the *Jewish Encyclopaedia* as having "originated in the Middle Ages" is not merely a discreditable memory of an ancient past, as that allusion might suggest; it is used in Hebrew schools today. It was a rabbinical production of the Talmudic era and repeated all the ritual of mockery of Calvary itself in a different form. Jesus is depicted as the illegitimate son of Mary, a hairdresser's wife, and of a Roman soldier called Panthera. Jesus himself is referred to by a name which might be translated "Joey Virgo." He is shown as being taken by his stepfather to Egypt and there learning sorcery.

The significant thing about this bogus life-story (the only information about Jesus which Jews were supposed to read) is that in it Jesus is *not* crucified by Romans. After his appearance in Jerusalem and his arrest there as an agitator and a sorcerer he is turned over to the Sanhedrin and spends forty days in the pillory before being stoned and hanged at the Feast of the Passover; this form of death exactly fulfils the Law laid down in *Deuteronomy* 21.22 and 17.5, whereas crucifixion would *not* have been in compliance with that *Judaic* Law. The book then states that in hell he suffers the torture of boiling mud.

The Talmud also refers to Jesus as "Fool," "sorcerer," "profane person," "idolator," "dog," "child of lust" and the like more; the effect of this teaching, over a period of centuries, is shown by the book of the Spanish Jew Mose de Leon, republished in 1880, which speaks of Jesus as a "dead dog" that lies "buried in a dunghill." The original Hebrew texts of these Talmudic allusions appear in Laible's *Jesus Christus im Talmud*. This scholar says that during the period of the Talmudists hatred of Jesus became "the most national trait of Judaism," that "at the approach of Christianity the Jews were seized ever and again with a fury and hatred that were akin to madness," that "the hatred and scorn of the Jews was always directed in the first place against the person of Jesus" and that "the Jesus-hatred of the Jews is a firmly-established fact, but they want to show it as little as possible."

This wish to conceal from the outer world that which was taught behind the Talmudic hedge led to the censoring of the above-quoted passages during the seventeenth century. Knowledge of the Talmud became fairly widespread then (it was frequently denounced by remonstrant Jews) and the embarrassment thus caused to the Talmudic elders led to the following edict (quoted in the original Hebrew and in translation by P.L.B. Drach, who was brought up in a Talmudic school and later became converted to Christianity):

"This is why we enjoin you, under pain of excommunication major, to print nothing in future editions, whether of the Mishna or of the Gemara, which relates whether for good or evil to the acts of Jesus the Nazarene, and to substitute instead a circle like this: O, which will warn the rabbis and schoolmasters to teach the young these passages only *viva voce*. By means of this precaution the savants among the Nazarenes will have no further pretext to attack us on this subject" (decree of the Judaist Synod which met in Poland in 1631. At the present time, when public enquiry into such matters, or objection to them, has been virtually forbidden by Gentile governments, these passages, according to report, have been restored in the Hebrew editions of the Talmud).

This vilification of the founder of another religion sets Judaism apart from other creeds and the Talmud from other literature published in the name of religion. Muslims, Buddhists, Confucians, Christians and others do not hate other creeds or their founders *as such*. They are content to differ and to believe that the paths may one day meet, God deciding the meeting-point.

For instance, the Koran describes Jesus as "strengthened with the Holy Spirit" and the Jews are reproached with rejecting "the Apostle of God," to whom was given "the Evangel with its guidance and light." Of his mother, the Koran says, "O Mary! verily hath God chosen thee and purified thee, and chosen thee above the women of the world," and, "Jesus, the son of Mary, illustrious in this world, and in the next, and one of those who have near access to God."

The central message of the Talmud, the newest "new Law," is plain: it specifically extended the Law to apply to Christianity and left no doubt about the duty of a Jew towards it.

Another motive for the new compendium was the problem created for the inner sect by the fact that the Gentiles had found much in the translated Torah that appealed to them (despite the obvious fact that it was lethally directed against them). The earlier Levitical scribes could not foresee that (because they could not foresee the translation itself). The ruling sect needed a new Law of its own, into which "stranger" eyes could not pry, and it needed to make the Jews understand that, though the heathen inexplicably had bound the racio-religious Law into the Christian Bible, this Law nevertheless still was the Law of the Jews alone, and inexorably in force.

Thus the Talmud set out to widen the gap and heighten the barrier between the Jews and others. An example of the different language which the Torah spoke, for Jews and for Gentiles, has previously been given: the obscure and apparently harmless allusion to "a foolish nation" *(Deuteronomy,* 32.21). According to the article on *Discrimination against Gentiles* in the *Jewish Encyclopaedia* the allusion in the original Hebrew is to "vile and vicious Gentiles," so that Jew and Gentile received very different meanings from the same passage in the original and in the translation. The Talmud, however, which was to reach only Jewish eyes, removed any doubt that might have been caused in Jewish minds by perusal of the milder translation; it specifically related the passage in *Deuteronomy* to one in *Ezekiel,* 23.20, and by so doing defined Gentiles as those "whose flesh is as the flesh of asses and whose issue is like the issue of horses"! In this spirit was the, "interpretation" of The Law continued by the Talmudists.

The Talmudic edicts were all to similar effect. The Law (the Talmud laid down) allowed the restoration of a lost article to its owner if "a brother or neighbour," but not if a Gentile. Book-burning (of Gentile books) was recommended (book-burning is a Talmudic invention, as the witch-hunt was prescribed by the Torah). The benediction, "Blessed be Thou ... who has not made me a goy," was to be recited daily. Eclipses were of bad augury for Gentiles only. Rabbi Levi laid down that the injunction not to take revenge (*Leviticus* 19.18) did not apply to Gentiles, and apparently invoked *Ecclesiastes* 8.4 in support of his ruling (a discriminatory interpretation then being given to a passage in which the Gentile could not suspect any such intention).

The Jew who sells to a Gentile landed property bordering on the land of another Jew is to be excommunicated. A Gentile cannot be trusted as witness in a criminal or civil suit because he could not be depended on to keep his word like a Jew. A Jew testifying in a petty Gentile court as a single witness against a Jew must be excommunicated. Adultery committed with a non-Jewish woman is not adultery "for the heathen have no lawfully wedded wife, they are not really their wives." The Gentiles are as such precluded from admission to a future world.

Finally, the Talmudic interpretation of the original moral commandment, "Thou shalt love the Lord thy God with all thine heart," is that "man shall occupy himself with the study of Holy Scripture and of the Mishna and have intercourse with learned and wise men." In other words, the man who best proves his love of God is he who studies the Talmud and shuns his Gentile fellow-man.

An illustrative glimpse from our present time sometimes best shows the effect produced on human minds by centuries of Talmudic rule. In 1952 a Mr Frank Chodorov published this anecdote: "One very cold night the rabbi tottered into our house in a pitiful condition; it took half a dozen glasses of boiling tea to thaw him out. He then told how a sympathetic goy had offered him a pair of gloves and why he had refused the gift; a Jew must not be the instrument of bringing a *mitvah*, or blessing, on a non-believer. This was the first time, I believe, that I came smack up against the doctrine of the 'chosen people', and it struck me as stupid and mean."

So much for the "hedge" which the Talmud set up between the Jews and mankind, and for the feeling of contempt and hatred for "strangers" which it set out to instil in the Jews. What did it do to the Jews themselves? Of this, the *Jewish Encyclopaedia* says, "The Talmudists made the Torah into *a penal code*." For once, in this painstakingly accurate work, the meaning is not quite clear; the Torah already *was* a penal code (as perusal of it today will show), and its penalties had sometimes been applied (by Ezra and Nehemiah against the Jews; and for that matter by the Romans, at the behest of the Sanhedrin, against the "prophet and dreamer of dreams," Jesus). Possibly the meaning is that, under the Talmudists, the penal code was regularly enforced, and its provisions strengthened.

That is certainly true; the rabbinical practice, previously cited, of "encouraging lynching as an extra-legal preventive," because they were not allowed by host-governments to pronounce death sentences, shows in how real a sense the Talmud could be applied as "a penal code." It was a very far cry from the few moral commandments of remote tradition to the multitudinous laws and regulations of the Talmud, which often forbade moral behaviour and assigned drastic punishments for "transgressions." Observance of these laws, not moral behaviour, remained the basis.

The Talmudic Law governed every imaginable action of a Jew's life anywhere in the world: marriage, divorce, property settlements, commercial transactions, down to the pettiest details of dress and toilet. As unforeseen things frequently crop in daily life, the question of what was legal or illegal (not what was right or wrong) in all manner of novel circumstances had incessantly to be debated, and this produced the immense records of rabbinical dispute and decisions in which the Talmud abounds.

Was it as much a crime to crush a flea as to kill a camel on the sacred day? One learned rabbi allowed that the flea might be gently squeezed, and another thought its feet might even be cut off. How many white hairs might a sacrificial red cow have and yet remain a red cow? What sort of scabs required this or that ritual of purification? At which end of an animal should the operation of slaughter be performed? Ought the high priest to put on his shirt or his hose first? Methods of putting apostates to death were debated; they must be strangled, said the elders, until they opened their mouths, into which boiling lead must be poured. Thereon a pious rabbi urged that the victim's mouth be held open with pincers so that he not suffocate before the molten lead enter and consume his soul with his body.

The word "pious" is here not sardonically used; this scholar sought to discover the precise intention of "the Law."

Was Dr. Johnson acquainted with or ignorant of the Talmud; the subject might prove a fascinating one for a literary debating society. He gave one argument its quietus by declaring, "There is no settling the point of precedence between a louse and a flea." Precisely this point had been discussed, and settled, among the Talmudic scholars. Might a louse or a flea be killed on the Sabbath? The Talmudic response was that the first was allowed and the second was a deadly sin.

"The Talmud became the unbreakable husk around a kernel determined to survive; it encased the heart of the Jew with a spirituality which though cold as ice was strong as steel to protect … The Talmud, which they carried with them everywhere, became their home," A home made of ice and steel, behedged and walled around, with all the windows stopped and the doors barred; the picture is Dr. Kastein's.

In this home the Jews, "owing to the acceptance of the idea of the Chosen People, and of salvation ... could interpret everything that happened *only from the standpoint of themselves as the centre.*" The planet swam in space, among the myriad stars, only to enthrone them on a mound of gold in a temple surrounded by heathen dead; "the Law raised an insuperable barrier against the outside world." No Jew, save a Talmudic scholar, could know all of this huge compendium. Probably no Gentile could gain access to an unedited version. A college of specialists and a lifetime of work would be needed to compare such translations as have been made with the originals, if they were made available. Many students, until recently, found the lack of translations significant, but the present writer cannot see that this is important. Enough is known of the Talmud (and most of this from Jewish or converted-Jewish sources) for its nature to be clear, and nothing is gained by heaping proof endlessly on proof. Ample enlightenment can be obtained from the *Jewish Encyclopaedia,* the German translation of the Jerusalem and Babylonian Talmuds (Zurich 1880 and Leipzig 1889), William Ruben's *Der alte und der neue Glaube im Judentum,* Strack's *Einleitung in den Talmud,* Laible's *Jesus Christus im Talmud,* Drach's *De l'Harmoni entre l'Eglise et la Synagogue,* and Graetz's *History of the Jews.*

The Talmud is *admittedly* manmade. The Torah was *attributed* to the voice of Jehovah, recorded by Moses. This is of great significance.

The reason for the difference is obvious: Mosaic manuscripts "hoary with the dust of ages" could not be indefinitely discovered. The scribes had to accept the responsibility, simply declaring that in doing so they used the absolute power of interpretation "orally" given to the first of their line. Thus they revealed the truth: that *They,* and none other, were God!

Dr. Kastein was accurate in saying, "It was not God who willed these people and their meaning; it was this people who willed this God and this meaning," or he would have been accurate had he said, "these scribes" instead of "this people." The earlier generation of scribes had willed the revelation made in *Deuteronomy;* the later one willed the Talmudic God and demanded that "these people" accept the Talmud as a continuation of the revelation earlier "willed."

When the Talmud was completed the question which the future had to answer was whether the central sect would succeed in imposing this New Law on the scattered Jews, as Ezra and Nehemiah, with Persian help, had inflicted the New Covenant on the Judahites in Jerusalem in 444 BC.

They did succeed. In 1898, at the Second World Zionist Congress at Basel, a Zionist from Russia, Dr. Mandelstamm of Kieff, declared, "The Jews energetically reject the idea of fusion with other nationalities and cling firmly to their historical hope, i.e., of world empire."

The Twentieth Century is witnessing the attempt to consummate that hope. Probably the institution of the ghetto chiefly helped the Talmudists to this success.

In the Twentieth Century the masses have been misled to think of "the ghetto" as a kind of concentration camp for Jews set up by Gentile persecutors. The same operation on fact has been performed on the entire history of oppression in the West; in the Twentieth Century all else has been drained away until what remains is presented solely as "the Jewish persecution."

The many persecutions of *men* during the last 1900 years have involved the Jews in proportion to their numbers, so that their share of the total mass of suffering was small (in the most notorious case of the present century, that of Russia, they were the oppressors, not the oppressed). I do not know if I should ever have elicited this fact, had not my own experience confronted me so sharply with it.

The ghetto was not something inflicted on the Jews by the Gentiles. It was the logical product of the Talmudic Law, and derived directly from the experiment in Babylon. Dr. Kastein describes the Talmud as "the home" which the Jews took everywhere with them. However, for physical life they also needed four walls and a roof. The Talmud itself decreed that the Gentiles were not "neighbours" and that a Jew might not sell landed property adjoining that of a Jew to a Gentile. The express object of such provisions as these was the segregation of Jews from others and their isolation in ghettoes.

The first ghetto was that which the Babylonian rulers allowed the Levites to set up in Babylon. The next was the Jerusalem around which Nehemiah, backed by the Persian king's soldiers, built new walls, wherefrom he drove out all non-Judahites. From those models the European ghetto took its shape. This institution is probably the most onerous part of the modern Jew's spiritual inheritance:

"The ghetto, friend, the ghetto, where all hopes at birth decay."

Jews who never saw a ghetto carry a half-conscious memory of it within them like a haunting fear, yet it was essentially a Talmudist conception, to which their ancestors surrendered. It was the perfect means of corralling a scattered congregation, imprisoning people's minds, and wielding power over them.

The demand for a ghetto often came from the Talmudists (that is to say, outside Poland, where all Jewish life, of course, was ghetto- life). The modern suggestion that the ghetto signified inferiority is part of the legend of "persecution," which is chiefly meant to intimidate Jews, so that they shall always fear to venture outside the fold; today's myth of "antisemitism" is intended to produce the same effect on them.

In ancient Alexandria (the New York of its day) and in medieval Cairo and Cordova the Jewish quarters were established at the insistence of the rabbis, intent on keeping their flock isolated from others. In 1084 the Jews of Speyer petitioned the ruling German prince to set up a ghetto; in 1412, at Jewish request, a ghetto law was enacted throughout Portugal. The erection of the ghetto walls in Verona and Mantua was for centuries celebrated annually by the Jews there in a festival of victory (Purim). The ghettoes of Russia and Poland were an essential and integral part of the Talmudic organization and any attempt to abolish them would have been denounced as persecution.

When the Roman ghetto was destroyed at Mussolini's order in the early 1930's the Jewish press (as Mr Bernard J. Brown records) lamented the event in such words as these:

"One of the most unique phenomena of Jewish life in Goluth is gone. Where but a few months ago a vibrant Jewish life was pulsating, there now remains a few half-destroyed buildings as the last vestige of the quondam ghetto. It has fallen victim to the Fascist passion for beauty and under Mussolini's order the ghetto has been razed...."

The implication of this is that the razing of the ghetto was "Fascism," just as the original creation of ghettoes (at Jewish demand) is presented as persecution by the Zionist historians of today.

With emancipation the ghetto disappeared; its maintenance would too blatantly have shown that the rulers of Jewry had no true intention of sharing in emancipation on an equal basis.

The *Jewish Encyclopaedia* recorded in its 1903 edition that "in the whole civilized world there is now not a single ghetto, *in the original meaning of the word:* The qualification is important, because in many places and ways the Jews continue the closed- community life, though without the identifying walls, and the law forbidding the sale of neighbour-land to Gentiles, without permission, has not lapsed (to give one instance, illustrative to those who know the city: in Montreal an entire district east of the Mountain has by such methods been made almost as solidly Jewish as if it were a ghetto).

The decline of the ghetto, during the century of emancipation, was a blow to the main prop of Talmudic power. A substitute had to be found unless the ghetto-spirit (as distinct from the physical ghetto) was to disintegrate altogether, and one was found in Zionism, which is the new method devised to re-corral the communities:

"There are many who *desire greater control over Jews by Jews,* and who resent the dissolution of this control in Russia, where once a ghetto made such control easy and absolute" (Rabbi Elmer Berger). "Only the intellectually blind can fail to note that the promotion of group life, centered around ancient religious traditions and cultures, *is a return to the ghetto* ... There can be no glory in a group of people striving *to perpetuate ghetto life* ... Even a cursory reading of history *shows that the Jew built his own ghettoes"* (Mr Bernard J. Brown).

Zionism is the true revival of Talmudic ghettoism, as these two Jewish authorities state. It is designed to undo the work of emancipation, to re-segregate the Jews, and to reimpose the creed of "severance" on them in full force. The chauvinist appeal of conquest and empire in the Middle East is being used to disguise this true meaning of the process.

The direction in which Jews were moving before Zionism set out to recapture them may be seen in this quotation from the article on *The Attitude of Modern Judaism* in the *Jewish Encyclopaedia*, 1916: "Modern Judaism as inculcated in the catechism and explained in the declarations of the various rabbinical conferences, and as interpreted in the sermons of modern rabbis, is founded on the recognition of the unity of the human races; the law of righteousness and truth being supreme over all men, without distinction of race, or creed, and its fulfilment being possible for all.

Righteousness is not conditioned by birth. The Gentiles may attain unto as perfect a righteousness as the Jews ... In the modern synagogues, 'Thou shalt love thy neighbour like thyself' *(Leviticus* 29) signified every human being."

Much has changed since 1916, and in 1955 these words are but the picture of what might have been. No doubt individual rabbis continue to "interpret their sermons" in this sense, but unless they are of the stuff of which heroes and martyrs are made they cannot long defy their congregations, and these have been taken back centuries by the appeal of Zionism.

The Zionists have gained political control over Gentile governments and the Jewish masses alike, so that what the individual remonstrant says is of little weight. The Zionists have restored the Levitical Law, in its Pharisaic and Talmudic interpretations, in full force. Their actions towards others in the past have been and in the future will be guided by that, and not by what "the attitude of modern Judaism" was in 1916.

The great change came in the year, 1917, which followed the publication of the words quoted above. The tradition of the Talmud and the ghettoes was still too strong, among the masses of Jewry, for "the attitude of modern Judaism" to prevail over the fanatical elders who then appeared.

Chapter 16

THE MESSIANIC LONGING

The Talmudic regime in the close confinement of the ghettoes was in its nature essentially rule by terror, and employed the recognizable methods of terror: spies-on-spies, informers, denunciants, cursing and excommunication, and death. The secret-police and concentration-camp regime of the Communist era evidently took its nature from this model, which was familiar to its Talmudic organizers.

During the many centuries of Talmudist government the terror, and the dogma which it enclosed, produced two significant results. These were recurrent Messianic outbursts, which expressed the captives' longing to escape the terror; and recurrent protests against the dogma, from the Jews themselves.

These were latterday symptoms of the feeling expressed on the ancient day when "the people wept" at the reading of The Law. The Talmud forbade the Jew almost every activity other than the amassing of money ("they only conceded just enough to the people about them to make their economic activities possible"; Dr. Kastein) and the study of the Talmud ("whenever the Law could not be unequivocally applied to the relations of life, they endeavoured to discover its interpretation").

The energies of the people were directed to spinning ever more tightly about themselves the net in which they were enmeshed: "They not only set a hedge about the Law, but, by cutting themselves off more definitely than ever from the outside world, and by binding themselves more exclusively to a given circle of laws, they set a hedge about themselves." With every breath they drew and movement they made, they had to ask themselves, "Does the Talmud allow or forbid this," and the ruling sect decided.

Even the most docile in time questioned the credentials of such a Law, asking "Can it be really true that every new edict and ban derives from God's revelation at Sinai?" That was their rulers' claim: "according to the Jewish view God had given Moses on Mount Sinai alike the oral and written Law, that is, the Law *with all its interpretations and applications,*" says Mr Alfred Edersheim. The people submitted to, but could not always inwardly accept so obviously political a claim, and this inner rebellion against something outwardly professed often led to strange happenings.

For instance, a Portuguese Marrano (a converted, or sometimes a secret Jew) called Uriel da Costa was once reconverted to Judaism, and then became appalled by the Talmud. In 1616, at Hamburg, he published his *Thesis against Tradition* in which he attacked "the Pharisees," charging that the Talmudic laws were *their* creation and not of any divine origin. The treatise was addressed to the Jews of Venice and the rabbi there, one Leo Modena, thereon by command pronounced the dreaded "Ban" on da Costa. At Rabbi Modena's death papers found among his effects showed that he had held exactly the same view as da Costa, but had not dared to declare that for which he excommunicated da Costa.

As a Communist Leo Modena would be a familiar figure in our own century. In effect, he sentenced to death the man whose beliefs he shared. Da Costa returned to the attack in 1624 with his *Test of the Pharisaical Tradition by Comparing it with the Written Law*. The Talmudists of Amsterdam, where da Costa then was, denounced him to the *Dutch* courts on the ground that his treatise was subversive of the *Christian* faith, and it was burned at the order of these Gentile authorities, who thus carried out the Talmudic Law!

This act of Gentile submission to the ruling sect recurs through all history from the time of Babylon to the present day. Da Costa was literally hounded to death and in 1640 shot himself.

Jewish history shows many such episodes. The student of this subject walks with terror as he turns its pages. The "Great Ban" was in effect a death sentence, and was so intended. It called down on the victim the "cursings" enumerated in *Deuteronomy*, and cursing was (and by the literal devotees of this sect still is) held to be *literally* effective.

The article on "Cursing" in the *Jewish Encyclopaedia* says, "Talmudic literature betrays a belief, amounting to downright superstition, in the mere power of the word ... *Not only is a curse uttered by a scholar unfailing even if undeserved* ... Scholars cursed sometimes not only with their mouths, but by *an angry, fixed look. The unfailing consequence of such a look was either immediate death or poverty.*"

This is recognizably the practice known today as "the evil eye," of which my encyclopaedia says, "This superstition is of ancient date, and is met with among almost all races, as it is among illiterate people and savages still." The *Jewish Encyclopaedia* shows that it is a *prescribed legal penalty* under the Judaic Law, for this same authority (as earlier quoted) states that "even the Bible" is secondary to the Talmud. Moreover, Mr M.L. Rodkinson, the scholar who was selected to make an English translation of the Talmud, says that "not a single line" of the Talmud has been modified. For that matter, the Talmud, in this case, only carries on the law of cursing as earlier laid down, by the Levites, in *Deuteronomy*.

The practice of cursing and of the evil eye, therefore, is still part of "The Law," as the quotations given above show. (The student may find a present-day example of the Talmudic "angry, fixed look" in operation if he refer to Mr Whittaker Chambers's description of his confrontation with the attorneys of Mr Alger Hiss; and the student may form his own opinion of the fact that soon afterwards Mr Chambers felt himself driven to commit suicide, failing in this attempt only through a chance).

Thus excommunication was a deadly thing. Mr Rodkinson makes this remarkable reference to it:

"We can conceive their" (the Talmudic rabbinate's) "terrible vengeance against an ordinary man or scholar who ventured to express opinions *in any degree at variance* with their own, or to transgress the Sabbath by carrying a handkerchief or drinking of Gentile wine, which in their opinion is against the law. Who, then, could resist *their terrible weapon of excommunication,* which they used for the purpose of making a man *a ravening wolf whom every human being fled from and shunned as the plague-smitten? Many who drank of this bitter cup were driven to the grave and many others went mad."*

This fate befell some of the great remonstrants. Moses Maimonides (born at the Talmudic centre, Cordova, in 1135) drew up a famous code of the principles of Judaism and wrote, "It is forbidden to defraud or deceive *any* person in business. *Judaist and non-Judaist are to be treated alike ... What some people imagine, that it is permissible to cheat a Gentile, is an error, and based on ignorance* ... Deception, duplicity, cheating and circumvention towards a Gentile are despicable to the Almighty, as 'all that do unrighteously are an abomination unto the Lord thy God' ."

The Talmudists denounced Maimonides *to the Inquisition,* saying, "Behold, there are among us heretics and infidels, for they were seduced by Moses Ben Maimonides ... you who clear your community of heretics, clear ours too." At this behest his books were burned in Paris and Montpellier, the book-burning edict of the Talmudic law thus being fulfilled. On his grave the words were incised, "Here lies an excommunicated Jew."

The Inquisition, like the Gentile rulers of the earlier period and the Gentile politicians of our day, often did the bidding of the inveterate sect. The falsification of history, insofar as it relates to this particular subject, has left the impression on Gentile minds that the Inquisition was primarily an instrument of "the Jewish persecution."

Dr. Kastein's presentation is typical: he says the Inquisition persecuted "heretics and peoples of alien creeds" and then adds, "that is to say, *principally* Jews," and from that point on he conveys the impression of a *solely* Jewish persecution. (In the same way, in our century, Hitler's persecution was through four stages of propagandist misrepresentation transformed from one of "political opponents" into one of "political opponents and Jews," then of "Jews and political opponents," and last, "of Jews").

The Inquisition sometimes burned the Talmud; it would have done better to translate and publish the significant parts, and that would still be wise. However, it also burned remonstrances against the Talmud, at the demand of the ruling sect. For instance, in 1240 the Talmud was denounced to it by a converted Jew, the Dominican Nicholas Donin, in Paris, and nothing was done, but in 1232, at the denunciation of the Talmudists, it had ordered the anti-Talmudic work of Maimonides to be publicly burned!

Another great expostulant against the Talmud was Baruch Spinoza, born at Amsterdam in 1632. The ban pronounced on him by the Amsterdam rabbinate derives directly from the "cursings" of *Deuteronomy:*

"By the sentence of the angels, by the decree of the saints, we anathematise, cut off, curse and execrate Baruch Spinoza, in the presence of these sacred books with the six hundred and thirteen precepts which are written therein, with the anathema wherewith Joshua anathematized Jericho; with the cursing wherewith Elisha cursed the children; and with *all the cursings which are written in the Torah;* cursed be he by day and cursed by night; cursed when he goeth out, and cursed when he cometh in; the Lord pardon him never; the wrath and fury of the Lord burn upon this man; and bring upon him all the curses which are written in the Torah. The Lord blot out his name under the heaven. The Lord set him apart for destruction from all the tribes of Israel, with all the curses of the firmament which are written in the Torah. There shall be no man to speak to him, no man write to him, no man show him any kindness, no man stay under the same roof with him, no man come nigh unto him."

Spinoza was banished from Amsterdam and exposed to "a persecution which threatened his life," as one encyclopaedia puts it. In fact it took his life, in the way depicted by Mr Rodkinson (as previously quoted). Shunned and destitute, he died at forty-four in a Gentile city, far from the centre of Talmudic government but not far enough to save him.

Two hundred years later, during the century of emancipation, Moses Mendelssohn proclaimed the heresy that Jews, while retaining their faith, ought to become integrated with their fellow men. That meant breaking free from the Talmud and returning to the ancient religious idea of which the Israelite remonstrants had glimpses. His guiding thought was, "Oh, my brethren, follow the example of love, as you have till now followed that *of hatred."* Mendelssohn had grown up in the study of the Talmud. He prepared for his children a German translation of the Bible, which he then published for general use among Jews.

The Talmudic rabbinate, declaring that "the Jewish youth would learn the German language from Mendelssohn's translation, more than an understanding of the Torah," put it under ban: "All true to Judaism are forbidden under penalty of excommunication to use the translation." They then had the translation publicly burned in Berlin.

The great remonstrants of Judaism always stirred Jewry, but always failed; the ruling sect always prevailed. There were two reasons for this: the invariable support given by Gentile governments to the dominant sect and its dogma, and an element of self-surrender among the Jewish masses. In this the Jewish mass, or mob, was not different from all mobs, or masses, at all periods in history. The mass passively submitted to the revolution in France, to Communism in Russia, to National Socialism in Germany, its inertia being greater than any will to resist or the fear of ensuing danger. So it has always been with the Jews and the Talmudic terror.

In our century remonstrant Jews affirmed, too soon, that the terror was no longer potent. In 1933 Mr Bernard J. Brown wrote, "The bite of excommunication has lost its sting ... The rabbis and the priests have lost their grip on human thought and men are free to believe as they please without let or hindrance"; and in 1946 Rabbi Elmer Berger said, "The average Jew is no longer subject to the punishment of excommunication."

Both were premature. The years which followed these statements show that the paramount sect was still able to enforce the submission of Jews throughout the world.

Nevertheless, the fierceness of the Talmudic rule, within the ghettoes, often produced a weeping, groaning and rattling of chains. This caused the Talmudists enough concern for them to introduce what seemed to be a mitigation. In about 900 AD "discussion about the Talmud and religious dogma became allowable" (Dr. Kastein). On the face of it this appeared to be in itself a reversion of the dogma, whereunder no dot or comma of any rabbinical ruling might be called in question, or any doubt expressed about the derivation from Mount Sinai.

Genuine debate would have let fresh air into the ghettoes, but if any intention to allow that had existed, Maimonides and Spinoza need never have been persecuted. What was actually permitted in the synagogues and schools was a unique form of dialectics, designed still further to strengthen the edifice of The Law. The disputants were merely allowed to prove that *anything* was legal under the Talmud; one debater would state a proposition and another the contrary, each demonstrating that The Law allowed it!

This practice (the brothers Thoreau give glimpses of it in their books) was called "pilpulism." It gives the key to a mystery which often baffles Gentiles: the agility with which Zionists are often able to justify, in themselves, precisely what they reproach in others. A polemist trained in pilpulism would have no difficulty in showing the Judaic law ordaining the enslavement of household Gentiles to be righteous and the Roman ban on the enslavement of Christians by Jewish masters to be "persecution"; the Judaic ban on intermarriage to be "voluntary separation" and any Gentile counter-ban to be "discrimination based in prejudice" (Dr. Kastein's terms); a massacre of Arabs to be rightful under The Law and a massacre of Jews to be wrongful under any law.

An example of pilpulism is provided by Dr. Kastein's own description of pilpulism: "A species of spiritual gymnastics which is frequently practised where men's intellects, *menaced with suffocation by the pressure of the outside world,* find no outlet for creative expression in real life."

The italicised words are the pilpulist's suggestive interjection; these debaters were stifled by pressure from *within* their communities, not from "the outside world" (which their Law excluded).

These pilpulist "discussions of the Talmud" may have given the closed communities a slight, and illusory, sense of participation in the despotism that ruled them (like the vote, which may be cast only for one party, in today's dictatorship states). Their real yearning, to escape from their captivity, found its outlet in the Messianic outbreaks; possibly the permission to "discuss the Talmud" was granted in the hope of checking these.

Ever and again the cry went up from the communities, held fast within the tribal palisade, "We *are* doing all the statutes and judgments; now give us the promised, miraculous End!" Thus he series of Messiahs appeared, and each time whipped the communities into a frenzy of anticipation. They were always denounced as "false Messiahs" (they had to be so denounced, as the ruling sect could not effect the triumphant enthronement in Jerusalem which The Law promised), and the people in the ghettoes fell back into hope deferred.

Early Messiahs were Abu Isa of Ispahan in the seventh, Zonarias of Syria in the eighth, and Saadya ben Joseph in the tenth century. The most famous of all was Sabbatai Zevi of Smyrna, who in 1648 proclaimed that the Millennium was at hand by pronouncing the dread name of God in the Synagogue, whereon the Ban was put on him and "to escape its effects" he fled, and stayed away for many years. However, his effect on the Jewish communities, pining for the promised End, was immense. They agreed that he *was* the Messiah; so that he returned to Smyrna in 1665 in defiance of the Talmudists, who in him perceived the greatest threat to their authority in many centuries.

Sabbatai Zevi next *declared himself to* be the Messiah. The desire to exchange the chains of the Talmud for the triumphant fulfilment in Jerusalem was so great that the congregation in Smyrna, followed by the Jewish masses all over the world, brushed aside the Talmudists' ban and acclaimed him. He then proclaimed that 1666 was to be the Messianic year, distributed the crowns of the world among his friends, and set out for Constantinople to dethrone the Sultan of Turkey (then ruler of Palestine). Jews everywhere began to sell their businesses, homes and chattels in preparation for "the return" and the day of world dominion. In London (as Samuel Pepys recorded in February 1666) bets were made among Jews on the prospects of his being acclaimed "King of the World and the true Messiah."

As was to be expected, he was arrested when he reached Constantinople and cast in jail. This merely increased his renown and following; the prison was besieged by clamorous throngs, so that he was removed to a fortress in Gallipoli, which in turn was transformed into a royal residence by gifts from Jews. Mass-emotions were fully aroused; in the imagination of a scattered nation, long isolated from mankind, he *was* the King of the World, come to liberate them by setting them over all mankind.

At that instant Sabbatai Zevi had done exactly what the elders of the sect themselves had done: he had promised what he could not fulfil (this is the basic flaw in the creed, which must eventually destroy it). Unlike the wary elders, he had set himself a time limit: the last day of the year 1666! As the year approached its end (and the Talmudic government in Poland, now sure of the outcome, through an emissary denounced him to the Sultan as "a false Messiah"), he decided, in his prison-palace, to save himself. With great ceremony he had himself converted to Islam and ended his days at the Sultan's court, like any present-day Zionist in New York. For a while he had shaken even the Talmudic government, which then put "the great Ban" on his followers. A tiny remnant of them survive to this day; they believe that Sabbatai will return and that his example must be copied, including conversion to Islam.

Zionism in our time is recognisably a new form of Messianism, leading to the same inevitable disappointment. After the passing of Sabbatai Zevi, and the hope they had put in him, the Jewish masses relapsed into the captivity of the ghettoes. Deprived of the hope of liberation, they reverted, beneath the stern gaze of their masters, to the study of The Law and its destructive message. They were being prepared for a task.

Douglas Reed

Chapter 17

THE DESTRUCTIVE MISSION

The study of hundreds of volumes, during many years, gradually brought realization that the essential truth of the story of Zion is all summed-up in Mr Maurice Samuel's twenty-one words: "We Jews, the destroyers, will remain the destroyer forever ... nothing that the Gentiles will do will meet our needs and demands."

At first hearing they sound vainglorious or neurotic, but increasing knowledge of the subject shows them to be honestly meant and carefully chosen. They mean that a man who is born and continues a Jew acquires a destructive mission which he cannot elude. If he deviates from this "Law" he is not a good Jew, in the eyes of the elders; if he wishes or is compelled to be a good Jew, he must conform to it.

This is the reason why the part played by those who directed "the Jews" in history was bound to be a destructive one; and in our generation of the Twentieth Century the destructive mission has attained its greatest force, with results which cannot even yet be fully foreseen.

This is not an opinion of the present writer. Zionist scribes, apostate rabbis and Gentile historians *agree* about the destructive purpose; it is not in dispute among serious students and is probably the only point on which agreement is unanimous.

All history is presented to the Jew in these terms: that destruction is the condition of the fulfilment of the Judaic Law and of the ultimate Jewish triumph.

"All history" means different things to the Jew and the Gentile. To the Gentile it means, approximately, the annals of the Christian era and any that extend further back before they begin to fade into legend and myth.

To the Jew it means the record of events given in the Torah-Talmud and the rabbinical sermons, and this reaches back to 3760 BC., the exact date of the Creation. The Law and "history" are the same, and there is only Jewish history; this narrative unfolds itself before his eyes exclusively as a tale of destructive achievement and of Jewish vengeance, in the present time as three thousand or more years ago. By this method of portrayal the whole picture of other nations' lives collapses into almost nothing, like the bamboo-and-paper framework of a Chinese lantern. It is salutary for the Gentile to contemplate his world, past and present, through these eyes and to find that what he always thought to be significant, worthy of pride, or shameful, does not even exist, save as a blurred background to the story of Zion. It is like looking at himself through the wrong end of a telescope with one eye and at Judah through a magnifying glass with the other.

To the literal Jew the world is still flat and Judah, its inheritant, is the centre of the universe. The ruling sect has been able, in great measure, to impose this theory of life on the great nations of the West, as it originally inflicted The Law on the Judahites themselves.

The command, "destroy," forms the very basis of the Law which the Levites made. If it be deleted, what remains is not "the Mosaic Law," or the same religion, but something different; the imperative, "destroy," is the mark of identity. It must have been deliberately chosen. Many other words could have been used; for instance, conquer, defeat, vanquish, subdue; but *destroy* was chosen, It was put in the mouth of God, but obviously was the choice of the scribes.

This was the kind of perversion which Jesus attacked: "teaching for doctrine *the commandments of men*"

It comes first at the very start of the story, being attributed directly to God in the original promise of the Promised Land: "I will ... *destroy* all the people to whom thou shalt come." Even before that the first act of destruction has been imputed to God, in the form of the first "vengeance" on the heathen: "I will stretch out my hand and smite Egypt ... I will smite all the first born in the land of Egypt... And Pharaoh's servants said unto him ... knowest thou not yet that Egypt is *destroyed?" (Exodus)*

From that beginning the teaching, "destroy," runs through all The Law, first, and all the portrayal of historical events, next. The act of destruction is sometimes the subject of a bargain between God and the chosen people, on an "If" and "Then" basis; either God offers to destroy, or the chosen people ask him to destroy. In each case the act of destruction is depicted as something so meritorious that it demands a high equivalent service. Thus:

"If thou shalt indeed ... do all that I speak, *then* I will be an enemy unto thine enemies ... and will *destroy* all the people to whom thou shalt come" *(Exodus).* (In this case God is quoted as promising destruction in return for "observance"; chief among the "statutes and judgments" to be observed is, "Ye shall utterly *destroy* all the places, wherein the nations which ye shall possess served other Gods"; *Deuteronomy).*

Conversely: "And Israel vowed a vow unto the Lord, and said, *If* thou wilt indeed deliver this people into my hand, *then* I will utterly destroy their cities; And the Lord hearkened to the voice of Israel, and delivered up the Canaanites; and they *utterly destroyed* them and their cities" *(Numbers).*

As will be seen, the bargain about "destruction" is conditional, in both cases, on performance of a counter-service by the people or by God.

The command, "utterly destroy," being high among the tenets of the inflexible Law, any exercise of clemency, or other shortcoming in utter destruction, is a grave *legal* offence, not merely an error of judgment. For this very crime (under this Law it *is* a crime, not a misdemeanour) Saul, the first and only true king of the united kingdom of Israel and Judah, was dethroned by the priests and David, the man of Judah, put in his place. This reason for David's elevation is significant, as the "king of the world," yet to come, is to be of the house of David. The same lesson is repeatedly driven home in the books of The Law, particularly by the allegorical massacre of the Midianites which concludes Moses's narrative (*Numbers*).

This was the basis on which all The Law, and all history of that time and later times, was built. From the moment when Israel rejected them and they were left alone with the Levites, the Judahites were ruled by a priesthood which avowed that destruction was Jehovah's chief command and that they were divinely chosen to destroy. Thus they became the only people in history specifically dedicated to destruction *as such*. Destruction as an *attendant result* of war is a familiar feature of all human history. Destruction as an avowed purpose was never before known and the only discoverable source of this unique idea is the Torah-Talmud.

The intention clearly was to organize a destructive force; therein lies the great truth of Mr Samuel's words in our time.

As long as any large body of people, distributed among the nations, submitted to such a Law their energies, wherever they were, were bound to be directed to a destructive end. Out of the experience of 458-444 BC, when the Levites with Persian help clamped down their law on a weeping people, the nation was born which ever since has performed its catalytic function of changing surrounding societies while remaining itself unchanged.

The Jews became the universal catalyst, and the changes they produced were destructive. This process caused much tribulation to the Gentiles (which they brought on themselves by their servience to the ruling sect) and no true gratification to the Jews (who inherited a melancholy mission).

The Gentiles have survived and will survive; despite the Daniels and Mordecais. and their latterday successors, the "full end" of those nations "whither I have driven thee" is further off than ever.

The Law specifically enjoined the chosen people to ruin other peoples among whom Jehovah "scattered" them as punishment for their own "transgressions."

For instance, *Exodus* cannot be regarded as more than a legend which received a priestly re-editing in Jerusalem and Babylon many centuries after any time at which anything resembling the events described in it could have occurred. Therefore the scribes had no need to attribute to the Egyptians fear of the destructive purpose nursed by the sojourners in their midst. If they did this, in the very first chapter of *Exodus*. ("Come, let us deal wisely with them; lest they multiply, and it come to pass, that, when there falleth out any war, *they join also unto our enemies and fight against us* ... ") it was evidently to fix the idea of this destructive mission in the minds of the people over whom they ruled.

Here the idea that "the people" should join with their hosts' enemies, in order to destroy their hosts, first appears. When the story reaches a more or less verifiable event (the fall of Babylon) it is portrayed in such a way as to foster this same notion. The Judahites are depicted as joining with the enemies of Babylon and exultantly welcoming the Persian invader. The destruction of Babylon is shown as an act of vengeance wreaked by Jehovah on behalf of the Judahites, exclusively; this vengeance is extended also to a king and the manner of his death (both apparently invented, but valid as historical precedents).

The presentation of history in the Old Testament ends with the next act of vengeance, on the Persian liberators! Western political leaders of our century, who often were flattered to be compared by Zionist visitors to good King Cyrus of Persia, the liberator of the Judahites, may not have read "The Law" with attention or have noted what then befell the Persians. Logically the Persians in their turn had to suffer for having Judahites among them.

For the purpose of this allegorical anecdote, a symbolic heathen "persecutor," Haman, was created, who advised the Persian king Ahasuerus: "There is a certain people scattered abroad and dispersed among the peoples in all the provinces of thy kingdom and their laws are diverse from those of every people; neither keep they the king's laws; therefore it profiteth not the king to suffer them" (*Esther 3*). Thus far, Haman's words are not much different from the opinion which any statesman might, and many statesmen through the centuries until our day did, proffer in respect of the "severed" people and their unique Law. But then, according to *Esther*, Haman adds, "If it please the king, let it be written that they may be *destroyed*," and king Ahasuerus gives the order. (Haman has to speak so, and king Ahasuerus to act so, in order that the ensuing Jewish vengeance may come about.) Letters go out to all provincial governors that all Jews are to be killed in one day, "even upon the thirteenth day of the twelfth month."

The later scribes who composed the book of Esther apparently wished to vary the theme of the powerful Judahite at the court of the foreign king, and conceived the character of Esther the secret Jewess, the favourite concubine of the Persian king who was raised to be his consort. At Esther's intercession the king cancels the order and has Haman and his ten sons hanged on gallows which Haman had built for Mordecai the Jew (Esther's cousin and guardian). The king also gives Mordecai carte blanche, whereon Mordecai instructs the governors of the "hundred twenty and seven provinces" from India unto Ethiopia to have the Jews in every city "gather themselves together and to stand for their life, to *destroy*, to slay and to cause to perish all the power of the people … both little ones and women…"

This countermanding decree being published, "the Jews had joy and gladness, a feast and a good day" and (a detail of interest) "many of the people of the land became Jews; for the fear of the Jews fell upon them."

Then, on the appointed day, the Jews "smote all their enemies with the stroke of the sword, and slaughter, and *destruction,* and did what they would unto those that hated them, slaying of their foes "seventy and five thousand." Mordecai then ordered that the fourteenth and fifteenth days of the month Adar should in future be kept as "days of feasting and joy," and so it has been, ever since.

Apparently Haman, Mordecai and Esther were all imaginary. No "king Ahasuerus" historically exists, though one encyclopaedia (possibly from the wish to breathe life into the veins of the parables) says that Ahasuerus "has been identified with Xerxes." In that case he was father of the king Artaxerxes who sent soldiers with Nehemiah to Jerusalem to enforce the racial "New Covenant," and in that event, again, Artaxerxes so acted after witnessing in his own country a massacre of 75,000 Persian subjects by Jews!

No historical basis for the story can be discovered and it has all the marks of chauvinist propaganda.

The perplexing fact remains that, if it was invented, it could be true in every detail today, when The Law founded on such anecdotes has been imposed on The West. Today people cannot "become Jews" (or very rarely), but a familiar picture of our time is conveyed in the words, "many of the people of the land became Jews; for the fear of the Jews fell upon them"; in our generation they become "Zionist sympathizers" from the same motive.

How faithful a portrait of the 20th Century politician in Washington or London is given in the passage, "and all the rulers of the provinces, and the lieutenants, and the deputies, and officers of the king, helped the Jews; because the fear of Mordecai fell upon them." If neither king Ahasuerus nor "Mordecai sitting in the king's gate" truly lived in 550 BC, nevertheless Mordecai in our century is real and powerful and two generations of public men have administered their offices from fear of him more than from care of their peoples' interest.

It is our today which makes this remote, implausible yesterday so plausible. On the face of it, Belshazzar and Daniel, Ahasuerus and Mordecai seem to be symbolic figures, created for the purpose of the Levitical political programme, not men who once lived. But ... the massacre of the Czar and his family, in our century, was carried out according to verse 30, chapter 5 of *Daniel*: the hanging of the Nazi leaders followed the precept laid down in verses 6 and 10, chapter 7, and verses 13 and 14, chapter 9, of *Esther*.

Whether these anecdotes were fact or fable, they have become The Law of our century. The most joyful festivals of the Jewish year commemorate the ancient legends of destruction and vengeance on which The Law is based: the slaying of "all the firstborn of Egypt," and Mordecai's massacre.

Perhaps, then, it is even true that within fifty years of their conquest by Babylon the Jews brought about the destruction of that kingdom by Persia;

and that within fifty years of their liberation by the Persian king they had in turn possessed themselves of the Persian kingdom, to such an extent that the king's governors "from India to Ethiopia" from fear of the Jews carried out a pogrom of 75,000 people, and that the death "accursed of God" was inflicted on some selected "enemies." In that case the Persian liberator fared rather worse at the captives' hands than the Babylonian captor, earlier.

As this tale goes along, with its inevitable allusions to "the Jews," it is important to remember that there have always been two minds in Judaism, and quotations from our time serve to illustrate this.

A Chicago rabbi, Mr Solomon B. Freehof, quoted by Mr Bernard J. Brown, considered the story of Haman, Mordecai and Esther to be "the essence of all the history of the Jewish people"; whereas Mr Brown himself (also of Chicago) says the celebration of Purim ought to be discontinued and forgotten, being in the present time "a travesty" even of "the festivals which were so disgusting" to the Israelite prophets. (Purim had not been invented when Isaiah and Hosea made their impassioned protests against the "appointed seasons" and "feast days").

Mr Brown wrote in 1933 and the event of 1946, when the Nazi leaders were hanged on a Jewish feast day, showed that his remonstrance was as vain as the ancient remonstrances cited by him. In 1946, as twenty-seven centuries earlier, the view expressed by Rabbi Freehof prevailed. The essential features of the event commemorated by Purim are those which invariably recur in earlier and later stages of the story of Zion: the use of a Gentile ruler to destroy Gentiles and give effect to the Judaic vengeance.

From the time of Mordecai, as the Old Testament provides no more history, the student must turn to Judaist authorities to learn whether later events also were presented to Jews in the same light; namely, as a series of Jewish ordeals suffered at the hands of "the heathen," each leading to the ruination of the heathen nation concerned and to a Judaic vengeance.

This research leads to the conclusion that all history, to the present time, is so seen by the elders of the sect and so presented to the Jewish masses. In the same way that Egypt, Babylon and Persia, in the Old Testament, exist only insofar as they capture, oppress or otherwise behave towards Jews, who are then avenged by Jehovah, so in the scholars' presentation of the later period does all else fall away. Rome, Greece and all subsequent empires have life and being, in this depictment, only to the extent that the behaviour of Jews towards them or their behaviour towards Jews gives them existence.

After Babylon and Persia, the next nation to feel the impact of the catalytic force was Egypt. The Jewish community in Alexandria (which had been large even before its reinforcement by fugitives from the Babylonian invasion) was at this period the largest single body of Jews in the known world; Egypt was in that respect in the position of Russia before the 1914-

1918 war and of the United States today. The attitude of the Jews, or at all events of the elders, towards the Egyptians was the same as their earlier attitude towards the Persians and Babylonians.

Dr. Kastein says, first, that Egypt was "the historic refuge" for Jews, which sounds like a grateful tribute until subsequent words show that "a refuge" is a place to be destroyed. He describes the feeling of the Jews towards the Egyptians in words very similar to those concerning the Jews which *Exodus* attributes to the Egyptians in respect of the earlier "captivity." He says, the Jews in Egypt "constituted a closed community ... they led a secluded life and built their own temples ... the Egyptians felt that the religious exclusiveness of the Jews showed that they despised and spurned their own form of faith." He adds that the Jews "naturally" upheld the Persian cause because Persia had formerly "helped them restore Judah.

Thus the fact that Egypt had given shelter, and was "the historic refuge" did not entitle Egypt to any gratitude or loyalty. Hostility to the host-people took the form of support for the Egyptians' enemy and therefore awoke Egyptian suspicion: "Other causes of hostility were the determination Shown by the Jews not to become assimilated with the people about them or *identify themselves with the country of their adoption* ... The profound spiritual necessity of keeping in touch with every branch of the nation, the call for loyalty towards every group of their own people, however fragmentary, *was bound to affect the integrity of their citizenship of a particular state."*

"As in Babylon of yore," concludes Dr. Kastein, the Jews in Egypt extended "open arms" to the Persian conqueror. Yet Egypt had shown the Jews only hospitality.

Babylon, Persia, Egypt ... then came Greece. In 332 BC. Greece conquered Persia and the Greek rule of Egypt began; Alexandria became the Greek capital. Many Alexandrine Jews would fain have followed Jeremiah's counsel to "seek the peace of the city." The power of the sect and the destructive teaching prevailed.

Dr. Kastein, the sect's devotee, says of Greece and its civilization merely that, "it was intellectually brilliant ... but the *prototype* of everything that was mendacious, cruel, slanderous, cunning, indolent, vain, corruptible, grasping and unjust." He dismisses the episode of Greece with the triumphant note. *"The Alexandrian Jews brought about the disintegration of Hellenic civilization."*

Babylon, Persia, Egypt, Greece ... Up to the start of the Christian era, therefore, history back to the Creation was presented to the Jews, by their scriptures and their scholars, as an exclusively Jewish affair, which took note of "the heathen" only insofar as they impinged on Jewish life, and as a record of destruction achieved against these heathen, in peace and war.

Was this portrayal true, of events in the pre-Christian era, and did it continue true of later events, down to our day?

The inference of our own generation, of which it is certainly true, is that is has always been true. In our century conflicts between nations, on the Babylonian-Persian model, even though they seemed at their start to be concerned with issues remote from any Jewish question, were turned into Judaic triumphs and Judaic vengeances, so that the destruction which accompanied them became an act of fulfilment under The Judaic Law, like the slaying of the Egyptian firstborn, the destruction of Babylon, and Mordecai's pogrom.

Rome followed Greece, and when Rome rose Cicero evidently shared the opinion, about the part played by the Jews in the disintegration of Greek civilization, which a Dr. Kastein was to express twenty centuries later, for at the trial of Flaccus Cicero looked fearfully behind him when he spoke of Jews; he knew (he said) that they all held together and that they knew how to ruin him who opposed them, and he counselled caution in dealing with them.

Fuscus, Ovid and Persius uttered similar warnings, and, during the lifetime of Jesus, Seneca said, "The customs of this criminal nation are gaining ground so rapidly that they already have adherents in every country, *and thus the conquered force their laws upon the conqueror.*" At this period too the Roman geographer Strabo commented on the distribution and number of the Jews (which in our time is patently so much greater than any statistics are allowed to express), saying that there was no place in the earth where they were not.

Greece and Rome, in the common Gentile view, created enduring values on which the civilization of Europe was built. Out of Greece came beauty and Greek foundations lie beneath all poetry and art; out of Rome came law and Roman ones lie beneath Magna Charta, Habeas Corpus and the right of a man to fair and public trial, which was the greatest achievement of The West.

To the Zionist scholar Greece and Rome were just transient heathen manifestations, equally repellent. Dr. Kastein says disdainfully that in Rome "from the very beginning Judea quite rightly saw merely the representative of unintellectual and stupid brute force."

For three hundred years after the lifetime of Jesus, Rome persecuted the Christians. After the conversion of the Emperor Constantine to Christianity in 320 AD, the Jews were forbidden to circumcise their slaves, keep Christian ones, or intermarry; this application of the Judaic Law in reverse is held by Dr. Kastein to be persecution.

After the division of the Roman Empire in 395 Palestine became part of the Byzantine Empire. The ban on Jews in Jerusalem had only been lifted after Rome became predominantly Christian, so that the city might still have been empty of Jews, but for Christianity. However, when the Persians in 614 carried their war against Byzantium into Palestine, the Jews "flocked to the Persian army from all sides" and then participated, "with the fury of men bent on avenging themselves for *three hundred years of oppression*," in "a wholesale massacre of Christians," (again according to Dr. Kastein, to whom, as above shown, the ban on the enslavement of Christians is oppression).

Enthusiasm for the Persians died with the vengeance on Christians; fourteen years later the Jews "were only too ready to negotiate with the Byzantine emperor Heraclitus," and to help him to reconquer Jerusalem.

Then came Muhammad and Islam. Muhammad shared the view of Cicero and other, earlier authorities; his Koran, in addition to the allusion previously cited, says, "Thou shalt surely find the most violent of all men in enmity against the true believers to be the Jews and the idolaters ..."

Nevertheless, Islam (like Christianity) showed no enmity against the Jews and Dr. Kastein has a relatively good word for it: "Islam allowed the infidel absolute economic freedom and autonomous administration ... Islam certainly practised toleration towards those of other faith ... Judaism was never offered such fine chances, such fine opportunities to flourish, from Christianity."

These "opportunities to flourish" were provided by Islam for the Jews on the soil of Europe, in Spain, as previously told; this was the entrance into the West, made possible by Islam to "the most violent of all men." In the wake of the Islamic conqueror the Talmudic government (after the Caliph Omar had taken Jerusalem in 637 and swept on westward with his armies) moved into Spain!

The Visigoth kings there had already developed similar feelings, about the Jews in their midst, to those expressed by Cicero, Muhammad and others. One of their last, Euric, at the Twelfth Council of Toledo, begged the bishops" to make one last effort to pull this Jewish pest out by the roots" (about 680). After that the Visigoth era quickly came to an end, the Islamic invader establishing himself in southern and central Spain in 712.

Dr. Kastein says, "The Jews supplied pickets and garrison troops for Andalusia." Professor Graetz more fully describes this first encounter between the Jews and peoples of Northern *European* stock:

"The Jews of Africa ... and their unlucky co-religionists of the Peninsula *made common cause with the Mohammedan conqueror,* Tarik ... After the battle of Xeres, July 711, and the death of Roderic, the last Visigoth king, the victorious Arabs pushed onward and *were everywhere supported by the Jews.* In every city that they conquered, the Moslem generals were able to leave but a small garrison of their own troops, as they had need of every man for the subjection of their country; *they therefore confided them to the safekeeping of the Jews. In this manner the Jews, who but lately had been serfs, now became the masters of the towns of Cordova, Granada, Malaga and many others. When Tarik appeared before the capital, Toledo, he found it occupied by a small garrison only ... While the Christians were in church, praying for the safety of their country and religion, the Jews flung open the gates to the victorious Arabs, receiving them with acclamations and thus avenged themselves for the many miseries which had befallen them ... The capital also was entrusted by Tarik to the custody of the Jews* ... Finally when Musa Ibn Nossair, the Governor of Africa, brought a second army into Spain and conquered other cities, *he also delivered them into the custody of the Jews* ..."

The picture is identical with that of all earlier historical, or legendary, events in which the Jews were concerned: a conflict between two "stranger" peoples was transformed into a *Judaic* triumph and a *Judaic* vengeance.

The Jews (as in Babylon and Egypt) turned against the people with whom they lived and once more "flung open the gates" to the foreign invader. The foreign invader, in his turn, "delivered" the cities taken by him to the Jews.

In war the capital city and the other great cities, the power and control over them, are the fruits of victory; they went to the Jews, not to the victor. The Caliph's generals evidently paid as little heed to the Koran's warnings as Western politicians of today pay to the teaching of the New Testament.

As to "the miseries" for which the Jews thus took vengeance, Professor Graetz specifically states that the cruellest of these was the denial of the right to keep slaves: "the *most oppressive* of them was the restraint touching the possession of slaves; henceforward the Jews were neither to purchase Christian slaves nor to accept them as presents"!

If the Arab conquerors counted on thankfulness from those to whom they had "entrusted the capital" and the great cities, they misreckoned. After the conquest Judah Halevi of Cordova sang: "... how fulfil my sacred vows, deserve my consecration, While Zion still remains Rome's thrall, and I an Arab minion? As trash to me all Spanish treasure, wealth or Spanish good, when dust as purest gold I treasure, where once our temple stood!"

This spirit disquietened the Caliph's advisers, as it had disquietened the Visigoth kings, Muhammad and the statesmen of Rome. Abu Ishak of Elvira spoke to the Caliph at Cordova in words which again recall those of Cicero:

"The Jews ... have become great lords, and their pride and arrogance know no bounds ... Take not such men for thy ministers ... for the whole earth crieth out against them; ere long it will quake and we shall all perish ... I came to Granada and I beheld the Jews reigning. They had parcelled out the provinces and the capital between them; everywhere one of these accursed ruled. They collected the taxes, they made good cheer, they were sumptuously clad, while your garments, O Muslims, were old and worn-out. All the secrets of state were known to them; yet is it folly to put trust in traitors!"

The Caliph, nevertheless, continued to select his ministers from among the nominees of the Talmudic government of Cordova. The Spanish period shows, perhaps more clearly than any other, that the Jewish portrayal of history may be nearer to historical truth than the narrative according to the Gentiles; for the conquest of Spain certainly proved to be *Judaic* rather than Moorish. The formal Moorish domination continued for 800 years and at the end, in keeping with precedent, the Jews helped the Spaniards expel the

Moors. Nevertheless, the general feeling towards them was too deeply distrustful to be assuaged. This popular suspicion particularly directed itself against the *conversos*, or Marranos. The genuineness of their conversion was not believed, and in this the Spaniards were right, for Dr. Kastein says that between the Jews and Marranos "a secret atmosphere of conspiracy" prevailed; evidently use was being made of the Talmudic dispensation about feigned conversion.

In spite of this public feeling the Spanish kings, during the gradual reconquest, habitually made Jews or Marranos their finance ministers, and eventually appointed one Isaac Arrabanel administrator of the state finances with instructions to raise funds for the reconquest of Granada. The elders, at this period, were dutifully applying the important tenet of The Law about "lending to all nations and borrowing from none," for Dr. Kastein records that they gave "financial help" to the Christian north in its final assault on the Mohammedan south.

After the reconquest the stored-up feeling of resentment against the Jews, born of the 800 years of Moorish occupation and of their share in it, broke through; in 1492 the Jews were expelled from Spain and in 1496 from Portugal.

Today's Zionist historians show a remarkable hatred of Spain on this account, and a firm belief in a Jehovan vengeance not yet completed. The overthrow of the Spanish monarchy nearly five centuries later, and the civil war of the 1930's, are sometimes depicted as instalments on account of this reckoning. This belief was reflected in the imperious words used by Mr Justice Brandeis of the United States Supreme Court, a leading Zionist, to Rabbi Stephen Wise in 1933: "Let Germany *share the fate of Spain!*" The treatment accorded to Spain in the subsequent decades of this century, in particular its long exclusion from the United Nations, has to be considered in this light.

At that point fifteen hundred years of the Christian era had passed and events had conformed to the pattern of the pre-Christian era, as laid down in the historical parts of the Old Testament, and to the requirements of the Judaic Law. The Jews in their impact on other peoples had continued, under Talmudic direction, to act as a destructive force…

"Captive" and "persecuted" everywhere they went (under their own Law, not through the fault of the peoples with whom they sojourned) their part was always what this Law ordained that it should be: to "pull down and *destroy.*" They were indeed used by their rulers to "abet disorder" between others, as the Koran said, and through the disorders thus abetted their rulers achieved civil power, wreaked vengeances, supported invaders and financed counter-blows.

During all this time this was the behest of their Talmudic masters, and constantly Jews rose to protest against it; but The Law was too strong for them. There was no happiness or fulfilment for the Jews in this mission, but they could not escape it.

At the end of this first encounter with the West, after eight centuries, the land "spewed them out."

This was the moment, so decisive for our present generation, to which a previous chapter alluded. But for the secret which was stored in the depths of Russia, this might have been the end of the catalytic force.

The experience of this expulsion was a very hard one for the body of Jews who experienced it, and they and their descendants gave many signs that they accepted the inference and would in time find some way to remain Jews and yet to become involved in mankind. That would have meant the end of the destructive idea and of the sect that fostered it.

Instead, the destructive idea survived and was projected into the affairs of the world through a new group of people, who had no physical descent from any Hebrews, or "children of Israel," or the tribe of Judah. They used the name "Jew" merely as a sign of allegiance to a political programme. The point now reached, in following the course of the destructive idea through the centuries, calls for some further description of these people (mentioned in the chapter on *The Movable Government*).

Even at the start of the 800 years in Spain (from 711 to 1492) the Jews there (the largest single community of Jews) were no longer Judahite or Judeans; not even they could claim to be of the pure line of Judah, or of Palestinian ancestry. Professor Graetz says of them, "The first settlement of Jews in beautiful Hesperia is buried in dim obscurity," and adds that the Jews there "desired to lay claim to high antiquity" for their ancestry, so that they simply asserted that "they had been transported thither after the destruction of the temple by Nebuchadnezzar."

Through many centuries the processes of nature and of man had enforced a mingling. The idea of a people chosen to rule the world over the bodies of fallen heathen appealed to primitive tribespeople in many places; the already-circumcised Arab could become a Jew and hardly notice any change; Rabbis in North African deserts and towns were remote from the "centre" and gladly extended their congregations. When the Roman emperors began to persecute "pagan religions" Judaism never fell under a general prohibition, so that many worshippers of Isis, Baal and Adonis, if they did not become Christians, entered the synagogues. The fierce law of tribal segregation could not at that time be enforced in places far from Babylon.

Thus the Jews who entered Spain with the Moors were, racially, already a mixed throng. During the 800 years *in* Spain the racial teaching was more strictly enforced, the "government" having been transferred to Spain, and in this way the "Sephardic" Jews took shape as a distinct national type. Then, at the expulsion from Spain, the government, as already told, was suddenly transplanted to Poland. What became, at that point, of these Sephardic Jews, who alone may have retained some faint trace of original Judahite or Judean descent?

The *Jewish Encyclopaedia* is explicit: "The Sephardim are the descendants of the Jews who were expelled from Spain and Portugal and who settled in Southern France, Italy, North Africa, Asia Minor, Holland, England, North and South America, Germany, Denmark, Austria and Hungary." *Poland is not mentioned;* the Talmudic Government went there, but the mass of these Sephardic Jews distributed themselves in Western Europe; they moved westward, not eastward. The "government" was suddenly separated from the people and the mass began to dissolve.

The *Jewish Encyclopaedia* says, of the Sephardim who were thus dispersed: "Among these settlers were many who were the descendants or heads of wealthy families and who, as Marranos, had occupied prominent positions in the countries they had left ... They considered themselves a superior class, the nobility of Jewry, and for a long time their co-religionists, on whom they looked down, regarded them as such ... The Sephardim never engaged in chaffering occupations nor in usury and they did not mingle with the lower classes. Although the Sephardim lived on peaceful terms with other Jews they rarely intermarried with them ... *In modern times the Sephardim have lost the authority which for several centuries they exercised over other Jews.*"

The Sephardim, then, neither went to Poland nor mingled with other Jews, when they left the Spanish Peninsula and spread over Western Europe. They remained aloof and apart, "looked down" on others professing to be Jews, and lost their authority. (The Judaists reference works also give curious estimates of the decline in their proportion of Jewry, from a large minority to a small minority; these seem beyond biological explanation *and probably are not trustworthy).*

Thus, at this removal of "the centre," the body of people, in whose name it had asserted authority for two thousand years, abruptly changed its nature as by magic.

The Jews hitherto known to the world, who had just emerged from their first impact between their Law and the peoples of *the West,* and were *in reflective mood,* suddenly began to lose caste in Jewry and to dwindle in numbers!

The Talmudic government set out to prepare its second encounter with the West from a new headquarters, planted among an Asiatic people, the Khazars, converted to Jehovah worship many centuries before. The ruling sect was thenceforward to operate through this different body of people; they were wild folk who had not known the cautionary experience in Spain.

In 1951 a New York publisher who contemplated issuing one of the present writer's books was strongly advised not to do this by the head of a Jewish political bureau, and was told, "Mr Reed invented the Khazars."

However, the *Judaist authorities agree about their existence* and conversion, and the historical atlases show the development of the Khazar kingdom, which at its greatest extent reached from the Black Sea to the Caspian (around 600 AD). They are described as a Tartar or Turco-Mongolian people and the *Jewish Encyclopaedia* says that their chagan, or chieftain, "with his grandees and a large number of his heathen people embraced Judaism, probably about 679 AD."

The fact is attested by correspondence between Hasdai ibn Shapnet, Foreign Minister to Abdel Rahman, Sultan of Cordova, and King Joseph of the Khazars, exchanged about 960 AD. The *Jewish Encyclopaedia* says that the Judaist scholars had *no doubts* as to the genuineness of this correspondence, in which the word *Ashkenazi* first occurs as denoting this sharply-outlined, hitherto unknown group of "Eastern Jews" *and as indicating Slav associations.*

This community of Turco-Mongolian Ashkenazim, then, was distinct in every element save that of the creed from the Jews previously known to the Western world, the Sephardim.

The hold of the Talmudic government, in the centuries that followed, became looser over the scattered communities of the West; but it ruled this new compact community in the East with a rod of iron.

The Jew of Semitic physiognomy became ever rarer (today the typical countenance of the Jew has Mongolian traits, as is natural).

No Gentile will ever know why this one mass-conversion of a numerous "heathen" people to Talmudic Judaism was permitted, thirteen hundred years ago. Was it chance, or were these elders able to foresee every mortal possibility? At all events, when the Sephardim were scattered and the destructive idea received, in Spain, its sharpest setback, this reserve force lay ready to hand and for the purpose of the destructive mission it was the best possible material.

Long before their conversion to Judaism the Khazars were hostile to the immigrant Russ from the north who eventually conquered them, established the Russian monarchy and accepted Christianity.

When the Khazars became converted the Talmud was complete, and after the collapse of their kingdom (in about 1000 AD) they remained the political subjects of the Talmudic government, all their resistance to Russia being governed by the Talmudic, anti- Christian Law. Thereafter they moved about in Russia, particularly to Kieff (the traditional "holy city" of Russian Christianity), elsewhere in the Ukraine, and to Poland and Lithuania.

Though they had no Judahite blood, they became under this Talmudic direction the typical nation-within-the-nation in Russia. The areas where they congregated, under Talmudic direction, became the centres of that anti-Russian revolution which was to become "the world revolution"; in these parts, and through these people, new instruments of destruction were forged, specifically for the destruction of Christianity and the West.

These savage people from the inmost recesses of Asia lived within the Talmud like any Babylonian or Cordovan Jew and for centuries "observed the Law" in order that they might "return" to a "promised land" of which their ancestors probably never heard, there to rule the world. In the Twentieth Century, when the politicians of the West were all agog with this project of the return, none of them had ever heard of the Khazars. Only the Arabs, whose lives and lands were directly at stake, knew of them, and vainly tried to inform the Peace Conference of 1919 and the United Nations in 1947.

After 1500, therefore, the Jews fell into two distinct groups: the scattered communities of the West, who were Sephardic in origin, and this closely corralled mass of Talmudic, Slav "Jews" in the East. Time had to show if the Talmudic centre would be able to make out of the Ashkenazim a destructive force as potent in the future as the earlier one in the past, and whether it could keep its hold over the communities in the West, with their different tradition and their memory of the Iberian expulsion.

About the year 1500, then, the Talmudic government moved from Spain to Poland, establishing itself among a body of "Jews" hitherto unknown to the West and relaxing its hold on the Sephardic Jews, who began to dwindle in numbers and to disintegrate as a cohesive force (in the judgment of the Judaic elders). Only about 450 years separate that event and that point in time from our present day, when the effects of the removal of the Talmudists to Poland have shown themselves, and have answered the two questions raised in the last paragraph.

These 450 years saw the *visible* Talmudic "centre" cease to exist (in Dr. Kastein's words) and the destructive idea simultaneously enter Europe in a new form, which bore the name "revolution."

The 450 years have seen three of these "revolutions" (counting only the chief ones). Each was more destructive than the last. Each was recognizable as the heir of the former one by its chief characteristics, and these, again, were the chief characteristics of the Judaic Law as laid down in the Torah-Talmud. The main assault in each case was on legitimate government, nationhood and Christianity. Under the Judaic Law the only legitimate government is that of Jehovah and the only legitimate nation is that of Jehovah's chosen people; under the Talmudic supplement of that Law Christianity is specifically the chief of those "other gods," after whom the chosen are for bidden to "go a-whoring"; and "destruction," as has been shown, is a supreme tenet of that Law.

When these revolutions began they were supposed to be aimed at "kings and priests," as the symbolic figures of oppression. Now that the power of kings and priests is gone, but the revolution is established in permanence, it may be seen that these were false words, chosen to delude "the multitude." The attack was on *nationhood* (the murdered king being in each case the symbol) and on *religion* (the destruction of churches being the symbolic act).

These were recognizable marks of authorship. The Torah-Talmud is the only original fount of such ideas that research can discover. "He shall deliver their kings into thine hand and thou shalt *destroy* their name from them ... ye shall utterly *destroy* all the places wherein the nations which ye shall possess served their gods." At the very moment when the Talmudic government vanished from sight, after setting itself among a barbaric Asiatic people, this creed of destruction entered Western Europe and began its ruinous march.

These three revolutions, then, like the historic events of the pre-Christian era depicted in the Old Testament, and of the Christian era up to the expulsion from Spain, also conformed with and fulfilled the Judaic Law. All three of them bear the common hallmark of a Judaic triumph, as their outcome. Were they originally instigated, organized and directed by the Talmudists?

In that respect there is a great difference between the first two and the last one.

Talmudic incitement and control of the English and French revolutions cannot be discovered, at any rate by the present writer's research. In each case the *results* bore the familiar signs of the Judaic triumph (the "return" of the Jews to England; the emancipation of the Jews in France), although at the start of both revolutions the Jewish question had not been present in the public mind as an issue at stake. As far as the student can ascertain at this distance of time, the projection of "the Jewish question" into these issues, and its elevation to a chief place among them, was something achieved while the revolutions went along, and the Judaic elders who accomplished this did not actually bring about the revolutions.

The third case, that of the Russian revolution, is entirely different. It culminated in the greatest Judaic triumph and Judaic vengeance on record, either in Old Testamentary history or in later history, and was organized, directed and controlled by Jews who had grown up in the Talmud-controlled areas. This is a fact of our present day, demonstrable and undeniable, and it is the most significant fact in the whole story of Zion, illuminating all the past and giving the key to all the future.

For our century, which produced that event has also seen the word "revolution" given a new meaning, or more accurately, given its *true* meaning: destruction without end until The Law is fulfilled. When the word "revolution" first became current in the West it was held to mean a limited thing: a violent uprising in a definite place caused by specific conditions there at a certain time. Unbearable oppression produced an explosive reaction, rather in the manner of a kettle blowing off its lid: that was the popular conception, instilled in "the multitude" by elders who knew better.

The Russian revolution revealed that the revolution had been organized as a *permanent* thing: a *permanently* destructive force,
permanently organized with a *permanent* headquarters and staff, and worldwide aims.

Thus, it had nothing to do with *conditions* here or there, or now and then, or local oppression. It stood for destruction as an aim in itself, or as a means of removing all legitimate government from the world and putting in its place some other government, other governors. Who could these be but the Talmudists themselves, given the Talmudic nature of the revolution in Russia and the obviously Talmudic aims of "the world revolution"?

What was aimed at was plainly the final consummation of The Law, in its literal form: "Thou shalt reign over every nation but they shall not reign over thee ... the Lord thy God shall set thee on high above all nations of the earth."

Without this motive the three revolutions would never have taken the course they took; the course they took prefigures the shape of the future. They represent stages in and steps towards the fulfilment of The Law, and, once again, those who in their day seemed to be great or powerful men in their own right, like King Cyrus and the mysterious King Ahasuerus, now look like mere puppets in the great drama of Judaic history as it moves towards its miraculous end in Jerusalem.

Cromwell was another such. To the average English schoolboy he lives only as the man who beheaded a king and brought back the Jews to England. Add to that his vaunted massacre of priests at Drogheda (an event which has not its like in British history) and what remains but a typical puppet-figure of Zionist history, created merely to help fulfil The Law?

Cromwell was one of the first of those many who since his day have called themselves Old Testamentary Christians, which figure of speech disguises the fact of anti-Christianity, as God and Mammon, on the best authority, cannot both be served. He forbade the celebration of Christmas Day, burned churches and murdered priors, and for an instant was a candidate for the Jewish Messiahship!

He was in power at the time when Sabbatai Zevi was whipping the Jewish masses into a frenzy of Zionist anticipation and shaking the Talmudic government to its foundations. Indeed, the alarm of the Talmudists about Sabbatai Zevi may have prompted the idea that they should use Cromwell to destroy him. In any case Jewish emissaries from Amsterdam were urgently despatched to England to discover whether Cromwell might be of Judaic decent! Had their research yielded positive results, Cromwell might have been proclaimed the Messiah, for he had one qualification most appealing to the elders: his zeal in "utter destruction." (If ever a Messiah should be proclaimed, the choice may prove surprising; when I was in Prague in 1939 a rabbi there was preaching that Hitler was the Jewish Messiah, so that a worried Jewish acquaintance asked me what I thought of this.)

Cromwell's pedigree disclosed no descent from David, or he would probably have been glad to play the part. His sword-and-Bible followers claimed by their bloodthirsty deeds to be fulfilling prophecy, and by restoring the Jews to England to be accomplishing the prescribed steps preparatory to the Millennium. They even proposed, on that account, that Cromwell's Council of State should follow the model of the ancient Sanhedrin and be composed of seventy members! (Cromwell himself had some contempt for these his "Millenarians," but as a "practical politician" of the kind familiar in our century he was glad to orate about "religious freedom" and the fulfilment of prophecy, while hunting down priests and clergymen).

For his part, Cromwell's real purpose was to enlist the financial support of the rich Amsterdam Jews (the entire history of the West seems to have been made under that tenet of the Judaic Law which commands lending unto all nations and borrowing from none). Mr John Buchan says of the Amsterdam Jews that "they controlled the Spanish, Portuguese and much of the Levant trade ... they commanded the flow of bullion; they would help him in the difficult finances of his government." Rabbi Manasseh ben Israel from Amsterdam (who had been foretelling the advent of the Messiah and the return of the Jews to Palestine) came to London and the matter was arranged.

Manasseh ben Israel's petition to Cromwell is reminiscent of the kind of argument, formally respectful and implicitly menacing, which was used in this century by Dr. Chaim Weizmann in his dealings with British Prime Ministers and American Presidents; he asked for "the readmission" of the Jews to England in one breath, alluded darkly in the next to the Jehovan retribution awaiting those who resisted such demands, and then depicted the rewards which would follow compliance. The picture is closely comparable with that of a New York Zionist informing an American presidential candidate in our generation that he can only expect the "New York State vote" if he commits himself to uphold the Zionist state in peace and war, by money and arms.

What was demanded from Cromwell was in fact an act of public submission to the Judaic Law, not "the readmission" of the Jews, for they had never left England! They had been expelled on paper but had remained where they were, and a formal legalization of that situation was required. Cromwell was prevented by public opposition from doing this (although according to a Judaist authority, Mr Margoliouth, he was offered £500,000 to sell to the Jews England's greatest Christian monument, Saint Paul's Cathedral, with the Bodleian Library thrown in!)

Then Cromwell's brief Interregnum came to an end (nevertheless, the popular mind insists on remembering him as the man who readmitted the

Jews!) and at this first bid in the West the destructive idea gained little ground. England was able to digest its revolution as if nothing very much had happened and to go on its way, if not refreshed, at any rate little the worse. Legitimate government was at once restored and religion was at all events not damaged more by this alien attempt on it than by the native inertia which began to weaken it at that time.

Nevertheless, this new phenomenon "revolution" had entered Europe, and 150 years after the expulsion from Spain "the Jewish question" dominated the event.

The sequel to Cromwell's Interregnum deserves brief comment because of the way the restored king was used for the Jewish purpose, as if nothing had happened. At Cromwell's death the Jews transferred their financial aid to Charles II who, soon after his restoration, made the necessary amendments, formally legalizing the position of the Jews in England. This did not in the least avail his dynasty, for the Amsterdam Jews next financed the expedition of William of Orange against his brother and successor, James II, who was dethroned and fled to France, the Stuart dynasty then coming virtually to an end. Thus the answer to the question, "Who has won?," as between Cromwell and the Stuarts, seems to have been, the Jews.

After a hundred and fifty years the revolution struck again, this time in France. It seemed a separate, different revolution at the time, but was it truly so? It bore the same distinctive features as the English revolution, earlier (and the Russian revolution, later): nationhood and religion were attacked under the pretext of curbing the tyranny of "kings and priests," and when that was done a much harsher despotism was set up.

At that time, after the partition of Poland, the Talmudic government had just "ceased to exist" (in Dr. Kastein's words), but obviously was operating from concealment; its activity would not have so abruptly ended after more than 2,500 years. Because of this withdrawal into obscurity today's student cannot trace what part it played, if any, in inciting and organizing the French revolution, through its followers in France. However, the revolution in Russia, 120 years later, gave proof of direct Talmudic-Jewish control in a measure never before suspected, so that this influence may have been greater, in the preparatory stages of the revolution in France, than history now reveals.

What is certain is that the French revolution, while it was brewing, was supposed to be for "the rights of man" (which presumably meant all men, equally), but when it began "the Jewish question," as by magic, at once came to the fore. One of the earliest acts of the revolution (1791) was the complete emancipation of the Jews (just as the law against "anti-semitism" was one of the first acts of the revolution in Russia).

Therefore the French revolution, in retrospect, assumes the look, common to its English predecessor and to so many violent events in history, of a Jewish triumph in its outcome; if it was not that in truth, then "history" has made it so. Presumably the masses concerned expected something quite different at its outset (and in that respect they resemble the masses which later were engaged in the two Twentieth Century wars).

The emancipation of the Jews was one enduring result of a revolution which achieved little else of permanence and left France in a condition of spiritual apathy from which it has never truly rallied. The history of France since the revolution is one of a long interregnum, in the course of which it has experimented, with almost every form of government known to man but has not until now again found happiness or stability.

From the downfall of Babylon to the revolution in France the ruling Talmudic Jews always acted as a destructive force among the peoples "whither I have driven thee." This was inevitable, given the creed to which they adhered and the fact that this religion was also The Law governing every act of their daily lives. Under the Judaic Law they could not act differently, and were indeed condemned to remain "the destroyers forever": "See, I have this day set thee over the nations and over the kingdom, to root out, and to pull down and to *destroy*."

The story of the Jews, under this control, was the same in Babylon, Persia, Egypt, Greece, Rome and Spain, and could not be anything else, given the unique Judaic Law.

Nevertheless not all "the Jews" wrote this story, nor is the story that of all "the Jews"; to omit this qualification would be like condemning "the Germans" for National Socialism or "the Russians" for an essentially alien Communism.

Resistance to the Law of destruction has been continual in Jewry, as this account has shown. At all times and places the Jews have given out a more embittered protest against this destiny of destruction, forced on them, than the Gentiles have made against the threat of destruction, aimed at them.

The words, "the Jews," wherever used in this discussion, need always to be read with this qualification.

Within three hundred years of the expulsion from Spain, then, "the Jewish question" twice came to the forefront during violent civil conflicts which seemed, when they began, to have been caused by the clash of native interests: the revolutions in England and France (this narrative will in its later course come to the all-significant matter of the revolution in Russia, and the Jewish part in it).

The aftermath of the revolution in France produced a man who also tried to settle the controversy of Zion. History records attempts to solve "the Jewish question" by almost every imaginable method, from force and suppression to placation, compromise and capitulation. They all failed, leaving this question still a thorn in the side of the Gentiles (and, for that matter, of the Jews, who were somewhat in the condition of people sent into the world with a burr beneath their skins).

The method he chose was the simplest conceivable and possibly for that reason is remembered even now with some consternation by the devotees of Zion; this upstart was very nearly too clever for them! He failed, apparently because this question cannot be solved by man at all, only by God in his good time. The man was Napoleon, whose attempt needs to be considered before the study of the revolution which threw him up is resumed.

Chapter 18

THE NAPOLEONIC INTERROGATION

When Napoleon reached his dizzy peak of power he presumably hoped to do great things for France and the French, as well as for himself (and his family).

Very soon after he became Emperor (or possibly even before) he found that one of the most difficult problems which would confront him was not a French affair at all but an alien one: "the Jewish question"! It had racked the lives of the people for centuries; no sooner was the Pope persuaded, and the imperial crown on Napoleon's head, than it popped up from behind Napoleon's throne, to harass him. In Napoleonic manner he took it by the throat and tried to extract an answer from it to the eternal question: did the Jews truly desire to become part of the nation and to live by its law, or did they secretly acknowledge another law which commanded them to destroy and dominate the peoples among whom they dwelt?

However, this famous Interrogation was Napoleon's *second* attempt to solve the Jewish riddle and the tale of the little known earlier one should briefly be told.

Napoleon was one of the first men to conceive the idea of conquering Jerusalem for the Jews and thus "fulfilling prophecy," in the currently fashionable phrase. He thus set an example imitated in the present century by all those British and American leaders who probably would most dislike to be compared with him: Messrs' Balfour and Lloyd George, Woodrow Wilson, Franklin Roosevelt and Harry Truman, and Sir Winston Churchill.

Napoleon's venture was so short-lived that history says almost nothing of it or of his motives. As he was at the time not yet ruler of France, only the commander in chief, he may have hoped by it merely to gain military support from the Jews of the Middle East for his campaign there. If he already pictured himself as First Consul and Emperor, he may (like Cromwell) have looked for monetary support from the Jews of Europe in that greater ambition.

In any case, he was the first European potentate (as supreme military commander he was really that) to court the favour of the Jewish rulers by promising them Jerusalem! In doing this he espoused the theory of separate Jewish nationhood which he later arraigned.

The story is authentic but brief. It rests entirely on two reports published in Napoleon's Paris *Moniteur* in 1799, when he was in command of the French expedition sent to strike at English power through Egypt.

The first, dated from Constantinople on April 17, 1799, and published on May 22, 1799, said: "Buonaparte has published a proclamation in which he invites all the Jews of Asia and of Africa to come and place themselves under his flag in *order to re- establish ancient Jerusalem.* He has already armed a great number and their battalions are threatening Aleppo."

This is explicit; Napoleon was undertaking to "fulfil prophecy" in the matter of "the return."

The second report appeared in the *Moniteur* a few weeks later and said, "It is not solely to give Jerusalem to the Jews that Buonaparte has conquered Syria; he has vaster designs …"

Possibly Napoleon had received news of the effect which the first report had produced in France, where this intimation that the war against England (like the revolution against "kings and priests") might be turned chiefly to Jewish advantage was not well received; alternatively, it may have done the English more good, among the other peoples of Arabia, than it could ever do Buonaparte among the Jews.

The bubble evaporated at that point, for Napoleon never reached Jerusalem. Two days before the first report was published by the distant *Moniteur,* he was already in retreat towards Egypt, thwarted by an obstinate Englishman at Acre.

Today's student feels somewhat resentful that Napoleon's Zionist bid was soon cut short, for if he had been able to press on with it a deputation of Zionist elders might soon have been examining his ancestry (like Cromwell's, earlier) for some trace of Davidic descent which would qualify him to be proclaimed the Messiah.

Thus all that remains today of this venture of Napoleon's is a significant comment made on it in our time by Mr. Philip Guedalla (1925): "An angry man had missed, as he thought, his destiny. But a patient race still waited; and after a century, when other conquerors had tramped the same dusty roads, it was seen that we had not missed ours."

The reference is to the British troops of 1917, who in this typical Zionist presentation of history are merely instruments in the fulfilment of Jewish destiny, a part missed by Napoleon. Mr. Guedalla uttered these words in the presence of Mr. Lloyd George, the British Prime Minister of 1917 who had sent those soldiers along those same "dusty roads." Mr. Lloyd George thus was able to sun himself in the approving gaze of an audience which looked on him as "an instrument in the hands of the Jewish God" (Dr. Kastein).

In 1804 Napoleon was crowned Emperor; and by 1806 "the Jewish question" was so large among his cares that he made his renowned second attempt to solve it.

Amid all his campaigns he was engrossed by it, like many potentates before him, and now he tried the reverse method of settling it: having briefly undertaken to restore "ancient Jerusalem" (and thus the Jewish nation), he now demanded that the Jews choose publicly between separate nationhood and integration in the nation wherein they dwelt.

He was in bad odour with the French at this time because of the favour which (they said) he showed to Jews. Complaints and appeals for protection against them poured in on him, so that he told the Council of State, "These Jews are locusts and caterpillars, they devour my France ... They are *a nation within the nation.*" Even *Orthodox* Judaism at that time strenuously denied this description.

The State Council itself was divided and in doubt, so that Napoleon summoned 112 leading representatives of Judaism, from France, Germany and Italy, to come to Paris and answer a list of questions.

The strange world in which Napoleon thus set foot is little understood by Gentiles. It is illumined by the following two quotations: "Owing to the acceptance of the idea of the Chosen People and of salvation, the Jewish world was Judeocentric, and the Jews could interpret everything that happened only from the standpoint of *themselves as the centre*" (Dr. Kastein).

'The Jew constructed a whole history of the world of which he made *himself the centre;* and from this moment, that is, the moment when Jehovah makes the covenant with Abraham, the fate of Israel forms the history of the world, indeed, the history of the whole cosmos, the one thing about which the Creator of the world troubles himself. It is as if the circles always become narrower; at last *only the central point remains: the Ego*" (Mr. Houston Stewart Chamberlain).

One of these authorities is a Zionist Jew and the other is what the first would call an anti-semite; the reader will see that they are in perfect agreement about the essence of the Judaic creed.

Indeed, the student of this question finds that there is really no disagreement about such matters between the Talmudic-Jewish scholars and those objectors whom they accuse of prejudice; what the Jewish extremists really complain of is that any criticism should be made from quarters "outside the law"; this is to them intolerable.

The questions devised by Napoleon show that, unlike the British and American politicians of this century who have taken up Zionism, he perfectly understood the nature of Judaism and the problem of human relationships thrown up by it. He knew that, according to the Judaic Law, the world had been created, at a date precisely determined, solely for the Jews and everything that happened in it (including such an episode as that of his own fame and power) was calculated simply to bring about the Jewish triumph.

Napoleon in his day comprehended the Judaic theory as it is expounded, in this century, by Dr. Kastein in relation to King Cyrus of Persia and his conquest of Babylon in 538 BC:

"If the greatest king of the age was to be *an instrument in the hands of the Jewish God,* it meant that this God was one who determined the date not only of one people *but of all peoples; that he determined the fate of nations, the fate of the whole world."*

Napoleon had tentatively offered to make himself "an instrument in the hands of the Jewish God" in the matter of Jerusalem, but had been foiled by the defender of Acre. Now he was Emperor and was not ready to be "an instrument," nor would he accept the proposition at all.

He set out to make the Jews stand up and declare their allegiance, and shrewdly devised questions which were equally impossible to answer without repudiating the central idea, or to evade without incurring the later reproach of falsehood. Dr. Kastein calls the questions "infamous," but that is only in the spirit earlier mentioned, that *any* question from a being outside the Law is infamous.

In another passage Dr. Kastein says, with involuntary admiration, that Napoleon in his questions "correctly grasped the principle of the problem," and this is higher praise than that accorded by Dr. Kastein to any other Gentile ruler.

Also, it is true; had mortal man been able to find an answer to "the Jewish question" Napoleon would have found it, for his enquiries went to the very heart of the matter and left truthful men only with the choice between a pledge of loyalty and an open admission of inveterate disloyalty.

The delegates, elected by the Jewish communities, came to Paris. They were in a quandary. On the one hand, they were all bred in the age-old faith that they must ever remain a "severed" people, chosen by God to "pull down and destroy" other nations and eventually to "return" to a promised land; on the other hand, they had just been foremost among those emancipated by the revolution, and the most famous general of that revolution, who interrogated them, once had undertaken to "re-establish ancient Jerusalem."

Now this man, Napoleon, asked them to say whether they were part of the nation he ruled, or not.

Napoleon's questions went, like arrows to a target, straight to the tenets of the Torah-Talmud on which the wall between the Jews and other men had been built. The chief ones were, did the Jewish Law permit mixed marriages; did the Jews regard Frenchmen as "strangers" (foreigners) or as brothers; did they regard France as their native country, the laws of which they were bound to obey; did the Judaic Law draw any distinction between Jewish and Christian debtors?

All these questions turned on the discriminatory racial and religious laws which the Levites (as earlier chapters showed) had heaped upon the moral commandments, thus cancelling them.

Napoleon with the utmost publicity and formality put *questions* before the Jewish representatives, which the world for centuries had been asking.

With this fierce light beating on them the Jewish notables had only two alternatives: to repudiate the racial Law in all sincerity, or to profess repudiation while secretly denying it (an expedient permitted by the Talmud).

As Dr. Kastein says, "The Jewish scholars who were called upon to refute the charges found themselves in an extremely difficult position, *for to them everything in the Talmud was sacred, even its legends and anecdotes.*" This is Dr. Kastein's way of saying that they could only evade the questions by falsehood, for they were not "called upon to refute charges"; they were merely asked to answer truthfully.

The Jewish delegates *ardently affirmed* that there was no longer any such thing as a Jewish nation; that they did not desire to live in closed, self-governed communities; that they were in every respect Frenchmen and nothing more. They hedged only on the point of mixed marriages; these, they said, were permissible "under the *civil* law."

Even Dr. Kastein is constrained to call Napoleon's next move "a stroke of genius."

It established historically that if forced publicly to answer these vital questions (vital to the peoples with whom they live) the representatives of Judaism will give answers which are either untrue or to which they cannot give effect.

The events of the decades that followed showed that the claim to separate nationhood-within-nations was never renounced by those who truly wielded power in Jewry.

Thus Napoleon, in failure, achieved a historic victory for truth which retains its value in our day.

He sought to give the responses obtained by him the most binding public form, which would commit Jews everywhere and for all the future to the undertakings given by their elders, by desiring that the Great Sanhedrin be convened!

From all parts of *Europe* the traditional 71 members of the Sanhedrin, 46 rabbis and 25 laymen, hastened to Paris and met among scenes of great magnificence in February 1807. Though the Sanhedrin, as such, had not met for centuries, the Talmudic "centre" in Poland had but recently ceased publicly to function, so that the idea of a directing body of Jewry was real and live.

The Sanhedrin went further than the Jewish notables in the completeness and ardour of its declarations; (incidentally, it began by recording thanks to the Christian churches for the protection enjoyed in the past, and this tribute is worth comparing with the usual Zionist version of history in the Christian era, which suggests that it was all a long ordeal of "Jewish persecution" at Christian hands). The Sanhedrin acknowledged *the extinction of the Jewish nation to be an accomplished fact.* This solved the central dilemma thrown up by the fact that the Law, which theretofore had always been held to be exclusively binding for Jews, allowed no distinction between religious and civil law. As "the nation" had ceased to exist, *the Talmudic laws of daily life were proclaimed to be no longer effective,* but the Torah, as the law of faith, remained immutable; thus said the Sanhedrists. If any clash or dispute were to occur, the religious laws were to be held *subordinate* to those of the state in which individual Jews lived. Israel thenceforward would exist *only as a religion,* and *no longer looked forward to any national rehabilitation.*

It was a unique triumph for Napoleon (and who knows how much it may have contributed to his downfall?). The Jews were liberated from the Talmud; the way to their re-integration in their fellow men, their involvement in mankind, was reopened where the Levites had closed it over two thousand years before; the spirit of discrimination and hatred was renounced and exorcised.

These declarations formed the basis on which the claim for full civil liberties was made and realized throughout the West in the years that followed. All sections of Judaism, known to the West, supported them.

Thenceforth Orthodox Judaism, with the face it turned toward the West, denied any suggestion that the Jews would form a nation within nations. Reform Judaism in time "eliminated every prayer expressing so much as even the suspicion of a hope or a desire for any form of Jewish national resurrection" (Rabbi Moses P. Jacobson).

The ground was cut from beneath those opponents of Jewish emancipation in the British Parliament who contended that "the Jews look forward to the coming of a great deliverer, to their return to Palestine, to the rebuilding of their temple, to the revival of their ancient worship, and therefore, they will always consider England not as their country, but merely as their place of exile" (quoted by Mr. Bernard J. Brown).

Yet these warning voices spoke the truth. In less than ninety years the declarations of the Napoleonic Sanhedrin had in effect been cancelled, so that Mr. Brown was brought to write:

"Now, although civil equalities have been firmly established by law in nearly every land, Jewish nationalism *has become the philosophy of Israel.* Jews should not be surprised if people charge that we obtained equality before the law under false pretences; *that we are still a nation within nations and that rights accorded us should be revoked.*"

Napoleon unwittingly did posterity a service in revealing the important fact that the replies obtained by him were valueless. The one- and-only Law, of all thought and action, was in the remainder of the Nineteenth Century reinflicted on the Jews by their Talmudic rulers, and by Gentile politicians who gave them the same help as King Artaxerxes gave to Nehemiah.

Were the responses sincere or false when they were given? The answer probably may be divided, just as Judaism itself has always been divided.

No doubt the delegates had much in mind the accelerating effect which their responses, as they were framed, would have on the grant of full equality in other countries. On the other hand, many of them must earnestly have hoped that the Jews, at long last, might enter into mankind without secret denials, for in Jewry this impulse to break through the tribal ban has always existed, though it has always been beaten back by the ruling sect.

The probability is that some of the delegates sincerely intended what they said, and that others "secretly broke" (Dr. Kastein's phrase) with the loyalties thus publicly affirmed.

Napoleon's Sanhedrin had a basic flaw. It represented the Jews of *Europe*, and these (who were in the main the Sephardim) were losing authority in Jewry. The Talmudic centre, and the great mass of "Eastern Jews" (the Slavic Ashkenazi) were in Russia or Russian-Poland, and not even Napoleon gave much thought to that fact if he even knew of it. These Talmudists were not represented in the Sanhedrin and the responses given were by their Law heresy, for they were the guardians of the traditions of the Pharisees and Levites.

The Sanhedrin's avowals brought to an end the third Talmudic period in the story of Zion. It was that which began with the fall of Judea in AD 70, when the Pharisees bequeathed their traditions to the Talmudists, and at the end of these seventeen centuries the eternal question seemed, by the Sanhedrin's responses, to have been solved.

The Jews were ready to join with mankind and to follow the counsel of a French Jew, Isaac Berr, that they should rid themselves "of that narrow spirit, of corporation and congregation, in all civil and political matters not immediately connected with our spiritual law. In these things we must absolutely appear simply as individuals, as Frenchmen, guided only by a true patriotism and by the general good of the nations." That meant the end of the Talmud, "the hedge around the Law."

It was an illusion. In the eyes of today's Gentile student it seems to have been a great opportunity missed. In the eyes of the literal Jew it was an appalling danger narrowly averted: that of common involvement in mankind.

The fourth period in this narrative then began, the century of "emancipation," the 19th Century. During it the Talmudists in the East set out to cancel what the Sanhedrin had affirmed, and to use all the liberties gained through emancipation, not to put Jews and all other men on one footing, but to corral the Jews again, to reaffirm their "severance" from others and their claim to separate nationhood, which in fact was one to be a nation above all nations, not a nation-within-nations.

The Talmudists succeeded, with results which we are witnessing in our generation, which is the fifth period in the controversy of Zion. The story of their success cannot be separated from that of the Revolution, to which this narrative now returns.

Douglas Reed

Chapter 19

THE WORLD REVOLUTION

For the sake of orderly sequence this narrative has been carried through to Napoleon's Sanhedrin; the answers given by it closed the third, and opened the fourth period in the story of Zion, which began with the public renunciation of separate-nationhood and ended, ninety years later, with the public re-affirmation of separate-nationhood in its extremest form.

Before it continues into that fourth phase, the narrative now must move back twenty years to the start of the *world-revolution*, and consider what part, if any, was played by "the Jews" in that.

The 19th Century, in the West, differed from the preceding eighteen centuries of the Christian era there in the emergence of two movements with a converging aim, which by the century's end dominated all its affairs.

The one movement, Zionism, aimed at reassembling a dispersed nation in a territory promised to it by *the Jewish god;* the second movement, Communism, aimed at the destruction of separate nationhood as such.

Thus these two movements appeared at first sight to be fixedly opposed to each other, for the one made nationalism its religion, even its god, and the other declared war to the death on nationalism. This antagonism was only apparent, and in truth the two movements ran on parallel tracks, not head on towards a collision on the same line. For the god who promised land to the nation to be gathered-in also promised to set it "above all people that are upon the face of the earth" and to destroy all other nations "with a mighty destruction until they be destroyed." The world-revolution, which pursued the second of these aims, thus fulfilled the condition set for the first of them; either by accident or by design, it too was doing the will of Jehovah.

That being so, the historian's task is to find out, if he can, what relationship existed between the organizers of Zionism and those of the world-revolution. If there was none, and the parallelism of purpose was coincidental, then history was evidently having a little joke with the West. If relationship can be shown, the pattern of the last 170 years prefigures the shape of coming events; in that case the world-revolution has been the handmaiden of Zion.

These 170 years have probably been the most profligate and least creditable in the history of the West. At the start of the 19th Century it had behind it seventeen centuries of Christian achievement; the world had never before seen man so much improve his own state and his conduct to others; even warfare was becoming subject to a civilized code, and the future seemed certain to continue this upward process. By the middle of the 20th Century much of this achievement had been lost; a large area of the West had been surrendered to Asiatic barbarism; the question whether the remaining West and its faith could even survive clearly hung in the balance and probably would be answered during the closing decades of the century.

The period which saw this deterioration was that of the rise of the Judaist power to a peak of influence in the affairs of the West which hardly any European potentate or pontiff, doctrine or dogma had ever attained. The picture of this swelling might, spreading over Europe like an eastern thundercloud, is given in two quotations from the beginning and end of the 19th Century. In 1791 the great German historian Johann Gottfried von Herder, looking back on the hundred years behind him, wrote:

"The ruder nations of Europe are *willing slaves* of Jewish usury ... The Jewish people is and remains in Europe an Asiatic people alien to our part of the world, *bound to that old law which it received in a distant climate*, and which according to its own confession it cannot do away with ... It is indissolubly bound to *an alien law that is hostile to all alien peoples.*"

The newspaper reader of 1807, when he learned of the Sanhedrin's ardent avowals of non-nationhood, would presumably have dismissed von Herder as a "bigot" (or even an "antisemite"), but the years and events have shown that he, like many before him, was but a scholar speaking truth. A hundred years later, in 1899, another, Mr. Houston Stewart Chamberlain, looked back on what Herder had written and recorded the further, continuing usurpation of power:

"A great change has taken place: the Jews play in Europe, and wherever European influence extends, a different part from that which they played a hundred years ago; as Viktor Hohn expresses it, we live today in a 'Jewish age'; we may think what we like about the past history of the Jews, their present history actually takes up so much room in our own history that we cannot possibly refuse to notice them: The 'alien' element emphasized by Herder has become more and more prominent ... The direct influence of Judaism on the 19th Century appears for the first time as a new influence in the history of culture; it thus becomes one of the burning subjects of the day. This alien people has become precisely in the course of the 19th Century a disproportionately important and *in many spheres actually dominant* constituent of our life ...... Herder said that 'the ruder nations of Europe were willing slaves of Jewish usury'. Today Herder could say the same of *by far the greatest part of our civilized world......our governments, our law, our science, our commerce, our literature, our art, practically all branches of our life, have become more or less willing slaves of the Jews and drag the feudal fetter, if not yet on two, at least on one leg... The direct influence of Judaism on the 19th century thus becomes one of the burning subjects of the day. We have to deal here with a question affecting not only the present, but also the future of the world... If the Jewish influence were to gain the upper hand in Europe in the intellectual and cultural sphere, we would have one more example of negative, destructive power.*"

Such was the development in a hundred years from von Herder to Chamberlain. The last three sentences are a brilliant prognosis, for Chamberlain had not seen the *proofs,* which our century has brought, of the truth of what he said; namely, that fantastic feat of international stage-management on the grand scale in October 1917 when Communism (the destroyer of nationhood) and Zionism (the creator of the dominant nation) triumphed at the same instant!

In the sixty years which have passed since Chamberlain wrote the process observed by him and Herder has gathered pace and power.

The question no longer simply "affects the future of the world"; it is with us every day and we have no *present* that is not shaped by it; it has already altered the nature of the world and of man's lot in it. "Our governments," in the half-century that has elapsed, have become such "willing slaves" of the Judaic master-sect that they are in fact the bailiffs or agents of a new, international ruling-class, and not true governors at all.

The West has come to this dilemma through the pressure of two millstones, Communism and Zionism, the nation-destroying world-revolution and the new, nation-creating, ruling-class. The one has incited the mob; the other has gained mastery over rulers. Are the organizers of both the same? This book seeks to answer the question in its remaining chapters. What is clear is that each stage in the ruination of the West, during these 170 years, has been accompanied by successive stages of "the return" to the Promised Land. That is an indication of common managership too strong to be set aside unless it can be conclusively disproved. To the "heathen" masses of Christendom the process which began with the emergence of the world-revolution in 1789 has been merely one of sound and fury, signifying nothing; but the student perceives that in majestic rhythm it fulfils The Law and The Prophets of Judah.

The 19th Century was one of conspiracy, of which the things we witness in the 20th Century are the results. Conspiracy bred Communism and Zionism, and these took the future of the West in a pincer-like clutch. What were their origins? Why did they germinate in darkness until they broke ground together in the 19th Century? Had they a *common* root? The way to answer that question is to examine the roots of each separately and find out if they join; and the purpose of this chapter and the next is to trace the root-idea of world-revolution.

The French revolution was the *world*-revolution in action, not a revolution *in* France. From the moment of the event in France no doubt remains on that score. Before then people might indulge notions about suffering peasants, stung to sudden uprising by arrogant aristocrats and the like, but diligent study of the background of the French revolution dispels such illusions. It was the result of a plan and the work of a secret organization revealed before it occurred; it was *not* merely a French outburst produced by

French causes. The plan behind it is the plan of Communism today; and Communism today, which is the world-revolution in permanence, has inherited the organization which evolved the plan.

The French revolution of 1789 is the one that provides the key to the mystery. It forms the link between the English one of 1640 and the Russian one of 1917 and reveals the whole process as a planned and continuing one which, having passed through these three stages, clearly will reach its final orgasm at some moment not far distant, probably during this century. That climax, foreseeably, will take the shape of an attempt to consummate and complete the world revolution by setting up a world-government under the control of the organization which has guided the revolutionary process from its start. This would establish the sway of a new ruling-class over the submerged nations. (As Dr. Kastein would say, it would "determine the fate of the whole world").

This picture, which only slowly emerged as the three centuries passed, is today clear in its historical perspective, where each of the three great revolutions is seen in the light thrown on it by the next:

The English revolution *appeared* at the time to be a spontaneous English episode, directed only against the pretensions, at that moment, of a particular royal house, the Stuarts, and a particular form of religion, called "Popery." No contemporary dreamed of considering it as the start of a *world*-movement against *all* religion and *all* legitimate government. (The ruling sect of Jewry supplied the revolutionary dictator with funds and by means of this, traditional "abetting" part the Jewish leaders became chief beneficiaries of the revolution; if they had any part in the original instigation of it, this cannot be shown, nor has any evidence of a long-term, master- plan behind the revolution survived).

The nature and course of the French revolution, however, puts the English one in a different light. It was *not*, and even at the time did not seem to be, a native French episode caused merely by French conditions. On the contrary, it followed a plan for *universal* revolution discovered and made public some years before; and the secret organization then exposed had members in many countries and all classes. Therefore its most characteristic acts (regicide and sacrilege), though they repeated those of the revolution in England, were seen not to be spontaneously vengeful deeds committed in the heat of a moment, but actions deliberately symbolic of a *continuing* plan and purpose: the destruction of *all* religion and *all* legitimate government, everywhere. Inevitably, this revelation leads to the surmise that the English revolution too may have been prepared by this secret organization with the aim of destroying all nationhood. (In the French revolution, as in the English one, the Judaist sect emerged as a chief beneficiary; the general emancipation of Jews, which came of it, was used by it as a cover for its conspiratorial work during the ensuing decades. Original Judaist instigation is not shown by any evidence now available.)

Thus the French revolution, unlike the English one, demonstrably was the product of a major conspiracy, with worldwide aims and deep roots. From this instant, the nature of the plan was plain, but the conspirators, wherever they were unmasked, seemed to be a horde of individuals with no bond of union between them save that of the arsonist's lust for destruction. The purpose was beyond doubt, but the identity of the organizers was still mysterious. This half-clarified scene was depicted in famous words by a classic authority on the subject, Lord Acton:

"The appalling thing in the revolution is not the tumult *but the design.* Through all the fire and smoke we perceive the *evidence of calculating organization. The Managers* remain studiously concealed and masked *but there is no doubt about their presence from the first.*"

The French revolution, then, revealed a *design* behind revolution, and it was the design of a set purpose in a *worldwide* field. What had seemed planless at the time of the English revolution now was seen to be, or had become the result of a plan and a pattern, and the conspiracy clearly was of such strength and age that its complicity in the earlier revolution had to be allowed for. However, this second revolution still left "the managers" masked, so that only half of the mystery had been solved (Lord Acton died in 1902 and thus did not see the third revolution).

The revolution in Russia, again, opened room for new theories about the French and English revolutions. Its acts of regicide and sacrilege were as unmistakable an identity-card as the Muslim's greeting is a token of his faith; by them it informed all who wished to hear that it was still working to "the design" of worldwide destruction first revealed by the French revolution. Moreover, the secret, for a hundred years called "a lie," was no longer even denied; from 1917 on the world-revolution was avowedly *permanent,* avowedly worldwide in purpose, and the erstwhile secret conspiracy became a political party, operating in all countries under orders from a central headquarters in Moscow.

Thus the Russian revolution threw a brighter light on the French one, clarifying its outlines and origins. However, in the matter of the "studiously concealed" and "masked" *managers,* the Russian revolution threw an entirely different light on the two earlier ones, or at the least it opened up conjectures about their possible origins which none had previously spent much thought upon. The "managers" of the revolution in Russia were nearly all Eastern Jews. On this occasion the significant, symbolic acts of regicide and sacrilege were committed by Jews and a law was enacted which in effect forbade all discussion of the part played by Jews, or by "the Jewish question," in these events or in public affairs at all.

Thus vital questions were answered and what was a great mystery in 1789 became plain in 1917. The great benefit which today's student derives from the French revolution is the proof, supplied by it, of the existence of a *design* for world-revolution, and of an *organization* which pursued that destructive ambition. Its existence and activity made the 19th Century the century of the grand conspiracy. A sense of evil things stirring in dark places, like the sounds which a prisoner in a dungeon awaits at night, disquietened men and nations. This was the feeling imparted by conspiracy to the enpested air around. From the moment of the French revolution men intuitively knew that they lived with conspiracy in their midst; in our day, which has suffered its effects, we can at least see with what we have to deal, if we look, and may say that it is the devil that we know.

Perhaps the greatest disservice that Napoleon did was, by his campaigns and glittering exploits to distract men's thoughts from the much greater danger that menaced them: the world-revolution and its secret "managers." But for him they might have paid more attention to the conspiracy, for they had the proof of its existence.

Chapter 20

THE DESIGN

This proof was given when the papers of Adam Weishaupt's secret society of "Illuminati" were seized by the Bavarian Government in 1786 and published in 1787. The original blueprint of *world*-revolution, and the existence of a powerful organization with members in the highest places, were then revealed. From that moment on no doubt remained that all countries and classes of society contained men who were leagued together to destroy *all* legitimate government and *all* religion. The conspiratorial organization burrowed underground again after its exposure, but survived and pursued its plan, bursting into full public view in 1917. Since then, as Communism, it has openly pursued the aims disclosed by the Bavarian Government's coup of 1786, by the methods then also revealed.

The publication of the Weishaupt documents came about by a chance as curious as that of the preservation of Mr. Whittaker Chambers's documents in 1948.[2] They were only a residue, remaining after the bulk had been destroyed, for something of the Illuminati's doings and designs had become known before 1786, partly through the boastings of its members, partly through the disclosures of some who (like Mr. Chambers 160 years later) revolted against the company in which they found themselves when they comprehended its true nature. Thus the Dowager Duchess Maria Anna of Bavaria in 1783 received information from former Illuminates that the order was teaching that religion should be regarded as nonsense (Lenin's "opiate for the people") and patriotism as puerility, that suicide was justifiable, that life should be ruled by passion rather than reason, that one

---

[2] Mr. Whittaker Chambers, an impressionable, rather morbid young American, was "captured" by the Communists at Columbia University, New York, in 1925 and became an agent and courier who, working under an alias, conveyed stolen official documents to his Communist superiors. In 1938 he sickened of his bondage and fled the party. In 1939, appalled by the alliance between Communism and Hitlerism, he tried to inform President Roosevelt of the infestation of government departments by Communist agents, and of the espionage that went on, but was rudely rebuffed, being told by a presidential emissary to "go jump in the lake." As a precaution, he had secreted his proofs (photographs of hundreds of secret official documents) in a disused lift-shaft and in the course of years forgot them, for he heard nothing more until 1948! Then his name was mentioned in the course of an enquiry arising out of disclosures made by another former Communist agent, and he was sub-poenaed to give evidence. He did this and was at once sued for libel by a high government official, Mr. Alger Hiss, whom he incriminated of stealing highly secret papers and conveying them, through Mr. Chambers, to the Communists. For his own protection he then sought out his relative in New York and asked if the package, secreted in the disused service-lift shaft ten years before, was still there. Covered with dust, it was, and the enormity of its contents, examined again after ten years, startled even Mr. Chambers. He hid the packet in a pumpkin on his farm, where at last it came to light of day when his defence against the libel charge had to be produced. This led to the conviction of his accuser, Mr. Hiss, and to the *partial* exposure of a condition of Communist infestation in the American Government so deep and widespread, that American state policy obviously must, during the entire period of the Second World War, have been to a great extent under the direct influence of the world-revolutionary leaders in Moscow.

might poison one's enemies, and the like. As a result of this and other information the Duke of Bavaria in 1785 issued an edict against the Illuminati; the order was indicted as a branch of Freemasonry, and government officials, members of the armed services, professors, teachers and students were forbidden to join it. A general ban was laid on the formation of secret societies (that is, bodies which banded together without making registration, as the law required).

This interdict (which obviously could not be made effective; *secret* organizations cannot be suppressed by decree) put the conspirators on guard, so that (as the two historians of the Illuminati relate, Messrs' C.F. Forestier and Leopold Engel) "a considerable amount of the most valuable papers of the order where either carefully concealed or burned" and "few documents survive, for most of them were destroyed and external relationships were broken off, in order to avert suspicion"; in other words, the order went deep underground. Thus the documents which *were* found, in 1786, represent only a minimum. M.Forestier says that in 1784 (the last year in which it tended rather to vaunt its power than to conceal it) the order stretched from its Bavarian base "over all Central Europe, from the Rhine to the Vistula and from the Alps to the Baltic; its members included young people who were later to apply the principles instilled into them, officials of all kinds who put their influence at its service, members of the clergy whom it inspired to be 'tolerant' and princes whose protection it was able to claim and whom it hoped to control." The reader will see that this is a picture of Communism today, save for the allusion to "princes"; the number of these has diminished almost to nothing since 1784.

However, the papers which were found and published, if they did not show the full range of the Illuminati's membership and connections, especially in France, Britain and America, nevertheless exposed the nature of the secret society and its all-destructive ambition. An Illuminist emissary was struck by lightning on a journey to Silesia in 1785. Papers found on him caused the houses of two Illuminist leaders to be searched. Correspondence between "Spartacus" (Adam Weishaupt) and the "Areopagites" (his closest associates in the order), and other papers then found revealed the full plan for world-revolution with which we of the 20th Century have become familiar through its results and under the name of "Communism."

None can believe today that this grandiose plan of destruction originated in the brain of one Bavarian professor, or resist the conclusion that (as Mrs Nesta Webster suggests) Weishaupt and his allies did not *create*, but only loosed upon the world a live and terrible force that had lain dormant for many centuries.

When he founded his Illuminati, on May 1, 1776, Weishaupt was dean of the faculty of law at Ingolstadt University (in our day university professors who are secret Communists are often to be found in the faculties of law). He had been brought up by the Jesuits, whom he came to hate, and he borrowed from them, and perverted to the opposite purpose, their secret of organization: the method which (as his associate Mirabeau said) "under one head, *made men dispersed over the universe tend towards the same goal.*" This idea, of leagueing men together in secret conspiracy and using them to achieve an aim which they do not comprehend, pervades the entire mass of letters and other Illuminist documents seized by the Bavarian Government.

The idea is presented with ardent fondness and the many ways of realizing it are of high ingenuity. The accumulated experience of ages, in conspiracy, must have been drawn on and Mrs Nesta Webster, in her search for the source of this morbid and perverse doctrine, found herself led back to the start of the Christian era and further. For instance, M. Silvestre de Sacy says that the method used by the Ismailis (a subversive sect within Islam in the 8th Century) was to enlist "partisans in all places and in all classes of society" in the attempt to destroy their professed faith and government; the Ismaili leader, Abdullah ibn Maymun, set out "to unite in the form of a vast secret society with many degrees of initiation freethinkers, who regarded religion only as a curb for the people, and bigots of all sects." The achievement of Abdulla ibn Maymun, according to another authority, M. Reinhart Dozy, was that "by means such as these the extraordinary result was brought about that a multitude of men of divers beliefs were all working together for an object known only to a few of them." These quotations exactly describe both the aims, methods and achievement of Adam Weishaupt and of Communism and they could be multiplied by extracts from the literature of the Cabalists, the Gnostics and the Manicheans.

The Weishaupt documents are incontestably authentic; the Bavarian Government unwittingly forestalled any attempt to cry "Forgery" (in the manner made familiar in our century) by inviting any who were interested to inspect the original documents in the Archives at Munich.

They revealed three main things: first, the aims of the society; second, the method of organization; and third, the membership, at least in a relatively restricted area (chiefly, the South German States). These three matters will be separately discussed here.

The basic idea, made abundantly clear in the correspondence between "Spartacus" and his pseudonymous fellow-conspirators, was to destroy all established authority, nationhood and religion, and thus to clear the way for the rise of a new ruling class, that of the Illuminates. The society's aims, as summed up by Henri Martin, were "the abolition of property, social authority and nationality, and the return of the human race to the happy state in which it formed only a single family without artificial needs, without useless sciences, every father being priest and magistrate; priest of we know not what religion, for in spite of their frequent invocations of the God of Nature, many indications lead us to conclude that Weishaupt had no other God than Nature herself."

This is confirmed by Weishaupt; "Princes and nations will disappear … Reason will be the only code of man." In all his writings he completely eliminated any idea of divine power outside Man.

The attack on "kings and princes" was merely "cover" for the true attack, on all *nationhood* (as time has shown; now that the supply of kings and princes has given out Communism impartially destroys proletarian prime ministers and politicians); and that on "priests" was a disguise for the real attack, on *all* religion. The true aim, in both cases, is revealed in Weishaupt's own correspondence with his intimates; the false one was professed to inferior agents of the society, or to the public if it ever got wind of Illuminist doings. Weishaupt's great skill in enlisting important people, who joined him in the belief that they were thus proving themselves "progressive" or "liberal," is shown by the number of princes and priests who were found in his secret membership-lists.

The best example of his success, and of his quick adaptability of method, is given by the case of religion. His attack on religion was a much more daring and startling thing in his day than in ours, when we have lived long enough with open Communism to become familiar with a proposition which in Weishaupt's day must have seemed scarcely credible: that man, having once found his way to the idea of God, should of his own will retrace his footsteps!

Weishaupt's original idea was to make Fire Worship the religion of Illuminism. This was unlikely ever to bring recruits from the rank s of the clergy, and he hit on a better idea, which brought them in numbers. He averred that Jesus had had "a secret doctrine," never openly revealed, which could be found by the diligent between the lines of the Gospels. This secret doctrine was to abolish religion and establish reason in its place: "when at last Reason becomes the religion of man so will the problem be solved." The idea of joining a secret society of which Jesus had been the true founder, and of following an example set by Jesus in using words to disguise meaning, proved irresistible to the many clerics who then passed through the door thus opened to them. They were figures of a new kind in their day; in ours the Communist cleric has become familiar.

The Illuminist leaders privately mocked them. "Spartacus's" chief collaborator "Philo" (the Hanoverian Baron von Knigge) wrote, "We say then, Jesus wished to introduce no new religion, but only to restore natural religion and reason to their old rights … There are many passages in the Bible which can be made use of and explained, and so all quarrelling between the sects ceases if one can find a reasonable meaning in the teaching of Jesus, *be it true or not* … Now therefore that people see that *we are the only real and true Christians,* we can say a word more against priests and princes, but I have so managed that after previous tests *I can receive pontiffs and kings in this degree*. In the higher Mysteries we must then (a) *disclose the pious fraud* and (b) reveal from all writings the origin of *all* religious lies and their connexion ..."

"Spartacus" happily commented, "You cannot imagine what sensation our Priest's degree is arousing. The most wonderful thing is that great Protestant and reformed theologians who belong to Illuminism still believe that the religious teaching imparted in it contains the true and genuine spirit of the Christian religion. Oh, man, of what cannot you be persuaded! I never thought that I should become the founder of a new religion."

Through this success in persuading clerics that irreligion was the true faith and antichrist the true Christianity Weishaupt made great strides in Bavaria. He recorded that all non-Illuminist professors had been driven from Ingolstadt University, that the society had provided its clerical members with "good benefices, parishes, posts at court," that the schools were Illuminist-controlled, and that the seminary for young priests would soon be captured, whereon "we shall be able to provide the whole of Bavaria with proper priests." Weishaupt's attack on religion was the most distinctive feature of his doctrine. His ideas about "the god of Reason" and "the god of Nature" bring his thought very close to Judaic thought, in its relation to the Gentiles, and as Illuminism became Communism, and Communism came under Jewish leadership, this might be significant. The Judaic Law also lays down that the Gentiles (who as such are excluded from the world to come) are entitled only to the religion of nature and of reason which Weishaupt taught. Moses Mendelssohn,[3] as quoted in his Memoirs, says:

---

[3] Moses Mendelssohn wrote this nearly two hundred years ago and it correctly defines the Judaist attitude toward Kipling's "lesser breeds without the Law." In our day (1955) a proposal was being bruited in Jewry to bring the lesser breeds nominally *within* the Judaist fold while perpetuating their inferiority and exclusion. As the reader of this book will recall, in the pre-Christian era proselytes were sought, but from the start of the Christian period Judaist hostility to conversion has been firm and even fierce (with the one exception of the mass-conversion of the Mongolian Khazars, from whom today's Ashkenazi sprang) and the Talmud says that "proselytes are annoying to Israel like a scab."

In 1955 a young Reform rabbi, born in Germany but living in America, suggested that the time had come for Judaism to undertake   missionary work among the Gentiles. The basis he laid down was identical with Moses Mendelssohn's dictum; this rabbi, Mr. Jakob Petuchowski, merely succeeded in finding a solution to what had seemed to Mendelssohn an insoluble difficulty ("Pursuant to the principles of my religion, I am not to seek to convert anyone who is not born according to our laws; the Jewish religion is diametrically opposed to it" i.e., conversion).

Mr. Petuchowski proposed, in fact, that conversions made by his proposed mission should be on a basis which would give the convert a status, in relation to the original Jews, rather comparable with that of the American Negro, during the slavery era, to the white folk in the big plantation house. The converts would be required (in other words, permitted) only to obey the "Seven Laws of Noah," (the allusion is presumably to the ninth chapter of *Genesis)*, and not the hundreds of commands and vetoes attributed to God by the "Mosaic Law." In this way the "lesser breeds" would apparently receive, at the hands of Judaism, the "religion of nature and of reason" recommended for them by Adam Weishaupt and Moses Mendelssohn alike. If they then called themselves "Jews," this would be rather as the plantation Negro took his owner's family-name.

This ingenious proposal may have been prompted by the reflection that Jewish power in the world is now so great that a solution to the problem of the status of the "lesser breeds" will have to be found, if "The Law" is to be literally "observed." Mr. Petuchowski's own words were, "Religious Jews do believe that the

"Our rabbis unanimously teach that the written and oral laws which form conjointly our revealed religion are obligatory *on our nation only:* 'Moses commanded us a law, even the inheritance of the congregation of Jacob'. We believe that all other nations of the earth have been *directed by God to adhere to the laws of nature* ... Those who regulate their lives according to the precepts of *this religion of nature and of reason* are called virtuous men of other nations ..."

In this authoritative view, then, God himself excluded the Gentiles from his congregation and commanded them to live merely according to the laws of nature and of reason. Thus Weishaupt was directing them to do just what the Jewish god directed them to do. If the Talmudic rabbis had no part in inspiring Illuminism (and research cannot discover any) the reason why they later took a directing part in Communism seems here to become plain.

So much for the *aims* of the Illuminati. They are those of Communism today, unchanged. As for the method, every baseness of which human beings are capable was listed for exploitation in the cause of recruitment. Among the papers were found two packets which particularly horrified public opinion at the time. They contained documents laying down the order's right to exercise the law of life and death over its members, a eulogy of atheism, the description of a machine for the automatic destruction of secret papers, and prescriptions for procuring abortion, counterfeiting seals, making poisonous perfumes and secret ink, and the like. Today, again, the contents of a Communist laboratory are familiar to any who follow such matters, but in 1787 the effect of this disclosure, in Catholic Bavaria, was like a glimpse of the antechamber of Hades.

Weishaupt's papers included a diagram illustrating the way in which he exercised control over his organization. It shows what might be a section of chain-mail, or of honeycomb, and is identical with the celebrated "cell" system on which Communism is built today. It is the product of an intelligence of the highest kind (and, obviously, of centuries of experience; methods of this sort cannot be devised without a long process of trial and error). The secret is that damage to such a structure cannot be more than local, the main fabric remaining always unimpaired and capable of repair. If a few links, or cells, are destroyed these can be made good in due time, and meanwhile the organization continues, substantially unharmed.

At the centre of this web sat Weishaupt, and held all threads in his hands. "One must show how easy it would be for one clever head to direct hundreds and thousands of men," he wrote above the diagram, and below it he added, "I have two immediately below me into whom I breathe my whole spirit, and each of these two has again two others, and so on. In this way I can

plans for God's kingdom on earth have been delivered into their keeping ... Those Gentiles, therefore, who have this larger salvation at heart, should be made acquainted with what Judaism has to offer, and should be invited to cast in their lot with the household of Israel."
What was here "offered" was in fact "the religion of nature and reason."

set a thousand men in motion and on fire in the simplest manner, and in this way one must impart orders and operate on politics."

When the Illuminist papers were published most of its members first learned that Weishaupt was its head, for he was known only to his close associates. The mass knew only that, somewhere above them, was a "beloved leader" or "big brother," a Being all-wise, kindly but stern, who through them would reshape the world. Weishaupt had in fact achieved the "extraordinary result" ascribed to Abdulla ibn Maymun in Islam: under him "a multitude of men of divers beliefs were all working together for an object known only to a few of them."

The fact that each dupe only knew his two neighbour dupes would not alone have been enough to bring about that result. How were the Illuminates *kept* together? The answer is that Weishaupt discovered, or received from some higher intelligence the secret on which the cohesive strength of the world-revolution rests today, under Communism: terror!

All Illuminates took "illuminated" names, which they used in their dealings with each other, and in all correspondence. This practice of the alias, or "cover name," has been continued to the present-day. The members of the Communist governments which usurped power in Russia in 1917 were known to the world, for the first time in history, by aliases (and are so known to posterity also). The exposures of 1945-1955 in America, England, Canada and Australia showed that the men who worked as Communist agents in the governments of these countries used "cover-names," in the way begun by Weishaupt.

Weishaupt organized his society in grades, or circles, the outer rings of which contained the new recruits and lesser dupes. Advancement through the grades was supposed to bring initiation into further chapters of the central mystery. Weishaupt preferred the enrolment of young men at their most impressionable ages, between 15 and 30. (This practice also was continued into our day; Messrs' Alger Hiss, Harry Dexter White, Whittaker Chambers, Donald Maclean, Guy Burgess and others were all "netted" at their American or English universities). Other grades or degrees were added as the circle of recruitment widened, or especial obstacles to it were discovered; the example of religion has already been given, and in this case also Communism, by making use of the suggestion that Jesus was the first Communist, has followed Weishaupt's precedent, merely changing "Illuminist" to "Communist." In this approach to prospective members the manner of the invitation, "Will you walk into my parlour?," was varied to meet individual cases.

The young men who were recruited for the conspiracy were sworn in with much intimidating ceremonial, including a significant mockery of the Christian sacrament. They were required to supply a dossier about their parents, listing their "dominant passions," and to spy on each other. Both these ideas are basic in Communism and one possibly original source of them is the "Mosaic Law," where the obligation to denounce kinsfolk who incur suspicion of heresy, and to place "a guard upon my guard," is included in the "statutes and judgments."

The young Illuminate was made to feel that he would never know how many eyes of unknown superiors might be on him (he only *knew* his immediate superiors); he was taught to inform on those around him and inferred that they informed on him. This is the basic principle of terror, which can never be completely established merely by killing, torture or imprisonment; only the knowledge that he can trust no man, not his own son or father or friend, reduces the human victim to utter submission. Since Weishaupt's day this secret terror has been resident in the West. Those who have no personal experience of it may gain understanding of the power it wields in our day, even many thousands of miles from its central headquarters, by reading Mr. Whittaker Chambers's description of his flight into concealment after he resolved to break with his Communist masters.

As to the membership of the Illuminati, the papers discovered showed that, after ten years of existence, it had several thousand members, many of them in important civil positions where they could exert influence on the acts of rulers and governments. They even *included* rulers: the contemporary Marquis de Luchet relates that some thirty reigning and non-reigning princes had gutlessly joined an order, the masters of which were sworn to destroy them! It included the Dukes of Brunswick, Gotha and Saxe-Weimar, princes of Hesse and Saxe-Gotha, and the Elector of Mainz; Metternich, Pestalozzi the educationist, ambassadors and politicians and professors. Above all others, it included the man who, twenty years later, was to write the world's most famous masterpiece on the theme of the youth who sold his soul to the devil. The inference that *Faust* was in truth the story of Goethe and Illuminism is hard to resist; its theme is essentially the same as that of *Witness* and other works which, in our day, have been written by men who escaped from Communism.

These lists were obviously not even complete, for the reason previously given, that precautions had already been taken before the Bavarian authorities raided the dwellings of Weishaupt's chief associates in 1786. For the same reason, the documents discovered only show a part of the area over which the Illuminati had spread; Weishaupt's own diagram showed that the secret order was constructed in such a way that detection should never uncover or damage more than a segment. It is possible, for the same reason again, that Weishaupt was but a group or area leader, and that the high directorate of what demonstrably was a world-revolutionary organization was never unmasked.

What is certain is that, although the Illuminist documents contained no names or other indications to show its power in France, the French revolution, when it began three years later, developed into an attack on all civil authority and all religion, exactly of the kind planned by Weishaupt and his associates. From that day to this writers in the service of the world-revolution (their name is legion, in all countries) have never ceased to deny all connexion whatsoever between Illuminism and the French Revolution; they artlessly argue that, as the secret society was forbidden in 1786, it cannot have had anything to do with an event in 1789.

The truth is that Illuminism, though forbidden, was no more extirpated than Communism would be by a legal ban today, and that its agents gave the French revolution those brandmarks which identify it as the work of the *world* revolutionaries, not of discontented French people. The acts of the Reign of Terror were of a nature unimaginable before they were committed, but they had long been familiar, in imagination, to the Illuminati. In what other minds could the idea have taken shape that the vessels of the sacramental supper should be borne by an ass in public procession through the streets of Paris? They were nurtured in the ancient tradition of such mockery, and their own initiates were admitted in a ceremony mocking the sacrament. In what brain but Weishaupt's could the notion of enthroning an actress as Goddess of Reason in Notre Dame have found birth?

"For the purpose of infernal evocation ... it is requisite ... to profane the ceremonies of the religion to which one belongs and to trample its holiest symbols underfoot"; this is Mr. A.E. Waite's description of the formula of black magic, and black magic and Satanism were two of the ingredients in the Illuminist brew.

Weishaupt and his intimates, or perhaps his masters, proposed to enter into France through their agents, secret Illuminates, in high places. In this century we have seen what great results can be achieved by this method, the aborted result of the Second World War, and the condition of armed truce in which it has left the world, was brought about by such men as Hiss and White and the higher men who protected them. Weishaupt selected the perfect way of gaining such power over French affairs and events: through another, very powerful secret society, which he permeated and captured by the methods laid down in his papers. This was Grand Orient Freemasonry.

The plan to acquire control of Freemasonry through Illuminist agents, and the success achieved, is plainly stated in Weishaupt's papers. First he records that, "I have succeeded in obtaining a profound glimpse into the secrets of the Freemasons; I know their whole aim and shall impart it all at the right time in one of the higher degrees." At a later stage he gave a general order for his "Areopagites" to enter Freemasonry: "Then we shall have a masonic lodge of our own ... we shall regard this as our nursery garden ... at every opportunity we shall *cover* ourselves with this ..." (i.e., Freemasonry).

This device of advancing "under cover" (which is still basic in Communism today) was the guiding principle: "If only the aim is achieved, it does not matter under what *cover* it takes place; and a *cover* is always necessary.

For in concealment lies a great part of our strength. For this reason we must always *cover* ourselves with the name of another society. The lodges that are under Freemasonry are in the meantime the most suitable cloak for our high purpose ... a society concealed in this manner cannot be worked against ... In case of a prosecution or of treason *the superiors cannot be discovered* ... We shall be *shrouded* in impenetrable darkness from spies and emissaries of other societies."

Today's Communist method, once again, may be clearly recognized in these words; they could be applied to the "capture" of parties, associations and societies in our day without change of a syllable. The extent of Weishaupt's success is best shown by quotation from the lament uttered, five years after the outbreak of the French revolution, by the Duke of Brunswick, Grand Master of German Freemasonry, who had also been an Illuminate. In 1794 he dissolved the order with words of pained surprise:

"... We see our edifice" (i.e., Freemasonry) "crumbling and covering the ground with ruins; we see *destruction* that our hands no longer arrest ... A *great sect* arose, which taking for its motto the good and the happiness of man, worked in the darkness of the conspiracy to make the happiness of humanity a prey for itself. This sect is known to everyone; its brothers are known no less than its name. It is they who have undermined the foundations of the Order to the point of complete overthrow; it is by them that all humanity has been poisoned and led astray for several generations ... They began by casting odium on religion ... the plan they had formed for breaking all social ties and *destroying all order* was revealed in all their speeches and acts ... they recruited apprentices of every rank and in every position; *they deluded the most perspicacious men by falsely alleging different intentions* ... Their masters had nothing less in view than the thrones of the earth, and the government of the nations was to be directed by their nocturnal clubs. This is what has been done *and is still being done.* But we notice that princes and people are unaware how and by what means this is being accomplished. That is why we say to them in all frankness: the misuse of our Order ... has produced all the political and moral troubles with which the world is filled today. You who have been initiated, you must join yourselves with us in raising your voices, so as to teach peoples and princes that *the sectarians, the apostates of our Order, have alone been and will be the authors of present and future revolutions* ... So as to cut out to the roots the abuse and error, we must from this moment dissolve the whole Order ..."

In this quotation the present narrative has jumped five years ahead of events, in order to show that one of the leading Freemasons of that generation, himself a penitent, identified the Illuminati as the authors of the French revolution and of *future* revolutions. Weishaupt's success in his declared intention of capturing Freemasonry from within, and the part then played by Illuminist agents inside Freemasonry in directing the revolution, could not be attested by a better authority than the Grand Master of German Freemasonry himself.

Under this injected influence Freemasonry, which was very strong in France, took an extreme course and produced the Jacobin clubs; these, again under Illuminist influence, presided over the Reign of Terror, when the masked authors of the revolution revealed its true nature by their deeds. Like the Russian revolution 130 years later, the one in France then displayed its hatred of the poor and defenceless more than of the rich, of the peasants of the Vendee more than their supposed oppressors, of all beauty as such, of churches and religion, of everything that might uplift the human soul above the level of animal needs and desires.

Adam Weishaupt himself became a Freemason in 1777, the year after he founded the Illuminati, being received into a Munich lodge. Count Mirabeau, the later revolutionary leader in France, was privy both to Weishaupt's intention to join and to the secret reason for it, for his *Memoirs* included a paper, dated 1776, which set out a programme identical with that of the Illuminati, and in his History of the Prussian Monarchy he refers to Weishaupt and to the Illuminati by name and says:

"The Lodge Theodore de Bon Conseil at Munich, where there were a few men with brains and hearts, was tired of being tossed about by the vain promises and quarrels of Masonry. The heads resolved to *graft on to their branch another secret association to which they gave the name of the Order of the Illuminés. They modelled it on the Society of Jesus, whilst proposing to themselves views diametrically opposed.*"

This is the exact intention and method described by Weishaupt in his own correspondence, and this is the proof that Mirabeau, the later revolutionary leader, knew of it at the time, that is in 1776. Moreover, his words suggest that the secret society of the Illuminati was founded with the express intention of gaining control of Freemasonry and of instigating and directing revolution through it. That Mirabeau was party to the whole undertaking from the start is suggested by the fact that the memoir of 1776 (the year in which the Illuminati were founded) ascribes to him the Illuminist "cover-name" of Arcesilas, so that he must have been a founder member, with Adam Weishaupt, and a leading Illuminate thereafter. Mirabeau, as the link between Weishaupt and the French Revolution, cannot be ignored. The editor of his *Memoirs*, M. Barthou, remarks that the "plan of reform" of 1776, found among Mirabeau's papers, "resembles very much in certain parts the work accomplished later by the Constituent Assembly" (the revolutionary parliament of 1789). That is another way of saying that the work of the Constituent Assembly very much resembled Adam Weishaupt's plan of 1776, when he and Mirabeau together were founding the Illuminati and planning together to gain control of Freemasonry.

The other stages in Weishaupt's underground capture of Freemasonry are also clear in the record. At the general congress of 1782 (seven years before the revolution) at Wilhelmsbad the Illuminati gained so many recruits that the Order of the Strict Observance, previously the most powerful body in Freemasonry, ceased to exist. The way to complete victory in the Masonic world was opened when the Illuminati enlisted the two most important personages in German Freemasonry, Duke Ferdinand of Brunswick (the later penitent) and Prince Carl of Hesse.

In 1785 Illuminist emissaries attended another general congress, in Paris, and from that moment the detailed planning of the revolution seems to have become the task of the Lodge of the Amis Reunis, which was a "cover" for the Illuminati. The blurring of traces at this point is the result of the notoriety which the order gained in Bavaria, its proscription in the following year, 1786, and the destruction of evidence. Nevertheless, in 1787, the same emissaries visited Paris at the invitation of the secret committee of the Lodge.

Even before the revolution had really developed, the fact that it was instigated and directed by Illuminism was known and published. The indictment and the warning uttered by the Marquis de Luchet stands out today as an astonishingly accurate prediction, not only of the course which the revolution would take in France, but of the continuing course of the *world* revolution down to our day. As early as 1789 he wrote:

"Learn that there exists a conspiracy in favour of despotism against liberty, of in capacity against talent; of vice against virtue, of ignorance against enlightenment ... This society aims at governing *the world* ... Its object is universal domination ... No such calamity has ever yet afflicted the world ..."

De Luchet precisely depicted the role which the monarch was to be forced to play during the Girondist phase ("see him condemned to serve the passions of all that surround him ... to raise degraded men to power, to prostitute his judgment by choices that dishonour his prudence"), and the plight in which the revolution would leave France ("We do not mean to say that the country where the Illuminés reign will cease to exist, but it will fall into such a degree of humiliation that it will no longer count in politics, that the population will diminish ..."). If his warning went unheeded, cried de Luchet, there would be "a series of calamities of which the end is lost in the darkness of time ... *a subterranean fire smouldering eternally and breaking forth periodically in violent and devastating explosions.*" The events of the last 165 years have not been better described than in these words of de Luchet, which foretold them. He also foresaw the "liberal and progressive" patron of the revolution who was to help greatly in bringing about the "violent and devastating explosions" of these 165 years: "there are too many passion interested in supporting the system of the Illumines, too many deluded rulers, imagining themselves enlightened, ready to precipitate their people into the abyss." He foresaw the continuing strength and clutch of the conspiracy: "the heads of the Order will never relinquish the authority they have acquired nor the treasure at their disposal." De Luchet called on Freemasonry to cleanse its stable while time remained: "would it not be possible to direct the Freemasons themselves against the Illumines by showing them that, whilst they are working to maintain harmony in society, those others are everywhere sowing seeds of discord and preparing the ultimate destruction of their order?" 165 years later, in Britain and America, men were calling on their governments in just such words, and just as vainly, to cleanse the public offices and services of the Illumines, by then called Communists.

The measure of de Luchet's foresight is given by the fact that he wrote in 1789, when the French revolution was hardly a revolution; it was universally held to be merely a mild, health-giving reform which would leave the monarch a wise meed of power, amend obvious evils, and establish justice and freedom for ever in a happy, regenerated France! That was still the general belief in 1790, when across the Channel another man saw the true nature of the revolution and "predicted with uncanny accuracy the course of events," to quote his biographer of more than a century later, Mr. John Morley.

Edmund Burke, an Irishman, was one of the greatest orators the British House of Commons ever saw. Time is the test of such a man's quality, and as the years pass the phrases of his attack on the French revolution ring ever more nobly; as in de Luchet's case, the remarkable thing is that it was published in 1790, when the names of Robespierre and Danton were hardly known, before the word "republic" had been heard, when the king looked forward to long years of constitutional reign, when all France was joyfully celebrating the peaceful improvement that had been effected. Across this happy scene fell suddenly the shadow of Burke's outstretched arm, pointing "like an inspired prophet" to the doom to come. His biographer says, "It is no wonder that when the cloud burst and the doom was fulfilled men turned to Burke as they turned of old to Ahitopheth, whose counsel was as if men enquired of the oracle of God."

Unhappily that is not a true picture of what occurred when Burke's warning was fulfilled. Very many men turned *against* Burke, not to him, precisely *because* he had spoken the truth; indeed, the power which the conspiracy even at that time wielded over the press and public debate is most clearly shown by the way flattery of him was suddenly turned into attack and defamation after he published his *Reflections* on the revolution. The Illumines, and the "liberal and progressive" organs and speakers controlled by them, had greatly counted on Edmund Burke, because he had upheld the cause of the American colonists a decade earlier. How could he support one revolution and attack another, they asked angrily, and Burke came under the kind of general attack which the united press, in our generation, keeps in its locker for any man who publicly demands the investigation of Communism-in-government.

Had Burke followed the "progressive" line, and pretended that the French revolution would help "the common man," the flattery of him would have continued, but in that case nothing he said would have been of enduring value, or have been remembered today. As it is, the inspired words of his attack on the revolution have the imperishable gleam of gold: "It is gone, that sensibility of principle, that chastity of honour, which felt a stain like a wound … The age of chivalry is gone. That of sophisters, economists and calculators, has succeeded; and the glory of Europe is extinguished for ever."

If these words, too, were inspired prophecy (and in 1955 they look truer than they were even in 1790) Christendom and the West at least found an eloquent and noble mourner in Edmund Burke. For he knew the difference between "revolutions" as clearly as he saw the true shape of the event in France. He was not to be bamboozled by the fact that somebody had miscalled a colonial war of independence, led by country squires, a "revolution." As a genuine friend of liberty, he had supported the colonists' bid to govern themselves and be masters in their own household. There was no resemblance whatever between their motives and those of the secret men who, as Burke saw, were behind the revolution in France. Therefore he stretched out his accusing hand and was as heedless of the reproaches of "liberal" and "progressive" as he had been of their flattery on the earlier occasion (assuredly Edmund Burke knew that their praise then had not been prompted by any sympathy with New England merchants or Southern plantation-owners).

In America, at that moment, the general feeling about the event in France was a deluded one, produced by the confusion of ideas which Burke rejected. There was, for the time being, a popular notion that another benign "revolution" had occurred, somewhat similar to the "American revolution." There was a transient "French Frenzy," when Americans wore cockades and liberty-caps, danced, feasted and paraded beneath intertwined French and American flags, and shouted "Liberty, Equality, Fraternity." With the Reign of Terror, this phase of illusion was followed by one of revulsion and horror.

The Jacobin leaders directed the Reign of Terror and, as good Illuminates, used classic pseudonyms in the manner initiated by "Spartacus" Weishaupt himself: Chaumette was Anaxagoras, Clootz (described as a Prussian baron) was Anacharsis, Danton Horace, Lacroix Publicola and Ronsin Scaevola. These terrorists, when they succeeded the Kerensky-phase, faithfully carried out the plan of the Illuminati, and by the killing of a king and the desecration of churches gave expression to its two chief ideas: the destruction of all legitimate government and of all religion. Yet even they were apparently only tools, for a contemporary, Lombard de Langres, wrote of that "most secret convention which directed everything after May 31, an occult and terrible power of which the other Convention became the slave and which was composed of the *prime initiates of Illuminism. This power was above Robespierre and the committees of the government* ... it was this occult power which appropriated to itself the treasures of the nation and distributed them to the brothers and friends who had helped on the great work."

It is this picture of men in high places doing the will of some hidden, but palpably directing, supreme *sect* that gives the revolution the aspect of a demoniac puppet-show, played against flickering red flames amid the odour of brimstone. *The* revolution, not the *French* revolution; whatever the true nature of the English one, since 1789 there has only been *one*, continuous revolution. There have not been episodic, disconnected outbreaks, in 1848 and 1905 and so on, but those recurrent eruptions of "a subterranean fire smouldering eternally" which de Luchet and Burke foresaw *before* the event. What is historically of great value in the annals of the French revolution, however, is the proof, which they afford, of the use of men for a purpose uncomprehended by them. This gives the revolution, then and now, its peculiar and satanic imprint; it is, as Lombard de Langres wrote, "the code of hell."

When the revolution was ebbing, three men arose, in France, England and America, who saw three things plainly: that its course had followed the chart revealed by the Illuminati papers in 1787; that this secret society had been able, through Freemasonry, to instigate and direct it; and that the secret league of conspirators, with its continuing plan for *world* revolution, had survived and was preparing the further "violent and devastating explosions" foretold by de Luchet. These three men were the Abbé Baruel, a Jesuit and eyewitness of the revolution; Professor John Robison a Scottish scientist who for over twenty years was general secretary of the Royal Society of Edinburgh; and the Rev. Jedediah Morse, a New England clergyman and geographer. They were all distinguished men. The Abbé Baruel's and Professor Robison's books and Mr. Morse's published sermons (all 1797-8) went into many editions and are still indispensable to students of the time. Their works and words gained much public attention and they were supported from Philadelphia, in his *Porcupine* 's *Gazette,* by William Cobbett, who seems to have been driven into exile by the same occult power which set out to destroy Messrs' Baruel, Robison and Morse.

The Abbé Baruel's' verdict on what had occurred was identical with de Luchet's earlier prophecy and Lord Acton's much later analysis:

"... We shall demonstrate that, even to the most horrid deeds perpetrated during the French revolution, everything *was foreseen and resolved on, combined and premeditated;* that they were the offspring of deep thought villainy, since they had been prepared and were produced by men, who alone held the clue of these plots and conspiracies, lurking in the secret meetings where they had been conceived ... Though the events of each day may not appear to have been combined, there nevertheless existed a secret agent and a secret cause, giving rise to each event and turning each circumstance to the long-sought-for end ... The grand cause of the revolution, its leading features, its atrocious crimes, will still remain one continued chain of deep laid and *premeditated* villainy."

The three men came to the same conclusion: "An anti-Christian conspiracy ... not only against kings, but against every government, against all civil society, even against all property whatsoever" (the Abbé Baruel); "An association has been formed for the express purpose of rooting out all the religious establishments, and overturning all the existing governments of Europe" (Prof. Robison); "The express aim is 'to root out and abolish Christianity and overthrow all civil governments'." (Mr. Morse). They agreed that what had happened was, not merely an episode in France, born of French circumstances, but the work of an organization with a continuing plan in all countries: a *universal* plan. They agreed that this organization was the secret society of the Illuminati, that it had inspired and controlled the terrorist phase of the revolution, that it had survived, and that it was established and strong in England and the United States. The Abbé Baruel in particular gave warning in this last respect.

The words and writings of these three men were supported by the leading public men of their day, and have been so fully borne out by events, particularly in our century, that historically they simply serve to show that the world-revolution was recognized by some, and its future course foretold, at the moment of its second appearance in the West. The efforts of these three men were as vain in averting the havoc which the conspiracy later wreaked, and for that reason the case of Messrs' Barruel, Robison and Morse is of especial interest.

What befell them proves more conclusively than any of their own words the very thing they strove to establish: the continued existence and strength of a secret society working, in all countries, for the destructive purpose which they described. Messrs' Barruel, Robison and Morse were smothered with vituperation. In their day newspapers were in their infancy, and were usually owned by one man, who also edited them. It must therefore have been much more difficult than it is today to gain control of a large proportion of them. The concentrated attack which was delivered against the three men from the moment when they said that Illuminism had brought about the French revolution and still existed shows that even in 1797 the Illuminés were in effective control of the press in America and England.

This was one of the most surprising discoveries yielded by the research which produced this book. In my own day I have been forced to realize that this control exists, and that a writer who writes about the world revolution in the vein of Edmund Burke will find all avenues of publication closing against him. Mrs Nesta Webster relates the same experience. When she first began to write on revolution, in the early 1920's, a well-known London publisher said to her, "Remember that if you take an anti-revolutionary line you will have the whole literary world against you." She says she thought this extraordinary but then found through experience that the publisher was right and that has been my observation too. However, I thought it was a condition that had arisen during the last thirty years until I studied the story of Messrs' Barruel, Robison and Morse; then I saw that "the whole literary world" fell as one man on them in 1798, when the Reign of Terror was recent. Nothing else so clearly showed, to me, that the line from Illuminism in 1789 to Communism today is but a line of inheritance; the *same* organization pursues the same aim with the same methods and even with the same *words*.

That was another curious thing about the attack on those three writers who took "an anti-revolutionary line." Soon after they gained the public eye the attacks in the newspapers began; nearly always anonymous. They made use of exactly the same language (Doublespeak) as that which is employed in similar assaults today. The three men were accused of starting a "witch-hunt," of being bigots and alarmists, of persecuting "freedom of opinion" and "academic freedom," of misrepresenting "liberal" and "progressive" thought, and the like. From that, the attack continued to slander and scurrilous innuendo, and I often found phrases which recurred in the campaign waged against an American Cabinet member, Mr. James Forrestal, in 1947-9; their private lives were said to be immoral and their financial habits shady; and at the last came the familiar suggestion that they were "mad." This suggestion is often made today, in the culminant stages of a campaign against any anti-revolutionary figure; it is evidently held to be especially strong medicine in defamation. This particular form of attack might have its original source in the Talmud, which uses it against Jesus (the *Jewish Encyclopaedia,* in its article on Jesus, refers its readers to the work of a Jewish writer who "agrees that there must have been abnormal mental processes involved in the utterances and behaviour of Jesus").

In short, these attacks on Messrs' Barruel, Robison and Morse made use of a limited political vocabulary which today is plainly recognizable as that of the revolution and its agents, and is now so hackneyed that it must be imparted to all initiates from some central place in the organization. The campaign against them was effective, so that their warnings, like those of Burke, were forgotten by the masses. However, the secret band (which must have the same horror of truth as the devil might have of the cross) continued to fear them, so that the defamation continued long after all three were dead! As recently as 1918 the Columbia University of New York allotted funds for a costly piece of research designed to show that the Illuminati truly died when they were proscribed in 1786 and thus could not have caused or survived the French revolution, and in this publication all the stock-in-trade epithets were brought out and used again, as if the three dead men were live "witch-hunters"!

In 1918 the Russian revolution was but a year old and the moment was evidently held apt for another attempt to show that the French revolution had been a self-contained affair, leaving no roots which might have erupted in Russia in 1917. Messrs' Barruel, Robison and Morse, if from some bourne they were able to watch these proceedings, no doubt observed that in 1918 and the following years Communism found the Columbia University of New York to be a very good hunting-ground. (Among the unlucky young men who were there entrapped for the cause was the Mr. Whittaker Chambers whose repentance and warning in 1939, had it been heeded by President Franklin Roosevelt, might have changed the whole course of the Second World War and of this century for the better).

The first two presidents of the American Republic, though they did not effectively act against the secret society, were deeply alarmed about it and well knew that what Barruel, Robison and Morse said was true. One of George Washington's last acts was, in a letter to Mr. Morse, to express the hope that his work would have "a more general circulation ... for it contains important information, as little known, *out of a small circle,* as the dissemination of it would be useful, if spread through the community." (Presumably General Washington would not have told a Whittaker Chambers to "go jump in the lake"). A little earlier Washington had informed another correspondent that he was fully satisfied that "the doctrines of the Illuminati and the principles of Jacobinism" had "spread in the United States."

Indeed, this was beyond doubt, for secret societies had appeared in the United States in 1793, that is, within ten years of the Republic's birth, under the guise of "Democratic Clubs." Their true nature was made plain by the attitude of the French Minister, Genet, towards them; he showed the open sympathy which Soviet Ambassadors, in our generation, display for Communist organizations, or perhaps more accurately, for those which serve as "cover" for Communism (the relationship between the Soviet embassies and the revolutionary party in the country of accreditation was established by massive documentary proof in the Canadian and Australian investigations of 1945-46 and 1954-55 respectively). George Washington, as president in 1794, charged these "self-created societies" with instigating the insurrectionary outbreak in Pennsylvania known as the Whiskey Rebellion. Washington's authority was too great for him to be attacked as a witch-hunter and the clubs burrowed quickly underground, but from that moment the presence on American soil of an organization for world-revolution was known to all who cared to know and were able to withstand the "brainwashing" of the press.

The part admittedly played by Grand Orient Freemasonry, under Illuminist permeation, in the French Revolution caused American Freemasonry also to fall under suspicion, but frank discussion of this question was hindered by the fact that the great Washington was head of the Masonic fraternity. The defenders of Freemasonry laid much emphasis on this (evidently on the principle of "innocence by association"), and on the occasion of Washington's funeral in 1799 made a great parade of fellowship with the dead hero. Out of respect for him, rather than from satisfied curiosity, the public debate then waned, but at least two prominent Masons, Amos Stoddard and the Rev. Seth Payson, like the Duke of Brunswick in Europe publicly stated that the Illuminati had permeated Freemasonry and were working under its name. Washington's successor, President John Adams, in 1798 addressed a stern warning to Freemasonry:

"... the society of Masons have discovered a science of government, or art of ruling society, peculiar to themselves, and unknown to all the other legislators and philosophers of the world; I mean not only the skill to know each other by marks or signs that no other persons can divine but the wonderful power of enabling and compelling all men, and I suppose all women, at all hours, to keep a secret. If this art can be applied, to set aside the ordinary maxims of society, and introduce politics and disobedience to government, and still keep the secret, it must be obvious that such science and *such societies may be perverted to all the ill purposes which have been suspected ...*"

After this public rebuke nothing but the death of Washington in the next year, probably, could have appeased the public desire for a thorough investigation; as so often in these affairs, the opponents of investigation profited from an irrelevant event which distracted or disarmed public attention. Nevertheless, public suspicion continued through three decades and led to the formation of an Anti-masonic Party in 1827, which at its State convention in Massachusetts in 1829 declared "there is evidence of an intimate connexion between the higher orders of Freemasonry and French Illuminism." That was almost the last kick of the party of investigation, for the next State convention, in Vermont in 1830, recorded the sequel with which our century has been made familiar: "... the spirit of enquiry ... was soon and unaccountably quelled; the press was mute as if the voice of the strangled sentinel and the mass of the people kept in ignorance that an alarm on the subject of Masonry had ever been sounded."

In other words, the cry for investigation had been drowned, as in our generation, by the counter-cry of "witch-hunt" and the like. From that moment until today the American people have never succeeded in moving any government to a full investigation and the secret infestation of government and the public departments continued, with results only partially revealed by the exposures of 1948 and after. The situation in England has been very similar.

In the last few paragraphs this narrative has jumped a few years to follow the course of American public uneasiness about Freemasonry to its end in 1830 (the Anti-masonic Party actually died in 1840). Now it returns to the immediate aftermath of the French revolution, and its effect on the world.

President Adams, as his *Works* show, was fully informed and persuaded about the existence of a *universal* and continuing conspiracy against all legitimate government and religion. He made the mistake, natural in his day, of thinking the plan a *French* one, just as people today, with no excuse, speak and think of *Russian* Communism, although the international nature of the revolution has long been made plain, beyond all doubt.

By his Sedition Act of 1798 President Adams tried to safeguard the future of the Republic, but time has since shown that laws against secret societies and conspiracies (although they *should* be enacted, to establish the illegality of the undertaking) are ineffective in checking them, especially as the secret organization has centuries of experience in eluding such laws. The one effective measure against secret conspiracy is investigation, public exposure and remedy, and this has never been fully used.

The American public man who most plainly perceived the entire shape of the future was Washington's confidant, Alexander Hamilton. He left among his papers an undated memoir (probably 1797-1800) which said:

"... the present era is among the most extraordinary which have occurred in the history of human affairs. Opinions, for a long time, have been gradually gaining ground, which threaten the foundations of religion, morality and society. An attack was first made upon the Christian revelation, for which natural religion was offered as a substitute ... The very existence of a Deity has been questioned and in some instances denied. The duty of piety has been ridiculed, the perishable nature of man asserted, and his hopes bounded to the short span of his earthly state. Death has been proclaimed an eternal sleep, the dogma of the immortality of the soul a cheat, invented to torment the living for the benefit of the dead ... A league has at length been cemented between the apostles and disciples of irreligion and anarchy. Religion and government have both been "stigmatized as abuses ... The practical development of this pernicious system has been seen in France. It has served as an engine to subvert all her ancient institutions, civil and religious, with all the checks that served to mitigate the rigour of authority; it has hurried her headlong through a series of dreadful revolutions, which have laid waste property, made havoc among the arts, overthrown cities, desolated provinces, unpeopled regions, crimsoned her soil with blood, and deluged it in crime, poverty, and wretchedness; ... This horrid system seemed awhile to threaten *the subversion of civilized society and the introduction of general disorder among mankind.* And though the frightful evils which have been its first and only fruits have given a check to its progress, it is to be feared that *the poison has spread too widely and penetrated too deeply to be as yet eradicated.* Its activity has been suspended, *but the elements remain, concocting for new eruptions as occasion shall permit.* It is greatly to be apprehended that *mankind is not near the end of the misfortunes which it is calculated to produce, and that it still portends a long train of convulsion, revolution, carnage, devastation and misery. Symptoms of the too great prevalence of this system in the United States are alarmingly visible.* It was by its influence that efforts were made to embark this country in a common cause with France in the early period of the present war; to induce our government to sanction and promote her odious principles and views with the blood and treasure of our citizens. It is by its influence that every succeeding revolution has been approved or excused; all the horrors that have been committed justified or extenuated; that even the last usurpation, which contradicts all the ostensible principles of the Revolution, has been regarded with complacency, and the despotic constitution engendered by it slyly held up as a model not unworthy of our imitation. In the progress of this system, impiety and infidelity have advanced with gigantic strides. Prodigious crimes heretofore unknown among us are seen...."

We of the 1950's are so familiar with the results here foreseen that we can scarcely realize what skill was needed, in the 1790's, so clearly to foresee them! From de Luchet before the Reign of Terror ("a series of calamities of which the end is lost in the darkness of time ... a subterranean fire smouldering eternally and breaking forth periodically in violent and devastating explosions") to Alexander Hamilton after it ("the elements remain, concocting for new eruptions as occasion shall permit ... mankind is not near the end of the misfortunes which it is calculated to produce ... a long train of convulsion, revolution, carnage, devastation and misery") the shape of our century was most plainly and accurately foretold.

The net result of all this prescience, in terms of precaution, was nothing.

Needlessly but massively, all came about as these men, and the Burkes and Barruels, Robisons and Morses foresaw; like a man sleepwalking, the West trod on all the charted landmines. The anti-revolutionary prophets were cried down; the revolutionary orators and writers took over the debate and were applauded.

Napoleon's wars helped to divert public attention from the plot and the organization that had been discovered. Ten years after the French revolution the documents of the Illuminati and the French revolution were being forgotten; the public masses either began to believe that the secret society truly was dead, or had never had part in the revolution, or did not care. Twenty years after the French revolution the Illuminati were as busy as ever. Nothing had changed, save that the sect's followers in England and America had succeeded, through their power over published information, in beguiling the public mind and in defaming all who gave warning.

This later knowledge about the Illuminati is recent; Mrs Nesta Webster's research discovered it. It comes from the boxes of Napoleon's police, which have now yielded their contents to the student and historian.

These show that, two decades after the revolution and on the eve of Napoleon's own downfall, the Illuminati were very much alive, and pursued their undeviating aim.

Francois Charles de Berckheim was a special commissioner of police at Mayence under the Empire, and a Freemason. He reported in 1810 that the Illuminati had initiates all over Europe and were working hard to introduce their principles into the lodges of Freemasonry: "Illuminism is becoming a great and formidable power ... kings and peoples will have much to suffer from it unless foresight and prudence break its frightful mechanism." A later report, of 1814, fully bears out the main contention of Messrs' Barruel, Robison and Morse in 1797-9 about the continuance of the secret society:

"The oldest and most dangerous association that which is generally known under the denomination of the Illuminés and of which the foundation goes back towards the middle of the last century ... the doctrine of Illuminism is subversive of every kind of monarchy; unlimited liberty, absolute levelling down, such is the fundamental dogma of the sect; to break the ties that bind the sovereign to the citizen of a state, that is the object of all its efforts."

Twenty years after the act of penance publicly performed by the Duke of Brunswick, Berckheim recorded that "among the principal chiefs ... are numbered men distinguished for their fortune, their birth, and the dignities with which they are invested." He believed that some of these were "*not* the dupes of these demagogic dreams" but "hope to find in the popular emotions they stir up the means of seizing the reins of power, or at any rate of increasing their wealth and credit; but the crowd of adepts believe in it religiously...."

The picture given in these words (which recall de Luchet's, of twenty-five years before) is, or should be, familiar today, for our generation has shown again that avarice for power still leads wealthy or well-known people to associate themselves with movements, apparently hostile to their wealth or renown, in the belief that through them they may become even richer or more notorious.

Berckheim then gives a description of the organization and methods of the Illuminati which reproduces the picture given by Weishaupt's correspondence of 1786, and could equally be a photograph of Communism at work in our century. The following extract shows a group of recognizable 20th Century characters, to which any attentive student of our times could fit names, yet it was written in 1813:

"As the principal force of the Illuminés lies in the power of opinions, they have set themselves out from the beginning to make proselytes amongst the men who through their profession exercise a direct influence on minds, such as litterateurs, savants and above all professors. The latter in their chairs, the former in their writings, propagate the principles of the sect by disguising the poison that they circulate under a thousand different forms. These germs, often imperceptible to the eyes of the vulgar, are afterwards developed by the adepts of the Societies they frequent, and the most obscure wording is thus brought to the understanding of the least discerning. *It is above all in the universities that Illuminism has always found and always will find numerous recruits; Those professors who belong to the Association set out from the first to study the character of their pupils.* If a student gives evidence of a vigorous mind, an ardent imagination, the sectaries at once get hold of him; they sound in his ears the words Despotism, Tyranny, Rights of the People, etc., etc. Before he can even attach any meaning to these words, as he advances in age, reading works chosen for him, conversations skilfully arranged, develop the germ deposited in his youthful brain. Soon, his imagination ferments ... At last, when he has been completely captivated, when several years of testing guarantee to the society inviolable secrecy and absolute devotion, it is made known to him that millions of individuals distributed in all the States of Europe share his sentiments and his hopes, that a secret link binds firmly all the scattered members of this immense family, and that the reforms he desires so ardently must sooner or later come about. This propaganda is rendered the easier by the existing associations of students, who meet together for the study of literature, for fencing, gaming or even mere debauchery. The Illuminés insinuate themselves into all these circles and turn them into hotbeds for the propagation of their principles. Such then is the Association's continual mode of progression from its origins until the present moment; it is by convening from childhood the germ of poison into the highest classes of society, in feeding the minds of students on ideas diametrically opposed to that order of things under which they have to live, in breaking the ties that bind them to sovereigns, that Illuminism has recruited the largest number of adepts...."

Thus Illuminism survived and flourished in darkness after its "adepts" in the editorial offices, university chairs and pulpits had beaten down the public clamour for its extirpation. For some five generations since then the thing has continued: a proportion of notable men and a proportion of young men at the universities have in each succeeding generation been enticed into this net. The only counter- measure which would give the seniors pause and open the eyes of the unwary younger ones would be full public information about the world revolution and its methods, and that has been denied from generation to generation, so that the secret sect has maintained its power and hold. There can be only one explanation for this refusal of governments, from generation to generation, to investigate and expose: namely, that in this day as in Weishaupt's the sect has its "adepts" in the governments themselves; of that our century has given sufficient evidence.

What of Weishaupt himself, twenty years and more after his exposure and the proscription of his order? In 1808 he was enquiring about a point of masonic ritual and his enquiry reached the notice of an eminent member of the Grand Orient, the Marquis de Chefdebien, who then wrote in a letter to a friend that Illuminism had supplied the men who "stirred up revolt, devastation, assassination": When Weishaupt died, in 1830, his order was probably stronger than it had ever been, but was about to change its name; the same organization, with the same aims, was in the 1840's to emerge as Communism. That further story belongs to later chapters, and at this point the present narrative takes leave of Adam Weishaupt, the man whose name is forever identified with the emergence of world-revolution as a permanent idea and ambition, propagated by a permanent organization of secret conspirators in all lands, and having nothing whatever to do with remedying oppression or injustice; these evils it desired to aggravate and perpetuate.

Whoever his prompters, whatever the original source of his great knowledge of human weakness, Weishaupt, as Mrs Nesta Webster says, "gathered into his hands the threads of all the conspiracies, was able to weave them together into a gigantic scheme for the destruction of France and the world." In his army men of all classes and of the most diverse views were welded together by bonds of infamy which seemed as strong as those of faith and honour: "Weishaupt's admirable system of watertight compartments precluded them from a knowledge of these differences and they all marched, unconsciously or not, towards the same goal."

If there were manifold currents of discontent before, Weishaupt fused them into one. With him and Illuminism, "vague subversive theory became active revolution"; the general staff was formed, the battle-operation laid down, the objective clarified. Today, nearly two hundred years later, the consequence of that is also clear: the all-destructive world-revolution must either prevail over Christendom and the West, reducing them both to ruins, or itself be crushed and broken up. There is now no third solution or middle course or different end to the conflict which was revealed in 1786. Leading public men and the sect's devotees both saw that from the start. By 1875 Mgr. Dillon tersely stated the unalterable fact:

"Had Weishaupt not lived, Masonry might have ceased to be a power after the reaction consequent on the French revolution. He gave it a form and character which caused it to outlive that reaction, *to energise it to the present day, and which will cause it to advance until its final conflict with Christianity must determine whether Christ or Satan shall reign on this earth in the end.*"

This book is a study of "the Jewish question" as the most important question in world affairs at the present time; yet the present chapter (the longest yet) on the world-revolution has made no mention of the Jewish question or of Jews. There is a reason for this. Fifty years *after* the French revolution the world-revolution was under Judaist direction, but original Judaist instigation of the world- revolution in its French phase *cannot* be shown. Therefore the possibility is open that the world-revolution was not at the start a Judaist undertaking, but one in which the ruling sect of Judaism later became the majority stockholder. Nothing definite can be established either way; the covering-up of tracks is the first principle of revolutionary tactics.

Apparently Jews played little or no part in the master-conspiracy (that of Weishaupt and his Illuminati) and simply a proportionate part, with all others, in the French revolution. As to the first, the leading authority on this subject, Mrs Nesta Webster, says "Jews appear to have been only in rare cases admitted to the Order." Leopold Engel, a mysterious character who reorganized the order in 1880, goes further, stating that the recruitment of the Jews was *forbidden*. On the other hand, Mirabeau, a leading Illuminate and revolutionary, identified himself with Judaist demands and pretensions, so that any restriction on the actual appearance of Jews in the Order may have been a "cover" device of the kind which Weishaupt held to be supremely important.

The best authorities at the time agreed that the Illuminati were the instigators of the revolution and that they were men of all countries. The Chevalier de Malet says, "The authors of the revolution are not more French than German, Italian, English, etc. They form a particular nation which took birth and has grown in darkness, in the midst of all civilized nations, with the object of subjecting them to its domination." This is the picture which today's student also gains from study of the literature of the French revolution; it is entirely different from the picture of the Russian revolution of 1917, to which the words could not be applied.

In the French revolution *itself* (as distinct from the foregoing conspiracy) the part played by Jews is fairly clear, but seems to have been that of "abetting disorder" ascribed to them by the Koran, rather than that of control or direction. Indeed, it is often difficult to distinguish Jews, as such, in the records of the time, because writers of the day did not so separate them. Moreover, the revolution in its French phase *appeared* to be against *all* religion and *all* nationhood (in the Russian phase, again, this was no longer the case). Thus, the mob which brought crosses and chalices to the revolutionary assembly, while the churches of Paris were being given over to "Feasts of Reason," also included Jews who contributed ornaments from the synagogue to the display of profanation. Again, at "the Temple of Liberty," a citizen "brought up in the prejudices of the Jewish religion" undertook to prove "that all forms of worship are impostures equally degrading to man." Alexandre Lambert *fils* then gave voice to this protest against the bondage of the Talmud:

"The bad faith, citizens, of which the Jewish nation is accused does not come from themselves but from their priests. Their religion, which would allow them only to lend to those of their nation at 5 percent, tells them to take all they can from Catholics; it is even hallowed as a custom in our morning prayers to solicit God's help in catching out a Christian. There is more, citizens, and it is the climax of abomination; if any mistake is made in commerce between Jews, they are ordered to make reparation: but if on 100 Louis a Christian should have paid 25 too much, one is not bound to return them to him. What an abomination! What a horror! *And where does that all come from but from the Rabbis?* Who have excited proscriptions against us? Our priests! Ah, citizens, more than anything in the world we must abjure a religion which ... by subjecting us to irksome and servile practices, makes it impossible for us to be good citizens."[4]

If the Jews are anywhere identified *as Jews* (not simply as participants) in the worst deeds of the revolution, this is in Jewish vaunt, not Gentile accusation. For instance, such a writer as M. Leon Kahn goes far out of his way to associate Jews, by name, with the attack on the king and on religion, and that a hundred years after the events. This is an example of the laboured effort, which may be traced in much Judaist literature, to show that nothing of this kind *can* happen in the world save by the hand of Jehovah, that is to say, of Jews.

M. Leon Kahn apparently could not picture the French revolution in any other terms than those of Daniel and Belshazzar. But for the Russian revolution, M. Leon Kahn might be forgotten; once again, it is our present-day that gives these depictments of old events their look of truth.

In the aftermath of the French revolution, the Jews, through their leaders, seem simply to have turned a situation to good account, as they were entitled to do. However, in the light of what followed later it is significant that the Jews who profited were the "Eastern Jews," and that these non-Semitic converts to Judaism at that point in time made their first breach in the walls of the West.

Most of the Jews in France were Sephardim, descended from those Spanish and Portuguese Jews who had some tenuous tradition, at least, linking them with Palestine. Any disabilities still suffered by these long-settled Jews were ended by the decree of 1790, which gave them all the rights of French citizens. In Alsace a community of Ashkenazim, the Slavic Jews, had appeared and these visitors from Russia were greatly disliked, so that the proposal to bestow citizenship on them provoked stormy debates, in the revolutionary Assembly and an insurrection among the Alsatian peasants. On

---

[4] The italicized line in this quotation gives a timely opportunity to remark that when Alexandre Lambert *fils* so spoke the *rabbinical* period in Judaist history had just begun. Before 1772, when Poland was partitioned, there had always been a visible, central, governing or directing authority for all of Jewry. At the start this was the Levitical priesthood, in Jerusalem and Babylon. Under Rome it was the dominant political party, the Pharisees, who were in effect the government. After the fall of Jerusalem and the dispersion it was the Talmudic "movable government" in Palestine, Babylonia, Spain and Poland. After this sank from sight in 1772 the "rabbinical" period began, where authority over the entire congregation of Jewry, as far as it was wielded, was exercised through the rabbis everywhere. Among these, naturally, were men of every degree of belief and temperament, from the most extreme to the most temperate; but the present century has shown that the majority of them, as at all earlier periods in Jewish history, followed the literal "Law" of Judaism, which from the Gentile point of view, of course, is extremism at its most extreme.

this occasion the warnings with which earlier centuries had made the West familiar again were heard. The Abbé Maury told the citizen deputies, "The Jews have traversed seventeen centuries without mingling with other nations … They must not be persecuted, they must be protected as individuals and not as Frenchmen, since they cannot be citizens … Whatever you do, they will always remain foreigners in our midst." The Bishop of Nancy concurred; "They must be accorded protection, safety, liberty; but should we admit into the family a tribe that is foreign to it, that turns its eyes unceasingly towards a common country, that aspires to abandon the land that bears it? The interest of the Jews themselves necessitates this protest."

The Sephardic Jews also protested: "We dare to believe that our condition in France would not today be open to discussion if certain demands of the Jews of Alsace, Lorraine and the Three Bishoprics had not caused a confusion of ideas which appears to reflect on us

… To judge by the public papers they appear to be rather extraordinary, since these Jews aspire to live in France under a special regime, to have laws peculiar to themselves, and to constitute a class of citizens separated from all the others."

This *Jewish* protest (a recurrent one through the ages down to our present day, and one always ignored by Gentile rulers) was as vain as that of the merchants of Paris thirty years before against the opening of their corporations to Jews:

"The French merchant carries on his commerce alone; each commercial house is in a way isolated; whilst the Jews are *particles of quicksilver, which at the least slant run together into a block.*"

Despite all opposition the decree emancipating the Jews of Alsace was passed in 1791. By the time Napoleon succeeded to power a Jewish problem of the first order had thus been created for him and (after his failure to solve it) for the world.

From this time on the ruling sect of Jewry bent all its efforts on reducing the authority of the original, Sephardic Jews and increasing that of their compact Ashkenazi in the East; from this moment on the Ashkenazi began to move into Europe (and later into America), to assume the leadership of the world-revolution and to carry with them everywhere the assault on all legitimate government, religion and nationhood.

That development followed the French revolution, or first phase of the world-revolution, which was like the opening of a door or the breaking of a dyke. At the time all that could fairly be said of the Jews in relation to the revolution was that they had been involved in it like other men, and had benefited from it rather more than other men. The sequel turned a different light on all this, and began to show Judaist *direction*, not mere involvement.

For in the half-century following the revelation of the blueprint for world-revolution and the outbreak in France, the historical processes of Jewry and of the world-revolution no longer remained separate or distinct; they converged. The continuing conspiracy and "the Jews" (in the sense of the dominant sect) then became identical and could no longer be considered apart. From the middle of the 19th Century the world-revolution was under Jewish leadership; whatever the fact had been before, it then passed into these hands. The authoritative witness, whose words (like the earlier ones of de Luchet, Alexander Hamilton and Edmund Burke) were fully borne out by events, was one Benjamin Disraeli, Prime Minister of England.

Chapter 21

THE WARNINGS OF DISRAELI

Benjamin Disraeli, later Lord Beaconsfield, repeatedly warned Christendom against the world-revolution. Like de Luchet, Alexander Hamilton and Edmund Burke fifty years before, he saw "the design" behind it; unlike Lord Acton, who fifty years later spoke only of anonymous "managers," Disraeli identified these organizers *as Jews*. The century that has passed since he uttered the plainest of these warnings has justified him; whatever its origins, the organized world-revolution was under Judaist leadership by the middle of the 19th Century and continued under Judaist leadership at least until the 1920's (in the present writer's opinion the condition continued after that and prevails today).

Why the Talmudic sect took over the leadership of the revolutionary organization established by Weishaupt, or whether it instigated the original revolutionary undertaking, are two questions which cannot be answered today.

If the ambition of Judaic world domination, instilled through the centuries by the Talmud and even more by the Cabala,[5] is ever to be realized the enslavement of "the heathen" to the Holy Nation will have to be accomplished through some destructive organization like that set up by Weishaupt; the fact that Weishaupt founded his Illuminati at the very moment when the Jewish "centre" in Poland sank from sight, after an unbroken life of more than two thousand years, might be more than a coincidence. On the other hand, it is equally possible that the dominant sect for the purpose of Talmudic fulfilment, took over control of a destructive organization already set up by non-Jews for a different end.

Disraeli's two most significant warnings preceded and followed the revolutionary outbreaks which occurred in many parts of Europe in 1848. Based on the experience gained in France a half-century before, these represented the second of the "eruptions, concocted as occasion shall permit," and "the periodical explosions" which (as de Luchet and Alexander Hamilton had foretold) the world- revolutionary organization was to bring about. They failed everywhere, possibly because the memory of the French revolution was recent enough for governments and peoples to deal resolutely with them. Their suppression left Disraeli in no illusion about the future. He

---

[5] The *Jewish Encyclopaedia* says that the Cabala (the oral, traditional lore, in contradistinction to the written law, or Torah) from the 13th century on branched out into an extensive literature alongside of and in opposition to the Talmud, being entrusted only to the few elect ones. Mrs. Nesta Webster, however, quotes another passage from the *Jewish Encyclopaedia* as saying that "the Cabala is not really in opposition to the Talmud" affairs, one who is "assisted by that absolute freedom from prejudice which is the compensatory possession of a man without a country."

had described what would happen before it occurred; after it, he foretold the continuance of the conspiracy and the recurrence of the violent outbreaks.

Disraeli wrote novels (with greater success than two later imitators, Colonel House of Texas and Mr. Winston Churchill when young), and depicted himself in them as the aloof, urbane, omniscient, slightly mocking impresario of human affairs. In *Coningsby* he is the chief character, Sidonia, a Spanish-Moslem Jew, the master financier, power behind all powers and passionless manipulator of Sidonia remarked in 1846 (the year when *Coningsby* was published): "That mighty revolution which is at this moment preparing in Germany and ... of which so little is as yet known in England, *is developing entirely under the auspices of the Jews.*"

Then, after the outbreaks of 1848, Disraeli returned to the subject, telling the House of Commons in 1852: "The *influence of the Jews* may be traced in the last outbreak of *the destructive principle* in Europe. An insurrection takes place against tradition and aristocracy, against religion and property. The natural equality of men and the abrogation of property are proclaimed by *the secret societies* who form provisional governments and *men of Jewish race are found at the head of every one of them*" (exactly the same thing recurred in Russia, in 1917, that is, seventy years after the 1848 outbreaks).

Disraeli added, "The most skilful manipulators of property ally themselves with Communists; the peculiar and chosen people touch the hands of all the scum and low castes of Europe." This, he said, was because they wished to destroy Christianity.

The task of research, in such a work as this, is arduous and has few compensations, but acquaintanceship with Disraeli was a solace. The reader has already met some true prophets among the many false ones, during this journey through the centuries, but he will not meet another quite like Benjamin Disraeli, whose liberation from Talmudic bonds gave him this "absolute freedom from prejudice." His name was significant, for he was of the breed of the Israelite prophets who denounced Judah. He was proud of his descent, and yet was enabled by his detachment to feel a love of England which those of native ancestry often cannot emulate. His ironical comments on public affairs and human events are refreshing to read today, when politicians shun the truth as the devil might shun holy water.

He candidly stated that "the world is governed by very different personages from what is imagined by those who are not behind the scenes," and in these words he publicly affirmed that real government is by the Hidden Hand. All informed observers know that this is the truth of affairs, but any present-day American president or British prime minister would denounce the statement as "witch-hunting." "I think," said Sidonia, "that there is no error so vulgar as to believe that revolutions are occasioned by economical causes." Thus spoke Disraeli; in our day the Lloyd Georges and Woodrow Wilsons, Roosevelts and Trumans have pretended that the revolutions in

France and Russia and elsewhere were spontaneous mass-eruptions by "the people," infuriate, against "tyranny." Disraeli practised the teaching of Christianity; he was not merely "a baptised Jew."

He would not have associated himself, or his country's name, with the Old Testamentary vengeance of Nuremberg, for this is what he said after the Indian Mutiny in 1857, when the spirit of revenge was ravening in the land: "I do without the slightest hesitation declare my humble disapprobation of persons in high authority announcing that upon the high standard of England 'vengeance' and not 'justice' should be inscribed ... I protest against meeting atrocities by atrocities. I have heard things said and seen things written of late which would make me almost suppose that the religious opinions of the people of England had undergone some sudden change, and that, instead of bowing before the name of Jesus, *we were preparing to revive the worship of Moloch.* I cannot believe that it is our duty to indulge in such a spirit."

These words contain an allusion which reaches every Jew and Gentile. Talmudic Judaism *is* "the worship of Moloch" and Disraeli knew this when he chose the words. The whole dispute between ancient Israel and Judah of the Levites raged round this false deity and his demands, and Israel turned its back on Judah on this very account; this is the root of the controversy of Zion, three thousand years ago and now.

It is reflected in the two most significant passages in the Old Testament: Jeremiah's charge that God had never commanded the children of Israel "to cause their sons and daughters to pass through the fire unto Moloch ... neither came it into my mind, that they should do this abomination, to cause Judah to sin"; and Ezekiel's answer that God *had* given Israel these "statutes that are not good" and the sacrifice of the firstborn. The god of love and mercy, the god of hatred, vengeance and human sacrifice: that was from the start the issue, and is today, and if Disraeli had lived a hundred years later Christendom might by this scion of Jewry have been spared the stigma of the Talmudic vengeance at Nuremberg.

Similarly, Disraeli cannot be imagined lending himself, his office and his country's strength to the support and spread of the world- revolution, as the leaders of Britain and America lent themselves in the first and second world wars; his whole public life was spent in forewarning his country against the destructive conspiracy which their acts promoted.

In 1955 a Lord Samuel (who in the heyday of Liberalism rose from plain Mr. Herbert Samuel, through various political offices, to ennoblement) proudly stated that he was the first Jew ever to have held Cabinet rank in England. This was presumably a jibe at Disraeli's conversion; nevertheless, the world in the 20th Century might have been the better for more Disraelis. The striking things about Disraeli, studied at the distance of a century, are his habit of speaking absolute truth, his accuracy of prediction, his vast instinctive and acquired knowledge, his deep though unimpassioned love for England,

and his Christian charity. In matters of fact he was always right; in those of opinion, he was ever on the side of the angels. His contempt for "Liberals" was great, though delicately phrased ("infanticide is practised as extensively and as legally in England as it is on the banks of the Ganges, a circumstance which apparently has not yet engaged the attention of the Society for the Propagation of the Gospel"). The present writer thinks he erred in one matter, namely, in his opinion that the doctrines of Jesus were the completion, not the repudiation, of Judaism. The contrary seems to me to be true, namely, that Judaism was that very heresy ("the worship of Moloch") which Disraeli spurned, and which Jesus came to change.

Disraeli was the product both of Sephardic Jewry and of England at that period; he could not, without *both* of these influences, have achieved that "absolute freedom from prejudice." His father, Isaac D'Israeli, wrote, "A religion which admits not *toleration* cannot be safely tolerated, if there is any chance of its obtaining a political ascendancy," and the *Encyclopaedia Britannica* says Isaac's reason for withdrawing from the synagogue was that Talmudic Judaism with its rigid laws "cuts off the Jews from the great family of mankind." His son's biographer, Mr. Hesketh Pearson, says the elders fined Isaac D'Israeli forty pounds when he declined election as Warden of the Congregation stating that he could never take part in their public worship "because, as now conducted, it disturbs, instead of exciting religious emotions." Isaac would not have been able so to challenge the elders, had he lived in a Talmudic community in Russia or Poland; he would have been outlawed, possibly killed.

Thus the father and the son (who became a member of the Church of England at the age of twelve) were formed by the free air of England at that time. Benjamin Disraeli, was to achieve the removal of the last disabilities put on Jews in England, and then publicly to proclaim that (in the immediate sequence to this emancipation) Jews were taking over control of the world-revolution everywhere. To a man of "absolute freedom from prejudice" the campaign against Jewish disabilities and the candid statement of this result were duties equally inescapable, even though the second development bore out the warnings of the enemies of that Jewish emancipation, which Disraeli had fought to complete.

Before concluding the tale of Disraeli's own warnings, the course of the world-revolution during his time needs to be traced, that is to say, during the century succeeding the outbreak in France. When Weishaupt died in 1830, leaving behind him the plan and the organization first revealed by the discovery of the Illuminati's documents in 1786, Disraeli was 26. The next fifty years were filled with the contest for Weishaupt's succession; during this period Disraeli uttered his many warnings. When it ended Jewish control of the world-revolution had nevertheless been firmly established and it had been given the imprint of the Eastern Jews, the Mongoloid Khazars, under their Talmudic rabbis.

The result might have been different, for men of various kinds struggled to succeed Weishaupt, and many of them were Gentiles. At the start there was no single, united revolutionary organization; there were revolutionary secret societies, not yet coalesced, in various countries. The chief of them, and the one in clearest line of descent from Weishaupt's Illuminati, was the Alta Vendita in Italy, some of the papers of which, seized and published by the Pontifical Government, revealed an identity of aim and method with the Illuminati documents of a half-century earlier (as Mrs Nesta Webster has established from the work of Cretineau Joly.)

In France Freemasonry continued to serve as the cloak used by the revolution, and in Germany the "League of Virtue" (Tugendbund) was directed by lieutenants of Weishaupt.

Various men worked to fuse these, apparently distinct national movements into one, and to assume the leadership, in succession to Adam Weishaupt. Among them were a Frenchman, Louis Blanc (whose name the reader is asked to bear in mind, for a reason which will appear later; at one moment he seemed likely to play the part of Lenin, even before Lenin was born), a Russian, Michel Bakunin, and a Jew, born in Germany, Karl Marx.

The struggle was fought between the last two, for Louis Blanc soon faded from the scene. Michel Bakunin and Karl Marx were as poles apart. Bakunin, "the father of Anarchy," was "a disciple of Weishaupt," according to the French revolutionary socialist, Benoit Malon. He represented that early breed of idealist revolutionaries who thought that they had found in revolution an instrument to destroy tyranny. He saw the danger that the confiscatory State, set up on the ruins of private property, would merely reproduce the tyrannical propensities of the private capitalist in gargantuan shape; therefore he looked for ways to reconcile the communal ownership of land and capital with the utmost possible diminution in the powers of the State and ultimately even with *the complete abolition of the State*. Thus he was the very opposite of Karl Marx, whose similar proposal, for the communal ownership of land and capital, was aimed simply at setting up a super-tyranny in place of petty tyrants.

The ruling passion (and original motive) of all Bakunin's work was a horror of despotism; Marx planned to destroy a ruling class in order to establish such a despotism as the world had never known. This was the profound difference between the two men, and it throws up a question never to be answered: what would the effect on the world have been if Bakunin's Anarchism, instead of Marx's Communism, had assumed leadership of the world-revolution? For Anarchism was opposed to every kind of forcible government, and to the State as the embodiment of the force employed in the government of the community; Communism was the deification of force wielded by the State.

Everything about Bakunin is genuine: his struggle, sufferings and death. Everything about Marx is bogus: his thirty years of incitement from the British Museum reading-room, his comfortable life on Friedrich Engels's bounty, his obviously calculated marriage to a *"von,"* his genteel funeral with graveside orations; all are typical of the petty bourgeois who so loudly declaimed against the *bourgeoisie*. The most bogus thing of all was his Communist Manifesto, which diagnosed an ailment ("The proletarian is without property") and prescribed suicide as the remedy ("The theory of the Communists may be summed up in the single sentence: Abolition of private property").

This was a plain intimation to the proletariat that it had nothing to gain but chains from Communism, and if revolutionary outbreaks all over Europe followed the publication of the Manifesto in January 1848, the oppressed masses cannot have roused to them by its logic. Within a few weeks of publication, revolts occurred all over Germany, in Austria, Hungary, Italy, France and Denmark. This was proof that the individual "secret societies" in the various countries were fusing together, that some means had been found to coordinate and synchronise their outbreaks, and thus, for the first time, to demonstrate *world*-revolution in action, through *simultaneous* eruptions in numerous countries.

Probably only one organization, already existing at that time, had at its disposal the international network which could make this synchronization and co-ordination possible, and that was the Talmudic rabbinate in Eastern Europe. Theoretically, the vast organization of the Catholic Church could have been put to the same purpose, but the Church saw its deadliest enemy in the revolution and was *not* so used; on that point history is clear. What Disraeli had known and stated two years before became historical fact: "that mighty revolution which is at this moment preparing in Germany ... is developing *entirely under the auspices of the Jews."* Karl Marx and his Communist Manifesto were the outward and visible signs of a significant historic event: Talmudic Judaism had taken over the world-revolution.

Of the three men who at that time appeared to contend for the generalship of the revolution, Louis Blanc quickly fell out of the running. He was a member of the provisional government set up in Paris after the 1848 revolt, and in the capacity of minister seemed to have the opportunity to put his theories into practice. He held that individualism and competition were cancers in the body social and, like Marx, wished to set up the all-despotic State (albeit of the "welfare" kind favoured by the British Socialists a century later). He was the herald of the "right to work" which, in Russia in the present century, proved to be the State's right to inflict forced labour. In his short-lived office he undertook "to guarantee the livelihood of the workers by work" and was authorized to call together an assembly of workers' delegates to prepare a plan for "full employment." This body was in form an anticipation of the Soviets, and it represents Louis Blanc's chief claim to be remembered. After the suppression of the revolt he fled to England and only returned twenty-three years later, bereft of importance.

That left Marx and Bakunin. Typically, Karl Marx, expelled from Prussia and France after 1848, settled comfortably in London until he died, thirty-four years later. Only Bakunin ran to man the "barricades." Bakunin was by birth a Russian aristocrat and had thrown up his ensignship in a Czarist regiment in 1832 after the suppression of the Polish insurrection of 1830; the spectacle of terrorized Poland inspired in the heart of this young Russian officer the horror of despotism which thenceforth dominated his life. He met Marx before 1848 and left a description of the difference between them: "Marx called me a sentimental idealist, and he was right; I called him a vain man, perfidious and crafty, and I also was right."

Bakunin was in Paris for the fighting of 1848, and in May 1849 was a member of the provisional government set up by the revolutionaries in Saxony, leading the defence of Dresden until the Prussian troops prevailed, when he was captured while trying to escape (with Richard Wagner). He was sentenced to death, and reprieved, successively by the Saxon and Austrian governments. He was kept in fetters and chained to a wall for a year and then surrendered to the Russian government. After six years imprisonment he was sent, toothless, scorbutic and prematurely aged, to "the comparative freedom of Siberia," whence, in 1861, after twelve years of captivity, he escaped to Japan, America and eventually England. Unbroken by his experiences, he at once resumed preaching the spirit of anarchist revolt and in 1864, in Switzerland, founded his International (the *Alliance Internationale Sociale Democratique).*

About the same time, Karl Marx founded *his* International (the International Working Men's Association) in London, and the next few years were filled with the decisive struggle between Bakunin and Marx for the soul of the revolution. During Bakunin's long absence in Saxon, Austrian and Russian jails and in Siberia, Marx in London had established his hold on the international revolutionary organization (in several countries he had sons-in-law as lieutenants, on the Napoleonic model), but Bakunin's renown was great and he was deprived of the leadership only by a series of tricks which Marx, through his control of the General Council, was able to use against his rival. In 1872 the General Council called a congress of the International at The Hague, where Bakunin and his friends could not go on account of governmental hostility. At this congress charges were made against Bakunin (reminiscent of those which sixty years later were to be raised against any Communist leaders of whom Stalin wished to rid himself and he was expelled from the International by vote of the Council, packed by Marx's hand-picked men.

Broken in health Bakunin died a few years later, and apparently brought on his end by refusing to take food. With him died any hope (if such hope ever existed) that the organized world-revolution might be used to overthrow tyranny and liberate men; from the moment that it came "entirely under the auspices of Jews" (Disraeli) its purpose was to enslave men and to establish an indestructible tyranny. Bakunin's idea was to organize force against oppression, and the worst oppressor of all, in his eyes, was The State. These are his words: "The State is not society, it is only an historical form of it, as brutal as it is abstract. It was born historically, in all countries, of the marriage of violence, rapine, pillage, in a word, war and conquest ... It has been from its origin, and it remains still at present, the divine sanction of brutal force and triumphant inequality. The State is authority; it is force; it is the ostentation and infatuation of force..."

Precisely such a State as that, Karl Marx designed to set up through his international revolutionary movement, and it was to be a *world* State. Bakunin in 1869, when his contest with Karl Marx was reaching its climax, like Disraeli in 1846 and 1852 identified the leadership of the world-revolution as Jewish and in this he saw the cause of the perversion, as he considered it, of the revolutionary idea. His *Polemique contre les Juifs*, written in 1869, was mainly directed against the Jews of the International, and from what we have since seen of these affairs we may assume that his expulsion by the Marxist General Council in 1872 became certain at the moment of that publication in 1869.

When Disraeli died in 1881 he had spent between thirty and forty years warning his countrymen and the world against "the secret societies":

"It was neither parliaments, nor populations, nor the course of nature, nor the course of events, that overthrew the throne of Louis Philippe ... The throne was surprised by the *secret societies*, ever prepared to ravage Europe ... Acting in unison with a great popular movement they may destroy society ..." (1852). "There is in Italy a power which we seldom mention in this House ... I mean *the secret societies*. It is useless to deny, because it is impossible to conceal, that a great part of Europe is covered with *a network of these secret societies, just as the superficies of the earth is now being covered with railroads* ... They do not want constitutional government; they do not want ameliorated institutions ... they want to change the tenure of land, to drive out the present owners of the soil, and to put an end to ecclesiastical establishments ..." (1856).

Disraeli plainly saw, and perhaps was the first to recognize the name, the fraudulent nature of Liberalism: "it is the manoeuvres of these men who are striking at property and Christ, which the good people of this country, who are so accumulative and so religious, recognize and applaud as the progress of the Liberal cause."

If it were in the power of man, by informed warnings to avert disastrous events, the repeated warnings of this unique authority would have averted the tribulation which the revolution brought on the millions of mankind in the next century. But, "by a divine instinct men's minds mistrust ensuing danger." The neglect of Disraeli's warnings proved what all preceding centuries had shown — that human beings will not be deterred from a dangerous undertaking, or aroused from a perilous inertia, by any spoken counsel. Experience alone can in time move them to act, and in that the 20th Century has made them rich.

In the middle decades of the last century Disraeli spoke in vain. He could not be merely defamed as a "witch-hunter," and therefore was derided with the mien of affectionate disdain: "it was generally thought" (says Mr. Hesketh Pearson) "that he had a bee in his bonnet on the subject of the secret societies, *the existence of which was denied;* but we can now see them as the seeds of a movement which, having found a formula, *fused and festered into Communism.*" That verdict of 1951 is obviously true and agrees with the contemporary one of the revolutionary eye-witness Benoît Malon: "Communism was handed down in the dark through the secret societies of the 19th Century."

Thus, when Disraeli died the thing he had striven to avoid had come about: the "secret societies" had been welded into one world- revolutionary movement under Jewish control, and this was preparing to blow up the foundations of the 20th Century. He had found the perfect description for this organization: "a network" which covered Europe "just as the superficies of the earth is now being covered with railroads." Informed men began more and more frequently to use this expression, "the network," and to speak of "the hidden hand" which ruled governments. In the years before the revolutions of 1848 the former Rabbi Drach, who like Disraeli foresaw what was coming, published his indictment of the Talmud as the source of this disruptive process; his ensuing persecution was described by a Jewish writer named Morel, who among other things said, "what can the wisest measures of the authorities of all countries do against *the vast and permanent conspiracy of a people which, like a network as vast as it is strong, stretched over the whole globe, brings its force to bear wherever an event occurs that interests the name of Israelite.*"

The sequence of events is significant. In 1772 Poland was partitioned and, after more than 2,500 years, the "centre" of Jewish Government "ceased to exist" (according to Dr. Kastein) or became a secret Jewish government (as the Russian authorities believed). In 1776 Adam Weishaupt founded his Illuminati. By 1846 Disraeli was writing that "the revolution is developing entirely under Jewish auspices." In 1869 Michel Bakunin, the disciple of Weishaupt, attacked the Jews in the revolutionary movement. In 1872 Bakunin was expelled and the united Communist movement plainly emerged, under Karl Marx (in 1917 it produced an almost exclusively Jewish Bolshevist government).

Such was the result, foretold by Disraeli, of the removal of Jewish disabilities and of a few decades of Jewish emancipation. The lowering of the barriers had not had the effect of amalgamating the Jews in the comity of peoples; its consequences had been to give "the most formidable sect" (Bakunin's words) freedom to work for the ruination of these peoples by revolution. The responses given by the Sanhedrin to Napoleon's questions at the century's start, by its middle-age had been shown to be void of force. Jews would *not* thenceforward be allowed to involve themselves with other men, in the nationhoods and laws of the lands where they dwelt; on the contrary, identification with the world revolution set them more apart from others than even they had ever been before. The century of emancipation had been turned into a fraud even before it ended.

During the 19th Century (as Dr. Kastein, again, records) the term "antisemitism" was born. As "persecution" could no longer be said to exist, some new word had to be found, capable of intimidating Gentiles and terrifying Jews, the second purpose being more important than the first, and "antisemitism" was invented. "Abracadabra" might have served as well, for the term "antisemitism" is patently absurd in relation to people who are demonstrably not Semites and whose Law commands the extirpation of Semites (the Arab peoples of Palestine; any expression of sympathy with the Semitic Arabs, expelled from their native land by the Zionist intruders in 1948, in time came to be attacked as "antisemitism").

Presumably the authors of this term desired to keep such words as Jew, Jewish and anti-Jewish out of the public controversy and counted on intimidating the mass-mind by the introduction of an obscurantist word. What the dominant sect meant by "antisemitism" was in fact a combination of lese majesty (offences against the dignity of the sovereign power) and heresy (opposition to the paramount religious doctrine); and by the middle of the present century the mass-mind had to a great extent submitted to this idea; that numerous breed which in earlier times would have doffed its cap at the approach of the squire's bailiff or have crossed itself when the priestly eye turned its way held its tongue and looked respectful when any Jewish affair was mentioned.

The word "antisemitism" was coined at the time when "men of Jewish race," as Disraeli and Bakunin pointed out, took over the direction of the world-revolution, and the main object of its invention was by intimidation to deter public discussion of that remarkable development; the events of the present century have abundantly proved that, as this book will show. In the recent time, a Jewish authority, Mr. Bernard Lazare, offered a definition of "antisemitism" in a book which bore the word as its title. This definition had nothing whatever to do with the prophet Shem and his tribe, with Semitic blood or speech or stock, or with anything Semitic whatsoever; Mr. Lazare related "antisemitism" entirely to an adverse opinion of the Jewish role in revolution. He wrote:

"This is what must separate the impartial historian from antisemitism. The antisemite says: 'The Jew is the preparer, the machinator, the chief engineer of revolutions'; the impartial historian confines himself to studying the part which the Jew, considering his spirit his character, the nature of his philosophy, and his religion, may have taken in revolutionary processes and movements."

What Mr. Lazare clearly meant was that nothing more than "a part" in revolutionary processes might be attributed to Jews, and that a man who said that The Jew is the preparer, the machinator, the chief engineer of revolutions" committed lese majesty and heresy.

However, it is substantially what Disraeli said (who may even have had a drop or two of Semitic blood, and in that differed from the Eastern Jews to whom he alluded): "that mighty revolution … is developing *entirely under the auspices of the Jews,*" "*the influence of the Jews* may be traced in the last outbreak of the destructive principle," "*men of Jewish race are found* at the head of every one of them" (i.e., the secret societies).

As he was himself racially Jewish, Disraeli presumably felt no need to labour the fact that many Jews were as stoutly opposed as he to the "mighty revolution" and to "the destructive principle." In his day this would have been apparent, and he would not have had to armourplate his words against the propagandist who, today, would accuse him of incriminating *all* Jews by his allusions to "the auspices of *the Jews*" and "the influence of *the Jews*" (which by Mr. Lazare's definition would make him "antisemitic"!).

From the French revolutionary period onward (when the long-resident Jews of France gave warning against the newcomers from the East who were making trouble in Alsace) the Sephardic Jews of the West strongly resisted the ill wind that was blowing towards them from the East. Emancipation had loosened their bonds; they stood to lose all they had gained if "the destructive principle," "engineered" by the Talmudic sect and the Ashkenazim in the East, were to prevail over the West.

The warnings of Disraeli were addressed to this, then the dominant section of Jewry as much as to the Gentiles; perhaps more. The Sephardic Jews may also be said to have paid more heed to them than the Gentile masses around them. Their punishment was to be excommunicated; by one of the most remarkable operations ever performed by statisticians on a body of people, the Sephardim were within a hundred years to be pronounced virtually extinct (like the "ten lost tribes" long before).

Chapter 22

THE MANAGERS

When Jewish direction of the world-revolution became discernible by the middle of the last century it was direction by the Ashkenazic (Eastern, or Slavic) Jews. The Sephardic (Western, or Iberian) Jews were in the mass strongly opposed to it. It was directed against them as much as against Christendom, for emancipation in Europe had led to a substantial measure of assimilation in their case; they were slipping from the grasp of the ruling elders of Judaism, who were faced with the loss of their power through Jewish integration in mankind. Segregation was vital to Talmudic Judaism, and integration was lethal.

At that point they threw the "Eastern Jews" into the contest, whose emergence as a separate body of Jews coincided with the start of the world-revolution. Before then the West knew only "Jews," and these were the Sephardic Jews. Alluding to the period when Disraeli began to speak of Jewish leadership of the revolution, Dr. Kastein says, "From this time onwards it is possible to speak of Western and Eastern Jews." In fact the separate breeds had existed for about a thousand years; what Dr. Kastein means is that the Eastern Jews at that moment emerged as a distinct body, mobilized by the rabbinical government for action against the emancipated Sephardic Jews of the West and against the West itself.

Up to that time the Western Jews had only been dimly aware of these Eastern Jews, and to the Christian West they were unknown. Their cohesion as a mass, and the energy which had been stored up in them by many centuries of rabbinical absolutism in the ghettoes, was to make of them, when they entered the West, the most powerful of all the forces which shaped the events of the 20th Century. They were good material for the purpose to which they were put. Racially of barbaric Asiatic origins, for centuries they had received a Talmudic training in a regimentation as strict as that of any ancient Oriental despotism.

In the grand strategy which unfolded during the 19th Century they were employed for a double purpose, and with skill were used to achieve ends, so contradictory, that their simultaneous accomplishment must have been held impossible, before it came about, by any rational observer. In Russia itself they were used, as a mass, to wreck emancipation (for there would have been no hope of reclaiming the emancipated Jews of Western Europe if these had seen that the Eastern Jews, too, were becoming emancipated). To the outer world they were simultaneously depicted, even while they blocked the process of emancipation in Russia, as being the victims of a cruel, "antisemitic" persecution which wantonly denied them emancipation!

Given the control of modern media of mass-propaganda and mass-suggestion it is possible to impress on the mind of the multitude these false images of what is happening elsewhere, and under the spell of such false notions to incite them into war itself. During the last century the politicians of the West began habitually to declaim against the persecution of the Jews in Russia, while those Jews, under a rigorous leadership, were being prompted to destroy emancipation by every conceivable means.

Lest the reader doubt, I must add that the picture here given is historically authentic, and is confirmed by the Judaist authorities. Among others Dr. Kastein says, "The great majority of Jews offered *bitter passive resistance* to all 'attempts at amelioration.'" However, this resistance was not simply "passive" but also took lethal forms. Dr. Chaim Weizmann is probably the best authority on this period, and his work will be extensively cited in what follows. The ghettoized Ashkenazim (both in their Communist and their Zionist organizations) were inspired to obstruct emancipation by every possible device (including assassination in the last resort) while the story of their persecution was hammered, as an intimidatory warning, into the consciousness of the Western Jews and, as a rightful claim for succour, into that of the Christian West.

The Gentile politicians of the West presented these fictions to their peoples as truth, for they had found that powerful Jews, in all countries, were able to assist parties favoured by them with money, press support and votes; the return they required was support for the cause of the "persecuted" Jews in Russia and for the "return" to Palestine. In effect this meant that politicians who sought these favours had to subordinate national interest to two causes ultimately destructive of all nation-states: the revolution and the ambition to acquire territory for the dominant race. This was the process by means of which, as Disraeli said in *Lothair* (1870) "democracy has degraded statesmen into politicians." In this way also that state of the mass-mind began to take shape which would not brook any confutation, no matter how fully proven, of the legend of a permanent Jewish persecution and of a disease endemic in Gentile man (an epidemic at that time in Russia called "antisemitism"). When it was dangerous to believe that the world was round, the multitude vocally agreed that it was flat; this condition was reproduced, in respect of Talmudic Judaism's propaganda, in the 19th century, with the results which have been seen in this one.

The Western Jews were much less responsive than the Western politicians to these two currents from the East. These original Jews, in whom the Sephardic tradition and strain continued, were moving towards integration, or at least towards an involvement, with diminishing frictions, in mankind. They intuitively feared the growing pressure from Russia and, recalling the unhappy end of the long, prosperous centuries in Spain, were filled with foreboding by the thought of its possible consequences. I recall, from my own time in Europe, how the Western Jews distrusted and feared these Eastern Jews, in whom they saw the spectral threat of an enforced return to the ghettoes and to rabbinical absolutism. The German Jew then was wont to refer to *"diese Ostjuden"* (these Eastern Jews!) with aversion; the Eastern Jew for his part, when after the first world war he made his way from Russia and Poland into Germany, spoke with contempt of the settled Jews there as *"diese Berliner"* (these Berliners!).

The rabbinical directorate of Jewry, in its Eastern fastnesses, set out to use these Judaized Tartars from Russia against the emancipated Jews of the West and against the West itself. The secretive life of Jewry has made the counting of Jewish heads impossible at all periods. This lack of any trustworthy figures of Jewish populations enabled the ruling sect a century ago to begin, and in our day almost to complete, an astonishing biological operation: they have transformed nearly all Jews into Ashkenazim!

At the end of the 18th century the Jews known to the West were the Sephardim, who inherited at least a tenuous tradition, a frail thread leading back through Spain to Africa, and fading then into a legend of Canaanitish origins. By the middle of the present century these Jews were declared by the elders of Jewry to have become almost extinct! A report presented to the Second World Sephardic Conference held in New York in 1954 stated that the Jewish world population was 11,763,491; that *only* 1,744,883 (or 15 percent) of these Jews were Sephardim; and that *merely* 52,000 of these Sephardim lived in Europe (which formerly knew *only* Sephardic Jews) and the entire Western Hemisphere.

Normal processes of birth and death could not have worked this magic. Evidently the Sephardim, like the ten tribes of Israel nearly three thousand years ago, have been declared to have "vanished" because they "ceased to believe that they had a destiny apart from their neighbours." The Ashkenazim have been awarded the inheritance of Judah, "an order of existence fundamentally different from that of the people about ... no process of assimilation to others ... absolute differentiation"; and nearly *all* Jews have now been declared to be Ashkenazim! Thus the elders of Judaism twice have expunged masses by strokes of the pen. The Sephardim have been excommunicated for the same reason as the Israelites, but obviously they live on in truth, some integrated in mankind, some segregated in original Judaism.

The identification of the Eastern Jews with the world-revolution, a century ago, cannot have come about by chance or by individual leanings, for they were despotically ruled. The regime of the rabbis in the East was nearly absolute and the ghettoized communities obeyed their commands, as God-empowered lawgivers and magistrates, in every act of daily life. During the 1930's, when I saw a good deal of such Eastern Jewish communities, in Poland and Ruthenia, they still lived a life of seclusion, unimaginable to the Western mind until it was beheld. A mass move of these Eastern Jews into the revolutionary camp (or any other camp) could not have occurred without rabbinical guidance, for the penalties of disobedience, in those Talmudic confines, were dire (I have quoted the Jewish authority who testifies that the rabbis sometimes encouraged lynching if local circumstances disabled them from openly pronouncing the death penalty prescribed by the Law.)[6]

Therefore the mass move into the revolutionary camp must be regarded as one of high policy, directed after full consideration by that Jewish government which was transferred to Poland after the expulsion from Spain and sank from the sight of men at the dissection of Poland in 1772. Contemplated in that historical perspective, the threefold purposes of the grand design become clear, and events have demonstrated them. First, through revolution the process of emancipation (and therewith of Jewish assimilation in the West) might be reversed and the supremacy of the ruling sect in Jewry maintained. Second, through revolution vengeance might be taken on Christendom for the expulsion from Spain, or perhaps for the existence of Christendom (for that is the affront to which the Talmud is in effect the answer). Third, revolution would promote the fulfilment of The Law, which ordained the ruination of the heathen and the triumph of the Chosen People, or at any rate of the sect which used that beguiling term.

An ambition which perhaps was not hugely foolish among Near Eastern tribes and in the small space of the known world in 500 BC, thus became the megalomaniac one of our global era, which is witnessing an attempt to impose an ancient tribal law, born in the petty feuds of little ancient lands, upon the world. The Gentile is apt to imagine that The Law which governs this undertaking is that which he can find in the Torah, or Old Testament, which he shares with the Jew, but this is not true. The Old Testament contains a lofty law of righteousness and neighbourly behaviour and inspired glimpses of the universal "house of prayer of all peoples." This

---

[6] This rabbinical administration of the Judaic Law within Jewish communities continues today in America, England and other Western countries. In 1955 a Jewish merchant of Leeds, in England, came under Jewish suspicion of having allowed some of 223 old British tanks, disposed of by him, to reach Egypt, a neighbour of the Zionist state. No complaint was raised in respect of their sale to other countries, and the transaction, whatever their destination, was legal under British law. The alleged Egyptian sale, *alone*, was brought before a Jewish court, the president of which stated in the British Press that if the man were cleared, the court's findings "will be accepted without question by the Jewish community," but if he were not "we have our ways as a community of dealing with a transgressor." The word "transgressor" relates to the Judaic rabbinical law, so that this was a public intimation that a man found to have "transgressed" that law would be punished, without regard to his innocence or guilt under the law of the country of which he was a citizen.

In this case the action taken cuts across State policy at its highest levels, those of foreign policy and national defence: for foreign policy and national defence cannot be conducted in the national interest if sections of the community are able to nullify governmental policy by dictating the choice of foreign countries to which arms may be sold, and punishing "transgressors." This case, however, was exceptional only in the publicity it received. As to that, as far as I was able to judge it aroused no great public interest or feeling, or if it did, this was not allowed to find expression in the newspapers. This was an example of the extent to which public discussion or criticism of any action taken by the ruling powers of Jewry had been silenced in the West by 1955.

Law was rejected by Judah, and the Torah includes the interpolations and cancellations which nullify it; but at any rate it contains *both;* it is two books, and any man may choose the one that seems to him to be the word of God. In fact that is what Christianity did; it took from the Old Testament, and applied to itself, those parts of the Torah which have a universal application, and it ignored the Levitical insertions which voided the moral commandments.

But the Judaic Law under which the Eastern rabbinate directed Eastern Jews into the revolutionary camp is that of the Talmud, of which "the modern Jew is the product" (Mr. Rodkinson, previously cited). The Talmud contains no lofty law of righteousness applicable to *all* men, but sets up the creed of Moloch, shorn of the universal applications; it is *one* book, not two. It is the uncompromising response to Christianity: "the precepts of justice, of equity, or charity towards one's neighbour, are not only not applicable with regard to the Christian, but constitute a crime in anyone who would act differently. The Talmud expressly forbids one to save a non-Jew from death ... to restore lost goods, etc. to him, to have pity on him" (the former Rabbi Drach, already quoted). This was The Law of the Slavic Ashkenazim in their ghettoes; the Ashkenazim, under stern direction, became the engineers of the world- revolution; and according to the Judaic authorities the Ashkenazim are now "the Jews," or 85 percent of them.

Thus a formidable, secret sect, in parts of Russia little known to the outer world, trained a compact mass of human beings for an onslaught on the nation-states of Christendom and the West, and in the 19th century began to unleash the force which it had generated. For the next hundred and fifty years (until the present day) the revolutionary force worked with spreading effect to disrupt the West, always following the plan originally disclosed in Weishaupt's papers, and "men of Jewish race" were constantly found at the head of it. The results have shown: Europe, once a land-mass of prosperous and virile nation-states, is now a place of bewildered peoples who struggle to make their way out of the new Dark Age and into the light again. The effects have spread far beyond Europe; Disraeli's "destructive principle" today beats on the doors of all the world. Possibly another hundred years must pass before the force let loose expends itself and the Ashkenazim (like the Sephardim before them) find the pull of mankind too strong for them, so that the Cabalist's dream of world dominion fades.

Under The Law this destruction was not an end in itself; it was a means *to* the end laid down in The Law. The extirpation of nation- states was to be the essential prelude to the establishment of the triumphant nation-State, that of the chosen people in their promised land. Thus, in the middle of the last century, a second force also was brought into being in those same Eastern, Talmudic-ruled areas where the world-revolution received its shape and impetus.

This was Zionism, the force that was set in movement to achieve "the return" and lay the foundations of the supreme Nation-State in Palestine. This, the force of domination, at every stage in the process of the last hundred years kept step with the force of revolution, and neither could have achieved what it did achieve without the other. The achievement is clear: the "return" *has* been accomplished and the nation-state of the chosen people *has* been founded; simultaneously the nation-states of other peoples, those breeds outside The Law, have been reduced or extinguished. The dominant-force corrupted the governments of these states at the top level; the revolutionary-force eroded their foundations at the bottom level.

Dr. Kastein, having affirmed that the Jewish government (the "centre," with its unbroken history of more than two thousand years) "ceased to exist" after the dissection of Poland in 1772, records that a hundred years later "a Jewish international" was in being. He evidently meant that the Jewish government *of Jews* had given way to a Jewish government *of governments*, and this is evidently the truth of our time.

Disraeli spoke of "a network" of revolutionary organizations which covered the earth like a system of railroads; it is the perfect description of the destructive mechanism which was constructed. To achieve the greater purpose there had to be another network at the top, and although Disraeli did not use the word in that case, he alluded to it when he said, "The world is governed by very different personages from what is imagined by those who are not behind the scenes." This is presumably "the Jewish international" of which Dr. Kastein speaks, a league of powerful and wealthy men at the top, under whose authority kings and princes, first, and republican presidents and politicians, next, equally found themselves.

These two machines worked in synchronization, each promoting the aim of the other. In their dealings with the masses, the Gentile rulers were forced by the threat of revolution from below to yield ever more authority, until they fell; in their dealings with foreign countries, and in the wars to which these led, they were constrained by the power of the purse to support the plan of the symbolic "return" to Palestine. The Gentile often asks why men of wealth should promote revolution. Disraeli put the same question, in order to give the answer: they wish to destroy Christianity. He knew precisely what he meant; to the Gentile the answer may be made more comprehensible by saying that they obey the Talmudic Law, which requires the destruction of heathen nation-states as the prelude to the triumphant "return."

Thus the story of the emergence of Zionism from the ghettoes of Russia and of the delicate interplay between the two forces, the one coiling itself round the rulers of the West and the other undermining the structure of the nation-states, forms the next chapter of the controversy of Zion.

Chapter 23

THE "PROPHET"

The 19th Century moved inexorably towards the repudiation of the Sanhedrin's avowals to Napoleon, towards the re-segregation of the Jews, towards the re-establishment of that theocratic state in the midst of states, the danger of which Tiberius had depicted before the Christian era began. The struggle was not between "the Jews" and "the Gentiles"; as on the ancient day when the Persian king's soldiers enabled Ezra and Nehemiah to enforce "the new Law" on the Judahites, it was once more between some Jews and some Gentiles and the other Jews and the other Gentiles. The mystery always was that at such junctures the Gentile rulers allied themselves with the ruling sect of Judaism against the Jewish masses and thus against their own peoples, among whom they fostered a disruptive force. This paradox repeated itself in the 19th century and produced the climacteric of our present day, in which all nations are heavily involved.

The emancipated Jews of the West were undone on this occasion, with the mass of Gentile mankind, by the Western politicians, who enlisted, like a Swiss Guard, in the service of Zionism. Therefore this narrative must pause to look "at the Liberals" of the 19th Century, who by espousing Zionism enabled it to disrupt the affairs and deflect the national policies of peoples.

They may best be studied through the founder of their line. "The Prophet" (he claimed the title which Amos angrily repudiated) was Henry Wentworth Monk, by few remembered today. He was the prototype of the 20th Century American president or British prime minister, the very model of a modern Western politician.

To account for this man one would have to revivify all the thoughts and impulses of the last century. It is recent enough for a plausible attempt. One effect of emancipation was to make every undisciplined thinker believe himself a leader of causes. The spread of the printed word enabled demagogues to distribute ill-considered thoughts: The increasing speed and range of transport led them to look for causes far outside their native ken. Irresponsibility might pose as Christian charity when it denounced its neighbours for indifference to the plight of Ethiopian orphans, and who could check the facts? Dickens depicted the type in Stiggins, with his society for providing infant negroes with moral pocket handkerchiefs; Disraeli remarked that the hideous lives of coalminers in the North of England had "escaped the notice of the Society for the Abolition of Negro Slavery."

The new way of acquiring a public reputation was too easy for such rebukes to deter those who were tempted by the beguiling term "liberal," and soon the passion for reform filled the liberal air, which would not brook a vacuum. The "rights of man" had to be asserted, and the surviving wrongs were most easily discovered among peoples faraway (and, for fervour, the further the better). It was the heyday of the self-righteous, of those who only wanted the good of others, and cared not how much bad they did under that banner. The do-gooders founded a generation, and also an industry (for this vocation was not devoid of material reward, as well as plaudits). In the name of freedom, these folk were in our day to applaud, and help bring about, the re-enslavement of half Europe.

Into such a time Henry Wentworth Monk was born (1827) in a farm settlement on the then remote Ottawa River in Canada. At seven he was wrenched from kith and kip and transported to the Bluecoat School in London, at that time a rigorous place for a lonely child. The boys wore the dress of their founder's day (Edward VI), long blue coat, priestly cravat, yellow stockings and buckled shoon. They lived as a sect apart, ate monastic fare and little of it, the rod was not spared, and they were sternly drilled in the Scriptures.

Thus young Monk had many emotional needs, crying to be appeased, and his child's mind began to find modern applications in the Old Testament, to which his infant mind was so diligently directed. By "swift beasts," he deduced, Isaiah meant railways, and by "swift messengers," steamships. He next decided, at this early age, that he had found the keys to "prophecy" and could interpret the mind of God in terms of his day. He ignored the warnings of the Israelite prophets and of the New Testament against this very temptation; what he found was merely the teaching of the Levitical priesthood, that one day the heathen would be destroyed and the chosen people re-gathered in their supreme kingdom in the promised land.

Men of rank and influence also were toying with this idea that the time had come for them to make up God's mind. When Monk was eleven a Lord Shaftesbury proposed that the great powers should buy Palestine from the Sultan of Turkey and "restore it to the Jews." England then had a statesman, Lord Palmerston, who did not let such notions disturb his duty, and nothing was done. But in young Monk an idea was ignited, and The Prophet was born; his life thenceforth held no other interest until it ended sixty years later.

At fourteen he obtained special leave to attend a sermon preached by "the first English Bishop in Jerusalem" (whose name, history records, was Solomon Alexander). The little boy returned to school with shining eyes, dedicated to his life's work of procuring Palestine, without regard to the people already in it, for some body of other people utterly unknown to him. The idea would not let him settle down on his father's Canadian farm when he returned to it; it stood between him and the Christian ministry, when he was made a candidate for this. He pored over the Old Testament and found it was but a code that cleared before his eyes.

Thus he fell into the irreverence which the study of the Levitical scriptures sometimes produces in men who describe themselves as Christians and yet ignore the New Testament. Once they accept the concept of foretellings to be *literally* fulfilled, they yield, in fact, to the Judaic Law of a political contract which leaves no latitude whatever to God, save in the one point of the *time* of completion. From that they proceed, in one bound, to the conclusion that *they* know the time (which God, presumably, has forgotten). At that stage such men believe that they are God. This is the end to which the process must lead them: the denial of Christianity, and of all divinity. This is the profanity to which all leading politicians of the West, in our century, lent themselves; Monk was the original of a multitude.

Even in his remote Canadian habitat he found other prophets. An American Jew, a Major Mordecai Noah, was trying to build a Jewish "city of refuge" on an island in the Niagara River, preparatory to "the return"; from what the Jews of North America needed refuge, until they "returned," he alone knew. Also, a Mr. Warder Cresson, the first United States Consul in Jerusalem, became so ardent for "restoration" that he embraced Judaism and published a book, *Jerusalem The Centre And Joy Of The Whole World*. Returning to America, he cast off his Gentile wife, renamed himself Michael Boas Israel, went to Palestine and there contrived to marry a Jewish girl with whom he could communicate only by signs.

All this fired Monk's ardour the more. He decided, in the Old Testamentary tradition, no more to cut his hair or adorn his body until "Zion is restored." As his hair grew abundantly, he became most hirsute; as he sold his small property and thereafter never laboured, he was for the rest of his days dependent on others. At twenty-six he set out for Jerusalem and reached it after much hardship. Having nothing but shagginess and shabbiness to testify to the truth of his message, he found few hearers.

Monk might have disappeared from the annals at that point but for a chance encounter which made him publicly known. In this century of world wars, trans-continental and trans-oceanic projectiles, and mass-destroying explosives, the 19th Century counts as a stable, peaceful period of time, unshadowed by fear for the morrow. The student, particularly of this controversy of Zion, is astonished to find how many educated men apparently lived in fright of annihilation and decided that they could only be saved if a body of the planet's inhabitants were transported to Arabia. The Prophet's path crossed that of another of these tremulous beings.

A young English painter, Holman Hunt, appeared in Jerusalem. He also was ready for "a cause," for he was waging the characteristic feud of the young artist against the Academicians, and that produces an inflammable state of mind. He enjoyed ill health and often thought his end near (he lived to be eighty-three). He had just painted *The Light of the World*, which depicted Jesus, lantern in hand, at the sinner's door, and the sudden apparition of the bearded

Monk caught his imagination. He grasped eagerly at the Prophet's idea of threatening mankind (including the Academicians) with extermination if it did not do what Prophecy ordained.

So these two, Prophet. and pre-Raphaelite, concerted a plan to startle the indifferent world. Monk depicted "the scapegoat" to Holman Hunt as the symbol of Jewish persecution by mankind. They agreed that Holman Hunt should paint a picture of "the scapegoat" and that Monk should simultaneously write a book explaining that the time had come for the persecuted to be restored, in fulfilment of prophecy.

(In fact the scapegoat was an ingenious Levitical device, whereby the priest was empowered to absolve the congregation of its sins by taking two kids of the goat, killing one for a sin-offering, and driving the other into the wilderness to expiate by its suffering "all their transgressions and all their sins ... putting them upon the head of the goat." The Prophet and Holman Hunt transformed the meaning into its opposite. The scapegoat for the sins of the Jews was to become the symbol of the Jews themselves; its tormentors, the Levitical priests, were by implication to be changed into Gentile oppressors!)

Holman Hunt went to work; this was a delightful way, both to take a swing at the Royal Academy ("problem pictures") and to identify himself with a cause. His picture would say more than any spoken word, and it would be followed by Monk's written word. The Picture and The Book, The Symbol and The Interpretation, The Herald and The Prophet — once the world beheld "The Scapegoat," Monk's work of revelation would find an audience, awakened to its transgressions and eager to make amends.

Hunt, wearing Arab robes and carrying easel and rifle, was then seen by the Bedouin driving a white goat to the Dead Sea. He painted an excellent picture of a goat (indeed, of two goats, as the first goat, with excessive zeal, died, and a substitute had to be found). For greater effect, a camel's skeleton was brought from Sodom and a goat's skull borrowed, and these were arranged in the background. The painting certainly produces the impression that the Levites must have been cruel (the animal's agony was graphically represented) and wicked, to pretend that by its suffering they could wash out all the iniquities of their people: Holman Hunt took it to England, first pledging himself, with Monk, "to the restoration of the Temple, the abolition of warfare among men, and the coming of the Kingdom of God upon the earth"; probably no painter ever had such large purposes in mind when he conceived a picture.

Monk then produced his *Simple Interpretation of the Revelation* and the joint undertaking was complete; the world had but to respond. In this first book Monk still tried to wed Levitical politics with Christian doctrine. Historically he stayed on safe ground; he pointed out, correctly, that "the ten tribes" could not have become extinct, but lived on in the mass of mankind. This led him to his "interpretation," which was to the effect that "the true

Israelites," Jewish and Christian, should migrate to Palestine and establish a model state there (at that point he was far from literal Zionism, and ran risk of being accounted an "antisemite"). His portrayal of the consequences was plain demagogy; if this were done, he said, war would come to an end. But then came the paramount idea (and who knows whence Monk got it?): an International Government must be set up in Jerusalem. Here Monk hit on the true intention of Zionism. Monk was only enabled to have his work published through an acquaintanceship which he owed to Holman Hunt: John Ruskin, the famous art critic, prevailed on the publisher Constable to print it. The Book (like The Picture) failed of effect, but Ruskin helped The Prophet with money and in other ways, and thus saved him from oblivion.

Ruskin, too, was the product of early pressures and inner disappointments. Like Wilkie Collins (an excellent craftsman who could not rest content with writing good novels and vainly tried to emulate Dickens's gift for arousing moral indignation), he was not happy to remain in the field where he was eminent but was ever ready to champion (and less ready to examine) anything that looked like a moral cause. Like Monk, he had been drilled in the Old Testament as a child (though by a possessive Puritan mother), and he was recurrently unlucky in love, sometimes humiliatingly so. He was therefore at all times in search of an outlet for unspent emotional impulses. He feared life and the future, so that The Prophet's incessant warnings of wrath to come unnerved him and made him put his hand in his pocket. He had a large audience and yielded to the same impiety as Monk and Holman; as his biographer says (Mr. Besketh Pearson), "he succumbed to the delusion, common to all messiahs, that his word was God's," and in the end his reason waned, but by then he had enabled The Prophet to preach and wander on.

After the failure of Monk's book Holman Hunt tried again. He began a painting of Jesus, in the synagogue, reading the messianic prophecies and announcing their fulfilment in himself. To make his meaning clear, he used Monk as the model for the figure of Jesus, and the indignation of the elders was to symbolize the world's rejection of The Prophet. Holman Hunt's preliminary study for this picture is in the National Gallery at Ottawa and shows Monk holding in one hand the Bible (open at the Book of the Revelation) and in the other: a copy of the *London Times*. (I was working in monastic seclusion in Montreal, somewhat bowed down by the nature and weight of the task, when I discovered the picture, and my neighbours were then surprised by the loud noise of mirth which burst from the usually silent room where a former correspondent of *The Times* bent over his labours).

Thereafter human nature slowly had its way. Holman Hunt sold a picture of the *Finding of Christ in the Temple* for £5,500 and his resentment against life (and the Academicians) mellowed. He found himself unable to ask the tattered Prophet to accompany him to fine houses like those of Val

Prinsep and Tennyson. Ruskin was busy with ill-starred loves, and was becoming sceptical as well. Nevertheless, these two sedentary men could not quite forget The Prophet's warnings that they would be destroyed unless they soon effected the restoration of the Jews to Palestine. He was always telling them that "the day" was at hand and pointing to some warlike episode, in Africa or Asia Minor or the Balkans or Europe, as the foretold beginning of the end; skirmishes and minor campaigns never lacked. At last Holman Hunt and Ruskin hit on a plan which seemed likely to allay their fears, appease their consciences and rid them of The Prophet: they urged him to go to Jerusalem and (like Sabbatai Zevi) proclaim the approach of The Millennium!

He was about to go when another war broke out, completely confounding him because it was not in any of the places where, interpreting prophecy, he had foretold the beginning of the end of days. It was in the very area from which, according to his published interpretation, salvation was to come: America.

After a glance at the authorities, The Prophet announced that he had located the error in his calculations: the Civil War was in fact the great, premonitory event. Now something must be done about Palestine without delay! John Ruskin put his foot down. If The Prophet were truly a prophet, he said, let him hasten to America before he went to Jerusalem, and call down some sign from heaven that would stop the Civil War. He, Ruskin, would finance the journey. And The Prophet went, to stop the Civil War.

The tradition then prevailed in America that a republican president must be accessible to all, and Mr. Abraham Lincoln was so beleaguered three days a week. One day, when the President's doors were open, The Prophet was swept in with a crowd of patronage- seekers, petitioners and sightseers.

His appearance gained him a few words of conversation with the President. Mr. Lincoln's harassed eye was arrested by the sight of something peering at him through the undergrowth. He asked who the visitor was, then learning that he was a Canadian come to end the war, asked for his proposal. The Prophet urged that the South free its slaves against compensation and the North agree to Southern secession, a suggestion which (Monk recorded) "appeared to amuse the President. Mr. Lincoln asked, "Do not you Canadians consider my Emancipation Proclamation as a great step forward in the social and moral progress of the world?"

Monk said this was not enough: "Why not follow the emancipation of the Negro by a still more urgent step: the emancipation of the Jew?" Mr. Lincoln was baffled (the Jews had always been emancipated in America) and asked in astonishment, "The Jew, why the Jew? Are they not free already?"

Monk said, "Certainly, Mr. President, the American Jew is free, and so is the British Jew, but not the European. In America we live so far off that we are blind to what goes on in Russia and Prussia and Turkey. There can be no permanent peace in the world until the civilized nations, led, I hope, by Great

Britain and the United States, atone for what they have done to the Jews, for their two thousand years of persecution, by restoring them to their national home in Palestine, and making Jerusalem the capital city of a reunited Christendom."

Characteristically, Monk had never been to "Russia, Prussia or Turkey"; he was that kind of "Liberal." In Russia the Talmudic rabbinate was opposing emancipation by every means, and two years before Monk saw Mr. Lincoln, the Czar Alexander II had been assassinated when he announced a parliamentary constitution; in Prussia the Jews *were* emancipated and for this very reason were the objects of attack by the Jews in Russia; the Jews under Turkish rule (which oppressed *all* subject nationalities impartially) were already *in* Palestine and thus could not be restored thither.

In Mr. Lincoln's day the notion that all wars, wherever fought and for whatever reason, ought to be diverted to the aim of establishing a Jewish state in Palestine was new (today it is generally accepted and put into practice, as the two world wars have shown), and the President was again amused. He had on hand the cruellest war in Western history up to that time. Being a man of resource, and versed in dealing with importuners, he rid himself of The Prophet with a good-humoured jest. "My chiropodist is a Jew," he said, "and he has so often put me on my feet that I would have no objection to giving his countrymen a leg up." Then, reminding Monk of the war in progress, he begged The Prophet to await its end: "then we may begin again to see visions and dream dreams." (Another topic for a debating society: was the use of this phrase chance or intention? Mr. Lincoln certainly knew what fate the Old Testament prescribes for "false prophets and dreamers of dreams.")

Monk returned to London and Ruskin paid his expenses to Palestine, whence, on arrival, he was deported as a nuisance in 1864. Destitute, he signed as seaman aboard a Boston-bound clipper and, being wrecked, swam the last part of the Atlantic. He was cast ashore bleeding and almost naked, so that, looking like a bear, he was shot as one, in semi-darkness, by a farmer. He lost his memory and mind, and in this condition at last came home. He recovered after some years and at once returned to his obsession. The "day of trouble," so long foretold, still had not come; the planet kept its accustomed place. He re-examined prophecy and decided that he had erred in recommending the union of Jews and Christians in the world-state to be set up in Jerusalem. Now he saw that what prophecy required God to do was first to put the Jews in possession of Palestine, *and then to set up a worldwide organization with power to enforce the submission of nations to its law.*

After a lifetime, Monk thus stumbled on the fullness of the political plan of world dominion which is contained in the Old Testament, and still thought that he was interpreting divine prophecy. No evidence offers that he ever came in contact with the initiates and illuminates of the grand design.

The only recorded Jewish money he was ever offered was a charitable gift of five pounds "if you are personally in want." He moved always in the company and at the cost of the bemused Gentile "Liberals."

He was forgotten in the Ottawa Valley when, in 1870, his hope (one must use the word) that "the day of troubles" was at last at hand was revived by a huge forest fire, which he took as a sign from heaven that the time had come. Somehow he made his way to London (1872) and to Hunt and Ruskin, who had thought him dead. Ruskin was wooing Rose La Touche, so that for the time he was unresponsive to warnings of doom and wrote to The Prophet, "I acknowledge the wonderfulness of much that you tell me, but I simply do not believe that you can understand so much about God when you understand so little about man … you appear to me to be mad, but for aught I know I may be mad myself" (these last words, unhappily, were prescient).

Such admonitions were not new to The Prophet. His relatives and friends had ever implored him, if he felt called to improve mankind, to look around him at home: the lot of the Canadian Indians, or even of the Canadians, might be bettered. To a man who held the key to divine revelation advice of this kind was sacrilegious, and Monk, by way of various pamphlets, came at length to the idea of a "Palestine Restoration Fund." For this he borrowed a notion of Ruskin's, originally devised to help Ruskin's own country; namely, that wealthy folk should forfeit a tithe of their incomes for the purpose of reclaiming English wastelands. Monk decided that the tithe should serve a better object: the "return"!

By this time (1875) Ruskin was once more unnerved, first by the death of Rose La Touche and next by the apparent imminence of one more distant war (this time a British-Russian one). Clearly The Prophet was right after all; the "day of troubles" *was* come. Ruskin signed Monk's manifesto and dedicated a tenth of his income to The Prophet's fund for the purchase of Palestine from the Sultan while the English wastelands stayed unreclaimed. When this was achieved, a congress of all nations was to set up a federation of the world in Jerusalem.

The Prophet, thus propped on his feet again, was further helped by Laurence Oliphant, a lion of the Victorian drawing rooms whom he had by chance met when he made his way about America, hobo-fashion. Oliphant was a man of different type, a bold, cynical venturer, or adventurer. The idea of buying Palestine appealed to him, but he had no illusions about it. He wrote to Monk, "Any amount of money can be raised upon it, owing to the belief which people have that they would *be fulfilling prophecy and bringing on the end of the world. I don't know why they are so anxious for the latter event, but it makes the commercial speculation easy.*" Oliphant, as will be seen, did not trouble to hide his disdain for The Prophet's message.[7]

In 1880 Holman Hunt, again enjoying deteriorated health, was so alarmed by small warlike episodes in Egypt and South Africa that he thought extinction at hand and joined with Monk in issuing a manifesto which anticipated the Zionist-ruled world-government schemes of this century. It was headed "The abolition of national warfare," called on all men of goodwill to subscribe a tenth of their income to the realization of "the Kingdom of God" in the form of a world government to be set up in Palestine and to be called "*the United Nations*," and proposed that the money be given to Mr. Monk for the purpose of acquiring Palestine.

That was the finish. Ruskin, approaching his end, rudely refused all further part in the fantasy. Oliphant dropped out. The "Bank of Israel" came to nothing. Samuel Butler showed The Prophet the door. Even Holman Hunt at last appealed to him to preach "that there is a God in heaven, who will judge every man on earth" and to desist from pretending in effect that he, Monk, was God. The Jews spoke similarly: one told him, "The land of our forefathers is dead, and Palestine is its grave ... *to attempt to form a nation from the polyglot people of Judaism today would only end in utter failure.*"

Monk was beyond redemption. In 1884 the Bluecoat boy returned to Ottawa for the last time and spent his final years canvassing, pamphleteering, and haranguing members of the Canadian House of Commons as they sat, between sessions, in their garden by the Ottawa River. They listened to him with amused indulgence; sixty years later Canadian Ministers, at Ottawa and New York, were to repeat all the things Monk said as the unassailable principles of high policy, and no Member would demur.

Monk's life was wretched and was not redeemed by any true faith or genuine mission. This account of it is given to show how false and foolish the great project was seen to be, and how misguided the men who took it up, against the background of the last century. The fallacy of the whole notion, of Zionism leading to the despotic world-government, is instantly displayed when it is considered in that setting, with Monk and his friends declaiming from the stage. The whole thing then is seen as a picaresque comedy; a farce, not merely because it was unsuccessful, but because it was never serious. What was recommended could not be seriously entertained because its consequences obviously had not been considered and, if calculated, at once were foreseen to be disastrous. Against the background of a time when debate

---

[7] Oliphant touched on an interesting point. One interpretation of the numerous prophecies is that the end of the world will follow the "return" of the Jews to Palestine, so that the folk who promote this migration presume even to determine the moment when Jehovah shall bring the planet to an end. The mystification expressed by Oliphant was felt by a perplexed French politician at the Peace Conference of 1919, who asked Mr. Balfour why he was so eager to bring about "the return" of the Jews to Palestine; if this truly was the fulfilment of prophecy, then prophecy also decreed that the end of the world would follow. Mr. Balfour replied languidly. "Precisely, that is what makes it all so very interesting."

was free and opinion, being informed, might be brought to bear on the matter, these men strut foolishly, leaving only the faint echo of clownish noises in the corridors of time.

Nevertheless, in the present century the entire vainglorious scheme, unchanged, was imported into the life of peoples as a serious and urgent undertaking, transcending the needs of nations. Indeed, it was made a sacrosanct one, for an unwritten law of heresy was set around it which in effect checked the antiseptic force of public discussion, and within this palisade the politicians of the West made a morality play out of The Prophet's claptrap. John Ruskin and Holman Hunt, from whatever bourne the Victorian friends of the oppressed may now inhabit, may look down and see the graves of many dead, and the living graves of nearly a million fugitives, as the first results of their great plan, now in accomplishment.

Monk, had he lived in this century, would have been qualified for important political rank, for support of this cause has become the first condition for admission to the high temporal places. His life was spent in pursuing the lure of an excessive vanity and in the very year of his death, 1896, the fantasy which led him became a political and practical reality, dominating our time. While he went his vagrant way between Ottawa, Washington, London and Jerusalem very different men, in Russia, built up the real force of Zionism. In 1896 it was launched into the lives of the peoples, and its explosive detonations have grown louder and more destructive until today even the newspaper scribes commonly allude to it as the issue which may set the spark to the third world war.

Chapter 24

THE COMING OF ZIONISM

In the second half of the last century when Communism and Zionism began their simultaneous assault on the West, Europe was a place of strong and confident states well able to withstand the effects of inner troubles and foreign wars. The revolutionary outbreaks of 1848 had been overcome without great exertion. Austria-Hungary and France were not much weakened by their Prussian defeats in 1866 and 1871; they resumed their national existences, as defeated countries for centuries had done, side by side with yesterday's victor, and soon were tranquil again. The Balkan people, emerging from five centuries of Turkish rule also were moving towards prosperity, in the kindlier air of national freedom. On the eastern borders of Europe Russia, under the flag of Christendom, appeared to be joining in this process of national and individual improvement.

The appearance was deceptive, for the two maggots were in the apple, and today's scene shows the result. The eighteen Christian centuries which, despite ups and downs showed a total sum of human betterment greater than that of any earlier time known to man, were coming either to an end or an interregnum; which, we still do not know, though believers have no doubt about the good resumption, somewhen. However, one eminent man of that period, from whom confidence in the outcome might have been expected, foresaw what was to come in our century and thought it would be the *end*, not a transient Dark Age.

This was Henry Edward Manning, the English clergyman who was converted to Rome, became Cardinal Archbishop of Westminster, and, had he accepted nomination by his fellow cardinals, might have become Pope. Edmund Burke, John Adams and Alexander Hamilton had all perceived the worldwide aims of the revolution and foretold its spreading eruptions. Disraeli, Bakunin and others, a half-century later, had testified to, and warned against, the Jewish usurpation of the revolutionary leadership. Manning joined in these warnings but also foresaw the coming of Zionism and the part it would play in the dual process.

Of the revolution he said, "The *secret societies* of the world, *the existence of which men laugh at and deny* in the plenitude of their self-confidence; the secret societies are forcing their existence and their reality upon the consciousness of those who, until the other day, would not believe that they existed" (1861). He expected the full success of Weishaupt's original plan and thought the time in which he lived was "the prelude of the anti-Christian period of the final dethronement of Christendom, and of the restoration of society without God in the world." Today the anti-Christian revolution holds temporal power in half of Europe, the Christian cross has been expunged from the flags of all great European nations save the British and from those of many small ones, and a "society without God" has been set up as a potential world-government, so that these words of ninety years ago are seen as an impressive forecast part- fulfilled.

Then (and in this he rose above the other seers) he depicted the part which Zionism would play in this process: "Those who have lost faith in the Incarnation, such as humanitarians, rationalists and pantheists, may well be deceived by any person of great political power and success, *who should restore the Jews to their own land* ... and there is nothing in the political aspect of the world which renders such a combination impossible."

Finally, he said that he expected the *personal* coming of Antichrist in the form of a Jew. (In these words he moved from the ground of political calculation, whereas events have shown he was expert, to that of interpreting prophecy; he related Saint Paul's message to the Thessalonians, 2.1.iii-xi, to the coming time, saying, "It is a law of Holy Scripture that when persons are prophesied of, persons appear.")

Thus, while Europe outwardly appeared to be slowly moving towards an improving future on the path which for eighteen centuries had served it well, in the Talmudic areas of Russia Zionism joined Communism as the second of the two forces which were to intercept that process. Communism was designed to subvert the masses; it was the "great popular movement" foreseen by Disraeli, by means of which "the secret societies" were to work in unison for the disruption of Europe. Zionism set out to subvert rulers at the top. Neither force could have moved forward without the other, for rulers of unimpaired authority would have checked the revolution as it had been checked in 1848.

Zionism was essentially the rejoinder of the Talmudic centre in Russia to the emancipation of Jews in the West. It was the intimation that they must not involve themselves in mankind but must remain apart.

Never since Babylon had the ruling sect ventured to play this card. It can never be played again, if the present attempt ultimately ends in fiasco. For that reason the Talmudists ever refrained from playing it, and only did this when emancipation confronted them with a vital emergency, the loss of their power over Jewry. Indeed, they had always denounced as "false Messiahs" those who clamoured that the day of fulfilment was come. Had Sabbatai Zevi, or for that matter Cromwell or Napoleon, been able to deliver Palestine to them, they might have proclaimed one of these to be the Messiah. On this occasion they proclaimed *themselves* to be the Messiah, and that bold enterprise can hardly be repeated. Historically therefore, we are probably moving towards the end of the destructive plan, because it obviously cannot be fulfilled, but the present generation, and possibly some generations to come, by all the signs have yet a heavy price to pay for having encouraged the attempt.

Dr. Chaim Weizmann's book is the best single fount of information about the twin roots of Communism and Zionism and their convergent purpose. He was present at the birth of Zionism, he became its roving plenipotentiary, he was for forty years the darling of Western courts, presidential offices and cabinet rooms, he became the first president of the Zionist state, and he told the entire tale with astonishing candour. He shows how, in those remote Talmudic communities nearly a hundred years ago, the strategy took shape which in its consequences was to catch up, as in a vortex, all peoples of the West. Americans and Britons, Germans and Frenchmen, Italians, Poles, Scandinavians, Balts, the Balkanic peoples and all others were to be implicated. The lifeblood and treasure of the West were to be spent on the promotion of these two complementary purposes like water from a running tap.

Millions, living and dead, were during two wars involved in their furtherance. Men now being born inherit a share in the final upheavals to which they must inexorably lead. The Jews shared in all that tribulation, in their small proportion to the masses affected. Dr. Weizmann's account enables today's student to see the beginnings of all this; and now this narrative reaches our own time, which receives daily shape from what then occurred.

He explains that the Jews in Russia were divided into three groups. The first group was that of the Jews who, seeking "the peace of the city," simply wanted to become peaceable Russian citizens, as the Jews of the West, in the majority, at that time were loyal German, French or other citizens. Emancipation was for this group the final aim, and it chiefly contained those Jews who, by talent, diligence and fear of Talmudic rule, had escaped from the ghettoes.

Dr. Weizmann dismisses it as small, unrepresentative and "renegade," and as it was swept away it must also disappear from this narrative, which belongs to the two other groups. By the edict of the Talmudists it has "disappeared from the face of the earth," or been excommunicated.

The remaining mass of Jews in Russia, (that is, those that lived in the ghettoes under Talmudic rule) were divided into two groups by a vertical line which split households and families, including Dr. Weizmann's own house and family. Both groups were revolutionary; that is to say, they agreed in working for the destruction of Russia. The dissension was solely on the point of Zionism. The "Communist-revolutionary" group held that full "emancipation" would be achieved when the world-revolution supplanted the nation- states everywhere. The "Zionist-revolutionary" group, while agreeing that the world-revolution was indispensable to the process, held that full "emancipation" would only be achieved when a Jewish nation was established in a Jewish state.

Of these two groups, the Zionist one was clearly the superior in Talmudic orthodoxy, as destruction, under the Law is but a means to the end of domination, and the dominant nation is that ordained to be set up in Jerusalem. In the households, dispute was fierce. The Communists maintained that Zionism would weaken the revolution, which professed to deny "race and creed"; the Zionists contended that revolution must lead to the restoration of the chosen people, of whom race *was* the creed. Individual members of these households probably believed that the point in dispute was valid, but in fact it was not. *Neither* of these groups could have taken shape, in those sternly ruled communities, against the will of the rabbinate. If the rabbis had given out the word that Communism was "transgression" and Zionism "observance" of "the statutes and judgments," there would have been no Communists in the ghettoes, only Zionists.

The ruling sect, looking into the future above the heads of the regimented mass, evidently saw that both groups were essential to the end in view; and Disraeli, in one of the passages earlier quoted, named the motive. From the middle of the last century the story of the revolution is that of Communism and Zionism, directed from one source and working to a convergent aim.

Dr. Weizmann gives an illuminating glimpse of this apparent dissension among the members of a conspiratorial, but divided, Jewish household where the ultimate shape of the high strategy was not seen and the issue between "revolutionary-Communism" and "revolutionary-Zionism" was fiercely argued. He quotes his mother, the Jewish matriarch, as saying contentedly that if the Communist-revolutionary son were proved right she would be happy in Russia, and if the Zionist-revolutionary one were correct, then she would be happy in Palestine. In the outcome both were by their lights proved right; after spending some years in Bolshevized Moscow she went to end her days in Zionized Palestine. That was after the two conspiracies, having grown in secrecy side by side, triumphed in the same week of 1917.

Communism was already an organized, though still a secret and conspiratorial party in the ghettoes when Zionism first took organized (though equally secret) form in the *Chibath Zion* (Love of Zion) movement. This was founded at Pinsk, where Dr. Weizmann went to school, so that as a boy his path led him into the Zionist-revolutionary wing of the anti-Russian conspiracy. In his childhood (1881) something happened which threatened to destroy the entire legend of "persecution in Russia" on which Talmudic propaganda in the outer world was based.

In 1861 Czar Alexander II, the famous Liberator, had liberated 23,000,000 Russian serfs. From that moment the prospect of liberty and improvement on the Western model opened out for Russian citizens of all nationalities (Russia contained about 160 nationalities and the Jews formed about 4 percent of the total population). Then, during the twenty years following the liberation of the serfs, the Jews began, under Talmudic direction, to offer "bitter passive resistance to all 'attempts at improvements'" (Dr. Kastein). In March 1881, Alexander II moved to complete his life's work by proclaiming a parliamentary constitution. Dr. Kastein's comment speaks for itself: "It is not surprising to find a Jewess taking part in the conspiracy which led to the assassination of Alexander II."

This event, the first of a similar series, was the first major success of the revolutionaries in preventing emancipation. It restored the ideal condition depicted by Moses Hess (one of the earliest Zionist propagandists) in the year *following* the liberation of the serfs: "We Jews shall always remain strangers among the nations; these, it is true, will grant us rights from feelings of humanity and justice, but they will never respect us so long as we place our great memories in the second rank and accept as our first principle, 'Where I flourish, there is my country.'"

During this period Leon Pinsker, another herald of Zionism, published his book *Auto-Emancipation*. The title was a threat (to the initiated); it meant, "We will not accept any kind of emancipation bestowed on us by others; we will emancipate ourselves and will give 'emancipation' our own interpretation." He said, "There is an inexorable and inescapable conflict between humans known as Jews and other humans," and he described the master-method to be used to bring about this "self-emancipation" and to "restore the Jewish nation": the struggle to achieve "these ends, he said, "*must be entered upon in such a spirit as to exert an irresistible pressure upon the international politics of the present.*"

These words of 1882 are some of the most significant in this entire story. They show foreknowledge of the highest order, as the reader may discern if he try to picture, say, some Polish or Ukrainian patriot-in-exile talking, then or now, of "exerting irresistible pressure upon international politics." The political emitter is a sad man of hope deferred, an habitué of the Café des Exiles who is usually thankful if the second secretary of an Under Secretary of State deigns to spare him half an hour. Pinsker was an obscure Jewish émigré in Berlin, little known outside revolutionary circles, when he wrote these words, which would seem to be of the most foolish pretension if the events of the next seventy years had not proved that he knew exactly what he meant. He knew *how* Zionism would prevail. Clearly the conspiracy, long before its nature was even suspected in the outer world, had powerful support far outside Russia and this unknown Pinsker was aware of the methods by which the affairs of the world were to be rearranged.

Such was the state of the two-headed conspiracy in Russia when Dr. Weizmann grew to manhood and began to play his part. The word "conspiracy," frequently used here, is not the author's; Dr. Weizmann candidly employs it. Loathing Russia, he went (without hindrance) to Germany. The sight of "emancipated" Jews there so repelled him that he longed for the ghettoes of Russia and returned to them during his holidays, then resuming his part in "the conspiracy," as he says. Then, at various universities in the emancipated West he continued his "open fight" to de-emancipate the Jews of Europe. They recognized the danger and turned faces of fear and enmity to these *Ostjuden*.

Thus in Germany Gabriel Rieser told the Zionist-revolutionaries from Russia, "We did not immigrate here, we were born here, and because we were born here, we lay no claim to a home anywhere else; we are either Germans or else we are homeless." Similarly, the rabbis of Reform Judaism resolved that "the idea of the Messiah deserves every consideration in our prayers, but all requests that we may be led back to the land of our fathers and the Jewish State be restored must be dropped out of them."

These Jews struggled to keep faith with the Sanhedrin's pledges. They had made peace with mankind, and it appeared impossible that the Talmudists could ever lead them back into a new Nehemiahan captivity. Dr. Kastein records with horror that towards the end of the 19th century "one Jew in five married a Gentile" and, with greater horror, that in war "on all fronts Jew stood opposed to Jew; this was a tragedy … which will be repeated … as long as Jews are *compelled* to fulfil their duties as citizens of the lands of their adoption." The shadow of the new Talmudic captivity was much nearer to the Jews of the West than even they could suspect. The elders in Russia had been organizing during all these decades and as the end of the century approached were ready to "exert irresistible pressure upon   the international politics of the present." The most successful specialist in this exertion of pressure; a roving Zionist prime minister, was young Chaim Weizmann, who during the last years of Monk's life moved about the European cities and universities, from Darmstadt to Berlin, and later from Berlin to Geneva, planting therein the time-bombs of the future and preparing for his 20th Century task.

As the century closed came a sudden acceleration in this process, as if a machine long in construction were completed and began to run at high power, and its throbbing pulsations were at once felt throughout all Jewry, though the Gentile masses, less sensitive to such vibrations, remarked them not at all. In the succession to Moses Hess another Jew from Russia, Asher Ginsburg (Ahad Ha'am) proclaimed that the Jews not only formed a nation but must have a Jewish state in Palestine. However, this was but one more voice from remote Russia, and the weakness of the Jews in the West was that they did not realize the power and strength of the compact, organized mass in the Eastern ghettoes, or at any rate, they could not see how it could make itself felt in Europe.

The warning to them came in 1896, the year of Prophet Monk's death, when Theodor Herzl published *The Jewish State*. With that, the cat was in their dovecot, and not very long afterwards the doves were in the cat. Their ranks were split, for this Theodor Herzl was not one of the Eastern Jews, not a Jew from Russia. He was one of themselves, or at all events they held him to be one. He appeared to be the very model of an emancipated Western Jew, yet he was on the side of the Zionists. A premonitory tremor ran through Jewry. Christendom, which had as much cause to be perturbed, remained blissfully unaware for another sixty years.

Douglas Reed

Chapter 25

THE WORLD ZIONIST ORGANIZATION

If mere chance, ever and again, produces men like Karl Marx and Dr. Theodor Herzl at moments when their acts can lead to destructive consequences out of proportion to their own importance, then chance in the past century has been enlisted in the conspiracy against the West. The likelier explanation is that a higher command was already in charge of these events and that it chose, or at all events used Herzl for the part he played. The brevity of his course across the firmament (like that of a shooting star), the disdainful way in which when his task was done he was cast aside, and his unhappy end would all support that explanation.

Those who have known Vienna and its atmosphere in our century will understand Herzl and his effect. A declining monarchy and a tottering nobility: a class of Jews rising suddenly and swiftly to the highest places; these things made great impression among the Jewish masses. Dr. Herzl, rather than the *Neue Freie Presse*, now told them how went the world and instructed politicians what to do. Obsequious *Obers* in the chattering cafés hastened to serve "Herr Doktor!" It was all new, exciting. Self-importance filled the Herzl's and de Blowitz's of that time and when Dr. Herzl emerged as the self-proclaimed herald of Zion the Western Jews were left awed and uncertain. If Dr. Herzl could talk like this to the Great Powers, perhaps he was right and the Napoleonic Sanhedrin had been wrong!

Could it be true that policy was made in Dr. Herzl's office, not in the Ballhausplatz? Had a Jew from Russia written *The Jewish State*, or attempted to set up a World Zionist Organization, the Western Jews would have ignored him, for they feared the conspiracy from the East and at least suspected its implications. But if Dr. Herzl, a fully emancipated Western Jew, thought that Jews must re-segregate themselves, the matter was becoming serious.

Herzl asserted that the Dreyfus case had convinced him of the reality of "antisemitism." The term was then of fairly recent coinage, though Dr. Kastein seeks to show that the state of mind denoted by it is immemorial by saying "it has existed from the time that Judaism came into contact with other peoples in something more than neighbourly hostility." (By this definition resistance in war is "antisemitism," and the "neighbours" in the tribal warfare of antique times, to which he refers, were themselves Semites. However, the words "contact exceeding neighbourly hostility" offer a good example of Zionist pilpulism.)

Anyway, Dr. Herzl stated that "the Dreyfus process made me a Zionist," and the words are as empty as Mr. Lloyd George's later ones, "Acetone converted me to Zionism" (which were demonstrably untrue). The

Dreyfus case gave the Jews complete proof of the validity of emancipation and of the impartiality of justice under it. Never was one man defended so publicly by so many or so fully vindicated. Today whole nations, east of Berlin, have no right to any process of law and the West, which signed the deed of their outlawry, is indifferent to their plight; they may be imprisoned or killed without charge or trial. Yet in the West today the Dreyfus case, the classic example of justice, continues to be cited by the propagandists as the horrid example of injustice. If the case for or against Zionism stood or fell by the Dreyfus case, the word should have disappeared from history at that point.

Nevertheless Dr. Herzl demanded that "*the sovereignty be granted us over a portion of the globe large enough to satisfy the rightful requirements of a nation*" (he specified no particular territory and did not especially lean towards Palestine). For the first time the idea of resurrecting a Jewish state came under lively discussion among Western Jews.[8] The London *Jewish Chronicle* described the book as "one of the most astounding pronouncements which have ever been put forward." Herzl, thus encouraged, went to London, then the focus of power, to canvass his idea. After successful meetings in London's East End he decided to call a Congress of Jews in support of it.

Consequently, in March 1897, Jews "all over the world" were invited to send delegates to a "Zionist congress," a counter-Sanhedrin, at Munich in August. The Western Jews were adamantly opposed. The rabbis of Germany, and then the Jews of Munich, protested, and the place of meeting was changed to Basel, in Switzerland. The Reform Jews of America two years earlier had announced that they expected "neither a return to Palestine ... nor the restoration of any of the laws concerning the Jewish State." (Most curious to relate today, when Rabbi Stephen Wise *in 1899* suggested a book about Zionism to the Jewish Publication Society of America its secretary replied, "The Society cannot risk a book on Zionism").

When Herzl's congress met most of the 197 delegates came from Eastern Europe. This group of men then set up a "World Zionist Organization," which proclaimed Jewish nationhood and "a publicly secured, legally assured home" to be its aims, and Herzl declared "The Jewish State exists." In fact, a few Jews, claiming to speak for *all* Jews but vehemently repudiated by many representative bodies of Western Jewry, had held a meeting in Basel, and that was all.

Nevertheless, the proposal, for what it was worth in those circumstances, was at last on the table of international affairs. The congress was in fact a Sanhedrin summoned to cancel the avowals made by the

---

[8] At that time it hardly reached the mind of the Gentile multitude. In 1841 a Colonel Churchill, English Consul at Smyrna, at the conference of Central European States called to determine the future of Syria had put forward a proposal to set up a Jewish state in Palestine, but apparently it was dismissed with little or no consideration.

Napoleonic Sanhedrin eighty years before. That Sanhedrin repudiated separate nationhood and any ambition to form a Jewish state; this one proclaimed separate nationhood and the ambition of statehood. Looking back fifty years later, Rabbi Elmer Berger observed, "Here was the wedge of Jewish nationalism, to be driven between Jews and other human beings. Here was the permanent mould of ghettoism into which Jewish life in the unemancipated nations was to remain compressed so that the self-generating processes of emancipation and integration could not come into play."

The Napoleonic Sanhedrin had a basic flaw, now revealed, of which Napoleon may well have been unaware. It represented the *Western* Jews, and Napoleon cannot reasonably be expected to have known of the strength of the compact, Talmudic-ruled mass of Jews in Russia, for Dr. Herzl, who surely should have known of this, was ignorant of it! He made the discovery at that first World Zionist Congress, called by him in such confident expectation of mass-support: "and then ... there rose before our eyes a Russian Jewry, *the strength of which we had not even suspected.* Seventy of our delegates came from Russia, and it was patent to all of us that they represented the views and sentiments of the five million Jews of that country. *What a humiliation for us, who had taken our superiority for granted!* "

Dr. Herzl found himself face to face with his masters and with the conspiracy, which through him was about to enter the West. He had declared war on emancipation and, like many successors, was unaware of the nature of the force he had released. He was soon left behind, a bugler whose task was done, while the real "managers" took over.

He had forged the instrument which they were to use in their onslaught on the West. Dr. Weizmann, who became the real leader, clearly sees that: "It was Dr. Herzl's enduring contribution to Zionism to have created one central parliamentary authority for Zionism ... This was the first time in the exilic history of Jewry that a great government had officially negotiated with the elected representatives of the Jewish people. The identity, the legal personality of the Jewish people, had been re-established."

Dr. Weizmann presumably smiled to himself when he included the words "parliamentary" and "elected." The middle sentence contains the great fact. The Jews who met at Basel, shunned by the majority of Western Jews, and its declarations, could only be lent authority by one event, which at that time seemed unimaginable; namely, their recognition by a Great Power. This inconceivable thing happened a few years later when the British Government offered Dr. Herzl Uganda, and that is the event to which Dr. Weizmann refers. From that moment all the Great Powers of the West in effect accepted the Talmudists from Russia as representing all *Jews*, and from that moment the Zionist-revolution also entered the West.

Thus ended the century of emancipation, which began with such bright prospect of common involvement, and the prescient words of Mr. Houston Stewart Chamberlain (written just before Dr. Herzl's congress met at Basel) at once became truth and living reality. Looking back on Gottfried von Herder's words of a hundred years before, "The ruder nations of Europe are willing slaves of Jewish usury," Chamberlain wrote that during the 19th Century "a great change has taken place ... today Herder could say the same of by far the greatest part of our civilized world ... The direct influence of Judaism on the 19th Century thus becomes one of the burning subjects of the day. We have to deal here with a question affecting not only the present, but also the future of the world."

With the formation of the World Zionist Organization, which the great governments of the West were to treat, in effect, as an authority superior to themselves, the burning subject began to mould the entire shape of events. That it affected "the future of the world" is plainly seen in 1956, when this book is concluded; from the start of that year the political leaders of the remaining great powers of the West, Britain and America, observed in tones of sad surprise that the next world war might at any time break out in the place where they had set up "the Jewish State," and they hastened to and fro across the ocean in the effort to concert some way of preventing that consummation.

Chapter 26

THE HERESY OF DR. HERZL

For the six years from 1897 to 1903 Dr. Theodor Herzl of the Vienna *Neue Freie Presse* was a world figure of an entirely new kind. He had created Zionism as an organized political force (and it was to be the death of him, as of some others who followed him on that path). He had launched it among the affairs of the West like a Chinese cracker. Yet he was an insubstantial shadow, the product of the cafés, of *Sacher Torte* and *Kaffee mit Schlagsahne*. He was like a man used for his "connections" by an astute company promoter and discarded when the flotation was well launched. He was never truly the leader and began to realize that, with a shock of alarm, at his first congress of 1897, when "there rose before our eyes a Russian Jewry, the strength of which we had not even suspected"; by 1904 the full realization of his captivity had killed him.

He once wrote that at Basel in 1897 "I founded the Jewish state ... *I founded the people* into the state sentiment and *conveyed to them the emotion that they were the national assembly.*" The next six years showed, in actual events, what Leon Pinsker had meant *in 1882* by "exerting irresistible pressure upon the international politics of the present."

Herzl, the Budapest-born Viennese journalist, began a triumphal tour of the great capitals; he was launched on a glittering flight, as from trapeze to trapeze, through the *haut monde*. Emperors, potentates and statesmen received him as the spokesman of all the Jews and the contrast between what they thought and what he must have known is impressive for, as his first lieutenant, Max Nordau, said after his death,: "Our people had a Herzl but Herzl never had a people"; the Talmudic rabbinate in the East, which scorned this false Messiah, stood between him and any mass following.

The world in which he moved seemed firm and well founded. The Widow at Windsor and the Old Gentleman at Schoenbrunn were beloved by their peoples; the Young Man in Berlin was growing older and mellowing; the Czar was still the father of his people; men's right to process of law was everywhere being asserted; gradually industrial serfdom was giving way to better conditions. But everywhere the rulers and politicians knew and feared the danger that this process, calculably good if given time, would be arrested and destroyed by the world-revolution, for by this time Weishaupt's secret society had grown, through Disraeli's "network of secret societies," into the Communist party organized in all countries.

Herzl's method was to exploit this general fear for his particular end, the Jewish State. He offered domestic peace if it were supported and revolution if it were not and he claimed to speak in the name of all the Jews.

It is, of course, implicit in this that he knew the revolutionary leadership to be Jewish, and he thus confirmed, several decades later, what Disraeli and Bakunin had said. His belief in the method he used is expressed in his famous phrase, "When we sink we become a revolutionary proletariat; when we rise there rises the terrible power of our purse."

Thus he told a Grand Duke of Baden that he would diminish revolutionary propaganda in Europe in proportion to the support that his territorial ambition received from high authority. Then he was received by the behelmeted Kaiser, mounted on a charger, at the very gates of Jerusalem, and the emperor agreed to present to the Sultan Herzl's proposal for a Zionist chartered company in Palestine under German protection. When nothing came of this Herzl threatened the Kaiser, too, with revolution: "If our work miscarries, *hundreds of thousands of our supporters will at a single bound join the revolutionary parties.*"

Then in Russia he was received by the Czar himself, to whom he spoke in similar terms. About this time the third Word Zionist Congress was held and the decision was taken that every Jew who became a member *acknowledged the sovereignty of the still mythical Jewish State.* Rabbi Elmer Berger says despondently that therewith "ghettoized, corporate Jewish existence became a reality again and now existed upon a greater scale that it had ever before achieved".

Next Herzl saw another potentate, the Sultan of Turkey. Nothing tangible came of all these journeys, but the great coup was at hand, for Herzl then transferred his activities to England. There, too, he evidently had access to the highest places, for one of the decisive actions of world history was prepared, British folk who were then in their cradles, and their children and grandchildren were to be caught up in the consequences of those unrecorded interviews.

Who enabled Dr. Herzl from Vienna to command reception by the great in all countries, and who ensured that they should listen to demands that were imperious, and intimidatory as well? Obviously "kingly portals" (his own phrase) would not have opened to him merely because he had called a meeting of 197 men at Basel and this had passed a resolution. Others, more powerful than he, must have interceded to set aside porters, doormen, footmen, secretaries, chamberlains and all those whose task it is to keep importuners from their masters.

At this point the present narrative enters the most secret and jealously guarded field of all. The origins of the world-revolution, its aims and the Jewish assumption of its leadership may now be shown from the mass of documentary evidence which has accumulated; the existence of Disraeli's "network," spreading over the superficies of the earth, is known to all; the nature of the "revolutionary proletarist" is clear. But there is also that second network, of influential men at the higher level where "the power of the purse" may be used to exert "irresistible pressure on the international politics of the present" through rulers and politicians. This network of men, working in all countries to a common end, is the one which must have enabled Herzl to penetrate, with his demands, to the highest places.

All experienced observers know of the existence of this force at the highest level of international affairs. The Zionist propagandists pretend that Jewish opposition to Zionism came only from "Jewish notables," "Jewish magnates" and "rich Jews" (these phrases repeatedly recur, for instance in Dr. Weizmann's book). In fact the division in Judaism was vertical, among rich and poor alike, and though the majority of Western Jews were at that time violently opposed to Zionism the minority contained rich and notable Jews. Only these can have enabled the spectre of Zionism, in the person of Dr. Herzl, to make its sudden, Nijinski-like leap into courts and cabinet-rooms, where he began to go in and out as if he were born to privilege. Those who helped him were plainly in alliance with the one compact, organized body of Zionists: the Talmudic communities in Russia.

Dr. Kastein says that the "executive" set up by the 197 men at Basel "was the first *embodiment* of a real *Jewish international.*" In other words, something that already existed received a visible expression. A "Jewish international" was already in being and this was powerful enough to command royal, princely and ministerial audiences for Dr. Herzl everywhere.

Of this international "network" of like-thinking men at the highest level, in Dr. Herzl's day, the student may only make a picture by carefully piecing together significant glimpses and fragments (its existence and concerted actions in our time are plainly demonstrable, as this book in its later chapters will show, from the growing mass of literature). For instance, Dr. Weizmann says he told Dr. Herzl that Sir Francis Montefiore (a leading Jew in England) was "a fool," whereon Herzl answered, "He opens kingly portals to me." Again, one Baron de Hirsch was Herzl's chief financial backer and supporter. Of this Baron de Hirsch Count Carl Lonyay (quoting from documents in the secret archives of the Imperial Court at Vienna) says that Crown Prince Rudolf of Austria, wishing to make provision for a woman friend before his suicide at Mayerling, obtained 100,000 gulden "from the banker, Baron Hirsch, in return for an act of friendliness he had performed in December, when he invited the banker to meet the Prince of Wales" (the future King Edward VII).

Baron de Hirsch, in the sequence to this introduction, became an intimate of the Prince of Wales, and private banker and financial adviser to the future King of England. He was also brother-in-law of a Mr. Bischoffsheim of the Jewish financial house of Bischoffsheim and Goldschmidt in London, of which a very rich German-born Jew, Sir Ernest Cassel, was a member. Sir Ernest, as Mr. Brian Connell says in a biographical study, fell heir to Baron de Hirsch's friendship with the future king: "where

Hirsch had been an intimate, Cassel was to become Edward VII's closest personal friend." He was indeed the last of the king's intimates to see him alive, the king, on the day of his death, insisting on keeping an appointment with Sir Edward and rising to dress himself for the purpose.

In the sequence to this account Mr. Connell says: "The *small international fraternity* of which he" (Sir Ernest Cassel) "became perhaps the leading member were all men with backgrounds similar to his own, people whom he approached in the course of his extensive travels. There was Max Warburg, head of the great private banking house in Hamburg; Edouard Noetzlin, honorary president of the Banque de Paris et des Pays Bas, in Paris; Franz Philippson in Brussels; Wertheim and Gompertz in Amsterdam and, above all, Jacob Schiff of the firm of Kuhn, Loeb and Company in New York. *Ties of race and interest bound these men together. The web of their communications quivered at the slightest touch. They maintained between them an incredibly accurate network of economic, political and financial intelligence at the highest level. They could withdraw support here, provide additional funds there, move immense sums of money with lightning rapidity and secrecy from one corner to another of their financial empires, and influence the political decisions of a score of countries."*

"Ties of race and interest ... web ... network ... intelligence at the highest level ... move immense sums of money ... influence political decisions ..."; there can be no reasonable doubt that this was the "Jewish international" of which Dr. Kastein wrote and the mechanism which operated, across all national boundaries, to support Dr. Herzl. Nothing less could explain the action which the British Government took and if there was doubt earlier, about the concerted action of this force, above and distinct from nations, the events of our mid-century have removed it. With such a power behind him Dr. Herzl was in a position to make demands and utter menaces. The powerful men who formed this international directorate (the term is not too large) at that time may not, as individuals, have believed in Zionism, and may even have been privately opposed to it. In the present writer's belief even they were not powerful enough to oppose, or to deny support to, a policy laid down by the elders of Jewry.

While the consequences of Dr. Herzl's journeys were secretly taking shape, he continued his travels. He took an innocent pride in his sudden elevation and liked the elegance of society, the tailcoats and white gloves, the chandeliers and receptions. The Talmudic elders in Russia, who had grown up to the kaftan and earlocks and were preparing to overthrow him, disdained but made use of this typical figure of "Western emancipation."

In 1903 he had astonishing experiences, resembling those of Sabbatai Zevi in 1666. He went to Russia and on his progress through Jewish cities was the object of Messianic ovations from the unenlightened masses. On this occasion he sought to persuade de Russia to bring pressure on the Sultan, in the matter of his proposal for a chartered company in Palestine. He made some impression on the Russian Minister of the Interior, von Plehve, to whom he said that he spoke for "all the Jews of Russia."

If he believed that he was soon undeceived. He did something that shows him either to have been recklessly brave or else quite unaware of what truly went on around him (this happens sometimes with such men). Presumably in order to strengthen his case with von Plehve, with whom he must have used the "Zionism or revolution" argument, he urged the Jews in Russia *to abstain from revolutionary activities* and discussed their "emancipation" with the Russian authorities!

Thus he wrote his own political death warrant, and indeed he soon died. To the Talmudic elders this was heresy; he had entered the forbidden room. They had been working to prevent Jewish emancipation in Russia, because they saw in it the loss of their power over Jewry. If his negotiations with the Russian Government succeeded, pacification in Russia would follow, and that would mean the end of the propagandist legend of "Jewish persecution" in Russia.

When he returned to address the Sixth Congress of his World Zionist Organization his fate rose to meet him in the form of a compact mass of Russian Jews no longer merely "humiliating" to him, but menacing. At this moment of his fiasco he thought he had the ace of trumps in his pocket and he produced it. As a result of those interviews in London and of the "irresistible pressure" which supported him, the British Government had offered Dr. Herzl of the Vienna *Neue Freie Presse* a territory in Africa, Uganda!

If history records a stranger thing, I have not discovered it. Yet the trump card proved to be a deuce. 295 delegates voted to accept the offer, but 175 rejected it; clearly Dr. Herzl did not speak for "all Jews." The great majority of the 175 Noes came from the Jews of Russia. The huddled Jewish throngs there had hailed Herzl as the Messiah; these 175 emissaries of the Eastern rabbinate imprecated him, for Uganda meant the ruin of their plan. They cast themselves on the floor in the traditional attitude of mourning for the dead or for the destruction of the temple. One of them, a woman, called the world-famous Dr. Herzl "a traitor" and when he was gone tore down the map of Uganda from behind the speakers' dais.

If what he said and wrote was fully candid, Dr. Herzl never understood why the Jewish emissaries from Russia refused to consider any other place than Palestine, and if that is so he must have been most guileless. He had built up his entire movement on the claim that "a place of refuge" was directly needed for "persecuted Jews," and these were the Jews of Russia; Jews were fully emancipated elsewhere. If that was true, then any good place would do, and he had now procured one for them; moreover, if any of them preferred to stay in Russia, and his negotiations with the Russian Government succeeded, they could have all they wanted in Russia too!

From the point of view of the Talmudic rabbinate in Russia the matter was entirely different. They, too, had built up the legend of "persecution in Russia," while they worked against emancipation there, but this was for the purpose of fulfilling the ancient Law, which meant possession of Palestine and all subsequent things that the Law ordained. Acceptance of Uganda would have meant Doomsday for Talmudic Judaism.

Dr. Weizmann describes Dr. Herzl's final humiliation. After the vote Herzl went to see the Jews from Russia, who had turned their backs on him and walked out, in their committee room. "He came in, looking haggard and exhausted. He was received in dead silence. Nobody rose from his seat to greet him, nobody applauded him when he ended … It was probably the first time that Herzl was thus received at any Zionist gathering: he, the idol of all Zionists."

It was also the last time. Within the year Dr. Herzl was dead, at the age of forty-four. No conclusion can be offered about his death. Judaist writers refer to it in cryptic terms. The *Jewish Encyclopaedia* says it was the result of what he endured and other authorities make similarly obscure, though significant, allusions. Those who during the centuries have been the object of anathema or excommunication by the ruling sect often have died soon and wretchedly. The student comes to feel that in this matter he approaches mysterious things, closed to all ordinary research.

The curious thing is that Herzl's intimate, right-hand man and leading orator saw the shape of things, at that time and to come, with complete clarity. He displayed a foreknowledge as great as that of Leon Pinsker when he depicted the series of events to which Pinsker's "irresistible pressure on international politics" would lead. At the very congress where Herzl suffered his humiliation Max Nordau (an alias or pseudonym; his name was Suedfeld) gave this exact prognosis:

"Let me tell you the following words as if I were showing you the rungs of a ladder leading upward and upward: Herzl, the Zionist congress, the English Uganda proposition, *the future world war, the peace conference where, with the help of England, a free and Jewish Palestine will be created*" (1903). Here spoke the initiate, the illuminate, the man who knew the strength and purpose of "the international." (Max Nordau helped the process, the course of which he foretold, by writing such best-sellers of the 1890's as *Degeneration,* in which he told the West that it was irredeemably corrupt). Even Max Nordau did not spell out his conclusion to its logical end. Another delegate did that, Dr. Nahum Sokoloff, who said: "*Jerusalem will one day become the capital of world peace.*" That the ambition is to make it the capital of the world is clear in 1956, when the Western governments stand in daily fear of its annexation to the Zionist state; whether mankind would find it to be the capital of *peace* remains to be seen.

After Dr. Herzl died Dr. Chaim Weizmann, the later Zionist leader, led the attack on the Uganda offer and at the Seventh Congress, of 1905, the acceptance, at his instigation, was revoked. From that moment Zionism was the instrument of the Talmudic rabbinate in the East.

The story of the Uganda offer and its scornful rejection shows the indifference of the ruling sect to the welfare and the wishes of the Jewish masses, for whom they pretended to speak; indeed, when the matter is carefully considered "hostility" suggests itself as a truer word than "indifference." This is seen by examining, in turn, the feeling expressed towards the offer by the three main groups of Jews: those of the West, those of Russia, and (a section of Jewry never even mentioned in all these loud exchanges) the Jews already in Palestine.

The Jews of the West at that time were strongly opposed to Zionism as such, whether it led to Uganda, Palestine or anywhere else; they just wanted to stay where they were. The Jews of Russia were depicted as needing simply "a place of refuge" from "persecution," and if that was true, Uganda might have appealed to them; anyway, the frenzied ovations with which they received Dr. Herzl suggest that they would have followed any lead he gave, had the rabbinate allowed them. That leaves the Jews who were already in Palestine. This one community of original Jews was ardently in favour of removal to Uganda, as research discovers, and for this reason they were denounced as "traitors" by the Judaized Chazars from Russia who had taken over Zionism! This is what the Zionist Organization at Tel Aviv still was saying about them *in 1945:*

"It was a degrading and distressing sight to see all these people who ... had been the first to build up the Jewish Palestine of that day, publicly denying and repudiating their own past ... *The passion for Uganda became associated with a deadly hatred for Palestine* ... In the community centres of the first Jewish colonies young men educated in the Alliance Israelite schools denounced Palestine as 'a land of corpses and graves,' a land of malaria and eye-diseases, a land which destroys its inhabitants. *Nor was this the expression of a few individuals.* Indeed, it was only a few individuals here and there ... who remained loyal ... The whole of Palestine was in a state of ferment ... *All opposition to Uganda came from outside of Palestine. In Zion itself all were against Zion.*"

What the masses of people wanted, Jewish or Gentile, was from 1903 of no account. Acceptance or refusal made no difference; the *offer* had been made, and by it the West and its future were involved in an enterprise foreseeably disastrous. As Dr. Weizmann says, a British government *by this act* committed itself to recognize the Talmudists from Russia as the government of all Jews; thereby it also committed future generations of its people, and the similar commitment of the American people was to follow a decade later, when the path had been prepared.

Out of that act of 1903 came the beginning of this century's tribulations. The story of Zion thereafter became that of Western politicians who, under "irresistible pressure," did the bidding of a powerful sect. 1903 was the conspiracy's triumphant year, and for the West it was to prove as ominous as 1914 and 1939, which years both took their shape under its shadow.

Chapter 27

THE "PROTOCOLS"

While Zionism thus took shape in the Eastern ghettoes during the last century and at the start of this one emerged as a new force in international affairs (when the British Government offered it Uganda), the world-revolution, in those same Talmudic areas, prepared its third "eruption." The two forces moved forward together in synchronization (for Zionism, as has been shown, used the threat of Communism in Europe to gain the ear of European rulers for its territorial demand outside Europe). It was as if twin turbines began to revolve, generating what was in effect *one* force, from which the new century was to receive galvanic shocks.

According to Disraeli and Bakunin the world-revolution had come under Jewish leadership around the middle of the century, and its aims then changed. Bakunin's followers, who sought to abolish the State as such because they foresaw that the revolutionary State might become more despotic than any earlier despotism, were ousted and forgotten. The world-revolution therewith took the shape of Karl Marx's Communist Manifesto, which aimed at the super-State founded in slave-labour and in "the confiscation of human liberty" (as de Tocqueville wrote in 1848).

This change in leadership and aims determined the course of the 20th Century. However, the *methods* by which the existing order was to be destroyed did *not* change; they continued to be those revealed by Weishaupt's papers published in 1787. Many publications of the 19th Century showed that the original Illuminist plan continued through the generations to be the textbook of the revolutionaries of all camps, as to *method*.

These works propagated or exposed the destructive plan in various ways, sometimes allegorical, but always recognizable if compared with the original, Weishaupt's documents. In 1859 Crétineau Joly assailed Jewish Leadership of "the secret societies." His book reproduced documents (communicated to him by Pope Gregory XVI) of the Italian secret society, the Haute Vente Romaine; their authenticity is beyond question. The Haute Vente Romaine was headed by an Italian prince who had been initiated by one of Weishaupt's own intimates (Knigge) and was a reincarnation of the Illuminati. The outer circle of initiates, the dupes, were persuaded that "the object of the association is something high and noble, that it is the Order of those who desire a purer morality and a stronger piety, the independence and unity of their country." Those who graduated into the inner degrees progressively learned the real aims and swore to destroy all religion and legitimate government; then they received the secrets of assassination, poison and perjury first disclosed by Weishaupt's documents.

In 1862 Karl Marx (whose Communist Manifesto is recognizably Illuminist) founded his First International, and Bakunin formed his Alliance Sociale Democratique (the programme of which, as Mrs Nesta Webster has shown by quoting correlative passages, was Illuminism undiluted). In the same year Maurice Joly published an attack on Napoleon III, to whom he attributed the identical methods of corrupting and ruining the social system (this book was written in allegorical form). In 1868 the German Goedsche reproduced the same ideas in the form of an attack on Jewish leadership of the revolution, and in 1869 the French Catholic and Royalist Gougenot Des Mousseaux took up the same theme. In that year Bakunin also published his *Polemic Against The Jews*.

In all these works, in one form or another, the continuity of the basic idea first revealed by Weishaupt's documents appears: namely, that of destroying all legitimate government, religion and nationhood and setting up a universal despotism to rule the enslaved masses by terror and violence. *Some* of them assailed the Jewish usurpation of, or succession to the leadership of the revolution.

After that came a pause in the published literature of the conspiracy first disclosed in 1787, until in 1905 one Professor Sergyei Nilus, an official of the Department of Foreign Religions at Moscow, published a book, of which the British Museum in London has a copy bearing its date-stamp, August 10, 1906. Great interest would attach to anything that could be elicited about Nilus and his book, which has never been translated; the mystery with which he and it have been surrounded impedes research. *One chapter* was translated into English in 1920. This calls for mention here because the original publication occurred in 1905, although the violent uproar only began when it appeared in English in 1920.

This one chapter was published in England and America as "The Protocols of the Learned Elders of Zion"; I cannot learn whether this was the original chapter heading or whether it was provided during translation. No proof is given that the document is what it purports to be, a minute of a secret meeting of Jewish "Elders." In that respect, therefore, it is valueless.

In every other respect it is of inestimable importance, for it is shown by the conclusive test (that of subsequent events) to be an authentic document of the world-conspiracy first disclosed by Weishaupt's papers. Many other documents in the same series had followed that first revelation, as I have shown, but this one transcends all of them. The others were fragmentary and gave glimpses; this one gives the entire picture of the conspiracy, motive, method and objective. It adds nothing new to what had been revealed in parts (save for the unproven, attribution to Jewish elders *themselves*), but it puts all the parts in place and exposes the whole. It accurately depicts all that has come about in the fifty years since it was published, and what clearly will follow in the next fifty years unless in that time the force which the conspiracy has generated produces the counter-force.

It is informed by a mass of knowledge (particularly of human weaknesses) which can only have sprung from the accumulated experience and continuing study of centuries, or of ages. It is written in a tone of lofty superiority, as by beings perched on some Olympian pinnacle of sardonic and ancient wisdom, and of mocking scorn for the writhing masses far below ("the mob" ... "alcoholized animals" ... "cattle" ... "bloodthirsty beasts") who vainly struggle to elude the "nippers" which are closing on them; these nippers are "the power of gold" and the brute force of the mob, incited to destroy its only protectors and consequently itself.

The destructive idea is presented in the form of a scientific theory, almost of an exact science, argued with gusto and eloquence. In studying the Protocols I am constantly reminded of something that caught my eye in Disraeli's dictum, earlier quoted. Disraeli, who was careful in the choice of words, spoke of "the destructive *principle*" (not idea, scheme, notion, plan, plot or the like), and the Protocols elevate the theory of destruction to this status of "a fundamental truth, a primary or basic law, a governing law of conduct" (to quote various dictionary definitions of "principle"). In many passages the Protocols appear, at first sight, to recommend destruction as a thing virtuous in itself, and consequently justifying all the methods explicitly recommended to promote it (bribery, blackmail, corruption, subversion, sedition, mob-incitement, terror and violence), which thus become virtuous too.

But careful scrutiny shows that this is not the case. In fact the argument presented begins at the end, world power, and goes backward through the means, which are advocated simply as the best ones to that end. The end is that first revealed in Weishaupt's documents, and it is apparent that both spring from a much earlier source, although the Protocols, in time, stand to the Weishaupt papers as grandson to grandsire. The final aim is the destruction of all religion and nationhood and the establishment of the super State, ruling the world by ruthless terror.

When the Protocols appeared in English the minor point, who was the author of this particular document, was given a false semblance of major importance by the enraged Jewish attack on the document itself. The asseveration of Jewish leadership of the revolutionary conspiracy was not new at all; the reader has seen that Disraeli, Bakunin and many others earlier affirmed it. In this case the allegation about a specific meeting of Jewish leaders of the conspiracy was unsupported and could have been ignored (in 1913 a somewhat similar publication accused the Jesuits of instigating a world-conspiracy resembling that depicted alike in the Protocols and in Weishaupt's papers; the Jesuits quietly remarked that this was false and the matter was forgotten).

The response of official Jewry in 1920 and afterwards was different. It was aimed, with fury, at the entire *substance* of the Protocols; it did not stop at denying a Jewish plot, but denied that there was *any* plot, which was demonstrably untrue. The existence of the conspiracy had been recognized and affirmed by a long chain of high authorities, from Edmund Burke, George Washington and Alexander Hamilton to Disraeli, Bakunin and the many others mentioned in an earlier chapter. Moreover, when the Protocols appeared in English conclusive proof had been given by the event in Russia. Thus the nature of the Jewish attack could only strengthen public doubts; it protested much too much.

This attack was the repetition of the one which silenced those earlier leaders of the public demand for investigation and remedy, Robison, Barruel and Morse, but on this occasion it was a Jewish attack. Those three men made no imputation of Jewish leadership, and they were defamed solely because they drew public attention to the *continuing* nature of the conspiracy and to the fact that the French revolution was clearly but its first "eruption." The attack on the Protocols in the 1920's proved above all else the truth of their contention; it showed that the standing organization for suppressing public discussion of the conspiracy had been perfected in the intervening 120 years. Probably so much money and energy were never before in history expended on the effort to suppress a single document.

It was brought to England by one of the two leading British correspondents of that day in Moscow, Victor Marsden of the *Morning Post* (the significant story of the other correspondent belongs to a later chapter). Marsden was an authority on Russia and was much under the enduring effect of the Terror. He was in effect its victim, for he died soon after completing what he evidently felt to be a duty, the translation of the Protocols at the British Museum.

Publication in English aroused worldwide interest. That period (1920 and onward) marks the end of the time when Jewish questions could be impartially discussed in public. The initial debate was free and vigorous, but in following years the attack succeeded in imposing the law of lese majesty in this matter and today hardly any public man or print ventures to mention the Protocols unless to declare them "forged" or "infamous" (an act of submission also foretold in them).

The first reaction was the natural one. The Protocols were received as formidable evidence of an international conspiracy against religion, nationhood, legitimate government and property. All agreed that the attribution to Jewish authorship was unsupported, but that the subject matter was so grave, and so strongly supported by events subsequent to the original publication, that full enquiry was needed. This remedy, "investigation," was the one advocated by many leading men 120 years earlier. In this instance the attack was in effect again on the demand for *investigation*, not simply on the allegation against "the Elders of Zion."

The Times (of London) on May 8, 1920 in a long article said, "An impartial *investigation* of these would-be documents and of their history is most desirable ... Are we to dismiss the whole matter without inquiry and to let the influence of such a book as this work unchecked?" The *Morning Post* (then the oldest and soberest British newspaper) published twenty-three articles, also calling for *investigation*.

In *The Spectator* on August 27, 1921, Lord Sydenham, a foremost authority of that day, also urged *investigation:* "The main point is, of course, the source from which Nilus obtained the Protocols. The Russians who knew Nilus and his writings cannot all have been exterminated by the Bolsheviks. His book ... has not been translated, though it would give some idea of the man ... What is the most striking characteristic of the Protocols? The answer is *knowledge* of a rare kind, embracing the widest field. The solution of this 'mystery,' if it is one, is to be found where this uncanny knowledge, *on which prophecies now literally fulfilled are based*, can be shown to reside." In America Mr. Henry Ford, declaring that "the Protocols have fitted the world situation up to this time; they fit it now," caused his *Dearborn Independent* to publish a series of articles of which a million and a half reprints were sold.

Within two years the proprietor of *The Times* was certified insane (by an unnamed doctor in a foreign land; a later chapter will describe this episode) and forcibly removed from control of his publications, and *The Times* published an article dismissing the Protocols as a plagiarism of Maurice Joly's book. The proprietor of the *Morning Post* became the object of sustained vituperation until he sold the newspaper, which then ceased publication. In 1927 Mr. Henry Ford published an apology addressed to a well-known Jew of America; when I was in the United States in later years I was told by credible informants that he was persuaded to do this, at a moment when a new-model Ford automobile was about to be marketed, by hostile threats from dealers on whom the fortunes of his concern depended.

The campaign against the Protocols has never ceased since then. In communized Russia all copies discoverable had been destroyed at the revolution and possession of the book became a capital crime under the law against "anti-semitism." In the direct sequence to that, though twenty-five years later, the American and British authorities in occupied Germany after the Second World War constrained the Western German government to enact laws against "anti-semitism" on the Bolshevik model; and in 1955 a Munich printer who reproduced the Protocols had his business confiscated. In England at the time of publication the sale of the book was temporarily stopped by authority, under the pressure described, and in the course of the years the attack on it continued so violent that publishers feared it and only small local firms ever ventured to print it. In Switzerland, between the wars, a

Jewish suit was brought against the book as "improper literature"; the case was won, but the verdict was set aside by a higher court.

The state of affairs thus brought about after 1920, and continuing today, was foretold by the Protocols *in 1905:* "Through the press we have gained the power to influence while remaining ourselves in the shade … The principal factor of success in the political" (field) " is the secrecy of its undertaking; the word should not agree with the deeds of the diplomat … We must compel the governments … to take action in the direction favoured by our widely-conceived plan, already approaching the desired consummation, by what we shall represent as public opinion, secretly prompted by us through the means of that so-called 'Great Power,' the press, which, with a few exceptions that may be disregarded, is already entirely in our hands … We shall deal with the press in the following way: … we shall saddle and bridle it with a tight curb; we shall do the same also with all productions of the printingpress, for where would be the sense of getting rid of the attacks of the press if we remain targets for pamphlets and books? … No one shall with impunity lay a finger on the aureole of our government infallibility. *The pretext for stopping any publication will be the alleged plea that it is agitating the public mind without occasion or justification* … We shall have a sure triumph over our opponents since they will not have at their disposition organs of the press in which they can give full and final expression to their views owing to the aforesaid methods of dealing with the press …"

Such is the history of the Protocols thus far. Their attribution to Jewish "Elders" is unsupported and should be rejected, without prejudice to any other evidence about Jewish leadership of the world-revolution as such. The Jewish attack on them was bent, not on exculpating Jewry, but on stopping the publication on the plea that it was "agitating the public mind without occasion or justification." The arguments advanced were bogus; they were that the Protocols closely resembled several earlier publications and thus were "plagiaries" or "forgeries," whereas what this in truth showed was the obvious thing: that they were part of the continuing literature of the conspiracy. They might equally well be the product of non-Jewish or of anti-Jewish revolutionaries, and that is of secondary importance. What they proved is that *the organization* first revealed by Weishaupt's documents was in existence 120 years later, and was still using the methods and pursuing the aim then exposed; and when they were published in English the Bolshevik revolution had given the proof.

In my opinion the Protocols provide the essential handbook for students of the time and subject. If Lord Sydenham, in 1921, was arrested by the "uncanny knowledge" they displayed, "on which prophecies now literally fulfilled are based," how much more would he be impressed today, in 1956, when much more of them has been as literally fulfilled. Through this book any man can see how the upheavals of the past 150 years were, and how those of the next fifty years will be brought about; he will know in advance just how "the deeds" of his elected representatives will differ from their "word."

In one point I am able from my own experience to test Lord Sydenham's dictum about fulfilled prophecies. The Protocols, speaking of control of published information, say: "Not a single announcement will reach the public without our control. Even now this is already being attained by us inasmuch as all news items are received by a few agencies, in whose offices they are focused from all parts of the world. These agencies will then be entirely ours and will give publicity only to what we dictate to them." That was not the situation in 1905, or in Lord Sydenham's day, or in 1926, when I became a journalist, but it was developing and today *is* the situation. The stream of "news" which pours into the public mind through the newspapers comes from a few agencies, as if from half a dozen taps. Any hand that can control those valves can control "the news," and the reader may observe for himself the filtered form in which the news reaches him. As to the editorial *views*, based on this supply of news, the transformation that has been brought about may be comprehended by referring to the impartially critical articles published in *The Times, Morning Post, Spectator, Dearborn Independent* and thousands of other journals some twenty-five years ago. This could not happen today. The subjugation of the press has been accomplished as the Protocols foretold, and by the accident of my generation and calling I saw it come about.

Comparative study of the Protocols and of the Weishaupt papers leads to the strong deduction that both derive from a common and much older source. They cannot have been the product of any one man or one group of men in the period when they were published; the "uncanny knowledge" displayed in them obviously rests on the cumulative experience of eras. In particular, this applies (in Weishaupt's papers and the Protocols alike) to the knowledge of human weaknesses, which are singled out with analytical exactitude, the method of exploiting each of them being described with disdainful glee.

The instrument to be used for the destruction of the Christian nation-states and their religion is "the mob." The word is used throughout with searing contempt to denote the masses, (who in public are flattered by being called "the people"). "Men with bad instincts are more in number than the good, and therefore the best results in governing them are attained by violence and terrorization

… The might of a mob is blind, senseless and unreasoning force ever at the mercy of a suggestion from any side." From this the argument is developed that "an absolute despotism" is necessary to govern "the mob," which is "a savage," and that "our State" will employ "the terror which tends to produce blind submission." The "literal fulfilment" of these precepts in communized Russia must be obvious to all today).

This "absolute despotism" is to be vested in the international super-State at the end of the road. In the meanwhile regional puppet- despots are depicted as essential to the process of breaking down the structure of states and the defences of peoples: "From the premier-dictators of the present day the peoples suffer patiently and bear such abuses as for the least of them they would have beheaded twenty kings. What is the explanation…? It is explained by the fact that these dictators whisper to the peoples through their agents that through these abuses the are inflicting injury on the States with the highest purpose - to secure the welfare of the peoples, the international brotherhood of them all, their solidarity and equality of rights. Naturally they do not tell the peoples that this unification must be accomplished only under our sovereign rule."

This passage is of especial interest. The term "premier-dictator" would not generally have been understood in 1905, when the peoples of the West believed their elected representatives to express and depend on *their* approval. However, it became applicable during the First and Second World Wars, when American presidents and British prime ministers made themselves, in fact, "premier-dictators" and used emergency powers in the name of "the welfare of peoples … international brotherhood … equality of rights." Moreover, these premier-dictators, in both wars, *did* tell the peoples that the ultimate end of all this would be "unification" under a world government of some kind. The question, who would govern this world government, was one which never received straightforward answer; so much else of the Protocols has been fulfilled that their assertion that it would be the instrument of the conspiracy for governing the world "by violence and terrorization" deserves much thought.

The especial characteristic of the two 20th Century wars is the disappointment which each brought to the peoples who *appeared* to be victorious. "Uncanny knowledge," therefore, again seems to have inspired the statement, *made in 1905 or earlier,* "Ever since that time" (the French Revolution) "we have been *leading the peoples from one disenchantment to another,*" followed later by this: "By these acts all States are in torture; they exhort to tranquillity, are ready to sacrifice everything for peace; *but we will not give them peace until they openly acknowledge our international Super-Government, and with submissiveness.*" The words, written before 1905, seem accurately to depict the course of the 20th Century.

Again, the document says "it is indispensable for our purpose that wars, so far as possible, *should not result in territorial gains.*" This very phrase, of 1905 or earlier, was made the chief slogan, or apparent moral principle, proclaimed by the political leaders of America and Britain in *both* world wars, and in this case the difference between "the word" and "the deed" of "the diplomat" has been shown by results. The chief result of the First War was to establish revolutionary-Zionism and revolutionary-Communism as new forces in international affairs, the first with a promised "homeland" and the second with a resident State. The chief result of the Second War was that further "territorial gains" accrued to, and *only* to, Zionism and Communism; Zionism received its resident State and Communism received half of Europe. The "deadly accuracy" (Lord Sydenham's words) of the Protocol's forecasts seems apparent in this case, where a specious phrase used in the Protocols of 1905 became the daily language of American presidents and British prime ministers in 1914-1918 and 1939-1945.

The reason why the authors of the Protocols held this slogan to be so important, in beguiling the peoples, is also explained. If the nations embroiled in wars are denied "territorial gains," the only victors will then be "our international *agentur* … our international rights will then wipe out national rights, in the proper sense of right, and will rule the nations precisely as the civil law of States rules the relations of their subjects among themselves." To bring about this state of affairs compliant politicians are needed, and of them the Protocols say: "The administrators whom we shall choose from among the public, with strict regard to their capacities for *servile obedience*, will not be persons trained in the arts of government, and will therefore easily become pawns in our game in the hands of men of learning and genius who will be *their advisers, specialists bred and reared from early childhood to rule the affairs of the whole world*."

The reader may judge for himself whether this description fits some of "the administrators" of the West in the last five decades; the test is their attitude towards Zionism, the world-revolution and world-government, and subsequent chapters will offer information in these three respects. But "deadly accuracy" appears to reside even more in the allusion to "advisers."

Here again is "uncanny knowledge," displayed more than fifty years ago. In 1905 the non-elected but powerful "adviser" was publicly unknown. True, the enlightened few, men like Disraeli, knew that "the world is governed by very different persons from what is imagined by those who are not behind the scenes," but to the general public the passage would have been meaningless.

In the First and Second World Wars, however, the non-elected, unofficial but imperious "adviser" became a familiar public figure. He emerged into the open (under "emergency powers") and became known to and was passively accepted by the public masses; possibly the contempt which the Protocols display for "the mob" was justified by this submission to behind-the-scenes rule even when it was openly exercised. In the United States, for instance, "advisers on Jewish affairs" became resident at the White House and at the headquarters of American armies of occupation. One financier (who publicly recommended drastic measures for "ruling the affairs of the world") was adviser to so many presidents that he was permanently dubbed "Elder Statesman" by the press, and visiting prime ministers from England also repaired to him as if to a supreme seat of authority.

The Protocols foretold this regime of the "advisers" when none understood what was meant and few would have credited that they would openly appear in the high places.

The Protocols repeatedly affirm that the first objective is the destruction of the existing ruling class ("the aristocracy," the term employed, was still applicable in 1905) and the seizure of property through the incitement of the insensate, brutish "mob." Once again, subsequent events give the "forecast" its "deadly accuracy":

"In politics one must know how to seize the property of others without hesitation if by it we secure submission and sovereignty ... The words, 'Liberty, Equality, Fraternity,' brought to our ranks, thanks to our blind agents, whole legions who bore our banners with enthusiasm. And all the time these words were canker-worms boring into the wellbeing of the people, putting an end everywhere to peace, quiet, solidarity and destroying all the foundations of the States ... This helped us to our greatest triumph; it gave us the possibility, among other things, of getting into our hands the master card, the destruction of privileges, or in other words the very existence of the aristocracy ... that class which was the only defence peoples and countries had against us. On the ruins of the natural and genealogical aristocracy ... we have set up the aristocracy of our educated class headed by the aristocracy of money. The qualifications of this aristocracy we have established in wealth, which is dependent upon us, and in knowledge ... *It is this possibility of replacing the representatives of the people which has placed them at our disposal, and, as it were, given us the power of appointment* .... . We appear on the scene as *alleged saviours of the worker* from this oppression when we propose to him to enter the ranks of our fighting forces; Socialists, Anarchists, Communists ... By want and the envy and hatred which it engenders we shall move the mobs and with their hands we shall wipe out all those who hinder us on our way ... The people, blindly believing things in print, cherishes ... a blind hatred towards all conditions which it considers above itself, for it has no understanding of the meaning of class and condition ... These mobs will rush delightedly to shed the blood of those whom, in the simplicity of their ignorance, they have envied from their cradles, and whose property they will then be able to loot. 'Ours' they will not touch, because the moment of attack will be known to us and we shall take measures to protect our own ... The word 'freedom' brings out the communities of men to fight against every kind of force, against every kind of authority, even against God and the laws of nature. For this reason we, when we come into our kingdom, *shall have to erase this word from the lexicon of life* as implying a principle of brute force which turns mobs into bloodthirsty beasts ... But even freedom might be harmless and have its place in the State economy without injury to the wellbeing of the peoples if it rested upon the foundation of faith in God … This is the reason why it is indispensable for us to undermine all faith, to tear out of the minds of the masses the very principle of Godhead and the spirit, and to put in its place arithmetical calculations and material needs …"

" … We have set one against another the personal and national reckonings of the peoples, religious and race hatreds, which we have fostered into a huge growth in the course of the past twenty centuries. This is the reason why there is not one State which would anywhere receive support if it were to raise its arm, for every one of them must bear in mind that any agreement against us would be unprofitable to itself. We are too strong, there is no evading our power. The nations cannot come to even an inconsiderable private agreement without our secretly having a hand in it … In order to put public opinion into our hands we must bring it into a state of bewilderment by giving expression from all sides to so many contradictory opinions and for such length of time as will suffice to make the peoples lose their heads in the labyrinth and come to see that the best thing is to have no opinion of any kind in matters political, which it is not given to the public to understand, because they are understood only by him who guides the public. This is the first secret. The second secret requisite for the success of our government is comprised in the following: to multiply to such an extent national failings, habits, passions, conditions of civil life, that it will be impossible for anyone to know where he is in the resulting chaos, so that the people in consequence will fail to understand one another … By all these means we shall so wear down the peoples that they will be compelled to offer us international power of a nature that by its possession will enable us without any violence gradually to absorb all the State forces of the world and to form a Super-Government. In place of the rulers of today we shall set up a bogey which will be called the Super-Government administration. Its hands will reach out in all directions like nippers and its organization will be of such colossal dimensions that it cannot fail to subdue all the nations of the world."

That the Protocols reveal the common source of inspiration of Zionism and Communism is shown by significant parallels that can be drawn between the two chief methods laid down in them and the chief methods pursued by Dr. Herzl and Karl Marx:

The Protocols repeatedly lay emphasis on the incitement of "the mob" against the ruling class as the most effective means of destroying States and nations and achieving world dominion. Dr. Herzl, as was shown in the preceding chapter, used precisely this method to gain the ear of European rulers.

Next, Karl Marx. The Protocols say, "The aristocracy of the peoples, as a political force, is dead … but as *landed proprietors* they can still be harmful to us from the fact that they are self-sufficing in the resources upon which they live. It is essential therefore for us at whatever cost *to deprive them of their land*

… At the same time we must intensively patronize trade and industry … what we want is that industry should drain off from the land both labour and capital and by means of speculation transfer into our hands all the money of the world.. …"

Karl Marx in his *Communist Manifesto* exactly followed this formula. True he declared that Communism might be summed up in one sentence, "abolition of private property," but subsequently he qualified this dictum by restricting actual confiscation to *land* and implying that other types of private property were to remain intact. (In the later Marxist event, of course, all private property was confiscated, but I speak here of the strict parallel between the strategy laid down *before* the event alike by the Protocols and Marx).

A passage of particular interest in the present, though it was written before 1905, says, "Nowadays if any States raise a protest against us, it is only *proforma* at our discretion and by our direction, for their anti-semitism is indispensable to us for the management of our lesser brethren." A distinctive feature of our era is the way the charge of "anti-semitism" is continually transferred from one country to another, the country so accused becoming automatically the specified enemy in the next war. This passage might cause the prudent to turn a sceptical eye on today's periodical reports of sudden "anti-semitic" turns in communized Russia, or elsewhere.

The resemblance to Weishaupt's documents is very strong in the passages which relate to the infiltration of public departments, professions and parties, for instance: "It is from us that the all-engulfing terror proceeds. We have in our service persons of all opinions, of all doctrines, restorating monarchists, demagogues, socialists, communists, and utopian dreamers of every kind. We have harnessed them all to the task: each one of them on his own account is boring away at the last remnants of authority, is striving to overthrow all established form of order. By these acts all States are in torture; they exhort to tranquillity, are ready to sacrifice everything for peace; but we will not give them peace until they openly acknowledge our international Super-Government, *and with submissiveness.*"

The allusions to the permeation of universities in particular, and of education in general, also spring directly from Weishaupt, or from whatever earlier source he received them: "… We shall emasculate the universities … Their officials and professors will be prepared for their business by detailed secret programmes of action from which they will not with immunity diverge, not by one iota. They will be appointed with especial precaution, and will be so placed as to be wholly dependent upon the Government." This secret permeation of universities (which was successful in the German ones in Weishaupt's day, as his documents show) was very largely effective in our generation. The two British government officials who after their flight to Moscow were paraded before the international press in 1956 to state that they had been captured by Communism at their universities, were typical products of this method, described by the Protocols early in this century and by Weishaupt in 1787.

Weishaupt's documents speak of Freemasonry as the best "cover" to be used by the agents of the conspiracy. The Protocols allot the function of "cover" to "Liberalism": "When we introduced into the State organism the poison of Liberalism its whole political complexion underwent a change. States have been seized with a mortal illness, blood-poisoning. All that remains is to await the end of their death agony."

The term "utopian dreamers," used more than once, is applied to Liberals, and its original source probably resides in the Old Testamentary allusion to "dreamers of dreams" with "false prophets," are to be put to death. The end of Liberalism, therefore, would be apparent to the student even if the Protocols did not specify it: "We shall root out liberalism from the important strategic posts of our government on which depends the training of subordinates for our State structure."

The "Big Brother" regimes of our century, are accurately foretold in the passage, "Our government will have *the appearance* of a patriarchal paternal guardianship on the part of our ruler."

Republicanism, too, is to be a "cover" for the conspiracy. The Protocols are especially contemptuous of republicanism, in which (and in liberalism) they see the weapon of self-destruction forged out of "the mob": "... then it was that the era of republics became possible of realization; and then it was that we replaced the ruler by a caricature of a government, by a president, taken from the mob, from the midst of our puppet creatures, our slaves. This was the foundation of the mine which we have laid under the peoples."

Then the unknown scribes of sometime before 1905 describe the position to which American presidents have been reduced in our century. The passage begins, "In the near future we shall establish *the responsibility of presidents.*" This, as the sequence shows, means *personal* responsibility, as distinct from responsibility curbed by constitutional controls; the president is to become one of the "premier-dictators" earlier foreseen, whose function is to be to break down the constitutional defences of states and thus prepare "unification under our sovereign rule."

During the First and Second World Wars the American presidents did in fact become "premier-dictators" in this sense, claiming that "the emergency" and the need for "victory" dictated this seizure of powers of *personal* responsibility; powers which would be restored to "the people" when "the emergency" was past. Readers of sufficient years will recall how inconceivable this appeared before it happened and how passively it was accepted in the event. The passage then continues:

"The chamber of deputies will provide cover for, will protect, will elect presidents, but we shall take from it the right to propose new, or make changes in existing laws, for this right will be given by us to the responsible president, a puppet in our hands ... *Independently of this we shall invest the president with the right of declaring a state of war. We shall justify this last right on the ground that the president as chief of the whole army of the country must have it at his disposal in case of need ... It is easy to understand that in these conditions the key of the shrine will lie in our hands. and that no one outside ourselves will any longer direct the force of legislation ... The president will. at our discretion, interpret the sense of such of the existing laws as admit of various interpretation; he will further annul them when we indicate to him the necessity to do so, besides this, he will have the right to propose temporary laws, and even new departures in the government constitutional working, the pretext both for the one and the other being the requirements for the supreme welfare of the state. By such measures we shall obtain the power of destroying little by little, step by step, all that at the outset when we enter on our rights, we are compelled to introduce into the constitutions of states to prepare for the transition to an imperceptible abolition of every kind of constitution, and then the time is come to turn every government into our despotism.*" This forecast of 1905 or earlier particularly deserves Lord Sydenham's tribute of "deadly accuracy." American presidents in the two wars of this century have acted as here shown. They did take the right of declaring and making war, and it has been used at least once (in Korea) since the Second World War ended; any attempt in Congress or outside to deprive them of this power, or curb them in the use of it meets with violently hostile attack.

So the Protocols continue. The peoples, on their progress "from one disenchantment to another," will not be allowed "a breathing- space." Any country "which dares to oppose us" must be met with war, and any collective opposition with "universal war." The peoples will not be allowed "to contend with sedition" (here is the key to the furious attacks of the 1790's, 1920 and today on all demands for "investigation," "Witch-hunting," "McCarthyism" and the like). In the Super-State to come the obligation will fall on members of one family to denounce dissident s within the family circle (the Old Testamentary dispensation earlier mentioned). The "complete wrecking of the Christian religion" will not be long delayed. The peoples will be kept distracted by trivial amusements ("people's palaces") from becoming troublesome and asking questions. History will be rewritten for their delusion (another precept since fulfilled in communized Russia), for "we shall erase from the memory of men all facts of previous centuries which are undesirable to us, and leave only those which depict all the errors of the national governments." "All the wheels of the machinery of all States go by the force of the engine, which is in our hands, and that engine of the machinery of States is Gold."

And the end of it all: "What we have to get at is that there should be in all the States of the world, beside ourselves, only the masses of the proletariat, a few millionaires devoted to our interests, police and soldiers ... The recognition of our despot ... will come when the peoples, utterly wearied by the irregularities and incompetence ... of their rulers, will clamour: 'Away with them and give us one king over all the earth who will unite us and annihilate the causes of discords, frontiers, nationalities, religions, State debts, who will give us peace and quiet, which we cannot find under our rulers and representatives' ."

In two or three of these passages I have substituted "people" or "masses" for "*Goyim*," because the use of that word relates to the unproven assertion contained in the book's title, and I do not want to confuse the issues; evidence about the identity of the authors of the conspiracy must be sought elsewhere than in an unsupported allegation. The authors may have been Jewish, non-Jewish or anti- Jewish. That is immaterial. When it was published this work was the typescript of a drama which had not been performed; today it has been running for fifty years and its title is *The Twentieth Century*. The characters depicted in it move on our contemporary stage, play the parts foretold and produce the events foreseen.

Only the denouement remains, fiasco or fulfilment. It is a grandiose plan, and in my estimation cannot succeed. But it has existed for at least 180 years and probably for much longer, and the Protocols provided one more proof in a chain of proofs that has since been greatly lengthened. The conspiracy for world dominion through a world slave state *exists* and cannot at this stage be abruptly checked or broken off; of the momentum which it has acquired it now must go on to fulfilment or failure. Either will be destructive for a time, and hard for those of the time in which the dénouement comes.

Chapter 28

THE ABERRATION OF MR. BALFOUR

As the first decade of the 20th Century grew older the signs of the coming storms multiplied. In 1903 the British Government had offered Uganda to Zionism and Max Nordau had publicly foretold "the future world war," in the sequence to which England would procure Palestine for Zionism. In 1905 the Protocols prophetically revealed the destructive orgy of Communism. Then in 1906 one Mr. Arthur James Balfour, Prime Minister of England, met Dr. Weizmann in a hotel room and was captivated by the notion of presenting Palestine, which was not his to give, to "the Jews."

The shape which "the future world war" would take was then determined. Mr. Balfour stood guard over the new century and yielded the pass. A different man, in his place, might have saved it; or another might have done the same, for by 1906 the hidden mechanism for exerting "irresistible pressure on the international affairs of the present" (Leon Pinsker, 1882) had evidently been perfected. Rabbi Elmer Berger says of that time, "that group of Jews which committed itself to Zionism … entered a peripatetic kind of diplomacy which took it into many chancelleries and parliaments, exploring the labyrinthine and devious ways of international politics in a part of the world where political intrigue and secret deals were a byword. Jews began to play the game of 'practical politics.'" The era of the malleable "administrators" and compliant "premier-dictators," all furthering the great plan, was beginning. Therefore any other politician, put in Mr. Balfour's place at that time, might have acted similarly. However, his name attaches to the initial misdeed.

His actions are almost unaccountable in a man of such birth, training and type. Research cannot discover evidence of any other motive than an infatuation, of the "liberal" sort, for an enterprise which he did not even examine in the light of duty and wisdom. "Hard- boiled" considerations of "practical politics" (that is, a cold calculation that money or votes might be gained by supporting Zionism) can hardly be suspected in him. He and his colleagues belonged to the oldest families of England, which carried on a long tradition of public service. Statesmanship was in their blood; understanding of government and knowledge of foreign affairs were instinctive in them; they represented the most successful ruling class in recorded history; and they were wealthy.

Why, then, did instinct, tradition and wisdom suddenly desert them in this one question, at the moment when their Conservative Party, in its old form, for the last time governed England, and their families still guided the country's fortunes from great houses in Piccadilly and Mayfair and from country abbeys? Were they alarmed by the menace that "the mob" would be incited against them if they did not comply? They realized that birth and privilege alone would not continue to qualify for the function of governing. The world had changed much in the century before, and they knew that the process would go on. In the British tradition they worked to ensure continuity, unbroken by violence and eased by conciliation. They were too wise to resist change; they aimed at guiding change. Perhaps they were too eager on that account to shake hands with Progress, when it knocked, without examining the emissaries' credentials.

Mr. Balfour, their leader, was a tall, aloof and scholarly bachelor, impassive and pessimistic; he was of chilly mien but his intimates contend that his heart was warm. His middle-aged love affair with Zionism might be a symptom of unwilling celibacy. In youth he delayed asking his ladylove until she became affianced to another; before they could marry her lover died; and as Mr. Balfour was about to make good his earlier tardiness *she* died. He then resolved to remain unmarried.

Women may not be good judges of a distinguished bachelor who wears a broken heart on his sleeve, but many of the contemporary comments about him come from women, and I quote the opinions of two of the most beautiful women of that day. Consuelo Vanderbilt (an American, later the Duchess of Marlborough) wrote, 'The opinions he expressed and the doctrines he held seemed to be the products of *pure logic* ... he was gifted with a breadth of comprehension I have never seen equalled"; and Lady Cynthia Asquith said, "As for his being devoid of moral indignation, I often saw him white with anger; any *personal injustice* enraged him."

The italicised words could not more completely misportray Mr. Balfour, if the result of his actions is any test. The one thought-process which cannot have guided him, in pledging his country to Zionism, was *logic,* for no *logical* good could come of this for any of the parties concerned, his own country, the native inhabitants of Palestine, or (in my opinion) the mass of Jews, who had no intention of going there. As for injustice (unless Lady Cynthia intended to distinguish between "personal" and mass injustice), the million innocent beings who today have been driven into the Arabian wilderness (in the manner of the Levitical "scapegoat") offer the obvious answer. Anyway, there he was, Prime Minister of England, having succeeded "dear Uncle Robert" (Lord Salisbury, of the great house of Cecil) in 1902. Clearly he cannot at that instant have conceived, from nowhere, the notion of giving Uganda to the Zionists, so that "irresistible pressure" must have been at work before he took office. What went on in that earlier period is all mystery or, in truth, conspiracy ("labyrinthine intrigue"). When he became prime minister the mine was already laid, and to the end of his days Mr. Balfour apparently never realized that it *was* the mine of which all are today aware.

Dr. Herzl, despairing of the Czar, the Kaiser and the Sultan (the three potentates had been amiable but prudent and non-committal; they knew, what Mr. Balfour never learned, that Zionism was dynamite[9]) had declared: "England, great England, free England, England commanding the seas will understand our aims" (the reader will perceive for what purpose, in this view, England had become

great, free, and commander of the seas). When the Uganda offer showed the Talmudic directorate in Russia that Dr. Herzl was wrong in thinking that England would "understand" their needs, Dr. Weizmann was sent to London. He was preparing to overthrow Dr. Herzl and now becomes our chief witness to the hidden events of that time.

A young Englishman, with some modest petition, would have great trouble even today in penetrating the janitorial and secretarial defences of a Cabinet minister's private room. Young Dr. Weizmann from Russia, who wanted Palestine, was quickly ushered into that of Lord Percy ("in charge of African affairs").

Lord Percy was another scion of a great ruling family with an ancient tradition of public service and wise administration. According to Dr. Weizmann, he "expressed boundless astonishment that the Jews should ever so much as have considered the Uganda proposal, which he regarded as impractical on the one hand, and, on the other, a denial of the Jewish religion. Himself *deeply religious*, he was bewildered by the thought that Jews could even entertain the idea of any other country than Palestine as the centre of their revival; and he was delighted to learn from me that there were so many Jews who had emphatically refused. He added, 'If I were a Jew, I would not give a halfpenny for the proposition.'"

Presumably Dr. Weizmann did not inform Lord Percy of the unanimous longing of *the Jews in Palestine* to remove to Uganda. What he had heard, if his record is correct, was virtually an invitation to get rid of Dr. Herzl and a promise to support the claim to Palestine. He went away to prepare Dr. Herzl's discomfiture. He did not go empty-handed.

Possibly, in the fifty years that have elapsed, British ministers have learned that official notepaper should be kept where only those authorized may use it. On leaving Lord Percy's room Dr. Weizmann took some Foreign Office notepaper and on it wrote a report of the conversation, which he sent to Russia (where, under the Romanoffs and the Communist Czars alike, government stationery is not left lying around). In Russia, this document, written on offical Foreign Office paper, must have aroused feelings akin to

---

[9] For that matter, the successors of the Czars were of just the same opinion. Lenin in 1903 wrote, "This Zionist idea is entirely false and reactionary in its essence. The idea of a separate Jewish nation, which is utterly untenable scientifically, is reactionary in its political implications… The Jewish question is: assimilation or separateness? And the idea of a Jewish people is manifestly reactionary." And in 1913 Stalin reaffirmed this dictum. The destiny of the Jews, he said, was assimilation (in a Communist world, of course, in this opinion).

those which a holy ikon would cause in a moujik. Clearly it meant that the British Government had no further use for Dr. Herzl and would procure Palestine for the Zionists in Russia. Lord Percy, in today's idiom, had started something.

All else followed as if arranged by Greek gods: the triumph of the Zionists from Russia over Dr. Herzl, his collapse and death, the rejection of the Uganda offer. Then Dr. Weizmann moved to England, "the one country which seemed likely to show a genuine sympathy for a movement like ours," and where he could "live and work without let or hindrance, *at least theoretically*" (any compilation of classical understatements might include this passage in first place).

Dr. Weizmann chose Manchester for his residence. He says "by chance," but credulity balks. Manchester held Mr. Balfour's constituency; Manchester was the Zionist headquarters in England; the chairman of Mr. Balfour's party in Manchester was a Zionist (today the British Conservative Party is still enmeshed in these toils).

The Greek drama continued. Mr. Balfour's prime-ministership ended in a fiasco for his party when in the 1906 election eight out of nine Manchester seats were lost to it. He then faded temporarily from office. At that moment another personage entered the present narrative. Among the triumphant Liberal candidates was a rising young man with a keen nose for political winds, a Mr. Winston Churchill. He also sought election in Manchester and commended himself to the Zionist headquarters there, first by attacking the Balfour government's Aliens Bill (which set a brake on large-scale immigration from such places as Russia) and next by supporting Zionism. Thereon "the Manchester Jews promptly fell into line behind him as though he were a kind of latterday Moses; one of their leaders got up at an all-Jewish-meeting and announced that 'any Jew who votes against Churchill is a traitor to the common cause' " (Mr. R.C. Taylor). Mr. Churchill, elected, became Under Secretary for the Colonies. His public espousal of Zionism was simply a significant episode at that time; three decades later, when Mr. Balfour was dead, it was to have consequences as fateful as Mr. Balfour's own aberration.

To return to Mr. Balfour: his private thoughts were much with Zionism. At no time, as far as the annals disclose, did he give thought to the native inhabitants of Palestine, whose expulsion into the wilderness he was to cause. By coincidence, the election was being mainly fought around the question of the allegedly cruel treatment of some humble beings far away (this is an instance of the method of stirring up the passions of "the mob," recommended by Dr. Herzl and the Protocols). The electors knew nothing of Zionism and when they later became acquainted with it felt no concern for the menaced Arabs, because that side of the matter was not put before them by a press then "submissive." However, in 1906 their feelings were being inflamed about "Chinese slavery" and (Manchester being Manchester) they were highly indignant about it. At that time Chinese Coolies were being indentured for three years work in the South African gold mines. Those chosen counted themselves fortunate, but for electoral and "rabble-rousing" purposes in Manchester this was "slavery" and the battle was fought and won on that score. The victorious Liberals forgot "Chinese slavery" immediately after the counting of the votes, (and when their turn in office came outdid the Conservatives in their enthusiasm for Zionism).

Thus, while shouts of "Chinese slavery" resounded outside his windows, Mr. Balfour, closeted with a Zionist emissary from Russia, prepared something worse than slavery for the Arabs of Palestine. His captivation was complete before the interview began, as his niece and lifelong confidante (Mrs Dugdale) shows: "His interest in the subject was *whetted* ... by the refusal of the Zionist Jews to accept the Uganda offer ... The opposition aroused in him *a curiosity* which he found no means to satisfy ... He had asked his chairman in Manchester to fathom the reasons for the Zionist attitude ... Balfour's interest in the Jews and their history ... originated *in the Old Testament training* of his mother and in his Scottish upbringing. As he grew up his intellectual admiration and sympathy for certain aspects of the Jews in the modern world seemed to him of immense importance. I remember in childhood imbibing from him the idea that Christian religion and civilization owed to Judaism *an immeasurable debt, ill repaid.*"

Such was Mr. Balfour's frame of mind when he received Dr. Weizmann in a room of the old Queen's Hotel in dank and foggy Manchester in 1906. The proposition before him, if accepted, meant adding Turkey, in 1906, to England's enemies in any "future world war" and, if Turkey were defeated in it, engaging in perpetual warfare thereafter with the Arab world.

But calculations of national interest, moral principle and statesmanship, if the above quotations are the test, had deserted Mr. Balfour's mind.

He was in the grip of a "whetted" interest and an unsatisfied "curiosity"; it sounds like a young girl's romantic feeling about love. He had not been elected to decide what "debt" Christianity owed to Judaism, or if he decided that one was owing, to effect its repayment, from a third party's funds, to some canvasser professing title to collect. If there *were* any identifiable debt and any rational cause to link his country with it, and he could convince the country of this, he might have had a case. Instead, he decided privately that there was a debt, and that he was entitled to choose between claimants in favour of a caller from Russia, when the mass of Jews in England repudiated any notion of such a debt. History does not tell of a stranger thing.

Dr. Weizmann, forty years later, recorded that the Mr. Balfour whom he met "had only the most naive and rudimentary notion of the movement"; he did not even know Dr. Herzl's name, the nearest he could get to it being

"Dr. Herz." Mr. Balfour was already carried away by his enthusiasm for the unknown cause. He posed formal objections, but apparently only for the pleasure of hearing them overborne, as might a girl object to the elopement she secretly desires. He was much impressed (as Dr. Weizmann says) when his visitor said, "Mr. Balfour, supposing I were to offer you Paris instead of London, would you take it?" "But, Dr. Weizmann, we have London," he answered. Dr. Weizmann retorted, "But we had Jerusalem when London was a marsh."

Mr. Balfour apparently felt this to be a conclusive reason why the Ashkenazic Jews from Russia should be removed to Palestine. However, the only body of Jews whose interest he had any right to consider, those of England, had been working hard to dissuade him from getting entangled in Zionism, and he made a last feeble objection: "It is curious, Dr. Weizmann, the Jews I meet are quite different." Dr. Weizmann replied, "Mr. Balfour, you meet the wrong kind of Jew."

Mr. Balfour never again questioned the claim of the Zionists from Russia to be the right kind of Jew. "It was from that talk with Weizmann that I saw that the Jewish form of patriotism was unique. It was Weizmann's absolute refusal even to look at it" (the Uganda proposition) "which impressed me"; to these words Mrs Dugdale adds the comment, "The more Balfour thought about Zionism, the more his respect for it and his belief in its importance grew. His convictions took shape before the defeat of Turkey in the Great War, *transforming the whole future for the Zionists*." He also transformed the whole future for the entire West and for two generations of its sons. In this hotel-room meeting of 1906 Max Nordau's prophecy of 1903 about the shape of "the future world war" was given fulfilment.

As that war approached, the number of leading public men who privily espoused Zionism grew apace. They made themselves in fact co-conspirators, for they did not inform the public masses of any intention about Palestine. None outside the inner circle of "labyrinthine intrigue" knew that one was in their minds and would be carried out in the confusion of a great war, when parliamentary and popular scrutiny of acts of State policy was in suspense. The secrecy observed stamps the process as a conspiratorial one, originating in Russia, and it bore fruit in 1917.

The next meeting between Dr. Weizmann and Mr. Balfour was on December 14, 1914.[10] Then the First World War had just begun. The standing British army had been almost wiped out in France, and France itself faced catastrophe, while only the British Navy stood between England

---

[10] An instance of the difficulty of eliciting facts in this matter: Mrs. Dugdale quoted Dr. Weizmann as saying, "did not see him again *until 1916*," but contradicts this statement by another of her own, "*On December* 14, 1914, Dr. Weizmann had an appointment to see Balfour." This *implicit* mention of a second meeting on that date appears to be confirmed by Dr. Weizmann's own statement, that after seeing Mr. Lloyd George on *December* 3, 1914, he "*followed up at once* Lloyd George's suggestion about seeing Mr. Balfour."

and the gravest dangers. A war, costing Britain and France some three million lives, lay ahead, and the youth of Britain was rushing to join in the battle. The great cause was supposed to be that of overthrowing "Prussian militarism," liberating "small nations," and restoring "freedom and democracy."

Mr. Balfour was soon to be restored to office. His thoughts, when he met Dr. Weizmann again, were apparently far from the great battle in France. His mind was not with his country or his people. It was with Zionism and Palestine. He began his talk with Dr. Weizmann by saying, "I was thinking about that conversation of ours" (in 1906) "and I believe that when the guns stop firing *you may get your Jerusalem.*"

People who lived at that time may recall the moment and see how far from anything which they supposed to be at stake were these thoughts of Mr. Balfour. In the person of Mr. Balfour the Prophet Monk reappeared, but this time armed with power to shape the destiny of nations. Obviously "irresistible pressure" behind the scenes had gained great power and was already most effective in 1914. By that time the American people were equally enmeshed in this web of "labyrinthine intrigue," hidden from the general view, though they did not suspect it. They feared "foreign entanglements"; they wished to keep out of the war and had a president who promised he would keep them out of it. In fact, they were virtually in it, for "irresistible pressure" by that time was working as effectively in Washington as in London.

Douglas Reed

Chapter 29

THE AMBITION OF MR. HOUSE

While Mr. Balfour and his associates in this still secret enterprise moved towards power in England during the First World War, a similar group of men secretly took shape in the American Republic. The political machine they built produced its full result nearly fifty years later, when President Truman in effect set up the Zionist state in Palestine.

In 1900 Americans still clung to their "American dream," and the essence of it was to avoid "foreign entanglements." In fact the attack on Spain in Cuba in 1898 had already separated them from this secure anchorage, and the mysterious origins of that little war are therefore of continuing interest. The American public was caused to explode in warlike frenzy, in the familiar way, when it was told that the *Maine* was blown up in Havana harbour by a Spanish mine. When she was raised, many years later, her plates were found to have been blown *out* by an *inner* explosion (but by then "the mob" had long lost interest in the matter).

The effect of the Spanish-American war (continuing American "entanglement" in the affairs of others) lent major importance to the question: who was to exercise the ruling power in America, for the nature of any "entanglements" clearly depended on that. The answer to this question, again, was governed by the effect of an earlier war, the American Civil War of 1861-1865. The chief consequences of it (little comprehended by the contending Northerners and Southerners) was sensibly to change the nature, first of the population, and next of the government of the Republic.

Before the Civil War the American population was predominantly Irish, Scots-Irish, Scottish, British, German and Scandinavian, and from this amalgam a distinctly "American" individual evolved. In the direct sequence to that war the era of unrestricted immigration began, which in a few decades brought to America many millions of new citizens from Eastern and Southern Europe. These included a great mass of Jews from the Talmudic areas of Russia and Russian Poland. In Russia the rabbinate had stood between them and "assimilation" and this continued when they reached America. Thus the 20th Century, at its start, threw up the question, what part would their leaders acquire in the political control of the Republic and of its foreign undertakings. The later events showed that the Eastern conspiracy, in both its forms, entered America through this mass-immigration. The process of acquiring an ever-increasing measure of political power began, behind the scenes, about 1900 and was to become the major issue of American national life in the ensuing fifty years.

Douglas Reed

The man who first involved America in this process was a Mr. Edward Mandell House (popularly known as Colonel House, but he had no military service), a Southern gentleman, chiefly of Dutch and English descent, who grew up in Texas during the bitter Reconstruction period that followed the Civil War. He is a remarkable character in this tale. As other connoisseurs might exult in the taste of rare brandy, he loved the secret exercise of power through others, and candidly confided this to his diary. He shunned publicity (says his editor, Mr. Charles Seymour) "from a sardonic sense of humour which was tickled by the thought that he, unseen and often unsuspected, without great wealth or office, merely through the power of personality and good sense, was actually *deflecting the currents of history*." Few men have wielded so much power in complete irresponsibility: "it is easy enough for one *without responsibility* to sit down over a cigar and a glass of wine and decide what is best to be done," wrote Mr. House.

His editor's choice of words is exact; Mr. House did not *guide* American State policy, but *deflected it towards* Zionism, the support of the world-revolution, and the promotion of the world-government ambition. The *fact* of his exercise of secret power is proven. *His motives* for exercizing it in those directions are hard to discover, for his thoughts (as revealed by his diary and his novel) appear to have been so confused and contradictory that no clear picture emerges from them.

His immense daily record of his secret reign (the *Private Papers*) fully exposed *how* he worked. It leaves unanswered the question of *what* he ultimately wanted, or if he even knew what he wanted; as to that, his novel shows only a mind full of half-baked demagogic notions, never clearly thought out. The highfalutin apostrophe on the flyleaf is typical: "This book is dedicated to the unhappy many who have lived and died lacking opportunity, because, in the starting, the worldwide social structure was wrongly begun"; apparently this means that Mr. House, who held himself to be a religious man, thought poorly of the work of an earlier authority, described in the words, "In the beginning God created the heaven and the earth."

In the search for the origins of Mr. House's political ideas (which at first were akin to Communism; in later life, when the damage was done, he became more moderate) the student is cast on significant clues. His editor finds in his early thought a note "reminiscent of *Louis Blanc and the revolutionaries of 1848*." With this in mind I earlier directed the readers attention to Louis Blanc, the French revolutionary who for a moment, in 1848, seemed likely to play Lenin's part and summoned the assembly of workers' delegates which was an anticipation of the 1917 Soviets.

Such notions, in a Texan of the late 19th Century, are as unexpected as Buddhism in an Eskimo. Nevertheless, Mr. House in youth acquired these ideas; someone had implanted them in him. His middle name, Mandell, was that of "a Jewish merchant in Houston, who was one of his father's most intimate friends; the fact that the elder House conferred a Jewish name upon his son *indicates the family's attitude towards the race*" (Mr. Arthur D. Howden, his biographer). In Mr. House's novel the hero refuses all preferment to go and live in a humble East Side room with a Polish Jew, come to America after anti-Jewish disturbances in Warsaw caused by the murder there, by "a young Jew, baited beyond endurance," of the son of a high government official. In later life Mr. House's brother- in-law and counsellor was a Jew, Dr. Sidney Mezes, who was one of the initiators of this century's world-government plan in its earliest form (The League to Enforce Peace).

That is about all that can be elicited about the intellectual atmosphere of Mr. House's mind-formative period. In one of his most revealing passages Mr. House himself comments on the suggestion of ideas to others and shows, apparently without realizing it, how powerless he ultimately was, who thought himself all-powerful: "With the President, as with all other men I sought to influence, it was invariably my intention to make him think that ideas he derived from me were his own ... Usually, to tell the truth, *the idea was not original with me ... The most difficult thing in the world is to trace any idea to its source* ... We often think an idea to be original with ourselves when, in plain truth, *it was subconsciously absorbed from someone else.*"

He began to learn about politics in Texas when he was only eighteen, then discerning during a presidential election (1876) that "two or three men in the Senate and two or three in the House and the President himself ran the government. The others were merely figureheads ... Therefore I had no ambition to hold office, nor had I any ambition to speak." (He puts the same idea into the mouth of a politician in his novel of 1912; "In Washington ... I found that the government was run by a few men; that outside of this little circle no one was of much importance. It was my ambition to break into it if possible and my ambition now leaped so far as to want, not only to be of it, but later, to be IT ... The President asked me to undertake the direction of his campaign ... He was overwhelmingly nominated and re-elected ... and I was now well within the charmed circle and within easy reach of my further desire to have no rivals... *I tightened a nearly invisible coil around the people, which held them fast...*")

In that spirit Mr. House entered Texan politics: "I began at the top rather than at the bottom ... it has been my habit to put *someone else nominally at the head,* so that I could do the real work undisturbed by the demands which are made on a chairman ... Each chairman of the campaigns which I directed received the publicity and the applause of both the press and the people during the campaign ... they passed out of public notice within a few months ... and yet when the next campaign came around, the public and the press as eagerly accepted another figurehead."

Mr. House used Texas somewhat as a rising actor may use the provinces. He was so successful as a party-organizer there that at the turn of the century he was the real ruler of the state and sat daily in the office of its governor (appointed by Mr. House and long forgotten) at the State Capitol, where he chose State senators and congressmen and handled the requests of the many office-holders who habitually besiege a State governor. The provincial tour accomplished, he prepared to conquer the capital. By 1900 he was "tired of the position I occupied in Texas" and was "ready to take part in national affairs." After further preparation he began, in 1910 as the First World War approached, *"to look about for a proper candidate for the Democratic nomination for President."*

Thus Mr. House, aged fifty, was a president-maker. Until I read his *Private Papers* I was much impressed by the "uncanny knowledge" displayed by a leading American Zionist, Rabbi Stephen Wise, who in 1910 told a New Jersey audience: "On Tuesday Mr. Woodrow Wilson will be elected governor of your State; he will not complete his term of office as governor; in November 1912 he will be elected President of the United States; he will be inaugurated for the second time as president." This was fore-knowledge of the quality shown by the Protocols, Leon Pinsker and Max Nordau, but further research showed that Rabbi Wise had it from Colonel House!

Evidently Mr. Wilson had been closely studied by the group of secret men which then was coalescing, for neither Mr. House nor Rabbi Wise at that moment had met him! But Mr. House "became convinced that he had found his man, although he had never met him ... 'I turned to Woodrow Wilson ... as being the only man ... who in every way measured up to the office'" (Mr. Howden). The standard measurement used is indicated by a later passage: "The trouble with getting a candidate for president is that the man that is best fitted for the place cannot be nominated and, if nominated, could not be elected. The People seldom take the best man fitted for the job; therefore it is necessary to work for the best man who can be nominated and elected, and just now Wilson seems to be that man." (This description, again, is qualified by the allusion in Mr. House's novel to the methods used by a powerful group to elect "its *creature*" to the presidency).

The Zionist idea coupled itself to the revolutionary idea, among the group of men which was secretly selecting Mr. Woodrow Wilson for the presidency, in the person of this Rabbi Stephen Wise (born in Budapest, like Herzl and Nordau). He was the chief Zionist organizer in America and as such still something of a curiosity among the Jews of America, who at that time repudiated Zionism and distrusted the "Eastern Jews." Until 1900, as Rabbi Wise says, Zionism in America was confined to the immigrant Jews from Russia, who brought it with them from the Talmudic ghettoes there; the mass of American Jews were of German origins and would have none of it. Between 1900 and 1910, a million new Jewish immigrants arrived from Russia and under Zionist organization began to form an important body of voters; here was the link between Mr. House (whose election-strategy will be described) and Rabbi Wise. Rabbi Wise, who was known chiefly as a militant orator, if not an agitator, in labour questions, was not then a representative Jewish figure, and nevertheless (like Dr. Weizmann in England) he was the man to whom the political potentates *secretly* gave access and ear.

The strength of this secret group is shown by the fact that in 1910, when Mr. House had privately decided that Mr. Wilson should be the next president, Rabbi Wise publicly proclaimed that he *would* be that, and for two terms. This called for a rearrangement of the rabbi's politics, for he had always supported the Republican party; after Mr. House's secret selection of Mr. Wilson, he changed to the Democratic one. Thus Mr. House's confused "revolutionary" ideas and Zionism's perfectly clear ones arrived together on the doorstep of the White House. Agreement between the group was cordial: Mr. Wise states that (after the election) "we received warm and heartening help from Colonel House, close friend of the president ... *House not only made our cause the object of his very special concern but served as liaison officer between the Wilson administration and the Zionist movement.*" The close parallel between the course of these hidden processes in America and in England is here shown.

The secret of Mr. House's hold over the Democratic Party lay in the strategy which he had devised for winning elections. The Democratic party had been out of office for nearly fifty unbroken years and he had devised a method which made victory almost a mathematical certainty. The Democratic party was in fact to owe its victories in 1912 and 1916, as well as President Roosevelt's and President Truman's victories in 1932, 1936, 1940, 1944 and 1948 to the application of Mr. House's plan. In this electoral plan, which in its field perhaps deserves the name of genius, lies Mr. House's enduring effect on the life of America; his political *ideas* were never clearly formed and were frequently changed, so that he forged an instrument whereby the ideas *of others* were put into effect; the *instrument* itself was brilliantly designed.

In essence, it was a plan to gain the vote of the "foreign-born," the new immigrants, solidly for the Democratic party by making appeal to their racial feelings and especial emotional reflexes. It was worked out in great detail and was the product of a master hand in this particular branch of political science.

The unique, fantastic thing about this plan is that Mr. House published it, anonymously, in the very year, 1912, when Mr. Wilson, secretly "chosen," was publicly nominated and elected. In that busy year Mr. House found time to write, in thirty days, a novel called *Philip Dru: Administrator* (the unusual word recalls the allusion in the Protocols to "The Administrators whom we shall choose

......"). The chapter entitled "The Making of a President," which is obviously not fiction, makes this almost unreadable novel a historical document of the first importance.

In this chapter of his novel (which Mr. House was prompted to publish by his assiduous mentor, Dr. Sidney Mezes) an American Senator called Selwyn is depicted as setting about to "govern the Nation with an absolute hand, and yet not be known as the directing power." Selwyn is Mr. House. Apparently he could not resist the temptation to give a clue to his identity, and he caused "Selwyn" to invite the man he selected as his puppet-president ("Selwyn seeks a Candidate") to "dine with me in my rooms at the *Mandell House.*" Before that, Selwyn has devised "a nefarious plan," in concert with one John Thor, "the high priest of finance," whereby "a complete and compact organization," using *"the most infamous sort of deception regarding its real opinions and intentions,"* might "elect *its creature* to the Presidency." The financing of this secret league was "simple." "Thor's influence throughout commercial America was absolute ... Thor and Selwyn selected the thousand" (millionaires) "that were to give each ten thousand dollars ... Thor was to tell each of them that there was a matter, appertaining to the general welfare of the business fraternity, which needed twenty thousand dollars, and that he, Thor, would put up ten and wanted him to put up as much ... There were but few men of business ... who did not consider themselves fortunate in being called to New York by Thor and in being asked to join him in a blind pool looking to the safeguarding of wealth." The money of this "great corruption fund" was placed by Thor in different banks, paid at request by Selwyn to other banks, and from them transferred to the private bank of Selwyn's son-in-law; "the result was that the public had no chance of obtaining any knowledge of the fund or how it was spent."

On this basis of finance Selwyn selects his "creature," one Rockland, (Mr. Wilson), who on dining with Selwyn at "Mandell House" is told, that his responsibility as president will be "diffuse": "while a president has a constitutional right to act alone, he has no moral right to act contrary to the tenets and traditions of his party, *or to the advice of* the party leaders, for the country accepts the candidate, the party and the party *advisers* as a whole and not severally" (the resemblance between this passage and the allusions in the Protocols to "the responsibility of presidents" and the ultimate authority of their "advisers" is strong).

Rockland humbly agrees to this. (After the election, "drunk with power and the adulation of sycophants, once or twice Rockland asserted himself, and acted upon important matters without having first conferred with Selwyn. But, after he had been bitterly assailed by Selwyn's papers ... *he made no further attempts at independence.* He felt that he was utterly helpless in that strong man's hands, and so, indeed, he was." This passage in Mr. House's novel *of 1912,* written before Mr. Wilson's inauguration, may be compared with one in Mr.

House's *Private Papers of 1926*, recording his actual relationship with the candidate during the election campaign. It states that Mr. House edited the presidential candidate's speeches and instructed him not to heed any other advice, whereon Mr. Wilson admitted indiscretions and promised "*not to act independently in future.*" In the novel Selwyn is shown as telling Thor of Rockland' s attempt to escape the thrall: "When he told how Rockland had made an effort for freedom, and how he brought him back, squirming under his defeat, they laughed joyously"; this chapter is called "The Exultant Conspirators").

Another chapter shows *how* the election of the "creature" was achieved. The plan described makes electioneering almost into an exact science and still governs electioneering in America. It is based on Mr. House's fundamental calculation that about 80 percent of the electors would in any circumstance whatever vote for one of the two opposed parties in roughly equal proportions, and that expenditure of money and effort must therefore be concentrated on "the fluctuating 20 percent." Then it analyzes this 20 percent in detail until the small residue is isolated, on which the utmost effort is to be bent. Every ounce or cent of wasteful expenditure is eliminated and a mass of energy released to be directed against the small body of voters who can sway the result. This plan has done so much to "deflect" the course of events in America and the world that it needs to be summarized here at some length.

Selwyn begins the nomination campaign by eliminating all states where either his party or the other was sure to win. In this way he is free to give his entire thought to the twelve doubtful States, upon whose votes the election would turn. He divides these into units of five thousand voters, appointing for each unit a man on the spot and one at national headquarters. He calculated that of the five thousand, four thousand, in equal parts, probably could not be diverted from his own or the other party, and this brought his analysis down to *one thousand* doubtful voters, in each unit of five thousand in twelve States, on whom to concentrate. The local man was charged to obtain all possible information about their "race, religion, occupation and former party ties," and to forward this to the national man in charge of the particular unit, who was then responsible for reaching *each individual* by means of "literature, persuasion or perhaps by some more subtle argument." The duty of the two agents for each unit, one in the field and one at headquarters, was between them to "bring in a majority of the one thousand votes within their charge."

Meanwhile the managers of the other party were sending out "tons of printed matter to their State headquarters, which, in turn, distributed it to the country organizations, where it was dumped into a corner and given to visitors when asked for. Selwyn's committee used one-fourth as much printed matter, but it went in a sealed envelope, along with a cordial letter, directed to a voter that had as yet not decided how to vote. The opposition was sending speakers at great expense from one end of the country to the other … Selwyn sent men into his units to personally persuade each of the one thousand hesitating voters to support the Rockland ticket."

By means of this most skilful method of analysis, elimination and concentration Rockland, in the novel, (and Mr. Wilson, in fact) was elected in 1912. The concentrated appeal to the "one thousand hesitating voters" in each unit was especially directed to the "race, creed and colour" emotion, and the objects of attention were evidently singled out with that in mind. "Thus Selwyn won and Rockland became the keystone of the arch he had set out to build."

The remainder of the novel is unimportant but contains a few other significant things. Its sub-title is "A Story of Tomorrow, 1920- 1935." The hero, Philip Dru, is a young West Pointer under the influence of Karl Marx, who is elected leader of a mass movement by acclamation at an indignation meeting after Selwyn's and Thor's conspiracy has become known. The manner of this exposure is also interesting; Thor has a microphone concealed in his room (something little known in 1912 but today almost as familiar in politics as the Statesman's Yearbook) and, forgetting to disconnect it, his "exultant" talk with Selwyn after Rockland's election becomes known to his secretary, who gives it to the press; a most implausible episode is that the press published it! Then Dru assembles an army (armed, apparently by magic, with rifles and artillery), defeats the government forces at a single battle, marches on Washington, and proclaims himself "Administrator of the Republic." His first major action (and President Wilson's) is to introduce "a graduated income tax exempting no income whatsoever" (Karl Marx's Communist Manifesto demanded "a heavy progressive or graduated income tax"; the Protocols, "a progressive tax on property").

Dru next attacks Mexico. and the Central American Republics, also defeating them in one battle and thereafter uniting them under the American flag, which in the next chapter becomes also "the undisputed emblem of authority" over Canada and the British, French and other Possessions in the West Indies. Selwyn and Philip Dru are obviously both Mr. House. Selwyn is the superbly efficient party- organizer and secret wielder of Power; Dru is the muddled "utopian dreamer" (the Protocols) who does not know what to do with Power when he gets it. Inevitably, at the end, Mr. House did not know what to do with two characters who were in truth one man, and was compelled to merge them, as it were, by making Selwyn, the original villain of the piece, the confidant and bosom companion of Dru. After that, equally clearly, he did not know what to do with Dru, short of having him chased off by bears. Therefore he put him on a ship bound for an unknown destination with Gloria (a love-hungry girl who for fifty chapters has had to listen to Dru's incoherent plans for remoulding the world), and concludes: "Happy

Gloria! Happy Philip! ... Where were they bound? Would they return? These were the questions asked by all, but to which none could give answer."

In fact hardly anybody can have persisted to the end of this novel, and nobody would have cared where Philip and Gloria went, with one exception. There was one solitary being in the world for whom the story must have held a meaning as terrible and true as Dorian Gray's Portrait for Dorian: Mr. Woodrow Wilson. In that respect *Philip Drew: Administrator* is a unique work. Two questions haunt the student. Did Mr. Wilson read it? What prompted Mr. House (or *his* prompter) to publish this exact picture of what was going on at the very moment when "the creature" was being nominated and elected? Considered in that light the book becomes a work of sadistic mockery, and the reader becomes aware that the group of men around Mr. House must have been as malevolent as they are depicted to be in the chapter, "The Exultant Conspirators."

Is it conceivable that Mr. Wilson did *not* read it? Between his enemies and his friends, during an election campaign, someone must have put it in his hands. The student of history is bound to wonder whether the perusal of it, either then or later, may have caused the mental and physical state into which he soon fell. A few contemporary descriptions of him may be given as illustration (although they anticipate the chronology of the narrative a little). Mr. House later wrote of the man he had "chosen" and had elected ("the only one who in every way measured up to the office"), "I thought *at that time*" (1914) "and on several occasions afterwards, that the President wanted to die; certainly his attitude and his mental state indicated that he found *no zest in life*." When Mr. Wilson had not long been president Sir Horace Plunkett, the British Ambassador, wrote to Mr. House, "I paid my respects to the President, and was *shocked* to see him looking so worn; the change since January last is terribly marked." Six years later Sir William Wiseman, a British governmental emissary, told Mr, House, "I was *shocked* by his appearance ... His face was drawn and of a grey colour, and frequently twitching in a pitiful effort to control nerves which had broken down" (1919).[11]

Apparently a sure way to unhappiness is to receive high office as the instrument of others who remain unseen. Mr. Wilson inevitably looks wraithlike when contemplated against this record, now unfurled. Mr. House, Rabbi Wise and others around him seem to have gazed on him as collectors

---

[11] Strong resemblances occur in contemporary descriptions of Mr. Roosevelt, whom Mr. House also believed that he chose as a "figurehead." Mr. Robert E. Sherwood says with emphasis that Mr. Roosevelt was ever haunted "by the ghost of Wilson," When Mr, Roosevelt had been president two years his party manager, Mr. James Farley, wrote, "The President looked bad ... face drawn and his reactions slow" (1935), and two years later he was "*shocked* at the President's appearance" (1937). In 1943 Madame Chiang Kai-shek was "*shocked* by the President's looks"; in 1944, says Mr. Merriman Smith, "he looked older than I have ever seen him and he made an irrelevant speech," and Mr. John T. Flynn says the President's pictures "*shocked* the nation." In 1945 Miss Frances Perkins, a member of his cabinet, emerged from his office saying, "I can't stand it, the President looks horrible."

might on a specimen transfixed by a pin. In the circumstances, he must have been guided by guesswork, rather than by revelation, when at the age of twenty he decided that he would one day be president. This was known and Rabbi Wise once asked him, "When did you first think or dream of the presidency?" As the rabbi knew so much more than the President of the way in which the dream had been realized, he may have spoken tongue in cheek, and was evidently startled out of his customary deference when Mr. Wilson answered, "There never was a time after my graduation from Davidson College in South Carolina when I did not expect to become president," so that the rabbi asked sardonically, "Even when you were a teacher in a girls' college!" Mr. Wilson, apparently still oblivious, repeated, "There never was a time when I did not expect and prepare myself to become president." Between Mr. Wilson's secret "choice" by Mr. House in 1910 and his public nomination for president in 1912 he was prompted to make public obeisance to Zionism; at that point the American people became involved, as the British people had in fact been committed by the Uganda offer of 1903. Mr. Wilson, under coaching for the campaign, made a speech on "The rights of the Jews," in which he said, "I am not here to express our sympathy with our Jewish fellow-citizens but *to make evident our sense of identity with them. This* is *not their cause; it is America's."*

This could only have one meaning; it was a declaration of foreign policy, if Mr. Wilson were elected. No need existed to "make evident the sense of identity" between Americans and Americans, and Jews in America were in every respect free and equal; only a refusal to identify *themselves* with America could alter that and Mr. Wilson in effect proclaimed this refusal. He was specifically stating that Jewish "identity" was different and separate and that America, under him, would support this self-segregation as a cause.

To the initiates it was a pledge to Zionism. It was also an oblique allusion and threat to Russia, for the implication of Mr. Wilson's words was that he recognized the Jews in Russia (who were then the only organized Zionists) as representing *all* Jews. Thus he took the Balfourean part in the American production of this drama.

At that time all the Zionist propaganda was directed against Russia. Some thirty years had passed since the assassination of Czar Alexander II, who had incurred the enmity of the revolutionaries by his attempt to introduce a parliamentary constitution (Dr. Kastein remarked that Jewish participation in the assassination was "natural"). His successor, Alexander III, was forced to devote himself to combating the revolution. In Mr. Wilson's time Czar Nicholas II was resuming Alexander the Liberator's attempt to pacify and unify his country by enfranchising the people, and once more was being fiercely opposed by the Talmudic Zionists.

Then, at the very moment when Mr. Wilson made his implicit attack on Russian "intolerance," assassination was again used in Russia to destroy

Nicholas II's work. During the revolution of 1906 he had issued an imperial decree making Russia a constitutional monarchy, and in 1907 he introduced *universal suffrage.* The revolutionaries feared this liberating measure more than they feared any Cossacks and used the People's Assembly, when it first met, for riotous uproar, so that it had to be dissolved. The Czar then chose as his prime minister an enlightened statesman, Count Stolypin, who by decree enacted a *land reform followed by new elections.* The result was that in the second parliament he received a great ovation and the revolutionaries were routed (some 3,000,000 landless peasants became owners of their land).

The future of Russia at that moment looked brighter than ever before. Stolypin was a national hero and wrote, "Our principal aim is to strengthen the agricultural population. The whole strength of the country rests on it ... *Give this country ten years of inner tranquillity* and you will not know Russia."

Those ten tranquil years would have changed the course of history for the better; instead, the conspiracy intervened and produced the ten days that shook the world. In 1911 Count Stolypin went to Kieff, where the Czar was to unveil a monument to the murdered Liberator, Alexander II, and was shot at a gala performance in the theatre by a Jewish revolutionary, Bagroff (in 1917 a Jewish commissar, discovering that a girl among some fugitives was Count Stolypin's daughter, promptly shot her).

That happened in *September* 1911; in *December* 1911 Mr. Wilson, the candidate, made his speech expressing "a sense of identity" with the Jewish "cause." In *November* 1911 Mr. Wilson had for the first time met the man, Mr. House, who had "chosen" him in 1910 (and who had then already "lined up all my political friends and following" on Mr. Wilson's behalf). Mr. House reported to his brother-in-law, "Never before have I found *both the man and the opportunity.*"

Before the election Mr. House drew up a list of cabinet ministers (see *Philip Dru)* in consultation with a Mr. Bernard Baruch, who now enters this tale. He might be the most important of all the figures who will appear in it during the ensuing fifty years, for he was to become known as "the adviser" to several Presidents and in the 1950's was still advising President Eisenhower and Mr. Winston Churchill: In 1912 he was publicly known only as a highly successful financier. His biographer states that he contributed $50,000 to Mr. Wilson's campaign.

Then during the election campaign Mr. Wilson was made to feel the bit. After initial indiscretions he promised Mr. House (as earlier quoted, and compared with *Philip Dru)* "not to act independently in future." Immediately after the election he received Rabbi Stephen Wise "in a lengthy session" at which they discussed *"Russian affairs with special reference to the treatment of Jews"* (Mr. Wise). At the same moment Mr. House lunched with a Mr. Louis D. Brandeis, an eminent jurist and a Jew, and recorded that *"his mind and mine are in accord concerning most of the questions that are now to the fore."*

Thus three of the four men around Mr. Wilson were Jews and all three, at one stage or another, played leading parts in promoting the re-segregation of the Jews through Zionism and its Palestinian ambition. At that time Mr. Brandeis and Rabbi Wise were the leading Zionists in America, and Mr. Brandeis, at his entrance into the story, deserves a paragraph.

He was distinguished in appearance and in intellect, but neither he nor any other lawyer could have defined what constituted, in him, "a Jew." He did not practise the Judaist religion, either in the Orthodox or Reformed versions, and once wrote, "During most of my life my contact with Jews and Judaism was slight and I gave little thought to their problems." His conversion was of the irrational, romantic kind (recalling Mr. Balfour's): one day in 1897 he read at breakfast a report of Dr. Herzl's speech at the First Zionist Congress and told his wife, "There is a cause to which I could give my life."

Thus the fully assimilated American Jew was transformed in a trice. He displayed the ardour of the convert in his subsequent attacks on "assimilation": "Assimilation cannot be *averted* unless there be re-established *in the Fatherland* a centre from which the Jewish spirit may radiate." The Zionists from Russia never trusted this product of assimilation who now wanted to de-assimilate himself. They detested his frequent talk about "Americanism." He said, "My approach to Zionism was through Americanism," and to the Talmudists this was akin to saying that Zionism could be approached through "Russianism," which they were bent on destroying. In fact it was illogical to advocate the fiercest form of racial segregation while professing to admire American assimilationism, and Mr. Brandeis, for all his lawyer's skill, seems never truly to have understood the nature of Zionism. He became the Herzl of American Zionists (Rabbi Stephen Wise was their Weizmann) and was rudely dropped when he had served his turn. However, at the decisive moment, in 1917, he played a decisive part.

Such was the grouping around a captive president as the American Republic moved towards involvement in the First World War, and such was the cause which was to be pursued through him and through his country's involvement. After his election Mr. House took over his correspondence, arranged whom he should see or not receive, told Cabinet officers what they were to say or not to say, and so on. By then he had also found time to write and publish that astonishing novel. He wanted *power*, and achieved it, but what else he wanted, in the sequence, he never decided. Thus his ambition was purposeless, and in retrospect he now looks like Savrola, the hero of another politician's novel, of whom its author, Mr. Winston Churchill, said "Ambition was the motive force, and Savrola was powerless to resist it." At the end of his life Mr. House, lonely and forgotten, greatly disliked Philip Dru.

But between 1911 and 1919 life was delightful for Mr. House. He loved the feeling of power for its own sake, and withal was too kind to want to hurt Rockland in the White House:

"It was invariably my intention, with the President as with all other men I sought to influence, to make him think that ideas he derived from me were his own. In the nature of things I have thought more on many things than had the President, and I had had opportunities to discuss them more widely than he. But no man honestly likes to have another man steer his conclusions. We are all a little vain on that score. Most human beings are too much guided by personal vanity in what they do. It happens that I am not. It does not matter to me who gets the credit for an idea I have imparted. The main thing is to get the idea to work. Usually, to tell the truth, *the idea was not original with me...*" (and as previously quoted, from Mr. Howden).

Thus someone "steered" Mr. House, who steered Mr. Wilson, to the conclusion that a body of men in the Talmudic areas of Russia ought to be put in possession of Palestine, with the obvious consequence that a permanent source of world warfare would be established there, and that the Jews of the world ought to be re-segregated from mankind. In this plan the destruction of Russia and the spread of the world-revolution also were foreseeably involved.

At that period (1913) an event occurred which seemed of little importance then but needs recording here because of its later, large consequence. In America was an organization called *B'nai B'rith* (Hebrew for "Children of the Covenant"). Founded in 1843 as a fraternal lodge exclusively for Jews, it was called "purely an American institution," but it put out branches in many countries and today claims to "represent all Jews throughout the world," so that it appears to be part of the arrangement described by Dr. Kastein as "the Jewish international." In 1913 B'nai B'rith put out a tiny offshoot, the "Anti-Defamation League." It was to grow to great size and power; in it the state-within-states acquired a kind of secret police and it will reappear in this story.

With the accession of Mr. Wilson and the group behind his presidential chair, the stage was set for the war about to begin. The function of America, in promoting the great supernational "design" through that war, was to be auxiliary. In that first stage England was cast for the chief part and the major objective, control of the British government, had not been fully attained when the war began. Thus the story now recrosses the Atlantic to England, where Mr. Balfour was moving again towards office. The leading men there were still resistant to the hidden purpose and plan and were intent on fighting the war, and winning it as quickly as possible, in the place where it began, Europe. They had to be brought into line if the process foretold by Max Nordau in 1903 was to be accomplished. Therefore the resistant men had to be disciplined or removed.

From 1914 to 1916, then, the story becomes that of the struggle to displace these men in England, and to supplant them by others who, like Mr. Wilson, would fall into line.

Chapter 30

THE DECISIVE BATTLE

The 1914-1918 war was the first war of nations, as distinct from armies; the hands that directed it reached into every home in most European, and many non-European countries. This was a new thing in the world, but it was foretold by the conspirators of Communism and Zionism. The Protocols of 1905 said that resistance to the plan therein unfolded would be met by "universal war"; Max Nordau in 1903 said that the Zionist ambition in Palestine would be achieved through "the coming world war."

If such words were to be fulfilled, and thus to acquire the status of "uncanny knowledge" revealed in advance of the event, the conspiracy had to gain control of the governments involved so that their acts of State policy, and in consequence their military operations, might be diverted to serve the ends of the conspiracy, not national interests. The American president was already (i.e., from 1912) the captive of secret "advisers," as has been shown; and if Mr. House's depiction of him (alike in the anonymous novel and the acknowledged *Private Papers)* is correct, he fits the picture given in the earlier Protocols, "... we replaced the ruler by a caricature of a president, taken from the mob, from the midst of our puppet creatures, our slaves."

However, Mr. Wilson was not required to take much active part in furthering the great "design" in the early stages of the First World War; he fulfilled his function later. At its start the main objective was to gain control of the British Government. The struggle to do this lasted two years and ended in victory for the intriguers, whose activities were unknown to the public masses. This battle, fought in the "labyrinth" of "international politics," was the decisive battle of the First World War. That is to say (as no decision is ever final, and can always be modified by a later decision), it produced the greatest and most enduring effects on the further course of the 20th Century; these effects continued to dominate events between the wars and during the Second World War, and in 1956 may be seen to form the most probable cause of any third "universal war." No clash of arms during the 1914-1918 war produced an effect on the future comparable with that brought about by the capture of the British Government in 1916. This process was hidden from the embroiled masses. From start to finish Britons believed that they had only to do with an impetuous Teutonic warlord, and Americans, that the incorrigible quarrelsomeness of European peoples was the root cause of the upheaval.

In England in 1914 the situation brought about in America by the secret captivity of President Wilson did not prevail. The leading political and military posts were held by men who put every proposal for the political and military conduct of the war to one test: would it help win the war and was it in their country's interest. By that test Zionism failed. The story of the first two years of the four- year war is that of the struggle behind the scenes to dislodge these obstructive men and to supplant them by other, submissive men.

Before 1914 the conspiracy had penetrated-only into antechambers (apart from the Balfour Government's fateful step in 1903). After 1914 a widening circle of leading men associated themselves with the diversionary enterprise, Zionism. Today the "practical considerations" (of public popularity or hostility, votes, financial backing and office) which influence politicians in this matter are well known, because they have been revealed by many authentic publications. At that time, a politician in England must have been exceptionally astute or far-sighted to see in the Zionists the holders of the keys to political advancement. Therefore the Balfourean motive of romantic infatuation *may* have impelled them; the annals are unclear at that period and do not explain the unaccountable. Moreover, the English have always tended to give their actions a guise of high moral purpose, and to persuade themselves to believe in it; this led Macaulay to observe that "we know no spectacle so ridiculous as the British public in one of its periodical fits of morality."

Possibly, then, *some* of the men who joined in this intrigue (which it undoubtedly was) *thought* they were doing right. This process of self-delusion is shown by the one statement, discoverable by me, which clearly identifies a group of pro-Zionists in high English places at that time, and offers a motive of the kind satirized by Lord Macaulay.

This comes from a Mr. Oliver Locker-Lampson, early in this century a Conservative Member of parliament. He played no great part and was notable, if at all, only for his later, fanatical support of Zionism in and outside parliament, but he was a personal friend of the leading men who fathered Zionism on the British people. In 1952, in a London weekly journal, he wrote:

"Winston, Lloyd George, Balfour and I were brought up vigorous Protestants, who believe in the coming of a new Saviour when Palestine returns to Jews." This is the Messianic idea of Cromwell's Millenarians, foisted on the 20th Century. Only the men named could say if the statement is true, and but one of them survives. Whether this is the true basis of Protestantism, vigorous or otherwise, readers may judge for themselves. None will contend that it is a sound basis for the conduct of State policy or military operations in war. Also, of course, it expresses the same impious idea that moved the Prophet Monk and all such men: that God has forgotten his duty and, having defaulted, must have it done for him. Anyway, a group had formed and we may as well use for it the name which this man gave it: the Vigorous Protestants.

The First World War began, with these Vigorous Protestants ambitious to attain power so that they might divert military operations in Europe to the cause of procuring Palestine for the Zionists. Dr. Weizmann, who had not been idle since we last saw him closeted with Mr. Balfour at Manchester in 1906, at once went into action: "now is the time ... the political considerations will be favourable," he wrote in October 1914. He sought out Mr. C.P. Scott, editor of the *Manchester Guardian*, which was much addicted (then as now) to any non-native cause. Mr. Scott was enchanted to learn that his visitor was "a Jew who hated Russia" (Russia, England's ally, at that moment was saving the British and French armies in the west by attacking from the east) and at once took him to breakfast with Mr. Lloyd George, then Chancellor of the Exchequer. Mr. Lloyd George (whom Dr. Weizmann found "extraordinarily flippant" about the war in Europe) was "warm and encouraging" about Zionism and suggested another meeting with Mr. Balfour. This ensued on December 14, 1914. Mr. Balfour, recalling the 1906 conversation, "quite nonchalantly" asked if he could help Dr. Weizmann in any practical way, receiving the answer, "Not while the guns are roaring; when the military situation becomes clearer I will come again" (Mrs Dugdale, with whose account Dr. Weizmann's agrees: "I did not follow up this opening, the time and place were not propitious." This was the meeting at which Mr. Balfour gratuitously said that "when the guns stop firing you may get your Jerusalem").

Dr. Weizmann did not grasp eagerly at Mr. Balfour's "quite nonchalant" offer for a good reason. The Zionist headquarters at that moment was *in Berlin* and Dr. Weizmann's colleagues there were convinced that Germany would win the war. Before they put any cards on the table they wished to be sure about that. When, later, they resolved to stake on the Allied card, "the guns" were still "roaring." Dr. Weizmann was not deterred by thought of the carnage in Europe from "following up the opening." As he truly told Mr. Balfour (and Mr. Balfour certainly did not understand just what was in his visitor's mind), "the time ... was not propitious," and Dr. Weizmann meant to wait "until the military situation becomes clearer."

Significantly, some of the men concerned in these publicly-unknown interviews seem to have sought to cover up their dates; at the time the fate of England was supposed to be their only preoccupation. I have already given one apparent instance of this: the confusion about the date of Mr. Balfour's second meeting with Dr. Weizmann, the one just described. Mr. Lloyd George, similarly, wrote that *his first* meeting with Dr. Weizmann occurred *in 1917*, when he was Prime Minister, and called it a "chance" one. Dr. Weizmann disdainfully corrected this: "actually Mr. Lloyd George's advocacy of the Jewish homeland *long predated his accession to the premiership and we had several meetings in the intervening years.*"

A third meeting with Mr. Balfour followed, "a tremendous talk which lasted several hours" and went off "extraordinarily well." Dr. Weizmann, once more, expressed his "hatred for Russia," England's hard-pressed ally. Mr. Balfour mildly wondered "how a friend of England could be so anti-Russian when Russia was doing so much to help England win the war." As on the earlier occasion, when he alluded to the anti-Zionist convictions of British Jews, he seems to have had no true intention to remonstrate, and concluded, "It is a great cause you are working for; you must come *again and again.*"

Mr. Lloyd George also warned Dr. Weizmann that "there would undoubtedly be strong opposition from certain Jewish quarters" and Dr. Weizmann made his stock reply, that in fact "rich and powerful Jews were for the most part against us." Strangely, this insinuation seems greatly to have impressed the Vigorous Protestants, who were mostly rich and powerful men, and they soon became as hostile to their fellow-countrymen, the Jews of England, as their importuner, Dr. Weizmann from Russia.

Opposition to Zionism developed from another source. In the *highest* places still stood men who thought only of national duty and winning the war. They would not condone "hatred" of a military ally or espouse a wasteful "sideshow" in Palestine. These men were Mr. Herbert Asquith (Prime Minister), Lord Kitchener (Secretary for War), Sir Douglas Haig (who became Commander-in-Chief in France), and Sir William Robertson (Chief-of-Staff in France, later Chief of the Imperial General Staff).

Mr. Asquith was the last Liberal leader in England who sought to give "Liberalism" a meaning concordant with national interest and religious belief, as opposed to the meaning which the term has been given in the last four decades (the one attributed to it by the Protocols: "When we introduced into the State organism the poison of Liberalism its whole political complexion underwent a change; States have been seized with a mortal illness, blood-poisoning ..."). With his later overthrow Liberalism, in the first sense, died in England; and in fact the party itself fell into decline and collapsed, leaving only a name used chiefly as "cover" by Communism and its legion of "utopian dreamers."

Mr. Asquith first learned of the intrigue that was brewing when he received a proposal for a Jewish state in Palestine from a Jewish minister, Mr. Herbert Samuel, who had been present at the Weizmann-Lloyd George breakfast in December 1914; these two were informed of it beforehand. Mr. Asquith wrote, "... Samuel's proposal in favour of the British annexation of Palestine, a country of the size of Wales, much of it barren mountain and part of it waterless. He thinks we might plant in this not very promising territory about *three or four million Jews* ... I am not attracted to this proposed addition to our responsibilities ... The only other partisan of this proposal is Lloyd George, and I need not say that he does not care a damn for the Jews or their part of the future ..."

Mr. Asquith (who correctly summed-up Mr. Lloyd George) remained of the same opinion to the end. Ten years later, when long out of office, he visited Palestine, and wrote, "This talk of making Palestine a Jewish National Home seems to me just as fantastic as it has always been." In 1915, by his adverse response, he made himself, and his removal from office, the object of the intrigue. As long as he could he kept his country out of the Palestinian adventure; he accepted the opinion of the military leaders, that the war could only be won (if at all) on the main battlefield, in Europe.

Lord Kitchener, who held this view, was of immense authority and public popularity. The paramount military objective at that stage, he held, was to keep Russia in the war (the Zionists wanted Russia's destruction and so informed the Vigorous Protestants). Lord Kitchener was sent to Russia by Mr. Asquith in June 1916. The cruiser *Hampshire,* and Lord Kitchener in it, vanished. Good authorities concur that he was the one man who might have sustained Russia. A formidable obstacle, both to the world-revolution there and to the Zionist enterprise, disappeared. Probably Zionism could not have been foisted on the West, had he lived. I remember that the soldiers on the Western Front, when they heard the news, felt that they had lost a major battle. Their intuition was truer than they knew.

After that only Asquith, Robertson, Haig and the Jews of England stood between Zionism and its goal. The circle of intrigue widened. The *Times* and *Sunday Times* joined the *Manchester Guardian* in its enthusiasm for Zionism, and in or around the Cabinet new men added themselves to Balfour and Lloyd George. Lord Milner (about to join it) announced that "if the Arabs think that Palestine will become an Arab country they are much mistaken"; at that moment Colonel Lawrence was rousing the Arabs to revolt against an enemy of the Allies, the Turk. Mr. Philip Kerr (Later Lord Lothian, at that time Mr. Lloyd George's amanuensis) decided that "a Jewish Palestine" must come out of the chastisement of "the mad dog in Berlin" (as the Kaiser was depicted to "the mob"). Sir Mark Sykes, Chief Secretary of the War Cabinet, was "one of our greatest finds" (Dr. Weizmann), and broadened the idea into "the liberation of the Jews, the Arabs and the Armenians."

By means of such false suggestions is "the multitude" ever and again "persuaded." The Arabs and Armenians were where they always had been and did not aspire to be removed elsewhither. The Jews in Europe were as free or unfree as other men; the Jews *of Palestine* had demonstrated their eagerness to go to Uganda, the Jews of Europe and America wanted to stay where they were, and only the Judaized Khazars of Russia, under their Talmudic directors, wanted possession of Palestine. Sir Mark's invention of this formula was one more misfortune for posterity, for it implied that the Palestinian adventure was but one of several, all akin. Unlike the other Vigorous Protestants, he was an expert in Middle Eastern affairs and must have known better.

Another recruit, Lord Robert Cecil, also used this deceptive formula, "Arabia for the Arabs, Judea for the Jews, Armenia for the Armenians" (Armenian liberation was quite lost sight of in the later events), and his case also is curious, for statesmanship is inborn in the Cecils. Zionism had strange power to produce aberrations in wise men. Mr. Balfour (a half Cecil) had a Cecilian wisdom in other matters; he produced a paper on the reorganization *of Europe* after the war which stands today as a model of prudent statesmanship, whereas in the question of Zionism he was as a man drugged.

Lord Cecil's case is similarly unaccountable. I remember a lecture he gave in Berlin (in the 1930's) about the League of Nations. Tall, stooped, hawk-visaged, ancestrally gifted, he uttered warnings about the future as from some mountain-top of revelation, and sepulchrally invoked "the Hebrew prophets." As a young journalist I was much impressed without comprehending what he meant. Today, when I have learned a little, it is still mysterious to me; if Jeremiah, for instance, was anything he was an anti-Zionist.

Yet Dr. Weizmann says specifically of Lord Robert, "To him the re-establishment of a Jewish Homeland in Palestine *and the organization of the world in a great federation were complementary features of the next step in the management of human affairs ... One of the founders of the League of Nations, he considered the Jewish Homeland to be of equal importance with the League itself.*" Here the great secret is out; but did Lord Robert discern it? The conquest of Palestine for the Zionists from Russia was but "the next step" in "*the management* of human affairs" (Lord Acton's dictum about "the design" and "the managers" recurs to mind). The "world federation" is depicted as a concurrent part of the *same* plan. The basic theory of that league, in its various forms, has proved to be that *nations* should surrender their *sovereignty*, so that separate nationhood will disappear (this, of course, is also the basic principle of the Protocols). But if nations are to disappear, why should the process of their obliteration begin with the creation of *one* new nation, unless it is to be the supreme authority in "the management of human affairs" (this conception of the one *supreme* nation runs alike through the Old Testament, the Talmud, the Protocols and literal Zionism).

Thus Lord Robert's espousal of Zionism becomes incomprehensible, for his inherited wisdom made him fully aware of the perils of world-despotism and at that very period he wrote to Mr. House in America:

"That we ought to make some real effort to establish a peace machinery when this war is over, I have no doubt ... One danger seems to me to be that too much will be aimed at... Nothing did more harm to the cause of peace than the breakdown of the efforts after Waterloo in this direction. It is now generally forgotten that the Holy Alliance was originally started as a *League to Enforce Peace*. Unfortunately, it allowed its energies to be diverted in such a way that it really became a *league to uphold tyranny*, with the consequence that it was generally discredited, *besides doing infinite harm in other ways* ... The example shows how easily the best intended schemes may come to grief."

The quotation shows that Lord Cecil should have been aware of the danger of "diverting energies"; it also shows that he misunderstood the nature of Zionism, if the opinion attributed to him by Dr. Weizmann is correct. When he wrote these words, a new "League to Enforce Peace" was being organized in America by Mr. House's own brother-in-law, Dr. Mezes; it was the precursor of the various world-government flotations that have followed, in which the intention of powerful groups to set up "a league to uphold tyranny" in the world has been plainly revealed.

Thus, as the second twelvemonth of the First World War ended, the Vigorous Protestants, who looked toward Palestine, not Europe, were a numerous band of brothers, husking the Russian-Zionist core. Messrs' Leopold Amery, Ormsby-Gore and Ronald Graham joined the "friends" above named. Zionism had its foot in every department of government save the War Office. Whatever the original nature of their enthusiasm for Zionism, material rewards at this stage undeniably beckoned; the intrigue was aimed at dislodging men from office and taking their places.

The obstructive prime minister, Mr. Asquith, was removed at the end of 1916. The pages of yesterday now reveal the way this was done, and the passage of time enables the results to be judged. The motive offered to the public masses was that Mr. Asquith was ineffective in prosecuting the war. The sincerity of the contention may be tested by what followed; the first act of his successors was to divert forces to Palestine and in the sequence to that Mr. Lloyd George nearly lost the war entirely.

On November 25, 1916 Mr. Lloyd George recommended that his chief retire from the chairmanship of the War Council in favour of Mr. Lloyd George. Normally such a demand would have been suicidal, but this was a coalition government and the Liberal Mr. Lloyd George was supported in his demand by the Conservative leaders, Mr. Bonar Law and Sir Edward Carson, so that it was an ultimatum. (These two presumably had honest faith in Mr. Lloyd George's superior abilities; they cannot be suspected of Tory duplicity deep enough to foresee that he would ultimately destroy the Liberal Party!)

Mr. Lloyd George also required that the incompetent (and Conservative) Mr. Balfour be ousted from the First Lordship of the Admiralty. The Liberal prime minister indignantly refused either to surrender the War Council or to dismiss Mr. Balfour *(December 4)*. He then received *Mr. Balfour's resignation,* whereon he at once sent Mr. Balfour a copy of his own letter refusing to dismiss Mr. Balfour. Thereon Mr. Balfour, though kept indoors by a bad cold, found strength to send another letter in which he *insisted* on resigning, as Mr. Lloyd George had demanded, and Mr. Lloyd George also resigned.

Douglas Reed

Mr. Asquith was left alone. On *December 6* Mr. Balfour (resigned at Mr. Lloyd George's dictate) felt well enough to receive Mr. Lloyd George. That afternoon the party leaders met and announced that they would gladly serve *under Mr. Balfour.* Mr. Balfour declined but offered gladly to serve *under Mr. Lloyd George.* Mr. Lloyd George then became Prime Minister and appointed the incompetent Mr. Balfour Foreign Secretary. Thus the two men privily committed to support Zionism moved into the highest political offices and from that moment the energies of the British Government were directed to the procurement of Palestine for the Zionists above all other purposes. (In 1952 I read a letter in the Jewish journal *Commentary,* of New York, intimating that the Jews of North Wales had by their votes played the decisive part in effecting Mr. Lloyd George's election. I am credibly informed, also, that in his attorney's practice he received much Zionist business, but cannot myself vouch for that. In his case the explanation of venal motives cannot be discounted, in my judgment; the inaccuracy of his statements about his relations with Zionism, which Dr. Weizmann twice corrects, is suggestive).

Thus the central figures on the stage regrouped themselves. Mr. Lloyd George, a small, smart-lawyer in a cutaway among taller colleagues, many still in the old frock coat, looked like a cocksparrow among crows. Beside him stood Mr. Balfour, tall, limp, ever ready with a wearily cynical answer to an honest question, given to a little gentle tennis; I see him now, strolling dreamily across Saint James's Park to the House. Around these two, the Greek chorus of cabinet ministers, junior ministers and high officials who had discovered their Vigorous Protestantism. Some of these fellow-travellers of Zion may have been honestly deluded, and not have realized in what chariot they rode. Mr. Lloyd George was the first major figure in a long line of others who knew a band-wagon when they saw one; through them the innocent words, "twentieth century politician," gained an ominous meaning and the century owes much of its ordeal to them.

As to the diversion of British military strength to an alien purpose, one stout resistant alone remained after the death of Lord Kitchener and removal of Mr. Asquith. The sturdy figure of Sir William Robertson faced the group around Mr. Lloyd George. Had he joined it, he could have had titles, receptions, freedoms, orders, gilt boxes, and ribbons down to his waistbelt; he could have had fortunes for "the rights" of anything he wrote (or any ghost for him); he could have had boulevards named after him and have paraded through cheering cities in Europe and America; he could have had Congress and the House of Commons rise to him and have entered Jerusalem on a white horse. He did not even receive a peerage, and is rare among British field marshals in this.

He was the only man ever to have risen to that highest rank from private. In England of the small professional army this was a great achievement. He was simple, honest, heavy, rugged in feature; he was of the

290

people and looked like a handsome sergeant-major. His only support, in his struggle, lay in the commander in France, Sir Douglas Haig, who was of the cavalry officer caste, good-looking and soldierly, the private soldier's ideal of what an officer should be. Robertson, the gruff old soldier, had (reluctantly) to attend some of the money-raising festivities with which society ladies, in wartime, keep themselves occupied, and at one such saw Lady Constance Stewart Richardson, who felt moved to perform dances in the draperies and manner of Isadora Duncan. A general, noticing Robertson's impatience, said, "You must admit she has a very fine leg." "Umph, just like any other damn leg," growled Robertson.

On this last man felt the task of thwarting the diversion of British armies to Palestine, if he could. He considered all proposals exclusively in their military bearing on the war and victory; if it would help win the war, motive was to him indifferent; if it would not, he opposed it without regard for any other consideration. On that basis he decided that the Zionist proposal was for a dangerous "sideshow" which could only delay and imperil victory. He never discussed and may not even have suspected any political implications; these were irrelevant to him.

He had told Mr. Asquith in 1915, "Obviously the most effective method" (of defeating the Central Powers) "is to *defeat decisively the main German armies, which are still on the Western Front.*" Therefore he counselled urgently against, "*auxiliary campaigns in minor theatres and the depletion of the forces in France ... The one touchstone by which all plans and proposals must be tested is their bearing on the object of the war.*"

Peoples engaged in war, are fortunate if their leaders reason like this, and unfortunate if they deviate from this reasoning. By that conclusive logic the Palestinian enterprise (a *political* one) was out. When Mr. Lloyd George became prime minister he *at once* bent all his efforts on diverting strength to a major campaign in Palestine: "When I formed my government I *at once* raised with the War Office the question of *a further campaign into Palestine.* Sir William Robertson, who was most anxious to avert the danger of any troops being sent from France to Palestine ... *strongly opposed this and for the time being won his point.*"

Sir William Robertson corroborates: "*Up to December 1916*" (when Mr. Lloyd George became prime minister) "operations beyond the Suez Canal had been essentially defensive in principle, *the government and General Staff alike ... recognizing the paramount importance of the struggle in Europe and the need to give the armies there the utmost support. This unanimity between ministers and soldiers did not obtain after the premiership changed hands ... The fundamental difference of opinion was particularly obtrusive in the case of Palestine ... The new War Cabinet had been in existence only a few days when it directed the General Staff to examine the possibility of extending the operations in Palestine ... The General Staff put the requirements at three additional divisions and these could only be obtained from the armies on the Western Front*

... The General Staff said the project would prove a great source of embarrassment and injure our prospects of success in France ... These conclusions were disappointing to Ministers, *... who wished to see Palestine occupied at once, but they could not be refuted* ... In February the War Cabinet *again* approached the Chief of the General Staff, asking what progress was being made with the preparation of an autumn campaign in Palestine."

These passages show how the course of State policy and of military operations in war may be "deflected" by political pressure behind the scenes. In this case, the issue of the battle between the politicians and the soldier affects the lives of nations at the present time, the 1950's.

Mr. Lloyd George then reinforced himself by a move which once more shows the long thought that must have gone into the preparation of this enterprise, and the careful selection of "administrators," to support it, that must have gone before. He proposed that the War Cabinet "take the Dominions into counsel in a much larger measure than hitherto in the prosecution of the war." Put in that way, the idea appealed greatly to the public masses in England. Fighting-men from Canada, Australia, New Zealand and South Africa were campaigning shoulder to shoulder with their own sons. The immediate response of the overseas countries to the "old country's" danger had touched the native Briton's heart, and he was very happy that their leaders should join more closely with his own in "prosecuting the war."

However, "the diplomat's word" (and his intention) differed greatly from his deed; Mr. Lloyd George's proposal was merely a "cover" for bringing to London General Smuts from South Africa, who was regarded by the Zionists as their most valuable "friend" outside Europe and America, and General Smuts was brought across to propose the conquest of Palestine!

The voting-population in South Africa is so equally divided between Afrikaners and English-speaking South Africans that the "fluctuating 20 percent" was, if anything, more decisive there than in America. The Zionists felt able, and possibly General Smuts believed they were able, to "deliver" an election-winning vote. One of his colleagues, a Mr. B.K. Long (a Smuts Member of Parliament and earlier of the London *Times)* wrote that "the substantial Jewish vote, which was firmly loyal to Smuts and his party," greatly helped him to such electoral victories. His biography mentions a large legacy from "a rich and powerful Jew" (an example of the falsity of Dr. Weizmann's charge against rich and powerful Jews; apropos, the same Sir Henry Strakosch bequeathed a similar gift to Mr. Winston Churchill) and gifts from some unnamed quarter of a house and car. Thus the party-political considerations which weighed with him were similar to those of Mr. Lloyd George, Mr. House and later others, and material factors are reasonably apparent in his case.

However, the religious (or pseudo-religious) motive is frequently invoked in his biographies (as it was sometimes claimed by Mr. Lloyd George). They state that he *preferred* the Old Testament to the New, and quote him as saying, "The older I get the more of an Hebraist I become." I met him many years later, when I knew how important a part he played in this earlier story. He was then (1948) much troubled about the declining situation in the world, and the explosive part of Palestine in it. He was of fine appearance, fit and erect when nearly eighty, keen-eyed, and wore a little beard. He was ruthless and on occasion could have been depicted in a cruel light (had the mass-newspapers been arrayed against instead of behind him) and his political astuteness equalled Mr. Lloyd George's. Propaganda portrayed him as the great architect of Anglo-Boer reconciliation; when he died at his lonely Transvaal farm the two races were more at variance than ever, so that true reconciliation remained for later generations to effect. In South Africa he was a divisive force and all knew that the real power behind his party was that of the gold and diamond mining group, not of England; Johannesburg was the base of his political strength. In 1948, when the test came, he was the first to support Zionism against a hard-pressed British Government.

On March 17, 1917 General Smuts reached London, amid unprecedented ovations, and the overthrow of Sir William Robertson at last loomed near. General Smuts's triumphant reception was an early example of the now familiar "build-up" of selected public figures by a push-button press. The method, in another form, is known among the primitive peoples of his native Africa, where "M'Bongo," the Praisemaker, stalks before the chief, proclaiming him "Great Elephant, Earth Shaker, Stabber of Heaven" and the like.

General Smuts was presented to the Imperial War Cabinet as "one of the most brilliant generals of the war" (Mr. Lloyd George). General Smuts had in fact conducted a small colonial campaign in South West Africa, and when he was summoned to London was waging an uncompleted one in East Africa against "a small but efficiently bush-trained army of 2,000 German officers and 20,000 native askaris" (his son, Mr. J.C. Smuts). The tribute thus was generous (Mr. Lloyd George's opinion of professional soldiers was low: "There is no profession where experience and training countless in comparison with judgment and flair").

By that time, the better to seclude themselves from "the generals" (other than General Smuts) Mr. Lloyd George and his small war- waging committee had taken a private house "where they sit twice a day and occupy their whole time with military policy, which is my job; a little body of politicians, quite ignorant of war and all its needs, are trying to run the war themselves" (Sir William Robertson). To this cloistered body, in *April 1917,* General Smuts by invitation presented his recommendations for winning the war. It was couched in this form: "*The Palestine campaign presents very interesting military and even political possibilities* ... There *remains* for consideration the far more important and complicated question of the Western Front. *I have always looked on it as a misfortune ... that the British forces have become so entirely absorbed by this front.*" (When this advice was tendered Russia was in collapse, the transfer of German armies to the Western Front was an obvious and imminent event, and the threat to that front had suddenly increased to the size of a deadly peril).

This recommendation gave Mr. Lloyd George the high military support (from East Africa) which he needed, and he at once had the War Cabinet order the military commander in Egypt to attack towards Jerusalem. General Murray objected that his forces were insufficient *and was removed.* Thereon the command was offered to General Smuts, whom Mr. Lloyd George considered "likely to prosecute a campaign *in that quarter* with great determination."

Sir William Robertson then won his greatest victory of the war. He had a talk with General Smuts. His visitor's qualities as a general can never be estimated because he never had an opportunity to test them, in the small campaigns in which he served. His qualities as a politician, however, are beyond all doubt; he was the wariest of men, and strongly averse to exchanging the triumphs of London for the risk of a fiasco in the field which might destroy his *political* future in South Africa. Therefore, after his talk with Sir William Robertson, he declined Mr. Lloyd George's offer. (As events turned out he would have been spared the fiasco, but that was unforeseeable, and thus one more conqueror missed the chance of entering Jerusalem on a charger. As politicians habitually love such moments, despite the comic aspect which time often gives them, he later regretted this: "To have entered Jerusalem! What a memory!"). At the time he told Mr. Lloyd George, "My strong conviction is that *our present military situation does not really justify an offensive campaign for the capture of Jerusalem and the occupation of Palestine.*"

Mr. Lloyd George was not to be deterred even by this volte-face, or by the collapse of Russia and the new danger in the West. In *September 1917* he decided that "the requisite troops for a big campaign in Palestine *could be spared from the Western Front during the winter of 1917-1918 and could complete the task in Palestine in time to be back in France for the opening of active work in the spring.*"

Only God can have preserved Mr. Lloyd George's fellow countrymen from the full penalties of this decision. The war could not be won in Palestine; it still could be lost in France, and the danger was grave. But Mr. Lloyd George, failed even by General Smuts, had found military support at last, for at this moment another figure, crying "mud-months," advanced from the wings of the central stage. This was one Sir Henry Wilson, who thus portrays himself during a wartime mission to Russia in January 1917: "Gala dinner at the Foreign Office ... I wore the Grand Officer of the Legion of Honour and the Star and Necklace of the Bath, also Russian shoulder- straps and grey astrakhan cap, and altogether I was a fine picture of a man. I created quite a sensation at the Foreign Office dinner and the reception afterwards. I was much taller than the Grand Duke Serge and altogether a 'notable,' as I was told. Superb!"

To this man, posturing against the tragic Russian background, Mr. Lloyd George and Zionism owed their golden opportunity, arrived at last, and England very nearly a catastrophe. Sir Henry Wilson was very tall, thin, smooth and smiling; one of those dapper, polished- leather-bound, red-tabbed, beribboned and brass-edged elegants of the Staff who discouraged the muddied, trenchweary soldiers in France. He spoke native French (by the chance of a French governess) and on this account "Henri" was beloved by the French generals, who thought him refreshingly free from English stiffness (indeed, he was an Irishman and on Irish questions disagreed with other Irishmen, by two of whom he was shot on his London doorstep in 1922, they being hanged).

Sir Henry earlier had agreed with all other military leaders about the paramountcy of the main front and the madness of wasteful "sideshows" and excelled others in the vigour with which he stated this principle: "The way to end this war is to kill Germans, *not Turks* ... The place where we can kill most Germans is *here*" (France) *"and therefore every pound of ammunition we have in the world ought to come here. All history shows that operations in a secondary and ineffectual theatre have no bearing on major operations except to weaken the forces there engaged"* (1915).

No staff graduate, or any fighting private, would dispute that. Sir Henry cannot by 1917 have discovered any *military* reason to abandon this basic principle of war for its opposite. The explanation of *his* volt-face can only be the obvious one. He had observed the rise of Zion and the nature of Mr. Lloyd George's dispute with his own chief, Sir William Robertson. Sir Henry saw the way to occupy Sir William's shoes. Hence Dr. Weizmann's account of his "discoveries of friends" at that period include an allusion to the "sympathy" of General Wilson, "a great friend of Lloyd George." On *August 23, 1917* Sir Henry reported to Mr. Lloyd George "the strong belief that if a really good scheme was thoroughly well worked out, we could clear the Turks out of Palestine and very likely knock them completely out *during the mud-months without in any way interfering with Haig's operations next spring and winter*" (in France).

In this report Mr. Lloyd George at long last found the support he needed for his order of *September 1917*, quoted six paragraphs back. He seized on the alluring phrase "mud-months"; it gave him a *military* argument! General Wilson explained to him that these "mud- months" in France, which by bogging down the armies would preclude a major German offensive while they continued, comprized "five months of mud and snow from the middle of November to *the middle of April*" (1918). On this counsel Mr. Lloyd George founded his decision to take from France "the requisite troops for a big campaign in Palestine" and to have them back in France in time for any emergency there. As to that, General Wilson, alone among military leaders, advised Mr. Lloyd George that the big German attack probably would never happen (it came in *the middle of March*).

Sir William Robertson vainly pointed out that the time-table was illusory; the movement of armies entailed major problems of transport and shipping, and by the time the last divisions landed in Palestine the first ones would be re-embarking! In *October* he again warned that troops taken from France could *not* be back there in time for summer fighting: "the right military course to pursue is to act *on the defensive in Palestine* ... and continue to seek a decision in the West ... *all reserves should be sent to the Western Front.*"

At that fateful instant chance, ever the arch-conspirator in this story, struck in favour of the Zionists. Cabinet Ministers in London (who apparently had almost forgotten the Western Front) were badgering Sir William Robertson to "give us Jerusalem as a Christmas box" (the phrase appears to reveal again the "extraordinary flippancy" about the war which Dr. Weizmann earlier attributed to Mr. Lloyd George). In Palestine General Allenby, under similar pressure, made a probing advance, found to his surprise that the Turks offered little opposition, and without much difficulty marched into Jerusalem.

The prize was of no military value, in the total sum of the war, but Mr. Lloyd George thenceforward was not to be restrained. Troops were diverted from France without regard to what impended there. On *January 6, 1918* Sir Douglas Haig complained of the weakening of his armies in France on the eve of the greatest battle; he was "114,000 infantry down." On *January 10,1918* the War Office was forced to issue orders to reduce all divisions from 12 to 9 battalions of infantry.

A free press might at that period have given Sir William Robertson the backing he needed, in public opinion, to avert all this. He was denied that, too, for at that stage the state of affairs foretold by the Protocols of 1905 was being brought about: "We must compel the governments ... to take action in the direction favoured by our widely-conceived plan ... by what we shall represent as public opinion, secretly prompted by us through the means of that so-called 'Great Power,' the Press, which, with a few exceptions that may be disregarded, is already entirely in our hands." Writers of great repute were ready to inform the public of the imminent danger; they were not allowed to speak.

Colonel Repington, of *The Times,* was the best-known military writer of that day; his reputation in this field was the highest in the world. He noted in his diary, "This is terrible and will mean the reduction of our infantry in France by a quarter and confusion in all our infantry *at the moment of coming crisis.* I have never felt so miserable since the war began ... I can say very little because the editor of *The Times often manipulates my criticisms or does not publish them* ...If *The Times* does not return to its independent line and act as watchdog of the public I shall wash my hands of it."

When the fulfilment of his warnings was at hand, Sir William Robertson was removed. Mr. Lloyd George, resolved to obtain authority for his Palestinian adventure, put his plan to the Supreme War Council of the Allies at Versailles, whose technical advisers, in January 1918, approved it "*subject to the Western Front being made secure*." Sir William Robertson, at M. Clemenceau's request, restated his warning that it would mortally *endanger* the Western Front. When the meeting broke up Mr. Lloyd George angrily rebuked him and he was at once supplanted by Sir Henry Wilson.

Before he left his post he used his last moments in it to make a final attempt to avert the coming disaster. He went (also in January) to Paris to ask help from General Pershing, the American commander, in replenishing the depleted front (only four and a half American divisions then had reached France). General Pershing, a soldier true to his duty, made the reply which Sir William expected and would himself have made in General Pershing's place: "He shrewdly observed that it was difficult to reconcile my request for assistance in defence of the Western Front *with Mr. George's desire to act offensively in Palestine.* There was, unfortunately, no answer to that argument, except that, so far as I was personally concerned, not a man or gun would be sent to Palestine from anywhere."

After that Sir William Robertson was no longer "concerned." His account differs from the memoirs of Mr. Lloyd George and other politicians in that it shows no rancour; his sole theme is *duty*. Of his treatment he merely says, "It had frequently been my unpleasant duty during 1917 to object to military enterprises which the Prime Minister wished the army to carry out and this opposition had doubtless determined him to try another Chief of the Imperial General Staff ... On the point of supersession, therefore, *there was nothing to say and I said nothing.*" Thus an admirable man passes from this story of many lesser men, but his work endured, because, up to the time of his dismissal, he may have saved just enough men and guns for the crumbling line to hold at the last extremity, in March, as a rending hawser may hold by a single thread.

When he was gone two men outside the government and army continued the struggle, and their efforts deserve record because theirs were among the last attempts to preserve the principle of free, independent and vigilant reporting. Colonel Repington was a former cavalry officer, an admirer of pretty women, a lover of good talk, a *beau sabreur.* His diaries give a lasting picture of the frothy life of the drawing-rooms that went on while armies fought in France and in London intriguers conspired in the political antechambers. He enjoyed it and although he felt its incongruity he realized that gloom alone was no remedy. He was as honest and patriotic as

Robertson, and incorruptible; lavish offers (which might have lured him into silence, and possibly were so intended) had no effect on him.

He wrote, "We are feeding over a million men into the sideshow theatres of war and are letting down our strengths in France *at a moment when all the Boche forces from Russia may come against us ... I am unable to get the support from the editor of The Times that I must have to rouse the country and I do not think I will be able to go on with him much longer.*" (I discovered Colonel Repington's diaries through my work on this book and then realized that his experience was identical with mine, just twenty years later, with the same editor). A month later he wrote, "In a stormy interview I told Mr. Geoffrey Dawson that his subservience to the War Cabinet during this year was *largely the cause of the dangerous position of our army ...* I would have nothing more to do with *The Times.*"

This left one man in England who was able and willing to publish the truth. Mr. H.A. Gwynne, of the *Morning Post,* printed Colonel Repington's article, which exposed the weakening of the French front on the eve of its attack, without submitting it to the censor. He and Colonel Repington then were prosecuted, tried and fined (public opinion was apparently too much on their side for harsher retribution). Sir William Robertson wrote to Colonel Repington, "Like yourself, I did what was best in the general interests of the country and the result has been exactly what I expected ... *But the great thing is to keep on a straight course and then one may be sure that good will eventually come of what may now seem to be evil.*"[12]

Thus the two wartime years of Mr. Lloyd George's leadership in England were momentous in their effects on the present time, and I believe I have shown how he achieved office and what paramount purpose he pursued through it. After eighteen months he had overcome all opposition, diverted a mass of men from France to Palestine, and was ready at last for the great venture.

On *March 7, 1918* he gave orders for "*a decisive campaign*" to conquer all Palestine, and sent General Smuts there to instruct General Allenby accordingly.

On *March 21, 1918* the long-awaited German attack in France began, embodying all the men, guns and aircraft released from the Russian front.

The "decisive campaign" in Palestine was immediately suspended and every man who could be squeezed out of Palestine was rushed to France. The

---

[12] In the sequel to all this Sir Edward Carson, who had unwittingly helped Mr. Lloyd George into the premiership, resigned from the government and told the editor of *The Times* that it was but Mr. Lloyd George's mouthpiece, the *Morning Post* being the truly independent paper. Mr. Gwynne told Colonel Repington that the government wished to destroy the *Morning Post* "as it is one of the few independent papers left." Before the Second War came it '*was*' "destroyed," as already related. After that only one weekly publication survived in England which, in my opinion, for many years sought to uphold the principle of impartial and independent reporting, but in 1953 *Truth* too, was by a change of ownership brought into line.

total number of men employed in Palestine was *1,192,511* up to October 1918 (General Robertson).

On *March 27, 1918* Colonel Repington wrote, "This is the worst defeat in the history of the army." By June 6 the Germans claimed 175,000 prisoners and over 2,000 guns.

At that point the truth was shown of the last words above quoted from Sir William Robertson's letter to Colonel Repington, and they are of continuing hopeful augury to men of goodwill today. By keeping on a straight course he *had* saved enough for the line to hold, at breaking point, until the Americans began to arrive in strength. Therewith the war was virtually at an end. Clearly, if Russia had been sustained, the Palestinian excursion avoided, and strength concentrated in France it could have been concluded earlier, and probably without the "entanglement" of America. However, that would not have furthered the great plan for "the management of human affairs."

At this point in the tale I write with the feelings of a participant, and they probably influence what I have written of the long earlier story, because the effects, as I have seen them in my generation, appear to me to be bad. I recall the great German attack of March 21, 1918; I saw it from the air and on the ground and was in the fighting for the first month, until I was removed by stretcher. I remember Sir Douglas Haig's order, that every man must fight and die where he stood; it was posted on the walls of my squadron's mess. I have no complaints about the experience, and would not delete it from my life if I could. Now that I have *come* to see by what ulterior means and motives it was all brought about, I think coming generations might be a little better able to keep Sir William Robertson's "straight course," and so to ensure that good will eventually come of what seems to them to be evil, if they know a little more of what went on then and has continued since. This is my reason for writing the present book.

As a result of the victory in Europe the coveted territory in Palestine was at length acquired. But it is one thing to acquire land and another to build something on it. On this land a Zionist "homeland" was to be erected, then a "state" (and last a "commonwealth"?). None of these things could be done by England alone. No precedent existed for the donation of Arabian territory, by a European conqueror, to an Asiatic beneficiary. For such a transaction other nations had to be co-opted, many nations, and a company promoted, so that it might be given the semblance of honest business. In fact, a "league of nations" was required, and America, above all, had to be "entangled." This other part of the plan was also in preparation; while British armies seized the tract of land desired, the smart lawyers had been looking for ways to amend the rightful title deeds to it, float a company and generally promote the undertaking.

Mr. Lloyd George had served his turn and his day was nearly done. The reader may now turn his eyes across the Atlantic and see what Mr.

House, Mr. Brandeis and Rabbi Stephen Wise have been up to. A Mr. Woodrow Wilson plays a shadowy part in these proceedings.

Chapter 31

THE WEB OF INTRIGUE

Such words as "conspiracy" and "intrigue," often used in this narrative, are not original with me; they come from authoritative sources. Mr. Arthur D. Howden, who wrote his biography in consultation with the man depicted, supplies the chapter title above; he describes the process of which Mr. House was (in America) the centre during the 1914-1918 war in the words, "*a web of intrigue was spun across the Atlantic.*"

In England the Lloyd George government and in America the president were at first separately enmeshed. Between 1914 and 1917 these "webs" in London and Washington were joined together by the transoceanic threads which Mr. Howden depicts in the spinning. Thereafter the two governments were caught in the same web and have never since freed themselves from it.

In President Wilson's America the real president was Mr. House ("liaison officer between the Wilson administration and the Zionist movement," Rabbi Wise). Mr. Justice Brandeis, who had decided to "give his life" to Zionism, was the president's "adviser on the Jewish question" (Dr. Weizmann); this is the first appearance in the Presidential household of an authority theretofore unknown in it and now apparently permanent. The chief Zionist organizer was Rabbi Wise, constantly in touch with the two other men.

Mr. House (and Mr. Bernard Baruch), chose the president's cabinet officers, so that one of them had to introduce himself to Mr. Wilson thus: "My name is Lane, Mr. President, I believe I am the Secretary of the Interior." The president lived at the White House in Washington but was frequently seen to visit a small apartment in East 35th Street, New York, where a Mr. House lived. In time this led to pointed questions and one party-man was told, "Mr. House is my second personality; he is my independent self. His thoughts and mine are one." Mr. House was often in Washington, where he conducted the president's interviews and correspondence, and, stopping cabinet officers outside the cabinet room, instructed them what to say inside it. Even from New York he directed America by means of private telephone lines linking him with Washington: "it is only necessary to lift off the receiver and I reach the Secretary of State's desk immediately."

The president's assent to acts of State policy was not required. Mr. House "did not expect affirmative commendation … if the President did not object, I knew that it was safe to go ahead." Thus Mr. Wilson had to express *dissent,* to delay or amend any action (and immediately after election he had been made to promise "not to act independently in future").

In 1914 Mr. House, who in 1900 had resolved to extend his power from Texan to *national* politics, prepared to take over *international* affairs: "he wanted to exercise his energy in a broader field ... From the beginning of 1914 he gave more and more thought to what he regarded as the highest form of politics and that for which he was peculiarly suited: international affairs." In fact, Texan upbringing did not so qualify Mr. House. In Texas the words "international affairs' had, in the public mind, a sound akin to "skunk," and there, more than anywhere in America, "the traditions of the 19th century still held the public mind; traditions which laid down, as the primary principle of American policy, *a complete abstention from the political affairs of Europe*" (Mr. Seymour). Mr. House, who somewhere in Texas had absorbed "the ideas of the revolutionaries of 1848" was to destroy that tradition, but this did not prove him "peculiarly suited" to intervene in "international affairs."

Mr. House was of different type from the languid Mr. Balfour, with his background of Scottish hills and mists, and Mr. Lloyd George, the Artful Dodger of Zionism from Wales, but he acted as if he and they had together graduated from some occult academy of political machination. In 1914 he began to appoint American ambassadors (as he says) and made his first calls on European governments as "a personal friend of the President."

Mr. Seymour, his editor, says: "It would be difficult in all history to find another instance of diplomacy so unconventional and so effective. Colonel House, a private citizen, spreads all the cards on the table and *concerts with the Ambassador of a foreign power the despatches to be sent to the American Ambassador and Foreign Minister of that power.*" Mr. Howden, his confidant, expatiates: "Mr. House had the initiative in what was done ... The State Department was *relegated to the status of an intermediary for his ideas, a depository of public records.* Much of the more confidential diplomatic correspondence passed directly through the little apartment in East 35th Street. The Ambassadors of the belligerents called on him when they *wanted to influence the Administration* or sought assistance in *the web of intrigue that was being spun across the Atlantic.*"

Mr. House: "The life I am leading transcends in interest and excitement any romance ... Information from every quarter of the globe pours into this little, unobtrusive study." Mr. Seymour again: "Cabinet members in search of candidates, candidates in search of positions made of his study a clearing house. Editors and journalists sought his opinion and despatches to the foreign press were framed almost at his dictation. United States Treasury officials, British diplomats ... and *metropolitan financiers* came to his study to discuss their plans."

A rising man across the Atlantic also was interested in "financiers." Mrs Beatrice Webb says that Mr. Winston Churchill, somewhat earlier, at a dinner party confided to her that "he looks to *haute finance* to keep the peace and for that reason *objects to a self-contained Empire* as he thinks it would destroy this cosmopolitan capitalism, the *cosmopolitan financier* being the professional peacemaker of the modern world and to his mind the acme of civilization." Later events did not support this notion that leading financiers ("metropolitan" or "cosmopolitan") were "professional peacemakers."

Such was the American picture, behind-the-scenes in 1915 and 1916. The purpose of the ruling group whose web now began to *span* the Atlantic is shown by the events which followed. Mr. Asquith was overthrown in the pretext that his incompetency imperilled victory; Mr. Lloyd George risked total defeat by diverting armies to Palestine. Mr. Wilson was re-elected in the pretext that he, in the old tradition, would "keep America out of the war"; elected, at once involved America in the war. "The diplomat's word" and his "deed" were different.

Mr. House privately "concluded that war with Germany is inevitable" on *May 30, 1915*, and in *June 1916* devised the election-winning slogan for Mr. Wilson's second campaign: "He kept us out of the war." Rabbi Stephen Wise, *before* the election, supported Mr. House's efforts: in letters to the President the rabbi "deplored his advocacy of a preparedness programme" and from public platforms he preached against war. All went as planned: "the House strategy worked perfectly" (Mr. Howden), and Mr. Wilson was triumphantly re-elected.

Mr. Wilson seems at that point to have believed the words put into his mouth. Immediately after the election he set up as a peacemaker and drafted a note to the belligerents in which he used the phrase, "*the causes and objects of the war are obscure.*" This was a culpable act of "independence" on the president's part, and Mr. House was furious. The harassed president amended the phrase to "the objects which the statesmen and the belligerents *on both sides* have in mind in this war *are virtually the same.*" This made Mr. House even angrier, and Mr. Wilson's efforts to expose the nature of "the web" in which he was caught thereon expired. He remained in ignorance of what his next act was to be for a little, informing Mr. House on *January 4, 1917*, "*There will be no war. This country does not intend to become involved in the war ... It would be a crime against civilization for us to go in.*"

The power-group moved to dispel these illusions as soon as Mr. Wilson's second inauguration was safely past *(January 20, 1917)*. Rabbi Stephen Wise informed the president of a change of mind; he was now "convinced that *the time had come for the American people to understand that it might be our destiny to have part in the struggle.*" Mr. House (who during the "no war" election had noted, "We are on the verge of war") confided to his diary on *February 12, 1917*, "We are drifting into war as rapidly as I expected" (which gave a new meaning to the word "drift").

Then on *March 27, 1917* President Wilson asked Mr. House "whether he should *ask Congress to declare war* or whether he should *say that a state of war exists*," and Mr. House "advised the latter," so that the American people were informed, on April 2, 1917, that a state of war *existed*.[13] Between November 1916 and April 1917, therefore, "the web of intrigue," spanning the ocean, achieved these decisive aims: the overthrow of Mr. Asquith in favour of Mr. Lloyd George, the commitment of British armies to the Palestinian diversion, the re-election of a president who would be constrained to support that enterprise, and the embroilment of America.

The statement of *existing war* made to Congress said the *purpose* of the war (which Mr. Wilson, a few weeks before, had declared in his draft to be "obscure") was *"to set up a new international order."* Thus a *new* purpose was openly, though cryptically revealed. To the public masses the words meant anything or nothing. To the initiates they carried a commitment to support the plan, of which Zionism and Communism both were instruments, for establishing a "world federation" founded on force and the obliteration of nationhood, with the exception of one "nation" to be recreated.

From this moment the power-groups in America and England worked in perfect synchronization, so that the two stories become one story, or one "web." The apparently powerful men in Washington and London co-ordinated their actions at the prompting of the inter- communicating Zionists on both sides of the ocean. Foreknowledge of what was to happen had earlier been displayed by Dr. Weizmann in London, who in *March 1915* wrote to his ally, Mr. Scott of the *Manchester Guardian*, that he "understood" the British Government to be willing to support Zionist aspirations at the peace conference to come (the event also foretold by Max Nordau in 1903). This

---

[13] Lord Sydenham, when he wrote of the "deadly accuracy" of the forecast in the "Protocols" of about 1900, might have had particularly in mind the passage, "... We shall invest the president with the right of declaring a state of war. We shall justify this last right on the ground that the president as chief of the whole army of the country must have it at his disposal in case of need." The situation here described became established practice during the present century. In 1950 President Truman sent American troops into Korea "to check Communist aggression," without consulting Congress. Later this was declared to be a "United Nations" war and they were joined by troops of seventeen other countries under an American commander, General MacArthur. This was the first experiment in a "world government"-type war and its course produced Senator Taft's question of 1952. "Do we really mean our anti-Communist policy?" General MacArthur was dismissed after protesting an order forbidding him to pursue Communist aircraft into their Chinese sanctuary and in 1953, under President Eisenhower, the war was broken off, leaving half of Korea in "the aggressor's" hands. General MacArthur and other American commanders later charged that the order forbidding pursuit was made known to the enemy by "a spy ring responsible for the purloining of my top secret reports to Washington" *(Life,* Feb. 7, 1956), and the Chinese Communist commander confirmed this *(New York Daily News,* Feb. 13, 1956). In June 1951 two British Foreign Office officials, Burgess and Maclean, disappeared and in September 1955 the British Government, after refusing information for four years, confirmed the general belief that they were in Moscow and "had spied for the Soviet Union over a long period." General MacArthur then charged that these two men had revealed the non-pursuit order to the Communist "aggressor" *(Life,* above-quoted).
On April 4, 1956 President Eisenhower was asked by a reporter at his regular news conference whether he would order a United States marine battalion, then recently sent to the Mediterranean, into war "without asking Congress first" (by that time war in the Middle East was an obvious possibility). He answered angrily. "I have announced time and time again I will never be guilty of any kind of action that can be interpreted as war until the Congress, which has the constitutional authority." On January 3, 1957, the first major act of his second term, he sent a draft resolution to Congress designed to invest him with unlimited, standing authority to act militarily in the Middle East "to *deter* Communist armed aggression."

was exactly what Mr. Asquith would not consider, so that Dr. Weizmann, in March 1915, was already describing Mr. Asquith's supplanters of December 1916 as "the British Government."

This "British Government," said Dr. Weizmann, would leave "the organization of *the Jewish commonwealth*" in Palestine "entirely to the care of the Jews." However, the Zionists could not possibly, even in a Palestine conquered for them, have set up "a commonwealth" against the native inhabitants. They could only do that behind the protection of a great power and its armies. Therefore Dr. Weizmann (foretelling in 1915 exactly what was to happen in 1919 and the following two decades) considered that a British "protectorate" should be set up in Palestine (to protect the Zionist intruders). This would mean, he said, that "the Jews take over the country; the *whole burden* of organization falls on them, but for the next ten or fifteen years they work under a *temporary* British protectorate."

Dr. Weizmann adds that this was "an anticipation of the mandate system," so that today's student also learns where the notion of "mandates" was born. The idea of ruling conquered territories under a "mandate" bestowed by a self-proclaimed "league of nations" was devised solely with an eye to Palestine. (Events have proved this. All the other "mandates" distributed after the 1914-1918 war, to give the appearance of a procedure generally applicable, have faded away, either by relinquishment of the territory to its inhabitants or by its conversion, in fact, into a possession of the conqueror. The concept of the "mandate" was maintained for just as long as was needed for the Zionists to amass enough arms to take possession of Palestine for themselves).

Thus, after the elevation of Mr. Lloyd George and the second election of Mr. Wilson, the shape of the future, far beyond the war's end, was fully known to Dr. Weizmann at the web's centre, who went into action. In a memorandum to the British Government he demanded that "*The Jewish population of Palestine* ... shall be officially recognized by the Suzerain government as *the Jewish Nation*." The "first full-dress conference leading to the Balfour Declaration" was then held. This committee, met to draft a British governmental document, met in a private Jewish house and consisted of nine Zionist leaders and one representative of the government concerned, Sir Mark Sykes (who attended "in his private capacity"). As a result Mr. Balfour at once arranged to go to America to discuss the matter.

Dr. Weizmann and his associates had to steer a very narrow course between two difficulties at that moment, and might have failed, had not "the web" enabled them to dictate what Mr. Balfour would be told by the men he crossed the ocean to see. The British Government, for all its zeal, took alarm at the prospect of acting as sole protector of the Zionists and wanted America to share the armed occupation of Palestine. The Zionists knew that this would violently upset American opinion, (had it come about America, from bitter experience shared, would have been much harder to win for the deed of 1948) and did not want the question of American co- occupation raised. Dr. Weizmann's misgivings were increased when, in "a long talk" he found Mr. Balfour, before his departure, eager for "an *Anglo-American* protectorate."

Dr. Weizmann at once wrote to Mr. Justice Brandeis warning him to oppose any such plan, but to assure Mr. Balfour of American support for the proposal of a solely British protectorate, (April 8, 1917), and this letter to Mr. Brandeis "must have reached him about the time of Balfour's arrival." Mr. Brandeis, risen to the United States Supreme Court, had retired from the *public* leadership of Zionism in America. In the tradition of his office, he should have remained aloof from all political affairs, but in fact, as Mr. Wilson's "adviser on the Jewish question," he informed the president that he was "*in favour of a British protectorate and utterly opposed to a condominium*" (that is, joint Anglo-American control).

When Mr. Balfour reached America (then in a state of "existing war" for just eighteen days) he apparently never discussed Palestine with the American President at all. Mr. Wilson's part at this stage "was limited to a humble undertaking to Rabbi Wise, "Whenever the time comes and *you and Justice Brandeis feel that the time is ripe for me to speak and act, I shall be ready*." By that time the rabbi had "briefed" Mr. House: "He is enlisted in our cause. There is no question about it whatever. The thing will go through Washington, I think, without delay" *(April 8, 1917*, six days after the "existing war" proclamation).

Mr. Balfour saw Mr. Brandeis. Clearly he might as well have stayed at home with Dr. Weizmann, as Mr. Brandeis merely repeated the contents of Dr. Weizmann's letters; Mr. Balfour simply moved from one end of "the web of intrigue" to the other. Mr. Brandeis (as Mrs Dugdale records) "became *increasingly emphatic* about the desire of the Zionists to see a *British administration in Palestine*." Mr. Balfour, his biographer adds, "pledged his own personal support to Zionism; he had done it before to Dr. Weizmann, *but now he was British Foreign Secretary*."

A later American comment on the part played by Mr. Brandeis in this affair is here relevant. Professor John O. Beaty of the Southern Methodist University of the United States says that the day when Mr. Brandeis's appointment to the Supreme Court was confirmed was "one of the most significant days in American *history, for we had for the first time,* since the first decade of the 19th Century, *an official of the highest status whose heart's interest was in something besides the United States*."

Mr. Brandeis "did more than press the idea of a Jewish Palestine under a British protectorate" (Dr. Weizmann). He and Mr. House issued (over the president's signature) the famous declaration repudiating secret treaties). This declaration was popular with the masses, who heard in it the voice of the Brave New World rebuking the bad old one. The words evoked pictures of becloaked diplomats climbing dark backstairs to secret chancelleries; now that America was in the war these feudal machinations would be stopped and all done above the board.

Alas for a pleasant illusion; the noble rebuke was another submission to Zionism. Turkey had still to be defeated so that the French and British governments (whose fighting men were engaged) wished to win over the Arabs and with them had made the "Sykes-Picot agreement," which foresaw an independent confederation of Arab States and, among them, an *international administration* for Palestine. Dr. Weizmann had learned of this agreement and saw that there could be no Zionist *state* if Palestine were under *international* control; exclusive British "protection" was essential. Pressure was applied and President Wilson's ringing denunciation of "secret treaties" was in fact aimed solely at the Arabs of Palestine and their hopes for the future. America *insisted* that England hold the baby.

Of this secret achievement Mr. Balfour's biographer happily records that it showed *"a Jewish national diplomacy was now in being"*; the words may be used as an alternative heading to this chapter, if any so desire. The British Foreign Office at last "recognized, with some slight dismay, that the British Government was virtually *committed.*" America, though in the war, was not at war with Turkey, and yet had been secretly committed (by Mr. Brandeis) to support the transfer of Turkish territory to an outside party. Therefore American participation in the intrigue had to remain publicly unknown for the moment, though Mr. Balfour had been informed of it in imperative tones.

The summer of 1917 passed while the Balfour Declaration was prepared, America thus having become secretly involved in the Zionist adventure. The only remaining opposition, apart from that of generals and a few high Foreign Office or State Department officials, came from the Jews of England and America. It was ineffective because the leading politicians, in both countries, were even more hostile to their Jewish fellow-citizens than were the Zionists. (The part played in all this by non-Jews was so great, even if it was the part of puppets, that one is constantly reminded of the need to regard with suspicion the attribution of the Protocols to solely Jewish authorship).

In England in 1915 the Anglo-Jewish Association, through its Conjoint Committee, declared that "the Zionists do not consider civil and political emancipation as a sufficiently important factor for victory over the persecution and oppression of Jews and think that such a victory can only be achieved by establishing a legally secured home for the Jewish people. The Conjoint Committee considers as dangerous and provoking anti-semitism the 'national' postulate of the Zionists, as well as special privileges for Jews in Palestine. The Committee could not discuss the question of a British Protectorate with *an international organization which included different, even enemy elements.*"

In any rational time the British and American governments would have spoken thus, and they would have been supported by Jewish citizens. In 1914, however, Dr. Weizmann had written that such Jews "have to be made to realize that *we and not they are the masters of the situation.*" The Conjoint Committee represented the Jews long established in England, but the British Government *accepted* the claim of the revolutionaries from Russia to be "the masters" of Jewry.

In 1917, as the irrevocable moment approached, the Conjoint Committee again declared that the Jews were a religious community and nothing more, that they could not claim "a national home," and that Jews in Palestine needed nothing more than "the assurance of religious and civil liberty, reasonable facilities for immigration and the like."

By that time such statements infuriated the embattled *Goyim* around Dr. Weizmann from Russia. Mr. Wickham Steed of *The Times* expressed "downright annoyance" after discussing "for a good hour" (with Dr. Weizmann) "the kind of leader which was likely to make the best appeal to the British public," produced "a magnificent presentation of the Zionist case."

In America, Mr. Brandeis and Rabbi Stephen Wise were equally vigilant against the Jews there. The rabbi (from Hungary) asked President Wilson, "What will you do when their protests reach you?" For one moment only he was silent. Then he pointed to a large wastepaper basket at his desk. "Is not that basket capacious enough for all their protests?"

In England Dr. Weizmann was enraged by "*outside* interference, *entirely from Jews.*" At this point he felt himself to be a member of the Government, or perhaps *the* member of the Government, and in the power he wielded apparently was that. He did not stop at dismissing the objections of British Jews as "outside interference"; he dictated what the Cabinet should discuss and demanded to sit in Cabinet meetings so that he might attack a Jewish minister! He required that Mr. Lloyd George put the question "on the agenda of the War Cabinet for *October 4, 1917*" and on *October* 3 he wrote to the British Foreign Office protesting against objections which he expected to be raised at that meeting "by a prominent Englishman of the Jewish faith."

Mr. Edwin Montagu was a cabinet minister and a Jew. Dr. Weizmann implicitly urged that he be not heard by his colleagues, or that if he *were* heard, Dr. Weizmann should be called in to reply! On the day of the meeting Dr. Weizmann appeared in the office of the prime minister's secretary, Mr. Philip Kerr (another "friend") and proposed that he remain there in case the Cabinet "decide to ask me some questions before they decide the matter." Mr. Kerr said, "Since the British Government has been a government, no private person has been admitted to one of its sessions," and Dr. Weizmann then went away.

But for that Mr. Lloyd George would have set the precedent, for Dr. Weizmann was scarcely gone when, after hearing Mr. Montagu, Mr. Lloyd George and Mr. Balfour sent out to ask Dr. Weizmann to come in. Mr. Montagu then succeeded, in the teeth of the Gentiles arrayed against him, in obtaining minor modifications in the draft, and Dr. Weizmann later rebuked Mr. Kerr for this petty compromise: "The Cabinet and even yourself attach undue importance to the opinion held by *so-called 'British Jewry.'* "Two days later *(October 9)* Dr. Weizmann cabled triumphantly to Mr. Justice Brandeis that the British Government had formally undertaken to establish a "national home for the Jewish race" in Palestine.

The draft experienced revealing adventures between October 9 and November 2, when it was published. It was sent to America, where it was edited by Mr. Brandeis, Mr. Jacob de Haas and Rabbi Wise before being shown to President Wilson for his "final approval." He simply sent it to Mr. Brandeis (who had already had it from Dr. Weizmann), who passed it to Rabbi Stephen Wise, "to be handed to Colonel House for transmission to the British Cabinet."

In this way one of the most fateful actions ever taken by any British Government was prepared. The draft, incorporated in a letter addressed by Mr. Balfour to Lord Rothschild, became "the Balfour Declaration." The Rothschild family, like many leading Jewish families, was sharply divided about Zionism. The name of a sympathetic Rothschild, as the recipient of the letter, was evidently used to impress Western Jewry in general, and to divert attention from the Eastern Jewish origins of Zionism. The true addressee was Dr. Weizmann. He appears to have become an habitué of the War Cabinet's antechamber and the document was delivered to him, Sir Mark Sykes informing him, "Dr. Weizmann, it's a boy!" (today the shape of the man may be seen).

No rational explanation for the action of leading Western politicians in supporting this alien enterprise has ever been given, and as the undertaking was up to that point secret and conspiratorial no genuine explanation *can* be given; if an undertaking is good conspiracy is not requisite to it, and secrecy itself indicates motives that cannot be divulged. If any of these men ever gave some public reason, it usually took the form of some vague invocation of the Old Testament. This has a sanctimonious ring, and may be held likely to daunt objectors. Mr. Lloyd George liked to tell Zionist visitors (as Rabbi Wise ironically records), "You shall have Palestine from Dan to Beersheba," and thus to present himself as the instrument of divine will. He once asked Sir Charles and Lady Henry to call anxious Jewish Members of Parliament together at breakfast "so that I may convince them of the rightfulness of my Zionist position." A *minyan* (Jewish religious quorum of ten) was accordingly assembled in the British Prime Minister's breakfast room, where Mr. Lloyd George read a series of passages which, in his opinion, prescribed the

Douglas Reed

transplantation of Jews in Palestine in 1917: Then he said, "Now, gentlemen, you know What your Bible says; that is the end of the matter."

On other occasions he gave different, and mutually destructive, explanations. He told the Palestine Royal Commission of 1937 that he acted to gain "the support of American Jewry" and that he had "a definite promise" from the Zionist leaders "that if the allies committed themselves to giving facilities for the establishment of a national home for the Jews in Palestine, they would do their best to rally Jewish sentiment and support throughout the world to the Allied cause."

This was brazen untruth at the very bar of history. America was already *in the war* when Mr. Balfour went there to agree the Balfour Declaration, and Mr. Balfour's biographer scouts the notion of any such bargain. Rabbi Elmer Berger, a Jewish commentator, says the alleged promise by Zionist leaders inspires in him, "… an irrepressible indignation, for myself, my family, my Jewish friends, all of whom are just ordinary Jews … it constitutes one of the most obscene libels in all history. Only callousness and cynicism could imply that Jews in the Allied nations were not already giving their utmost to the prosecution of the war."

Mr. Lloyd George's *third* explanation ("Acetone converted me to Zionism") is the best known. According to this version Mr. Lloyd George asked Dr. Weizmann how he could be requited for a useful chemical discovery made during the war (when Dr. Weizmann worked for the government, in any spare time left by his work for Zionism). Dr. Weizmann is quoted as replying, "I want nothing for myself, but everything for my people," whereon Mr. Lloyd George decided to give him Palestine! Dr. Weizmann himself derides this story ("History does not deal in Aladdin's lamps. Mr. Lloyd George's *advocacy of the Jewish homeland long predated his accession to the premiership*"). For that matter, it is British practice to make cash awards for such services and Dr. Weizmann, far from wanting nothing for himself, received ten thousand pounds. (If chemical research were customarily rewarded in land he might have claimed a minor duchy *from Germany* in respect of a patent earlier sold to the German Dye Trust, and presumably found useful in war as in peace; he was naturally content with the income he received from it for several years).

The conclusion cannot be escaped: if any honest explanation of his actions in this matter could be found Mr. Lloyd George would have given it. From this period in 1916-1917 the decay of parliamentary and representative government can be traced, both in England and America. If secret men could dictate major acts of American state policy and major operations of British armies, then clearly "election" and "responsible office" were terms devoid of meaning. Party distinctions began to fade in both countries, once this hidden, supreme authority was accepted by leading Western politicians, and the American and British electors began to be deprived of all true choice. Today this condition is general, and now is public. Leaders of *all* parties, before elections, make obeisance to Zionism, and the voter's selection of president, prime minister or party makes no true difference.

In November 1917 the American Republic thus became equally involved with Great Britain in Zionism, which has proved to be a destructive force. However, it was only one agency of "the destructive principle." The reader will recall that in Dr. Weizmann's Russian youth the mass of Jews there, under their Talmudic directors, were united in the revolutionary aim, and only divided between revolutionary-Zionism and revolutionary-Communism.

In the very week of the Balfour Declaration the other group of Jews in Russia achieved their aim, the destruction of the Russian nation- state. The Western politicians thus bred a bicephalous monster, one head being the power of Zionism in the Western capitals, and the other the power of Communism advancing from captive Russia. Submission to Zionism weakened the power of the West to preserve itself against the world-revolution, for Zionism worked to keep Western governments submissive and to deflect their policies from national interests; indeed, at that instant the cry was first raised that opposition to the world-revolution, too, was "anti-semitism." Governments hampered by secret capitulations in any one direction cannot act firmly in any other, and the timidity of London and Washington in their dealings with the world-revolution, during the four decades to follow, evidently derived from their initial submission to "the web of intrigue" spun across the Atlantic between 1914 and 1917.

After 1917, therefore, the question which the remainder of the 20th Century had to answer was whether the West could yet find in itself the strength to break free, or prise its political leaders loose, from this double thrall. In considering the remainder of this account the reader should bear in mind what British and American politicians were induced to do during the First World War.

Douglas Reed

Chapter 32

THE WORLD REVOLUTION AGAIN

The simultaneous triumphs of Bolshevism in Moscow and Zionism in London in the same week of 1917 were only in appearance distinct events. The identity of their original source has been shown in an earlier chapter, and the hidden men who promoted Zionism through the Western governments also supported the world-revolution. The two forces fulfilled correlative tenets of the ancient Law: "Pull down and destroy ... rule over all nations"; the one destroyed in the East and the other secretly ruled in the West.

1917 gave proof of Disraeli's dictum about the revolution in its 1848 phase, when he said that Jews headed "everyone" of the secret societies and aimed to destroy Christianity. The controlling group that emerged in 1917 was so preponderantly Jewish that it may be called Jewish. The nature of the instigating force then became a matter of historical fact, not of further polemical debate. It was further identified by its deeds: the character of its earliest enactments, a symbolic mockery of Christianity, and a special mark of authorship deliberately given to the murder of the monarch. All these bore the traits of a Talmudic vengeance.

In the forty years that have passed great efforts have been made to suppress public knowledge of this *fact*, which has been conclusively established, by non-sequential rebukes to any who claim to discuss history. For instance, in the 1950's an able (and deservedly respected) Jewish writer in America, Mr. George Sokolsky, in criticizing a book previously cited wrote, "It is impossible to read it without reaching the conclusion that Professor Beaty seeks to prove that Communism is a Jewish movement." In respect of the leadership it *was* that for a long period before 1917 (as to later and the present situation, subsequent chapters will look at the evidence). It was *not* a conspiracy of all Jews, but neither were the French revolution, Fascism and National Socialism conspiracies of all Frenchmen, Italians or Germans. The organizing force and the leadership were drawn from the Talmudic-controlled Jewish areas of Russia, and in that sense Communism was demonstrably Eastern Jewish.

As to the purposes revealed when the revolution struck in 1917, these showed that it was not episodic or spontaneous but the third "eruption" of the organization first revealed through Weishaupt. The two main features reappeared: the attack on all legitimate government of any kind whatsoever and on religion. Since 1917 the world-revolution has had to cast aside the earlier pretence of being directed only against "kings" or the political power of priests.

Douglas Reed

One authority of that period knew and stated this. In the tradition of
Edmund Burke and John Robison, George Washington and Alexander
Hamilton and Disraeli, Mr. Winston Churchill wrote:
"It would almost seem as if the gospel of Christ and *the gospel of anti-
Christ* were designed to originate among the same people; and that this mystic
and mysterious race had been chosen for the supreme manifestations, both of
the divine *and the diabolical* ... From the days of 'Spartacus' Weishaupt to those
of Karl Marx, and down to Trotsky (Russia), Bela Kun (Hungary), Rosa
Luxembourg (Germany) and Emma Goldman (United States), *this worldwide
conspiracy for the overthrow of civilization and for the reconstitution of society on the basis of
arrested development, of envious malevolence and impossible equality, has been steadily
growing.* It played, as a modern writer, Mrs Nesta Webster, has so ably shown,
a definitely recognizable part in the tragedy of the French Revolution. *It has
been the mainspring of every subversive movement during the nineteenth century; and now at
last this band of extraordinary personalities from the underworld of the great cities of
Europe and America have gripped the Russian people by the hair of their heads and have
become practically the undisputed masters of that enormous empire. There is no need to
exaggerate the part played in the creation of Bolshevism and in the bringing about of the
Russian Revolution by these international and for the most part atheistical Jews. It is
certainly a very great one; it probably outweighs all others."*
This is the last candid statement (discoverable by me) from a leading
public man on this question. After it the ban on public discussion came down
and the great silence ensued, which continues to this day. In 1953 Mr.
Churchill refused permission (requisite under English law) for a photostat to
be made of this article *(Illustrated Sunday Herald*, February 8, 1920), without
saying why.
The fact of Jewish leadership was a supremely important piece of
knowledge and the later suppression of it, where public debate would have
been sanative, produced immense effects in weakening the West. The
formulation of any rational State policy becomes impossible when such major
elements of knowledge are excluded from public discussion; it is like playing
billiards with twisted cues and elliptical balls. The strength of the conspiracy is
shown by its success in this matter (as in the earlier period, of Messrs'
Robison, Barruel and Morse) more than by any other thing.
At the time, the facts were available. The British Government's White
Paper of 1919 (Russia, No. 1, a Collection of Reports on Bolshevism) quoted
the report sent to Mr. Balfour in London in 1918 by the Netherlands Minister
at Saint Petersburg, M. Oudendyke: "Bolshevism is organized and worked by
Jews, who have no nationality and whose one object is *to destroy* for their own
ends the existing order of things." The United States Ambassador, Mr. David
R. Francis, reported similarly: "The Bolshevik leaders here, most of whom are
Jews and 90 percent of whom are returned exiles, care little for Russia or any
other country but are internationalists and they are trying to start a *worldwide*

social revolution." M. Oudendyke's report was deleted from later editions of the British official publication and all such authentic documents of that period are now difficult to obtain. Fortunately for the student, one witness preserved the *official* record.

This was Mr. Robert Wilton, correspondent of the London *Times*, who experienced the Bolshevik revolution. The *French* edition of his book included *the official Bolshevik lists* of the membership of the ruling revolutionary bodies (they were *omitted* from the English edition).

These records show that the Central Committee of the Bolshevik party, which wielded the supreme power, contained 3 Russians (including Lenin) and 9 Jews. The next body in importance, the Central Committee of the Executive Commission (or secret police) comprized 42 Jews and 19 Russians, Letts, Georgians and others. The Council of People's Commissars consisted of 17 Jews and five others. The Moscow Che-ka (secret police) was formed of 23 Jews and 13 others. Among the names of 556 high officials of the Bolshevik state officially published in 1918-1919, were 458 Jews and 108 others. Among the central committees of small, supposedly "Socialist" or other non-Communist parties (during that early period the semblance of "opposition" was permitted, to beguile the masses, accustomed under the Czar to opposition parties) were 55 Jews and 6 others. All the names are given in the original documents reproduced by Mr. Wilton. (In parentheses, the composition of the two short-lived Bolshevik governments *outside* Russia in 1918- 1919, namely those of Hungary and Bavaria, was similar).

Mr. Wilton made a great and thankless effort to tell newspaper readers what went on in Russia (broken, he survived only a few years and died in his fifties). He did hot choose the task of reporting the most momentous event that ever came in any journalist's path of duty; it devolved on him. Educated in Russia, he knew the country and its language perfectly, and was held in high esteem by the Russians and the British Embassy alike. He watched the rioting from the window of *The Times* office, adjoining the Prefecture where the ministers of the collapsing regime took refuge. Between the advent of the Kerensky government in the spring of 1917 and the seizure of power by the Bolsheviks in November 1917, his duty was to report an entirely new phenomenon in world affairs: the rise of a Jewish regime to despotic supremacy in Russia and to overt control of the world-revolution. At that moment he was made to realize that he would not be allowed faithfully to report the fact.

The secret story is told, with surprising candour, in the *Official History* of his paper, *The Times*, published in 1952. It shows the hidden mechanism which operated, as early as 1917, to prevent the truth about the revolution reaching the peoples of the West.

This volume pays tribute to the quality of Mr. Wilton's reporting, and his standing in Russia, *before 1917*. Then the tone of the references to him abruptly changes. Mr. Wilton's early warnings of what was to come in 1917, says the book, "*did not at once affect the policy of the paper, partly because their writer did not command full confidence.*"

Why, if his earlier work and reputation were so good? The reason transpires.

The narrative continues that Mr. Wilton began to complain about the "burking" or suppression of his messages. Then *The Times* began to publish articles about Russia from men who had little knowledge of that country. As a result the editorial articles about Russia took on the tone, exasperating to Mr. Wilton, with which newspaper-readers became familiar in the following decades: "those who believe in the future of Russia as *a free and efficient democracy will watch the vindication of the new regime with patient confidence and earnest sympathy.*" (Every incident of Mr. Wilton's experience in Moscow, which Colonel Repington was sharing in London, was repeated in my own experience, and in that of other correspondents, in Berlin in 1933-1938).

The "interregnum of five months began, during which a Jewish regime was to take over from Kerensky. At this very moment his newspaper lost "confidence" in Mr. Wilton. Why? The explanation emerges. The *Official History* of *The Times* says, "It was *not happy for Wilton* that one of his messages … should spread to *Zionist circles,* and even into the Foreign Office, the idea *that he was an anti-semite.*"

"Zionist circles," the reader will observe; not even "Communist circles"; here the working partnership becomes plain. Why should "Zionists" (who wanted the British government to procure them "a homeland" in Palestine) be affronted because a British correspondent in Moscow reported that a Jewish regime was preparing to take over in Russia? Mr. Wilton was reporting the nature of the coming regime; this was his job. In the opinion of "Zionists," this was "anti-semitism," and the mere allegation was enough to destroy "confidence" in him at his head office. How, then, could he have remained "happy" and have retained "confidence." Obviously, only by misreporting events in Russia. In effect, he was expected not to mention the determining fact of the day's news!

When I read this illuminating account I wondered by what route "Zionist circles" had spread to "the Foreign Office," and the Foreign Office to Printing House Square the "idea" that Mr. Wilton was "an anti-semite." The researcher, like the lonely prospector, learns to expect little for much toil, but in this case I was startled by the large nugget of truth which I found in *The Times Official History* thirty- five years after the event. It said that "*the head of propaganda* at the Foreign Office sent to the Editor a paper by one of his staff" repeating the "allegation," (which apparently was first printed in some Zionist sheet). The *Official History* revealed even the identity of this assiduous "one."

It was a young Mr. Reginald Leeper, who three decades later (as Sir Reginald) became British Ambassador in Argentina. I then looked to *Who's Who* for information about Mr. Leeper's career and found that his *first* recorded employment began (when he was twenty- nine) *in 1917*: "entered International Bureau, Department of Information in 1917." Mr. Leeper's memorandum about Mr. Wilton was sent to *The Times* early in *May 1917*. Therefore, if he entered the Foreign Office on New Year's day of 1917, he had been in it just four months when he conveyed to *The Times* his "allegation" about the exceptionally qualified Mr. Wilton, of seventeen years' service with that paper, and the effect was immediate; the *Official History* says that Mr. Wilton's despatches thereafter, during the decisive period, either miscarried or "were *ignored.*" (The editor was the same of whom Colonel Repington complained in 1917-1918 and to whom the present writer sent his resignation in 1938 on the same basic principle of reputable journalism.)

Mr. Wilton struggled on for a time, continually protesting against the "burking" and suppression of his despatches, and then as his last service to truthful journalism put all that he knew into his book. He recognized and recorded the acts which identified the especial nature of the regime: the law against "anti-semitism," the anti-Christian measures, the canonization of Judas Iscariot, and the Talmudic fingerprint mockingly left in the death-chamber of the Romanoffs.

The law against "anti-semitism" (which cannot be defined) was in itself a fingerprint. An illegal government, predominantly Jewish, by this measure warned the Russian masses, under pain of death, not to interest themselves in the origins of the revolution. It meant in effect that the Talmud became the law of Russia, and in the subsequent four decades this law has in effect and in growing degree been made part of the structure of the west.

The short-lived anti-Christian deeds of the French phase of the revolution reappeared in more open form. The dynamiting of churches and the installation of an anti-God museum in the Cathedral of Saint Basil were the most ostentatious indications of the nature of the regime, which Mr. Wilton indicated: "Taken according to numbers of population, the Jews represented *one* in ten; among the commissars that rule Bolshevist Russia they are *nine* in ten; if anything the proportion of Jews is still greater." This was plain reporting, and if the report had related to "Ukrainians," for instance, instead of "Jews," none would have objected; the mere act of reporting a fact became the ground for secret denunciation because the fact related to Jews.

The memorial to Judas Iscariot, recorded by Mr. Wilton, was another deliberate intimation to Christendom. If the Jewish rulers merely wanted to bring about an equalitarian society in 1917, there was no relevance in bestowing a halo of heroism on a deed of AD 29; the revolution in Russia cannot be understood at all unless the symbolism of this act is comprehended.

The aspect of a Talmudic vengeance on "the heathen" was unmistakably given to the massacres of that period. In August 1918 a Jew, Kanegisser, shot a Jew, Uritsky; thereon a Jew, Peters, at the head of the Petrograd Cheka ordered "mass terror" on *Russians* and another Jew, Zinovieff, demanded that ten million Russians be "annihilated"; the British Government's White Book on Bolshevism (1919) records the massacre of Russian peasants which followed.

By far the most significant act was the form given to the murder of the Romanoff family. But for Mr. Wilton this story would never have reached the world, which to this day might believe that the Czar's wife and children ended their lives naturally in "protective" custody.

The Czar acted *constitutionally* to the end, abdicating at the advice of his ministers (March 5, 1917). Thereafter (during the Kerensky period and its first aftermath) he was relatively well treated for a year as the prisoner at Tobolsk of a *Russian* commandant and *Russian* guards. In April 1918, when the Jewish regime had gained control, he was transferred, by order from Moscow, to Ekaterinburg. The Russian guards were then withdrawn and their place inside his prison house was taken by men whose identity has never been established: The local Russians later recalled them as "Letts" (the only foreign-speaking Red soldiers known to them), but they seem to have been brought from Hungary.

The Russian commandant's place was taken by a Jew, Yankel Yurovsky (July 7). That completed a chain of Jewish captors from the top, Moscow, through the regional Urals Soviet, to his prison at Ekaterinburg (which is in the Urals). The real ruler of Russia then was the terrorist Yankel Sverdloff, president of the Moscow Cheka, who was a Jew. The Ekaterinburg Cheka was run by seven Jews, one of them Yankel Yurovsky. On July 20 the Urals Soviet announced that it had shot the Czar and sent his wife and son to "a place of security." The Moscow Cheka issued a similar announcement, signed by Sverdloff, "approving the action of the Regional Soviet of the Urals." At that time the entire family was dead.

The truth only became known through the chance that Ekaterinburg fell to the White armies on July 25, that Mr. Wilton accompanied them, and that their commander, General Diterichs, a famous Russian criminologist, M. Sokoloff, and Mr. Wilton uncovered the buried evidence. When the White troops withdrew Mr. Wilton brought away the proofs; they appear in his book and include many photographs.

The murders had been carried out by order from and in constant consultation with Sverdloff in Moscow; records of telephone conversations between him and the Chekists in Ekaterinburg were found. Among these was a report to him from Ekaterinburg saying "Yesterday a courier left with the documents that interest you." This courier was the chief assassin, Yurovsky, and the investigators believed that the "documents" were the heads of the Romanoffs, as no skulls or skull-bones were found.

The deed was described by witnesses who had not been able to escape, and at least one was a participant. At midnight on July 16 Yurovsky awoke the Czar and his family, took them to a basement room and there shot them. The actual murderers were Yurovsky, his seven unidentified foreign accomplices, one Nikulin from the local Cheka, and two Russians, apparently professional gunmen employed by the Cheka. The victims were the Czar, his wife, ailing son (who was held in his father's arms as he could not walk), four daughters, Russian doctor, manservant, cook and maid. The room was still a shambles, from the shooting and bayoneting, when M. Sokoloff and Mr. Wilton saw it, and his book includes the picture of it.

The circumstances having been determined, the investigators almost despaired of finding the bodies, or their remains; they learned that Yurovsky, before escaping the town, had boasted that "the world will never know what we did with the bodies." However, the earth at length gave up its secret. The bodies had been taken by five lorries to a disused iron pit in the woods, cut up and burned, 150 gallons of petrol being used; one Voikoff of the Urals Cheka (a fellow-passenger of Lenin in the train from Germany) as Commissar of Supplies had supplied 400 lbs. of sulphuric acid for dissolving the bones. The ashes and fragments had been thrown down the shaft, the ice at the bottom having first been smashed so that the mass would sink; then a flooring had been lowered and fixed over the place. When this was removed the search reached its end. On top lay the corpse of a spaniel belonging to one of the princesses; below were fragments of bone and skin, a finger, and many identifiable personal belongings which had escaped destruction. A puzzling find was a small collection of nails, coins, pieces of tinfoil and the like. This looked like the contents of a schoolboy's pockets, and was; the little boy's English tutor, Mr. Sidney Gibbes, identified it. The precautions taken to dispose of the bodies and of other evidence were of the kind that only criminals of long experience in their trade could have devised; they resemble the methods used in gang warfare, during the Prohibition period, in the United States.

These discoveries, becoming known in the outer world, exposed the untruth of Sverdloff's announcement that only the Czar had been "executed" and his family sent to "a place of security." The murderers staged a mock trial of "28 persons on the accusation of having murdered the Czar and his family." Only eight names were published, all of them unknown in connection with the crime, and five persons were said to have been shot, who if they existed at all cannot have had any part in it. The arch-assassin, Sverdloff, was soon afterwards killed in some party dispute and thousands of innocent people died in the indiscriminate massacres which followed.

Ekaterinburg was renamed Sverdlovsk to give enduring fame to his part in the symbolic deed.

The chief reason for recounting the details of the pogrom of the Romanoffs is to point to the "fingerprint" which was left in the room where it was done. One of the assassins, presumably their leader, stayed to exult and put a significant signature on the wall, which was covered with obscene or mocking inscriptions in Hebrew, Magyar and German. Among them was a couplet which deliberately related the deed to the Law of the Torah-Talmud and thus offered it to posterity as an example of the fulfilment of that law, and of Jewish vengeance as understood by the Levites. It was written in German by someone who parodied the Jewish poet, Heinrich Heine's lines on the death of Belshazzar, the imaginary potentate whose murder is portrayed in *Daniel* as God's punishment for an affront offered to Judah:

Belsazar ward aber in selbiger Nacht Von selbigen Knechten umgebracht.[14]

The parodist, sardonically surveying the shambles, adapted these lines to what he had just done:

Belsa*tsar* ward in selbiger Nacht Von *seinen* Knechten umgebracht.

No clearer clue to motive and identity was ever left behind.

The revolution was not Russian; the eruption was brought about in Russia, but the revolution had its friends in high places everywhere. At this period (1917-1918) the student for the first time is able to establish that leading men began to give that secret support to Communism which they were already giving to its blood brother, Zionism. This happened on *both* sides of the fighting-line; once the secret, but overriding purposes of the war came into play the distinction between "friend" and "foe" disappeared. The Zionists, though they concentrated "irresistible pressure" on the politicians of London and Washington, long kept their headquarters in *Berlin;* the Communists obtained decisive support from Germany at one moment and from Germany's enemies the next.

For instance, Germany when the 1914-1918 war began started "sending back to Russia Russians of revolutionary tendencies who were prisoners here, with money and passports, in order that they may stir up trouble at home" (Ambassador Gerard in Berlin to Mr. House). Mr. Robert Wilton says the decision to *Foment the revolution* in Russia was formally taken at a German and Austrian General Staff meeting at Vienna late in 1915. The German Chief-of-Staff, General Ludendorff, later regretted this: "By sending Lenin to Russia our government assumed ... a great responsibility. From a *military* point of view his journey was justified, for Russia had to be laid low; but our government should have seen to it that we were not involved in her fall."

---

[14] ["But ere the morning came again, Belshazzar was slain by his own men."]

That, taken as an isolated case, might be a simple human error: what appeared to be a sound *military* move produced catastrophic *political* consequences not foreseen when it was made. But what explanation can be found for American and British politicians, whose foremost *military and political* principle should have been to sustain Russia and yet who supported the alien revolutionaries who "laid Russia low"?

I have already quoted the editorial about the revolution ("... a free and efficient democracy ... the vindication of the new regime ...") which appeared in *The Times* of London while its experienced correspondent's despatches were being "ignored" and "confidence" withdrawn from him because the newspaper had received "an allegation" that he was "an anti-semite." On the other side of the Atlantic the true ruler of the Republic, Mr. House was confiding to his diary similar sentiments. For him the alien revolutionaries smuggled into Russia during wartime *from the West* ("this band of extraordinary personalities from the underworld of the great cities of Europe and America," Mr. Churchill) were honest agrarian reformers: "the Bolshevists appeared to the peace-hungry and land- hungry Russians as the first leaders who made a sincere effort to satisfy their needs."

Today all know what happened to the Russians' "land-hunger" under Bolshevism. In 1917 the Czars and their ministers for fifty years had been toiling to satisfy this "land-hunger" and by assassination had been thwarted. Apparently Mr. House was ignorant of that. When the revolution was accomplished he instructed the shadow-president: "that literally nothing be done further than that an expression of sympathy be offered for *Russia's* efforts to weld herself into *a virile democracy* and *to proffer our financial, industrial and moral support in every way possible.*"[15]

The resemblance between the first phrase of this sentence and the editorial of *The Times* in London may be noted; powerful behind- scene groups in both capitals evidently were agreed to present the public masses with this false picture of a "virile" and "efficient" *democracy* in the making. The second phrase cancelled the policy initially recommended of "literally doing nothing" beyond uttering sympathetic words, by giving the order literally to do *everything;* for what more can be done than to give "financial, industrial and moral support in every way possible"? This was American state policy from the moment that Mr. House so instructed the president, and it exactly describes the policy pursued by President Roosevelt during the *Second* World War, as will be shown.

---

[15] It might be significant of the influences which continued to prevail in the entourage of American presidents during the next two generations that President Eisenhower in 1955, from his hospital room in Denver, sent a personal message of congratulations to the Soviet Premier, Bulganin, on the anniversary of the *Bolshevik* revolution, November 7. The democratic and parliamentary revolution, legitimized by the Czars abdication, occurred in March 1917; November 7 was a day on which the Bolsheviks overthrew the legitimate regime. By 1955 American presidents *were* habitually warning their people against the menace of "Soviet" or "Communist" (i.e., Bolshevik) aggression.

Thus the West, or powerful men in the West, began to range itself with the world-revolution against the Russians, which meant, against all men who abhorred the revolution. Not all the powerful men, or men later to become powerful, lent themselves to this hidden undertaking. At that time Mr. Winston Churchill again stated the nature of the revolution:

"Certainly I dispute the title of the Bolshevists to represent Russia … They despise such a mere commonplace as nationality. Their ideal is a worldwide proletarian revolution. The Bolsheviks robbed Russia at one stroke of two most precious things: peace and victory, the victory that was within her grasp and the peace which was her dearest desire. The Germans sent Lenin into Russia with the deliberate intention of working for the downfall of Russia … No sooner did Lenin arrive there than he began *beckoning a finger here and a finger there to obscure persons in sheltered retreats in New York, in Glasgow, in Berne and other countries*" (the reader will perceive whence the "Russian" revolutionaries were brought to Russia) "*and he gathered together the leading spirits of a formidable sect, the most formidable sect in the world* … With these spirits around him he set to work with demoniacal ability to tear to pieces every institution on which the Russian state and nation depended. Russia was laid low. Russia had to be laid low … Her sufferings are more fearful than modern records hold and she had been robbed of her place among the great nations of the world." (House of Commons, 5 November 1919.)

Mr. Churchill's description remains valid, particularly the phrase, "the most formidable sect in the world," which resembles the phrase used by Bakunin in his attack on Jewish usurpation of the revolution fifty years earlier. The passage quoted from Mr. Churchill's article earlier in this chapter shows that he was equally aware of the identity of this sect.

Thus Dr. Chaim Weizmann's youthful fellow-conspirators from the Talmudic area of Russia triumphed in Russia at the very moment when he triumphed in London and Washington. The only difference between him and them, from the start, was that between "revolutionary-Zionism" and "revolutionary-Communism," as he shows. In his student days in Berlin, Freiburg and Geneva, he had waged many a hot debate about this point of difference, which for those who reject revolution as such is a distinction without meaning. Mr. Balfour's amanuensis, Mrs Dugdale, portrays the blood-brothers of the revolution in argument during the years when their simultaneous triumph was in preparation:

"Lenin and Trotsky took power in the same week of November 1917 that Jewish nationalism won its recognition. Years before, in Geneva, Trotsky and Weizmann had night after night expounded from rival cafés in the university quarter their opposed political beliefs. Both of them Russian-born … they had swayed *the crowds of Jewish students* from one side of the street to the other; Leon Trotsky, apostle of Red revolution; Chaim Weizmann, apostle of a tradition unbroken for two thousand years. Now by a most strange coincidence in the same week each of them accomplished the fulfilment of his dream."

In truth, the pincers in which the West was to be gripped had been forged, and each handle was held by one of two groups of revolutionaries "Russian-born" (but not Russian).

For Dr. Weizmann and his associates in London and Washington, the event in Moscow was a passing embarrassment, in one respect. They had based their demand for Palestine on the legend that "a place of refuge" must be found for Jews "persecuted in Russia" (an obvious *non sequitur* but good enough for "the mob"), and now there *was* no "persecution in Russia." On the contrary, in Moscow a Jewish regime ruled and "anti-Semitism" was a capital offence. Where, then, were the Jews who needed "a place of refuge"? (This is evidently the reason why Mr. Robert Wilton had to be prevented from reporting the nature of the new regime in Moscow).

Rabbi Elmer Berger says, "The Soviet government *even privileged Jews as Jews* ... at a single stroke, the revolution emancipated those very Jews for whom, previously, no solution other than Zionism would be efficacious, *according to Zionist spokesmen. Soviet Jews no longer had need of Palestine, or any other refuge.* The *lever* of the suffering of Russian Jewry, which Herzl had often used in attempts to prise a charter for Palestine from some power, *was gone.*"

That did not deter Dr. Weizmann. At once he informed the Jews that they must not expect any respite:

"Some of our friends ... are very quick in drawing conclusions as to what will happen to the Zionist movement after the Russian revolution. Now, they say, the greatest stimulus for the Zionist movement has been removed. Russian Jewry is free ... Nothing can be more superficial and wrong than that. *We have never built our Zionist movement on the sufferings of our people in Russia or elsewhere. These sufferings were never the cause of Zionism.* The fundamental cause of Zionism was, and is, the ineradicable striving of Jewry to have a home of its own."

Dr. Weizmann spoke truth in untruth. It was true that the organizers of Zionism, in their private hearts, had never in reality built their movement on "the sufferings of our people in Russia or elsewhere"; they were indifferent to any suffering, Jewish or other, caused by Zionism. But they *had* beyond all dispute *used* "the sufferings of our people in Russia" as their argument in beleaguering Western politicians, who from Mr. Wilson in 1912 onward repeatedly alluded to it.

In this crucial week, the falsity of the entire contention, though revealed, made no difference, for the British Government, as Mrs Dugdale recorded, was at length *committed.* Not even a pretence could be maintained that any Jews needed "a place of refuge" but Mr. Lloyd George had undertaken to conquer Palestine for "the Jews."

The basic fallacy of the enterprise was exposed at the very instant when it was clamped like a millstone round the neck of the West. Although this irreparable flaw in its foundation must cause its ultimate collapse, like that of Sabbatai Zevi's messiahship in 1666, the tragi-comedy thenceforth had to be played to its ruinous end.

But for one later event, the undertaking would have died a natural death within a few years and would survive today in the annals merely as Balfour's Folly. This event was the coming of Hitler, which for a while filled the gap left by the collapse of the legend of "persecution in Russia" and produced in some Jews a desire to go even to Palestine. For the Zionists Hitler, had he not arisen, would have needed to be created; a collapsing scheme was made by him to look almost lifelike for some time. The Hitlerist episode belongs to a later chapter in this narrative.

Chapter 33

THE LEAGUE TO ENFORCE PEACE

At the same moment in 1917 when the two kindred forces from Russia, revolutionary-Communism and revolutionary-Zionism, emerged into the full open, the third secret purpose of the war, the one of which they were the instruments, also was revealed. This was the project for a "federation of the world" to take over "the management of human affairs" and to rule *by force.*

The masses then (as in the Second War, twenty-five years later) were being egged on to destroy a "madman in Berlin" on this very ground, that he sought to rule the world by force. In England Mr. Eden Philpotts (one of many such oracles then and in the next war) thundered:

"You thought *to grasp the world;* but you shall keep its curses only, crowned upon your brow ..." and that was the universal cry. Yet the secret plan promoted in the West was equally one to "grasp the world by force" and to put new "warlords" over it.

It was merely dressed in other words. What was reactionary Prussian militarism in Germany was one of Mr. House's "advanced ideas" in Washington; what was megalomaniac ambition in the Kaiser was an enlightened concept of "a new world order" in London. The politicians of the West became professional dissimulators. Even Disraeli could not foresee in 1832 ("The practice of politics in the East may be defined by one word: dissimulation") that this would become the definition of political practice in the *West* in the 20th Century; but this happened when Western political leaders, by supporting Zionism and the world-revolution, yielded to the prompting of Asiatics; their acts took on an Asiatic duplicity in place of native candour.

Strangely, Mr. Woodrow Wilson, the most compliant of them all, at the start rebelled most fretfully against the secret constraints. He tried, as has been shown, to declare that "the causes and objects of the war are obscure," and when this was forbidden by Mr. House, still avowed that the belligerents on both sides pursued "the same" objects. He went further at the very start of his presidency, when he wrote, "It is an intolerable thing that *the government of the Republic should have got so far out* of the hands of the people; should have been *captured by interests which are special and not general.* We know that *something intervenes* between the people of the United States *and the control of their own affairs* at Washington." Presumably he learned the nature of these "interests" and this "control," and the galling knowledge may have caused his collapse (and that of Mr. Roosevelt in the later generation).

Nevertheless, he was used to launch the plan for setting up "a federation of the world," based on force. The idea was "oozed into his brain" by others; the phrase is used by Mr. House's biographer to describe the method by which Mr. House prompted the actions of other men (and by which his own were prompted). In *November* 1915, when the American people were still ardent for the president who was keeping them out of the war, Mr. House instructed him:

"We must throw the influence of this nation in behalf of a plan by which international obligations must be kept and maintained and in behalf of some plan by which *the peace of the world* may be maintained."

This was always the sales-talk: that "the plan" would "maintain world peace." Mr. House had long been discussing the plan with Sir Edward Grey (Mr. Asquith's Foreign Secretary; he became blind in 1914 but in a moment of spiritual clairvoyance used the words which have become truer ever since, "The lights are going out all over Europe"). Sir Edward Grey was captivated by "the plan," and wrote to Mr. House, "International law has hitherto had *no sanction;* the lesson of this war is that the Powers must bind themselves to give it *sanction.*" "Sanction" was the euphemism used by the dissimulators to avoid alarming the masses by the sound of "war" or "force." The dictionary definition, in such a context, is "a coercive measure," and the only means of coercion between nations is, ultimately, war: no "sanction" can be effective unless it is backed by that threat. Therefore Sir Edward Grey thought war could be ended by making war. He was an incorruptible but apparently deluded man; the originators of the great "idea" knew what they meant (and in our day this also has been revealed).

By 1916 Mr. House had instructed Mr. Wilson as to his duty and in May the president publicly announced support for "the plan" at a meeting of a new body candidly called "The League to *Enforce* Peace." Mr. Wilson knew nothing of its nature: "*it does not appear that Woodrow Wilson studied seriously the programme of the League to Enforce Peace*" (Mr. House's *Private Papers*).

This was a reincarnation of the earlier "League to enforce peace" which (as Lord Robert Cecil had reminded Mr. House) "really became a *league to uphold tyranny.*" In 1916 the name gave away the game; American opinion was not then ready to walk into so obvious a trap. Senator George Wharton Pepper recalls: "*A heavily-financed organization* aptly entitled 'The League F Peace' was making our task easier by emphasizing, as its title indicated, that the Covenant" (of the League of Nations) "was intended to be made effective *by force* ...Our constant contention, in opposition to theirs, was that *the appeal to force* was at the best futile and at the worst dangerous ... I contrasted the certain futility of *an appeal to international force* with the possible hopefulness of reliance upon international conference, and declared myself favourable to any association of the latter type and unalterably opposed to a league which was based on the former."

The dissimulators soon dropped the name, "The League to Enforce Peace," but the "plan," which produced "The League of Nations," transparently remained the same: it was one to transfer the control of national armies to some super-national committee which could use them for "the management of human affairs" in ways serving its own special ends, and that has continued the motive to the present day. As in the earlier case of Zionism, President Wilson was committed long before the crucial moment (by his public declaration of May 1916) and as soon as America was in the war (April 1917) announced that it was involved in an undertaking to set up "*a new international order*"; this statement was made at the moment of the first revolution in Russia and of the preparation of the Balfour Declaration.

Thus the three great "plans" moved together into the West, and this was the project which was to crown the work of the other two. Its basic principle was the destruction of nation-states and nationhood so that it gave expression, in modern form, to the ancient conflict between the Old Testament and the New, between the Levitical Law and the Christian message. The Torah-Talmud is the only discoverable, original source of this *idea* of "destroying nations"; Mr. House thought it almost impossible to trace any "idea" to its fount, but in this case the track *can* be followed back through the centuries to 500 BC, and it is nowhere obliterated during those twenty-five hundred years. If before that time anybody in the known world had made this "destructive principle" into a code and creed they and it have faded into oblivion. The *idea* contained in the Torah-Talmud has gone unbroken through all the generations. The New Testament rejects it and speaks of "the *deception* of nations," not of their destruction. *Revelation* foretells a day when this process of deception of nations shall end. Those who seek to interpret prophecy might very well see in The League to Enforce Peace, under its successive aliases, the instrument of this "deception," doomed at the end to fail.

Mr. House having decided, and Mr. Wilson having declared, that "a new international order" must be established, Mr. House (according to Mr. Howden) set up a body known as "The Inquiry" to draft a plan. Its head was his brother-in-law, Dr. Sidney Mezes (then president of the College of the City of New York), and its secretary a Mr. Walter Lippmann (then writing for *The New Republic*). A Dr. Isaiah Bowman (then director of the American Geographical Society) gave "personal advice and assistance."

The group of men placed in charge of The Inquiry therefore was predominantly Jewish (though in this case not Russian-Jewish: this might indicate the true nature of the superior authority indicated by Dr. Kastein's allusion to "a Jewish international") and Jewish inspiration may thus reasonably be seen in the plan which it produced. This (says Mr. Howden) was a draft "Convention for a League of Nations" to which *Mr. House* put his signature in July 1918: "President Wilson *was not*, and never pretended to be, *the author of the Covenant.*" Here, then, are the origins of the League of Nations.

The Peace Conference loomed ahead when Mr. House prepared to launch this "new world order," and its first acts pointed to the identity of the controlling-group behind the Western governments. Zionism and Palestine (issues unknown to the masses when the 1914-1918 war began) were found to be high, if not paramount among the matters to be discussed at the conference which ended it.

President Wilson, for this reason, seems to have known moments of exaltation between long periods of despondency. Rabbi Stephen Wise, at his side, depicted the Palestinian undertaking in such terms that the president, entranced, soliloquised, "To think that I, a son of the manse, should be able to help restore the Holy Land to its people." While he thus contemplated himself in the mirror of posterity the rabbi beside him compared him with the Persian King Cyrus, who had enabled the exiled Jews of his land to return to Jerusalem." King Cyrus had allowed native Judahites, if they wished, to return to Judah after some fifty years; President Wilson was required to transplant Judaized Chazars from Russia to a land left by the original Jews some eighteen centuries before.

Across the Atlantic Dr. Weizmann made ready for the Peace Conference. He was then evidently one of the most powerful men in the world, a potentate (or emissary of potentates) to whom the "premier-dictators" of the West made humble obeisance. At a moment in 1918 when the fate of England was in the balance on the stricken Western Front an audience of the King of England was postponed. Dr. Weizmann complained so imperiously that Mr. Balfour at once restored the appointment; save for the place of meeting, which was Buckingham Palace, Mr. Weizmann seems in fact to have given audience to the monarch. During the Second World War the Soviet dictator Stalin, being urged by the Western leaders to take account of the influence of the Pope, asked brusquely, "How many divisions has the Pope?" Such at least was the anecdote, much retold in clubs and pubs, and to simple folk it seemed to express essential truth in a few words. Dr. Weizmann's case shows how essentially untrue it was. He had not a single soldier, but he and the international he represented were able to obtain capitulations never before won save by conquering armies.

He disdained the capitulants and the scene of his triumphs alike. He wrote to Lady Crewe, "We hate equally anti-semites *and philo-semites.*" Mr. Balfour, Mr. Lloyd George and the other "friends" were philo-semites of the first degree, in Dr. Weizmann's meaning of the word, and excelled themselves in servience to the man who despised them. As to England itself, Dr. Weizmann two decades later, when he contemplated the wild beasts in the Kruger National Park, soliloquised, "It must be a wonderful thing to be *an animal* on the South African game reserve; much better than being a Jew in Warsaw *or even in London.*"

In 1918 Dr. Weizmann decided to inspect his realm-elect. When he reached Palestine the German attack in France had begun, the depleted British armies were reeling back, and "most of the European troops in Palestine were being withdrawn to reinforce the armies in France." At such a moment he demanded that the foundation stone of a Hebrew University be laid with all public ceremony. Lord Allenby protested that "the Germans are almost at the gates of Paris!" Dr. Weizmann replied that this was "only one episode." Lord Allenby obdured; Dr. Weizmann persisted; Lord Allenby under duress referred to Mr. Balfour *and was at once ordered by cable to obey.* With great panoply of staff officers, troops and presented arms (disturbed only by the sounds of distant British-Turkish fighting) Dr. Weizmann then held his ceremony on Mount Scopus. .

(I remember those days in France. Even half a million more British soldiers there would have transformed the battle; a multitude of lives would have been saved, and the war probably ended sooner. The French and British ordeal in France made a Zionist holiday in Palestine).

When the war at last ended, on November 11, 1918, none other than Dr. Weizmann was at luncheon the *sole* guest of Mr. Lloyd George, whom he found "reading the Psalms and near to tears." Afterwards the Zionist chieftain watched from historic Ten Downing Street as the prime minister disappeared, borne shoulder high by a mafficking mob towards a Thanksgiving service in Westminster Abbey.

Masses and "managers"; did any among the crowd notice the high, domed head, with bearded face and heavy-lidded eyes watching from the window of Ten Downing Street?

Then Dr. Weizmann led a Zionist delegation to the Peace Conference of 1919 where "the new world order" was to be set up. He informed the august Council of Ten that "the Jews had been *hit harder by the war than any other group";* the politicians of 1919 made no demur to this insult to their millions of dead. However, a remonstrant Jew, Mr. Sylvain Levi of France, at the last moment tried to instil prudence in them. He told them:

First, that Palestine was a small, poor land with an existing population of 600,000 Arabs, and that the Jews, having a higher standard of life than the Arabs, *would tend to dispossess them;* second, that the Jews who would go to Palestine would be *mainly Russian Jews, who were of explosive tendencies;* third, that the creation of a Jewish national home in Palestine would introduce *the dangerous principle of Jewish dual loyalties.*

These three warnings have been fulfilled to the letter, and were heard with hostility by the Gentile politicians assembled at the Peace Conference of 1919. Mr. Lansing, the American Secretary of State, at once gave M. Lévi his quietus. He asked Dr. Weizmann, "What do you mean by a Jewish national home?" Dr. Weizmann said he meant that, *always safeguarding the interests of non-Jews*, Palestine would ultimately become "*as Jewish as England is English.*" Mr. Lansing said this absolutely obscure reply was "absolutely clear," the Council of Ten nodded agreement, and M. Levi, like all Jewish remonstrants for twenty-five centuries, was discomfited. (He was only heard at all to maintain a pretence of impartial consideration; Rabbi Wise, disquietened by "the difficulties we had to face in Paris," had already made sure of President Wilson's docility. Approaching the president privately, he said, "Mr. President, *World Jewry* counts on you in its hour of need and hope," thus excommunicating M. Levi and the Jews who thought like him. Mr. Wilson, placing his hand on the rabbi's shoulder, "quietly and firmly said, 'Have no fear, Palestine will be yours.'")

One other man tried to avert the deed which these men, with frivolity, were preparing. Colonel Lawrence loved Semites, for he had lived with the Arabs and roused them in the desert against their Turkish rulers. He was equally a friend of Jews (Dr. Weizmann says "he has *mistakenly* been represented as anti-Zionist") and believed that "a Jewish homeland" (in the sense first given to the term, of a *cultural* centre) could well be incorporated in the united Arab State for which he had worked.

Lawrence saw in Paris that what was intended was to plant Zionist nationalism like a time-bomb among a clutter of weak Arab states, and the realization broke him. Mr. David Garnett, who edited his *Letters* , says, "Lawrence won his victories without endangering more than a handful of Englishmen and they were won, not to add subject provinces to our empire, but that the Arabs whom he had lived with and loved should be a free people, and that Arab civilization should be reborn."

That was Lawrence's faith during his "Revolt in the Desert," and what the men who sent him to Arabia told him. When the Paris Conference began he was "fully in control of his nerves and quite as normal as most of us" (Mr. J.M. Keynes). He arrived believing in President Wilson's pledge (speech of the Fourteen Points, January 8, 1918), "The nationalities under Turkish rule should be assured *an undoubted security of life and an absolutely independent opportunity of autonomous development.*" He could not know that these words were false, because Mr. Wilson was secretly committed to Zionism, through the men around him.

After Dr. Weizmann's reply to Mr. Lansing, and its approval by the Council of Ten, the betrayal became clear to Lawrence and he showed "the disillusion and the bitterness and the defeat resulting from the Peace Conference; he had complete faith that President Wilson would secure self-determination for the Arab peoples when he went to the Peace Conference; he was completely disillusioned when he returned."(Mr. Garnett) Lawrence himself later wrote, "We lived many lives in those whirling campaigns" (in the desert) "never sparing ourselves any good or evil; yet when we achieved and the new world dawned *the old men came out again and took from us our victory and remade it in the likeness of the former world they knew* ... I meant to make a new nation, to restore to the world a lost influence, to give twenty millions of Semites the foundations on which to build an inspired dream-palace of their national thoughts."

Lawrence, who was broken by this experience, was then among the most famous men in the world. Had he joined the dissimulators hardly any rank or honour would have been refused him. He threw up his rank, and away his decorations, and tried from shame even to lose his identity; he enlisted under an assumed name in the lowest rank of the Royal Air Force, where he was later discovered by an assiduous newspaper man. This last phase of his life, and the motor-bicycle accident which ended it, have a suicidal look (resembling the similar phase and end of Mr. James Forrestal after the Second War) and he must be accounted among the martyrs of this story.

The leading public men were agreed to promote the Zionist adventure through the "international world order" which they were about to found, at any cost in honour and human suffering. In nearly all *other* questions they differed, so that, the war hardly ended, reputations began bursting like bubbles and friendships cracking like plaster, in Paris. Some breach occurred between President Wilson and his "second personality, independent self" (a similar, mysterious estrangement was to sever President Roosevelt and *his* other self, Mr. Harry Hopkins, at the end of another war).

Mr. House was at his zenith. Prime ministers, ministers, ambassadors and delegates besieged him at the Hotel Crillon; in a single day he gave forty-nine audiences to such high notables. Once the French Prime Minister, M. Clemenceau, called when Mr. Wilson was with Mr. House; the president was required to withdraw while the two great men privately conferred. Perhaps humiliation at last broke Mr. Woodrow Wilson; he was stricken by mortal illness in Paris (as Mr. Franklin Roosevelt at Yalta, though Mr. Wilson survived rather longer). Apparently the two never saw or communicated with each other again! Mr. House merely recorded, "My separation from Woodrow Wilson was and is to me a tragic mystery, a mystery that now can never be dispelled for its explanation lies buried with him."

The illusions of power were dissolving. These men were never truly powerful, because they acted as the instruments of others. They already look wraithlike in the annals, and if the squares and boulevards named after them still bear their names, few remember who they were. Mr. Wilson returned to America and soon died. Mr. House before long was lonely and forgotten in the apartment in East 35th Street. Mr. Lloyd George found himself in the political wilderness and was only able to complete the ruin of a once-great Liberal party; within a decade he found himself at the head of four followers.

Mr. Balfour, for a few more years, absent-mindedly haunted Saint James's Park.

They were not able to accomplish all that their mentors wished. Shaken by the violence of American objections, Mr. Wilson "absolutely declined to accept the French demand for the creation of an international force that should operate *under the executive control of the League.*" The American Constitution (the president suddenly recollected) did not permit of any such surrender of sovereignty.

Thus the worst was averted, in that generation. The secret men, who *continued* to be powerful when these "premier-dictators" and pliable "administrators" were shorn of their *semblance* of power, had to wait for the Second World War to get their hands on the armies of the nation-states. Then they achieved their "League to enforce peace" almost (but still not quite) in the fullness of despotic power coveted by them. In 1919 they had to content themselves with a modest first experiment: The League Of Nations.

The United States would not even join it; the masses of America, disquietened by the results of the war and instinctively striving to regain the safe haven of "no foreign entanglements," would have none of it. Britain joined, but under other prime ministers than Mr. Lloyd George would not hand over control of its armies. The way to the kind of "new world order" envisaged by Mr. House and his prompters was blocked for the time being. Nevertheless a way was found, through the League of Nations, to effect one fateful, and possibly fatal breach in British sovereignty.

The authority of this "League of Nations," whatever it amounted to, was used to cover the use of British troops as a bodyguard for the Zionists intending to seize Palestine. The device employed to give this mock-legal air to the deed was called "the mandate," and I have earlier shown where it was born. By means of it the League of Nations was able to install the Zionists from Russia in Arabia, where they revealed the "explosive tendencies" foretold by M. Sylvain Levi in 1919 and apparent to all today, in 1956. This was the sole, enduring accomplishment of the "new world order" set up in 1919 and by the ancient test, *Cui bono?*, the authorship of this "idea" may be judged.

The story of "The mandate" (and of a man who tried to avert it) therefore forms the next chapter in this narrative.

Chapter 34

THE END OF LORD NORTHCLIFFE

During the three years which followed the Peace Conference of 1919 the way had to be found to keep British armies in Palestine, make them look as if they performed an honourable duty there, and in fact use them as cloak for a deed which had the character of an assassination. This problem, of infinite complexity, was efficiently solved. An impressive picture of the secret manipulation of great governments for a nefarious purpose emerges from the records; the method of exerting "irresistible pressure upon international politics" constantly improved with practice.

After the Peace Conference had approved the Zionist claim to Palestine (and thereby disowned the mass of emancipated Western Jews, personified by M. Sylvain Levi) the next step was taken at the San Remo Conference of 1920, where the victor powers met to dismember the conquered Turkish Empire. This conference adopted the ingenious deception invented by Dr. Weizmann in 1915 and agreed that Britain should administer Palestine under "a mandate."

Protests against the undertaking then were growing loud, because its true nature was beginning to be realized, but Mr. Balfour assured Dr. Weizmann that "they were regarded as without importance and would *certainly not affect policy, which had been definitely set.*" Here is the cryptic statement, often to recur later, that policy in this one question must not, cannot and never will alter, so that national interest, honour and all other considerations are irrelevant. I know of no other case where an unalterable tenet of high State policy has been fixed without regard to State interest or consultation of public opinion at any stage. At San Remo Mr. Lloyd George was worried lest "the frost" of peace should set in before the secret purpose was accomplished, and told Dr. Weizmann, "You have no time to waste. Today the world is like the Baltic *before a frost.* For the moment it is still in motion. But if it gets set, you will have to batter your heads against the ice blocks and wait for a second thaw." Had Mr. Lloyd George said "second war" he would have been correct and possibly that was what he meant by "thaw." In these circumstances the San Remo Conference "confirmed the Balfour Declaration *and the decision to give the mandate to Great Britain.*" After that only one step remained between the Zionists and their goal; the League of Nations had to invent "mandates," bestow on itself the right to bestow mandates, and then "ratify" *this* Mandate.

That happened in 1922, as will be seen, but during the interval protests against the deed came from *every responsible authority or community directly involved.* The forces engaged in promoting it were three: the directing Zionists from Russia, the "philo-semites" in high places whom Dr. Weizmann "hated" while he used them, and, among the masses, that body of sentimental liberals scathingly depicted in the Protocols. Against it was ranked authoritative and experienced opinion in such overwhelming measure that, had the question been any other than this one to which the "administrators" were secretly committed, it would have collapsed. The mass of protest was so great that it is enumerated in its parts here for comparison with the summary which follows. It came from (1) the Palestinian Arabs; (2) the Palestinian Jews; (3) the chief *Zionist* leader in America, as well as the anti-Zionist Jews of America and England; (4) the British officials and soldiers in Palestine; (5) British and American official investigators; (6) a large body of the press, then still free of occult control in this matter.

(1) The Arabs saw from the start what was in store for them, for they knew the Torah. Dr. Weizmann had told the Peace Conference "The Bible is our mandate," and they knew about "the God of the Jews" and his promises of pogrom and reward: "When the Lord thy God shall bring thee into the land whither thou goest to possess it, and shall cast out many nations before thee ... seven nations greater and mightier than thou; and when the Lord thy God shall deliver them up before thee, and thou shalt smite them; *then thou shalt utterly destroy them; thou shalt make no covenant with them, nor show mercy unto them*" *(Deuteronomy* 7, 1-3).

Thus Zionism, and Western support of it, meant extermination for them under a Law of 2,500 years earlier (and the events of 1948 proved this). In 1945 King Ibn Saoud told President Roosevelt, "You have fought two world wars to discover what we have known for two thousand years" and in 1948 the intention *literally* to fulfil the above-quoted "statute and commandment" was proved by deed. Significantly, even anti-Zionist Jews could not believe, before it happened, that this literal "fulfilment" was intended. In 1933 Mr. Bernard J. Brown correctly cited the above-mentioned passage as the reason for Arab fears and said, "Of course, the uncultured Arabs do not understand that *the modern Jew does not take his Bible literally and would not be so cruel to his fellow man*, but he suspects that if the Jews bottom their claim to Palestine on the strength of their historic rights to that land, *they can only do so on the authority of the Bible, and the Arab refuses to reject any part of it.*" Mr. Brown of Chicago did not know the Chazars).

The Arabs in 1920 were not deceived by Mr. Balfour's *public* pledge (in the Declaration) that their "civil and religious rights" would be protected or by Mr. Wilson's *public* pledge (the Fourteen Points) that they would have "undoubted security of life" and "absolutely independent opportunity of autonomous development." If they did not know, they guessed that Mr. Balfour, Mr. Lloyd George and Mr. Wilson had *secretly* promised the Zionists *Palestine.* Knowing the Torah, they equally disbelieved the *public* statement of Mr. Winston Churchill in 1922 (when he was Colonial Secretary), "Unauthorized statements have been made to the effect that the purpose in view is to create a wholly Jewish Palestine. Phrases have been used such as 'Palestine is to become as Jewish as England is English'" (a direct rebuke to Dr. Weizmann). "His Majesty's government regard any such suggestion as impracticable and have no such aim in view. Nor have they at any time contemplated the disappearance or subordination of the Arabic population, language or culture in Palestine" (in the Second World War, as Prime Minister, and after it as Opposition leader Mr. Churchill gave his support to the process here denied).

The original Jewish community of Palestine (never taken into consideration at any stage in all these proceedings) was violently anti-Zionist. Dr. Weizmann, almost alone among his fellow-Zionists and the Western politicians associated with them, had slight acquaintance with these original Jews, having made one or two brief visits to Palestine; he says most of his fellow-Zionists from Russia were "*completely ignorant*" of them. At this period in 1919-1922 the Zionist leaders first learned that the Jews of Palestine held them to be "heathen, impious, heartless, ignorant and malevolent." Dr. Weizmann (whose attitude is the familiar one that he was only acting for their good; "we were only anxious to make conditions a little modern and comfortable for them") was "rather horrified to discover *how remote from them we remained.*" He dismisses them as old fogies who, annoyingly, bombarded the Jewish organizations in America with complaints about the Zionists, "quite ninety percent" of their letters being violently hostile. (Typically, Dr. Weizmann learned of the contents of these letters from a British censor, derelict in his duty, who showed them to him). These protests of the native Arabs and native Jews of Palestine were ignored by the politicians of Paris and San Remo.

Mr. Louis Brandeis in 1919 visited the country which then, for twenty years, had formed the object of his revived interest in Judaism. He was at once disillusioned by actual acquaintance with the unknown land and decided that "it would be *wrong* to encourage immigration." He urged that the World Zionist Organization should be greatly reduced, if not abolished, and that future activity should be restricted to the modest task of building up a "Jewish Homeland" through separate Zionist associations in the various countries. In effect this would have been simply a "cultural centre" in Palestine, consisting perhaps of a university and academies, and of somewhat more numerous farm settlements, with reasonable means of immigration for the small number of Jews who, of their own volition, might wish to go to Palestine.

This meant abandoning the concept of separate Jewish nationhood symbolized by a Jewish *State*, and was treason. It was (as Dr. Weizmann says) a revival of the old cleavage between "east" and "west"; between "*Ostjuden*" and emancipated Western Jews; between "Washington" and "Pinsk" (the name of the author of the phrase about "international pressure" was significant, not coincidental).

The Zionists from Russia overthrew Mr. Brandeis as easily as Dr. Herzl in 1903-4. Mr. Brandeis made the proposal summarized above to the Cleveland Congress of American Zionists in 1921. Dr. Weizmann, opposing, insisted on "a *national* fund" (that is, revenue to be raised by the self-appointed government of a Jewish *nation* from obligatory tithe-payments by members of the Zionist organization) and "a *national* budget." Mr. Brandeis's weakness was precisely that of Dr. Herzl in 1903; the great Western governments were *committed* to the Zionists from Russia. The congress, which if it was in any way "elected" was elected by about one-tenth of the Jews of America, upheld Dr. Weizmann and Dr. Brandeis fell from his high place.

In Palestine the British soldiers and officials saw that an impossible task was to be inflicted on them. They were of a stock that had gained more experience in the administration of overseas territories than any other in history, and experience and instinct alike warned them. They knew how to administer a country justly on behalf of all its native peoples and had often done this. They knew that no country could be justly administered, or even kept quiet, if alien immigrants were to be forced into it and the native peoples compelled to allow this. Their protests, too, began to flow towards London and until the end, thirty years later, were ignored. The Arabs from the start accepted the bitter truth and began (in 1920) to resist by riot, rising and every means at hand; they have never since ceased and obviously will not until their grievance is amended or they are all put in permanent, armed captivity.

As the "front-rank politicians" (Dr. Weizmann's phrase) in London and Washington were resolved at any cost to implant the Zionists in Palestine, without regard to any protest, opinion or counsel whatever, today's student might wonder why President Wilson and Mr. Lloyd George sent commissions of investigation to the land bartered about by them. If they hoped to receive encouraging reports (in the manner of Sir Henry Wilson's "mud-months" advice) they were deceived, for these investigators merely confirmed what the Arabs, Jews and British in Palestine all had said. President Wilson's King-Crane Commission (1919) reported that "the Zionist look forward *to a practically complete dispossession of the present non-Jewish inhabitants of Palestine.*" This commission added, "by various forms of *purchase*"; the more experienced British officers heard by it correctly informed it that "the Zionist programme could not be carried out except *by force of arms.*" Mr. Lloyd George's Haycraft Commission (1921) reported that the real root of the trouble then starting in Palestine lay *in the justified* Arab belief that the Zionists *intended to dominate in Palestine.*

By far the greatest obstacle to the Zionist ambition came from factual reporting in the press of what was happening in Palestine and from editorial comment adverse to Zionism. At any time up to the 1914-1918 war the American and British governments, before they went too far, would have had to reckon with public opinion, accurately informed by the newspapers. The corruption of the press (foretold by the Protocols) began with the censorship introduced during the First World War; the rise of the directing power behind the scenes had been shown by the cases of Colonel Repington, Mr. H.A. Gwynne and Mr. Robert Wilton in 1917-1918; experienced correspondents were driven to resign or to write books because their reports were ignored, burked, or suppressed; an editor who published the faithful report without submission to the censorship was prosecuted.

In 1919-1922 the censorship was ending and the newspapers naturally reverted, in the main, to the earlier practice of true reporting and impartial comment on the facts reported. This re-established the former check on governmental policies, and if it had continued would undoubtedly have thwarted the Zionist project, which could not be maintained if it were open to public scrutiny. Therefore the entire future for the Zionists, at this crucial moment when "the Mandate" still was not "ratified," turned on the suppression of adverse newspaper information and comment. At that very juncture an event occurred which produced that result. By reason of this great effect on the future, and by its own singular nature, the event (denoted in the heading to the present chapter) deserves relation in detail here. At that stage in the affair England was of paramount importance to the conspirators (I have shown that Dr. Weizmann and Mr. House both used this word) and in England the energetic Lord Northcliffe was a powerful man. The former Alfred Harmsworth, bulky and wearing a dank Napoleonic forelock, owned the two most widely read daily newspapers, various other journals and periodicals, and in addition was majority proprietor of the most influential newspaper in the world, at that time, *The Times* of London. Thus he had direct access to millions of people each day and, despite his business acumen, he was by nature a great newspaper *editor*, courageous, combative and patriotic. He was sometimes right and sometimes wrong in the causes he launched or espoused, but he was *independent* and unpurchasable. He somewhat resembled Mr. Randolph Hearst and Colonel Robert McCormick in America, which is to say that he would do many things to increase the circulation of his newspapers, but only within the limits of national interest; he would not peddle blasphemy, obscenity, libel *or sedition*. He could not be cowed and was a force in the land.

Lord Northcliffe made himself the adversary of the conspiracy from Russia in two ways. In May 1920 he caused to be printed in *The Times* the article, previously mentioned, on the Protocols. It was headed, "The Jewish Peril, A Disturbing Pamphlet, Call for Enquiry." It concluded, "An impartial *investigation* of these would-be documents and of their history is most desirable ... are we to dismiss the whole matter *without inquiry* and to let the influence of such a book as this work unchecked?"

Then in 1922 Lord Northcliffe visited Palestine, accompanied by a journalist, Mr. J.M.N. Jeffries (whose subsequent book, *Palestine: The Reality*, remains the classic work of reference for that period). This was a combination of a different sort from that formed by the editors of *The Times* and *Manchester Guardian*, who wrote their leading articles about Palestine in England and in consultation with the Zionist chieftain, Dr. Weizmann. Lord Northcliffe, on the spot, reached the same conclusion as all other impartial investigators, and wrote, "In my opinion we, without sufficient thought, guaranteed Palestine as a home for the Jews despite the fact that 700,000 Arab Moslems live there and own it … The Jews seemed to be under the impression that all England was devoted to the one cause of Zionism, enthusiastic for it in fact; and I told them that this was not so and to be careful that they do not tire out our people by *secret importation of arms to fight 700,000 Arabs … There will be trouble in Palestine … people dare not tell the Jews the truth here. They have had some from me.*"

By stating *this* truth, Lord Northcliffe offended *twice;* he had already entered the forbidden room by demanding "inquiry" into the origins of the Protocols. Moreover, he was able to publish this truth in the mass-circulation newspapers owned by him, so that he became, to the conspirators, a dangerous man. He encountered one obstacle in the shape of Mr. Wickham Steed, who was editor of *The Times* and whose championship of Zionism Dr. Weizmann records.

In this contest Lord Northcliffe had an Achilles heel. He particularly wanted to get the truth about Palestine into *The Times,* but he was not *sole* proprietor of that paper, only chief proprietor. Thus his own newspapers published his series of articles about Palestine but *The Times,* in fact, refused to do so. Mr. Wickham Steed" though he had made such large proposals about the future of Palestine, declined to go there, and denied publicity to the anti-Zionist case.

These facts, and all that now follows, are related (again, with surprising candour) in the *Official History* of *The Times* (1952). It records that Mr. Wickham Steed "evaded" visiting Palestine when Lord Northcliffe requested him to go there; it also records Mr, Wickham Steed's "inaction" following Lord Northcliffe's telegraphed wish "for a leading article attacking Balfour's attitude towards Zionism." In what follows the reader's attention is particularly directed to dates.

In May 1920 Lord Northcliffe had caused publication of the article about the Protocols in *The Times.* Early in 1922 he visited Palestine and produced the series of articles above mentioned. On February 26, 1922 he left Palestine, after his request, which was ignored, to the editor of *The Times.* He was incensed against the incompliant editor and had a message, strongly critical of his editorial policy, read to an editorial conference which met on March 2, 1922. Lord Northcliffe wished that Mr. Wickham Steed should resign and was astonished that he remained after this open rebuke. The editor, instead of resigning, decided "to secure a lawyer's opinion on the degree of provocation necessary to constitute unlawful dismissal." For this purpose he consulted *Lord Northcliffe's own special legal adviser* (March 7, 1922), who informed Mr. Wickham Steed that Lord Northcliffe was "abnormal," "incapable of business" and, judging from his appearance, "unlikely to live long" and advised the editor *to continue in his post!* The editor then went to Pau, in France, to see Lord Northcliffe, in his turn decided that Lord Northcliffe was "abnormal" (March 31, 1922), and informed a director of *The Times* that Lord Northcliffe was "going mad."

The suggestion of madness thus was put out by an editor whom Lord Northcliffe desired to remove and the impressions of others therefore are obviously relevant. On May 3, 1922 Lord Northcliffe attended a farewell luncheon in London for a retiring editor of one of his papers and "*was in fine form*." On May 11, 1922 he made "*an excellent and effective speech*" to the Empire Press Union and "*most people who had thought him 'abnormal' believed they were mistaken.*" A few days later Lord Northcliffe telegraphed instructions to the Managing Director of *The Times* to arrange for the editor's resignation. This Managing Director saw nothing "abnormal" in such an instruction and was not "*in the least anxious about Northcliffe's health.*" Another director, who then saw him, "*considered him to have quite as good a life risk as his own;* he "*noticed nothing unusual in Northcliffe's manner or appearance*" (May 24, 1922).

On *June* 8, 1922 Lord Northcliffe, from Boulogne, asked Mr. Wickham Steed to meet him in Paris; they met there on *June* 11, 1922, and Lord Northcliffe told his visitor that he, Lord Northcliffe, would assume the editorship of *The Times.* On *June* 12, 1922 the whole party left for Evian-les-Bains, a doctor being secreted on the train, as far as the Swiss frontier, by Mr. Wickham Steed. Arrived in Switzerland "a brilliant French nerve specialist" (unnamed) was summoned and in the evening certified Lord Northcliffe insane. On the strength of this Mr. Wickham Steed cabled instructions to *The Times* to disregard and not to publish anything received from Lord Northcliffe, and on *June* 13, 1922 he left, never to see Lord Northcliffe again. On *June* 18, 1922 Lord Northcliffe returned to London and was in fact removed from all control of, and even communication with his undertakings (especially *The Times;* his telephone was cut). The manager had police posted at the door to prevent him entering the office of *The Times* if he were able to reach it. All this, according to the *Official History,* was on the strength of certification in a foreign country (Switzerland) by an unnamed (French) doctor. On August 14, 1922 Lord Northcliffe died; the cause of death stated was ulcerative endocarditis, and his age was fifty-seven. He was buried, after a service at Westminster Abbey, amid a great array of mourning editors.

Such is the story as I have taken it from the official publication. None of this was known outside a small circle at the time; it only emerged in the *Official History* after three decades, and if it had all been published in 1922 would presumably have called forth many questions. I doubt if any comparable displacement of a powerful and wealthy man can be adduced, at any rate in such mysterious circumstances.

For the first time, I now appear in this narrative as a personal witness of events. In the 1914-1918 war I was one participant among uncomprehending millions, and only began to see its true shape long afterwards. In 1922 I was for an instant in, though not of the inner circle; looking back, I see myself closeted with Lord Northcliffe (about to die) and quite ignorant of Zionism, Palestine, Protocols or any other matter in which he had raised his voice. My testimony may be of some interest; I cannot myself judge of its value.

I was in 1922 a young man fresh from the war who struggled to find a place in the world and had become a clerk in the office of *The Times*. I was summoned thence, in that first week of June when Lord Northcliffe was preparing to remove Mr. Wickham Steed and himself assume the editorship of *The Times*, to go as secretary to Lord Northcliffe who was at Boulogne. I was warned beforehand that he was an unusual man whose every bidding must be quickly done. Possibly for that reason, everything he did seemed to me to be simply the expression of his unusual nature. No suspicion of anything more ever came to me, a week before he was "certified" and, in effect, put in captivity.

I was completely ignorant of "abnormal" conditions, so that the expert might discount my testimony. Anyway, the behaviour I observed was just what I had been told to expect by those who had worked with him for many years. There was one exception to this. Lord Northcliffe was convinced that his life was in danger and several times said this; specifically, he said he had been poisoned. If this is in itself madness, then he was mad, but in that case many victims of poisoning have died of madness, not of what was fed to them. If by any chance it was true, he was *not* mad. I remember that 1 thought it feasible that such a man should have dangerous enemies, though at that time I had no inkling at all of any particular hostility he might have incurred. His belief certainly charged him with suspicion of those around him, but if by chance he had reason for it, then again it was not *madness;* if all this had transpired in the light of day such things could have been thrashed out.

I cannot judge, and can only record what I saw and thought at the time, as a young man who had no more idea of what went on around him than a babe knows the shape of the world. When I returned to London I was questioned about Lord Northcliffe by his brother, Lord Rothermere, and one of his chief associates, Sir George Sutton. The thought of madness must by that time have been in their minds (the "certification" had ensued) and therefore have underlain their questions, but not even then did any such suspicion occur to me, although I had been one of the last people to see him before he was certified and removed from control of his newspapers. I did not know of that when I saw them or for long afterwards. In such secrecy was all this done that, although I continued in the service of *The Times* for sixteen years, I only learned of the "madness" and "certification" *thirty years late* , from the *Official History*. By that time I was able to see what great consequences had flowed from an affair in which I was an uninitiated onlooker at the age of twenty- seven.

Lord Northcliffe therefore was out of circulation, and of the control of his newspapers, during the decisive period preceding the ratification of "the mandate" by the League of Nations, which clinched the Palestinian transaction and bequeathed the effects of it to our present generation. The opposition of a widely-read chain of journals at that period might have changed the whole course of events. After Lord Northcliffe died the possibility of editorials in *The Times* "attacking Balfour's attitude towards Zionism" faded. From that time the submission of the press, in the manner described by the Protocols, grew ever more apparent and in time reached the condition which prevails today, when faithful reporting and impartial comment on this question has long been in suspense.

Lord Northcliffe was removed from control of his newspapers and put under constraint on June 18, 1922; on July 24, 1922 the Council of the League of Nations met in London, secure from any possibility of loud public protest by Lord Northcliffe, to bestow on Britain a "mandate" to remain in Palestine and by arms to install the Zionists there (I describe what events have shown to be the fact; the matter was not so depicted to the public, of course).

This act of "ratifying" the "mandate" was in such circumstances a formality. The real work, of drawing up the document and of ensuring that it received approval, had been done in advance, in the first matter by drafters inspired by Dr. Weizmann and in the second by Dr. Weizmann himself in the ante-chambers of many capitals. The members of Mr. House's "Inquiry" had drafted the Covenant of the League of Nations; Dr. Weizmann, Mr. Brandeis, Rabbi Stephen Wise and their associates had drafted the Balfour Declaration; now the third essential document had to be drafted, one of a kind that history never knew before. Dr. Weizmann pays Lord Curzon (then British Foreign Secretary) the formal compliment of saying that he was "in charge of the actual drafting of the mandate" but adds, "on our side we had the valuable assistance of Mr. Ben V. Cohen ... one of the ablest draughtsmen *in America*." Thus a Zionist in America (Mr. Cohen was to play an important part in a much later stage of this process) in fact drafted a document under which "the new world order" was to dictate British policy, the use of British troops and the future of Palestine.

Lord Curzon's part was merely to moderate the terms of the "mandate" if he could, and he did achieve minor modifications, though these had little effect on events in the long run. An able statesman *(not* a politician) who looked like a Roman emperor, he was "entirely loyal to the policy adopted and meant to stand by the Balfour Declaration" (Dr. Weizmann), but was known personally to disapprove the project which duty required him to further (this might be the reason why he never became Prime Minister, for which office he was highly qualified). He contrived to delete one word from the draft. Dr. Weizmann and Mr. Cohen desired it to begin, "Recognizing *the historic rights* of the Jews to Palestine ..." Lord Curzon said, "If you word it like that, I can see Weizmann coming to me every day and saying he has a *right* to do this, that and the other in Palestine! I won't have it." Thus "historical rights" became "historical connection," a lesser misstatement; Lord Curzon, a scholar certainly did not believe that the Chazars from Russia had any historical connection with the Arabian Peninsula.

Dr. Weizmann, while the draft was thus being prepared, set off on another international tour, to ensure that all members of the Council of the League of Nations would inaugurate "the new world order" by voting for "the Mandate." He called first on the Italian Foreign Minister, one Signor Schanzer, who said the Vatican was worried about the future, under Zionism, of the Room of the Last Supper in

Jerusalem. Dr. Weizmann, in the tone habitual among his associates when they spoke of things holy to others, says, "My education in Church history having been deficient, I did not know why the Italians laid such stress on the Room of the Last Supper."[16]

Dr. Weizmann was able to reassure Signor Schanzer and left Rome assured of Italian support. After that the thing became a landslide and from that time on the "votes" of the League of Nations (and of the later "United Nations") in vital questions were always arranged beforehand by this method of secret canvassing, lobbying and "irresistible pressure" in general. Dr. Weizmann went on to Berlin and found a famous Jewish minister there, Dr. Walter Rathenau, to be violently opposed to Zionism. He "deplored any attempt to turn the Jews of Germany 'into a foreign body on the sands of the Mark of Brandenburg'; that was all he could see in Zionism." Dr. Rathenau was murdered soon after this, so that the cause of the emancipated Western Jews was deprived of another notable champion.

By his journeys and visits Dr. Weizmann at last assured himself, in advance of the meeting, of all votes at the Council table save two, those of Spain and Brazil. He then called in London on the Spanish dignitary who was to represent Spain and said, "Here is Spain's opportunity to repay *in part* that

---

[16] By 1950 the Zionists had opened a "Cellar of the Catastrophe" on a lower floor of the same building as a place of pilgrimage for Jews. A legend at the entrance said, "Entrance forbidden to those who have not strong nerves." The Chief Rabbi of South Africa after inspecting this place, wrote. "Everything is being done to develop and foster this new cult of Mount Zion; to provide a substitute for the Wailing Wall and an emotional outlet for the religious feelings of the people. There seemed to me to be something un-Jewish in it, something which belonged rather to superstition than to true religions faith, ... I tremble to think of the effect of these completely apocryphal stories" (of miraculous cures) "on the simple, pious and superstitious Jews of Yemen. Is there being developed a Jewish Lourdes? I hope not, but the signs are ominous."

long-outstanding debt which it owes to the Jews. The evil which your forefathers were guilty of against us you can wipe out *in part.*"

Dr. Weizmann was cautious, twice using the words "in part." His host, whose duty was to contemporary Spain, was being allured with the suggestion which had earlier fascinated Mr. Balfour; that Spain owed some indeterminate "debt" to "the Jews," for all of whom his visitor claimed to speak, and that by wiping out Arab hopes in Palestine he could wipe out (in part) this debt said to have been incurred by Spain. Considered by standards of reason these conversations read like something from the Mad Hatter's Tea-Party. In any case, the Spanish representative promised the vote of Spain and, for full measure, *also that of Brazil,* so that the chain of yesses was complete. Even Dr. Weizmann could not tell whether this happy ending to his visit was the result of his own eloquence or of pressure applied at a higher level (that of the Spanish delegate's superiors in Madrid).

In England, as the moment approached, a last bid was made to avert British embroilment in this enterprise. Lords Sydenham, Islington and Raglan led an attack on "the mandate" in the House of Lords and *by a large majority carried their motion for the repeal of the Balfour Declaration.* However, the upper house, its earlier powers abolished, by that time could only protest, and Mr. Balfour (soon to become a lord) at once reassured Dr. Weizmann: "What does it matter if a few foolish lords pass such a motion?"

After all this secret preparation the stage was set for the meeting of the League Council in London on July 24, 1922 and "everything went off smoothly when Mr. Balfour introduced the subject of the ratification of the Palestine Mandate." Without any demur Britain was awarded "the mandate" to remain in Palestine and to provide an armed cordon for the Zionists when they arrived there.[17]

Thus in 1922 the British future was left burdened with an undertaking which had never received public scrutiny and during the next three decades the growing bills began to pour in. Early in the process America also was re-involved, although the general public there did not realize this for another thirty years.

President Wilson was dead and his Democratic party was out of office. President Harding was at the White House and the Republican party was back in power. It had been swept back by the wave of popular feeling against the

---

[17] The "mandates" also bestowed on Britain in respect of Iraq and Transjordan, and to France in respect of Syria, were soon relinquished, these territories becoming independent states. Other countries received "mandates" in respect of various colonial and oceanic territories, which in time and in fact became their possessions. These other "mandates" were from the start fictitious and served in the office of chaperones to tile dubious one which needed respectable company. Of the entire bogus arrangement only the Palestinean "mandate" continued until the Zionists being numerous enough and sufficiently supplied with arms, it was abandoned and the country left to the invaders then able to take and hold it by force. The later "United Nations," for obvious reasons, did not resurrect the word "Mandate." It found another word, "Trusteeship," for the same idea, which is transparently that of transferring territories from one ownership to another through a sham process of "international law" and legality.

disappointing outcome of the war and of instinctive desire to be free from "entanglements" overseas. The country felt itself well out of the League of Nations and its mysterious activities all over the world.

Then the Republican party led the Republic back in to the embroilments in which the Democratic party first had involved it. Presumably the party-managers, those architects of public misfortune, thought to compete with the other party for the favour of those powerful groups, and the "fluctuating vote" controlled by them, described in Mr. House's diary and novel.

In June 1922, just before the League Council in London bestowed the Palestinian "Mandate" on Britain, the United States Congress passed a joint resolution of both houses, the wording of which was *almost identical with that of the Balfour Declaration of* 1917. Thereafter the Zionist halter was firmly reaffixed round the neck of American State policy, and though the American voter only realized this, it became immaterial to him which party prevailed at elections.

Chapter 35

THE NATIONAL HOME

For ten years after the foisting of "the Mandate" on the British people the pretence was continued that the "Jewish National Home" in Palestine, under their protection, would be simply "a cultural centre" of Judaism, harmless to the Arabs; a Judaist Mecca with university, library and farm-settlements. The Arabs were never beguiled; they saw that they were the objects of an attempt to reinforce, in the 20th Century AD, the Law of violent dispossession set up by the Levites in the 5th Century BC They responded with riotous protest and warlike uprising which have never since ceased, so that "the war to end war" started warfare without end.

At once it became apparent that Zionism had been inserted like a blasting charge into the life of peoples and that in "a small country the size of Wales or Vermont" (just "liberated" from the Turk) the time-fuse of a future world-conflict had been planted. Nevertheless, a new British Colonial Secretary, Mr. Leopold Amery, went to Palestine in 1925 and (he says) "frankly told the Arabs that there was *no possibility of change* in the British policy" *(Jewish Telegraph Agency)*.

These words (like Mr. Balfour's earlier statement that British policy in this question was "*definitely set*") contain the central mystery and challenge. In what other issue in history was a reversal of policy ever declared to be *impossible?* This policy had been proved impossible of *fulfilment*, and disastrous. What power dictated that it must be pursued in those or any circumstances whatever? No British or American political leader ever explained this secret capitulation to the electorate, to Parliament or to Congress (in the 1950's statements similar to those of Mr. Balfour and Mr. Amery were often made in America, as will be seen).

During this decade, when the project of the "national home" proved a fiasco, the Western politicians continued to congratulate themselves on what they had done. Mr. Lloyd George told an applauding Zionist audience in London: "I was brought up in a school where I was taught more about the history of the Jews than about the history of my own land." His day was ending, but candidates for his shoes hastened to declare their allegiance. A coming prime minister, Mr. Ramose Macdonald, though unable to attend this meeting, sent a message declaring support for Zionism; another, Mr. Stanley Baldwin, joined the circle of "friends" (Dr. Weizmann); In South Africa General Smuts saw in his "work for the Jews the justification of his life."

Lord Balfour considered his Declaration the great achievement of his life and in 1925 first went to see the country he had been privately bartering for twenty years. He was (characteristically) a bad sailor and emerged pale from his cabin at Alexandria. At Tel Aviv he said (with intention to flatter) that the Herzliah High School boys "might have come from Harrow" and the mayor "might easily be the mayor of Liverpool or of Manchester," and he "opened" the still unbuilt Hebrew University. He toured Palestine under strong guard and said his cordial reception reminded him of a general election "with everybody on the same side." Then (against Dr. Weizmann's pressing advice) he continued to Syria, where he was besieged by an Arab mob, clamant for his life, in the Victoria Hotel in Damascus, being rushed to the coast amid a strong escort of French cavalry and restored (still seasick) by ship to England.

Mr. J.M.N. Jeffries records what went on in Palestine during this decade. The Zionists began to buy up Arab land (which under the Talmudic Law might never under any conditions be resold to Arabs). The Arabs cheerfully sold them *some* land but too well knew the Torah to yield enough for Palestine ever to be taken from them by simple purchase (as the too-simple King-Crane Commission had foreseen). Moreover, they bred fast and soon showed that Zionist immigration, in any normal circumstances, could never produce a population nearly equal to them. From the start it was clear, as all experienced observers had stated, that they could only be dispossessed through a new world war.

The intention to dispossess them was not admitted at that time. Mr. Churchill's White Paper of 1922, indeed, proposed that they should be allowed to hold elections in their own country! Dr. Weizmann forbade this and thus was placed "in the curious position of *seeming* to oppose democratic rights to the Arabs"; he then complains that the Arabs, who drew the obvious conclusion from his denial of elections, were the victims of "the deliberate misrepresentation of Zionist aims."

The uproar in Palestine caused the British government to send out more "investigators" (and again, one wonders why, if there was "no possibility of change" in British policy). The Shaw and Simpson Commissions followed the earlier King-Crane and Haycraft Commissions and, once they saw the facts, produced substantially the same reports. On this account Dr. Weizmann asks plaintively why "as often as a commission went out to Palestine to investigate" it was "an almost universal rule that such administrators as came out favourably inclined turned against us in a few months."

The fiasco of the "national home" was so clear that even the politicians began to hedge. Mr. Lloyd George in 1925 told the Zionists publicly "any policy of expropriation or anything that suggests it will only make difficulties in the path of Zionism." Dr. Weizmann at once replied: "Mr. Lloyd George will believe me when I say that the Jews are the last people in the world to *build their home on the back of somebody else.* The Jews have suffered so much from injustice *that they have learned their lesson* and I can assure you that *the Arabs will not suffer at our hands.*" Again "the word" invites comparison with "the deed" that ensued later.

However, what happened in Palestine during this decade was all incidental to the greater purpose of retaining control over the politicians of London and Washington, so that "policy" there should continue to be "impossible to change." That, and not the success or failure of the "national home" in Palestine, was decisive, and Dr. Weizmann at the end triumphed again.

At this period he had to deal with a greater difficulty than any offered by the Western politicians: the alarm, and hostility, of that "World Jewry" which he and his associates from Russia claimed to represent. The emancipated Jews could have offered effective opposition to the Zionists if they had formed an anti-Zionist organization. They feared to do so, and this was their undoing. They did not want Zionist nationalism and a Jewish state, but they *did* want the Judaist Mecca, the cultural and religious centre, and feared that the term "anti-Zionist" would imply antagonism to that. Through this chink in their armour Dr. Weizmann unerringly reached.

His whole undertaking in Palestine was then near collapse. The "Mandate" provided that the British government would recognize his Zionist Organization as "an appropriate Jewish agency for the purpose of advising and co-operating with the administration of Palestine" in matters affecting "the establishment of the Jewish National Home." However, there was a qualification: this agency was "to take steps in consultation with His Britannic Majesty's government *to secure the co-operation of all Jews* who are willing to assist in the establishment of the Jewish National Home."

As masses of Jews were openly opposed to Dr. Weizmann's Zionism, even he could not pretend that he spoke for them. Thus he transferred his canvassing from the antechambers of the Gentiles to the Jews and for *eight years* sped about the world in search of a solution to this problem, The great mass of emancipated Jews of the West resolutely opposed any project that might turn out to be one for the recreation of "a Jewish nation."

Then Dr. Weizmann found the riddle's answer. He coined the term "non-Zionist." The Jews in Britain remained aloof but those in America fell into the trap. "Non-Zionist" seemed to offer the best of both worlds; it would enable them to oppose Zionist nationalism while supporting the Judaist-Mecca idea. In 1928 a group of Jews announced that they represented "the non-Zionists" and would work with Dr. Weizmann for "the upbuilding of Palestine." On this basis Dr. Weizmann in 1929 set up his "*Enlarged* Jewish Agency," thereafter claiming that, by including "non-Zionists," it fulfilled all provisions of "the Mandate" and that he once more represented "all Jews." The dilemma from which Dr. Weizmann was rescued is shown by his words: he says he regarded the Zionist situation as "*hopeless and helpless* unless the non-Zionists came to the rescue,"

The Arabs at once saw that this "enlarged" Jewish agency would be the true government of Palestine and intensified their resistance. The result was that at last a British government felt forced to admit the fiasco and in 1930 the Passfield White Paper undertook to *suspend Zionist immigration and to curtail the authority of the Jewish Agency.* The "set" policy *was* "changed"! Dr. Weizmann, his authority reinforced by the recruitment of the "non-Zionists," struck at once. He gave audience to the British prime minister, then Mr. Ramsay Macdonald, who behaved like a man held up by a gun; he not only revoked the White Paper but humbly asked Dr. Weizmann whom he should appoint as the next High Commissioner in Palestine.

Thus the years that the Zionists have eaten continued. What these politicians feared, none can confidently say; their memoirs are uniformly silent on this central mystery and their capitulations are unique in history. Mr. Macdonald's surrender re-established the principle that "policy" in this matter was "set" and immutable, and during the ensuing twenty years this became the paramount principle of all British and American state policy. The politicians of both countries evidently held Dr. Weizmann to be the emissary of a power which they dared not disobey; their demeanour resembled the African Native's rolling-eyed fear of the witchdoctor.

Mr. Macdonald's submission restored the situation in London to its former shape, but in Palestine the "national home," an artificial growth forcibly implanted in a hostile soil, continued to wither. In ten years the Jewish population increased by less than a hundred thousand immigrants. In 1927 three thousand more emigrants departed than immigrants came. A small revival followed in 1928, but the average yearly exodus from Palestine, up to 1932, was almost a third of the immigration.

The Zionist adventure was in collapse, as all qualified parties had foretold. Left alone, the Jews of the world clearly would never in any substantial numbers go to Palestine; if events took their natural course the Arab population evidently would increase its preponderance. Nothing was to take its natural course. At that very moment the mysterious Hitler arose in Germany (and at the same instant Mr. Roosevelt in America) and the Second World War loomed up ahead.

Chapter 36

THE STRANGE ROLE OF THE PRESS

The years which followed, 1933-1939, were those of the brewing of the Second World War. "Prussian militarism," supposed to have been laid low in 1918, rose up more formidable than ever and the spectacle so absorbed men's minds that they lost interest in the affair in Palestine, which seemed unrelated to the great events in Europe. In fact it was to loom large among those "causes and objects" of the second war which President Wilson had called "obscure" in the first one. The gap left by the collapse, in 1917, of the legend of "Jewish persecution in Russia" was filled by "the Jewish persecution in Germany" and, just when Zionism was "helpless and hopeless," the Zionists were able with a new cry to affright the Jews and beleaguer the Western politicians. The consequences showed in the outcome of the ensuing war, when revolutionary-Zionism and revolutionary-Communism proved to be the sole beneficiaries.

My own experience during those years ultimately produced this book. When they began, in 1933, I had climbed from my clerkship to be a correspondent of *The Times* in Berlin and was happy in that calling. When they ended, in 1939, I was fully disenchanted with it and had felt compelled to throw up my livelihood. The tale of the years between will show the reason.

From 1927 on I reported the rise of Hitler, and by chance was passing the Reichstag when it burst into flames in 1933. This event (used to set up the secret-police-and-concentration-camp system in Germany, on the Bolshevist model) cemented Hitler in power, but some prescience, that night, told me that it meant much more than that. In fact the present unfinished ordeal of the West dates from that night, not from the later war. Its true meaning was that the area of occupation of the world-revolution spread to the middle of Europe, and the actual transfer to Communist ownership in 1945 merely confirmed an accomplished fact (theretofore disguised from the masses by the bogus antagonism between National Socialism and Communism) which the war, at its outset, was supposed to undo. The only genuine question which the future has yet to answer is whether the world-revolution will be driven back or spread further westward from the position which, in effect, it occupied on the night of February 27, 1933.

From the start of Hitler's regime (on that night) all professional observers in Berlin, diplomats and journalists, knew that it meant a new war *unless this were prevented.* Prevention at that time was relatively simple; Mr. Winston Churchill in his memoirs rightly called the Second War "the unnecessary war." It could have been prevented by firm Western opposition to Hitler's preliminary warlike forays (into the Rhineland, Austria and

Czechoslovakia) at any time up to 1938 when (as Mr. Churchill also confirms) the German generals, about to overthrow Hitler, were themselves undone by the Western capitulation to him at Munich.

The trained observers in Berlin were agreed that he would make war if allowed and so advised their governmental or editorial superiors in London. The Chief Correspondent of *The Times* in Berlin, Mr. Norman Ebbutt (I was the second correspondent) reported early in 1933 that war must be expected *in about five years* unless it were forethwarted, and this particular report was printed. He, I and many other reporters during the following years grew alarmed and perplexed by the suppression, "burking" and ignoring of despatches, and by the depictment of Hitler, in Parliament and the newspapers, as an inherently good man who would remain peaceable if his just grievances were met (at others' expense).

This period has become known as that of "the policy of appeasement" but *encouragement* is the truer word, and the policy changed the probability of war into certainty. The strain brought Mr. Ebbutt to physical collapse. From 1935 on I was Chief Correspondent in Vienna, which was then but another vantage-point for surveying the German scene. From there, late in 1937, I informed *The Times* that both Hitler and Goering had said that the war would begin "by the autumn of 1939"; I had this information from the Austrian Chancellor. I was in Vienna during Hitler's invasion and then, after brief arrest by Storm Troops on the way out, transferred to Budapest, where I was when the supreme capitulation of Munich followed in September 1938. Realizing then that a faithful reporter could do nothing against "the policy of appeasement," and that his task was meaningless, I resigned by expostulant letter, and still have the editor's discursive acknowledgement.

Fourteen years later *The Times* publicly confessed error, in respect of its "policy of appeasement," in that curiously candid *Official History* of 1952. This contains a grudging reference to me: "There were resignations from junior members of the staff" (I was forty- three in 1938, was Chief Correspondent for Central Europe and the Balkans, had worked for *The Times* for seventeen years, and I believe I was the only correspondent to resign). In this volume *The Times* also undertook never so to err again: "it is not rash to say that aggression will never again be met at Printing House Square in terms of mere 'Munich.'" The editorial articles and reports of *The Times* about such later events as the bisection of Europe in 1945, the Communization of China, the Zionization of Palestine and the Korean war seem to me to show that its policies did not change at all.

Thus my resignation of 1938 was inspired by a motive similar to that of Colonel Repington (of whom I then had not heard) in 1918. There was a major military danger to England and qualified reporters were not allowed to make this plain to the public; the result, in my opinion, was the Second World War. The journalist should not regard himself too seriously, but if his reports are disregarded in the most momentous matters of the day he feels that his calling is a sham and then he had best give it up, at any cost. This is what I did, and I was comforted, many years later, when I read Sir William Robertson's words to Colonel Repington: "The great thing is to keep on a straight course and then one may be sure that good will eventually come of what may now seem to be evil."

When I resigned in 1938 I had a second reason, not present in 1933, for perplexity about the way the press is conducted. In that matter, too, I could only assume that some infatuation worked to distort the truthful picture of events. The outcome of the ensuing war, however, showed that a powerful motive had lain behind this particular misrepresentation.

In the case of "the Jewish persecution" in Germany I found that impartial presentation of the facts gradually gave way to so partisan a depictment that the truth was lost. This transformation was effected in three subtle stages. First the persecution of "political opponents and Jews" was reported; then this was imperceptibly amended to "Jews and political opponents"; and at the end the press in general spoke only of "the persecution of Jews." By this means a false image was projected on to the public mind and the plight of the overwhelming majority of the victims, by this fixing of the spotlight on one group, was lost to sight. The result showed in 1945, when, on the one hand, the persecution of Jews was made the subject of a formal indictment at Nuremberg, and on the other hand half of Europe and all the people in it were abandoned to the self-same persecution, in which the Jews had shared in their small proportion to populations everywhere.

At that period I, typical of Englishmen of my generation, had never thought of Jews as different from myself, nor could I have said what might make a Jew, in his opinion, different from me. If I later became aware of any differentiation, or of the desire of a powerful group to assert one, this was not the result of Hitler's deeds but of the new impediment to impartial reporting which I then began to observe. When the general persecution began I reported it as I saw it. If I learned of a concentration camp containing a thousand captives I reported this; if I learned that the thousand included thirty or fifty Jews I reported that. I saw the first terror, spoke with many of the victims, examined their injuries, and was warned that I incurred Gestapo hostility thereby. The victims were in the great majority, certainly much over ninety percent, Germans, and a few were Jews. This reflected the population-ratio, in Germany and later in the countries overrun by Hitler. But the manner of reporting in the world's press in time blocked-out the great suffering mass, leaving only the case of the Jews.

I illustrate this by episodes and passages from my own experience and reporting. Rabbi Stephen Wise, writing *in 1949*, gave the following version of events personally reported by me *in 1933*, and undoubtedly purveyed the

351

same version in the presidential circle of which he was a familiar during those years: "The measures against the Jews continued *to outstrip in systematic cruelty and planned destruction the terror against other groups.* On January 29, 1933 Hitler was summoned to be chancellor ... *at once* the reign of terror began *with beatings and imprisonment of Jews* ... We planned a protest march in New York on May 10, the day of *the ordered burning of Jewish books* in Germany ... *the brunt* of the attack was borne *by Jews* ... concentration camps were established and *filled with Jews.*"

All these statements are false. The measures against the Jews did *not* outstrip the terror against other groups; the Jews were involved in a much larger number of others. The reign of terror did *not* begin on January 29, 1933, but in the night of the Reichstag fire, February 27. No "burning of Jewish books" was ordered; I attended and reported that bonfire and have looked up my report published in *The Times,* to verify my recollection. A mass of "Marxist" books was burned, including the works of many German, English and other non-Jewish writers (my books, had they then been published, would undoubtedly have been among them); the bonfire included *some* Jewish books. The "brunt" of the terror was *not* borne by Jews, nor were the concentration camps "filled with Jews." The number of Jewish victims was in proportion to their ratio of the population.

Nevertheless this false picture, by iteration, came to dominate the public mind during the Second War. At the time of my resignation, which was provoked solely by the "policy of appeasement" and the imminent advent of "the unnecessary war," this other hindrance to faithful reporting was but a secondary, minor annoyance. Later I discerned that the motive behind it was of major importance in shaping the course and outcome of the Second War." When I came to study the story of Mr. Robert Wilton I perceived that there was also a strong resemblance between my experience and his. He sought to explain the nature of an event in Russia and thus was inevitably led into "the Jewish question." Twenty years later I observed that it was in fact impossible to draw public attention to the misreporting of the nature of the persecution of Germany and to explain that the Jews formed only a small fraction of the victims.

That matter had nothing to do with my resignation, but I was becoming aware of it around that time, and this widening perception is reflected in the two books which I published after renouncing journalism. The first, *Insanity Fair,* was devoted entirely to the menace of war. I thought, somewhat vaingloriously, that one voice might still avert it, and today's reader may still verify that motive. To account for this excess of zeal in me, the indulgent reader, if he be old enough, might recall the feeling of horror which the thought of another world war caused in those who had known the first one. This feeling can never be fully comprehended by those of later generations, who have become familiar with the thought of a series of wars, but it was overpowering at the time.

The second book, *Disgrace Abounding,* on the eve of war continued the warning theme, but in it, for the first time, I gave some attention to "the Jewish question." My experience was widening and I had begun to discern the major part it would play in forming the shape and issue of the Second War which then was clearly at hand. My thought from then on was much given to it; in this way I came in time to write the present book and in that light the remaining chapters on the brewing, course and aftermath of the Second War, are written.

Douglas Reed

Chapter 37

THE MANAGERS, THE MESSIAHS AND THE MASSES

Amid jubilant scenes in Washington and Berlin on two successive days (March 4 and 5, 1933) the two twelve-year reigns began which were to end at almost the same instant in 1945. Today an impartial historian could hardly compute which reign produced the greater sum of human suffering. At the start the two men who appeared on the central scene were both hailed as Messiahs. In America a Rabbi Rosenblum described President Roosevelt as "a Godlike messenger, the darling of destiny, the Messiah of America's tomorrow"; there spoke a political flatterer in words intended to "persuade the multitude." In 1937, in Prague menaced by Hitler, a Jewish acquaintance told me his rabbi was preaching in the synagogue that Hitler was "the Jewish Messiah" (a pious elder who sought to interpret events in terms of Levitical prophecy). All through these years the masses in both countries (and for that matter in Russia too) had their particular "premier-dictator" depicted to them in such terms, or in those of "Big Brother," "Papa," "Uncle," "Beloved Leader" or the fireside-loving "Friend." The apparent antagonists, Mr. Roosevelt and Herr Hitler, both in different ways promoted "the destructive principle" in its three recognizable forms: revolutionary-Communism, revolutionary-Zionism and the ensuing "world government to enforce peace."

Mr. Roosevelt's reign began with a significant deception. He used a wheeled chair but the public masses were never allowed to see him, in flesh or picture, until he had been helped to an upright position. His infirmity was known; nevertheless, some directing intelligence decreed that the false picture of a robust man must to his last day be presented to the multitude (and even afterwards, for the sculptor who later made his London monument had to depict him in this sturdy pose).

Mr. Roosevelt created precedent by having his cabinet sworn in by the hand of a distinguished Jew, Mr. Justice Cardozo, who was a committed Zionist, having yielded in 1918 to Mr. Brandeis and Rabbi Stephen Wise, with the despondent-sounding words, "Do what you please with my name"; he then received his Supreme Court judgeships, Rabbi Wise requesting them for him, first from Governor Al Smith of New York State and then from President Herbert Hoover. Thus the shadow of "dual allegiance" fell on Mr. Roosevelt's administration at its start (as on Mr. Wilson's, from the figure of Mr. Brandeis).

Mr. Roosevelt, after the Republican interregnum of 1921-1933, resumed the Wilson policies and in that spirit approached the major problem of America's future at that moment: namely, whether the forces represented by the great Jewish immigration from Eastern Europe, which had occurred in the six decades following the Civil War, should or should not *govern* America. All competent authorities had observed, usually with foreboding, the rapid rise of this new problem in American life, and had depicted the effects of the transplantation to American soil of a large population-mass which, under its religious directors, rejected the concept of "the melting-pot" and of "assimilation." Mr. James Truslow Adams referred to it in his *Epic of America,* and Rudyard Kipling, who lived in New England in the 1890's, wrote:

"The land was denuding itself of its accustomed inhabitants and their places had not yet been taken by the wreckage of Eastern Europe... Immigrants were coming into the States at about a million head a year ... Somewhere in the background, though he did not know it, was the 'representative' American, who traced his blood through three or four generations and who, controlling nothing and affecting less, protested that ... all foreign elements could and would soon be assimilated into 'good Americans.' And not a soul cared what he said ... What struck me ... was the apparent waste and ineffectiveness, in the face of the foreign inrush, of all the indigenous effort of the past generation. It was then that I first began to wonder whether Abraham Lincoln had not killed too many autochthonous 'Americans' in the Civil War, for the benefit of their hastily imported Continental supporters. This is black heresy, but I have since met men and women who have breathed it. The weakest of the old-type immigrants had been sifted and salted by the long sailing- voyage of those days. But steam began in the later sixties and early seventies, when human cargoes could be delivered with all their imperfections in a fortnight or so. And one million more-or-less acclimatized Americans had been killed."

This problem was only new *to America;* it was the oldest problem in recorded history and, as this narrative has shown, had recurred in country after country, down the ages, whenever Jewish immigration reached flood levels. Dr. Weizmann is a witness to it, for he discusses it in relating his beleaguerment of a British official, Sir William Evans Gordon, who grappled with it in England twenty years before it excited the alarm of United States Congresses. In 1906 Sir William sought to solve it through an Aliens Bill (as the 67th and 68th United States Congresses by quota laws). Dr. Weizmann says that in performing his duty Sir William (like Senator Pat McCarran and Representative Francis E. Walter in America in the 1950's) came to be "generally regarded as responsible for all the difficulties placed in the way of Jewish immigrants into England." Dr. Weizmann then continues:

"Whenever the quantity of Jews in any country reaches the *saturation point,* that country *reacts against them* ... England had reached the point where she could or would absorb so many Jews and no more ... The reaction against this *cannot be looked upon as anti-semitism* in the ordinary or vulgar sense of that word; it is a universal social and economic concomitant of Jewish immigration and we cannot shake it off. Sir William had no particular anti-Jewish prejudice. He acted ... in the most kindly way, *in the interests of his country ... In his opinion it was physically impossible for England to make good the wrongs which Russia had inflicted on its Jewish population* ... .I am fairly sure he would equally have opposed mass influx of any foreign element; but, as it happened, no other foreign element pressed for admission in such numbers." (Forty years later Dr. Weizmann spoke similarly to Jews in America: "Certain countries can digest a certain number of Jews; once that number has been passed, *something drastic must happen; the Jews must go*").

Dr. Weizmann thus soberly presented the valid argument against unrestricted Jewish immigration only because he was speaking chiefly to Jews and was drumming into them the Talmudic argument that Jews *cannot* be assimilated; this argument is essential to Zionism, but is not inherently true. The quoted passages show that in 1906 a man in authority was still able to state that his country could not make good "wrongs" supposed to have been inflicted on Jews in another country, and to let "the interests of his country" govern his duty. In the ensuing decades all the premier-dictators of the West made it State policy to remedy alleged wrongs, done by a third party, at the expense of an innocent fourth party. The absurdity is shown by Dr. Weizmann's own last-quoted remark, that when the number of digestible Jews is exceeded in any country "something drastic must happen; the Jews must go." He and his associates for half a century had been using all their power in America to gain unrestricted access for Jews, so that, according to his own words, they were deliberately leading the Jews there to disaster; the time must come, if what he said was true, when governments elsewhere in the world will be under pressure to admit large numbers of Jews from America because of "the wrongs" done them there.

Such was the background of the dominant issue in American life when Mr. Roosevelt became president. Between 1881 and 1920 over three million legally-recorded immigrants entered the United States from Russia, most of them Jews. According to the United States Census Bureau the country contained 230,000 Jews in 1877 and about 4,500,000 in 1926. Only "estimates" are at any time obtainable in matters of Jewish population, as the "elders" oppose head-counting by others, and these figures are generally held to have been largely under-estimated. In the ensuing decade the figures eluded all verification, chiefly owing to changes in immigrant-classification ordered by President Roosevelt, and even the competent authorities will not attempt to estimate the extent of unrecorded and illegal immigration (competent observers judge that the total number of Jews in the United States now may be around ten million). In any case, the greatest single community of Jews in the world today is in the American Republic, having been transplanted thither during the last two generations.

In proportion to the total American population even the highest estimate would not reach one-tenth. In itself this is a relatively small group; politically organized to tip the balance of power it is of decisive importance. This problem was recognized and the Congressional Committee on Immigration in 1921 declared:

"The processes of assimilation and amalgamation are slow and difficult. With the population of the broken parts of Europe headed this way in ever-increasing numbers, why not peremptorily check the stream with this temporary measure, and in the meantime try the unique and novel experiment of enforcing all the immigration laws on our statutes?"

A quota law then passed limited the number of any nationality entering the United States to three percent of the foreign-born of that nationality resident in the United States in 1910. The next Congress went much further than the general statement above quoted; it was specific about the danger, the same Committee reporting:

"If the principle of individual liberty, guarded by a constitutional government, created on this continent nearly a century and half ago *is to endure*, the basic strain of our population must be maintained and our economic standards preserved … The American people do not concede the right of *any foreign group … to dictate the character of our legislation.*"

The years which then followed showed that the effect of Mr. Roosevelt's presidency would be further to break down the principle stated, to alter "the basic strain," and to enable "a foreign group" to dictate State policy.

Mr. Roosevelt (like Mr. Wilson, Mr. Lloyd George and General Smuts) evidently was selected before he was elected. Mr. Howden says that Mr. House "picked Roosevelt as a natural candidate for the presidency long before any other responsible politician," chose him as Assistant Secretary of the Navy in 1913, and then through the years groomed him for the presidency, expecting to govern through him, as through President Wilson. Then something went wrong. Mr. House was confident that President Roosevelt would call on him but then realized that "certain people don't want the president to listen to me." These people were evidently too strong, for Mr. House was dropped without any courtesy and at this point (1933) disappears from the story.

One can only offer a reasonable surmise about the reasons. Mr. House, at seventy-five, regretted young *Philip Dru* of 1912, who had thought the American Constitution "outmoded and grotesque," had seized power by force and then governed by emergency decree. He had a new set of more sober and responsible ideas ready for Mr. Roosevelt and, from relegation, then "watched with forbidding" the concentration of irresponsible power in Mr. Roosevelt's hands. Mr. House had caused President Wilson, as his first major act, to write into the American Constitution (as the Sixteenth

Amendment) the chief destructive measure proposed in Karl Marx's Communist Manifesto of 1848, the "progressive income tax," but in the 1930's Mr. House was alarmed by the completely untrammelled control of the public purse which his second "Rockland" obtained.

Presumably, then, Mr. House was discarded because he had retreated from his earlier ideas, for those original ideas governed Mr. Roosevelt's policy throughout his twelve years. He supported the world-revolution; his first major act of State policy was to recognize the Communist Government and in the ensuing war he resumed the House-Wilson policy of "all support." He supported revolutionary-Zionism. Finally, he took up the old "league to enforce peace" idea and re-foisted it on the West under a new name, that of the "United Nations."

Thus Mr. Roosevelt put "Philip Dru's" ideas into further practice. Of Mr. Wilson in the earlier generation his Secretary of the Interior, Mr. Franklin K. Lane, had said, "All Philip Dru had said should be comes about; the President comes to Philip Dru in the end." As to Mr. Roosevelt, twenty years later, Mr. House's biographer (Mr. Howden) says, "It is impossible to compare Dru's suggested legislation with Mr. Roosevelt's and not be impressed by their similarity".

This is an illustrative example of the transmission of ideas from generation to generation, among a governing group. Mr. House's ideas were those of "the revolutionaries of 1848," which in turn derived from Weishaupt and the revolutionaries of 1789, who had them from some earlier source. When Mr. House abandoned them they were transmitted without a hitch to the ruling group around another president, and the one man who had modified these ideas was left behind.

Mr. House was the only casualty in the inner circle. Mr. Bernard Baruch was adviser to Mr. Roosevelt even before he became president. Mrs Eleanor Roosevelt records that "Mr. Baruch was a trusted adviser to my husband both *in Albany* and in Washington," that is, during Mr. Roosevelt's four-year term as Governor of New York State, before his presidential nomination. During this pre- presidential period Mr. Roosevelt (according to one of Mr. Baruch's biographers, Mr. Morris V. Rosenbloom), although America had repudiated the League of Nations, drafted the plan for a new body to be called the United Nations. Rabbi Stephen Wise and Mr. Brandeis, of the earlier group around President Wilson, regrouped themselves around President Roosevelt (Hitler's anti-Jewish measures in Germany at this time revived Mr. Brandeis's desire to drive Arabs out of Palestine).

Right at the start of Mr. Roosevelt's twelve years some doubt may have arisen about his docility, and means have been found to ensure it (the reader will recall "Rockland's" attempt to assert independence in 1912 and the "exultant conspirators" mirth about his capitulation). That would explain the curious fact that Rabbi Stephen Wise, who had campaigned for Mr. Roosevelt as senator in 1914 and as governor of New York State in 1928, did *not* support him for the presidency in 1932. Then something happened to reassure the rabbi, for immediately after Mr. Roosevelt's election he proclaimed that the new president had "rewon my unstinted admiration," and by 1935 was again an intimate of the White House.

In the light of earlier experience, the identity of the men surrounding President Roosevelt plainly pointed to the policies he would pursue. He made this clearer by widening the circle of his Jewish advisers. In 1933 this had a new significance. In 1913 President Wilson's Jewish advisers were publicly accepted as Americans like any other Americans, and simply of the Jewish faith. In 1933 the question of their allegiance had been raised by the Zionist adventure in Palestine. In addition, the issues of the world-revolution and of world-government had arisen since 1913, and both of these also threw up the question of American *national* interest, so that the feelings entertained about them in the president's immediate circle became a matter of first importance.

All this lent a specific significance to the earlier Congressional pronouncement (1924), denying the right of "any foreign group" to "dictate the character of our legislation." Among the president's "advisers" many were of foreign birth or in effect became "foreign" by their devotion to Zionism or their attitude towards the world-revolution and world-government. In this sense a "foreign group," embodying the mass-immigration of the preceding hundred years, formed itself around the American president and "steered" the course of events. The twelve years which followed showed that any "advice" acted on by the president must have been to the benefit of the destructive principle in its three interrelated forms: Communism, Zionism, world-government.

Prominent among his advisers (in addition to the three powerful men above named) was the Viennese-born Professor Felix Frankfurter. Mr. House's biographer Mr. Howden, who expresses Mr. House's opinion, thinks he was the most powerful of all: "Professor Frankfurter duplicated with Mr. Roosevelt, more than anyone else … the part played by Mr. House with President Wilson." The part played by unofficial advisers is always difficult to determine and this opinion may place Professor Frankfurter too high in the hierarchy. However, he was undoubtedly important (he, too, first came into the advisory circle under Mr. Wilson).

Like Mr. Brandeis and Mr. Cardozo, he became a Supreme Court Justice and never *openly* appeared in American politics; yet the effects of his influence are plainer to trace than those of other men, which have to be deeply delved for. He was head of the Harvard Law School during the 1930's and in that capacity trained an entire generation of young men who were to give a definite shape to the events of the 1940's and 1950's. They received marked preference for high employment in their later careers.

They include in particular Mr. Alger Hiss, who by trial and conviction was revealed as a Communist agent, though he was a high "adviser" of President Roosevelt, (Mr. Justice Frankfurter voluntarily appeared at the trial to testify to Mr. Hiss's character), and Mr. Dean Acheson, who as American Secretary of State at that time declared he would not "turn his back" on Mr. Hiss, and others. Mr. Hiss played an important part at the Yalta Conference, where the abandonment of half Europe to the revolution was agreed; Mr. Acheson's period of office coincided with the abandonment of China to the revolution.

Apart from this distinct group of young men apparently trained during President Roosevelt's early years in office to take over the State Department, the president was accompanied by a group of Jewish advisers at the highest level. Mr. Henry Morgenthau junior (a leading Zionist, whose "Morgenthau Plan" of 1944 was the original basis for the bisection of Europe in 1945) was his Secretary of the Treasury for eleven of the twelve years. Other intimate associates were Senator Herbert Lehman (another leading Zionist who took great part in promoting the "second exodus" from Europe in 1945-1946, which led to the war in Palestine), Judge Samuel Rosenmann (a resident inmate of the White House, who helped write Mr. Roosevelt's speeches), Mr. David Niles (of Russian-born parentage, and for many years "adviser on Jewish affairs" to Mr. Roosevelt and his successor), Mr. Benjamin Cohen (a drafter of the Balfour Declaration in 1917 and another important Zionist), and three Jews from Russia, Messrs' Sidney Hillman, Isador Lubin and Leo Pasvolsky.

These leading names, from the personal entourage of the president, represent only the pinnacle of an edifice that was set around all American political life. This sudden growth of Jewish influence, behind the scenes of power, obviously was not a spontaneous natural phenomenon. The selection was discriminatory; anti-Zionist, anti-revolutionary and anti-world-government Jews were excluded from it. The formation of this "palace guard" was unpopular, but unofficial advisers are difficult to attack on specific grounds and Mr. Roosevelt ignored all protests, and so escorted began his thrice-renewed presidency. Hitler simultaneously appeared as the symbol, at that moment, of the mathematically-recurrent Jewish persecution, and in the calculations of President Roosevelt's advisers took the place occupied by "the Czar" twenty years before in those of Mr. Wilson's.

Mr. Roosevelt's long continuance in office was chiefly due to Mr. House's master-plan for winning elections. Under this strategy of the intensive appeal to the "fluctuating" vote "discrimination" became the chief slogan. It was raised on behalf of the Negroes, who were used as a stalking-horse[18]; and in fact was used to crush objection to the excessive influence of the "foreign group" represented by "the palace guard." Coupled with it was the appeal to the poor in the form of promises to soak the rich. This strategy proved so effective that the Republicans beat a retreat and began to compete with the Democrats for the favour of "the foreign group," who were held to be the arbiters of elections. In this way the secret grip on power was made secure, and the American elector was in fact deprived of true choice between parties. Mr. Roosevelt fortified himself by his policy of "deficit-spending," the basic theory of which was that the amount of public debt was unimportant, as the State only owed it to itself. At that point the American people lost and have never since regained control of the public purse, and the occupant of the White House became able by a stroke of the pen to command expenditures which in earlier times would have covered the annual budgets of half-a-dozen thrifty States. Mr. Roosevelt gained these powers by invoking the need to beat "The Crisis," and he produced The Permanent Emergency in which his country still lives.

His presidency followed a design obviously predetermined and the course of events in the world might have been entirely different if it had been shorter. However, the hidden mechanism was so efficient, and the hold of his mentors on it so secure, that he was maintained in office through three re-elections. Only once was his tenure threatened with unexpected interruption, dangerous to these plans.

In a Southern State, Louisiana, arose a politico of Mr. Roosevelt's type. Mr. Huey Long, a young demagogue with a fleshy face and curly hair from a poor hillbilly home, grew popular (like Mr. Wilson and Mr. Roosevelt) by attacking "the interests" (in his particular countryside, the oil interests in

---

[18] The agitation about the lot of the American Negro, of which so much is heard in the outer world, is kept going, from New York, almost entirely by the two chief Jewish publicity organizations (the American Jewish Committee and the Anti-Defamation League, both of which dispose of large funds) and the National Association for the Advancement of Coloured People, which from its inception has been largely Jewish-directed. The Negro himself plays a passive part in it. His wish is for better opportunities of advancement *alongside* the white population; he does *not* desire to interbreed. The energy of the Jewish organizations which claim to intercede in his cause is entirely directed towards a compulsory *intermingling* which neither race desires. Thus the influence of these non-Negro groups was the chief one behind the litigation leading to the Supreme Court ruling of 1955, which held the existing separate-school system to be illegal and ordered its abolition and compulsory mixed-schooling (this judgment can hardly be enforced in the South without civil war and it has been followed by various violent episodes, including the use of the National Guard and of tanks to *enforce* mixed-schooling). I was able to see the American Jewish Committee's budget for 1953, the estimates for which were $1,753,000. This stated, in respect of the Negroes, "The status of Jews is more secure in most of the civil and political rights areas than that of some other groups, especially Negroes. But so long as a successful threat is made to the enjoyment of rights by Negroes, the rights of Jews are riskfully in balance. Accordingly, a large proportion of our work has been directed towards securing greater equalization of opportunities for such other groups, rather than for ourselves ... An example of this is our relationship with the N.A.A.C.P., which comes to us for assistance in certain matters where we have a special competence ... A fruitful weapon is court action ... We participate directly in litigation ... We have filed briefs attacking segregation ... and have prepared briefs challenging discrimination against Negroes." The Supreme Court is composed of political appointees, not of professional jurists; this is an important factor in what might develop into a grave situation.

general and Standard Oil in particular). The idol of the poor whites, he was elected governor in 1928 and at once tried to raise money for building schoolhouses by putting a tax on oil, whereon at the opening of the Louisiana Legislature one Rabbi Walter Peiser refused to invoke a blessing, calling him "an unworthy governor."

Mr. Long grew more popular and was elected to the United States Senate where (March 1935) he devoted "a large part" of a speech to "an attack on Mr. Bernard Baruch," in whom he apparently saw the supreme representative of the "interests" (about the only charge never made against Mr. Long, who had many Jewish associates, was that he was "anti-semitic"). Mr. Long was becoming a force in the land and wrote a book called *My First Week in the White House*, containing illustrations which showed Mr. Roosevelt, looking much like the Roosevelt of Yalta, listening humbly to the wisdom of a hale and ebullient Huey Long.

He set out to undo Mr. Roosevelt by outdoing him in Mr. Roosevelt's especial skill: lavish spending and lavish promises. He did this in an ingenious way (he was possibly trickier than even Mr. Roosevelt). Mr. Long, with his "Share the Wealth" and "Every Man a King" programme, controlled the political machine in Louisiana. When the Roosevelt money began to flow into the States (for expenditure on all manner of crisis "projects," and incidentally on votes) Mr. Long calmly diverted it to his own similar ends. He forced through the Louisiana Legislature a law prohibiting local authorities from receiving any Washington money without the consent of a Louisiana State Board. As he controlled this board, he intercepted the cornucopian stream and the money was spent to enhance his, not Mr. Roosevelt's voting strength. He did with public money what Mr. Roosevelt was doing, but for his own political account.

In 1935 Mr. Roosevelt's second election campaign loomed ahead. Suddenly his advisers became aware that Mr. Long was popular far beyond his native Louisiana; he was a national figure. The Democratic National Committee "was astonished when a secret poll revealed that Long on a third-party ticket could poll between three and four million votes and that his Share The Wealth plan had eaten deeply into the Democratic strength in the industrial and farm States" (Mr. John T. Flynn).

Therefore Mr. Long, although he could not have become president at that time, certainly *could* have prevented Mr. Roosevelt's re- election, and the ruling few suddenly beheld a disturber of their regime. However, as Mr. Flynn says, "Fate had gone Democratic and remained so"; on September 8, 1935 Mr. Long was shot in the Louisiana State Capitol by a young Jew, Dr. Carl

Austin Weiss. The motive will never be known because Dr. Weiss, who might have explained it, was shot by Mr. Long's tardy bodyguard.[19]

The political effect was clear; Mr. Roosevelt's re-election was ensured. The usual suggestion of "a madman" was conveyed to the public mind and various other motives, not entailing insanity, also were suggested. No public investigation was made, as in the cases of other political assassinations of the last hundred years, in respect of which investigation was denied or curtailed. Such investigations as have been made (for instance, in the cases of President Lincoln, the Archduke Franz Ferdinand and King Alexander of Yugoslavia) have never supported the theory (always put forward) of the lonely "madman," but have revealed thorough organization with powerful support. The removal of Mr. Long determined the pattern of events for a decade, so that it was as important in its effects as the murders of more highly-placed men.

Mr. Roosevelt was re-elected in 1936. His allotted task evidently was to re-involve his country in the "foreign entanglements" of Mr. House and Mr. Wilson, and, like Mr. Wilson, he promised from election to election to keep it out of these. Meanwhile, the uproar about Hitler grew and, as I have shown, his persecution of men was subtly transformed into a "persecution of Jews." Mr. Roosevelt, just two years before the Second War, made *public,* through cryptic statement which to the initiated was an undertaking to involve his country in war and to wage it primarily for the cause represented by his palace guard. Mr. Wilson made his public statement, with its menace to Russia, in December 1911, about three years before the First World War; Mr. Roosevelt made his, with its menace to Germany, in October 1937, about two years before the Second World War. The two statements are implicitly identical in identifying the American cause with the Jewish cause as misrepresented by the Zionists.

Mr. Roosevelt said (October 5, 1937), "Let no one imagine that America will escape ... that this Western hemisphere will not be *attacked* ... *When an epidemic of physical disease* starts to spread, the community approves and *joins in a quarantine of patients* in order to protect the health of the community against the spread of the disaster."

The president's speech-writers on this occasion were not cryptic enough. The allusion to "joining in a quarantine" was instantly understood by the public masses also as a threat of war. This caused such consternation that Mr. Roosevelt was obliged up to the very moment, four years later, when America was actually involved in war to promise "again and again and again"

---

[19] Mr. Long had foretold his assassination in July, saying in the Senate that enemies bad planned his death with "one man, one gun, and one bullet" as the medium. He said that a dictograph, concealed in a New Orleans hotel room where his "enemies" had met, recorded this conversation. A contemporary writer who claims to have been present at the meeting, Mr. Hodding Carter, says, "The 'plotting' was limited to such hopefully expressed comments as, 'I wish somebody would kill the ....'"

that "your sons will not be sent into any foreign war." (In October 1937 he certainly knew that war was coming in the autumn of 1939; at that very moment I had informed *The Times* from Vienna that Hitler and Goering had said so, and the American president would not have been less accurately informed).

By 1937 the falsification of the news-picture from Germany, which was described in the last chapter, had been going on for four years. I gave several instances, and here adduce another. Rabbi Stephen Wise relates that the American Jewish Congress immediately after Hitler's advent to power started the boycott-Germany movements on the basis of "cable reports" from Germany that "*a nationwide pogrom*" of Jews was being "planned."[20] He then mentions, casually, that the "reported" pogrom "did not come off," but the boycott did.[21]

Starting with this imaginary pogrom in Berlin, the propagandist campaign in America formed the basis on which Mr. Roosevelt rested his "quarantine" speech. The Zionists around the president were not truly concerned about the suffering of Jews at all; on the contrary, it was necessary to their politics in America and to the entire undertaking, and they feared its alleviation. In this they continued the policy of the Talmudic revolutionaries in Czarist Russia, who went to the length of assassination to prevent the emancipation of Jews, as has been shown.

Thus Rabbi Wise records that he and his fellow Zionists were not deterred by urgent protests and appeals from the Jews in Germany to stop the boycott. The prospect of an accommodation between Hitler and the Jews of Germany, indeed, appalled them and Rabbi Wise informed his associates of his "two fears" in this respect: "… that our Jewish brothers in Germany might feel moved or compelled to accept a peace agreement or pact *that might mean some slight amelioration or mitigation of their wrongs* … that the Nazi regime might decide to prevent some of the evil consequences of its regime *by such palliative treatment of the Jews as would disarm worldwide Jewish protest*." (He describes the second possibility as the "graver" danger).

---

[20] The Nazis always claimed that their one-day Jewish boycott of April 1, 1933 was in reply to this provocation from New York, and Rabbi Wise's book of 1949 thus bears out their statement.

[21] The word "pogrom" (a Russian one meaning "'massacre"') plays an especial part in this propaganda. It is applied to any kind of disturbance in which Jews are involved and has by suggestion been given this specific, though false significance, so that the casual reader might suspect a misprint if he were to read of "a pogrom of Russians" (or of Arabs). Dr. Weizmann says "'there were never any pogroms" in his native Russian countryside but uses the word continually, explaining that "'it is not necessary to live among pogroms to know that the Gentile world is poisoned." In inciting a British military governor of Palestine to harsh measures against Arabs Dr. Weizmann said he "had had some experience with the atmosphere which precedes pogroms," though by his own earlier statement he had none. He describes as a pogrom disorders in which five or six Jews were injured, and as "'Arab terrorism" the events of 1938, in which 69 British, 92 Jews and 1500 Arabs were killed. A distinguished British officer, Sir Adrian Carton de Wiart V.C., who lived in Poland between the two wars, says 'The Jewish question seemed unanswerable … Pogroms *were rumoured* to be taking place, but I considered the rumours to have been grossly exaggerated for there were no ocular proofs of the massacre of thousands of Jews."

Douglas Reed

Thus they *feared* that "the persecution" would collapse; the words are specific. Rabbi Wise, in New York, preferred that Jews in Germany should suffer rather than this should happen: "To die at the hands of Nazism is cruel; *to survive by its grace were ten thousand times worse. We* will survive Nazism unless *we* commit the inexpiable sin of bartering or trafficking with it *in order to save some Jewish victims"* (1934, to the world Jewish Conference). *"We* reject out of hand with scorn and contempt any and every proposal *which would ensure the security of some Jews* through the shame of all Jews" (1936). Mr. Brandeis, in Washington, was equally resolute for martyrdom in Germany: "Any arrangement which results in making a market abroad for German goods strengthens

Hitler.... ...To thus relieve Hitler's economic distress *in order to save by emigration some of Germany's Jews* would be .... deplorable statesmanship."[22]

For the Zionists in America the spectral danger of a reconciliation between Hitler and the Jews became most acute in 1938. General Smuts then sent his Defence Minister, Mr. Oswald Pirow, to Germany to ease tension in the Jewish question, if he could. The British prime minister, Mr. Neville Chamberlain, welcomed the attempt; he told Mr. Pirow that the pressure of international Jewry was one of the principal obstacles to an Anglo-German understanding and said he would be helped in resisting this pressure (Leon Pinsker's "irresistible pressure") if Hitler could be induced to moderate his spleen.

Mr. Pirow then went to Germany. He says that he made a specific proposal, that Hitler responded favourably, and that agreement was in sight.

At that very instant fate again intervened, as in the case of Mr. Huey Long, Count Stolypin, Czar Alexander II and others; whenever a chance of pacification appeared fate intervened. A young Jew shot a German diplomat, Herr von Rath, in Paris. Riots followed in Germany, synagogues were burned, and Mr. Pirow's mission abruptly ended. No investigation into the murder, or any organization that might have been behind it, was held, or if one was begun it never produced any informative result; Rabbi Wise presents the familiar picture (found also in Mr. House's novel) of the "half-crazed youth," maddened beyond endurance.

---

[22] In fact, these Zionists were quite ready to "'traffic with the Nazis" and make financial deals with them when it suited their purpose. Seven years later, when the Second War was at its climax, Rabbi Stephen Wise received an offer from "'a group of Nazi functionaries" to allow Jews to go from Poland to Hungary, against payment. Both these countries were German-occupied, so that the advantage to the Jews involved is not apparent, and Mr. Wise must have had some ulterior reason (possibly connected with the later "'exodus" to Palestine) for wishing to transfer Jews from occupied Poland to occupied Hungary *in wartime* when he had so fiercely opposed their *liberation from Germany in peacetime.'* He requested President Roosevelt to release dollars for the bribe, to be deposited to these Nazis' account in Switzerland, whereon the president "'immediately" answered, "'Why don't you go ahead and do it, Stephen!" Instructions were then given to another prominent Zionist, Mr. Henry Morgenthau at the Treasury, and despite State Department and British Foreign Office protests the money was transferred to the Geneva office of the World Jewish Congress for crediting to the Nazi leaders!

366

Mr. Roosevelt responded immediately: "The news of the past few days from Germany has deeply shocked public opinion in the United States ... *I myself could scarcely believe that such things could occur in a twentieth century civilization* ... I asked our Ambassador in Berlin to return at once for report and consultation".

The words referred to the synagogue-burning. (Mr. Roosevelt did not comment on the murder) and the central sentence is demonstrably untrue, because Mr. Roosevelt, and all his contemporaries, had earlier seen the wanton destruction of religious edifices. True, they had not been synagogues, but Mr. Roosevelt had "seen" the dynamiting of Christian churches and cathedrals in Communized Russia, and on becoming president had rushed to recognize the government that did it. Moreover, when he made this declaration he had just sent a telegram cordially approving the enforced capitulation of Czechoslavakia to Hitler and in that deed had found nothing incongruous with 20th Century civilization. This was the moment when I threw up my post, feeling unable to continue in journalism at a time when untruth was master of "the news."

The United States in effect became involved in the Second War when President Roosevelt made these declarations in 1937 and 1938, not on the day of Pearl Harbour, and a straight line led from them to his later statement of July 17, 1942, when he implicitly promised vengeance on Germany solely on account of its treatment of Jews; the men who prompted him to that public threat had from the start vehemently opposed any mitigation of Jewish suffering in Germany.

The murder of von Rath in Paris was the shot of Sarajevo which in effect opened the second war, as the developing fluid, time, now reveals. Unlike Mr. Wilson, Mr. Roosevelt never privately believed that he would keep his country neutral; in 1938 his mentor, Mr. Bernard Baruch, declared "We are going to lick that fellow Hitler; he isn't going to get away with it" (General George C. Marshall). Unless some change occurs, and none is foreseeable yet, the American president in any third war would find himself held in the same coils as his predecessors of 1914-1918 and 1939-1945.

During these six years when "the unnecessary war" was brewed I watched the turbulent, darkening scene from Berlin and Vienna and all the great cities on which the long night was soon to fall: Prague and Budapest, Belgrade and Bucharest, Sofia and Warsaw. I saw as much as any man, I suppose, of the stoking of the furnace from which the ingot, war, was produced; and more than most, because I was not confined to any one country or faction, but had the run of them all. I knew the noise of the bravoes in the Storm Troopers' *Stammkneipen*, the furtive, bitter talk of their adversaries in private dwellings, and the nervous murmur of men on the run, who glanced ever over their shoulders. I saw the face of the mob, that dinosaur without a cerebral cavity, in both its moods: the inflamed one of illusory hope (in Berlin) and the hollow-cheeked, sunken-eyed one of hopeless disillusionment (in Moscow). I met fear at every level, from the street-cleaner to the head of state or of government; I saw the terror in both its headquarter cities.

I knew or met many of the men who *appeared* to be powerful and to uphold opposing causes, and yet by their acts all brought "the unnecessary war" nearer and nearer. I talked with Hitler, Goering and Goebbels; I lunched quietly by the Geneva lakeside with chubby Maxim Litvinoff, a typical figure of the Café des Exiles, and wondered what he knew of Russia who so little Russia knew, though he was Foreign Minister of that communized land. I saw Mussolini, and Ramsay Macdonald, one of the British prime ministers who passed shadow-like across the blind during these years. I talked for long hours with Edouard Benesh in the old castle at Prague, with Austrian chancellors and Hungarian prime ministers, with Balkan kings and politicians. I went to watch the League of Nations, with high expectations then (for I was still callow) and was repelled by the manner of its proceedings, which was without dignity, by the lobbying and canvassing behind the scenes, and by the throng of hangers-on and intriguers which infringed it; I think few enthusiasts for the "United Nations" would be found among those who knew the League of Nations. I went to Moscow, in the journalistic bodyguard of a rising young minister named Anthony Eden, and there saw a regime which was the facsimile of the National Socialist one in Germany in every major respect save the status of the Jews, who appeared to me to be predominant in the key-positions of the Soviet state.

It was all a whirling confusion, at the centre of which was one plain fact: that Hitler would make war unless he were prevented and that this war was coming, because he would not be prevented. There was another British prime minister, Mr. Stanley Baldwin (a source of grief to the newspaper correspondents in Germany) who withheld the truth of Hitler's warlike intentions from his countrymen because, as he later said, he would have "lost the election" if he had told it. If his successor, Mr. Neville Chamberlain, thought that by continuing the policy of encouragement to Hitler he could "steer" Hitler to direct his war against the Soviet (I have no proof of this, but it may have been Mr. Chamberlain's calculation) that was at least *a policy*, where before was no policy at all. But it was a mistaken policy, for all qualified observers in Germany foresaw that when he struck Hitler would join hands with Stalin in waging war, not wage war against him (I wrote this in my pre-war books).

When I experienced Hitler's first two invasions, of Austria and Czechoslovakia, I realized that the last hope of averting the unnecessary war was gone. I felt that I lived in a mad world and this explains the title, *Insanity Fair,* which I gave to the book I wrote at that time. I could see only a lunatic lack of policy then. Eighteen years later, in the light of all that has come about and been made known, the possibility that the unnecessary war was not in all quarters held to be unnecessary obviously cannot be written off.

Chapter 38

THE LITTLE COUNTRY FAR AWAY

In forgotten Palestine during the 1930-1940 decade, while "The Chief" and "*Der Fuehrer*" reigned in Washington and Berlin, matters went from bad to worse and at the end a British government was about to abandon the hopeless task foisted on it by Mr. Balfour (who died in 1930 after a deathbed leave-taking from Dr. Weizmann) when, on the eve of another war, a Mr. Winston Churchill recommitted his country to it. Thus the British people, believing that their business was solely with Hitler, once more went into war under sealed orders, among which was the purpose, unsuspected by them, that had brought them to the brink of defeat in 1918.

Successive British governments, in this affair, found themselves in the plight of the circus clown who cannot rid himself of the fly- paper; each time they thought they had shaken it off, Dr. Weizmann affixed it in a new place. In Palestine the British administrators and soldiers, on whom "the Mandate" had been thrust, could not do their duty. The Arabs obdurately rebelled; the Zionists in London importuned the government there to use force against the Arabs; if the men on the spot tried to act impartially between the parties orders from home restrained them.

British history overseas is probably vindicated by results in every case but this. It produced free overseas nations in empty lands, and in conquered ones populated by others the oft-proclaimed (and ever-derided) intention to upraise the conquered and then depart is being carried out; India is only one proof of that. In the case of Palestine all the rules previously followed by Britain overseas were broken and all experience set at naught, under the "pressure" exercized in London, or from other capitals if London ever baulked.

Thus the British officials and troops sent to Palestine were the unluckiest in British history (characteristically, the only man among them who was publicly honoured after their departure was a traitor). They knew how to administer a genuine "protectorate"; the word has an honest meaning as well as the false one mockingly given to it by Hitler in Czechoslovakia. Occupation with the consent, or at the invitation of native inhabitants can be an admirable thing. I have travelled in one such genuine "protectorate," Basutoland. The British went there at Basuto request and the consequence was that the Basuto survived as a free nation, where they would otherwise have been enslaved by stronger neighbours. Their lot and prospect today are better than they could have become in any other way and they realize this, so that a few dozen white administrators govern 660,000 Basuto in mutual esteem.

The British in Palestine, for the first time in their nation's history, were required to repress the people they had come to "protect" and to protect others who were in fact invaders from Russia. The corruption of "the civil power" in England, from Mr. Balfour's time on, achieved this result. The supreme maxim of Western constitutionalism is that "the civil power" must always be superior to the military one, so that militarist regimes may not arise. But if the civil power yields to the dictates of a secret third party with military aims, it becomes in fact *inferior* to a military power, though not to its native generals. In this way the supreme maxim is stood on its head, because a nation's armed forces can then be put at the service of interests alien to, and destructive of, its own. This happened in Palestine.

The repression of native Arabs as "rebels" did not help Zionism *in Palestine*. At the start of the 1930-1940 decade the rise of Hitler strengthened its position in the lobbies of London and Washington, but this improvement was counterbalanced by the further deterioration which occurred in Palestine itself as the decade wore on. During this later period Dr. Weizmann, who from 1904 to 1919 had concentrated his efforts on the British government extended his activities to two new places; his orbit covered "Jerusalem, London and New York" and he dealt with British prime ministers like a man whittling sticks.

His next victim was, once more, Mr. Ramsay Macdonald, who after desertion by his Socialist colleagues became prime minister of a coalition government of all other parties. Young Jimmy Macdonald from Lossiemouth, Scotland's poor boy made good, was by this time Mr. Ramsay Macdonald of the graying, floating hair. He made his son, Mr. Malcolm Macdonald, Under-Secretary for the Colonies, and therewith both Macdonalds left the happy dreamland of Socialist platform oratory for the cold, hard world of "irresistible pressure." Mr. Macdonald again set out to stop the endless fighting and rioting in Palestine, which by this time had claimed many British lives, and soon announced that his government would suspend Zionist immigration, regulate Zionist land purchases, and punish incitements to disorder *"in whatever quarter they may originate."*

Mr. Macdonald at once became the object of violent attack and began to wear the bewildered mien for which he became famous (and which I observed when I met him in 1935). He received the visit of Dr. Weizmann and three Zionist associates and was accused of "dealing rather frivolously" with "the *moral implications of promises* given to Jews" (Dr. Weizmann). Leading politicians in his own country, America and South Africa began a furious campaign against him. Intimidated a second time, he appointed a special Cabinet Committee to reconsider the oft-considered "Palestine policy." A Socialist minister, Mr. Arthur Henderson, was chairman and Mr. Malcolm Macdonald was secretary; Dr. Weizmann and six leading Zionists formed "the committee"; the Arabs, as usual, were not represented.

Dr. Weizmann violently attacked the undertaking to punish incitements to disorder *from whatever quarter;* disorder, violence and massacre, he said, originated *only* with the native Arabs. Mr. Macdonald again surrendered in a letter to Dr. Weizmann, under the terms of which Zionist immigration to Palestine in 1934 and 1935 exceeded all previous figures. Having dealt with Mr. Macdonald Dr. Weizmann undertook the grand tour. As the Second War approached he was everywhere, in South Africa, Turkey, France, Italy, Belgium and other lands. In France he met "every premier between the two wars" and of these he found M. Leon Blum, a co- religionist, to be especially sympathetic. M. Aristide Briand, the Foreign Minister, was also well-disposed "although a little vague as to what was going on" (Dr. Weizmann often refers in such terms to the Western politicians who did his bidding). He saw Mussolini three times. He spoke to distinguished audiences about the iniquities of Hitler and told them it was "the responsibility of the civilized world" on this account to expel the Palestinian Arabs (he did not put it so plainly).

Nevertheless, by the later 1930's Zionism in Palestine was disintegrating again. But for the Second War it would have faded into oblivion, an Arabian Jameson Raid undertaken in irresponsibility and ignominiously ended.

In 1936 Arab rioting became even more violent. By then successive British governments for fourteen years, at Zionist behest, had refused to allow the Arabs to hold elections. With time Dr. Weizmann's argument that this refusal was of the essence of "democracy" lost appeal and the British government found itself in an increasingly difficult dilemma. Mr. Stanley Baldwin (after succeeding Mr. Macdonald) resorted to the old "pending-basket" procedure; he sent one more commission of investigation (the fifth?) to Palestine, and at this point the thing became plain farce.

Mr. Macdonald had been cowed by Dr. Weizmann and his bodyguard into cancelling a "Palestine policy" announced after full consultation with his responsible advisers. Now that Mr. Baldwin sent a commission to Palestine to discover an alternative policy it was received by Dr. Weizmann! With agility he hopped from London to Jerusalem and back, telling the British government in London what to do, their Commissioners in Palestine what to report, and the British government in London, again, what it should do with the report when it arrived. (Betweenwhiles he visited New York to arrange for more "pressure" from that quarter).

This Peel Commission received from some quarter a proposal that the eternal dilemma might be solved by partitioning Palestine, and promptly consulted Dr. Weizmann. Until that moment the pretence had been kept up, all through the years, that the Zionists did not claim a Jewish state, only the "national home." Dr. Weizmann knew that if a British government could

Douglas Reed

once be brought to support "partition" it would at last be committed to a separate Jewish *state*.

His Asiatic mastery of the art of negotiation compels admiration. By invoking the Old Testament he firmly nailed down the *idea* of partition without committing himself to any boundaries. He said that he might be able to make some concession about the actual area to be taken for his Zionists, as Jehovah had not indicated precise frontiers in his revelations to the Levites. This accepted the offer of territory while leaving the entire question of boundaries open so that even "partition," obviously, was to be no solution. The words with which Dr. Weizmann supported partition are of interest in the light of later events: "The Arabs are afraid that we shall absorb the whole of Palestine. Say what we will about *the preservation of their rights,* they are dominated by fear and will not listen to reason. A Jewish state with definite boundaries internationally guaranteed would be something final; the transgressing of these boundaries would be *an act of war which the Jews would not commit, not merely because of its moral implications, but because it would arouse the whole world against them.*"

The Peel Commission recommended partition and stated that "the Mandate" was unworkable. Had the British Government acted on that report and promptly withdrawn from Palestine much might have been spared mankind, but within two years the Second World War reinvolved it in the insoluble problem.

As it approached Dr. Weizmann continued to beleaguer the Western politicians with the argument that "the Jewish National Home would play a very considerable role in that part of the world as the one reliable ally of the democracies." By this he meant that the Zionist demand for arms for the forcible seizure of Palestine, which was about to be made, would be presented in that way, through the politicians and the press, to the public masses of the West. In 1938 he then proposed to Mr. Ormsby-Gore, British Secretary for the Colonies, that the Zionists should be allowed to form a force of something like 40,000 men. This presupposed that the unnecessary war would come about (an anticipation in which the leading men behind the scenes apparently were all agreed), and Dr. Weizmann did all he could to ensure this, using the case of the Jews as his sole argument. After the murder of von Rath and the anti-Jewish disorders in Germany he told Mr. Anthony Eden:

"*If a government is allowed to destroy a whole community which has committed no crime ... it means the beginning of anarchy and the destruction of the basis of civilization. The powers which stand looking on without taking any measures to prevent the crime will one day be visited by severe punishment.*"

Hitler's persecution of *men* was ignored in these private, fateful, interviews in political antechambers; the plight of one "community" *alone* was advanced as the argument for war. The Zionists, as events have shown, were intent on destroying "a whole community which had committed no crime"

374

(the Arabs of Palestine, who knew nothing of Hitler) and the arms they demanded were used for that purpose. Significantly, Dr. Weizmann put his argument in terms of the *Christian* creed; under that teaching the destruction of a community innocent of crime *is* itself a crime which will bring "severe punishment." Under the Levitical Law, however, which Dr. Weizmann invoked as the basis of his demand for Palestine, it is the chief "statute and commandment," to be rewarded by power and treasure, not punished.

In the last twelvemonth before the Second War the secret arbiters of power exerted their maximum effort to gain control of men and events. Mr. Roosevelt was "committed" but could only be made use of at a later stage. In England Mr. Baldwin, the Worcestershire squire and manufacturer, gave way to the Birmingham business-man, Mr. Neville Chamberlain, in whom a serious obstacle to the exercise of "irresistible pressure" behind the scenes arose.

Mr. Chamberlain's name is linked with the final, fatal act of encouragement to Hitler: the abandonment and enforced surrender of Czechoslovakia at Munich. For a few weeks the public masses thought he had saved the peace by this deed and at that moment I, in Budapest and Prague, first understood what Thomas Jefferson meant when he said, "I really look with commiseration over the great body of my fellow citizens who, reading newspapers, live and die in the belief that they have known something of what has been passing in the world of their times."

Nevertheless, Mr. Chamberlain may have calculated that he was compelled to do what he did by the state of British weakness and unpreparedness which his predecessor, Mr. Baldwin, had allowed to come about. I believe he was wrong if he so calculated; even at that late moment firmness would have saved the day, because the German generals were ready to overthrow Hitler; but he may have been honestly convinced that he could not act otherwise. Where he unforgivably erred was in depicting the deed of Munich as something *morally* right and in bolstering up this contention with allusions to "a small country a long way away with which we have nothing to do," or similar words.

However, he was at least consistent in this last attitude. He wanted to disentangle England from its imbroglio in another small country far away where it had found only tribulation bequeathed to it by Mr. Balfour. What he did incurred the bitter enmity of those who were powerful behind the political scenes, and in my opinion the true source of his overthrow may have been the same as that of Mr. Asquith in 1916.

1938, when the word "partition" rang out, was the bloodiest year in Palestine up to that time; 1500 Arabs were killed. The Peel Commission had recommended partition but could not suggest how it might be effected. Yet another body of investigators was sent out, this time in search of a means of bisecting the infant without killing it. This Woodhead Commission reported in October 1938 that it could not devise a practical plan; in November the von Rath murder and the anti-Jewish disorders which followed it in Germany were used by the Zionists to intensify their incitements against the Arabs in Palestine.

Mr. Chamberlain then did an extraordinary thing, by the standards prevailing. He called a Palestine conference in London at which *the Arabs* (for the first time since the Peace Conference of 1919) were represented. From this conference emerged the White Paper of March 1939 in which the British government undertook *"the establishment within ten years of an independent Palestine state"* and *"the termination of the Mandate."* In this state the native Arabs and immigrant Zionists were to *share* the government in such a way as to ensure that the essential interests of *each* community were safeguarded. Jewish immigration was to be limited to 75,000 annually for five years and the irrevocable land-purchases were to be restricted.

This plan, if carried out, meant peace in Palestine at last, but no separate Jewish state. At that moment the figure of Mr. Winston Churchill advanced to the forefront of British affairs. He had for ten years been in political eclipse and the future student may be interested to know what contemporaries have already forgotten: that during this period he was a highly unpopular man, not because of any specific acts or quality, but because he was consistently given that "bad press" which is the strongest weapon in the hands of those who control political advancement. This organized hostility was made particularly plain during the abdication crisis of 1937, when his pleas for time received much more bitter attack than they inherently deserved and he was howled down in the House of Commons. His biographers depict him as suffering from depression during these years and thinking himself "finished" politically. His feeling in that respect may be reflected in his published words (privately written) to Mr. Bernard Baruch early in 1939: "War is coming very soon. We will be in it and you will be in it. You will be *running the show* over there, but I *will be on the sidelines over here."*

Very soon after he wrote this Mr. Churchill's political fortunes took a sudden turn for the better and (as in the case of Mr. Lloyd George in 1916) his attitude towards Zionism appears to have had much to do with this, to judge from what has been published. His record in this matter suggests that Mr. Churchill, the product of Blenheim and Brooklyn, is something of "a riddle inside a mystery wrapped in an enigma," to use the words employed by him about the Communist state in 1939. In 1906, as has been shown, he was among the earliest of the politicians who supported Zionism on the hustings, so that a Zionist speaker said any Jew who voted against him was a traitor. However, in office during the First War he took little part in that affair and Dr. Weizmann only mentions him once at that period, and then not as a "friend." Then, as Colonial Secretary in 1922, he gave offence to Zion by his White Paper, which Dr. Weizmann calls "a serious whittling down of the

Balfour Declaration." It proposed for Palestine "a Legislative Council *with a majority of elected members*," and this would have meant, not only holding those elections which Dr. Weizmann to the end forbade, but allowing the native Arabs of Palestine to govern their own country!

Thus Mr. Churchill's ten years in the political wilderness, 1929-1939, were also ones during which he was in disfavour with the Zionists and Dr. Weizmann's narrative never mentions him until the eve of the Second War, when he is suddenly "discovered" (as the playwrights used to say) in it as a most ardent champion of Zionism. This is the more curious because, as late as October 20, 1938, Mr. Churchill was still talking like the author of the White Paper of 1922: "We should ... give to the Arabs a solemn assurance ... that the annual quota of Jewish immigration should not exceed a certain figure for a period of at least ten years." Very soon after that he re- emerges in Dr. Weizmann's account as a man implicitly and *privately* agreed to support a Zionist immigration of millions.

Quite suddenly Dr. Weizmann says that in 1939 he "met Mr. Winston Churchill" (ignored in his story for seventeen years) "and he told me he would take part in the debate, speaking *of course against the Proposed White Paper.*" The reader is left to guess why Mr. Churchill should have undertaken "of course" to speak against a document which, in its emphasis on the need to do justice to the Arabs, was in accord with his own White Paper of 1922 and with his speeches for seventeen years after it.

Then, on the day of this debate, Dr. Weizmann was invited to lunch with Mr. Churchill "who read his speech out to us" and asked if Dr. Weizmann had any changes to suggest. The reader will recall that editors of *The Times* and *Manchester Guardian* wrote editorial articles about Zionism after consultation with the chieftain of one interested party; now Mr. Churchill approached a debate on a major issue of state policy in the same manner. He was renowned for the quality of his speeches, and became so in America on account of the strange fact (as it was considered there) that he wrote them himself. However, in the circumstances above described by Dr. Weizmann, the point of actual penmanship appears of minor importance.

At that moment Mr. Churchill's "championship" (Dr. Weizmann) was vain; the great debate ended in victory for Mr. Chamberlain and his White Paper by a majority of 268 to 179. It was substantial, but many politicians already smelt the wind and their sail-trimming instinct is reflected in the unusually large number of abstentions: 110. This gave the first warning to Mr. Chamberlain of the method, of dereliction within his own party, by which he was to be overthrown. The debate showed another interesting thing, namely, that the Opposition party by this time held Zionism to be a supreme tenet of its policy, and, indeed, the ultimate test by which a man could prove whether he was a "Socialist" or not! The rising Socialist party had long forgotten the wrongs of the working man, the plight of the oppressed and the sad lot of "the underdog"; it was caught up in international intrigue and wanted to be on the side of the top-dog. Thus Mr. Herbert Morrison, a Socialist leader, pointed accusingly at Mr. Malcolm Macdonald (whose department was closely identified with the White Paper) and mourned the heresy of a man who "was once a Socialist." Socialism, too, by this time meant driving Arabs out of Palestine, and the trade union notables, with their presentation gold watches, did not care how poor or oppressed those distant people were.

The Second War broke out very soon after the issuance of the White Paper and the debate. At once all thought of "establishing an independent Palestine" and "terminating the Mandate" was suspended, for the duration of the war (and at its end a very different picture was to be unveiled). At its start Mr. Roosevelt in America was "publicly and privately committed" to support Zionism (Mr. Harry Hopkins). In England Mr. Chamberlain was an impediment, but he was on his way out. Mr. Churchill was on his way in. The people wanted him, because he was "the man who had been right" about Hitler and the war; they knew nothing of his talks with Dr. Weizmann and the effects these might produce.

Chapter 39

THE ARMING OF ZION

For six years the grappling masses surged to and fro over three continents, and at the end those who thought themselves the victors were further from the Holy Grail than at the start; at the victor-politicians' parleys the cock crowed a second time. Three decades earlier President Wilson had striven to cry that "the causes and objects are obscure ... the objects of the statesmen on both sides are virtually the same," and the outcome justified him. The German leaders then had decided to "foment" and Mr. House to "support" the world-revolution; the Zionists kept their headquarters in Berlin as long as they thought that a victorious Germany might set up the "Jewish homeland" in Palestine, and only transferred them when victory was seen to lie with the West.

The Second War again bore out the truth of Mr. Wilson's stifled cry. It could not have begun at all without the complicity of the world-revolution in the onslaught of the new "madman in Berlin," and the peoples then overrun could discern no difference between the Communist and the Nazi oppression. Then, when the two turned against each other, Mr. Hopkins (in Mr. House's stead) began to "support" the world-revolution again, so that victory could bring no "liberation." Hitler wanted to re-segregate the Jews; Mr. Brandeis in America similarly, and imperially, decreed that "No Jew must live in Germany." Mr. Churchill desired that "three or four million Jews" should be transplanted to Palestine; the Communist state, by profession anti-Zionist, supplied the first contingent of these.

When the smoke of battle cleared only three purposes had been achieved, none of them disclosed at its start: the world-revolution, with Western arms and support, had advanced to the middle of Europe; Zionism had been armed to establish itself in Palestine by force; the "world-government," obviously the result which these two convergent forces were intended to produce, had been set up anew in embryo form, this time in New York. The war behind the war was the true one; it was fought to divert the arms, manpower and treasure of the West to these purposes. Through the dissolving fog of war the shape of the great "design" first revealed by Weishaupt's paper, and exposed again in the Protocols, showed clear.

When the war began the intention to abandon the unworkable "Mandate" and withdraw from Palestine, after ensuring the equitable representation of all parties there, was official British policy, approved by Parliament. The Zionists saw that no British government, in any foreseeable future, could be brought to perform the actual deed of assassination: that is to say, to expel the Arabs from their own Palestine by arms. They set about to obtain arms for themselves under cover of the war.

The war was hardly begun when Dr. Weizmann appeared in Mr. Churchill's office. Unknown to the general public, this remarkable man for thirty-three years (from the day of his interview with Mr. Balfour) had exercised mastery over the politicians of England and America. His person cannot have inspired such awe, so that they must have seen in him the representative of a force which cowed them; the one which Dr. Kastein called "the Jewish international" and Mr. Neville Chamberlain "international Jewry."

Mr. Churchill, returned to office after ten years as First Lord of the Admiralty, presumably should have been absorbed by the war at sea, but Dr. Weizmann was concerned with other things. He said, "after the war we would want to build *up a state of three or four million Jews in Palestine*" and states that Mr. Churchill replied, "*Yes, indeed, I quite agree with that.*" Mr. Churchill, twelve months earlier, had called for "solemn assurances" to the Arabs that Zionist immigration would be regulated and restricted. Even today, in 1956, Palestine has but 1,600,000 Jews and a state of permanent warfare exists in Arabia in consequence of their introduction; if their number is to be doubled or trebled the shape of the future is apparent and Mr. Churchill, in 1939, presumably saw it.

Mr. Churchill then had no responsibility for Palestine. Dr. Weizmann evidently expected that Mr. Churchill would soon be Prime Minister. He then went to America and expounded his plan to President Roosevelt, finding him "interested" but cautious (his third election campaign impended), and returned to England, where Mr. Churchill had supplanted Mr. Chamberlain in the highest office.

Thus the situation of 1916 was recreated, with a small difference. Mr. Lloyd George was required to divert British *armies* to Palestine, for the initial conquest of the coveted land, and did so. Mr. Churchill was asked to divert *arms* to the Zionists there so that they could establish themselves, and sought to comply. Indeed, he had been giving orders in that sense for five months when he next saw Dr. Weizmann, and records them in appendices to his war memoirs.

He became prime minister on May 10, 1940 as France collapsed and the British island stood alone, defended only by the remnant of its air forces and its navy; the army had been destroyed in France. On May 23 he instructed his Colonial Secretary, Lord Lloyd, that the British troops in Palestine should be withdrawn and "*the Jews armed* in their own defence and properly organized as speedily as possible." He repeated the order on May 29 (while the evacuation from Dunkirk was in progress) and on June 2. On June 6 he complained of military opposition to it, and at the end of June of "difficulties" with two responsible ministers, particularly Lord Lloyd ("who was a convinced anti-Zionist and pro-Arab; I wished *to arm* the Jewish colonists").

Thus the matter was already being discussed in terms, not of national interest, but of "pro" this and "anti" that, the language of the soap-box. Mr. Churchill continued in this strain, telling Lord Lloyd that the large numbers of troops in Palestine were "the price we have to pay for the *anti-Jewish policy* which has been persisted in for some years" (the policy of his own White Paper of 1922). If the Jews were properly armed, he said, British troops would be released for service elsewhere "*and there would be no danger of the Jews attacking the Arabs.*" He refused to acquaint Parliament with the views of the *responsible* minister: "I could certainly not associate myself with such an answer as you have drawn up for me."

At that moment arms were more precious than diamonds in England. The armies rescued from France were without weapons and disorganized; Mr. Churchill records that the whole island contained barely 500 field guns and 200 tanks of any age or kind; months later he was still urgently appealing to President Roosevelt for 250,000 rifles for "trained and uniformed men" who had none. In those days I scoured the countryside to obtain, at last, a forty-year old pistol which would fire only single shots. Mr. Churchill's rousing words about fighting forever on the beaches and in the streets and never giving up did not thrill me, because I knew that, if an invasion once gained foothold, they were empty; men cannot fight tanks with bare hands. The unarmed state of the land was dire. I should have been bewildered had I known that Mr. Churchill, at such a time, gave his mind so persistently to the arming of Zionists in Palestine.

The danger of invasion was receding when Dr. Weizmann next saw Mr. Churchill, in August 1940. He then proposed that the Zionists should form an army of 50,000 men, and in September presented Mr. Churchill with "a five-point programme," the main point of which was "the recruitment of the greatest possible number of Jews in Palestine for the fighting services." He says that Mr. Churchill "consented to this programme."

Lord Lloyd (like Sir William Robertson, Mr. Edwin Montagu and many others in the First War) fought hard to avert all this. He was pursued by the untimely fate which dogged many of the men who tried to do their duty in this matter: he died in 1941, aged only 62. However, responsible officials and soldiers never ceased to try and restrain the "top-line politicians" from this new diversion. Dr. Weizmann complains that, despite Mr. Churchill's support, "exactly four years were to pass before, in September 1944, the Jewish Brigade was officially formed," and attributes this delay to the obstinate resistance of "*experts*" (his word). Mr. Churchill similarly complained: "I wished to *arm the Jews* at Telaviv ... Here I encountered every kind of resistance" (July 1940, just before the air attack on Britain began).

Dr. Weizmann evidently thought the time was come to subdue this resistance by "pressure" from another quarter, for in the spring of 1941, he went again to America. At this time (as in the First War) he was nominally giving the British "war effort" the benefit of his scientific knowledge, on this occasion in the field of isoprene. He says he was "absorbed in the work," but he contrived to make himself free from it and, as he was Dr. Weizmann, no difficulties arose about crossing the Atlantic in wartime.

The ground had been prepared for him in America, where Rabbi Stephen Wise was instructing President Roosevelt (as he had instructed the long-dead President Wilson) about his duty towards Zionism: "On May 13, 1941 I found it necessary to send the president first-hand reports from Palestine" (the rabbi's first-hand reports about a "reported" pogrom in 1933 had produced the boycott in New York) "and write about the imperilled status of the unarmed Jews ... The British Government *ought to be made to understand how enormous would be the shock and how damaging its effect upon the democratic cause*, if there should be a general slaughter because of failure adequately to *arm the Jews* as well as to strengthen the defences of Palestine with *guns, tanks and planes*."

The president replied, "I can merely call to the attention of the British our deep interest in the defence of Palestine and our concern for *the defence of the Jewish population there;* and, as best I can, supply the British forces with the material means by which the maximum protection to Palestine will be afforded." Equipped with this letter (as Dr. Weizmann once with a report of an interview written on British Foreign Office letter-paper) Rabbi Stephen Wise "the next day left for Washington, and after conference with high government officials felt more confident that the British *would be made to understand* that there must be *adequate equipment (guns, tanks and planes) for our people in Palestine* ... And probably thanks to the intervention of Mr. Roosevelt, the business of *parity* had been dropped to a large extent" (the last allusion is to the insistence of responsible British administrators that, if arms were being handed around, Arabs and Zionists *in equal numbers* should be armed in Palestine; even Mr. Churchill had found difficulty in resisting this proposal).

These Zionist potentates in the various countries applied "irresistible pressure on international politics" in perfect synchronization. If London lagged in compliance, it was "made to understand" by Washington; had the positions been reversed the procedure would have been the opposite. Thus the mechanism had been well oiled when Dr. Weizmann arrived and he soon satisfied himself that "the top political leaders" showed "real sympathy for our Zionist aspirations."

In Washington, as in London, he found the responsible officials a nuisance: "The trouble always began when it came to *the experts* in the State Department." Below the "top-line politician" in Washington level ministers and high officials, and in Palestine American professors, missionaries and businessmen, all tried to keep American state policy free of this incubus. The chief responsible official in Washington is described by Dr. Weizmann in the identical terms used by Mr. Churchill to Lord Lloyd: "The head of the Eastern Division of the State Department was an avowed *anti-Zionist* and *pro-Arab*"; this indicates the original source of political vocabulary at the top level.

Dr. Weizmann realized that from this period on Washington was the place whence pressure might best be maintained on London, and early in 1942 transferred himself thither. His liberation from the scientific work which "absorbed" him in England was easily arranged, President Roosevelt discovering that Dr. Weizmann was urgently needed in America to work on the problem of synthetic rubber. The American Ambassador in London, Mr. John G. Winant, scented trouble and "earnestly advised" Dr. Weizmann, when he reached America, to devote himself "as completely as possible to chemistry." Mr. Winant was alarmed about the consequences of all these machinations, and foreboding eventually broke him; his death, soon afterwards, was of tragic nature. As for his counsel, Dr. Weizmann remarks that "actually, I divided my time almost equally between science and Zionism," and if that was so "chemistry" came off better than any who knew Dr. Weizmann would have expected.

Before he left he "dropped in" at Ten Downing Street, where by 1942 he had been on dropping-in terms for nearly thirty years, to bid goodbye to Mr. Churchill's secretary, as he says. Not surprisingly, he saw Mr. Churchill, who said (according to Dr. Weizmann): "When the war is over, I would like to see Ibn Saud made lord of the Middle East, the boss of the bosses, *provided he settles with you*... of course we shall help you. Keep this confidential, but you might talk it over with Roosevelt when you get to America. There's nothing he and I cannot do if we set our minds on it." (Dr. Weizmann, after the interview, made a note of this confidence and gave it to the Zionist political secretary with instructions to disclose it to the Zionist executive if anything befell Dr. Weizmann; also, he published it in his later book).

Mr. Churchill erred if he expected Dr. Weizmann to help set up an Arabian "lord of the Middle East," for that potentateship is obviously reserved to Zionism. Hence Dr. Weizmann did not even convey Mr. Churchill's message when he saw President Roosevelt and talked only about his scientific work. In other quarters he pressed for "America to send *the maximum number of planes and tanks to that theatre*" (Africa, where they would be most accessible to the Zionists in Palestine). At this stage he began close co-operation with Mr. Henry Morgenthau, junior, of the president's inner circle, who was to prove of "peculiar assistance" at the later, decisive moment.

Dr. Weizmann again encountered irritating hindrances: "Our difficulties were *not connected with the first-rank statesmen*. These had, for by far the greatest part, always understood our aspirations, and their statements in favour of the Jewish *National Home* really constitute a literature. It was always *behind the scenes,* and on the lower levels, that we encountered an *obstinate, devious and secretive opposition* … *All the information supplied from the Middle East to the authorities in Washington worked against us.*"

For nearly forty years, at that time, Dr. Weizmann had worked "behind the scenes," deviously and in secret; history shows no comparable case. At one more behind-the-scenes meeting with President Roosevelt he then imparted Mr. Churchill's message, or rather (according to his own account) a different one: he said Mr. Churchill had assured him that "the end of the war would see a change in the status of the Jewish National Home, and that the White Paper of 1939 would go." He describes this as Mr. Churchill's "plan" but it is not the message previously quoted, although it might depict Mr. Churchill's mind. What is significant is that Dr. Weizmann omitted Mr. Churchill's main proposal, to make King Ibn Saoud "lord of the Middle East … provided he settles with you." Dr. Weizmann says that President Roosevelt's response to Mr. Churchill's plan (as thus misrepresented to him) was "completely affirmative," which in Zionese means that he said "Yes" to a Jewish *state* ("a change in the status of the Jewish National Home"). The president, according to Dr. Weizmann, then himself introduced the name of Ibn Saoud, and showed himself "aware of the Arab problem." Dr. Weizmann, if his account is correct, did *not* then say that Mr. Churchill recommended "a settlement" with Ibn Saoud. On the contrary, Dr. Weizmann "maintained the thesis that *we could not rest our cause on the consent of the Arabs.*"

That was the opposite of Mr. Churchill's envisaged "settlement" and was specific: it meant *war* against the Arabs and American support for such a war. Thereon Mr. Roosevelt merely "again assured me of his sympathies and of his desire to settle the problem." There is some mystery in this reserve of President Roosevelt in the matter of "the Arab problem" which might have had important consequences had he not died, two years later, almost immediately after *meeting* Ibn Saoud. However, what he cautiously said and privately thought was no longer of vital importance in 1943, because the real decision had been taken. Behind the scenes, under cover of a war in Europe, arms were on their way to the Zionists, and this secret process was to determine the shape of the future. From this moment neither the top-line politicians, if they rebelled, nor the hard-pressed responsible officials had the power to prevent Zionism from planting in Palestine a time-bomb which may yet blow up the second half of the 20th Century.

For the time being Dr. Weizmann, in July 1943, returned to London, assured that "pressure" from Washington would be maintained.

Chapter 40

THE INVASION OF AMERICA

While military invasions and counter-invasions multiplied during the six years of the Second War, absorbing all thought and energy of the masses locked in combat, a silent invasion went on which produced more momentous effects than the armed ones. This was the political invasion of the American Republic and its success was shown by the shape of American state policy at the war's end, which was so directed as to ensure that the only *military* invasions that yielded enduring "territorial gains" were those of the revolution into Europe and of the Zionists into Arabia. Historically surveyed, Mr. Roosevelt's achievement may now be seen to have been threefold and in each respect perilous to his country's future: he helped to arm Zionism, he armed the revolution in its Moscow citadel, and he opened the doors of his American citadel to its agents.

He began the process at the start of his presidency by his recognition of the Soviet, when the ambassador of the revolution, Maxim Litvinoff, undertook that the revolutionary state would keep its nose out of American domestic affairs; Mr. Roosevelt's mentors were not the men to remind him that when once the fox gets in his nose he'll soon find ways to make his body follow. The story of his support of the revolutionary state by money and arms belongs to a later chapter; this one aims to tell the tale of its penetration of the American Republic on its own soil during his long presidency.

Mr. Roosevelt began by breaking down the barriers against uncontrolled immigration which the Congresses immediately before him strove to set up, because they saw in it the danger of the capture of the American administration by "a foreign group." Under various of his edicts the supervision of immigration was greatly weakened. Immigration officials were forbidden to put questions about Communist associations, and the separate classification of Jewish immigrants was discontinued. This was supported by a continuous press campaign against all demands for enquiry into loyalty or political record as "discrimination against the foreign-born."

None can say how many people entered the United States during that period. By 1952 Senator Pat McCarran, chairman of the United States Senate Judiciary Committee, estimated that, apart from legal immigration, five million aliens had *illegally* entered the country, including large numbers of "militant Communists, Sicilian bandits and other criminals." The chief investigating officer of the Immigration Service declined even to estimate the number of illegal entrants but said that at that time (when some measure of control had been re-established) "over half a million a year" were being intercepted and sent back at the Mexican border *alone*. The Social Security authorities, who supplied the cards necessary to obtain employment, were forbidden to give any information about applicants to the immigration or police authorities.

This mass of immigrants went to swell the size of the "fluctuating vote" on which Mr. Roosevelt's party (still following Mr. House's strategy) concentrated its electoral effort and its cry of "no discrimination." Under the president's restrictions on loyalty-interrogations the way into the civil service and armed forces was opened to American-born or legally-domiciled alien Communists. The results to which this led were shown in part by the many exposures of the post-war period, the literature of which would fill an encyclopaedia of many volumes. The entire West was also involved (as the Canadian, British and Australian exposures in time showed) and the significant thing is that, with the Canadian exception, no governmental investigation ever led to these partial revelations, which were always the work of persistent private remonstrants; nor was genuine remedial action ever taken, so that the state of affairs brought about during the 1930's and 1940's today continues not much changed, a source of grave weakness to the West in any new war.

The renewal of large-scale immigration formed the background to the political invasion of the Republic. This was a three-pronged movement which aimed at the capture of the three vital points of a state's defences: state policy at the top level, the civil services at the middle level and "public opinion" or the mass-mind at the base. The way in which control over acts of state policy was achieved (through the "adviserships" which became part of American political life after 1913) has already been shown, this part of the process having preceded the others. The methods used to attempt the capture of government services will be discussed later in this chapter. In what immediately follows, the capture of the mass-mind in America, through control of published information, will be described; it was indispensable to the other two thrusts.

This form of political invasion is called by Dr. Weizmann, who exhaustively studied it in his youth, when he was preparing in Russia for his life's work in the west, "the technique of propaganda and the approach to the masses." The operation so described may now be studied in actual operation:

Far back in this book the reader was invited to note that "B'nai B'rith" put out a shoot. B'nai B'rith, until then, might be compared with such groups of other religious affiliation as the Young Men's Christian Association or the Knights of Columbus; its declared objects were the help of the poor, sick and fatherless and good works in general. The little offshoot of 1913, the "Anti-

Defamation League," had by 1947 become a secret police of formidable power in America.[23]

In Doublespeak "anti-defamation" means "defamation" and this body lived by calumny, using such terms as anti-semite, fascist, rabble-rouser, Jew-baiter, Red-baiter, paranoiac, lunatic, madman, reactionary, diehard, bigot and more of the like. The vocabulary is fixed and may be traced back to the attacks on Barruel, Robison and Morse after the French revolution; the true nature of any writer's or newspaper's allegiance may be detected by keeping count of the number of times these trade-mark words are used. The achievement of this organization (usually known as the A.D.L.) has been by iteration to make fetishes of them, so that party politicians hasten to deny that they are any of these things. Under this regime reasoned debate became outlawed; there is something of sorcery in this subjugation of two generations of Western men to the mumbo-jumbo of Asiatic conspirators.

When the A.D.L. was born *in 1913* it had merely desk-room in the parent B'nai B'rith office and a tiny budget. *In 1933* Mr. Bernard J. Brown wrote, "Through the intervention of the A.D.L. we have succeeded in *muzzling the non-Jewish press* to the extent that newspapers in America abstain from pointing out that any person unfavourably referred to is a Jew." *In 1948* the Jewish *Menorah Journal* of New York wrote, "Should but one phrase in a reprinted *literary classic* reflect unjustly upon Jews, the A.D.L. will promptly belabour the innocent publisher until he bowdlerizes the offending passage. Let one innocent movie-producer incorporate a Jewish prototype, however inoffensive, in his picture and the hue and cry raised by the A.D.L. will make him wish he's never heard of Jews. But when Jews are subtly propagandized into accepting Communist doctrine ... *the A.D.L. remains silent. No word, no warning, no hint of caution, much less exposure and condemnation*; although there are men *high in the councils of the organization who should know by their own experience how the Communists 'infiltrate.'"* (The *Menorah Journal* spoke for the many Jews who were alarmed because the A.D.L. was attacking *anti-Communism* as *anti-semitism*).

These quotations show the growth of the A.D.L.'s power in thirty-five years. It has imposed the law of heresy on the public debate in America. No criticism of Zionism or the world-government plan is allowed to pass without virulent attack; criticism of Communism is only tolerated in the tacit understanding that any war with Communism would lead to the communized

---

[23] In fact though not in form. The secret police in countries where the institution is native (Hitler's Gestapo was copied from the Asiatic model, which had a century-old tradition in Russia and Turkey) have the entire power and resources of the state behind them; indeed, they *are* the state. In America Zionism built the nucleus of a secret police nearly as effective in many ways as those prototypes. It could only become *equally* effective if it gained full control of the state's resources, including the power of arrest and imprisonment, and in my judgment that was the *ultimate* goal.

world-state; and as to that, "Jerusalem is the capital of the world no less than the capital of Israel" (the Zionist mayor of Jerusalem, 1952).

America has today a few surviving writers who fight on for independent debate and comment. They will discuss any public matter, in the light of traditional American policy and interest, save Zionism, which hardly any of them will touch. I have discussed this with four of the leading ones, who all gave the same answer: it could not be done. The employed ones would lose their posts, if they made the attempt. The independent ones would find no publisher for their books because no reviewer would mention these, save with the epithets enumerated above.

The A.D.L., of such small beginnings in 1913, in 1948 had a budget of three million dollars (it is only one of several Jewish organizations pursuing Zionist aims in America at a similar rate of expenditure). The *Menorah Journal*, discussing "Anti-Defamation Hysteria," said, "Fighting anti-semitism has been built up into a big business, with annual budgets running into millions of dollars." It said the object was "to continue beating the anti-semitic drum" and "to scare the pants off prospective contributors" in order to raise funds. It mentioned some of the methods used ("outright business blackmail; if you can't afford to give $10,000 to this cause, you can take your business elsewhere"), and said American Jews were being "stampeded into a state of mass-hysteria by their self-styled defenders."[24]

The *Menorah Journal* also drew attention to the falsification of news by Jewish newsagencies subsidized by the big organizations. It showed that some minor brawl among juveniles in Manhattan had been depicted in "front-page scare headlines which would have led a stranger to believe that a Czarist pogrom was going on" (by these same means the "Czarist pogroms" earlier, and Rabbi Stephen Wise's "reported pogrom in Berlin" in 1933 reached the world). Out of this particular "scare headline" grew a mass-meeting in Madison Garden, where another politician aspiring to presidential office (a Mr. Wendell Willkie at that moment) declared, "The mounting wave of anti-semitism at home shocks me ... etc., etc."

"Mass-hysteria" is not only produced among Jews and band-wagon politicians by this method; it produces another kind of mass- hysteria among earnest but uninformed people of the "Liberal" kind: the mass-hysteria of self-righteousness, which is a tempting form of self-indulgence. The late Mr. George Orwell was of those who helped spread "mass-hysteria" in this way. He was a good man, because he did not merely incite others to succour the weak and avenge injustice, but went himself to fight when the Civil War

---

[24] The reader need not find any contradiction between this quotation and my statement in the preceding paragraph. Debate and comment are largely free in the *Jewish* press, which is intended chiefly for perusal "among ourselves," and the newspaper-reader, anywhere in the world, who takes the pains regularly to obtain Jewish newspapers of all opinions will find himself much better informed about what goes on in the world. The black-out is in the non-Jewish press.

broke out in Spain, then discovering that Communism, when he saw it, was worse than the thing which (as he thought) he set out to destroy. He died before he could go to Palestine and experience any similar enlightenment, so that what he wrote about "anti-semitism" was but the echo of "anti-defamationist hysteria." It is so good an example of this that I quote it; here a man of goodwill offered, as his own wisdom, phrases which others poured into his ear.

He explored "anti-semitism in Britain" (1945) and found " a perceptibly anti-semitic strain in Chaucer." Mr. Hilaire Belloc and Mr. G.K.Chesterton were "literary Jew-baiters." He found passages in Shakespeare, Smollett, Thackeray, Shaw, T.S. Eliot, Aldous Huxley and others "which *if written now* would be *stigmatized* as anti-semitism" (he was right without knowing it; if written *now* they would have been *stigmatized*). Then he suffered what Americans call a pratfall. He said that "offhand, the only English writers I can think of who, before the days of Hitler, made a definite effort to stick up for Jews are Dickens and Charles Reade." Thus he extolled one of the A.D.L.'s "Jew-baiters" as a champion of Jews; in America the film of *Oliver Twist* was banned because of Fagin! This was the work of the A.D.L.; its representative, a Mr. Arnold Forster, announced:

"American movie-distributors refused to become involved in the distribution and exhibition of the motion picture after the A.D.L. and others expressed the fear that the film was harmful; the Rank Organization *withdrew* the picture in the United States." Later the picture was released after censorship by the A.D.L.; "seventy two eliminations" were made at its command and a prologue was added assuring beholders that they might accept it as "a filmization of Dickens without anti-semitic intentions." (In occupied Berlin the A.D.L. ban was final; the *British* authorities ordered *Dickens* withdrawn from *German* eyes).

I was in America at this time and thus saw the fulfilment of a prediction made in a book of 1943, when I wrote that, as the secret censorship was going, Chaucer, Shakespeare and Dickens would one day be defamed as "anti-semites." I thought to strain probability, to make a point, but it happened in all three cases: a Shakespearean actor-manager visiting New York was ordered not to play *The Merchant of Venice,* Dickens was banned, and the defamationists put Chaucer on their black-list.

A private organization which can produce such results is obviously powerful; there is nothing comparable in the world. Mr. Vincent Sheehan wrote in 1949, "There is scarcely a voice in the United States that dares raise itself for the rights, any rights, of the Arabs; any slight criticism of the Zionist high command is immediately labelled as anti-semitic." Miss Dorothy Thompson, whose picture and articles at that time were published every day in hundreds of newspapers, similarly protested. Mr. Sheehan's popularity with book- reviewers immediately slumped; Miss Thompson's portrait and writings are seldom seen in the American press today.

How is the oracle worked? By what means has America (and the entire West) been brought to the state that no public man aspires to office, or editor feels secure at his desk, until he has brought out his prayer-mat and prostrated himself to Zion? How have presidents and prime ministers been led to compete for the approval of this faction like bridesmaids for the bride's bouquet? Why do leading men suffer themselves to be paraded at hundred-dollar-a-plate banquets for Zion, or to be herded on to Zionist platforms to receive "plaques" for services rendered?

The power of money and the prospect of votes have demonstrably been potent lures, but in my judgment by far the strongest weapon is this power to control published information; to lay stress on what a faction wants and to exclude from it all that the faction dislikes, and so to be able to give any selected person a "good" or a "bad" press. This is in fact control of "the mob." In today's language it is "the technique of propaganda and the approach to the masses," as Dr. Weizmann said, but it is an ancient, Asiatic art and was described, on a famous occasion, by Saint Matthew and Saint Mark: "The chief priests and elders *persuaded the multitude...* The chief priests *moved the* people ..."

In forty years the A.D.L. perfected a machine for persuading the multitude. It is a method of thought-control of which the subject-mass is unconscious and its ability to destroy any who cry out is great. One of the first to be politically destroyed was the head of the Congressional Committee charged to watch over sedition (the Un-American Activities Committee). The Protocols of 1905 foretold that the nation-states would not be allowed to "contend with sedition" by treating it as crime and this "forecast" also was fulfilled. Mr. Martin Dies relates that he was required by the secret inquisition to restrict the definition of "subversion" to "fascism," and to equate "fascism" with "anti-semitism." "Subversion," had these importuners had their way with him, would have been any kind of resistance to "the destructive principle," not the subverting of the nation-state. He would not yield, but was driven out of political life by defamation.

The A.D.L. (and the American Jewish Committee) "set out to make the American people *aware* of anti-semitism." It informed Jews that "25 out of every 100 Americans are *infected* with anti-semitism," and that another 50 might develop the disease. By 1945 it was carrying out "a high-powered educational program, geared to reach every man, woman and child" in America through the press, radio, advertising, children's comic books and school books, lectures, films, "churches" and trade unions. This programme included "219 broadcasts a day," full-page advertisements in 397 newspapers, poster advertizing in 130 cities, and "persuasions" subtly incorporated in the printed matter on blotters, matchbox covers, and envelopes. The entire national press ("1900 dailies with a 43,000,000 circulation") and the provincial, Negro, foreign-language and labour newspapers were kept supplied with, "and used," its material in the form of "news, background material, cartoons and comic strips." In addition, the A.D.L. in 1945 distributed "more than 330,000 copies of important books *carrying our message* to libraries and other institutions," furnished authors with "material and complete ideas," and circulated nine million pamphlets "all tailored to fit the audiences to which they are directed." It found "comic books" to be a particularly effective way of reaching the minds of young people, soldiers, sailors and airmen, and circulated "millions of copies" of propaganda in this form. Its organization consisted of the national headquarters, public relations committees in 150 cities, eleven regional offices, and "2,000 key men in 1,000 cities."

The name of the body which supplied this mass of suggestive material never reached the public. During the 1940's the system of "syndicated writers" in New York or Washington enveloped the entire American press. One such writer's column may appear in a thousand newspapers each day; editors like this system, which saves them the cost of employing their own writers, for its cheapness. Through a few dozen such writers the entire stream of information can be tinctured at its source (the method foretold in the Protocols). By all these means a generation has been reared in America (and this applies equally to England) which has been deprived of authentic information about, and independent comment on, the nature of Zionism, its original connection with Communism, the infestation of administrations and capture of "administrators," and the relationship of all this to the ultimate world-government project.

The opposition to this creeping control was strong at first and was gradually crushed during two decades (I have given examples in England) by various methods, including the purchase of newspapers, but chiefly by unremitting and organized pressure, persuasive or menacing. In America a newspaper which prints reports or comment unacceptable to the A.D.L. may expect to receive a visit from its representatives. Threats to withdraw advertizing are frequently made. The corps of "syndicated" writers joins in the attack on any individual writer or broadcaster who becomes troublesome; many American commentators have been driven from the publishers' lists or "off the air" in this way. An illustrative example:

The *Chicago Tribune* in 1950 reported the view of *a senior official of the State Department* that the United States was ruled by "a secret government" consisting of three members of the deceased Mr. Roosevelt's circle: Mr. Henry Morgenthau junior, Justice Felix Frankfurter and Senator Herbert Lehman. The word "Jew" was not used; the article expressed the opinion of a high public servant on a matter held by him to be of great national importance. This article raised much commotion in the Zionist and Jewish press throughout the world (few non-Jewish newspapers paid attention to it, for the obvious reason). I was in South Africa but guessed what would follow and when I next went to America learned that I was right; the *Tribune* Tower in Chicago was besieged by the A.D.L. with peremptory demands for an apology. On this particular occasion none was made; the newspaper was at that time a lonely survivor from the days of independent reporting and comment. (A piquant detail; the writer of this "anti-semitic" report had interested himself, not long before, in efforts to obtain the release on parole of a Jew serving a life-term for murder, on the ground that expiation might reasonably be held to have been made).

Even the figures for expenditure, staff and activities, above given, convey no true idea of the power and omnipresence of the A.D.L. I myself would not have believed, until I saw it, that a body of such might could almost invisibly operate in a state still nominally governed by president and Congress. Its numerous offices and sub-offices are clearly only the centres of a great network of agents and sub-agents, for its eye is as all-seeing as that of the N.V.D. in captive Russia or of the Gestapo once in Germany, as I found through personal experience:

I am a fairly obscure person and when I went to America in 1949 was almost unknown to the public there, the publication of most of my books having been prevented by the methods above described. I found that the A.D.L. watched me like a hawk from my arrival and from this first realized its immense spread and vigilance; I had not suspected that it scrutinized every roof for every sparrow. An American acquaintance who had read some of my books introduced me to a colleague who expressed pleasure at meeting their author. This man asked me to dine with him and a friend, whom he presented as "my cousin." The cousin was an entertaining fellow; I learned a year later that he was head of the A.D.L.'s New York office and the true organizer of the little dinner-party.[25] This happened a few days after I landed and thereafter the A.D.L. knew my every movement. They knew about the book I was writing and when it was ready for publication the "cousin" approached

---

[25] By this means material for dossiers and for "smearing" attacks is often obtained. In 1956 the A.D.L. published such a "smear" volume called *Cross-Currents*, described as "the book that tells how anti-semitism is used today as a political weapon." It was filled with attacks on "anti-semites" and contained numerous extracts from letters and conversations supposed to have passed between the persons named. The reviewer of the book in the *New York Times*, though sympathetic (writing for that journal he would not be antagonistic) said "the authors do not let the reader in on the secret of how they came into possession of these intriguing papers ... *this reticence about sources is a major weakness and it is particularly serious where statements are quoted from an oral interview.*" Who were these interviewers, he asked, and how did they go about their assignment? I could have told him, and the reader of this book has the answer. If my "oral interview" with the "cousin," who purported to be a strong "anti-semite," did not provide material for this volume, the reason is of interest. Late in a convivial evening he asked me suddenly how strong I thought "anti-semitism" to be in the United States. Believing him to be what he professed to be, I answered just as I would have answered, had I known his identity. I said that I had travelled in more than thirty of the forty-eight States and had never once heard the word "Jew" mentioned by any of the thousands of people I had met, which was the fact.

the American publisher of an earlier book of mine with a pointed request to know if he *contemplated* issuing this one; a man of discretion, he answered No.

Three years later, in 1952, when this book had appeared in England, the American Legion's magazine at Hollywood published some five hundred words from it. The A.D.L. at once demanded a retraction from the Hollywood commander of the Legion, who referred to the magazine's editor. No inaccuracy was alleged; the deputation just called the book "anti-semitic." The editor refused to retract unless false statement or other valid reason were proved, and resigned when the commander, ignoring him, published the familiar "apology" in face of threats that "all Jews" would boycott the Hollywood Stadium, which was operated by the Legion. The editor, departing, said this proved the truth of what was stated in the book. The apology availed the commander nothing for the nationwide American Broadcasting Company, which had been televising the Legion's events at the Stadium, at once announced that it would terminate its contract with the Legion and televise rival events; the commander ruefully said that this "comes as a complete shock to me."

When I next visited America, in 1951, another acquaintance, who thought my books informative and wished me to write for American newspapers, refused to credit what I told him. He said he was sure a certain publication would welcome an article from me on a subject then topical (not Zionism) and wrote to its editor. He was told, to his astonishment, that the publication of anything of mine, was "*verboten*," and when he suggested publication without my name was informed that this would not avail: "there is probably a representative of the A.D.L. on our payroll" (I have the letter).

Another acquaintance, head of a large bookselling concern, ordered his office to obtain a book of mine from Canada and was told that the Toronto wholesaler reported inability to supply. I made enquiry and learned that no order had reached Toronto. My acquaintance then investigated and could not find out who, *in his own office*, had intercepted the order, telling me he now realized that my books were "on the index."

The reader need only multiply these few examples from the personal experience of one man to see the effect on the total sum of information supplied to the public masses. The peoples of the Western nation-states are deprived of information in the matters most vitally affecting their present and future, by a press which (they are constantly told) is "the freest in the world."

Another method used by the A.D.L. to keep Jews in "mass hysteria" and non-Jews in a state of delusion is that of the *agent provocateur*, the bogus "anti-semite" (the "cousin" above mentioned is an example). Part of this method is the distribution of "documents" exposing "the whole world plot" and usually attributed to some unverifiable gathering of rabbis. The serious student of the real Talmudic enterprise, which can be documented from authentic Talmudic sources, at once recognizes these fabrications. An "admirer" once sent me such a "document," found (he said) in a secret drawer of an old family bureau which could not have been opened for a hundred years. I had the paper examined and then asked my correspondent to tell me how his long dead great grandfather had contrived to obtain paper manufactured in the 1940's. The correspondence closed.

An example of the employment of the bogus "anti-semite" by the A.D.L. is on record, authenticated by the organization itself. A prolific writer of books attacking "anti-semitism" in America is a man of Armenian origins, one Avedis Boghos Derounian, whose best known alias is John Roy Carlson. Several libel actions were brought against one of his books published during the Second War, in which he attacked over seven hundred persons, and one judge, awarding damages, said "I think this book was written by a wholly irresponsible person who was willing to say anything for money; I would not believe him on oath, nor at any time hereafter; I think that book was published by a publisher who was willing to publish anything for money." In November 1952 a radio-interviewer confronted this man with a well-known American foreign correspondent, Mr. Ray Brock, who taxed Carlson with having formerly edited "*a viciously antisemitic* sheet called *The Christian Defender.*" This could not be denied, as the fact had become known, so Carlson said he had done it "*with the approval of the Anti-Defamation League.*" The host-interviewer then interrupted to say that the A.D.L., on enquiry by him, confirmed this (the confirmation was unavoidable, the A.D.L. having admitted to the *Chicago Tribune* in 1947 that it had employed the man between 1939 and 1941 and "found his services satisfactory").

The fact that this man then was able (1951) to publish another book *attacking* "anti-semites" and to have it loudly praised in the leading New York newspapers (in face of the judicial comment above quoted) is a sign of the great change which this organization has brought about in American life in the last twenty years. The web of which the A.D.L. formed the centre stretched to other English- speaking countries, so that no independent writer anywhere could escape it. I give instances from my own experiences in that larger setting:

In March 1952 *Truth* (which was then unsubjugated), reported that the Canadian Jewish Congress had requested a Canadian bookseller to remove from his shelves a book of mine. When I visited Canada that year I made enquiry and found that this pressure was general on Canadian booksellers, many of whom had yielded to it. At that time also a Zionist journal in South Africa stated, "Until such time as racial groups receive protection in law, *no bookshop is entitled to say that it will sell books ... like some of Reed's books*"; I later spent some time in South Africa and found the position there to be identical with the one in Canada. The "racial protection" foretold in the above quotation is the Zionist-drafted "Genocide Convention" of the United Nations, which contains a provision prescribing legal penalties for anything said by some faction to cause "mental harm"; this provision, if enforced during another war, would make the

A.D.L. censorship permanent and worldwide. I never went to Australia but think I would have found there the secret interference prevailing in the bookshops of Canada and South Africa. However, about the same time an Australian senator, unknown to me even by name, in attacking an "anti-semitic" organization equally unheard of by me, said it was "in close touch" with me; Australian newspapers published this defamationist message but refused to print the factual correction. During these years I received many complaints from readers that the chief librarian of a large Toronto library had pasted on the flyleaves of books of mine a "warning" to readers about them; protests had no effect.

In all these ways a curtain was lowered between the public masses and factual information about their affairs. The capture of the mass- mind became as complete as that of "the top-line politicians."

This left one position unconquered at the middle-layer between the captive politicians and the persuaded-multitude. It was the class of which Dr. Weizmann repeatedly complains: the permanent officials, the professionals and experts. From the start the strongest opposition to Zionism's encroachment came from this group (and from the "outside interference, entirely from Jews" of which Dr. Weizmann also complained). The non-elected official, the career civil servant, the professional soldier, the foreign expert all are almost impossible to suborn. The permanent official does not depend on election and feels himself an integral part of the nation. The professional soldier instinctively feels that the nation and his duty are one, and recoils at the thought that military operations are being perverted for some ulterior, political motive. The expert cannot smother his knowledge at the bidding of party-men any more than an expert craftsman can be tempted to make a watch that goes backward.

In fact, only the *complete* capture of a state, including the power of dismissal, disqualification from employment and arrest can ever fully overcome the resistance of public servants, professionals and experts to something that clearly conflicts with their duty. The A.D.L., in my judgment, showed that it looked forward to a day when it would overcome this obstacle by an attempt that was made in 1943.

The high directing intelligence behind this body evidently knows that the best moment to attain its aims is in the later stages and aftermath of a great war. At the start the embroiled masses are still intent on the objects professed and after the period of confusion which follows the war they regain some clarity of vision and begin to ask questions about what has been done under cover of the war; if the secret purpose has not then been attained the opportunity has been lost. These secret purposes were advanced between 1916 and 1922 (not between 1914 and 1918) in the First War, and between

1942 and 1948 (not 1939-1945) in the Second War. If a third war were to begin, say, in 1965 and continue until 1970, ostensibly for the purpose of "destroying Communism," the secret effort to realize the full ambition of Zionism and of the communized world-state would come during the period of greatest confusion, say, from 1968 to 1974.

The bid to capture the civil service in America was made in 1943, the fourth year of the Second War, and was partially exposed (by chance) in 1947, when the fog was clearing. The aim was to interpose between the American people and their public services a secret, defamationist black-list which would prevent men of patriotic duty from entering them, and open them wide to approved agents of the conspiracy. The lists then compiled were at one period being so rapidly extended that they would soon have included every person in the United States whose employment in public office was not desired by the secret arbiters. The defamatory dossiers of the A.D.L. were being incorporated in the official files of the American Civil Service. This could have provided the basis for secret police action at a later stage ("political opponents" were rounded up on the strength of such lists by Goering's new secret police on the night of the Reichstag fire). All unknown to the American people, then and now, a coup of the first order was far advanced in preparation.

Mr. Martin Dies once described the A.D.L., which supplied these lists, as "a terrorist organization, using its resources, not to defend the good name of Jews, but to force and compel compliance with the objectives of their organization by terrorist methods; it is a league of defamation."[26] The description was borne out by the disclosures of the Subcommittee to Investigate the Civil Service Commission set up by the Committee on Expenditures of the American House of Representatives, which met on October 3, 6 and 7, 1947 under the chairmanship of Representative Clare E. Hoffman of Michigan.

This investigation also was brought about solely by the efforts of individuals; the whole effort of government was bent on averting it. Some loyal civil servant saw what was secretly being done and informed certain Congressmen that black lists were being inserted in the Civil Service files. Even that might not have led to any action, had not these Congressmen learned that they themselves were among the blacklisted! Under the restraints bequeathed by the long Roosevelt administration investigation, even then, could only be set in motion on grounds that "funds voted by Congress were being misused" (hence the intervention of the Committee on Expenditures). About a hundred American Senators and Congressmen then learned that they (and some of their wives) were shown as "Nazis" on cards in the Civil Service

---

[26] In 1956 President Eisenhower sent the annual convention of the A.D.L. a eulogistic message commending it for "reminding the nation that the ideals of religion must apply in all areas of life."

files. They succeeded in securing copies of these cards, which bore a note saying that the defamationist information on them was "copied from the subversive files" of a private firm of Zionist lawyers. These files, the note continued, *"were made up in co-operation with the American Jewish Committee and the Anti-Defamation League; the sources of this information must not be disclosed under any circumstances;* however, *further* information concerning above may be obtained …" (from the Zionist attorneys).

The senior officer of that department of the United States Civil Service Commission which was charged with investigating applicants for employment appeared before the sub-committee on subpoena. As the official directly responsible, he said the files were secret ones, the existence of which had only just become known to him (presumably, when he received the subpoena). The only files theretofore known to him were those normally kept by his department; they recorded persons investigated who for various reasons were to be rejected if they sought employment. He had ascertained that the secret files contained "750,000 cards" and had been prepared in the Commission's *New York office* (his own headquarters office was in Washington), and that copies of the cards had been sent to and incorporated in the files of *every branch office of the Civil Service Commission throughout the United States.* He said he had no power to produce the secret files; power to do this lay solely with the three Civil Service Commissioners (the very heads, under the president, of the Civil Service).

These Commissioners (a Mr. Mitchell, Mr. Flemming and Miss Perkins), then subpoenaed, refused to produce the files, stating that the president had forbidden this (the secret files had been introduced under President Roosevelt; this order not to divulge came from President Truman). Thereon Mr. Hoffmann said, *"This is the first time I have ever heard the acknowledgement that we have in this country a Gestapo."*

The Commissioners made no protest. Mr. Hoffmann then asked if persons *who had no intention even of applying for a Civil Service post* were black-listed. The senior Commissioner, Mr. Mitchell, confirmed that this was the case, thus explicitly admitting that the black list was of *unlimited* range. Mr. Hoffmann said, "Then it has nothing to do with the immediate case of a person applying for a job?," and Mr. Mitchell agreed. Mr. Hoffmann continued, "You claim the right to list in your files the names of *anyone and everyone in this country?* Is that not correct?" and the three Commissioners silently assented.

The investigators discovered that in June and July of 1943 *alone* (that is, in the confusion-period of a great war) 487,033 cards had been added to the secret files, this work having occupied scores of clerks. A Congressman reminded the Commissioners that in the very year (1943) when these secret cards were incorporated the Civil Service Commission had specifically forbidden its investigators even to ask questions about any applicant's

Communist associations (the policy generally introduced by President Roosevelt). The Commissioners showed great anxiety to avoid discussing the part played by the Anti-Defamation League in this affair and repeatedly evaded questions on that point.

The official report, so astonishing by earlier standards, shows that the A.D.L. was in a position secretly to introduce into official records defamatory dossiers, quickly extensible into secret police files covering the entire country. This was recognizably an attempt to gain control of the American Civil Service and to make loyalty, by the earlier standards, a disqualification. As no assurance of remedial action was obtained, the result of this public investigation may be compared with a surgical examination by doctors who, having opened the patient and found a malignant growth near a vital organ, declare that they have order not to remove it and sew up the incision. Thus the unhealthy condition remained.

The uses which could conceivably be made of such secret, nation-wide black-lists were illustrated by some strange episodes of 1951 and 1952, when bodies of troops suddenly swooped on small towns in California, New York State and Texas and "occupied" them in the name of "the United Nations" or of "Military Government." City halls, police headquarters and telephone exchanges were taken over; mayors, officials and private individuals were arrested; bands of the "enemy" (garbed by some costumier in "Fascist" uniforms) were paraded around; trials were held by military courts and concentration camps were set up; proclamations were made threatening "resisters" and "conspirators" with dire penalties, and so on.

These proceedings look very much like a rehearsal of the kind of thing the world might well see, in the confusion-period of any third war, if "the league to enforce peace" were making its third bid for world-authority. On this occasion, too, indignant private investigators were quite unable to discover what authority ordered these affairs. The official military spokesman, a colonel at the Pentagon, when hard pressed by an inquirer, was only allowed to say that the question was "one of local *and political significance, over which the military exercises no control"!* That pointed to the president, government and State Department, but all these authorities remained as silent as the Civil Service Commissioners had been uninformative.

By the end of the Second War this secret invasion, in all its forms, had impaired the inner structure of the American Republic to such an extent that some change in its outer form, as known to the world for 150 years, was likely during the confusion-period of any third war. The instinctive struggle of the original population to maintain itself and its traditions against a usurpation, the nature of which it was not allowed to comprehend, was failing. This resistance would gain strength, and mend some of the breaches, as the Second War receded, but grave weaknesses remained which were bound to show themselves under the strain of the new war, with the thought of which the American mass-mind was daily made familiar by the politicians and the controlled press.

From 1943 onward the weakness of the American Republic lay more in its own impaired foundations than in any foreign air forces or fleets.

Douglas Reed

Chapter 41

THE REVOLUTION "EXTENDS"

The Second World War, much more clearly than the First, followed the course charted by the Protocols of 1905. The embroiled masses wreaked destruction and vengeance on each other, not for their own salvation, but for the furtherance of a plan of general enslavement under a despotic "world government." The aims initially proclaimed ("liberation," "freedom" and the destruction of "militarism," "Nazism," "Fascism," "totalitarian dictatorship" and the like) were not achieved; on the contrary, the area where these conditions prevailed was greatly enlarged.

Lenin, in his *Collected Works,* wrote: "The World War" (1914-1918) "will see the establishment of Communism in Russia; *a second world war will extend its control over Europe;* and a third world war will be necessary to make it worldwide." The central phrase of this forecast was almost literally fulfilled by the outcome of the Second War. The revolution extended its frontiers to the middle of Europe and thus was put in a position to extend its *military* control over all Europe, at least at the outset of any third war. In 1956 the American General Gruenther, who then bore the rank, apparently made permanent by some untraceable act of the "premier-dictators" in wartime; of "Supreme Allied Commander," told a West German newspaper, "If it should come to a battle on the ground at all, then we are, of course, not strong enough to hold the present front in Europe."

By 1956 the Western people, for ten years, had been made accustomed by almost daily intimations from their leaders to the thought that war with "Russia" was inevitable. This was the consequence of the outcome of the Second War; this outcome, again, was the result of the diversion of acts of state policy and of military operations to the purposes of destroying nation-states and of general enslavement; and this diversion, in turn, was the consequence of the process described in the previous chapter as "the invasion of America." The strength and wealth of America were decisive in the Second War and they were used to bring about a denouement which made a third war a permanent peril.

Thus the story of America's embroilment in the Second War demonstrated the power of the "foreign group" which had come to dictate in Washington, and gave living reality to the farewell address of George Washington himself: "Against the insidious wiles of foreign influence, I conjure you to believe me, fellow-citizens, the jealousy of a free people ought to be constantly awake, since history and experience prove that foreign influence is one of the most baneful foes of republican government." Washington spoke in 1796, when the Reign of Terror had shown the true nature of the revolution in France and when the presence of the conspiracy's agents in America was first realized.

The published records of the Second War show that the conspiracy had obtained power to dictate major acts of American state policy, the course of military operations and the movement of arms, munitions, supplies and treasure. Its conscious agents were numerous and highly-placed. Among the leading men who supported or submitted to them many may have been unaware of the consequences to which their actions were bound to lead.

This chapter in the republic's story occupied three and a half years, from Pearl Harbour to Yalta. A significant resemblance occurs between the manner of America's entry into war in 1898 and 1941. In both cases the provocation necessary to inflame the masses was supplied, and difficult problems of convincing Congress or "public opinion" were thus eluded. In 1898 the *Maine* was "sunk by a Spanish mine" in Havana harbour, and war followed on the instant; many years later, when the *Maine* was raised, her plates were found to have been blown *out* by an *inner* explosion. In 1941 the Japanese attack on Pearl Harbour "on a day that will live in infamy" enabled President Roosevelt to tell his country that through a completely unexpected attack it was "at war." The later disclosures showed that the government in Washington had long been warned of the impending attack and had not alerted the Pearl Harbour defenders. In both cases the public masses remained apathetic when these revelations ensued. (They are of continuing relevance in 1956, when another American president has publicly sworn that he will "never be guilty" of sending his country to war "without Congressional authority," but has added that American troops might have to undertake "*local warlike acts* in self-defence" without such parliamentary approval).

In the First War President Wilson, re-elected on the promise to keep his country out of war, immediately after his re-inauguration declared that "a state of war *exists*." In the Second War President Roosevelt was re-elected in 1940 on the repeated promise that "your boys are not going to be sent into any foreign wars." His electoral programme, however, included a five-word proviso: "We will not send our armies, navies or air forces to fight in foreign lands outside the Americas *except in case of attack*." These five words were added (says one of Mr. Bernard Baruch's approved biographers, Mr. Rosenbloom) "by Senator James F. Byrnes, who was so close to Baruch that it was sometimes impossible to tell which of the two originated the view that both expressed."

The importance of the proviso was shown on *December 7, 1941*, when the Japanese attacked Pearl Harbour. Twelve days earlier Mr. Henry L. Stimson, the Secretary for War, after a cabinet meeting on *November 25, 1941*, had noted in his diary: "The question was how we should *manoeuvre them*" (the

Japanese) *"into the position of firing the first shot"* without allowing too much danger to ourselves; it was a difficult proposition."

The pre-history of this notation, again, is that on *January 27, 1941* the United States Ambassador in Tokyo had advised his government that "in the event of trouble breaking out between the United States and Japan, the Japanese intended to make a surprise attack against Pearl Harbour"; that the Soviet spy in Tokyo, Dr. Richard Sorge, informed the Soviet Government in *October* 1941 that "the Japs intended to attack Pearl Harbour within sixty days" and was advised by the Soviet Government that his information had been transmitted to President Roosevelt (according to Sorge's confession, *New York Daily News*, May 17, 1951); that the Roosevelt government delivered a virtual ultimatum to Japan on *November 26, 1941*; that secret Japanese messages, from *September 1941* up to the very moment of the attack, which were intercepted and decoded by United States intelligence units, gave unmistakable evidence of a coming attack on Pearl Harbour but were not transmitted to the American commanders there; that on *December 1* the Head of Naval Intelligence, Far Eastern Section, drafted a despatch to the Commander-in-Chief of the Pacific Fleet saying "war between Japan and the United States is imminent," which was cancelled by superior authority; that on *December 5* Colonel Sadtler of the U.S. Signal Corps, on information received, drafted a despatch to commanders, "War with Japan imminent; eliminate all possibility of another Port Arthur" (an allusion to the similar "surprise attack" that began the Russo-Japanese war), which was similarly suppressed; that a Japanese reply, obviously tantamount to a declaration of war, to the Roosevelt ultimatum was received in Washington on *December 6, 1941* but no word was sent to the Pearl Harbour defenders. A message stating that "the Japanese are presenting at one p.m., eastern time today what amounts to an ultimatum ... be on the alert" was at last despatched about noon on *December 7, 1941*, and reached the commanders at Pearl Harbour between six and eight hours *after* the Japanese attack.

The record now available suggests that the Americans on Hawaii *alone* were left without knowledge of the imminent onslaught which cost two battleships and two destroyers (apart from many vessels put out of action), 177 aircraft and 4575 dead, wounded or missing.

A direct and immediate consequence was also the disaster suffered by the British navy off Malaya, when the battleships *Prince of Wales* and *Renown* were sunk with great loss of life.

Political leaders who are ready to obtain their country's entry into war by facilitating an enemy attack on it cannot be depended on to wage it in the national interest. The American people as a whole still is unaware of the truth of Pearl Harbour, an ominous beginning which led in unbroken line to the ominous end.

Eight investigations were held, seven naval or military ones during wartime and one Congressional one at the war's end. Thus wartime secrecy enshrouded them all and none of them was truly public or exhaustive; moreover, all were conducted under the aegis of the political party whose man was president at the time of Pearl Harbour. The vital facts (that the president knew at the latest eight weeks earlier, from an intercepted Japanese despatch, that "a surprise attack was being planned and that these intercepted messages were withheld from the Pearl Harbour commanders over a long period) were burned throughout. The Secretary of War's diary (with the significant entry above quoted) was not admitted in evidence and Mr. Stimson himself was not called, being in ill health. Control of the press enabled the long proceedings (six months) to be presented to the public in bewildering and confusing form.

However, the three naval commanders chiefly concerned have published their accounts. Rear Admiral Kimmel, Commander-in-Chief of the Pacific Fleet at the time, says of another admiral's belief that "President Roosevelt's plans *required* that no word be sent to alert the fleet in Hawaii," that "the individuals in high position in Washington who *wilfully* refrained from alerting our forces at Pearl Harbour should never be excused. The Commanders at Pearl Harbour were never informed of ... the American note delivered to the Japanese Ambassadors on November 26, 1941, which effectually ended the possibility of further negotiations and thus made the Pacific war inevitable ... No hint of vital intercepts received, decoded and delivered to responsible officials in Washington on December 6 and 7, 1941, was sent to the Navy and Army Commanders in the Hawaiian area."

Fleet Admiral Halsey, who at that time was one of Admiral Kimmel's three senior commanders, says, "All our intelligence pointed to an attack by Japan against the Philippines or the southern areas in Malaya or the Dutch East Indies. While Pearl Harbour was considered and not ruled out, the mass of the evidence *made available to us* pointed in another direction. *Had we known* of Japan's minute and continued interest in the exact location and movement of our ships in Pearl Harbour" (indicated by the withheld message) "it is only logical that we would have concentrated our thought on meeting the practical certainty of an attack on Pearl Harbour."

Rear Admiral Theobald, commanding destroyers of the Battle Force at Pearl Harbour, writing in 1954 says, "Dictates of patriotism requiring secrecy regarding a line of national conduct *in order to preserve it for possible future repetition* do not apply in this case because, in this atomic age, *facilitating an enemy's surprise attack, as a method of initiating a war,* is unthinkable." (The admiral presumably means that he *hopes* a repetition is "unthinkable"). He adds. "The recurrent fact of the true Pearl Harbour story has been the repeated withholding of information from Admiral Kimmel and General Short" (the naval and military commanders at Pearl Harbour, who were made scapegoats)

"... never before in recorded history had a field commander been denied information that his country would be at war in a matter of hours, and that everything pointed to a surprise attack upon his forces shortly after sunrise." Admiral Theobald quotes the later statement of Admiral Stark (who in December 1941 was Chief of Naval Operations in Washington and who refused to inform Admiral Kimmel of the Japanese declaration of war message) that all he did was done on the order of higher authority, "which can only mean President Roosevelt. The most arresting thing he did, during that time, was to withhold information from Admiral Kimmel."

Fleet Admiral Halsey, writing in 1953, described Admiral Kimmel and General Short as "our outstanding military martyrs." They were retired to conceal from the public, amid the confusion and secrecy of war, the true source of responsibility for the disaster at Pearl Harbour, but they were rather "the first" than the "outstanding" military martyrs, in the sense used by Admiral Halsey. They originated a line, now long, of American naval and military commanders who experienced something new in the history of their calling and country. They found that they courted dismissal or relegation if they strove for military victory by the best military means or objected to some strategy dictated from above which was obviously prejudicial to military victory. Their operations had to conform to some higher plan, the nature of which they could not plainly perceive, but which was patently not that of military victory in the national interest, taught to them from their earliest days as the sole ultimate reason for a soldier's being.

What, then, was this superior plan, to which all American military effort from Pearl Harbour to Yalta and after was made to conform? It was in fact Lenin's "extension" of the revolution. The story of the three-and-a-half years only becomes explicable in that light.

In the First World War, American entry coincided with the revolution in Russia, and Mr. House at once instructed the president "to proffer our financial, industrial and moral support in every way possible" to the new "democracy." In the Second War Hitler's attack on his Moscovite accomplice followed quickly on Mr. Roosevelt's second re-inauguration and before Pearl Harbour America was in the war as far as support of the "new democracy" was concerned, for "financial, industrial and moral support," by way of "Lend- Lease," was being prepared for the Revolutionary state in a measure never before imagined possible.[27]

<hr>

[27] The three forms of such support enumerated by Mr. House include "financial" support. The most difficult of all questions to answer is, how much *financial* support then was given. Innumerable books allude to large financial support by "Wall Street banking houses" and the like, but I have quoted none of these here because I could not verify, and therefore do not quote these; such transactions, in any case, are almost impossible to uncover, being conducted in the greatest secrecy. However, a significant allusion appears in a letter from Lenin himself to Angelica Balabanoff (his representative in Stockholm at the period when Communism was "establishing" itself in Moscow): "Spend millions, tens of millions, if necessary. There is plenty of money at our disposal." No doubt remains about the *German* financial support given to the

By June of 1942 President Roosevelt's intimate, a Mr. Harry Hopkins, publicly told the Communist state (at a mass meeting in Madison Square Garden), "*We are determined that nothing shall stop us from sharing with you all that we have and are.*" These words reflected a presidential order earlier issued (March 7, 1942) to American war agencies (and much later made public) that preference in the supply of munitions should be given to the Soviet Union over *all other Allies and over the armed forces of the United States*. The Chief of the American Military Mission in Moscow, Major General John R. Deane, in a book of 1947 described his vain efforts to stem this tide and said this order of President Roosevelt was "the beginning of a policy of appeasement of Russia from which we have never recovered and from which we are still suffering."

The word "appeasement" was incorrectly used by General Deane, for the policy went far beyond simple "appeasement," and was obviously aimed at *increasing* the military and industrial strength of the revolutionary state *after* the war.

It is explicit in the above passages that Mr. Roosevelt intended to give the revolutionary state greater support than any other ally, free or captive, and implicit that he was resolved to support Poland's aggressor and was indifferent about the "liberation" of other countries overrun. The high causes held out to the Western masses, until they were fully involved in the war, had in fact been abandoned, and the supra-national project of extending the revolution, destroying nation-states and advancing the world-government ambition had been put in their place. (I began to write in this sense in 1942 and my elimination from daily journalism then began; up to that time I was one of the highly-paid "names" in the newspapers).

In 1941 this policy of supporting the revolutionary state was clearly bound to produce much greater effects than in 1917. In 1917 American support could only effect "the *establishment*" of Communism in Russia.

Bolshevik conspirators. The German Foreign Office documents captured by the Allies in 1945 include a telegram sent by the German Foreign Minister, Richard von Kuehlmann, to the Kaiser on Dec. 3, 1916 which says, "It was not until the Bolsheviks had received from us a steady flow of funds through various channels and under varying labels that they were in a position to be able to build up their main organ, the *Pravda*, to conduct energetic propaganda and appreciably to extend the originally narrow basis of their party." The Foreign Minister, anticipating the illusions of Western politicians in the next generation, added "It is entirely in our interest that we should exploit the period while they are in power, which may be a short one ..." (someone added a note in the margin, "There is no question of supporting the Bolsheviks in the future," a dictum which did not reckon with Hitler). The German papers include a report made in August 1915 by the German Ambassador in Copenhagen, Count Brockdorff-Rantzau, on the activities of "an expert on Russia," one Dr. Helphand, who was helping to organize the Bolshevik conspiracy. This says, "Dr. Parvus" (Helphand's pseudonym) "has provided the organization with a sum to cover running expenses ... not even the gentlemen working in the organization realize that our Government is behind it." Helphand then estimated the cost of organizing the revolution "completely" at "about twenty million roubles." Brockdorff-Rantzau received authority from Berlin to make an advance payment and Helphand's receipt is in the documents: "Received from the German Embassy in Copenhagen on the 29th of December 1915 the sum of one million roubles in Russian bank notes for the promotion of the revolutionary movement in Russia; signed, Dr. A. Helphand" (Royal Institute of International Affairs journal, London, April 1956).

In 1941 the situation was entirely different. Communism was long since *"established."* Support, if given in the boundless measure promised by Mr. Hopkins, was bound to enable it to *"extend,"* in accordance with Lenin's dictum. The support given was so prodigious that it enabled Communism to "extend" over a vast area and to prepare for another war as well; the prospect of this third war, arising immediately the second one ended, was then depicted to the Western masses as the consequences of Soviet perfidy.

The values transferred to the revolutionary state from America are almost beyond human comprehension. Elected in 1932 to abolish "deficits," President Roosevelt in twelve years spent more than all former American presidents together, and in sovereign irresponsibility. Public expenditure in America today, eleven years after his death, is still beyond the understanding of an academy of accountants; it is a balloon world of noughts with a few numerals scattered among them. In this zero-studded firmament the amount "lent-leased" to the revolutionary state by President Roosevelt might seem insignificant: 9,500,000,000 dollars. In fact arms and *goods* to that value were shipped, in theory on a sale-or-return basis; it was a vast transfer of treasure, and a few decades earlier would have enabled several new states to set up housekeeping without fear of the future.

This stream of wealth was directed by one man, described by his official biographer (Mr. Robert E. Sherwood) as "the second most important man in the United States." Mr. Harry Hopkins thus played the potentate's part, in the distribution of war materials, first filled by Mr. Bernard Baruch in 1917. The original idea was Mr. Baruch's, who in 1916 insistently demanded that "one man" be appointed as the "administrator" of the all-powerful War Industries Board which, when America entered that war, grew out of an earlier "Advisory Commission" attached to the president's Cabinet "Defence Council."

This pre-history of Mr. Hopkins's appointment is significant, because it shows the continuing power and method of the group around the American presidents of both world wars. A Congressional Investigating Committee of 1919, headed by Mr. William J. Graham, said of the "Advisory Commission" which produced the 1918 War Industries Board, that it "served as *the secret government of the United States* ... A commission of seven men chosen by the president seems to have devised the entire system of purchasing war supplies, planned a press censorship, designed a system of food control ... and in a word designed practically every war measure which the Congress subsequently enacted, *and did all this behind closed doors* weeks and even months before the Congress of the United States declared war against Germany ... There was not an act of the so-called war legislation afterwards enacted that had not before the actual declaration of war been discussed and settled upon by this Advisory Commission."

Mr. Baruch himself, testifying before a Select Committee of Congress on the wartime activities of the "one-man" authority which he himself had caused to be set up, said, "The final determination rested with me ... whether the Army or Navy would have it ... the railroad administration ... or the Allies, or whether General Allenby should have locomotives, or whether they should be used in Russia or in France ... I probably had more power than perhaps any other man did ..." (This was the First War background to Mr. Churchill's words to Mr. Baruch in 1939, "War is coming ... you will be running the show over there." The extent of Mr. Baruch's power in the First War is further illustrated by an incident in 1919, when President Wilson was brought back to America a completely incapacitated man. Mr. Baruch then "became one of the group that made decisions during the President's illness" (Mr. Rosenbloom). This group came to be known as "the Regency Council," and when the ailing president's senior Cabinet officer, Mr. Robert Lansing, Secretary of State, called Cabinet meetings on his own authority the president, from his sickbed, dismissed him; though he broke also with other associates, including Mr. House, "Wilson clung to his trust in Baruch").

In the Second War President Roosevelt revived President Wilson's power to establish a "Defence Council" with an "Advisory Commission" (1940), and in 1942 this was enlarged into a "War Production Board," the counterpart of the 1918 "War Industries Board." Mr. Baruch again advised that "one man" be put in charge of this all-powerful body, but in the event he was not the one man appointed. His biographer says that he was disappointed, but the reader may keep an open mind about that.

The rare references to Mr. Baruch in this narrative do not denote the extent of his influence. The best observers known to me all believed that he was the most powerful of the men around American presidents over a period of more than forty years, up to now. His biographer states that he continued to act as adviser to every American president (including the three Republican ones of 1920, 1924 and 1928) from President Wilson on, and, writing in 1952, predicted that he would also "advise" President Eisenhower and even gave an outline of what this advice would be. Mr. Baruch's true place in this story, or the present writer's estimate of it, will be shown at a later stage, when he made his most significant *open* appearance.

Even though Mr. Baruch, with evident accuracy, described himself as the most powerful man in the world in 1917-1918, his power actually to shape the events and map of the world was much less than that of any man who occupied the same place in the Second War, for the obvious reason that "the determination of what anybody could have" now extended to the revolutionary state *established as a great military power with obvious and vast territorial* aims. Even the War Production Board became of secondary importance when the "Lend-Lease Administration" was set up, and Mr. Harry Hopkins was appointed "Administrator" and also chairman of President Roosevelt's

"Soviet Protocol Committee" with power *"to determine supply quotas to be dispatched to Russia."* From that moment the fate and future of the West were in the hands of a man known to a wide circle as "Harry the Hop."

Mr. Hopkins could only have occupied so elevated a place in the Twentieth Century; public opinion, if informed by a free and impartial press, would hardly have suffered him, for he had no qualification to handle great affairs, least of all foreign ones. Even his biographer, though well-disposed to a fellow-inmate of the White House (in which respectable precincts Mr. Hopkins, according to his own diary, once acted as pander to a visiting Communist notable, a Mr. Molotov), wonders how this man, "so obscure in origin and so untrained for great responsibility," could have become "Special Adviser to the President."

As to that, today's student cannot discover who "chose" Mr. Hopkins for his role. However, he finds that Mr. Hopkins in his youth had absorbed the same kind of ideas (those of "Louis Blanc and the revolutionaries of 1848") which Mr. House acquired in *his* Texan boyhood. Mr. Hopkins had studied at the feet of a Fabian Socialist from London (who held that nation-states should disappear in a "United States of the World") and from a Jewish teacher of Bohemian and Russian origins who had been a pupil of Tolstoy, the Bolshevists' hero. The transmission of "ideas," again. Presumably these were the qualifications which cause Mr. Sherwood to call him "the *inevitable* Roosevelt favourite." Earlier he had been known as a "fixer" and fund-raiser and "little brother of the rich." The University of Oxford conferred on him one of the most ill-fitting doctorates in its history and Mr. Churchill's fulsome references to him, in the war memoirs, are strange to read.

When Mr. Hopkins took his place as chairman of President Roosevelt's Soviet Protocol Committee he found among its members some who greatly mistrusted the policy of unconditional supply to the revolutionary state. He issued to them the following imperial fiat: "The United States is doing things *which it would not do for other United Nations* without full information from them. This decision to act without full information was made ... after due deliberation ... There was *no reservation* about the policy at the present time but the policy was constantly being brought up by various persons for rediscussion. He proposed that *no further consideration be given to these requests for rediscussion*" (1942).

Thus the revolutionary state, through Mr. Hopkins, was shown to be "the inevitable Roosevelt favourite." In this passage the mystery recurs to which I drew attention in the case of British Ministers and Zionism: the "policy" has been "settled" and *cannot* be altered. By whom this policy had been "deliberated," and who had decreed that it must not be re-examined in any circumstances whatever, were Mr. Hopkins's secrets, and all this was again "behind closed doors" as far as the embroiled masses were concerned. In vain the Republican leader, Senator Robert E. Taft, protested when he saw what was going on: "How can anyone swallow the idea that Russia is battling for democratic principles … To spread the four freedoms throughout the world we will ship aeroplanes and tanks to Communist Russia. But no country was more responsible for the present war and Germany's aggression." A violent campaign was immediately begun in the press which continued until Senator Taft's death. Today's map and state of affairs vindicate his warning, and those who today read Mr. Hopkins's fiat, quoted above, may see that the outcome of the war was determined by these secret actions of 1942 and earlier.

Of "aeroplanes and tanks" 15,000 and 7,000, respectively, were *donated*. A navy of 581 vessels was also given (over many years 127 of these were returned and in 1956 the Soviet offered to pay for 31; the remaining ships, over 300, were declared to have been lost, sunk or declared unseaworthy). A merchant fleet was also presented.

This was only the smaller part of the total transfer of wealth in many forms. The American Government has never published the details of its deliveries. The fact that these are known, and that the greater part of them consisted of supplies obviously designed to strengthen the industrial and war-making capacity of the revolutionary state *after the war's end*, is due to one of the accidents which assist the historian, although, in the condition of the press today, they never reach the general public mind and therefore produce no remedial result.

In May 1942 a Captain George Racey Jordan reported for duty at the great Newark Airport in New Jersey. He was a First War soldier rejoined and had never forgotten the advice of a sergeant given to him in Texas in 1917: "Keep your eyes and ears open, keep your big mouth shut, and *keep a copy of everything*." To the last five words posterity owes the most astonishing book (in my opinion) of the Second World War.

Captain Jordan was instructed to report to "United Nations Depot No. 8," as he found Newark Airport to be described on his orders. The body known as the "United Nations" was set up three years later, and this was an anticipation, revealing the intention of the men around the president. Captain Jordan, when he reported for duty as Liaison Officer, had no suspicion of the power of the Soviet in America and was soon enlightened in three ways. In May 1942, after an American Airlines passenger aircraft on the apron brushed the engine housing of a Lend-Lease medium bomber waiting to be flown to the Soviet Government, a Soviet officer angrily demanded the banishment of American Airlines from this great American airport. When this was refused the Soviet officer said he would "call Mr. Hopkins," and in a few days an order from the United States Civil Aeronautic Board banished *all* American civil airlines from the field.

Captain Jordan then began to keep a very full diary, and by means of it was later able to show (when he and the rest of the world learned about "atomic bombs") that during 1942 about fifteen million dollars' worth of graphite, aluminium tubes, cadmium metal and thorium (all materials necessary for the creation of an atomic pile) were sent to the Soviet Government from Newark. At this time the "Manhattan Project" (the production of the first atom bomb) was supposed to be of such intense secrecy that its chief, Major General Leslie R. Groves, later testified that his office would have refused, without his personal approval, to supply any document even to President Roosevelt. In 1942, when he made these entries in his diary, Captain Jordan had no idea of the use to which these materials might be put, for he had never heard of the "Manhattan Project" or of "the atom bomb."

His next experience of the authority wielded by the Soviet officers came when one of them took affront on seeing a red star on an aeroplane belonging to the Texaco Oil Company and threatened to "phone Washington" and have it removed. Captain Jordan had difficulty in explaining that the Texas Oil Company had been using the emblem of its home state (the "Lone Star State") for many years before the 1917 revolution!

At this time Captain Jordan began to realize that the mass of material that was going to the Communist state was not in the least covered by the terms of the master Lend-Lease agreement ("The Government of the United States will continue to supply the U.S.S.R. with such *defence* articles, *defence* services and *defence* information as the President ... shall authorize to be transferred or provided") but included many things that had nothing to do with "defence" and everything to do with the post-war strengthening of the Soviet. He noted, for instance, the supply of "tractors and farm machinery, aluminium manufacturing plant, railway car shops, steel mill equipment" and the like more. These shipments (which, an enthusiastic interpreter told him, "will help to Fordize our country") are indicated in the round totals which are the only information on the subject provided by the American Government. President Truman's "Twenty First Report to Congress on Lend-Lease Operations" shows under the head of "Non-munitions" the enormous figures of $1,674,586,000 for *agricultural products* and $3,040,423,000 for *industrial materials and products*.

In 1943, when heavy losses to the ocean convoys caused a much greater proportion of Lend-Lease materials to be sent by air, an American air terminus for the movement of these supplies was set up at Great Falls, Montana, and Captain Jordan was transferred there as "Lend-Lease Expediter." Once more his orders from the United States Army Air Force designated him "United Nations Representative," though no such body existed, and he found awaiting him a *Presidential* directive, headed "Movement of Russian Airplanes," which said that " ... *the modification, equipment and movement of Russian planes have been given first priority, even over planes for U.S. Army Air Forces.*" He also had his third experience of Soviet power: the Soviet officer with whom he dealt held that his rank of captain was too low and asked for his promotion to major; when the gold oak leaves duly arrived they were pinned on Major Jordan's shoulders by Colonel Kotikov, an event probably unprecedented in American military history.

Major Jordan then noticed that an extravagant number of black suitcases, roped and sealed, was passing through his "pipeline to Moscow." His misgivings were by this time heavy and he used a favourable opportunity (and the sole power remaining to him, that of giving or withholding clearance for American-piloted Lend-Lease aircraft on the last stretch to Fairbanks in Alaska) to thrust past armed Soviet secret policemen into an aeroplane and open about eighteen suitcases out of fifty. He made a rough note of the contents of the opened ones.

Among the mass of papers, plans, correspondence and blueprints were two discoveries which, years later, proved to fit neatly into the picture of espionage and conspiracy which was revealed by the various exposures of 1948-1956. One was a bundle of State Department folders, each with a tab. One of these read, "From Hiss," and another, "From Sayre." Major Jordan had never heard either name, but they were the names of the chief State Department official later convicted (Alger Hiss) and of another State Department official involved in the same affair. These folders contained copies of secret despatches from American attaches in Moscow, forwarded by diplomatic pouch to Washington, and now returning in duplicate to those from whom they were to be held secret.

The more important discovery was one which affects all men living in the West as much today as if it were now detected. It was a letter addressed to the Soviet Commissar of Foreign Trade, Mikoyan. Major Jordan noted down an excerpt from it: " ... had a hell of a time getting these away from Groves" (the chief of the atomic-bomb project). The letter was signed "H. H." Attached to it were a map of the Oak Ridge atomic plant in Tennessee and a carbon copy of a report, rubber-stamped "Harry Hopkins," containing a number of names so strange to Major Jordan that he also made a note of them, intending to look up their meaning. Among them were "cyclotron," "proton" and "deuteron," and phrases like "energy produced by fission" and "walls five feet thick, of lead and water, to control flying neutrons." Mr. Hopkins, as already shown, was "the inevitable Roosevelt favourite," "the Special Adviser to the President," "the second most important man in the United States."

(For some years after the Second War the public masses in America and England were told by their leaders that their best protection against a new war, and the most effective deterrent to "Soviet aggression," was Western possession of the atom bomb. On September 23, 1949 the Soviet Union exploded an atom bomb, to the surprise of none who carefully followed affairs. Major Jordan then could contain himself no longer and approached a

Senator, who was stirred enough to induce a leading broadcaster, Mr. Fulton Lewis, to make the story known. In that form, and in his later book, it thus became public, and it was the subject of two Congressional hearings, in December 1949 and March 1950. The press unitedly misrepresented the gravamen of the matter and, as in all these cases, no true remedial effect was produced; nothing effective has been done to prevent the recurrence of a similar state of affairs in another war).

In 1944 Major Jordan, more worried than ever, attempted to see the Lend-Lease liaison officer at the State Department but was intercepted by a junior official who told him "Officers who are too officious are likely to find themselves on an island somewhere in the South Seas." Not long after he was removed from White Falls. His book contains the complete list of Lend-Lease shipments which, as liaison officer, he was able to see and copy. This shows all the chemicals, metals and minerals suitable for use in an atomic pile which were transferred, and some of them may also be suitable for use in the hydrogen bomb; they include beryllium, cadmium, cobalt ore and concentrate (33,600 lbs), cobalt metal and cobalt-bearing scrap (806,941 lbs), uranium metal (2.2 lbs), aluminium tubes (12,766,472 lbs), graphite (7,384,482 lbs), thorium, uranium nitrate, oxide and urano-uranic oxide, aluminium and alloys (366,738,204 lbs), aluminium rods (13,744,709 lbs), aluminium plates (124,052,618 lbs), brass and bronze ingots and bars (76,545,000 lbs), brass or bronze wire (16,139,702 lbs), brass and bronze plates (536,632,390 lbs), insulated copper wire (399,556,720 lbs), and so on.

These lists also include the "purely postwar Russian supplies" (General Groves), such as an oil-refinery plant, forging machinery and parts ($53,856,071), lathes, precision boring-machines, canning machinery, commercial dairy equipment, sawmill machinery, textile machinery, power machines ($60,313,833), foundry equipment, electric station equipment, telephone instruments and equipment ($32,000,000), generators ($222,020,760), motion picture equipment, radio sets and equipment ($52,072,805), 9,594 railway freight cars, 1,168 steam locomotives ($101,075,116), merchant vessels ($123,803,879), motor trucks ($508,367,622), and endlessly on.

Among the major donations obviously intended to strengthen the Soviet Union industrially *after* the war, Major Jordan's records include one repair plant for precision instruments ($550,000), two factories for food products ($6,924,000), three gas generating units ($21,390,000), one petroleum refinery with machinery and equipment ($29,050,000), 17 stationary steam and three hydro-electric plants ($273,289,000). The Soviet lists reproduced by Major Jordan suggest that a spirit approaching hysteria in giving moved Mr. Hopkins and his associates, for they include items for which no rational explanation can be found, for instance: eyeglasses ($169,806), teeth ($956), 9,126 watches with jewels ($143,922), 6,222 lbs of toilet soap $400 worth of lipsticks, 373 gallons of liquor, $57,444 worth of fishing tackle, $161,046 worth of magic lanterns, $4,352 worth of "fun fair" devices, 13,256 lbs of carbon paper, two "new pianos," $60,000 worth of musical instruments and (an item which conjures up visions of the "Beloved Leader," Mr. Roosevelt's and Mr. Churchill's "Uncle Joe"), "one pipe," valued at ten dollars!

Mr. Hopkins's past as a professional fund-raiser and welfare-worker seems to show in the donation of $88,701,103, over four years, for "relief or charity"; those who have visited Soviet Russia may try to imagine this money being doled out by the Commissars to the poor! This was not the end of cash-giving under "Lend-Lease." In 1944 Mr. Henry Morgenthau junior, Mr. Roosevelt's Secretary of the Treasury, and his Assistant Secretary, Mr. Harry Dexter White (later shown to have been a Soviet agent) ordered the shipment to the Soviet Government of duplicates of the United States Treasury plates to be used for printing money for the use of the forces occupying Germany *after* the war. This meant that the money printed by the Soviet Government for the use of its troops was redeemable by the American Government as there was no distinction whatever between the paper printed. By the end of 1946, when public protests caused the American Government to stop paying its own troops with these notes, so that the Soviet Government could make no further use of them, the United States Military Government in Germany found that it had redeemed about $250,000,000 *in excess of the total of notes issued by its own Finance Office*. (The Soviet Government ignored a request to pay the modest sum of some $18,000 for the plates and materials delivered to it, which had enabled it to draw $250,000,000 straight from the United States Treasury).

Thus for four or five years there was an unlimited transfer of the wherewithal of war, of supplies for post-war industrial use, and of wealth in manifold forms to the revolutionary state, and "re-discussion" of this policy lay under ban at the highest level. Moreover, "preference" and "priority" for this policy, in relation to American needs or those of other allies, was explicitly ordered at that level.

There were two other ways in which the revolutionary state could be "supported" and helped to "extend": (1) the conduct of military operations; (2) the direction of State policy at high-level conferences issuing from these military operations. As the policy of delivering arms and wealth was so firmly, even fanatically pursued in favour of the revolutionary state, it was logical to expect that the *same* policy would be pursued through military operations and the conferences resulting from them. In fact, this happened, as good observers foresaw at the time and as the receding picture of the war now plainly shows. It also was the inevitable result of the capture of a great measure of power behind the scenes, in the American Republic, by means of the invasion described in the last chapter.

The effort to turn all military operations to the advantage of the revolutionary state, which in complicity with Hitler had started the war by the joint attack on Poland, began soon after Pearl Harbour. It failed then but was entirely successful in the last stages of the war, as the outcome showed. The leading part in this process was taken by the most enigmatic figure of the Second War, General George C. Marshall, Chief of Staff of the United States Army. To him Senator Joseph McCarthy, in his oration before the Senate on June 14, 1951 (a carefully-documented indictment which is a major reference-source in this matter) attributed "the *planned* steady retreat from victory which commenced long before World War II ended" and the fact that America, having power to tip the balance, operated between the policies advocated by Mr. Churchill and the Soviet dictator Stalin "almost invariably in support of the Russian line."

In view of the vast consequences which General Marshall's interventions produced the circumstances of his original elevation are of interest. President Roosevelt appointed him Chief of Staff in 1939 over the heads of twenty major generals and fourteen senior brigadiers (six years earlier his nomination to general, being adversely reported on by the Inspector General, had been barred by the then Chief of Staff, General Douglas MacArthur). One of General Marshall's earliest acts was, in 1940, to ask Senator James F. Byrnes (an intimate of Mr. Bernard Baruch) to propose an amendment to an army estimates bill authorizing the Chief of Staff to override seniority rules in favour of younger officers held by him to be "of unusual ability." Senator Byrnes's amendment, then adopted, provided that "in time of war or national emergency ... any officer of the Regular Army may be appointed to higher temporary grade ...," and under this empowerment General Marshall during 1940 made 4,088 promotions, among them that of the fifty-year old Colonel Dwight Eisenhower, who then had no battle or command experience but within three years was to become Supreme Allied Commander. The combination of General Marshall and General Eisenhower was decisive in shaping the outcome of the war in 1945.

Immediately after Pearl Harbour and the American entry into the war in December 1941 the Soviet propagandists in Moscow and in the West began loud clamour for the Western allies to invade Europe forthwith. Mr. Churchill, when he saw President Roosevelt soon after Pearl Harbour, had obtained general agreement that an invasion before 1943, at the earliest, was a military impossibility. By April 1942 General Eisenhower, at General Marshall's instruction, had prepared a plan for an invasion *in 1942*, and Mr. Roosevelt had been persuaded to cable Mr. Churchill in this sense *(The Hinge of Fate)*. General Marshall, with Mr. Hopkins, then went to London and was told by Mr. Churchill that disaster on the French coast due to a hasty and reckless invasion was probably "the only way in which we could possibly lose the war" (Mr. Sherwood).

General Marshall, in view of his appointment, was presumably entitled to be regarded as the best military brain in the United States. What he proposed was in fact that the only great fighting ally, at that time, should commit suicide and that the war should be lost, at all events for England. Mr. Churchill said that if such an attempt were made the Channel would be turned into "a river of Allied blood," but in truth it would have been three-fourths British blood; the American Commander in the British Isles, later asked what forces he could contribute, "pointed out that all we could count on using would be the 34th division then in Ireland." General Clark added that even this one division lacked anti-aircraft support, tanks and training (the first American troops to engage in combat, in North Africa late in 1942, proved to be quite unready for battle). The leading American military critic, Mr. Hanson W. Baldwin, later wrote, "In retrospect it is now obvious that our concept of invading Western Europe in 1942 was fantastic."

In spite of all this General Marshall, on return to Washington, proposed to President Roosevelt that the United States *withdraw from the war in Europe unless the British acceded to his plan,* (Secretary Stimson). General Marshall was sent again to England to see Mr. Churchill (he brusquely refused to stay at Chequers). His plan then collapsed under the weight of General Mark Clark's report from Ireland, that he could put only one untrained and under-equipped division into the venture. But the proposal, and the threat, had been made, and all that followed later in the war must be considered in the light of this action of the highest military officer in the United States.

In the spring of 1942 the Germans still had 1,300,000 troops in France and the Low Countries, and the Western allies had no comparable force to throw against them, even if they had possessed air superiority, landing craft, amphibious vehicles, and invasion- training. Mr. Roosevelt had to withdraw from General Marshall's menacing plan, and England, for the third time in that war, survived a mortal danger. The war went on through 1942 and 1943, while British, and later American armies crushed the Germans in North Africa, and then the decisive turn in the war came. The Western Allies were ready to strike; how and where were they to strike? At that juncture General Marshall's second great intervention determined the outcome of the war.

Mr. Churchill's own account, and the narratives of all other authorities, agree that he was from first to last consistent, at all events in this major issue. He was the only man among the Western leaders with great military and political experience, and he clearly saw that the war would bring neither true victory nor peace if the revolutionary state, the aggressor at the war's start, were enabled to spread deep into Europe. He desired that military operations should be so conducted that it should not extend beyond, or far beyond its natural frontiers.

In this controversy his great antagonist proved to be General Marshall more than President Roosevelt, whose state of health in the last year of the war may have incapacitated him from clear thought, unless he was simply the helpless captive of the pressures around him. Mr. Churchill desired to strike from the south as well as from the north and to bring the Balkan and Central European countries under Allied occupation before they could pass merely from Hitlerist enslavement into that of the Red armies; this policy would have led to true victory, have given the world a prospect of peace for the rest of the 20th Century and have largely fulfilled the original "aims" of the war, among which "liberation" was the greatest. General Marshall was resolved to concentrate on the invasion of France and to leave the whole of Eastern, Central and Balkan Europe to the armies of the revolutionary state, and Mr. Roosevelt, whether clear- minded or confused, pursued this policy to the bitter end which the world saw at Yalta, where "defeat was snatched from the jaws of victory."

The struggle continued for eighteen months, but the die was cast, as events proved, at the first Quebec Conference of August 1943, when the Anglo-American armies, having completed the conquest of North Africa, had returned to Europe and were driving the German armies out of Italy. At Quebec, under General Marshall's insistence, the decision was taken to withdraw troops from Italy for a secondary invasion of France, auxiliary to the main invasion of Normandy. This meant the disruption of Field Marshal Alexander's Allied force in Italy (which after the capture of Rome had become "a tremendous fighting-machine ... with horizons unlimited"; General Clark), halting the advance there, and, above all, abandoning all idea of a thrust from Italy across the Adriatic which would have carried the Allied armies to Vienna, Budapest and Prague. This would have altered the entire post-war picture to the advantage of the West and of peace; a glance at the map will make the matter plain to any reader. At that moment true "victory" was within reach, and it was thrown away in favour of the invasion of Southern France, a dispersion of military strength even graver in its consequences than that of British armies to Palestine in the First War.

The secondary, southern invasion offered no military advantage to justify this decision which was obviously political; the document on which General Marshall based his arguments in favour of it at the Quebec Conference reveals this. It was called "Russia's Position" and was ascribed to "a very high-level United States military estimate" (Mr. Sherwood), which indicates General Marshall himself. It said, "Russia's post-war position in Europe will be a dominant one ... Since Russia is the decisive factor in the war, she must be given every assistance and every effort must be made to obtain her friendship. Likewise, since without question she will dominate Europe on the defeat of the Axis, it is even more essential to develop and maintain the most friendly relations with Russia."

Here the overriding "policy" laid down in respect of Lend-Lease deliveries reappears in respect of *military operations;* it is that of unconditional surrender to the paramountcy of Soviet aims and interests. Stalin had opposed the thrust through the Balkans and averred that "the only direct way of striking at the heart of Germany was through the heart of France"; the "high level military estimate" produced at Quebec in fact propounded Stalin's plan. The document, as the reader will see, twice states an *assumption* as a fact, namely, that after the war "Russia's position in Europe will be dominant ... without question she will dominate Europe." That was precisely the question which, in 1943, had yet to be decided by nearly two more years of military operations, and Mr. Churchill's policy was designed to prevent the very thing that was stated as an accomplished fact. He wished to see the Soviet victorious, but *not* "dominating" Europe. He was overborne, and at that moment in 1943 the Second World War, by means of political decisions taken in secrecy, was politically lost to the West.

This was General Marshall's most momentous intervention. Mr. Churchill, though he never criticized General Marshall, refers cryptically to him in his war memoirs, and in *Triumph and Tragedy* mourned the lost opportunity. General Mark Clark, in 1943 the American Commander in Italy, in 1950 wrote, "If we switched our strength from Italy to France, it was obvious to Stalin ... that we would turn away from Central Europe. Anvil" (the invasion of Southern France) "led into a dead-end street. It was easy to see why Stalin favoured Anvil ... After the fall of Rome, Kesselring's army could have been destroyed if we had been able to shoot the works in a final offensive. Across the Adriatic was Yugoslavia ... and beyond Yugoslavia were Vienna, Budapest and Prague ... After the fall of Rome we 'ran for the wrong goal,' both from a political and a strategical standpoint ... Save for a high level blunder that turned us away from the Balkan States and permitted them to fall under Red Army control, the Mediterranean campaign might have been the most decisive of all in post-war history ... A campaign that might have changed the whole history of the relationships between the Western World and Soviet Russia was permitted to fade away ... The weakening of the campaign in Italy ... was one of the outstanding political mistakes of the war."

General Mark Clark (a brilliant American soldier who was subsequently relegated to secondary commands and resigned from the Army) says "blunder" and "mistake," but the document above quoted and many other sources now available show that the decision was neither blunder nor mistake in the ordinary sense of those words: that is, an error made in miscalculation of the consequences. The consequences were foreseen and were intended; that is now beyond doubt. The decision was political, not military, and it was made by the men who formed the group around the president. It was, in the field of military operations, the exact parallel of the decision taken in respect of Lend-Lease operations: to subordinate all other considerations to the interest of the revolutionary state.

Thus the war, which could have been ended (probably in 1944) by the Allied liberation of the countries overrun by Hitler, leaving the Soviet state within the natural Russian boundaries or a little more, and Europe in balance, dragged on through 1944 into 1945; while the German armies in Italy were given respite and the wasteful invasion of Southern France lent no impetus to the main invasion of Normandy.

The shape which the war took in its last ten months then was that dictated by the Soviet Government and superimposed on Western military strategy through its agent in the American Government, the man known as Harry Dexter White. Being dead, he cannot testify, but he is commonly held by the best authorities known to me to have been the author of the plan, for the destruction of Germany and the abandonment of Europe to Soviet "domination," which is known to posterity as the "Morgenthau plan."

Under the shadow of this plan (as will be seen) the Western armies gradually broke their way through to the edge of Germany. To the last moment Mr. Churchill who had been defeated by General Marshall in his earlier plea to have the right arm of the Allied armies strike through the Balkans at "the soft underbelly" of the enemy) strove to make good something of what had been lost by a massive, last-minute thrust of the left arm to Berlin and beyond. The story is told both in his and in General Eisenhower's memoirs.

General Eisenhower describes his refusal of Field Marshal Montgomery's proposal, late in 1944, to strike hard with all available forces for Berlin. He considers that the idea was too risky, or reckless; earlier in his book he gently criticizes Montgomery for being too cautious. He continued through the following months with a sprawling general advance which left the Red Armies time to press into Europe, and in March 1945 (when the Yalta Conference was over and the Soviet intention to annex, rather than liberate, Rumania and Poland had already been shown, and President Roosevelt was cabling formal protests to Stalin) General Eisenhower informed the Soviet dictator *by direct cable* of his plan, marking it "Personal to Marshal Stalin." Its communication to Stalin before it had even been endorsed by the Allied Chiefs of Staff brought angry protest from Mr. Churchill, who to the last strove to save what could yet be saved from the fiasco which was being prepared by urging that at least Vienna, Prague and Berlin be taken."

This was all in vain. General Marshall, in Washington, notified London that he fully approved both General Eisenhower's "strategic concept" and his "procedure in communicating with the Russians." Thereafter the Allied advance in the West was, in fact, arranged to receive Soviet approval, and British counsel was disregarded. General Eisenhower had informed Stalin *directly* on March 28 that he would stop *short of Vienna*. On April 14 he informed the Chiefs of Staff that he would stop seventy miles *short of Berlin*, on the Elbe line, adding "If you agree, I propose to inform Marshal Stalin"; as

British objections had already been overridden, the first three words were but a matter of form. There still remained Prague, capital of captive Czechoslovakia. General Eisenhower advised Stalin that he would advance to Prague "if the situation required"; he had substantial forces standing idle on the Czech border. Stalin replied (May 9, 1945) requesting General Eisenhower "to refrain from advancing the Allied forces in Czechoslovakia beyond the … Karlsbad, Pilsen and Budweis line." General Eisenhower at once ordered his General Patton to halt on that line.

Thus "the hideous bisection" of Europe was brought about; to this description of it Mr. Churchill added the platitudinous comment, "it cannot last." "General Eisenhower five years later claimed that he *alone* was responsible for these three fatal decisions: "I must make one thing clear. Your question seems to imply that the decision not to march into Berlin was *a political decision.* On the contrary, there is only one person in the world responsible for that decision. That was I. There was no one to interfere with it in the slightest way." This statement was made in reply to a question at a dinner of the Association of the Bar of the City of New York on March 3, 1949; The questioner said "the general feeling is that if our Army had marched into Berlin and … Prague the picture in the post-war period might have been different … Had our political leaders … refrained from interfering with you in going through your regular military procedure of taking as much as our armies might take … don't you think the postwar picture might have been different?"

General Eisenhower's statement *cannot* have been true, even if he thought it was. The order to hold back the Allied advance until the Red armies had taken possession of Germany and Central Europe, with its three chief capitals, obviously followed the "policy" which, demonstrably, governed Lend-Lease: that of giving preference to the demands of the Soviet state over all other allies, and even over the needs of America itself. For that matter, General Eisenhower's own naval aide and biographer, Captain Harry C. Butcher, specifically states that when General Eisenhower (against Mr. Churchill's protest) opened direct communication with Moscow about the halting-line for the Allied advance, the question of "boundaries and areas to be occupied *had gone beyond the sphere of military headquarters.*" General Eisenhower's actions clearly followed a predetermined political plan agreed at the highest level; by the time he became president its consequences were plain to see and he might have felt "haunted" by President Roosevelt's example (as Mr. Roosevelt was always "haunted" by that of President Wilson).

Mr. Churchill supplied (on May 11, 1953) the conclusive comment on this military outcome of the Second War, which was the second great "disenchantment" for troops who thought themselves victorious: "If our advice had been taken by the United States after the armistice in Germany, the Western Allies would not have withdrawn from the front line which their armies had reached to the agreed occupation lines, *unless and until agreement had been reached with Soviet Russia* on the many points of difference about the occupation of enemy territories, of which the German zone is only, of course, a part. Our view was not accepted and a wide area of Germany was handed over to Soviet occupation *without any general agreement between the three victorious powers.*"

Thus the policy followed in the transfer of arms, wealth and goods and in the conduct of military operations during the Second War served to "extend" the revolution. One other way remained in which this process of extension could be advanced through the war: by the capitulation of Western state policy, at the highest political level, in the pourparlers and conferences of leaders which were held as the military picture unfolded.

The feelings of readers might be needlessly harrowed if the story of all these meetings (Atlantic, Cairo, Casablanca, Teheran, Yalta) were told. The contrast, between the initial declaration of high purposes and the final surrender to all the abominations initially denounced, is shown bleakly enough if the first (the Atlantic meeting) and the last (the Yalta Conference) are briefly described.

The "Atlantic Charter" was preceded by President Roosevelt's third post-election oration, on January 6, 1941, when he told an America not yet at war that he "looked forward to a world founded upon four essential freedoms … freedom of speech, freedom of worship, freedom from want, freedom from fear." Then the Atlantic Charter of August 14, 1941, the joint product of Mr. Roosevelt and Mr. Churchill, reproduced the phraseology with which students of the Protocols of 1905 had long been familiar (one wonders if the "premier-dictators" ever read them). It stated "certain basic principles," said to govern the "respective policies" of America and Britain, on which the two signatories "base their hopes for a better future for the world"; the first of these was "no aggrandisement, territorial or otherwise," and the next, "no territorial changes that do not accord with the freely expressed wishes of the peoples concerned." The third principle was "the right of all peoples to choose the form of government under which they will live; and the wish to see sovereign rights and self-government restored to all those who have been forcibly deprived of them."

The retreat from these lofty purposes followed in the Casablanca and Teheran Conferences of 1943 (at Teheran Stalin was present, and was included in the "Declaration" as being "dedicated … to the elimination of tyranny and slavery, oppression and intolerance"), and culminated at Yalta in February 1945, just three and a half years after the "Atlantic Charter."

At the time of this conference the Anglo-American armies were being held back in Europe so that the Red armies might embed themselves deep in the heart of Europe. The far fall of Western diplomacy (if the word is not too genteel) from its earlier high estate was made brutally clear by the Yalta meeting, and perusal of the records might make today's Westerner long for old days when plenipotentiaries and ambassadors, in formal dress and conscious of their responsibilities, gathered in dignity to arrange the affairs of nations after a war; in comparison with the Congress of Vienna and Berlin, the Yalta conference looks somewhat like a smoking- concert in a pothouse.

The Western leaders, on the refusal of the Soviet dictator to leave his domains, foregathered with him in the Crimea; in dealings with Asiatics, this is from the start a surrender. The American president and his intimate, Mr. Hopkins, were dying men, and in Mr. Roosevelt's case this was apparent from the news-reel pictures which the masses saw; I recall the exclamation of shock that sprang from an audience among which I sat. Some of the leading dignitaries were accompanied by relatives, so that the affair took on the look of a family excursion, a rather pleasant escape from the burdensome trammels of war. But much the worst feature of all was that the visitors were subjected to (and many of them fell victim to) one of the oldest tricks in negotiation known to wily Asiatic mankind: plying with liquor. A high delegate, Major General Laurence S. Kuter, who represented the United States Army Air Force, says:

"The first course *at breakfast* was a medium-sized tumbler containing ...Crimean brandy. Following the opening toasts and the brandy there were repeated servings of caviar and vodka ... Then assorted cold cuts were served ... and with them, a white wine ... Finally, small hard Crimean apples and with them bountiful glasses of a quite sweet Crimean champagne ... The final course of this breakfast consisted of tall thin tumblers of boiling hot tea with which brandy was served in snifters. That was just breakfast! How could any man with his stomach full of the above described stuffings make one rational or logical decision in relationship to the welfare of the United States of America ... Elliott Roosevelt, who went with his father to the conference, said that practically everyone was drunk." As to dinner in the evening, Mr. Charles E. Bohlen, who was present as Assistant Secretary of State and interpreter to President Roosevelt, says of one such meal that "Marshal Stalin acted as host. The atmosphere of the dinner was *most cordial*, and forty-five toasts in all were drunk."

On top of all this, the dying President Roosevelt arrived at Yalta as the signatory of the "Morgenthau Plan," drafted by a Soviet agent in his own Treasury Department (Mr. Harry Dexter White); and was accompanied by another Soviet agent, later exposed and convicted, Mr. Alger Hiss of his State Department, who at this vital moment was the president's special adviser about "political affairs." In effect, therefore, the Soviet government was represented on two sides of the three-sided table, and the outcome of the conference was the logical result. Up to the very eve of the meeting Mr. Churchill continued his effort to save something of Central Europe and the Balkans from the fate to which they were abandoned at Yalta. When he met

President Roosevelt at Malta, on the way to Yalta, he once more proposed some operation from the Mediterranean; General Marshall, in the tone of his threat of 1942, then "announced that if the British plan were approved ... he would recommend to Eisenhower that he had no choice but to be relieved of his command" (Mr. Sherwood).

A month before the meeting at Yalta Mr. Churchill cabled to President Roosevelt, "At the present time I think the end of this war may well prove to be more disappointing than was the last." He had come a long way from the "finest hour" of 1940, during which year, on acceding to the prime ministership, he wrote, "Power in a national crisis, when a man believes he knows what orders should be given, is a blessing." He now knew how little true power the "premier-dictators" have and could only hope, at the utmost, to salvage a little from the ruins of victory, which at that moment was being thrown away just before it was won.

What he knew, and told President Roosevelt, was all unknown to the embroiled masses. That complete control of the press, of which the Protocols arrogantly boast, prevented the truth from reaching them, and they were being swept along from day to day on a high tide of inflamed enthusiasm for the great "victory" which they were about to gain. Mr. Churchill's "power" was quite impotent to alter that. A few months earlier (August 23, 1944) he had asked his Minister of Information, "Is there any *stop on the publicity for the facts about the agony of Warsaw*, which seem, from the papers, to have been *practically suppressed?*" *(Triumph and Tragedy)*. The enquiry sounds genuine, and in that case Mr. Churchill was ignorant of what any independent journalist could have told him, that such facts *were* "practically suppressed." He does not record what answer he received, if any.

The "agony" to which Mr. Churchill refers is the heroic rising of General Bors's underground army of Poles against the Germans as the Red armies approached Warsaw. The Soviet advance was immediately halted by order from Moscow, and Stalin refused to allow British and American aircraft to use Soviet airfields for the purpose of succouring the Poles. Mr. Churchill says "I could hardly believe my eyes when I read his cruel reply" and records that he urged President Roosevelt to order American aircraft to use the fields, as "Stalin would never have dared fire on them." Mr. Roosevelt refused and the Poles were abandoned to Hitler's SS. troops, who razed Warsaw, killed 200,000 of its inhabitants, and deported the surviving 350,000. On October 1, after resisting for eight weeks, Radio Warsaw made this last broadcast, "This is the bitter truth; we have been worse treated than Hitler's satellites; worse than Italy, worse than Rumania, worse than Finland ... God is righteous and in his omnipotence he will punish all those responsible for this terrible injury to the Polish nation" (words which recall the Czech broadcast "bequeathing our sorrows to the West" after the abandonment of Czechoslovakia to Hitler in 1939).

The power which the revolution had gained in the infested West was enough to prevent the publication of facts like these during the Second War, and Mr. Churchill's enquiry of his Minister of Information vanished into air. The "agony of Warsaw" came just three years after Mr. Roosevelt signed the "declaration of principles" stating that he wished "to see sovereign rights and self-government restored to those who have been forcibly deprived of them."

Such was the background to the Yalta Conference where, at his first meeting with Stalin, President Roosevelt, a man on the grave's edge, told the Soviet dictator that he "was more bloodthirsty in regard to the Germans than he had been a year ago, and he hoped that Marshal Stalin *would again* propose a toast to the execution of 50,000 officers of the German Army." The word "again" alludes to the Teheran Conference of December 1943, where Stalin had proposed such a toast and Mr. Churchill had angrily protested and left the room. Thereon President Roosevelt had suggested that only 49,500 be shot, and his son, Elliott, in convivial mood, had expressed the hope that "hundreds of thousands" would be mown down in battle; "Uncle Joe," beaming with pleasure, then had risen from his seat to embrace Mr. Elliott Roosevelt.

Mr. Roosevelt wished by this prompting of Stalin to annoy Mr. Churchill (whom by 1945 he apparently regarded as an adversary); he had told his son Elliott at Teheran, "Trouble is, the P.M. is thinking *too much of the postwar,* and where England will be; he's scared of *letting the Russians get too strong"),* and made this plain to Stalin by saying he would "now tell him something indiscreet, since he would not wish to say it in front of Prime Minister Churchill." Among the things which were not told in front of Mr. Churchill was this: "The President said he felt that the armies were getting close enough to have contact between, *and he hoped General Eisenhower could communicate directly with the Soviet staff rather than through the Chiefs of Staff in London and Washington as in the past" (February* 4, 1945).

Here is the explanation for the fate of Vienna, Berlin and Prague; in *March, April* and *May* General Eisenhower, in the messages accordingly sent *direct* to Moscow of which Mr. Churchill complained, submitted his plan of advance and agreed to halt the Allied armies west of these capitals.

Stalin did not again propose the shooting of 50,000 Germans. The Yalta records suggest that he showed some reserve towards Mr. Roosevelt's private proposals to him (which included one that the British should give up Hong Kong), and the picture of him which emerges from these papers is, that of a more dignified, and in spoken words at least more scrupulous man, than the president! The reasons may be, on the one hand, that Mr. Roosevelt's talk was so callous and cynical that it produces a feeling of repugnance in the reader; on the other, even Stalin may have hesitated to believe that the American president would go as far as he said in supporting Soviet aggrandizement and have suspected some trap, so that he showed more than his usual reserve. In any case, the murderer of millions appears, in these particular pages, rather less repellent than his visitor.

The supreme test of Western honour at Yalta lay in the treatment of Poland. The invasion of Poland by the Soviet and Nazi states in partnership had begun the Second War; it was clearly the country chiefly covered by Mr. Roosevelt's and Mr. Churchill's declaration of 1941 (the Atlantic Charter) that "sovereign rights and self-government" must be "restored to those who have been forcibly deprived of them." At the time of the Yalta Conference, when the European war had only ten weeks to run, Poland had in fact been abandoned to the revolution; that was implicit in the desertion of the Warsaw Poles and as explicit as it could be in Mr. Roosevelt's order to General Eisenhower to subordinate his plan of advance to Soviet wishes. This meant that Poland, and with it all the European countries east and south-east of Berlin, would in fact be annexed to the Soviet, or incorporated in the area of the revolution.

Though Mr. Churchill had not given up the last hope of averting it, the imminence of this annexation was apparent at Yalta, and the final degradation of the West lay in the acceptance of it, at the end even by Mr. Churchill. For *acceptance* it was: the pretence that merely half of Poland's territory would be abandoned to the Soviet, that Poland would be "compensated" by amputations from Germany, and that "free elections" would be held in the state thus produced, was abhorrent when everyone knew that *all* of Poland, and the half of Germany from which Poland was to be "compensated," were to pass alike from Nazi enslavement into Communist enslavement, and that the Allied armies were to be held back to ensure this.

Thus when Mr. Roosevelt asked leave to "bring up Poland" he had abandoned the high "principles" of the Atlantic Charter. He began by saying "there are six or seven million Poles in the United States," thus intimating that for him the only problem was that of votes in American elections, not of Poland, and then he proposed the amputation of Poland along the Curzon line, adding the strange remark that "Most Poles, like the Chinese, want to save face" (many observers of this period noted that he was sometimes incoherent, and he did not explain how the loss of Polish territory would save the Polish face). Mr. Roosevelt had been well briefed for this proposal. Mr. Edward Stettinius, who was nominally his Secretary of State at that time but seems to have had no part in forming policy, records that "the President asked me to get a lawyer to consult with him over the wording of the Polish boundary statement; I called *Alger Hiss*." Mr. Churchill was left alone to make the last protest on behalf of the original "principles" and objects of the Second World War: "This is what we went to war against Germany for: that Poland should be free and sovereign. Everyone here knows the result to us, unprepared as we were, and that it nearly cost us our life as a nation. Great Britain had no material interest in Poland. Her interest is only one of honour because we drew the sword for Poland against Hitler's brutal attack. Never could I be content with any solution that would not leave Poland as a free and independent state" ... (later, when the pressure of Mr. Roosevelt and Stalin were proving too strong for him) "It would be said that the British Government had given way completely on the frontiers, had accepted the Soviet view and had championed it ... Great Britain would be charged with forsaking the cause of Poland ..."

But in the end he signed (and later Polish troops, the first to fight Hitler, remained mourning in their quarters while the great "Victory Parade" was held in London).

Thus the deed was done, and instead of freedom of speech and worship, freedom from want and fear, the peoples of Eastern Europe were abandoned to the secret police and concentration regime which Hitler had first introduced there on the night of the Reichstag fire. It would seem that nothing worse than this could be done, and yet one even worse thing *was* done. Under the "Protocol on German Reparations" the basic device of Soviet terrorism, *slave labour,* was approved and extended to the conquered peoples, for this document authorized "the three governments" to obtain reparation from Germany in the form of "the use of German labour."

Under some subsidiary agreement the Western Allies agreed to regard *all* Russian prisoners as "deserters," to be driven back to the Soviet state. All these matters read soberly on paper; the picture of their *results* for human beings appears in such words as those of the Rev. James B. Chuter, a British Army chaplain and one of 4,000 prisoners from a disintegrated German prisoner-of-war camp who made their way towards the advancing Allies in 1945: "Along the eastern bank of the river Mulde was encamped a great multitude ... This was the end of the journey for the tens of thousands of refugees who had passed us. The Mulde was the agreed line at which the Americans halted and to which the Russians would advance. The Americans would let none save German military personnel and Allied prisoners of war cross the river. From time to time some desperate soul would fling himself into the flood in a vain attempt to escape from the unknown fury of the Russian arrival. *It was to avoid such incidents and to discourage them that the occasional splutter of American machine guns on the Western banks was heard ... sounding, in that most frightening manner, a plain warning to all who thought to cross the river line."*

Such was the outcome of the Second World War, and the agreement which sanctified it all, (in which Stalin's signature was added to those of the two signatories of the Atlantic Charter of 1941) said, "By this declaration *we reaffirm our faith in the principles of the Atlantic Charter."*

This was the end of the Yalta Conference, but for a significant footnote. At a last "man-to-man" meeting between President Roosevelt and Stalin, on the eve of the president's departure to visit King Ibn Saoud, Stalin said "the Jewish problem was a very difficult one, that they had tried to establish a national home for the Jews in Birobidzhan but that they had only stayed there two or three years and then scattered to the cities." Then President Roosevelt, in the manner of a man who is a member of an exclusive club and is sure his host must also belong, "said he was a Zionist and asked if Marshal Stalin was one."

This exchange produces on the reader the effect of two men getting down to the real business at last. Stalin replied that "he was one in principle *but he recognized the difficulty.*" In this passage, again, the Georgian bank-robber sounds more like a statesman and speaks more prudently than any Western leader of the last forty years, none of whom have admitted any "difficulty" (Mr. Churchill was wont to denounce any talk of "difficulty" as anti-Jewish and anti-semitic). This was not the whole conversation on the subject, although it is all that the official record discloses. On the same, last day of the full conference Stalin asked Mr. Roosevelt if he meant to make any concessions to King Ibn Saoud, and the President replied "that there was only one concession he thought he might offer "and that was to give him" (Ibn Saoud) "*the six million Jews in the United States.*" (This last quotation is authentic but was *expunged* from the official record).

All the statements cited above, with the one exception, are taken from the official publication, "The Conferences at Malta and Yalta, 1945," issued by the American State Department on March 16, 1955. The newspapers next morning broke out in headlines, of which one in the *Montreal Star* is typical: "World Capitals Dismayed, Shocked over Disclosures of Yalta Secrets." This was nonsense; by 1955 the masses were apathetic about such things, having been brought by control of the press to the condition of impotent confusion foretold in the Protocols of 1905.

Historically regarded, the revelations of these Yalta documents are incriminating enough, *but they are not complete.* Much was expunged (I have given one example) and presumably it was the worst. In May 1953, under pressure from the United States Senate, the American State Department undertook to publish in unexpurgated form, by June 1956, the documents of *all twelve* wartime conferences. Only the Yalta papers had been published by May 1956, and these in expurgated form. Two State Department officials charged with preparing the papers for publication, Dr. Donald M. Dozer and Mr. Bryton Barron, pressed for prompt and full publication and were dismissed and retired, respectively, early in 1956, in the face of President Eisenhower's statement in April 1955, "I think that to hold secret any document of the war, including my own mistakes ... is foolish. Everything ought to be given out that helps the public of the United States to profit from past mistakes and make decisions of the moment."

Mr. Barron, before his retirement, was "subjected to gruelling brain-washing sessions to secure his consent to the deletion of important documents" and informed his superiors that the compilation they were preparing to issue would be "a distorted, incomplete, badly expurgated one that tends to shield the previous Administration and will mislead the American people."

This history of the Yalta papers shows that, ten years after the Second World War, power was still in the hands of the essentially "foreign group" which during the war had been able to divert supplies, military operations and State policy to the purpose of "extending" the revolution. They were still able to override the public undertakings of presidents and to frustrate the will of Congress; they still held the reins. This meant that the infestation of the American government and its departments by agents of the revolution, which began with Mr. Roosevelt's first presidency in 1933, had not been remedied in 1955, despite many exposures; and that, as this was the case, American energies in any third war could in the same way be diverted to promote the overriding plan for a communized world-society (Lenin's third stage in the process). Once more the embroiled masses would fight to bring about results, the direct opposites of the causes held out to them at any new "Pearl Harbour."

This undermining of the West was not confined to the United States; it was general throughout the Western world and this chapter dwells on the American case only because, in the conditions of today, the strength and wealth of America are so great that their use or misuse probably will decide the issue. A similar condition was shown to exist in the country, Britain, from which the great overseas nations originally sprang, and in the two greatest of these, Canada and Australia.

The first exposure came in Canada, immediately after the war's end, and this is the only one of the four Cases in which full governmental investigation and full public disclosure of the results followed; also, it lit the fuse which in time led to all the other exposures, in America, Australia and Britain. A *Russian,* at the risk of his life, disclosed to the Canadian Government the network of governmental infestation and espionage of which the Soviet Embassy at Ottawa was the centre (despite the leading part taken by *Russians* in this process of warning Western politicians and the press continued to incite their peoples against "Russians," not against the revolutionary conspiracy of which Russia was the captive). The full public investigation, which would otherwise be surprising, seems to be accounted for by the fact that the Canadian Prime Minister of that day, Mr. Mackenzie King, although a wily politician, was in all else a simple man, more interested in communing with the spirit world than anything else. When he was convinced by documents of the truth of Igor Gouzenko's statements he saw that they revealed "*as serious a situation as ever existed in Canada at any time*" and flew at once to inform the American president (Mr. Roosevelt's successor) and the British Prime Minister (then Mr. Clement Attlee) that this situation was shown by them to be "*even more serious* in the United States and England."

At that time Mr. Whittaker Chambers's documentary proof that Mr. Alger Hiss was the centre of a Soviet network in the American State Department had been available to, but ignored by, two American presidents for six years, and three years later Mr. Truman was publicly to deride all such stories as "a Red herring." The exposure of Mr. Hiss and his associates followed in a trial which was entirely the result of efforts by individual patriots (including Mr. Richard Nixon, a later Vice-President) to wring the truth from a reluctant government and to compel exposure. In the sequence to the Hiss affair a mass of disclosures followed, which showed American government departments to have been riddled with Soviet agents at all levels. The literature of this period and subject is now too great even to summarize here, but it is conclusive, and much of it is official, though reluctant.

In England, for six years after the Canadian Prime Minister's warning, nothing was done to remedy a condition revealed by the highest authority. Then in 1951 two Foreign Office officials, one of them a senior and rising young man, and both of them notorious characters who had evidently been protected and advanced in their official careers by some powerful hand, suddenly disappeared. It was known that they had fled to Moscow, fearing exposure on the Hiss model. For four more years British governments (Socialist and Conservative) refused all public investigation or any information beyond the bland statement that "all possible inquiries are being made." Then in 1955 the British Foreign Office suddenly announced that the two men had been under suspicion of conveying secret information to the Soviet Government *from 1949* (they disappeared in 1951). This belated announcement was not spontaneous; it was extorted from the British government only by the fact that one more *Russian,* Vladimir Petrov of the Soviet Embassy at Canberra, had fled his captivity and had revealed that these two men, Burgess and Maclean, had been recruited as spies for the Soviet during their student days at Cambridge University twenty years earlier (1930-1935; this is the method, of capturing men in their unwary youth, on which the Weishaupt documents and the Protocols alike lay emphasis; the career of Alger Hiss affords an exact parallel in America). Immediately after this tardy Foreign Office admission Burgess and Maclean were proudly paraded before international newspapermen in Moscow as officials of the Soviet Foreign Ministry (and immediately after that the Soviet leaders of the moment, Kruschev and Bulganin, were invited to pay a ceremonial visit to London).

The Petrov disclosures brought about an investigation in Australia, the fourth great country infested, by a Royal Commission of three judges. Of the entire series, only this investigation can be compared with the Canadian one of nine years earlier. It *was* fairly thorough and the "public report (September 14, 1955) stated that the Soviet Embassy in Canberra from 1943 on "controlled and operated an espionage organization in Australia" and gave warning that Soviet intelligence agents were still operating in Australia through undercover agents entering the country as immigrants. The Australian Foreign Minister, Mr. R. Casey, at that time stated that there was "a nest of traitors" among Australian civil servants. His words confirmed what Mr. Mackenzie King had said ten years before, and in that decade nothing truly effective had been done in any of the four great countries affected, or infected, to remedy the mortally dangerous condition exposed.

A chief reason for this was that all the governmental, parliamentary and judicial investigations of the decade (with one exception) misinformed public opinion more than they informed it, by concentrating on the issue of "espionage," which in fact is a *minor* one. The fact that great countries try to obtain knowledge, through spies and agents, of military and other matters which other great countries try to keep secret is generally known so that the masses probably were not much moved even by the extent of espionage which was revealed; this, they told each other, was something for counter-intelligence to handle.

Thus the investigations diverted public attention from the truly grave condition which was exposed. This was not the mere theft of documents, *but the control of state policy at the highest level* which was gained by the infestation of the Western countries. It was this that enabled arms, supplies, wealth, military operations and the conduct of Western politicians at top-level conferences all to be guided into a channel where they would produce the maximum gain, in territory and armed strength, for the revolutionary state.

Exposure of this condition came only in the Hiss trial and its numerous attendant investigations and disclosures. These showed that the revolution had its agents at the top-levels of *political power*, where they could direct State policy and the entire energies of nations; the two men both purveyed secret papers, but this was a small function auxiliary to their major accomplishment, which was to produce the map of and the situation in Europe with which the world is confronted today.

The names of Mr. Alger Hiss and Mr. Harry Dexter White are inseparable from that denouement. Mr. Hiss, from his university days in the 1930's, rose as rapidly in the public service, under some protection, as Mr. Donald Maclean in the British one. He was denounced as a Soviet agent in 1939 by a fellow-Communist who awoke to his duty when the Communist state joined with Hitler in the attack on Poland, and the proof then lay disregarded for many years while two American presidents continued to advance him. He was constantly at Mr. Roosevelt's side (sometimes in separate meetings with Stalin) at Yalta and the abandonment of Eastern Europe to the revolution cannot be dissociated from his name; the disclosures about his activity made at his trial make that conclusion inescapable. After Yalta, and evidently as a sign of the especial confidence placed in him by the international group which was in control of events during that confusion-period, he was made first Secretary General of the

United Nations, which thus came in to being at San Francisco in April 1945 under the directorship of an agent of the revolution.

The decisive part played by Hiss at Yalta is indicated by a few significant quotations. The nominal Secretary of State, Mr. Edward Stettinius, on the eve of Yalta instructed his State Department staff that "all memoranda for the President on topics to be discussed at the meeting of the Big Three *should be in the hands of Mr. Hiss* not later than Monday, January 15." In this way Hiss was put in charge of the State Department's briefing papers for the President on all questions expected to arise at Yalta. Mr. James F. Byrnes, an earlier Secretary of State who was present at Yalta in a later capacity (director of the Office of War Mobilization and Reconversion) says, "So far as I could see, the President had made little preparation for the Yalta Conference ... Not until the day before we landed at Malta did I learn that we had on board a very complete file of studies and recommendations prepared by the State Department ... Later, when I saw some of these splendid studies I greatly regretted that they had not been considered on board ship. I am sure the failure to study them while en route was *due to the President's illness.*"

These papers prepared by the experts and professionals of the State Department expressed views about future relations with the Soviet which Mr. Roosevelt's utterances at Yalta did not reflect, and as he had not looked at them this was natural. Mr. Hiss in fact made American policy at Yalta. Mr. Stettinius records Hiss's presence "behind the President" at the formal conferences, and says that he himself always "conferred" with Hiss before and after these meetings. The official, but expurgated American report of the Yalta Conference apparently was edited with an eye to the concealment of Hiss's part; it contains only notes and jottings made by him which mean nothing when separated from their essential background: his membership of the conspiracy. Mr. Bryton Barron (one of the two State Department historians whose refusal to "distort history" and "suppress official data" led to their dismissal, as earlier mentioned) at Chicago in February 1956 publicly stated that, if he were allowed, he could "relate incidents to demonstrate the power Alger Hiss exercised ... and how he operated at high levels," adding that the official publication "failed to list many of his more significant activities at that fateful conference."

The name of Alger Hiss is the best known in this context, because of his public trial and conviction. The first authority in this question, Mr. Whittaker Chambers, thinks that the man known as "Harry Dexter White," whom he calls "one of the most influential men on earth," may have played an even greater part in shaping American State policy in the Soviet interest.

According to the American newspapers, no birth certificate of any man called "Harry Dexter White" exists and none knows who he was! Mr. Henry Morgenthau junior (the only Cabinet officer to continue in office through nearly the entire twelve years of Mr. Roosevelt's presidency), very soon after his appointment introduced "Harry Dexter White" (1934) into the United States Treasury. His rise there (like Mr. Hiss's in the State Department) was of the rapid kind which indicates influential backing. Immediately after Pearl Harbour he was invested with "full responsibility for all matters with which the Treasury Department has to deal *having a bearing on foreign relations*," and later was appointed Assistant to the Secretary himself.

During all these years the man whose true identity apparently will never be known was a Soviet agent, and the proof was proffered to but refused by President Roosevelt. Mr. Whittaker Chambers states that he first received secret Treasury documents from Mr. White (for transmission to the Soviet Government) *in 1935*, and *in 1939* (after the Hitler-Stalin alliance) was ready to produce the papers proving Mr. White's (and Mr. Hiss's) activities; these papers then had to be left in safe hiding by him for another *nine years*, when he brought them out to demolish Mr. Hiss's libel action against himself. From first to last, no governmental body would look at them. In 1941 the F.B.I. interviewed Mr. Chambers and was given Mr. White's name by him, but no action followed; the F.B.I. was equally unable to move any governmental authority to action in this matter, and the eventual exposure, through *private* agency, came only *in 1948*.

Mr. White's first decisive intervention in American State policy came in 1941. According to two unimpeachable authorities (the Harvard Professors William Langer and S. Everett Gleason in *The Undeclared War*) he drafted the American ultimatum of November 26, by means of which Japan was "manoeuvred into firing the first shot" at Pearl Harbour (Secretary Stimson's phrase). Thus his hand may be plainly traced in the initial act of America's involvement in the Second War, as may Soviet prompting of it.

Having shaped the beginning, he also shaped the end of the Second War, in the interest of the same party, his masters. He is generally credited with the drafting of the "Morgenthau Plan." In both cases, therefore, American State policy was fashioned by the United States Treasury, not by the State Department or the War Department, which, under the President, are the departments constitutionally responsible for the conduct of foreign policy in time of war; and at the Treasury, as has been shown, Mr. White was "fully responsible" for all matters bearing on foreign relations.

The general tendency in America since the Second War has been to point to Mr. White as the original author of these fateful actions. This may be token reluctance to point a finger at the responsible Cabinet officer himself, Mr. Henry Morgenthau junior. Mr. Morgenthau originally appointed Mr. White, signed both the draft ultimatum to Japan of November 1941 and the draft plan for dismembering Germany of September 1944, and in both cases President Roosevelt acted on the plan submitted. It is therefore difficult to see how Mr. Morgenthau's and Mr. White's responsibility can be separated, and the most that might be assumed is that the directing brain was the pseudonymous Mr. Harry Dexter White's.

The genesis of the "Morgenthau Plan" for the dismemberment of Germany into petty provinces, the destruction of its industry and flooding of its mines and its reduction to the status of "a goat pasture" was described by another Assistant Secretary to the Treasury, Mr. Fred Smith, in 1947. He said it was first discussed at a meeting (at which he was present) between General Eisenhower, Mr. Morgenthau and Mr. White in the general's mess tent in the south of England on August 7, 1944. Mr. White (says Mr. Smith) raised the subject of Germany; General Eisenhower said he would like to "see things made good and hard for them for a while ... the whole German population is a synthetic paranoid"; and Mr. White remarked, "We may want to quote you on the problem of handling the German people," whereon General Eisenhower said he could do this. Mr. Morgenthau, on this basis, devised the "plan" and went to London to canvass it with Mr. Churchill and Mr. Eden, then returning by air to America to put it before President Roosevelt.

Up to that point, says Mr. Smith, the State Department had not been informed of Mr. Morgenthau's activities in the matter. Mr. Roosevelt apparently had misgivings and formed a committee to develop the plan, in which committee the Secretaries of State and War at last joined Mr. Morgenthau of the Treasury. The disclosure of the Morgenthau Plan before this committee "resulted in as violent an explosion as has ever occurred in the hallowed chambers of the White House"; Mr. Hull and Mr. Stimson both violently attacked it. Nevertheless, when President Roosevelt then went to Quebec to meet Mr. Churchill Mr. Morgenthau "happened" to be with him, and Mr. Hull and Mr. Stimson were left behind. Mr. Churchill records his surprise at that, but both he and Mr. Roosevelt then signed "the Morgenthau Plan," which possibly might more accurately be called the White-Morgenthau plan.

Thus President Roosevelt (against the strong protests of his responsible Cabinet officers, the Secretaries of State and of War) and Mr. Churchill (in contradiction of many declarations) approved a peace of vengeance. Both men later spoke as if they had not understood what they did. Mr. Churchill said he "regretted" his signature, but never explained how he came to give it (Mr. James F. Byrnes mildly comments that this is "difficult to understand"). Mr. Roosevelt spoke as if he had inadvertently initialled an inter-office memorandum without looking at it. He said he had yielded to the importunities of "an old and valued friend" (Mr. Sherwood), and this indicates Mr. Morgenthau; he also said that he was "frankly staggered" and "had no idea how he could have initialled this; he had evidently done it without much thought" (Mr. Stimson).

The public masses were left to infer that error had been realized in time and that "the Morgenthau Plan" was abandoned; the factories were *not* blown up and the mines were *not* flooded. This was soothing-syrup, not truth. The *spirit* of the peace of vengeance, proposed in the White-Morgenthau plan, *did* prevail. Mr. Morgenthau did not succeed with his proposal (the one jocularly made by Mr. Roosevelt to Stalin at Yalta) that "archcriminals" should be put to death by the military without provision for any trial, but the trials which were held remain a blot on Western justice. The bisection of Germany (which in fact was the bisection *of Europe,* friend or foe) was more perilous to the future than any dismemberment of Germany into provinces. Above all, the West, by approving slave labour, put the civilizing process of nineteen centuries into reverse. (Significantly, eleven years after the war's end the United States Government withheld its adherence to an international convention, proposed by the International Labour Organization, *outlawing forced labour;* it was obviously debarred from adhering by its signature to the Yalta agreements).

Thus the ghost of "Harry Dexter White" still haunts the scene, for the shape which this Soviet agent and his associates gave to American government policy left the future of the West more troubled than it had ever been. When the war ended he was still rising in the esteem of American presidents, for he was appointed to preside over the second of the two great international planning conferences at which the future of the nation-states was to be submerged in that of an international directorate. The first was the organizing conference of the United Nations, where Mr. Alger Hiss occupied the directorial chair. The second was the monetary conference at Bretton Woods, which set up the World Bank and the International Monetary Fund. Mr. White was the organizer of that pilot conference and then was appointed American executive director of the International Monetary Fund. Thus the chief representative of the United States Government, at each of these preparatory meetings of the new international directorate, was a Soviet agent.

Before Mr. White received this last appointment (publicly announced by Mr. Roosevelt's successor, Mr. Harry Truman, on January 23, 1946), the F.B.I. had several times given warning at the White House about Mr. White's secret activities, the last time in a special message to the President's personal military aide on November 8, 1945, in which Mr. White was specifically named as a Soviet agent and spy. After the President's public announcement of Mr. White's new appointment, the head of the F.B.I, Mr. J. Edgar Hoover, sent a further strong warning (February 1, 1946), saying that White, if his appointment were confirmed, "would have the power to influence in a great degree deliberations on all international financial arrangements." Despite this, Mr. White's appointment was confirmed on May 1, 1946, (this history was made public by the Attorney General of the United States, Mr. Herbert Brownell junior, on November 17, 1953); Mr. Truman's reply made no reference to the warning of November 1945 and stated that he allowed

White's appointment to stand *after* consideration of the warning of February 1946).

In April 1947 (by which time the exposure of Mr. Hiss was drawing near) Mr. White resigned "for reasons of health." In August of 1948, when the proof of his guilt was conclusive and was about to be made public, he was called before the Un-American Activities Committee of Congress and denied ever having been a member of the conspiracy. He was then privately confronted with some of the most damning evidence (now all on record) and three days later was found dead, receiving Jewish burial. No autopsy report is on record and the circumstances of his death remain as mysterious as his identity.

Nearly seven years later (January 3, 1955) the Internal Security Committee of the United States Congress reported:

"1. Alger Hiss, Harry Dexter White, and their confederates in the Communist underground in Government, had power to exercise *profound influence on American policy and the policies of international organizations during World War II and the years immediately thereafter;* (this is the vital, and supremely dangerous "confusion-period" to which I earlier alluded; the later years of a war and the early years of its aftermath);

"2. They had power to exercise profound influence on *the creation and operation of the United Nations and its specialized agencies;* "3. This power was not limited to their officially designated authority. It was inherent in their *access to and influence over higher officials, and the opportunities they had to present or withhold information on which the policies of their superiors might be based;*

"4. Hiss, White and a considerable number of their colleagues who helped make American foreign policy and the policies of international organizations during crucial years, have been exposed as secret Communist agents."

This might appear to record the good ending to a bad story, for at earlier times the discovery and publication of such a state of affairs by a parliamentary authority would have meant, first, impeachment proceedings and the like, and second, remedial action. In fact, as I can testify (for I was in America during many of these years) the remedial effect was very small, if any. The chief reason for this was, that the entire process of investigation and disclosure was accompanied by a most violent press campaign against the investigators and disclosers, not against the culprits and the conspiracy.

Here the history of the period after the French revolution ... and of the ordeal-by-smearing suffered by Messrs' Morse, Barruel and Robison, repeated itself. If any future historian should examine the yellowing newspaper pages of these years he will find ten thousand abusive words directed against those who called for investigation and remedy for every one aimed at an exposed or convicted member of the conspiracy; he will find columns of praise for Mr. Hiss, for example, alongside columns of vituperation directed against the penitent agent, Mr. Whittaker Chambers, whose self-defence brought about Mr. Hiss's conviction. In time this storm centred around the head of one Senator Joseph McCarthy (as in the earlier decade it raged over that of Mr. Martin Dies, until he was driven out of political life), and a new epithet was coined for the delusion of the masses: "McCarthyism" (the demand for investigation and remedy) was by endless iteration made to sound to them more repugnant than "sedition."

Because of this the most significant moment in American history after the Second War was one in 1954, when the Senate censured Senator McCarthy. In 1952, for the first time in twenty years, the candidate nominated by the Republican party, was elected, General Eisenhower. The return to office, after two decades, elated the Republicans and General Eisenhower's victory was very largely due to his undertaking to stamp out the Communist infiltration of government, which had been revealed to have occurred during the long Roosevelt administration and had been inherited by his successor. In 1954 the new President allowed it to be known that he looked with disfavour on Senator McCarthy's "methods" and thus implicitly gave his nod to the censure motion (the American Jewish Committee also imperiously demanded that the Senate approve it), which then carried. Senator McCarthy, like many before him, then began to fade from the political scene and the principle that "investigation" was pernicious was re-established.

Thus the American voter found that the apparent choice between candidates, at a presidential election, gave him no true choice at all in the matter of combating sedition. With this censure motion, approved by the President of the day, all the investigations and exposures ended in sand. From that moment the agents of the conspiracy were implicitly left free to resume the burrowing process which resulted in the state of affairs represented, during the Second War, chiefly by Messrs' Alger Hiss and Harry Dexter White. It is this which makes the policy of America an incalculable and dangerous explosive force in any future war.

In the matter of sedition the "premier-dictators" of our time perform a function allotted to them by the Protocols of 1905, that major document of a conspiracy of which such men as Harry Dexter White were demonstrably part. Protocol No. 19 says that when the super-government has been established sedition will be placed in the category of "thieving, murder and every kind of abominable and filthy crime" and adds that "we have done our best to obtain that *the nation-states should not arrive at this means of contending with sedition.* It was for this reason that through the Press and in speeches and indirectly ... *we have advertised the martyrdom alleged to have been accepted by sedition-mongers for the idea of the commonweal.*"

Mr. Hiss was presented as a martyr, over a long period, in the press of the world, of no matter what party; Senator McCarthy, who "arrived at this means of contending with sedition," was presented as a brute. This control of the press, established in the last two decades, enables the conspiracy to stand between the nation-states and their wish to root out sedition. The Protocols of 1905 foretold: "We shall have a sure triumph over our opponent since they will not have at their disposition organs of the press in which they can give full and final expression to their views."

In America, which today is the key to the future of the West, the matter is further complicated by the existence of a body which is able to make drastic interventions in this field. The Supreme Court of the United States, by sitting in judgment on constitutional issues between the Federal Government and the forty-eight separate State Governments, frequently decides matters which in other parliamentary countries would be ones for the legislature, not the judiciary. Moreover, the members of this court are political (which is to say, party) appointees, not necessarily professional jurists or men of any judicial training. The danger of political control of such a body is obvious, and it was made plain by a majority judgment handed down on April 2, 1956, when the Supreme Court set aside the conviction of a Communist under the Pennsylvania State law against sedition. In this judgment the Supreme Court stated the "the field of sedition" was that of Congress alone and that "no room has been left" for State legislation or action against sedition. Forty-two of the forty-eight States at that time had sedition laws and this judgment, if it is not overridden by special act of Congress, will at a blow reduce the obstacles to sedition in America by the separate powers of those forty-two States, leaving, as the sole defence, the national administration, which had been repeatedly shown by the events of the preceding ten years to have been infested with seditionists. This judgment, too, may be compared with the passage previously quoted from the Protocols.

Lastly, the Second War led to the revival of the League of Nations, which had sprung from the "League to Enforce Peace." This body was obviously never an alliance of nations, but an instrument for the control of nations, to be wielded by whomever gained command of it. The conclusions of the Senate Committee quoted above testify to the part which Messrs' Alger Hiss, Harry Dexter White and their associates played in organizing and fashioning it. Clearly, in their minds it was intended to "extend the revolution" universally, following Lenin's dictum, and to become the "Super-Government" foreseen by the Protocols. The shadow of the universal concentration-camp regime looms already in its "Genocide Convention," where the causing of "mental harm" is defined as a crime against unspecified "groups."

What it will become depends on the future success or failure of the nation-states in "contending with sedition." In the Second War, as in the first, all the "top-line leaders" and "premier-dictators" appear from the start to have been secretly agreed in the resolve to set up a "world-organization" and to subordinate their nation-states to it. This was their own project, not that of their peoples, who were never consulted. No nation has ever evinced a desire to sink its identity in some world-state, ruled by who knows whom. On the contrary, the continuing love of nationhood, despite all ordeals and defeats, is the clearest human feeling evinced by the 20th Century, and this clearly will increase until "the deception of nations" ends and the idea of obliterating nations collapses.

Nevertheless, the wartime leaders, free from all public supervision in their meetings, their cabled exchanges and their telephone talks, all through the war pressed on with the project for a new world order, which at the war's end was to be found in the secretarial hands of Messrs' Hiss and White. Mr. Baruch's biographer records that Mr. Roosevelt was busy with the idea long before he became president, and selected the name, "United Nations." Mr. Baruch. himself, the permanent adviser of presidents, was of cosmic ambition; the same biographer quotes him as saying on many occasions, "Of course we can fix the world."

The absence of humility is the most striking thing about all these mortals. Mr. Churchill is as disappointing to the student, in this matter, as he is reassuring in that of the sorry end of the war in Europe, which he unquestionably tried to avert. In the matter of re- moulding the world he was as incorrigible as all the others, and the brave phrases he sometimes used ("I have not become His Majesty's first minister in order to preside over the liquidation of the British Empire") are not easy to reconcile with his enthusiasm for a concept based on the eventual "liquidation" of all nation-states.

Thus, at a time when a disastrous end to the war then in progress was being prepared, these wartime leaders were busy with world- government notions. They could not or would not conduct the war to true victory, but they were ready to reorganize the world! "The questions of World Organization" (says Mr. Churchill in October 1944) "were now thrusting themselves upon all our minds." From faraway South Africa, once more, General Smuts raised his voice, saying that Soviet Russia must be included, and from Washington President Roosevelt agreed that the revolutionary state which had helped Hitler start the war must be "a fully accepted and equal member of any association of the Great Powers formed for the purpose of *preventing international war.*" Mr. Roosevelt foresaw a period of "differences" and "compromises" during which "the child" would learn how to toddle. Mr. Churchill comments that the child was "the World Instrument" and thenceforth this term seems to have been the favourite one among the wartime leaders.

In this way, through one more world war, the "league to enforce peace" again came into existence, and the agents of the conspiracy were numerously entrenched in the commanding posts of the central body and of its auxiliary agencies, as was to be expected in the circumstances now known;

Messrs' Hiss and White were the chiefs of a great clan. The first major act of the new "World Instrument" was in effect to give sanction to the revolution's annexation of half Europe by electing the puppet-governments of the communized captive countries there to membership.

Thus in all fields Lenin's dictum about the "extension" of the revolution through a second world war was fulfilled. This was not the result of the persuasion of peoples (in the two cases so far, those of Hungary in 1919 and of Spain, where nation-states have been allowed to fight Communism it was thrown out). It was the result of the infestation of the West by members of the conspiracy, of the virtual suspension of sedition laws which they were able to effect, and of the command of policy, supplies and military operations which they gained.

Douglas Reed

Chapter 42

THE TALMUDIC VENGEANCE

Despite the protests of the responsible American Cabinet officers, Messrs' Hull and Stimson, and the professionals in the British Foreign Office, the Second War ended in "a peace of vengeance"; or rather (as vengeance is the denial of, and can never beget peace) in a vengeance which planted the seeds of new war.

The two "premier-dictators" of the West, Messrs' Roosevelt and Churchill, took responsibility for the vengeance, for, despite their later disavowals of it, they both signed the document which was its charter: the Protocol of the Yalta Conference. Under this the Christian West joined with the barbaric East to wreak a barbaric vengeance on Europe. The aim of this chapter is to discover where the original responsibility lay (for the avowal that they acted at the promptings or under the pressure of shadowy others, or in ignorance of what they signed, occurs in the statements of both men; here the ultimate powerlessness of these seemingly all-powerful wartime potentates is shown).

In January 1943 Mr. Roosevelt, at Casablanca, first struck the note of "blind vengeance," when he "suddenly stated the principle of unconditional surrender" (Mr. Hull). The words, with their Old Testamentary ring, meant that the enemy would not be granted peace at any price whatever, and this was the absolute reversal of all "principles" previously proclaimed by the Western leaders. The responsible American Cabinet member, Mr. Hull, states that he and his department had not been informed of this somersault in policy and that "Mr. Churchill was dumbfounded"; also that the British Foreign Office appealed for the term to be avoided. Mr. Churchill (as he stated after the war in the House of Commons) nevertheless supported the use of the term "but only after it was used by the President without consultation with me." Mr. Churchill added that "if the British Cabinet had considered these words they would have advised against it" (but for, many years he continued to urge the desirability of "summit" conferences between the Moscovite dictator and the two Western leaders, despite this experience).

Thus at Casablanca in 1943 the decision to wreak *vengeance* was first taken. This was the background to the "Morgenthau Plan" of September 1944 (obviously first devised in Moscow, then drafted by Mr. Harry Dexter White for his superior, then forwarded by Mr. Morgenthau to Mr. Roosevelt, who with Mr. Churchill initialled it), the spirit of which pervaded the Yalta Conference and its Protocol. Mr. Roosevelt's later expression of astonishment ("he had no idea how he could have initialled this") and Mr. Churchill's words of regret ("I had not time to examine the Morgenthau Plan in detail ... I am sorry I put my initials to it") are both voided by the fact that both then signed the Yalta document, its child and the charter of vengeance.

By giving their names to it the two Western leaders did greater harm to the West than any it could have suffered by war; what is destroyed by explosive can be rebuilt, but spiritual values achieved by the efforts of nations during nineteen centuries, once ruined are harder to restore. The East lost nothing because vengeance was its barbaric tradition, partly discarded during the last century of the Czars' rule but re-established in 1917. In the West, the area of Christendom, the case was different.

During the centuries the West had gradually improved the conduct of warfare from the savagery of primitive times to the civilized code which it reached by the end of the reign of Louis XIV. The nations came ever more to accept this overriding code, which outlawed the insensate killing or maltreatment of non-combatants and the plunder of their property, which provided for the immunity of a flag of mercy, and laid down that enemy dead, wounded and prisoners must be cared for as the combatant's own. Out of all this, in time, came an international organization, under the sign of the cross, which took thought and care for every soldier alike, without regard to nationality or rank. Probably this code of civilizing warfare formed the best possible first step towards the abolition of war for which men ultimately hope. The records of war waged under this code are uplifting to study; those of wars which denied it repel.

The wars of the 19th Century in Europe were fought, in increasing measure, under this code, so that their stories show man's effort to dignify himself even in war. This holds good of the Crimean war, and of the three Prussian wars, against Denmark, Austria and Prussia. They were honourably waged and concluded. (The only great Western war of that century in which the picture darkened was the civil one in America, where vengeance *was* wreaked, after victory, on the defeated party. This would not have happened but for the assassination of President Lincoln, the pacifier and unifier, within a few days of the victory; in the unlit shadows of that crime the same revolutionary conspirators may lurk, who demonstrably have shaped the events of our country).

With that exception, war continued to be waged under this civilizing code throughout the West and wherever the West set its foot. At this century's beginning came the Anglo-Boer War in South Africa. A few extracts from the journal of the Boer Colonel Deneys Reitz, written immediately after the fighting, show how men at war behaved towards each other, under this code, only fifty years ago:

In a British prisoner-of-war camp: "One prisoner asked for an interview with my father. His name was Winston Churchill … he said he was not a combatant but a war-correspondent and asked to be released on that account. My father replied that he was carrying a Mauser pistol when taken and so must remain where he was. Winston Churchill said that all war-correspondents *in the Soudan* carried weapons for self-protection, and the comparison annoyed my father, who told him the Boers were not in the habit of killing non- combatants …"

After the Boer victory at Spion Kop: "We spent the next hour or two helping the English Red Cross doctors and bearer parties bury their dead and carry away their wounded …"

After the Boer capture of Dundee: "I saw General Penn Symons, the Commander of the English troops. He was mortally wounded and the nurses told me he could not last out the night. Next morning … I met a bearer-party carrying his body, wrapped in a blanket, and I accompanied them to where they buried him behind the little English chapel …."

At the Boer siege of Ladysmith: "One of our men was shot through both legs and another pluckily carried him back to the sprit on his shoulders, the English firing all around him, until they realized that he was helping a wounded comrade, after which they let him go in peace and were even sporting enough to allow him to return to us without a shot fired"; "… A huge soldier loomed up in the dark … he lunged at me with his bayonet, but his insecure footing deflected the thrust and brought him stumbling against me. The man was at my mercy now, for I had my carbine against his side, but there came over me an aversion to shooting him down like a dog, so I ordered him to put up his hands instead …"

"I found the soldier whom I had killed and was horrified to see that my bullet had blown half his head away, the explanation being that during one of our patrols I had found a few explosive Mauser cartridges at a deserted trading station and had taken them for shooting game. I kept them in a separate pocket of my bandolier but in my excitement had rammed one of them into the magazine of my rifle without noticing it. I was distressed at my mistake … I would not knowingly have used this type of ammunition. I flung the remainder into the brook …"

After a battle: "The serious casualties were left for the British ambulances to pick up … the English soldiers, officers and men, were unfailingly humane. This was so well known that there was never any hesitation in abandoning a wounded man to the mercy of the troops, in the sure knowledge that he would be taken away and carefully nursed.

"We saw the lights of a train, but General Smuts would not allow us to pile boulders on the metals nor to fire as the engine thundered by, for fear of killing civilians, so we stood aside, catching a glimpse of officers and others seated in the dining-car … all unaware of the men looking at them from the darkness."

On the way to the Boer surrender: "On board the British battleship *Monarch* we spent a week in comfort, for officers and men vied with each other in their efforts to welcome us. The British, with all their faults, are a generous nation … throughout the time that we were amongst them there was no word said that could hurt our feelings or offend our pride, although they knew that we were on an errand of defeat."

This is a picture of civilized men at war. Today's parrot-phrase about "the next war destroying civilization" is empty, because civilization is a state of mind and spirit and cannot be destroyed by explosives, though it *can* be destroyed by such deeds as the vengeance of 1945. The war depicted by Colonel Reitz was fought when I was a boy and the code observed by such men as he, on all sides and in war or peace, was the one which Englishmen of my generation were taught to honour.

It was honoured in the First World War. I remember the British treatment of prisoners-of-war and I remember the liberation of British prisoners from German ones in the final advance; the treatment was similar in both. A wounded man had no nationality; he received as good care, if he were a captive, as if he were hit on his own side of the line. Non-combatants and civilian populations were respected; plunder and rape were outlawed.

What, then, caused the sudden abandonment of this civilized code of warfare by the West after the Second World War? The peoples had not changed in the twenty-seven years that had passed, from the Armistice of 1918. They were not more cruel or less kindly than before. They were blinded by a propaganda which hid from them the real nature of their leaders' deeds; and these leaders, by their own words, were prompted by others or did not know what they signed. In that way the vengeance of 1945 was wreaked and civilized men were left to say, with Edmund Burke, "It is gone, that sensibility of principle, that chastity of honour, which felt a stain like a wound." The significant prelude came, even before the fighting ceased, with the indiscriminate bombing of civilian populations in a country already defeated but denied the refuge of surrender. The killing of non-combatants was the reproach most loudly raised against Germany, in both wars, by the British and American politicians. On February 10, 1944 the Yalta Conference ended, where Mr. Roosevelt, in private parley with Stalin, had said he was feeling "more bloodthirsty" than before about the Germans. On February 13 and 14 British and American bombers for hours on end rained explosive on Dresden, a city crowded with fugitives, mostly women and children, from the advancing Red armies. The number of people killed, burned and buried that day and night will never be known; estimates vary between 50,000 and 250,000.[28] The war documents so far issued do not disclose who ordered this act, and strict measures were apparently taken to prevent the affair from ever being brought under public discussion.

---

[28] The number therefore may have been greater than at Hiroshima or Nagasaki, where the new atom-bombs were used, for the first time, on an utterly defenceless civilian population; and this against the protests of both the American and the British military commanders, General MacArthur and Lord Louis Mountbatten, who advised that the defeat of Japan was already effectively imminent.

After that came General Eisenhower's order to halt the Anglo-American advance on the Elbe line, and therewith to abandon Berlin, Vienna and Prague, and all East Europe to the Soviet armies. This was vengeance against friend and foe alike, for it meant the abandonment of half a continent to Asiatic enslavement. It was made more barbaric by the order (the effect of which was earlier shown in an eye-witness's words) to the Allied armies to prevent fugitives from the abandoned area, *by force,* from escaping to the West; at that point British and American gun-muzzles were turned against many of Hitler's victims, as well as German women and children. The culminating deed came later when, from the camps where hundreds of thousands of these refugees were gathered, having reached the West earlier or despite the cordon, many were picked out to be *driven back* to their pursuers.

England had abolished slavery, in its overseas colonies, more than a century before this; in America, President Lincoln had abolished it during the Civil War of 1861-1865. By these acts the wartime leaders of England and America re-introduced slavery *in Europe* in 1945!

The trials of "war criminals" formed the peaks of the vengeance and the Everest of them all was reached in the Nuremberg trial of the chief Nazi leaders.

The "wicked man" whom the masses had for six years been incited to destroy was not named in the indictment at all, even *in absentia,* although his deputy Martin Bormann (whose death was no more or less proven than Hitler's) *was* included. This significant gap at the end of Hitler's career may be as significant as many earlier gaps in what is generally known about him. In these days, when the infiltration of all parties, classes and governments by the agents of the revolution is a known and proven thing, it is of interest that the mass of literature about him ignores his early associations and the strong evidence of his Communist background. The Viennese police dossier of his early days has apparently disappeared. His later Brown Army commander, Captain Roehm, told a Storm Troop leader (who told me) that when the Bavarian troops drove the Bolshevist Government out of Munich in 1919 the unknown Adolf Hitler was taken prisoner with the bodyguard of the Moscow emissary Levine, and saved his skin by turning informer (this might explain why Roehm, the possessor of incriminating knowledge, was killed by Hitler after he came to power). Hitler's own original proposal for the name of the National Socialist party was "the Social Revolutionary Party"; he described himself as "the executor of Marxism" (not its executioner); and he told Hermann Rauschning that he had built his organization on the model of Communism. I met Hitler once or twice and studied him at close quarters for many years, before and after his rise to power; I believe that no genuinely informative work about him and the part he played has yet appeared.

This period was marked by a series of acts which evidently were deliberately devised to give it a nature of mockery especially humiliating to the

Christian West; it was as if captives were made to perform clownish tricks for the amusement of their captors. This was shown at Nuremberg when *the Soviet judge was selected to read the part of the judgment which condemned the Germans for taking men and women away from their homes and sending them to distant camps where they worked as slave labour.* The British, American and French members of the court listened while Western justice, their inheritance and trust, was mocked. At that time, under the Yalta agreement, Germans, Poles and many more were being taken from their homes and sent to slave-camps; behind the Soviet judge loomed the shadow of the Moscow cellars where men were shot without trial and of the vast Siberian prisonland where, for thirty years then, millions of uncharged and untried human beings wasted in slavery.

So much for the peaks of the vengeance. In the foothills unnumbered smaller deeds were committed which make up the darkest pages in the recent story of the West. It was a reversal to barbarism; where lay the inspiration of it? What directing hand made the Western leaders abet the revolution from the East in a vengeance of the kind practised by savage, primitive tribes? This vengeance was not "the Lord's" in the Christian interpretation. Whose vengeance was it?

Certain symbolic deeds were evidently meant to establish the authorship, or nature, of the vengeance. These crowning acts of symbolism were the reproductions, after nearly thirty years, of the similar acts committed during the revolution in Russia: the Talmudic boast left on the wall of the Romanoffs' death chamber and the canonization of Judas Iscariot. After the Second World War the Nazi leaders were hanged on the Jewish Day of Judgment in 1946, so that their execution was presented to Jewry in the shape of Mordecai's vengeance on Haman and his sons. Then in the Bavarian village of Oberammergau, where the world-famous Passion Play had been performed for three centuries, the players of the chief parts were put on trial for "Nazi activities" before a Communist court. Those who appeared as Jesus and the apostles were all declared guilty; the one performer acquitted was he who took the part of Judas. These things do not happen by accident, and the vengeance on Germany, like the earlier one on Russia, was in this way given the imprint of a Talmudic vengeance (that is, a vengeance on Christendom, the Talmud being the specifically anti-Christian continuation of the pre-Christian Torah). The vengeful writ ran on both sides of the line which by that time was supposed to be an "Iron Curtain" dividing "the free world" from the enslaved Asiatic one; in this matter of vengeance there was no iron curtain. Nuremberg was in the Western zone; Oberammergau in the Soviet one.

By the choice of the Jewish Day of Judgment for the hanging of the Nazi leaders and German commanders the Western leaders gave the conclusion of the Second War this aspect of a vengeance exacted specifically in the name of "the Jews." The shape which the trial took showed the purpose of the immense propaganda of falsification conducted during the war, which I have earlier described. "Crimes against Jews" were singled out as a separate count, as if Jews were different from other human beings (and when the judgment was delivered a hundred million human beings in Eastern Europe had been handed over to the general persecution of all men, from which Jews in their proportion suffered in Germany). This particular indictment was made "the crux of the case" against the defendants (Captain Liddell Hart's words) and was based on the assertion that "six million Jews" had been killed (as time went by the word "perished" was substituted for "killed"). An impartial court would at the outset have thrown out any suit based on this completely unverifiable assertion: At Nuremberg lawyers, who in a private case would have demanded acquittal on the strength of an unproven statement in respect of a decimal point or digit, used this fantastic figure as the basis of their demand for conviction.

I earlier described, with illustrations from Jewish sources, the process by means of which, over the years, the Jews were "singled out" from the mass of Hitler's victims and their number inflated at will from day to day (Hitler's book-bonfire became "the burning of *Jewish* books"; his concentration camps where ninety percent of the inmates were Germans became concentration camps for Jews; a wartime report about the killing of" 150,000 White Russians, Ukrainians and Jews at Kieff" was changed to "150,000 *Jews*"; and so on interminably).

The statement about the "six million Jews," allowed to pass without question by the men on the bench, was the end-product of this process. In six years of war the Germans, Japanese and Italians, using every lethal means, killed 824,928 British, British Commonwealth and American fighting-men, merchant sailors and civilians. Assuming that the Germans killed, say, half of these in Europe, they killed (according to this assertion) *fifteen times as many Jews* there. To do that, they would have needed such quantities of men, weapons, transports, guards and materials as would have enabled them to win the war many times over.

The figure would not even deserve scrutiny if it had not been used to give the Second War the brand of "a Jewish war" and if that, again, did not foreshadow the shape of any third war. Because of that, it may be examined here.

At no time in history, from antiquity to this day, can the number of Judahites, Judeans or Jews, living at any given time, be determined; for that reason the number afflicted in any calamity also cannot be determined, and there are many more reasons why the number of Jewish victims in the Second World War cannot be fixed. The process of mystification begins in *Genesis* and continues through the Torah (the seventy people taken by Jacob to Egypt, for instance, apparently increased to two or three million within 150 years). At all periods large, and sometimes huge variations occur in the "estimates," and only estimates are possible, as the present term, "Jew," is legally indefinable and statistically elusive.

An eminent Jewish authority, Dr. Hans Kohn, in his article on "the distribution of Jews" in the *Encyclopaedia Britannica Book of the Year for 1942*, writes:

"In view of the fact that in several of the countries where the largest number of Jews were living in 1941 *the census did not contain any questions regarding religion* ... the exact number of Jews in the world in 1941 *could not be ascertained*. The definition of persons falling under the classification of 'Jewish race' *is in no way agreed upon* ... In countries where the census *included* questions of religious origins, *even this religious criterion of Jewish faith is difficult to define exactly*.

Thus the *assumption* which generally varied around the figure of 16 million" (for the entire world) "*cannot claim any foundation on exact 'figures*. To this uncertainty about the number of Jews in the world was added in recent years *a growing uncertainty about their numerical distribution in the different countries and continents*. Probably more than 6,000,000 Jews lived in Poland and the U.S.S.R." A weaker basis than that even for "estimates" (not to speak of "statistics") can hardly be imagined, yet in the ensuing period, when all the additional confusions of war and occupation were piled on this infirm foundation, precise numbers of Jewish casualties were produced day by day, circulated by thousands of assiduous propagandists, and at the end declared to amount to six millions!

Dr. Kohn says that "probably" more than 6,000,000 Jews lived in Poland and U.S.S.R. *in 1941*. In respect of the U.S.S.R. this might corroborate another Jewish authority (Prof. H.M.T. Loewe), who said in the *Encyclopaedia Britannica of 1937* that 2,700,000 Jews then lived there. Similarly, four years earlier (1933) the Jewish journal *Opinion* had stated that the Jewish population of the U.S.S.R. was under 3,000,000; and the Soviet official *Encyclopaedia* in 1953 stated that "the Jewish population of the Soviet Union *in 1939* was 3,020,000."

This near agreement among four authorities in respect of the period 1933-1941 might lead the reader to think that the number of *Jews* in one country at least (the U.S.S.R.) was established with reasonable accuracy at a given time. On the contrary, this is a statistical jungle where *nothing* is ever established. In 1943 the Jewish Commissar Mikhoels said in London (according to the Johannesburg *Jewish Times* of 1952), "Today we have in the Soviet Union 5,000,000 Jews." That is two million more than two years before, and if it was true presumably meant that most of the *Jews* in Poland, after Hitler and Stalin fell out, moved into Soviet territory. However, in the same issue of the *Jewish Times* a leading Jewish writer, Mr. Joseph Leftwich, stated that the Jewish population of the U.S.S.R. in 1952 was 2,500,000, "a loss *since* 1943 of 2,500,000." He asked, "where and how did they disappear?";

the answer, in my judgment, is that most of them disappeared into the statistics.

That is not the end of the confusion in this one section of the question. The *Encyclopaedia Britannica* of 1937 (in giving the above- cited figure of 2,700,000 Jews in Russia on Jewish authority) said they formed about six percent of the total population. The total population was elsewhere given in the same encyclopaedia as 145,000,000 and six percent of that would be 8,700,000!

The encyclopaedias, statistical yearbooks and almanacs are in this one question all at odds with each other and untrustworthy. I could multiply examples (for instance, the Jewish World Congress in 1953 announced that the Jewish population of the U.S.S.R. was 1,500,000) but wandering in a maze without an outlet is profitless. All published figures are "estimates" made at the estimators' pleasure, and are without value. A professional accountant might write a book on the efforts of the encyclopaedists to make the post-war figure of Jewish population in the world conform with the pre-war "estimates," minus six million. Figures are tricky things: a few examples:

The leading American reference yearbook, the *World Almanac*, in 1947 gave the 1939 Jewish world-population as 15,688,259. In later editions up to 1952 it increased this pre-war estimate (without explanation) by a million, to 16,643,120. It gave the *1950* population as 11,940,000, which, if subtracted from the first figure given for 1939, gives a reduction of nearly four millions (though not of six). However, it based even this "estimate" on another estimate, namely, that in 1950 the Jewish population of the U.S.S.R. was 2,000,000. This still left unanswered Mr. Leftwich's question in respect of Commissar Mikhoels's statement, that in 1943 the Jewish population of the U.S.S.R. was 5,000,000.

In England *Whitaker's Almanac*, of similar eminence, struggled with the same problem. In its 1949 and 1950 issues it gave the 1939 "estimated" Jewish world population as 16,838,000 and that of 1949 as 11,385,200, a reduction of nearly 5,500,000. However, the figures given for Jewish population in separate countries added up to 13,120,000 (not 11,385,200). Incidentally, *Whitaker's* in 1950 gave the Jewish population of the U.S.S.R. as 5,300,000, against the *World Almanac's* figure for the same year, of 2,000,000.

Both these publications are of the highest repute for painstaking accuracy and the fault is not theirs; in this one matter alone *only* Jewish "estimates" are available, and for obvious reasons no dependence can be placed on these. I pointed out the discrepancies in a book of 1951 and observed that *Whitaker's* in 1952 no longer contained these "estimates of Jewish populations"; apparently it had abandoned the statistical quest as hopeless, and was right to do so. Another encyclopaedia in its 1950 edition also dropped the subject. Finally, the *New York Times*, which may be described as the world's leading Jewish newspaper (it is Jewish-owned and New York is today primarily a Jewish city) in 1948 published what claimed to be an authoritative statistical article, computing the Jewish population of the world (three years after the war's end) between 15,700,000 and 18,600,000. If either figure was near truth this meant that the Jewish world-population had remained stationary or increased during the war years.

Newspaper articles are soon forgotten (unless some diligent student preserves them) but the great propagandist fabrications are handed on. Thus the historians, those men of precision in other questions, passed on the legend of "mass-extermination" to posterity. At the war's end Professor Arnold J. Toynbee was producing his monumental *Study of History* and in its eighth volume (1954) said that "the Nazis ... reduced the Jewish population of Continental Europe, west of the Soviet Union, from about 6,5 million to about 1,5 million by a process of mass-extermination." He called this "a bare statistical statement" and then added a footnote showing that it was *not* a statistical statement: "it is *not possible to give exact figures based on accurate statistics* and it seemed improbable in 1952 that the necessary information *would ever be obtainable*." Professor Toynbee explains that his figure was based on Jewish "calculations, in which there were several possible sources of error." He concludes that "it might be estimated" that five million Continental Jews had been done to death by the Nazis.

The estimate is historically valueless. The starting-point for consideration of this question is the fact that six million Jews, or anything approaching that number, cannot possibly have been "done to death" or caused to "perish," for the reasons given at the start of this discussion; the very assertion, made before the Nuremberg court, was an affront to their 825,000 fighting-men, sailors and civilians, killed in *all* theatres of war, of which only the Western politicians of this century would have been capable.

The number of Jews who were killed or perished will never be known, for the reasons already stated and partly discovered by Professor Toynbee in his footnote to history. The very term "Jew" is indefinable; Jews are often not isolated in statistics; and at no time can the number of *living* Jews in the world be ascertained with any approach to accuracy. Indeed, any attempt to reach statistical clarity through census or immigration data is attacked as "discrimination" and "anti-semitism." For instance:

"Immigrants seeking to settle in Australia will from now on not be asked on application forms if they are Jewish, it was made known in Sydney by the executive committee of Australian Jewry, which *protested against this practice* to the immigration authorities" (the *Jewish Times,* Johannesburg). In England, "it is impossible, *in the absence of official statistics,* to do more than make an intelligent guess ... the exact number of Jews in Britain *remains a mystery*" (the *Zionist Record,* Johannesburg). In America, President Roosevelt was brought under unremitting pressure to abolish the requirement to state "Jewish" on immigration forms, and in 1952 a major campaign was waged by the Anti-Defamation League and the American Jewish Committee against the McCarran-Walter Act because it sought to restore this requirement. This act was in the event passed over President Truman's veto, but even a rigorous application of the reinstated requirement would not lead to clarification, as applicants, if they wish, may insert "British" or any similar description, instead of "Jewish."

This state of statistical affairs is now well-nigh universal, so that the whole question is a mystery and has deliberately been made one. None can even guess the number of Jews whose deaths, during the war, were not natural or the result of bombing and the like, but who were done to death by the Nazis. My opinion is that, whatever was the number of Jews in the countries overrun by Hitler, the number of their victims was in roughly that proportion to the total population stricken, Polish, Czech and other. I have found this to be the opinion of all persons known to me who survived the concentration camps and occupations. Having suffered themselves, their feeling for Jewish victims was as strong as for all others, but they could not understand why the one case of the Jews was singled out and the number of Jewish victims monstrously exaggerated.

The reason, hidden from them, became clear with the hangings on the Jewish Day of Judgment, for this symbolic act set the pattern for the entire conduct of the occupation, on both sides of the line, in its early years, and even for the future conduct of Western foreign policy far outside the bounds of Europe. The Talmudic vengeance was the start of a new era in the history of the West, during which all national considerations were to be subordinated to the cause of Jewish nationhood, as represented by the Talmudists from Russia.

I have a description, from a person who was present, of the manner in which the Nuremberg judgment came to be delivered on September 30 and October l, 1946 (between the Jewish New Year, September 26, and the Jewish Day of Atonement, October 5), and was *executed* immediately after midnight in the morning of October 16, Hoshana Rabba, the day when the Jewish god, after an interval during which he considers his verdict on every single human being, and may still pardon sinners, *delivers his final judgment*. This description says, ." . . all thought the judgment would be delivered sooner than it was, and *a number of trifling circumstances delayed it, till the date was fixed somewhere round September 15* ... Then X, one of the member judges, objected to the literary form of part of the judgment ... it was roughly calculated how long it would take to recast it and to recopy the recasting; and the date was fixed by this."

I have deleted the name of the member judge. As a result of this delay for literary improvement the judgment fell midway through the holiest ten days of the Jewish Year and was executed on the day of Jehovah's vengeance. I had foretold some such denouement, in a book published during the war, after Mr. Anthony Eden, on 17 December 1942 in the House of Commons, had made a "Declaration" about the Jews, in which he implicitly limited to the Jews the threat that "Those responsible for these crimes shall not escape retribution." Mr. Roosevelt, in America, had made a declaration of similar implication.

The Nuremberg trial formed the model for many lesser "war crimes" trials; these have been discussed, from the legal and moral point of view, in the books of Mr. Montgomery Belgion, Mr. F.J.P. Veale and the late Captain Russell Grenfell. A little of the truth about them filtered out in the course of years. In 1949, an American Administration of Justice Review Board, appointed after numerous protests, reported on some of the American military court trials at Dachau, where 297 death sentences had been approved. The report spoke of "mock trials" to which the defendants had been brought hooded, with ropes round their necks, and "tried" before mock-altars with crucifixes and candles; they were subjected to brutal treatment in the effort to extort confessions which then could be produced before the real trial (the prisoners were led to believe that the mock-trial was the genuine one).

The biggest of these trials was the "Malmedy trial" of 1945-1946, at which forty-three prisoners were sentenced to death. This trial related to the killing of American prisoners by SS. troops near Malmedy in 1944, and bitter feeling against any proved guilty was to be expected from American prosecutors. However, the tormentors of these prisoners were not Americans, as those who remember the admirable bearing of American troops in Germany after the First World War might expect. They were Jews from Austria who had entered the United States just before the Second War and, under Mr. Roosevelt's regime, had quickly been taken into the American army and American uniform. A genuine American who was present at these mock-trials (a veteran court reporter) stated that he left the service of the War Crimes Branch in disgust after witnessing the "brutal sadism" practised by one of the inquisitors. Then the chief American prosecutor in this trial, a colonel, admitted to a Senate subcommittee that he had known about the mock-trials; he thought they were proper if the trial court itself was informed of the method used to obtain the defendants' confessions, and said the prisoners should have known that the black-mass trial was a false one because they were not assigned defence counsel.

A Judicial Commission was sent to investigate and reported in 1949 that the confessions "admittedly" had been obtained by "the use of mock trials in which one or more persons *attired* as American officers pretended to preside as judges and others *attired* in American uniforms pretended to be the prosecutor and defender of the accused." In consequence some of the death sentences were commuted. The chairman of this commission, Justice Gordon Simpson of Texas, told the Senate Subcommittee that the trial procedures followed were "not American" (they certainly were not British) and had been agreed "at the London Four-Power Conference that fixed the terms of the war crimes trials," so that responsibility, once more, goes back to the politicians of London and Washington and the groups which exercised pressure on them. Justice Simpson also testified that the American Army "could not find enough qualified Americans" for these war crimes trials, in which the good name of the West was involved, "and therefore had to draw on some of the German refugees."

This aspect of the trials was further illuminated by an event of January 1953, when two men were arrested by the American military authorities in occupied Vienna on charges of conspiring with a secretary of the Soviet Embassy in Washington to transmit secret American military documents to the Soviet state. They were both Viennese-born Jews who had reached America in 1938 and 1940, at the ages of 16 and 26. In any previous war they would have been kept under observation as "enemy aliens"; under Mr. Roosevelt they had received American army commissions as "friendly aliens." In 1945 they were made "members of the American prosecution team at the war crimes trials." When they were arrested as Communist agents and spies a high official of the American Military Government in Vienna said, "This ties in with information showing that too many of *the Americans* employed at Nuremberg were either Communists or were being used by Communists." He added that "the American prosecution staff at Nuremberg went off in hundreds of directions when the trials were over, many into the American State Department or the United Nations."

At this time the further disclosure was made that in 1949 Mr. John J. McCloy (an American High Commissioner particularly feared by the Germans during the war-crimes trials period) had been given legal briefs "showing that serious errors in translation from German and other languages into English were introduced *into evidence;* these errors, in some cases, were made by persons whose Communist ties have since been proved by loyalty checks." This material has never been made public, but if it should ever be used in an impartial investigation of the trials grave embarrassment for the Western leaders would be caused. At the war's end Communists were everywhere in control of the Nazi concentration camps (as will be shown later in this chapter); in the manner above described they became prosecutors and judges of the very crimes which they had committed!

On both sides of the line vengeance was wreaked in the same spirit. Mongolian soldiers from the East, as they entered Germany, were incited by the recorded voice of Ilya Ehrenburg, from Moscow, to fall in particular on *pregnant* women; what else could the rabid injunction mean, not to spare "even *unborn* Fascists." An American woman living in Berlin, Mrs Frances Faviell, described her horror when she read the diary kept by her housekeeper, Lotte, and its description of "the raping of Lotte and thousands of women, even old women of 65, by the filthy Mongol troops, not once but time after time, women with their children clinging to their skirts ..." The diary recorded "every date and detail, written by the light of Lotte's torch, the murders of those who had tried to protect the old women, the apology of the *Russian* officer who had found the bodies ... his explanation to Lotte that the troops had been given forty- eight hours *Plunderfreiheit* ... It was one of the most horrible documents I had ever read and I felt icy cold as I put it down." *Plunderfreiheit;* loot-liberty! This was the human result of the political arrangement made, to the drinking of forty-five toasts, at Yalta. On the Western side of the line the same vengeance continued. In August 1947 a British M.P., Mr. Nigel Birch, found nearly four thousand Germans still in one concentration camp, held indefinitely without charge or trial. He reported that the first question put to them, if they ultimately came to trial, was always the same: "Did you know *the Jews* were being persecuted?" The story continued in that vein; no other persecution mattered (and at that time legions of human beings had been driven back to the Soviet terror which they tried to escape).

The British and American Governments left the Germans in no doubt as to the nature of the vengeance they were exacting. One of the first acts of the Allied High Commissioners was to enact a law "against anti-semitism." Thus they extended into the West the law which identified the nature of the first Bolshevist administration in Russia, the "law against anti-semitism" introduced on July 27, 1918. Under this British-American edict Germans were being imprisoned and their property confiscated ten years later, in 1955; and in 1956 a Jew from Austria, by that time domiciled in England and a naturalized British subject, brought action against a German under a Western German law (inherited from the Allied High Commissioners) which made it an offence "to utter anti-semitic remarks or be unduly prejudiced against Jews."

These laws prevent public discussion, but cannot suppress thought. Their object, plainly, was to suppress all public enquiry about the nature of the regime, west of the "Iron Curtain" as east of it. The effect was to give *carte blanche* to *Plunderfreiheit* in the Anglo- American zone, too. For instance, the Anglo-American law against anti-semitism explicitly made a criminal offence of public discussion of the following affair, which I quote in the words of the *Jewish Herald* of Johannesburg:

"Philip Auerbach was a man of extraordinarily strong character, courageous in the extreme, burning with Jewish pride and lit up with a sense of *hate* of German Nazism ... He was *ruthless and merciless in the days when the American forces were still haters of Germany and were still ready to do his bidding, to co-operate with him in relieving the Germans of their loot, giving him a virtual carte-blanche for signing documents, for searching, causing arrests and striking terror ... In those days when Philip Auerbach appeared at the head of immense Jewish demonstrations in Germany after the war, the high-ranking American officers usually accompanied him, thereby indicating his authority. With the Jewish flag at the head of these demonstrations, Auerbach would take the salute,* the band playing Hatikvah and the tens of thousands of D.P.'s joining in what was a constant political offensive for opening the gates of Palestine before the restoration of the state … *No one will ever be able to estimate the value in money of assets of all kinds, equipment, clothing, furniture, motor-cars and every variety of commodity which Auerbach helped out of Germany … He wielded a power in Germany only second to that of the military authorities."*

The man described was a private person, and was able to use the armed forces of America for his looting. His crimes were so flagrant that in time Jewish organizations dissociated themselves from him (he robbed Jews and Gentiles impartially), though on grounds of expediency more than morals. Seven years later (1952), when West German political support for "the free world" was becoming important again, he was arrested on charges "embracing interminable lists of goods which had been carried out of Germany *by forged documents, possibly involving also Jewish officers in the American Army and Jewish welfare organizations."*

In 1952 the West German government was being forced to pay "reparations" to the new Zionist state and a full public disclosure of Auerbach's looting activities, conducted with American Army support, would have been embarrassing. Therefore the above-quoted charge was dropped, "no doubt because of repercussions of a political character," as the *Jewish Herald* remarked. Had it been maintained even a bogus case for the payment of German tribute to Zionists from Russia in Palestine would have been hard to make plausible. Consequently Auerbach was tried (with a rabbi) merely on minor counts of embezzling some $700,000 of funds, blackmail, accepting bribes and forging returns. He received thirty months imprisonment and later committed suicide.

The American and British press published brief, unintelligible reports of this affair, with the insinuation that it denoted the revival of "anti-semitism" in Germany. This was the echo of the tone taken in the Jewish press, which after Auerbach's suicide asked "On whose head this blood?," and the like; the suggestion that any conviction of any Jewish defendant on any charge, whether guilty or innocent, was a sign of "anti-semitism" was by then general. The *Jewish Herald,* for instance, considered the charges morally iniquitous because they related to a period when "normal regulations were disregarded by everyone, *above all by Jews,* who *justifiably* ignored *German* considerations of right and wrong." The principles ignored were not German but universal in Christian communities, or had been theretofore. The only protest against these falsifications, seen by me, came from a Jewish correspondent of the *New York Daily News,* who by chance had suffered from Auerbach's crimes; had it come from a German victim, or an American or British eyewitness, I believe no Western newspaper would have printed it.

The Western masses knew nothing of these happenings in British-American-occupied Germany at the time, and might not have objected violently if they had known, for at that period they were still under the influence of wartime propaganda, particularly in the matter of the Nazi concentration camps. They seemed to me completely to have forgotten that the concentration camp was originally a Communist idea, copied by Hitler, and that the further the Red armies were allowed into Europe the more certain its perpetuation became. Their feelings were inflamed by the horrifying news-reel pictures, shown to them on a million screens as the Allied armies entered Germany, of piles of emaciated corpses stacked like firewood in these camps.

I was a member of those audiences and heard the comments around me with misgiving. Wartime propaganda is the most insidious poison known to man, and I believe these picture-goers of 1945, deprived of truthful information for years, had lost all ability, perhaps all desire to judge what they saw. I think most of them thought the human remains they saw were those of Jews, for this was the suggestion hammered into their minds by the press day by day. They constantly read of "Nazi gas chambers for *Jews* … Nazi crematoria for *Jews*," and few of them in later years troubled to read the stories of inmates and find out who these victims truly were. One instance: a German woman who spent five years in Ravensbruck camp (Frau Margaret Bubers Newmann) says the first victims were the *sick or afflicted*, or those *incapable of work*, and the next ones were "*the inferior races*," among whom *the Poles* were placed first, and the Czechs, Balts, Hungarians and others next.

Thus the piles of dead received as little true compassion as the living who were driven back by the Western Allies into the concentration-camp area, and today it may be only a matter of historical interest, pertaining to such a book as this, to show that the "Nazi" concentration camps, at the time when the Anglo-American armies entered Germany, were predominantly under *Communist* control, that Jews were among the tormentors, and that anti-Communism was a surer qualification for the death-chamber than anti-Hitlerism!

Ten years ago this statement (which I substantiate below) would have been sunk by mere weight of derision, if it could have been published at all. Today enough has been revealed about the Illuminist Communist method of infiltrating every class, party, church, organization and institution for some people at least to await the proof with open mind; or so I suppose. Lenin's dictum was that all wars must in their course be turned into revolutionary wars, which means that the members of the conspiracy must fight for the success of the revolution, not for their country's victory. The capture of the concentration camps was more helpful to this strategy than anything else could have been, because the camps were full of people who, if they survived, would have fought Communism, as they fought Hitlerism, to the death. The world has never understood this aspect of the resistance to Hitler, because it never understood Hitler himself. Those who have persisted with this book may see the deep significance of his words to Hermann Rauschning: "I got *illumination and ideas from the Freemasons* that I could never have obtained from other sources" (almost exactly Adam Weishaupt's words)." I have learnt a great deal from Marxism ... The whole of National Socialism is based on it."

The Communists, in their capture of the concentration camps, were aided by the policy of unconditional support of the revolution which the Western leaders pursued; it gave them power and prestige among the captives which they used for their own ends. I was appalled when a young British officer, parachuted into Yugoslavia, described to me the drops of containers filled with golden sovereigns (which a British subject may not legally possess) to Tito.[29] The same thing happened in Greece. Major W. Stanley Moss, dropped into Greek Macedonia as a British commando-leader and liaison officer, found the Communists usurping control of the guerrillas by means of the golden rain that dropped on them and says, "When the Great Day came" (victory in Europe) "the world was amazed at the wealth of gold which the Communists found at their disposal. None of the money came from Russia; *it was presented to the Communists by the Allies.* For years money had been poured into the country for the maintenance of guerrilla forces and the general pursuance of the war, *but the Communists had used only a small proportion of it in the fight against the Germans.* We knew long before the event of the turn the future would take ... *and yet we were unable to do anything to prevent it.*" (Major Moss makes one factual misstatement; "the world" was never "amazed at the wealth of gold" which the Allies had dropped on the Communists, because the world was never informed of it).

The picture was the same in every occupied country. Wing-Commander Yeo-Thomas, sent secretly into France to study the methods and organization of the French resistance movement, vainly warned London: "The avowed aim of the Communist Party was *the mass uprising of Frenchmen on D-Day ... to dominate all others after liberation.* Meanwhile B.B.C. broadcasters *jeered* at Frenchmen who feared the 'Communist bogey.'" The consequences of this were described by Mr. Sisley Huddleston in 1952; during the "liberation" of France the Communists killed in cold blood more than a hundred thousand anti-Communists.

---

[29] Mr. Winston Churchill's efforts to reduce the area of Soviet incursion into Europe, after the fighting, by an invasion from the South which would have given the Western Allies command at least of Austria and Czechoslovakia and very probably of Hungary and the whole of Germany, were weakened by his insistence on setting up Communism in Yugoslavia. That action, for which his Memoirs give no sufficient explanation, also weakens his post-war argument, recalling his vain attempts to gain American support for the blow from the South and maintaining that the outcome of the war would have been different and better had he been heard. His emissary to the Communist leader, Tito, has recorded his own misgiving in this matter and Mr. Churchill's instruction to him: "The less you and I worry about the form of government they set up the better." The effect of Mr. Churchill's actions was to "set up" the Communist form of government and to abandon the anti-Communist leader and British ally, General Mihailovitch, who was later executed by Tito.

In these circumstances it was inevitable that the Communists should come to power in the "Nazi" concentration camps too, so that the Western masses, when they saw the pictures of these camps being "liberated" in fact beheld something which their armies were to make permanent in Europe east of the Elbe line. The truth came out in 1948 but if one in a million of the people who saw those pictures knows of it I shall be surprised.

In that year the revolutionary chieftain in Yugoslavia, the pseudonymous "Marshal Tito," was at odds with the rulers in the Kremlin. This was dangerous for a Communist and he may have thought to protect himself, better than by armed bodyguards, by making public something of what he knew, calculating that Moscow might then leave him alone rather than provoke further revelations. The trial he staged was reported in Yugoslavia and ignored in the West. He had thirteen of his Communist intimates shot (senior governmental and party officials) *for taking part in the mass-murder of captives at the most infamous camp of all, Dachau.*

Truth outs in the strangest ways, though in our age of press-control it does not out very far. In this case the releasing instrument was an elderly Austrian general, Wilhelm Spielfried, who emerged alive from Dachau. He wanted the world to know what had transpired there, and in the confusion attending the breakup of the camp (on the arrival of Western troops) he extracted from the commandant's office a Gestapo card-index recording the people done to death, and the manner, signed by the Gestapo agent responsible in each case.

Among these agents were several of "Marshal Tito's" leading collaborators. In time General Spielfried gained publication for this small section of his material; the remainder still awaits a publisher bold enough to print it.

"Tito" (one Joseph Brosz) had himself been a Kremlin agent from 1934 on. By putting his nearest collaborators on public trial (at Ljubljana on April 20, 1948) he poised the sword of further disclosures over the Kremlin domes. The accused men included Oskar Juranitsch (Secretary General in Tito's Foreign Ministry); Branko Dil (Inspector General of Yugoslav Economy); Stane Oswald (a senior official, with ministerial rank, in the Ministry of Industry); Janko Pufler (head of Tito's State Chemical Trust); Milan Stepischnik (head of Tito's State Metallurgical Institute); Karl Barle (an official with ministerial rank); Professors Boris Kreintz and Miro Koschir of the University of Ljubljana; and other Communist notables. All were former members of the International Brigade in Spain, and agents of the MVD (Soviet secret police).

All made the customary confessions; the defence they advanced is of prior interest. They justified themselves simply by claiming that they had *never killed or injured* a Communist: "I never endangered one *of ours;* I never did anything to a party-comrade." They said they invariably chose for death anyone who could be classified as a Conservative, Liberal, Catholic, Protestant, Orthodox, Jew or Gipsy, *provided* that the victim was not a Communist.

This collaboration in the concentration camps between Hitler's Gestapo and its prototype, Stalin's MVD,[30] came about in the following way. "Anti-Fascist Committees" were formed in the camps. If Hitler and his Gestapo had been genuine in their professions, these committees would obviously have furnished the first victims of the gas-chambers. Instead, they were accepted as representing the camp inmates and were given privileged status, then agreeing to take part in the killings. This was the perfect way of ensuring that anti-Communists should be few in post-war Germany.

In this manner the piles of corpses grew, which the outer world later beheld on screens in darkened rooms. This pictorial journalism fulfilled to the letter Mr. G.K. Chesterton's dictum of many years earlier: "Journalism is a false picture of the world, thrown upon a lighted screen in a darkened room so that the real world is not seen."

The Communist Juranitsch, the chief accused, said, "Yes, I killed hundreds and thousands of people, and took part in the 'scientific experiments'; that was my task in Dachau." Dil explained that his work had been to experiment with "blood-stilling preparations; he had shot the subjects point-blank in the chest for the purpose. Pufler described the injection of selected inmates with malaria bacilli for the purposes of observation, stating that "they died like flies, and we reported to the doctor or SS. officer the results." These confessions were *not* false. They were corroborated and could not be denied, for the reports made were the ones abstracted by General Spielfried from the commandant's office. Pufler explained how these Communist trusties of the Gestapo hid their collaboration from other inmates; when they themselves reappeared from the laboratories and crematoria they told some invented story of a trick or miracle to explain their escape; as none of the victims ever returned, they could not be challenged.

These men ended against a wall, but not for their crimes. They were discarded like pawns by their master in his game against the Kremlin. They

---

[30] In this matter, too, the Western masses were hopelessly misled by years of propaganda, presenting "the Nazis" and "our Soviet allies" as opposites, whereas a close affinity always existed. Mr. Karl Stern, a Jew from Germany who migrated to North America and became a convert to Roman Catholicism, records his own misunderstanding of this, during German days when he was on the staff of a psychiatric institute: "A couple of Nazi doctors held forth on the so-called 'Theory of Permanent Revolution' of Trotzky. This theory was new to me ... but that it should be propounded by these people was something entirely new and quite astonishing ... I said, 'Gentlemen, I understand that you draw a good deal of your theory on political strategy from Trotzky. Does it not strike you as extraordinary that you, Nazis, quote Trotzky, a Bolshevist and a Jew, as if he were your evangelist?' They laughed and looked at me as one would look at a political yokel, which I was ... They belonged to a then quite powerful wing in the Nazi party which was in favour of an alliance of Communist Russia and Nazi Germany against what they called Western Capitalism ... When one was not listening very carefully, one was never quite sure whether they were talking Nazism or Bolshevism, and in the end it did not matter much."

had strictly obeyed the master-tenet of the revolution ("all wars are revolutionary wars") by using the opportunity given to them to destroy political opponents, and not "the enemy." They did, in another form, what the rulers in Moscow did when they massacred the 15,000 Polish officers in Katyn Forest; they attacked the nation-states and laid the foundations for the all-obliterating revolution.

The revelations of the Ljubljana trial have received corroboration, in various points, from many books of survivors from the concentration camps. Mr. Odo Nansen, son of the famous Norwegian explorer, wrote of his experience in the Sachsenhausen camp, eighteen months before the war ended:

It's extraordinary how the Communists have managed things here; they have all the power in camp next to the SS., and they attract all the other Communists, from other countries, and place them in key positions ... Many of the Norwegian prisoners here have turned Communist. Besides all the immediate *advantages* it offers, most likely they expect Russia to be the big noise after the war, and then I suppose they think it may be handy to have one's colour right. Last night I was talking to our *Blockaeltester*, a Communist. When he and his mates came into power, there would be not merely retaliation but even more brutality and greater cruelty than the SS. uses to us. I could make no headway with my humanism against that icy block of hate and vengefulness, that hardboiled, hidebound focussing on a new dictatorship."

Wing Commander Yeo-Thomas, who was parachuted into France to help the French resistance, was captured and taken to Buchenwald. He was told on arrival by a British officer already there: "Don't let on that you are officers, and if any of you held any executive position in peacetime keep it to yourselves. The internal administration of the camp is *in the hands of Communists*... Buchenwald is the worst camp in Germany; your chances of survival are practically nil." Wing Commander Yeo-Thomas says, "The three chief internal administrators of the camp, called *Lageraeltester*, were Communists." Under the supervision of these men, "prisoners were inoculated with typhus and other germs and their reactions, almost always ending in death, under the various vaccines, studied." Only three of this officer's group of thirty-seven captives survived, the others being hanged on hooks in the crematorium wall and slowly strangled to death. The three survivors "had to fear their fellow-prisoners almost as much as they had *formerly* feared the Germans; for the *Communists*, if they learned that officers had managed to cheat the gallows, would certainly denounce them." Communists ran these camps, tortured and murdered the victims. If there was any difference between them and the Gestapo jailers it was only that they were more villainous, because they denounced and killed men who were supposed to be their comrades in battle against a common foe. As the

Eastern Jews, in particular, play so large a part in Communism, Jews logically appear among the persons implicated in these deeds. That is not in itself surprising at all, for Jews, like all other men, are good and bad, cruel or humane; but it was kept hidden from the public masses, who received a picture of torture-camps inhabited almost entirely by Jews, tormented by depraved "Nazi" captors. In fact, the Jews formed a small proportion of the entire camp-population; the tormentors in the last three years of the war were largely Communists, whose motives have been shown; and among these tormentors were Jews.

My files include a number of reports from *Jewish* newspapers of "trials" of Jews denounced by former Jewish inmates of the Auschwitz, Vlanow, Muhldorf and other camps.

I have given the word "trials" in inverted commas in this case, for a good reason. These "trials," with one exception, were held before *rabbinical* courts, in Western countries and before magistrates' courts in Tel Aviv. They were treated as Jewish affairs, of no concern to other mankind, and if any sentences were passed they were not recorded in any journal seen by me, though the deeds charged resembled those of the Ljubljana trial. The implication was plainly that, if any such deeds were committed, they had to be judged under the Jewish law, if at all, and that Gentile law had no writ. (This indeed appears nowadays to be the governing assumption since Zionism recreated the "Jewish nation" and it is reflected in a report published in the *Zionist Record* during 1950, which stated that the function of the "chief Public Relations Office of the Executive Council of Australian Jewry" was to "screen from public view the misdemeanours of individual Jews who commit some minor *or major* indiscretion." The screening here mentioned goes on at all times and in all countries of the West).

At Tel Aviv a Jewish doctor and two Jewish women were accused by Jewish witnesses of administering lethal injections to prisoners at Auschwitz, mutilating sexual organs, carrying out "scientific experiments," sending victims to the death chambers. In another case at Tel Aviv in 1951 a Jewish doctor (then employed in the Tel Aviv municipal hospital) was accused by several Jewish witnesses of brutal acts committed at Vlanow camp, where he had acted as "assistant to the German camp commandant." A Jewish woman witness said he had beaten her unconscious and when she recovered she found her three sons, aged 12, 15 and 18, shot dead; a fortnight earlier, she said, she had seen the accused give order to the Ukrainian camp police to take away thirty prisoners, including her husband, who were then shot. The bare heads of these two cases were reported but, as I say, if any result was published it escaped my research,

In New York a Jewish board of three members (the composition laid down by the Levitical Law) heard charges by a Jew against a synagogue official whom he accused of killing an inmate at Muhldorf, where he was a block warden. The report stated that the board would send its findings "to the Jewish community" in the accused's town "without recommendations or sanctions," which meant that, if he were a "war criminal," he would be left to his congregation to deal with. In all these cases it was implicit that only charges of maltreating *other Jews* came under consideration, and that if the persons accused had committed similar acts against non-Jewish captives these would not have formed part of the case.

Of a different kind but the same basic nature was a case heard before an Israeli district court in 1954-1955. A Jew from Hungary distributed a pamphlet alleging that one Dr. Israel Kastner, a high Israeli Government official and a leading candidate (at the 1955 election) of the government majority-party, in Hungary during the war had collaborated with the Nazis, prepared the ground for the murder of Jews, saved a Nazi war criminal from punishment, and so on. Dr. Kastner brought suit for criminal libel against his accuser, and the Israeli judge after nine months handed down a judgment stating that the charges had been substantiated. This judgment said that Dr. Kastner was a collaborator "in the fullest sense of the word" and had "sold his soul to the devil," and the Israeli Premier at that time, Mr. Moshe Sharett, commented, "A man is justified in taking any action, even in selling his soul to the devil, in order to save Jews" (the accusation was that he *betrayed* Jews to the Nazis). The *Government* then announced that it would appeal the judgment, through its Attorney General, and I could never learn what transpired, if anything.

Thus, while much was heard of "war criminals" and their trials, these Jewish "war criminals" appeared only before Jewish tribunals and if they were punished, the world was not told. I know of only one case (others may have escaped my notice) where such Jews were included in a "war criminals trial." The *Jewish Telegraph Agency* (May 8, 1946) reported, "The verdict in the trial of 23 guards at the Breendouck concentration camp at Antwerp, one of the lesser-known Nazi hells, was announced here yesterday. Among the guards are 3 Jews, Walter Obler, Leo Schmandt and Sally Lewin. Obler and Lewin have been sentenced to death and Schmandt to 15 years imprisonment."

Mr, Joseph Leftwich, in his discussion of "anti-Semitism" with Mr. A.K. Chesterton, asked of this trial, "What does it prove? That the human beast is found everywhere, and that Jews are no more immune than any other human group." That is correct but beside the point of this argument, which is that the mass-mind, during the Second War, was given the false picture of a solely Jewish persecution conducted by non-Jews and that events in the world in this century are consistently so misrepresented, to the general misfortune.

The chapter of Hitler's Jewish helpers was not a small one. Lord Templewood, British Ambassador to Spain during the war, says, "For month after month General Franco" (himself of Jewish origin) "allowed the Spanish press to act as the loudest possible speaker for German propaganda. None of the well-established papers were permitted any liberty of action. Each alike had to re-echo his master's voice. In this case the master was a very sinister Eastern Jew, Lazare by name … In Vienna he faithfully served Hitler as a fanatical propagandist in support of the Anschluss. Since then he had become an important figure in the Nazi world … From the German Embassy, where he had more authority than the Ambassador himself, he daily directed not only the general course of the Spanish press, but even the actual words of the news and articles. His subordinates had their desks in the Spanish offices and not a word reached the Spanish public that had not been subject to his sinister approval. By a cunning mixture of brutal dictation and unabashed corruption, he succeeded in making the Spanish papers even more venomous than the papers actually published in Germany."

I knew this Lazare, a conspirator of the suave, smiling and debonair type, and through him first became aware of the Jewish element among Hitler's higher initiates. When I met Lazare, in 1937, he was "Press Secretary" of the Austrian Legation in the Rumanian capital, Bucharest. Austria, then my headquarters, was living in daily fear of the Nazi invasion which came in 1938, and its official representatives abroad were by all presumed to be staunch Austrians and stout anti-Nazis; in the case of Jews this appeared to be doubly sure. I was struck first by the fact that impoverished little Austria could even afford the luxury of a "Press Secretary" in a Balkan capital and next by Lazare's lavish style of life and entertainment. I assumed that, like many men on this fringe of diplomatic life ("press secretaryships" in the Balkans were somewhat dubious) he was "doing well on the side," which in Bucharest was not unusual.

He was; though not through the deals in furs or carpets which I vaguely suspected. His affluence, as events soon showed, came from a political source, the Nazi one. When Hitler marched into Austria the newspapermen of the world were summoned to a press conference at the historic Ballhausplatz to hear the Nazi version of this event. The door opened to admit the spokesman of the new regime, Hitler's "Press Chief" in captive Austria, the apologist (or propagandist) for the annexation. It was Herr Lazare, the "Austrian" (he was born a Turkish subject). He saw me at once and a quick smile flashed from the brazen face of guilt; waving his hand gaily to me, he said "Hullo, Mr. Reed, nice to meet you again." Then he explained the Fuehrer's benevolent motives for the invasion, and its beneficent effects for Germany, Austria and mankind,"

The reader may see that "the real world" is very different from "the false picture" which the masses receive, especially in wartime, when such men as this control the flow of information into the mass-mind.

Against this background, the vengeance raged and reached its Talmudic climax in two symbolical movements of people, one eastward and one westward. From the "free world" escaped fugitives were driven back by the

Allied armies into Communist slavery; from the Communist area (where a man may not even leave his town without police permission) a great mass of Eastern Jews freely emerged and was ushered, beneath an Allied umbrella, through Europe towards Palestine. This two-way process gave the vengeance its final stamp of identity and may be studied in the following quotations:

The *Saturday Evening Post* of April 11, 1953, said, "With this shameful agreement" (Yalta) "as their authority Soviet MVD agents strode through the displaced-persons camps after the war and put the finger on thousands who had managed to escape the Soviet tyranny. These miserable victims were herded into boxcars and driven back to death, torture or the slow murder of the Siberian mines and forests. Many killed themselves on the way. Also under a Yalta agreement, the Soviet was permitted to use German prisoners in forced labour in 'reparations account.' For such inhumanities there is no excuse."

Miss Kathryn Hulme, a Californian, was deputy director (1945-1951) of a refugee camp at Wildflecken in Bavaria, administered by the organization known as UNRRA (United Nations Relief and Rehabilitation Administration). She writes in her book, "Londa" (a colleague) "had been assigned for a time to a southern camp when its Russian refugees, mainly prisoners of war, had been sent back to Russia under terms of the Yalta Agreement. She told us how the Russian prisoners of war had slashed their wrists, stripped naked and hanged themselves. Even after every destructive object was taken from them they still found ways to suicide. She could never understand how Stalin had sold his idea to Roosevelt and Churchill that there had been no Russian prisoners of war taken by the Germans, only deserters."

Now the opposite side of the picture: the treatment given to *one* group of people "singled out" from the entire mass of Hitler's victims and Stalin's captives. Miss Hulme says, "… and then the Jews came. We had never had a Jewish camp in our northern area … The Jews numbered *less than one-fifth* of our Zone's total DP [displaced person, ed.] population but they were such an articulate minority that *if you only read the newspapers to learn about Occupation affairs, you gained the impression that they were the whole of the DP problem* … You had to handle them with kid gloves, it was said, especially when transferring them from one camp to another, and heaven help the IRO worker who left a loop of barbed wire visible in any camp to which they were to be transferred. They were classified 'persecutees,' *the only DP's except medical cases who got a special food ration because of a non-worker status* …There was a small German community set down on the highway that divided the two halves of the camp. The Jewish delegates … said this was the most dangerous feature of all; the IRO must agree *to arm their Jewish police* to protect their people from these Germans living in their midst … That nearly every German in that village would be cheerfully in the employ of the Jews within a fortnight after their arrival never even entered my head as I soothingly promised to plead for authorization to arm a

DP police ... The Jewish DP police were in woolly green tunics, with the Star of David on their caps ... Nothing had been left to chance or last-minute improvization ... Their welfare office was hung with martial posters *depicting young Jewish girls in trenches hurling grenades at Arabs.* The Jewish DP police practised marksmanship with the carbines we had secured for them as 'defence' against the Germans who were now gainfully employed in the heavy manual labour of the camp. The Jewish workshops swung into swift production of fine woollen greatcoats and stout leather shoes heavily hob-nobbed for rough terrain. We could only guess that this too was all for Israel and, through some mysterious channels, was ultimately delivered there; we never saw any of our Jewish DP's wearing the useful clothing ... Over all the ferment and frenzy flapped a flag we had never seen before, pale blue stripes on a white ground with the Star of David."

Miss Hulme describes the Jewish camp: "We showed off the big camp which we were making ready for them like rental agents proud of an accommodation that was without doubt the handsomest DP housing in all Bavaria ... The rabbis shook their heads; it didn't seem to be good enough." She explains that the American DP Act, subsequently passed, was full of traps which debarred the ordinary DP; "only the Jews, who could claim and prove persecution in any Eastern European country in which they had set foot, could get out of that trap." She records that American semi-governmental or officially supported organizations supplied the machinery and other workshops, the materials, and the "special food reinforcements" which were given only to Jews.

The means by which this privileged class was established in the camps of misery were described by Lieut.-Col. Judah Nadich in the South African *Jewish Times* (February 4, 1949). Rabbi Nadich was "Jewish adviser to General Eisenhower with the U.S. forces in Europe, and worked closely with him in matters relating to DP and other Jewish problems." He says, "To Eisenhower's credit it should be said that when the appalling conditions in the DP camps were brought to his attention" (in 1945) "he moved quickly to improve conditions. Important directives were issued, increasing the food ration *for the persecuted, as distinct from other DP's;* special camps were set up for Jews; Jewish DP's living outside camps *were given preferential treatment;* an adviser on Jewish affairs was appointed and full co-operation was granted to the Joint Distribution Committee and later to the Jewish Agency. Few if any of these conditions were granted by Montgomery in the British zone, and a constant stream of Jewish DP's flowed into the American zone. Eisenhower made frequent visits to the camps for inspection purposes and his personal visits lifted the morale of the DP's *and served to remind officers on lower levels of the attitude of their Commander-in-Chief. Officers at fault were censured, including one of the highest ranking generals."*

General Eisenhower's "attitude," according to this authoritative account, was that the Jews were to be treated as a privileged class. If he accepted the advice of his Jewish adviser this was natural, for Rabbi Nadich, as will be seen, claimed that the few Jews among every hundred DP's were the only "persecuted" and in this were "distinct from other DP's." The statement reveals the function of that now established figure of our times, the Jewish adviser.

Thus by 1945 only "the persecution of Jews" remained of Hitler's all-embracing "persecution of political opponents" begun in 1933. Propaganda had eliminated all but this one small section; the last quotation shows, why Miss Hulme, from her DP camp, wrote that "if you only read the newspapers ... you gained the impression that the Jews were the whole of the DP problem." While the huge mass of sufferers was forgotten or driven back to the persecution from which some had escaped, this one group, under the protection and escort of the West, was clothed, supplied, equipped, armed and conducted towards its invasion of a small country in Arabia.

The Asiatic East supplied these invaders; the Christian West convoyed them. In this undertaking there was no difference at all between "the free world" and the enslaved world behind "the Iron Curtain"; on the contrary, there was identity of purpose and synchronization in its execution. A directing intelligence was obviously at work which cared nothing for nation-states and frontiers, for wartime friend or wartime foe, or for any of the "principles" so often proclaimed by the premier-dictators. The West shared the vengeance with the East, but the *pattern* was set by the East, and it was the same pattern that had showed in Russia in 1917, in the Protocols of 1905 and in the revolutions of 1848. Therefore the authors of the vengeance of 1945 must be sought in the revolutionary area, and for this reason the nature of the revolution in 1945 may be examined, to discover whether it, and its leadership, had changed from 1917 (when it was ninety percent Jewish) and 1848 (when Disraeli said it was led by Jews).

Research into the events of the three decades 1917 -1945 leads to the conclusion that by 1945 the revolution had for a hundred years been a Jewish-controlled revolution, for that space of time having passed since Disraeli first identified the nature of the leadership. I use the words "Jewish-controlled revolution" to denote a movement under the direction of the Talmudic rabbinate in the East, *not* a movement generally supported by Jews; as I have repeatedly shown, the staunchest opposition came from those Western Jews who were furthest from the reach of the Talmudic directorate. The distinction is that which the careful student must make between "National Socialism" and "Germans," between "Communism" and "Russians."

In the sense of that definition, the revolution, in my judgment, continued through the thirty years that followed 1917 to be Jewish. The Jewish nature of the first Bolshevist governments and of their deeds was earlier shown. The same characteristics appeared in the two short-lived offshoot governments which the Bolshevists set up in 1919, in Bavaria and Hungary. In both cases the terrorists were, in the main, imported into these countries in the guise of returning "prisoners of war," and had been trained as Communist agitators in Russia. In Germany the Communist movement then was headed by the "Spartacus League" ("Spartacus" was Adam Weishaupt's code-name), the leaders of which were nearly all Jews: Rosa Luxembourg, Leo Jogiches (from Poland), Paul Lévi, Eugene Levine (from Russia), and Karl Liebknecht. Thus the Bolshevist Government of Bavaria (which counted one Adolf Hitler among its soldiers) logically proved to be headed by Jews: Kurt Eisner, Ernst Toller and Eugene Levine.

In Hungary the chief terrorist leaders were all Jews trained in Russia: Matyas Rakosi, Bela Kun, Erno Geroe and Tibor Szamuely. The ostentatiously anti-Christian acts of this regime again showed its underlying purpose. Of this government the historian of the Communist International, Herr F. Borkenau, says, "Most of the Bolshevik and left Socialist leaders and a considerable percentage of their executive staff had been Jews ... anti-semitism was therefore the natural form of reaction against Bolshevism." In this typical passage the reader may see that "reaction against Bolshevism" is classified as "anti-semitism"; clearly the epithet could only be escaped by *not* "reacting against Bolshevism."

The following ten years were inactive ones and the matter can next be tested in Spain, where the revolution made its bid in 1931. It was directed by emissaries from Moscow, many of them Jews, and this accounted for the disillusionment of many ardent republicans, Spanish and foreign; for instance, many of the clergy and Catholic laity voted for the republic, then finding that the reforming impulse, once more, was perverted into an attack on the Christian *faith*, as such. Churches, monasteries and any building carrying the Cross were destroyed, priests and nuns murdered; the specific mark of identification again appeared, seen in similar acts in Bavaria, Hungary, Russia, France and England.

Fatherhood of the attack on Christianity in Spain was formally proclaimed by the official organ of the Komintern: "*the flames ascending from the burning churches and monasteries of* Spain have shown *the true character* of the Spanish revolution"; the pedigree was traced through one more generation. Ecclesiastical property was confiscated, but the Spanish masses were not enriched thereby; the gold reserve of the Bank of Spain (about 700 million dollars) was transferred to Moscow by the last Republican premier, one Juan Negrin (as related by General Walter Krivitsky). The revulsion of those Spaniards who had hoped to set up a constitutional republic, and found themselves under an alien, anti-Christian tyranny, was inflamed by the murder of the monarchist leader, Calva Sotelo, in 1936, and in the sequence Spain "spewed out" the revolution (as every country has done where the Red Army, with its "political commissars," could not enter to establish it).

Leading Zionist and anti-Zionist Jews in America alike, implicitly or explicitly, attributed Jewish authorship to the revolution in Spain.

Mr. Justice Brandeis, at the time when efforts were being made to reach an accommodation with Hitler in the question of the Jews, strongly opposed them and imperiously told Rabbi Stephen Wise: "Let Germany *share the fate of Spain.*" Mr. Bernard J. Brown wrote, "… the Jews were as responsible for the establishment of a republic in Spain *and the overthrow of the authority of the church* in that country as in any other country where freedom reigns."

During these two decades (that is, the period between the First and Second Wars) Jewish heads became ever fewer among the row that dotted the Kremlin wall on great occasions (when, alone, the imprisoned Russian masses saw their rulers; even the tumultuous cheers came from disks played through loudspeakers). Jews appeared, too, in the dock at great show trials, or disappeared from the political scene without explanation. No substantial diminution in Jewish control or direction of the revolution seems to have occurred during that period, to judge by the following figures:

In 1920 official Bolshevik statements showed that 545 members of the chief ruling bodies included 447 Jews. In 1933 the American Jewish journal *Opinion* stated that Jews occupied almost all important ambassadorial posts and that in White Russia 61 percent of all officials were Jews; it also stated that the Jewish percentage of the population (then given as 158,400,000) was "less than 2 percent." If this was true it meant that Russia at that time contained less than 3,000,000 Jews. In 1933 the *Jewish Chronicle* stated that one-third of the Jews in Russia had become officials. If this was the case, they plainly formed the new governing class.

At that time the nature of the *teaching* had not been modified at all. The Commissar for Public Instruction, Lunatscharsky, was one of the few *Russians* in high office but he spoke like a Talmudist: "*We hate Christianity and Christians; even the best of them must be looked upon as our worst neighbours. They preach the love of our neighbours and mercy, which is contrary to our principles. Down with the love of our neighbour; what we want is hatred. We must learn how to hate and it is only then that we shall conquer the world.*" This is but one specimen of an entire literature of that period, and the only original source for such ideas, known to me, is the Talmud, which itself is the continuation of an ancient, savage, pre-Christian idea, and contains such precepts as "You are human beings but the nations of the earth are not human beings but beasts." Presumably Lunatscharsky qualified by such orations for his choice as Ambassador to Spain during the revolutionary attempt there.

In 1935 I went to Moscow for the London *Times*, accompanying Mr. Anthony Eden. He was the first British Minister to visit the revolutionary capital. *The Times* had previously refused to send a correspondent, so that I was its first representative to appear there after Mr. Robert Wilton, whose story I earlier told. The fifteen-year vacuum had been filled by a correspondent residing in Riga, Latvia, Mr. R.O.G. Urch, who was the object of constant defamation behind the scenes. I knew of this but, being callow in these affairs, did not then understand its significance.

I was at once struck by something I had never met in any other country. My first report said that Mr. Eden drove from the station through streets lined with "drab and silent crowds" and a Jewish censor demanded excision of these words. At first I thought this merely fatuous (I asked if he wished me to say that the throng was composed of top-hatted *bourgeois)* but in following days I saw more and in my book of 1938 wrote:

"The censorship department, and that means the whole machine for controlling the game and muzzling the foreign press, was entirely staffed by Jews, and this was a thing that puzzled me more than anything else in Moscow. There seemed not to be a single non-Jewish official in the whole outfit ... I was told that the proportion of Jews in the government was small, but in this one department that I got to know intimately they seemed to have a monopoly, and I asked myself, where were the *Russians?* The answer seemed to be that they were in the drab, silent crowds which I had seen but which must not be heard of."

I soon learned from older hands that "the proportion of Jews in the government" was in effect not small but that they retained a large measure of control, if they were not predominantly in control. I was unable to meet any Russians in Moscow, this was the other side of the same unique experience. I had never before beheld a ruling caste so completely segregated from the slave-mass.

At the time of this visit to Moscow I had no cause to look for a predominance of Jews; the thing forced itself on my notice. I had hardly begun to think about "the Jewish question" in 1935. The impression I have recorded above was the first one of a trained observer who had never before seen Moscow or Russia. I find it confirmed by an equally experienced man who lived there for twelve years, from 1922 to 1934. Mr. William Henry Chamberlain's book remains today authoritative about that period. He wrote, "Considerable number of Jews have made careers in the Soviet bureaucracy. Of perhaps a dozen officials whom I knew in the Press Department or the Commissariat for Foreign Affairs I recall only one who was not a Jew. Indeed, the predominance of Jews in this Commissariat at the time of my stay in Russia was almost ludicrous; the Russians were mainly represented by the grizzled doorkeeper and the unkempt old women who carried around tea. One also found many Jews in the Gay-Pay-Oo," (Secret Police) "in the Communist International and in departments connected with trade and finance."

Mr. Chamberlain reaches a different conclusion from mine about the original cause of this effect. He says, "After I left Russia I sometimes received letters inquiring as to 'what the Jews were doing under the Soviet regime,' implying that the Jews were acting *as a solid compact* body and that the whole Revolution was a Jewish conspiracy. There is not the slightest historical warrant for such an assumption … No theory that the Jews as a racial bloc worked for the triumph of Bolshevism will stand serious historical analysis." Two things are confused in this dictum: the directing force of Jewry and the entire body of people called "Jews." Neither the Germans nor the Russians, as "a racial bloc," worked for "the triumph" of National Socialism or Communism, but each got it. Masses and mobs never consciously "work for" the triumph of anything; they are pushed around by whatever highly-organized group obtains power over them. The "solid compact body" of workers never "works for" a general strike, but general strikes are proclaimed in their name. This book has shown throughout that the staunchest opposition to Zionism, for instance, came from Jews, but today the "racial bloc" has had Zionism thrust on it like a straitjacket. In my opinion the directing force of the revolution was from 1848 onward demonstrably that of the Talmudic rabbinate in the East, and in *that* sense "the revolution" was "a Jewish conspiracy."

In Moscow in 1935 I came to know some of the Jewish oligarchs. One was the portly Maxim Litvinoff, a most typical figure of the Romanisches Café or the Café Royal, become a grandee of the revolution. Another was Oumansky, a smooth, smiling and deadly young man who came (I think) from Rumania but could not have been more un-Russian if he had been born in Africa. I felt as if I travelled through Russia (like Lenin towards it) in a sealed train.

In 1937 the state of affairs, I believe, had not much changed. Mr. A. Stolypine (whose father, the last of the persevering emancipators, had been assassinated in 1911) wrote that the substitution of Russians or others for Jews "on the highest rungs of the Soviet official ladder" was patently a tactical move and that the Jews "still have in their hands the *principle levers of control; the day they are obliged to give them up the Marxist edifice will collapse like a house of cards.*" He enumerated the high offices still occupied by Jews and in particular pointed out that the key-positions of real control, *through terror,* all remained in Jewish hands. These were the concentration and slave-labour camps (controlled by a Jewish triumvirate; they contained perhaps seven million Russians); the prisons (all Soviet prisoners were governed by a Jewish commissar); the entire news-publication-and-distribution machinery, including the censorship; and the essentially Talmudic system of "political commissars," through which the armed forces were kept under terrorist discipline.

In 1938 a Mr. Butenko, who held a lower-rank post in the Soviet diplomatic service, fled to Italy rather than obey an order of recall from Bucharest to Moscow. He stated in the *Giornale d'Italia* that the new ruling class in his country was almost exclusively Jewish. Particularly in the Ukraine, the entire administration and all industry were in such hands, and this was a policy deliberately followed by Moscow.

Thus the identity of the managers of the revolution did not change substantially between 1917 and 1939; they withdrew from most of the frontal places but retained the true "levers of control." Then the fog of war came down and the next point in time at which the matter may be tested is the closing period and aftermath of the Second War, 1945 and the following years.

Before the Second War even began the "war aims" of the revolution were publicly stated by Stalin at the Third Komintern Congress in Moscow in May 1938:

"The *revival of revolutionary action* on any scale sufficiently vast will not be possible unless we succeed in utilizing the existing disagreements between the capitalistic countries, *so as to precipitate them against each other into armed conflict …* *All war* truly generalized should terminate automatically by revolution. The essential work of our party comrades in foreign countries consists, then, *in facilitating the provocation of such a conflict.*"

The reader will observe that this is the sole statement of "war aims" which was undeviatingly pursued through the ensuing conflict, successfully "provoked" by the Hitler-Stalin pact. The Western leaders, by defaulting on their own earlier-declared "war aims" and abandoning half of Europe to the revolution, ensured the accomplishment of the "war aims" above stated in that area.

What "managers," then, did the revolution impose on the Eastern European countries thus left prey to it in 1945? Here once more the opportunity offers to test the identity of the directing force behind the revolution. The choice was free; the revolution had no *need* to impose Jewish governments on the dozen countries abandoned to it unless this was its deliberate policy.

In communized Poland the United States Ambassador, Mr. Arthur Bliss Lane, saw and recorded the prevalence of Jews, many of them alien, in the key-posts of terrorism. Major Tufton Beamish, a Member of the British Parliament, wrote, "Many of the most powerful Communists in Eastern Europe are Jews … I have been surprised and shocked to discover the large proportion of Jews to be found in the ranks of the Secret Police forces."

To communized Hungary the terrorist of 1919 Matyas Rakosi (born Roth, in Yugoslavia) returned as Premier in 1945, and on this occasion had the Red Army to keep him in that office. *Eight years later* (1953) the Associated Press reported that "90 percent of the high officials in the Hungarian

Communist regime are Jews, including Premier Matyas Rakosi"; the London *Times* in that year said Mr. Rakosi's cabinet was "predominantly Jewish"; *Time* magazine of New York spoke of "the strongly Jewish (90 percent in the top echelons) government of Communist Premier Matyas Rakosi, who is himself a Jew." In Hungary, as in the other communized countries, the specific attack on Christianity began at once with the imprisonment of high ecclesiastics. The case which attracted most attention in the outer world was that of the Hungarian Cardinal Mindszenty, imprisoned on charges of treason. The Source of this deed was indicated by a statement addressed to the Jews of the world in 1949 by "the Central Board of Jews in Hungary, the Hungarian Zionist Organizatian and the Hungarian Section of the World Jewish Congress" which said, "It is with great relief that the Hungarian Jews received the news of Cardinal Mindszenty's arrest. With this action the Hungarian Government has sent the head of a pogrom- clique ... to his well-deserved place."

Of communized Czechoslovakia the London *New Statesman* (a trustworthy authority in such questions) wrote *seven years after the war's end*, "In Czechoslovakia, as elsewhere in Central and South-Eastern Europe, both the party intellectuals and *the key men in the secret police* are largely Jewish in origin." Of Rumania the *New York Herald-Tribune* reported in 1953, eight years after the war's end, "Rumania, together with Hungary, has probably the greatest number of Jews in the administration."

In Rumania the terror raged under Ana Pauker, a Jewess, whose father, a rabbi, and brother were in Israel. This is an interesting case of the dissension in a Jewish family described by Dr. Weizmann in his account of his boyhood in Russia, where Jewish households were split between "revolutionary" Communism" and "revolutionary-Zionism," and only in that question. Mrs Pauker used her office to enable her father to leave Rumania for Israel, although (as her brother said) "it is party policy to keep the Jews in Rumania."

The part played by, and evidently given with considered intention to women in the revolution, since the days of the beldames who knitted around the guillotine, is of particular interest to the student who cares to trace comparisons between the methods of the revolution and the customs of savage African tribes. In communized East Germany the reign of terror was presided over by one Frau Hilde Benjamin, who was first made vice-president of the Supreme Court there and then Minister of Justice. "Red Hilde" is frequently described as a Jewess in the press and her atrocious regime is beyond dispute, even the London *Times* having gone so far as to call her "the dreaded Frau Benjamin." In two years nearly 200,000 East Germans were convicted under her direction for "political crimes" and she presided over several Soviet-model "show trials" of people charged with such offences as belonging to the sect of Jehovah's Witnesses.

Communized Eastern Germany contained 17,313,700 people according to the 1946 census, and among these are only between 2,000 and 4,000 Jews, if Jewish "estimates" are correct. Of this tiny minority the Johannesburg *Zionist Record* in 1950 reported that "life in the Eastern Zone has brought changes for the better. Not a few of them today occupy high positions in the Government and Administration, positions which no Jew had ever before held in Germany and which, despite all talk of democracy, they cannot even today hold in Western Germany. Several Jews hold important posts in the Ministries of Information, Industry and Justice. The Supreme Judge in the Eastern sector of Berlin is a Jew, and so are several senior judges in the provinces outside Berlin. In the press, too, as well as in the theatre, quite a considerable number of Jews have been given responsible positions."

Even four thousand Jews presumably could not occupy all those high places and the same journal in another issue said, "When the Russian occupation authorities were established shortly after the end of the war, there were many Jews occupying *key* positions and holding high ranks in the Soviet administration. They included Jews *who had lived in Russia* ... and who came to Germany and Austria in the ranks of the Red Army, and Jews from areas annexed by Russia in the last ten years, the Baltic states Latvia and Lithuania."

This brings the story nearly down to our present day and what remains will be discussed in a concluding chapter. When the revolution spread outward into the area abandoned to it by the West in 1945 the history of 1917-1918 in Russia was repeated. A Talmudic vengeance was wreaked and Jewish governments were with obvious intent set up everywhere. There was no great change in that state of affairs, either real or apparent, for another eight years. What was done reaffirmed once more the nature of the revolution and of its directing force and Talmudic purpose.

Chapter 43

THE ZIONIST STATE (1)

The revolution, having spread into the half of Europe held clear for it by the Western Allies, did one more thing: in the manner of a serpent striking, it thrust out a tongue that reached to the southern shores of Europe, across the Mediterranean and into the tiny land called Palestine. The money, equipment, escort and convoy were provided by the West, but the revolution supplied the two indispensable constituents of the Zionist State: *the people* to invade it and *the arms* which made its conquest certain.

The West connived, but the Zionist state in the last analysis was the creation of the revolution, which in this manner fulfilled the Levitical doctrine of "the return." These incursions into Europe and into Arabia were the sole "territorial gains" reaped from the Second War, in the early stages of which the Western "premier-dictators" for a second time had publicly renounced all thought of territorial gain. The result of these two developments was to leave, in bisected Europe and bisected Palestine, two permanent detonation point s of new war, which at any moment could be set off by any who might think to further their ambitions by a third war. The reader will recall that in the years preceding the Second War Zionism was in collapse in Palestine; and that the British Parliament in 1939, having been forced by twenty years of experience to realize that the "Jewish National Home" was impossible to realize, had decided to abandon the unworkable "Mandate" and to withdraw after ensuring the parliamentary representation of *all* parties in the land, Arab, Jews and others. The reader then beheld the change which came about when Mr. Churchill became Prime Minister in 1940 and privately informed Dr. Weizmann (according to Dr. Weizmann's account, which has not been challenged) that he "quite agreed" with the Zionist ambition "after the war … to build up a state of three or four million Jews in Palestine."

Mr. Churchill always expressed great respect for parliamentary government but in this case, as a wartime potentate, he privily and arbitrarily overrode a policy approved, after full debate, by the House of Commons. After that, the reader followed Dr. Weizmann in his journeys to America and saw how Mr. Churchill's efforts "to arm the Jews" (in which he was opposed by the responsible administrators on the spot) received support from there under the "pressure" of Dr. Weizmann and his associates.

That was the point at which the reader last saw the Zionist state in gestation. Throughout 1944, as Mr. Churchill records in his war memoirs, he continued to press the Zionist ambition. "It is well known I am determined not to break the pledges of the British Government to the Zionists expressed in the Balfour Declaration, as modified by my subsequent statement at the

Colonial Office in 1921. *No change can be made in policy* without full discussion in Cabinet" (June 29, 1944). The policy *had* been changed after full discussion in Cabinet and Parliament, in 1939. Here Mr. Churchill simply ignored that major decision on policy and reverted to the earlier one, echoing the strange words of another Colonial Secretary (Mr. Leopold Amery, earlier quoted) that this policy *could not change*.

Again, "There is no doubt that this" (the treatment of Jews in Hungary) "is probably the greatest and most horrible crime ever committed in the whole history of the world ... all concerned in *this* crime who may fall into our hands, including the people who only obeyed orders by carrying out the butcheries, *should be put to death* after their association with the murders has been proved ... Declarations should be made in public, so that everyone connected with it will be hunted down and put to death" (July 11, 1944). Here Mr. Churchill, like President Roosevelt and Mr. Eden, implicitly links the execution of captives *solely* with their crimes against Jews, thus relegating all other sufferers to the oblivion in to which, in fact, they fell. Incidentally, the reader saw in the last chapter that Jews were among the tormentors, as well as among the victims.

To continue: "I am anxious to reply *promptly* to Dr. Weizmann's request for the formation of a Jewish fighting force put forward in his letter of July 4" (July 12, 1944). "I like the idea of the Jews trying to get at the murderers of their fellow-countrymen in Central Europe and I think it would give a great deal of satisfaction in the United States. I believe it is the wish of the Jews themselves to fight the Germans everywhere. It is with the Germans they have their quarrel" (July 26, 1944). If Mr. Churchill, as stated by Dr. Weizmann, had agreed to the building up "of a state of three or four million Jews in Palestine," he must have known that the Zionists had a much larger quarrel with the population of Arabia, and that any "Jewish fighting force" would be more likely to fall on these innocent third parties than on the Germans.

Mr. Churchill's last recorded allusion (as wartime prime minister) came after the fighting in Europe ended: "The whole question of Palestine *must be settled at the peace table* ... I do not think we should take the responsibility upon ourselves of managing this very difficult place while the Americans sit back and criticise. Have you ever addressed yourselves to the idea that we should ask them to take it over? ... I am not aware of the slightest advantage which has ever accrued to Great Britain from this painful and thankless task. Somebody else should have their turn now" (July 6, 1945).

This passage (considered together with President Roosevelt's jocular remark to Stalin, that the only concession he might offer King Ibn Saoud would be "to give him the six million Jews in the United States") reveal the private thoughts of these premier-dictators who so docilely did the bidding of Zion. Mr. Churchill wished he could shift the insoluble problem to the

American back; Mr. Roosevelt would gladly have shifted it on to some other back. In this matter the great men, as an unwary remark in each case shows, behaved like the comedian who cannot by any exertion divest himself of the gluey flypaper. Mr. Churchill, in this inter-office memorandum, was not aware "of the slightest advantage that has ever accrued to Great Britain from this painful and thankless task." But in public, when Zion was listening, he continued (and to the moment of writing this book continues) to applaud the Zionist adventure in a boundless manner which aroused the curiosity even of *Jewish* critics (as will be seen).

At the time when Mr. Churchill dictated this last memorandum his words about "settling the question of Palestine at the peace table" were so irrelevant that he might have had humorous intent in using them. The issue was closed, for the Zionists had arms, the men to use these arms were to be smuggled through Europe from the revolutionary area by the West (as shown in the last chapter), and both major political parties in England and America were ready to applaud any act of aggression, invasion or persecution the transmigrants committed with the arms they had obtained.

This was particularly evident in the case of the Socialist party in England, which at that time was still the country chiefly involved in the fate of Palestine. The Labour party (as it called itself) in England presented itself as the champion of the poor, defenceless and oppressed; it had been born and bred in the promise of old-age pensions, unemployment relief, free medicine and the care and relief of the destitute, poor or humble generally. As the war drew towards its end this party at long last saw before it the prospect of office with a substantial majority. Like the Conservative party (and both parties in America) it apparently calculated that victory was even at this stage not quite certain and that it could be ensured by placating Zion. Thus is placed at the head of its foreign policy the aim to drive from a little country far away some people who were poorer, more friendless and longer oppressed than even the British worker in the worst days of the Industrial Revolution. In 1944 its leader, Mr. Clement Attlee, proclaimed the new, crowning tenet of British Socialism: "Let the Arabs be encouraged to move out" (of Palestine) "as the Jews move in. Let them be handsomely compensated for their land, and their settlement elsewhere be carefully organized and generously financed" (twelve years later nearly a million of these people, encouraged to move out by bombs, still languished in the neighbour Arab countries of Palestine; and the British Socialist Party, at every new turn of events, was more clamant than ever for their further chastisement).

The British Socialists, when they made this statement, knew that the Zionists, under cover of the war against Germany, had amassed arms for the conquest of Palestine by force. General Wavell, the commander in the Middle East, had long before informed Mr. Churchill that "left to themselves, the Jews would beat the Arabs" who had no source of arms-supply). General

Wavell's view about the Zionist scheme was that of all responsible administrators *on the spot,* and for that reason he was disliked by Dr. Weizmann. The reader has already seen, as far back as the First War, that Dr. Weizmann's displeasure was dangerous even to high personages and it may have played a part in General Wavell's removal from the Middle East command to India. The official British *History of the War in the Middle East* describes General Wavell as "one of the great commanders in military history" and says tiredness, caused by his great responsibilities, was aggravated by the feeling that he did not enjoy the full confidence of Mr. Churchill, who bombarded his Middle East commander with "irritating" and "needless" telegrams about "matters of detail." By his relegation General Wavell may have been another victim of Zionism, and British military prowess have suffered accordingly in the war; this cannot be established but it is a reasonable surmise.

In 1944 assassination again appeared in the story. Lord Moyne, as Colonial Secretary, was the Cabinet minister then responsible for Palestine, the post earlier held by Lord Lloyd (who had been rudely rebuked by Mr. Churchill for tardiness in "arming the Jews" and had died in 1941). Lord Moyne was the friend of all men, and sympathetic to Judaism, but he shared the view of all his responsible predecessors, that the Zionist enterprise in Palestine would end disastrously. For that reason, and having sympathy for suffering mankind in general, he was inclined to revive the idea of providing land in Uganda for any Jews who truly needed to find a new home somewhere.

This humane notion brought him the mortal hatred of the Zionists, who would not brook any diversion of thought from the target of their ambition, Palestine. In 1943 Lord Moyne modified his view, according to Mr. Churchill, who suggested that Dr. Weizmann should go to Cairo, meet Lord Moyne there and satisfy himself of the improvement. Before any meeting could come about Lord Moyne was assassinated in Cairo (November 1944) by two Zionists from Palestine, one more peacemaker thus being removed from a path strewn with the bones of earlier pacifiers. This event for a moment disturbed the flow of Mr. Churchill's memoranda to his colleagues about "arming the Jews," and the responsible men in Palestine once again urgently recommended that Zionist immigration thither be suspended. Mr. Churchill's reply (November 17, 1944) was that this would "simply play into the hands of the extremists," whereon the extremists were left unhindered in their further plans and their tribe increased.

As the Second War approached its end in Europe Mr. Churchill's hopes of some spectacular transaction which would happily integrate the Chazars in Arabia faded. If his suggestion (that Ibn Saoud be made "lord of the Middle East, provided he settles with you," i.e. Dr. Weizmann) was ever conveyed by Dr. Weizmann to President Roosevelt, an episode of 1944 may have been the result of it. An American, Colonel Hoskins, ("President Roosevelt's personal representative in the Middle East"; Dr. Weizmann) then visited the Arab leader. Colonel Hoskins, like all qualified men, had no faith in the plan to set up a Zionist state but was in favour of helping Jews to go to Palestine (if any so wished) *in agreement with the Arabs*. He found that King Ibn Saoud held himself to have been grossly insulted by Dr. Weizmann of whom he spoke "in the angriest and most contemptuous manner, asserting that I" (Dr. Weizmann), "had tried to bribe him with twenty million pounds to sell out Palestine to the Jews"; and he indignantly rejected any suggestion of a deal on such terms. Therewith all prospect of any "settlement" vanished and Colonel Hoskins also passed from the story, another good man defeated in his attempt to solve the insoluble problem posed by Mr. Balfour.

Thus, as the war entered its last months, only two alternatives remained. The British Government, abandoning the decision of 1939, could struggle on, trying to hold the scales impartially between the native inhabitants and their besiegers from Russia; or it could throw up "the Mandate" and withdraw, whereupon the Zionists would expel the native inhabitants with arms procured from the European and African theatres of war.

This second great moment in the Palestinian drama approached. Mr. Roosevelt had been told by Dr. Weizmann that the Zionists "could not rest the case on the consent of the Arabs" but had remained non-committal. Mr. Churchill, according to Dr. Weizmann, *had* committed himself, in private, and in 1944 Dr. Weizmann grew impatient to have from Mr. Churchill a *public* committal in the form of an amended Balfour Declaration which would award *territory* (in place of the meaningless phrase, "a national home") to Zion (in 1949 he was still very angry that Mr. Churchill, on the "pretext" that the war must first be finished, refrained from making this final public capitulation).

Like Macbeth, Dr. Weizmann's "top-line politicians" flinched and shrunk as the moment for the deed approached. Neither Mr. Churchill nor Mr. Roosevelt would openly command their soldiers to do it and the Zionists furiously cried "Infirm of purpose!" Then Mr. Roosevelt went to Yalta, wearing the visage of doomed despair which the news-reel pictures recorded, arranged for the bisection of Europe, and at the end briefly informed Mr. Churchill (who was "flabbergasted" and "greatly disturbed" by the news, according to Mr. Hopkins) that he was going to meet King Ibn Saoud on board the U.S. cruiser *Quincy*.

What followed remains deeply mysterious. Neither Mr. Roosevelt nor Mr. Churchill had any right to bestow Arab land on the lobbyists who beleaguered them in Washington and London; nevertheless, what was demanded of them was, in appearance, so small in comparison with what had just been done at Yalta, that Mr. Roosevelt's submission and same harsh ultimatum to King Ibn Saoud would have surprised none. Instead, he suddenly stepped out of the part he had played for many years and spoke as a statesman; after that he died.

He left Yalta on February 11, 1945, and spent February 12, 13 and 14 aboard the *Quincy*, receiving King Ibn Saoud during this time. He asked the king "to admit some more Jews into Palestine" and received the blunt answer, "No." Ibn Saoud said that "there was a Palestine army of Jews all armed to the teeth and … they did not seem to be fighting the Germans but were aiming at the Arabs." On February 28 Mr. Roosevelt returned to Washington. On March 28 Ibn Saoud reiterated by letter his verbal warning (since confirmed by events) of the consequences which would follow from American support of the Zionists. On *April* 5 President Roosevelt replied reaffirming his own pledge verbally given to Ibn Saoud that:

"*I would take no action,* in my capacity as Chief of the Executive Branch of this Government *which might prove hostile to the Arab people.*" On *April 12* he died. This pledge would never have become known but for the action of an American statesman, Secretary of State James G. Byrnes, who published it six months later (October 18, 1945) in a vain attempt to deter Mr. Roosevelt's successor, President Truman, from taking the very "action hostile to the Arabs" which President Roosevelt swore he would never commit.

Mr. Roosevelt's pledge was virtually a deathbed one, and another of history's great unanswered questions is, did he mean it? If by any chance he *did*, then once more death intervened as the ally of Zionism. His intimate Mr. Harry Hopkins (who was present at the meeting and drafted a memorandum about it) sneered at the suggestion that it might have been sincerely intended, saying that President Roosevelt was "*wholly committed publicly and privately and by conviction*" to the Zionists (this memorandum records Mr. Roosevelt's statement that he had learned more from Ibn Saoud about Palestine in five minutes than he had previously learned in a lifetime; out of this, again, grew the famous anecdote that Ibn Saoud said, "We have known for two thousand years what you have fought two world wars to learn"). However, Mr. Hopkins may conceivably not be a trustworthy witness on this one occasion, for immediately after the meeting he, the president's shadow, mysteriously broke with Mr. Roosevelt, whom he never saw again! Mr. Hopkins shut himself in his cabin and three days later, at Algiers, went ashore, "sending word" through an intermediary that he would return to America by another route. The breach was as sudden as that between Mr. Wilson and Mr. House.

What is clear is that the last few weeks and days of Mr. Roosevelt's life were overshadowed by the controversy of Zion, not by American or European questions. Had he lived, and his pledge to Ibn Saoud become known, Zionism, which so powerfully helped to make and maintain him president for twelve years, would have become his bitter enemy. He died. (The pledge was *categorical;* it continued, "no decision will be taken with regard to the basic situation in Palestine *without full consultation with both Arabs* and Jews"; this was direct repudiation of Dr. Weizmann, who had told him, "we could not rest the case on Arab consent").

Thus, cloaked in a last-moment mystery, Mr. Roosevelt too passed from the story. A parting glimpse of the throng which had gathered round him during his twelve-year reign is given by the senior White House correspondent, Mr. Merriman Smith; this description of a wake shows that the carousing of Yalta accompanied the president even to his grave: "Most of the people on the train were members of the Roosevelt staff. Before the train was out of sight of the crepe-hung Hyde Park depot, they started what turned out to be a post- funeral wake. Liquor flowed in every compartment and drawing-room. The shades were drawn throughout the train and from the outside it looked like any train bearing mourners home. But behind those curtains, the Roosevelt staff had what they thought was a good time. Their Boss would have approved ... I saw one of the top New Dealers hurl a tray of empty glasses into a toilet and shout in mock bravado, 'Down the hatch, we won't need you anymore.' Porters and club stewards bustled up and down the corridors with gurgling, sloshing trays. If you hadn't known the people in the drawing room, you would have thought they were on their way home from a football game. Some of the people were using whisky as an antidote for worry over their jobs ... I could hear an alcoholic chorus of Auld Lang Syne ..."

Such were the trappings of statesmanship, during those last days when "the boys" toiled towards another "victory," when the Communist armies seized half of Europe, and the Zionists from Russia were convoyed by the West towards the invasion of Palestine.

In this question of Palestine, Mr. Roosevelt was liberated from his dilemma by death. Mr. Churchill was left to face his. He had courted Zionist favour from the days of the 1906 election. He had been a member of the British Government in 1917, of which another member (Mr. Leopold Amery, quoted in a Zionist paper in 1952) said, "We thought when we issued the Balfour Declaration that *if the Jews could become a majority* in Palestine they would form *a Jewish state* ... We envisaged *not a divided Palestine,* which exists only west of the Jordan."

Mr. Churchill never publicly stated any such intention (indeed, he denied it), but if it was his view this means that even the Zionist state set up after the Second World War by no means fulfils the intention of those who made the Balfour Declaration, and that further conquests of Arab lands have yet to be made by war.

The governing word in the passage quoted is "if"; "if the Jews could become a majority ..." By 1945 three decades of Arab revolt had shown that the Zionists never would *become a majority*" unless the Arabs were driven out of their native land by arms. The question that remained was, who was to drive them out? Mr. Roosevelt had sworn not to. Dr. Weizmann, ever quick to cry "I stay here on my bond," liked to claim that Mr. Churchill was committed as far as Dr. Weizmann wanted him to go.

Even Mr. Churchill could not do this deed. He, too, then was liberated from his dilemma; not by death, but by electoral defeat. His memoirs express wounded pride at this rebuff; "All our enemies having surrendered unconditionally or being about to do so, I was immediately dismissed by the British electorate from all further conduct of their affairs."

It was not as simple as that. The future historian has to work from such material, but the living participant knows better, and I was in England and saw the election when Mr. Churchill was "dismissed." In truth the British electorate could hardly have been expected to see in the outcome of the war (of which Mr. Churchill is the bitterest critic) cause for a vote of thanksgiving to Mr. Churchill, but there were other reasons for his defeat than mere disillusionment.

As in American elections, so in this British one of 1945 the power to "deliver the vote" was shown. Mr. Churchill had gone far in "arming the Jews" and in privately committing himself to Zionism, but not far enough for Dr. Weizmann. In England at the mid- century control of the press was virtually complete, in this question; Zionist propaganda at the election turned solidly against Mr. Churchill and was waged in behalf of the Socialists, who had given the requisite promise of support for "hostile action" against the Arabs ("The Arabs should be encouraged to move out as the Jews move in …"). The block of Jewish Members of Parliament swung over in a body to the Socialist party (and was strongest in the left wing of it, where the Communists lurked). With high elation the Zionists saw the discomfiture of their "champion" of 1906, 1917 and 1939. Dr. Weizmann says that the Socialist victory (and Mr. Churchill's "dismissal") "delighted all liberal elements." This was the requital for Mr. Churchill's forty years of support for Zionism; he had not actually ordered British troops to clear Palestine of Arabs and, for a while, was an enemy.

Thus Mr. Churchill was at least reprieved from the task of deciding what to do about Palestine and should not have been so grieved as he depicts himself, when he was dismissed soon after "victory." The British Socialists, at last provided with a great majority in parliament, then found at once that they were expected by forcible measures to "encourage the Arabs to move out." When they too shrank from the assassin's deed the cries of "betrayal" fell about their ears like hailstones. Dr. Weizmann's narrative grows frantic with indignation at this point; the Socialist government, he says, "within three months of taking office repudiated *the pledge* so often and clearly, even vehemently, repeated to the Jewish people." During forty years Lord Curzon seems to have been the only leading politician caught up in this affair to realize that even the most casual word of sympathy, uttered to Dr. Weizmann, would later be held up as "a pledge," solemnly given and infamously broken.

Among the victorious Socialists a worthy party-man, one Mr. Hall, inherited the Colonial Office from Lord Lloyd, Lord Moyne and others dead or defamed, and was barely in it when a deputation from the World Zionist Congress arrived:

"I must say the attitude adopted by the members of the deputation *was different from anything which I have ever experienced.* It was not a request for the consideration by His Majesty's Government of the decisions of the Zionist conference, *but a demand that His Majesty's Government should do what the Zionist Organization desired them to do.*" Ten years later an American ex-president, Mr. Truman, recalled similar visits during his presidency in similar terms of innocent surprise; in 1945 the thing had been going on since 1906 without disturbing Mr. Hall's political slumbers. Soon after this he was ousted from the Colonial Office, his suitability for a peerage suddenly being realized.

The Socialist government of 1945, which in domestic affairs must have been nearly the worst that a war-weary country, in need of reinvigoration, could have received, in foreign affairs did its country one service. It saved, of honour, what could be saved. Under pressure from the four corners of the world it refused to play the assassin's part in Palestine; if it did not protect the Arabs, and by that time it probably could not protect them, at least it did not destroy them for the Zionist taskmaster.

This achievement was the sole work of a Mr. Ernest Bevin, in my estimation the greatest man produced in British political life during this century. According to report, King George VI, the most unobtrusive of monarchs, urged the incoming Socialist prime minister, Mr. Attlee, to make his best and strongest man Foreign Secretary, because the state of the world so clearly demanded this. Mr. Attlee thereon revised a list already drafted, expunging the name of some worthy "liberal" who might have involved his country in the coming pogrom of Arabs, and inserting that of Mr. Bevin.

By 1945 Palestine was clearly too big an issue for Colonial Secretaries to handle; it was, and will long remain, the major preoccupation of Prime Ministers and Foreign Secretaries, Presidents and Secretaries of State in England and America, because it is the most inflammable source of new wars. In 1945, as soon as "victory" was won, it was seen to dominate and pervert the politics of all nation- states. Without awe, Ernest Bevin, the farm lad from Somerset and the dockers' idol, took up the bomb and sought to remove the fuse. Had he received support from one leading man in any Western country he might have saved the day. They all fell on him like wolves; there was something of the camp-meeting and of revivalist hysteria in the abandon of their surrender to Zionism.

He was a robust man, with the beef and air of the West Country in his bones and muscle and its fearless tradition in his blood, but even he was physically broken within a few years by the fury of unremitting defamation. He was not spiritually daunted. He realized that he had to do with an enterprise essentially conspiratorial, a conspiracy of which the revolution and Zionism were linked parts, and he may be unique among politicians of this century in that he used a word ("conspiracy") which has a dictionary meaning plainly applicable to this case. He bluntly told Dr. Weizmann that he would not be coerced or coaxed into any action contrary to Britain's undertakings. Dr. Weizmann had not experienced any such instruction, at that high level, since 1904, and his indignation, surging outward from him through the Zionist organizations of the world, produced the sustained abuse of Mr. Bevin which then followed.

Mr. Churchill, had he remained prime minister, would apparently have used *British* arms to enforce the partition of Palestine. That seems to be the inescapable inference from his memorandum to the Chiefs of Staff Committee (January 25, 1944), in which he said "the Jews, left to themselves, would beat the Arabs; there cannot therefore be any great danger *in our joining hands with the Jews to enforce the kind of proposals about partition* which are set forth." The reader may see how greatly circumstances alter cases. The bisection *of Europe* was for Mr. Churchill "a hideous partition, which cannot last." Partition *in Palestine* was worthy to be enforced by "joining hands with the Jews."

Mr. Bevin would have no truck with such schemes. Under his guidance the Socialist government announced that it "would not accept the view that *the Jews should be driven out of Europe or that they should not be permitted to live again* in these" (European) *"countries without discrimination,* contributing their ability and talent towards rebuilding the prosperity of Europe."

The words show that this man understood the nature of Zionist chauvinism, the problem posed by it and the only solution. They depict what will inevitably happen one day, but that day has been put back to some time after another ruinous era in Palestine, which will probably involve the world. He was either the first British politician fully to comprehend the matter, or the first to act with the courage of his knowledge.

The Socialist government of 1945 was driven, by responsible office, to do what all responsible governments before it had equally been forced to do: to send out one more commission of enquiry (which could but repeat the reports of all earlier commissions) and in the meantime to regulate Zionist immigration and to safeguard the interest of the native Arabs, in accordance with the pledges of the original Balfour Declaration.

Dr. Weizmann considered this "a reversion to the old, *shifty* double emphasis *on the obligation towards the Arabs of Palestine*" and the Zionist power went to work to destroy Mr. Bevin, on whose head, for the next two years, a worldwide campaign was turned. It was concentric, synchronised and of tremendous force. First, the Conservative party was sent into action. The

Socialists had defeated them by capitulations to Zionism, which brought them the help of the controlled press. The Conservatives, being out of office, played this trump card against the Socialists, and in turn made their capitulations to Zion. This was at once made clear: the party proclaimed that it would *combat* the *domestic* and *support* the *foreign* policy of the Socialists, but from the moment of the Socialist declaration about Palestine it made *one* exception to the second rule; it began a sustained attack on the Socialist government's policy *about Palestine*, which meant, on Mr. Bevin.

At that point Mr. Churchill, safe in opposition, demeaned himself by accusing Mr. Bevin of "anti-Jewish feelings," a shot taken from the locker of the Anti-Defamation League (which added a new epithet, "Bevinism," to its catalogue of smearwords). No such traducement of a political adversary ever came from Mr. Bevin, Mr. Churchill's outstanding colleague during the long war years. Thus Mr. Bevin, at the post of greatest danger, received the full support of the opposition party in all matters of foreign policy save one, Palestine. He might yet have saved the day but for the intervention of the new American president, Mr. Harry S. Truman, with whose automatic elevation (on the death of the incumbent) from the Vice-Presidency the story of the 20th Century resumed the aspect of Greek tragedy (or of a comedy of errors). Mr. Truman involved his country up to the neck in the Palestinian imbroglio at the very moment when in England, at long last, a man had arisen who was able and staunch enough to liquidate the disastrous venture.

Unless a man has that genius which needs no basis in acquired knowledge, a small town in the Middle West and Kansas City are poor places for learning about world affairs. Mr. Truman, when the presidency was thrust upon him, had two major disqualifications for the office. One was native remoteness from world politics, and the other was too close acquaintance with ward politics, of which he had seen much. In Kansas City he had watched the machine at work; he knew about patronage, ward bosses and stuffed ballot-boxes. He had received the impression that politics were business, and essentially simple in the basic rules, which allowed no room for high-falutin' ideas.

A middle-sized, hale, broadly-smiling man who was to sign the order for an act of destruction unprecedented in the history of the West, he strode briskly on to the stage of great events. He decided at Potsdam that "Uncle Joe" was "a nice guy" and there completed Mr. Roosevelt's territorial rearrangements in Europe and Asia. He arranged for the atom-bombing of defenceless Hiroshima and Nagasaki. No comparable series of acts ever fell to the lot of a once-bankrupt haberdasher precipitated into the office of a "premier- dictator." Then he turned his gaze on domestic affairs and the next Congressional and presidential elections. In these, he knew (and said), the Zionist-controlled vote was decisive.

While Mr. Bevin strove to undo the tangle, Mr. Truman undid Mr. Bevin's efforts. He demanded that a hundred thousand Jews be admitted immediately to Palestine, and he arranged for the first *partisan* commission of enquiry to go to Palestine. This was the only means by which any commission could ever be expected to produce a report favourable to the Zionist scheme. Two of its four American members were avowed Zionists; the *one* British member was Zionist propagandist and a left-wing enemy of Mr. Bevin. This "Anglo-American Commission" went to Palestine, where Dr. Weizmann (for perhaps the tenth time in some thirty years) was the chief personage heard. It recommended (though "cautiously") the admission of one hundred thousand "*displaced persons*" (the term was presumably meant to mislead the public masses and was at the moment of some importance; no truly displaced persons wanted to go to Palestine).

Therewith the fat of the next war was in the fire, and an American president publicly supported "hostile action" against the Arabs, for it was that. The next Zionist Congress (at Geneva in 1946) joyfully recorded this new "pledge" (Mr. Truman's "suggestion" and the partisan commission's "cautious recommendations"). This was a characteristic Zionist Congress, being composed chiefly of Jews from Palestine (who had already migrated there) and from America (who had no intention of going there); the herded-mass, to be transported thither, was not represented. Dr. Weizmann's description of the decisions taken are of great significance.

He says the congress "had a special character" and showed "a tendency to rely on methods ... referred to by different names: '*resistance*,' '*defence*,' '*activism*.' " Despite these "shades of meaning" (he says) "one feature was common to all of them: the conviction of the need *for fighting against British authority in Palestine, or anywhere else*, for that matter."

Dr. Weizmann's guarded remarks must be considered in the context of his whole book and of the entire history of Zionism. What he means is that the Zionist World Congress at Geneva in 1946 decided to resume the method of terror and assassination which had proved effective in Russia in the germinating stage of the two-headed conspiracy. The congress knew this to be the method "referred to by different names" during its discussions, for it had *already* been resumed in the assassination of Lord Moyne and many terrorist exploits in Palestine. The prompting impulse for the Congress's decision (which in fact it was) came from the American president's recommendation that a hundred thousand people should be forcibly injected into Palestine. The Zionists took that to be another "pledge," committing America to approval of anything they might do, and they were right.

Dr. Weizmann knew exactly what was at stake and in his old age shrank from the prospect that re-opened before him: reversion to the worship of Moloch, the god of blood. He had seen so much blood shed in the name of revolutionary-Communism and revolutionary- Zionism, the two causes which had dominated his parental home and home town in the Pale. In his youth he had exulted in the riots and revolutions and had found the assassinations a natural part of the process; in his maturity he had rejoiced in the ruin of Russia despite the decades of bloodshed which ensued. For fifty-five years he had cried havoc and unloosed dogs of war. Almost unknown to the masses embroiled in two wars, he had become one of the most powerful men in the world. Beginning in 1906, when he first wheedled Mr. Balfour, he had gradually risen until his word in the lobbies was law, when he could command audience of monarchs and obedience of presidents and prime ministers. Now, when the enterprise he had so long schemed for was on the brink of consummation, he recoiled from the blood-stained prospect that opened immeasurably before him; blood, and more blood, and at the end ... what? Dr. Weizmann remembered Sabbatai Zevi.

He was against "truckling to the demoralizing forces in the movement," the cryptic phrase he uses to cover those referred to by Mr. Churchill as "the extremists," and by the administrators on the spot as "the terrorists." This meant that he had changed as his end approached, for without terrorism Zionism would never have established itself at all and if, in 1946, his Zionist state *was* to be achieved, this could only be done by violence. Thus at the last Dr. Weizmann realized the futility of his half-century of "pressure behind the scenes" and no doubt saw the inevitable fiasco that lay ahead, after the Zionist state had been born in terror. Psychologically, this was a moment of great interest in the story. Perhaps men grow wise in their old age; they tire of the violent words and deeds which seemed to solve all problems in their conspiratorial youth, and this revulsion may have overtaken Chaim Weizmann. If it did, it was too late to alter anything. The machine he had built had to continue, of its own momentum, to its own destruction and that of any in its path. The remaining future of Zionism was in the hands of "the demoralizing forces in the movement," and he had put it there.

He was denied a vote of confidence and was not re-elected president of the World Zionist Organization. Forty years after Herzl, he was cast aside as he had cast Herzl aside, and for the same essential reason. He and his Chazars from Russia had overthrown Herzl because Herzl wanted to accept Uganda, which meant renouncing Palestine. He was overthrown because he feared to re-embark on the policy of terror and assassination, and that also meant renouncing Palestine.

The note of despair sounded even earlier, in his allusions to Lord Moyne's murder: "Palestine Jewry will ... cut out, root and branch, *this evil* from its midst ... this utterly un-Jewish phenomenon." These words were addressed to Western ears and were specious; political murder was *not* "an utterly un-Jewish phenomenon" in the Talmudic areas of Russia where Dr. Weizmann spent his revolutionary and conspiratorial youth, as he well knew, and a series of similar deeds stained the past. Indeed, when he spoke to a

Zionist audience he candidly admitted that political murder was *not* an "utterly un-Jewish phenomenon" but the opposite: "What was the terror in Palestine but *the old evil* in a new and horrible guise."

This "old evil," rising from its Talmudic bottle to confront Dr. Weizmann at Geneva in 1946, apparently accounts for the note of premonition which runs through the last pages of his book of 1949 (when the Zionist state had been set up by terror). The Moyne murder, he then forebodingly said, "illumines the abyss into which terrorism leads." Thus in his last days Dr. Weizmann saw whither his indefatigable journey had led: to an abyss! He lived to see it receive a first batch of nearly a million victims. From the moment of his deposition effective control passed into the hands of "the terrorists," as he calls them, and his belated cry of "Back!" fell on empty air. The "activists" (as they prefer to call themselves) were left with power to ignite a third world conflict when they pleased. Dr. Weizmann survived to play a determining part in the next stage of the venture but never again had true power in Zionism.

From 1946 the terrorists took command. They set to work to drive the British from Palestine first, and knew they could not fail in the state of affairs which had been brought about during the Second War. If the British defended either themselves or the semitic Arabs the cry of "anti-semitism" would rise until the politicians in Washington turned on the British; then, when the British left, the terrorists would drive out the Arabs.

The terror had been going on for many years, the Moyne murder being only one incident in it; indeed, one of the harassed Colonial Secretaries, Mr. Oliver Stanley, in 1944 told the House of Commons that it had sensibly impeded "the British war effort," or in other words, prolonged the war (he is a trustworthy witness, for he was hailed by the Zionists at his death as "a staunch friend"). In 1946 and 1947, after the Geneva Congress, it was intensified, hundreds of British soldiers being ambushed, shot while asleep, blown up and the like. The terror was deliberately given the visible appearance of "the old evil" when two British sergeants were slowly done to death in an orchard and left hanging there. The choice of this Levitical form of butchery ("hanging on a tree," the death "accursed of God") signified that these things were done under the Judaic Law.

The British government, daunted by the fury of the American and British press, under common constraint, feared to protect its officials and soldiers, and one British soldier wrote to *The Times:* "What use has the army for the government's sympathy? It does not avenge those who are murdered, nor does it prevent any further killings. Are we no longer a nation with sufficient courage to enforce law and order where it is our responsibility to do so?"

This was the case. The great Western governments had fallen, under "irresistible pressure," into a nerveless captivity, and Britain and America had ceased, anyway for the time, to be sovereign nations. At length the British government, in despair, referred the problem of Palestine to the new organization in New York called "the United Nations" (which had as little right to dispose of Palestine as the League of Nations before it).

Delegates from Haiti, Liberia, Honduras and other parts of "the free world" thronged to Lake Success, a forlorn, suburban pond outside New York. There was an hissing in the world at this time and from the parent UNO bodies called COBSRA, UNRRA, UNESCO uncoiled. On this particular day something called UNSCOP (United Nations Special Committee on Palestine) rendered to UNO its report recommending "the partition of Palestine."

Dr. Weizmann (though deposed by the Zionist Organization for his warnings against terrorism) was once more the chief authority heard by UNSCOP in Jerusalem, and then quickly returned to New York where, in October and November of 1947, he dominated the hidden scene as lobbyist supreme. "Irresistible pressure" operated with relentless force. The delegates whom the public masses saw on the moving-picture screens were puppets; the great play was all behind the curtain and in that, Chesterton's "real world," of which the multitude saw nothing, two great operations were in progress, by means of which the fate of Palestine was settled far from the debating halls of the United Nations. First, hundreds of thousands of Jews from Russia and Eastern Europe were being smuggled across Western Europe to invade Palestine. Second, the approach of an American presidential election was being used by the Zionists as a means to set the rival parties there bidding against each other for Zionist support, and thus to ensure that the decisive American vote in the United Nations would be cast for the invasion.

In each case, and as in the preceding three decades, men arose who strove to disentangle their countries from its consequences. The secret convoying of the Eastern Jews across Western Europe was revealed by a British general, Sir Frederick Morgan (to whose work in planning the invasion of Normandy General Eisenhower's book pays tribute). When the fighting ended General Morgan was lent by the British War Office to "UNRRA," the offspring-body of the United Nations which was supposed to "relieve and rehabilitate" the sufferers from the war. General Morgan was put in charge of the most hapless of these (the "displaced persons") and found that "UNRRA," which cost the American and British taxpayer much money, was being used as an umbrella to cover the mass-movement of Jews from the eastern area to Palestine. These people were *not* "displaced persons." Their native countries had been "liberated" by the Red Armies and they were able to live in them, their welfare ensured by the special law against "anti-semitism" which all these communized countries received from their Communist overlord. They had not been "driven from Germany," where they had never lived. In fact, these were, once more, the *Ostjuden*, the Chazars, being driven by their Talmudic masters to a new land for a conspiratorial purpose.

In this way a new war was being cooked over the embers of the dying one and General Morgan twice (in January and August 1946) publicly stated that "a secret organization existed to further a mass movement of Jews from Europe, a second Exodus." Senator Herbert Lehman, a prominent Zionist who was Director General of UNRRA, said this warning was "anti-semitic" and demanded General Morgan's resignation. He relented when General Morgan disclaimed "anti-semitic" intent, but when the general repeated his warning eight months later he was *summarily dismissed* by the new Director General, a Zionist sympathizer and former Mayor of New York, Mr. Fiorello La Guardia, known to New Yorkers as The Little Flower. Mr. La Guardia then appointed a Mr. Myer Cohen in General Morgan's place. The British government hastened to punish General Morgan by retiring the celebrated invasion-planner, stating (falsely) that this was at his request.

Two independent bodies of high status confirmed General Morgan's information; in the servient condition of the press their disclosures received little publicity. A Select Committee on Estimates of the British House of Commons reported (November 1946) that "very large numbers of Jews, *almost amounting to a second Exodus,* have been *migrating from Eastern Europe* to the American zones of Germany and Austria with the intention in the majority of cases of finally making their way to Palestine. It is clear that it is *a highly organized movement, with ample funds and great influence behind it,* but the Subcommittee were unable to obtain any real evidence who are the real instigators." A War Investigating Committee sent to Europe by the United States Senate said that "heavy migration of Jews *from Eastern Europe* into the American zone of Germany is part of *a carefully organized plan financed by special groups in the United States.*"

The picture, once again, is of a conspiracy supported by the Western governments, in this case the American one in particular. The "organization" in America disposed of American and British public funds lavishly, and effected the mass-transfer of population under the cloak of war-relief. Its leaders were able summarily to dismiss high officials, publicly-paid, who exposed what went on, and the British government supported this action. Although by that time (1946-1947) the perfidy of the revolutionary state was supposed to have been realized by the Western politicians (so that "cold war" was waged with it), the three governments of Washington, London and Moscow acted in perfect accord in this one matter. The "exodus" came from Russia and from the part of Europe abandoned by the West to the revolution. No man may leave the Soviet state without permission, most rarely granted, but in this one case the Iron Curtain opened to release a mass of people, just large enough to ensure immediate war and permanent unrest in the Near

East. Just as smoothly, thirty years before, the frontiers and ports of Germany (an enemy), England (an ally) and America (a neutral) had opened to allow the revolutionaries to go to Russia. On both occasions, at this supreme level of policy, the super-national one, there were no allies, enemies or neutrals; all governments did the bidding of the supreme power.

One of the British Colonial Secretaries earliest involved in Zionism and the Balfour Declaration of 1917, Mr. Leopold Amery, had said: "We thought when we issued the Balfour Declaration that *if the Jews could become a majority in Palestine they would form a Jewish state.*" In 1946-1948, at last, this thought was being realized, in the only way possible: by the mass-transplantation of Eastern Jews to Palestine. Only one thing still was needed: to obtain from "the United Nations" some act of mock-legalization for the invasion about to occur. To ensure that, the capitulation of the American president was necessary; and the way to bring that about was to threaten his party-advisers with the loss of the approaching presidential election, which lay a year ahead.

A third war was in truth being hatched, in the thinning fog of the second war, by this clandestine movement of population, and in America (after the dismissal of General Morgan in Europe) the two men whose offices made them directly responsible tried to nip the peril in the bud. One was General Marshall, whose interventions in the question of invading Europe and later in that of China have been shown by their consequences to have been most ill-omened. In the question of Palestine he showed prudence. In 1947 he was Secretary of State and was thus chiefly responsible, under the president, for foreign policy. He strove to ward off his country's involvement in the Palestinian fiasco and, as in all such cases, his relegation soon followed.

The other man was Mr. James Forrestal, Secretary for Defence. He was a successful banker, brought in to government in wartime for his executive ability; he was wealthy and only the impulse to serve his country can have moved him to take office. He foresaw disastrous consequences from involvement and died believing he had utterly failed in his effort to avert it. Of all the men concerned during two generations, he alone left a diary which fully exposes the methods by which Zion controls and manipulates governors and governments.

Mr. Truman went further than even President Roosevelt in taking foreign policy and national security out of the province of the responsible ministers, and in acting contrary to their counsel under the pressure applied through electoral advisers. The story is made complete by Mr. Forrestal's *Diary,* Mr. Truman's own memoirs, and Dr. Weizmann's book.

The struggle behind the scenes for control over the American president, and therewith of the Republic itself, lasted from the autumn of 1947 to the spring of 1948, that is, from the United Nations debate about the partition of Palestine to the proclamation of the Zionist state after its forcible seizure.

Dates are important. In November 1947 the Zionists wanted the "partition" vote and in May 1948 they wanted recognition of their invasion. The presidential election was due in November 1948, and the essential preliminary to it, the nomination contests, in *June and July* 1948. The party-managers instructed Mr. Truman that re-election was in the Zionist gift; the opposition candidate received similar advice from his party-managers. Thus "the election campaign took on the nature of an auction, each candidate being constantly under pressure from his organizers to outbid the other in 'supporting the invasion of Palestine. In these circumstances the successful candidate could only feel that election was a reward for "supporting partition" in November 1947 and "granting recognition" in May 1948; nothing could more clearly illustrate the vast change which the mass-immigration of Eastern Jews, in the period following the Civil War, had brought about in the affairs of the American Republic. Mr. Forrestal left a full account of the chief moves in this fateful, hidden contest.

The time-bomb planted by Mr. Balfour thirty years earlier reached its explosion-moment when the British government in 1947 announced that it would withdraw from Palestine if other powers made impartial administration there impossible; this was the reply to President Truman's proposal that 100,000 "displaced persons" be allowed to enter Palestine immediately. Mr. Truman's responsible advisers at once informed the American government of the consequences which would flow from a British withdrawal. General Marshall told the American Cabinet that such a British withdrawal "would be followed by a bloody struggle between the Arabs and Jews" (August 8, 1947), and his Under Secretary of State, Mr. Robert Lovett, pointed to the danger of "solidifying sentiment among all the Arabian and Mohammedan peoples" against the United States (August 15, 1947).

This warning was at once answered by the voice of party-politics. At a Cabinet lunch Mr. Robert Hannegan (Postmaster General, but previously national chairman of the President's party, the Democratic Party) urged the President to "make a statement of policy on Palestine" demanding "the admission of *150,000* Zionists." Thus the party-man's counsel was that President Truman should respond to the British warning by *increasing* his bid for Zionist electoral support, from 100,000 to 150,000 persons. Mr. Hannegan said this new demand *"would have a very great influence and great effect on the raising of funds for the Democratic National Committee"* and, as proof of what he promised, added that the earlier demand (related to 100,000 immigrants) had produced the result that *"very large sums were obtained from Jewish contributors and they would be influenced in either giving or withholding by what the President did on Palestine."*

Thus the issue from the outset was presented to the President in the plainest terms of national interest on the one hand and party- contributions, party-votes and party-success on the other. It was argued throughout the months that followed and finally determined on that basis, without any gloss.

Mr. Forrestal's alarm became acute. He held that if state policy and national security (his province) were to be subordinated to vote- buying the country would pass under Zionist control and earlier (in 1946) had asked the President if Palestine could not be "taken out of politics." Mr. Truman at that time had "agreed about the principle" but evinced the feeling "that not much will come of such an attempt, that political manoeuvring is inevitable, *politics and our government being what they are.*"

In September 1947, Mr. Forrestal spurred by his misgivings, laboured tirelessly to have Palestine "taken out of politics." His idea was that both contending parties must contain a majority of people who could be brought to agree, in the paramount national interest, that major foreign issues be set above dispute, so that Palestine could not be used for huckstering at election-time. He found only disdain for this idea among the men of "practical politics."

Deeply disturbed by Mr. Hannegan's above-quoted remarks of September 4, Mr. Forrestal at a Cabinet lunch on September 29, 1947 openly asked President Truman "whether it would not be possible to lift the Jewish-Palestine question out of politics." Mr. Truman said "it was worth trying to do, although he was obviously sceptical." At the next Cabinet lunch (October 6) the party-boss rebuked the responsible Cabinet officer:

"Mr. Hannegan brought up the question *of* Palestine. He said many people who had *contributed* to the Democratic campaign *were pressing hard for assurances from the administration of definitive support for the Jewish position in Palestine.*"

Mr. Forrestal foresaw Mr. Truman's capitulation and his alarm increased. He saw the Democratic party-manager, Mr. J. Howard McGrath (November 6, 1947) and again could make no headway. Mr. McGrath said, "There were two or three pivotal states *which could not be carried without the support of people who were deeply interested in the Palestine question.*" Mr. Forrestal made no impression with his rejoinder, "I said I would rather lose those states in a national election than run the risks which I felt might develop in our handling of the Palestine question."

The next day he again received support from General Marshall, who told the Cabinet that the Middle East was "another tinder box," and Mr. Forrestal then "repeated my suggestion ... that a serious attempt be made to lift the Palestine question *out of American partisan politics ... Domestic politics ceased at the Atlantic Ocean and no question was more charged with danger to our security than this particular one*" (November 7, 1947).

The "partition" vote was by this time near and Mr. Forrestal made another appeal to Mr. McGrath, the Democratic party-manager, showing him a secret report on Palestine provided by the governmental intelligence agency.

Mr. McGrath brushed this aside, saying Jewish sources were responsible for a substantial part of the contributions to the Democratic National Committee and many of these contributions were made *"with a distinct idea on the part of the givers* that they will have an opportunity to express their views and have them seriously considered on such questions as the present Palestine question. There was a feeling among the Jews that the United States was not doing what it should to *solicit votes* in the United Nations General Assembly in favour of the Palestine partition, and beyond this the Jews would *expect* the United States to do its utmost to implement the partition decision if it is voted by the United Nations *through force if necessary."*

This quotation reveals the process of progressively raising the bid for Zionist funds and the Zionist vote which went on behind the scenes. At the start only United States support for the partition proposal had been "expected." Within a few weeks this "expectation" had risen to the demand that the United States should "solicit" the votes of other countries in support of partition *and should use American troops to enforce partition,* and the party-manager was quite accustomed to such notions (if American troops in the 1950's or 1960's find themselves in the Near East, any of them who have read Mr. Forrestal's *Diaries* should know how they came to be there). Mr. Forrestal must have acted from a sense of duty, not of hope, when he implored Mr. McGrath "to give a lot of thought to this matter because it involved not merely the Arabs of the Middle East, but also might involve the whole Moslem world with its four hundred millions of people: Egypt, North Africa, India and Afghanistan."

While Mr. Forrestal fought this losing battle behind the curtained windows of the White House and of party-headquarters, Dr. Weizmann, in Washington, New York and Lake Success was indefatigably organizing "the vote" on partition. He was having his difficulties, but was rescued from them at this culminant moment when he found "a welcome and striking change" among some of those "wealthy Jews" who formerly had opposed Zionism. At this belated stage in his narrative he first mentions Mr. Bernard Baruch, saying that Mr. Baruch had *formerly* been "an oppositionist Jew," one of the "rich and powerful Jews who were against the idea of the Jewish National Home, but they did not know very much about the subject."

One can only speculate about the exact composition and nature of the "Jewish International" which Dr. Kastein described as having come into existence around the start of this century. It is permissible, in the light of all that has happened in these fifty years, to envisage it as a permanent, high directorate, spread over all nation-state boundaries, the membership of which probably changes only when gaps are left by death. If that is its nature, a reasonable further inference would be that Dr. Weizmann was a very high functionary, perhaps the highest functionary, subordinate to it, but that undoubtedly there was a body superior to him. In that case, I would judge that its four most important members, in the United States at that period, would have been Mr. Bernard Baruch, first, and Senator Herbert Lehman, Mr. Henry Morgenthau junior and Justice Felix Frankfurter, next. If there were a doubt, it would previously have attached to Mr. Baruch, who had never publicly associated himself with "leftist" causes or with Zionism. His great crony, Mr. Winston Churchill, quoted Mr. Baruch's "negative view" about Zionism to Dr. Weizmann, who in consequence (as he says) "took great care not to touch on the Jewish problem" when he earlier met Mr. Baruch in America.

Nevertheless, at this decisive moment Mr. Baruch suddenly "changed a great deal" (Dr. Weizmann) and *his* support, added to the Zionist "pressure" that was being exerted on American politics, was determining. Dr. Weizmann, as he hurried round the lobbies at Lake Success, learned that the American delegation was *opposed to* the partition of Palestine. Thereon he enlisted the "particularly helpful" support of Mr. Baruch (until then, for forty years or more, regarded as an opponent of Zionism even by such intimates as Mr. Winston Churchill!), and also of the junior Mr. Henry Morgenthau (whose name attaches to the plan of "blind vengeance" adopted by Mr. Roosevelt and Mr. Churchill at Ottawa in 1944).

Mr. Baruch presumably did not hold Dr. Weizmann in the awe which seems to have seized the Western politicians at the Zionist leader's approach. Therefore his sudden support of Zionism must denote either an abrupt conversion or the revelation of a feeling earlier concealed; in either case, his intervention was decisive as will be seen.

Dr. Weizmann was well supported by the other powerful Jews in the Democratic Party. Senator Lehman was head of UNRRA when it was used to smuggle the Eastern Jews across Europe to Palestine, and had demanded General Morgan's resignation for publicly calling attention to this mass-movement of people; his part in the drama was already plain. Mr. Justice Frankfurter was equally busy; Mr. Forrestal was told by Mr. Loy Henderson (in charge of Middle Eastern Affairs in the State Department) that "very great pressure had been put on him as well as Mr. Lovett to get active American *solicitation* for United Nations votes for the Palestine partition; he said Felix Frankfurter and Justice Murphy had both sent messages *to the Philippines delegate* strongly urging his vote" (this is the same Mr. Frankfurter who called on Mr. House at the 1919 Peace Conference in Paris "to talk about the Jews in Palestine"; he was also the devoted instructor of Mr. Alger Hiss at the Harvard Law School).

Having such support, Dr. Weizmann was a besieging general backed by superior armies when he called on the citadel's commander, President Truman, on November 19, 1947, to *demand that* the United States support the partition of Palestine, and furthermore, that the Negev district (to which Dr. Weizmann attached "great importance") be included in the Zionist territory.

Mr. Truman's discipline was exemplary: "*he promised me that he would communicate at once with the American delegation*" (Dr. Weizmann). Out at Lake Success the chief American delegate, Mr. Herschel Johnson, as he was about to inform the Zionist representative of the American decision to vote against the inclusion of the Negev, was called to the telephone and received, through President Truman, Dr. Weizmann's orders. With that the deed was done and on November 29, 1947 the General Assembly of the United Nations *recommended* (Zionist propaganda always says "decided") that "independent Arab and Jewish states, *and the specific international régime for the City of Jerusalem*" should come into existence after termination of the British "Mandate" on August 1, 1948.

The vote was 31 against, 13 with, 10 abstentions. The manner in which the American vote was procured has been shown. As to some of the other votes, Under Secretary Robert Lovett said at the next Cabinet lunch (December 1, 1947) that "he had never in his life been subject to so much pressure as he had been in the last three days." The Firestone Tire and Rubber Company, which had a concession in Liberia, reported (he said) that it had been asked by telephone to instruct its representative in Liberia "*to bring pressure on the Liberian Government to vote in favour of partition.*" (Mr. Loy Henderson's account of the "great pressure" used to get American "solicitation" of the votes of small countries has already been quoted). Thus was the "vote" of "the United Nations" produced in the most explosive issue of this century's world affairs.

At the Cabinet lunch immediately after this "vote" Mr. Forrestal returned to the attack: "I remarked that many thoughtful people of the Jewish faith had deep misgivings about the wisdom of the Zionists' *pressures* for a Jewish state in Palestine ... The decision was fraught with *great danger for the future security of this country.*" He then discussed the question (December 3, 1947) with Mr. James

F. Byrnes, who had ceased to be Secretary of State earlier in the year (his relegation was foreseeable; it was he who disclosed President Roosevelt's pledge to Ibn Saoud).

Mr. Byrnes said President Truman's actions had placed the British Government "in a most difficult position" and added that Mr. David

K. Niles and Judge Samuel Rosenman "were chiefly responsible" for it. Both these men had been brought into the White House among the "Palace Guard" with which Mr. Roosevelt surrounded himself; Mr. Niles (of Russian-Jewish descent) was the "adviser on Jewish affairs" and Judge Rosenman had helped write presidential speeches. These men (said Mr. Byrnes) told Mr. Truman "that Dewey was about to come out with a statement favouring the Zionist position on Palestine, and had insisted that unless the President anticipated this moment *New York State would be lost to the Democrats.*"

Here Mr. Byrnes gave another glimpse of the behind-the-scenes auction. The two candidates for the highest office in the United States (Mr. Thomas Dewey was the prospective nominee of the other party," the Republican) in these portrayals look like children, incited against each other by the offer of a dangling bag of sweets. Mr. Truman, by doing the Zionist bidding in the matter of partition, had by no means ensured the Democrats of the prize, for the election was still a year distant and during that time the Zionists were to demand more and more, and the Republican party to bid higher and higher for the dangling reward.

Mr. Forrestal, in desperation, now tried to convince the Republican Mr. Dewey: "I said the Palestine matter was a matter of the deepest concern to me *in terms of the security of the nation*, and asked, once more, if the parties could not agree to take this question out of their electoral campaigning." Governor (of New York State) Dewey's response was much the same as President Truman's: "It was a difficult matter to get results because of the intemperate attitude of the Jewish people who had taken Palestine as the emotional symbol, *because the Democratic party would not be willing to relinquish the advantages of the Jewish vote*." Thereon Mr. Dewey continued to try and outdo the Democratic politicians in his bid for "the Jewish vote" (and to his own surprise nevertheless lost the election).

Mr. Forrestal next tried to strengthen the hand of the State Department, in its resistance to the President, by a memorandum (January 21, 1948) in which he analyzed the dangers to American national security flowing from this entanglement: "It is doubtful if there is any segment of our foreign relations of greater importance *or of greater danger ... to the security of the United States* than our relations in the Middle East." He warned against doing "permanent injury to our relations with the Moslem world" and "a stumble into war." He said he had found "some small encouragement" among individual Republicans for his proposal to take the question "out of party-politics," but among the Democrats had met a feeling *"that a substantial part of the Democratic funds come from Zionist sources inclined to ask in return for a lien upon this part of our national policy."*

The last nine words are explicit and are literally correct. The Zionists demanded the submission of American state policy and offered in return a four year tenure of the presidency to the highest bidder. Whether they were in truth able to deliver what they offered has never been tested; the party-managers took them at their word and the candidates of *both* parties put on the sackcloth of submission before they were nominated, knowing (or believing) that they would not even achieve nomination unless they wore it.

Mr. Forrestal urged the Secretary of State (General Marshall) to remonstrate with the President, pointing out that a large body of Jews "hold the view that the present zeal of the Zionists can have most dangerous consequences, not merely in *their divisive effects in American life, but in the long run on the position of Jews throughout the world."*

Under-Secretary Lovett, on reading Mr. Forrestal's memorandum, produced one already prepared by the Planning Staff of the State Department. This informed the President that the partition plan was "not workable" (exactly as British governments had been warned by their colonial administrators that "the Mandate" was "not workable"); that the United States was *not* committed to support it if it could not be effected without force; that it was against American interest to supply arms to the Zionists while refusing them to the Arabs; that the United States should not take on itself to enforce the "recommendation" of partition *and should try to secure withdrawal of the partition proposal.*

Mr. Lovett added, "the use of the United Nations by others as a propaganda platform is complicating our conduct of foreign relations" and said the State Department was "seriously embarrassed and handicapped by the activities of Niles at the White House in going directly to the President on matters involving Palestine." On that very day, the Under-Secretary complained, he had once more been under "pressure"; Mr. Niles had telephoned from the White House "expressing the hope that the embargo on the sales of arms to the Zionists would be lifted."

At that point Mr. Forrestal evidently became an acute annoyance to the powers behind the White House and his elimination was decided. First he received a visit from Mr. Franklin D. Roosevelt junior. Whatever the father's deathbed pledge not to take "hostile action against the Arabs," the son (a New York politician, with presidential hopes) was an extreme Zionist partisan. Mr. Forrestal pointedly said, "I thought the methods that had been used by people *outside* of the Executive branch of the government to bring *coercion and duress on other nations in the General Assembly bordered closely on scandal."* He records (as if with surprise) that his visitor "made no threats" in response to this, and he then explained his proposal to "lift the question out of politics" by agreement between the parties.

Mr. Roosevelt, his father's son, replied that "this was *impossible,* that the nation was *too far committed,* and that, furthermore, the Democratic Party would be bound to lose and the Republicans to gain by such an agreement." Mr. Forrestal answered that "failure to go along with the Zionists might lose the states of New York, Pennsylvania and California;" (the "pivotal states" earlier mentioned by party-manager McGrath) "I thought it was about time that somebody should pay some consideration to whether we might not lose the United States."

No comment by Mr. Roosevelt is recorded, but he was a harbinger of ill for Mr. Forrestal because on this same day (February 3, 1948) came the intervention of Mr. Bernard Baruch. Mr. Baruch, earlier an opponent of Zionism, was now so zealous in the cause that he advised Mr. Forrestal "*not to be active in this* matter … I was already identified, *to a degree that was not in my own interests*, with opposition to the United Nations policy on Palestine."

Ominous words for Mr. Forrestal! The annals here record for the first time a specific intervention by Mr. Baruch in high affairs, and its nature. His counsel was that Mr. Forrestal, a Cabinet officer, consider his *own* interest, which was endangered; until that time Mr. Forrestal as a responsible Cabinet officer had considered only the interest of his country. Mr. Forrestal does not say whether he saw in this advice anything threatening; his allusion to Mr. Roosevelt on the same day shows that the thought of "threats" was in his mind.

He then gave way to the fear which in the end cowed nearly all men who strove against the thrall of Zion. Four days later (February 7, 1948) he drew up a last paper on the subject which he never submitted to the President, but which contains something of historical importance. He said that on February 6, "Eisenhower told me that effective United States participation in a Palestine police force would involve about one division with appropriate supporting units." At that time, therefore, General Eisenhower (then Chief of Staff) was drafting plans for the potential engagement of American troops in Palestine. Mr. Forrestal put away this last memorandum. On February 12 and 18 he made two final appeals to General Marshall to contend with the President and the party-managers and at that point his efforts ceased.

His desisting availed him nothing for within a twelvemonth he was literally hounded to death. His end needs to be described here, before the armed seizure of Palestine is recorded; it is the classic case of persecution by defamation, leading to death.

I first went to America early in 1949 and was perplexed by the venom of the attacks, in the press and radio, on one Mr. James Forrestal, Secretary for Defence. I knew nothing of him but his name, and the part he played in this affair (as above recorded) was then entirely unknown to the public. Nevertheless they read or heard daily that he was insane, a coward who had left his wife to be attacked by a burglar, a tax defaulter, and all manner of other things. By chance I met a friend of his who told me that he had been so reduced by this persecution that those near to him were gravely alarmed. A few weeks later he threw himself from a high window, leaving in his room some copied verses from Greek tragedy which ended with the refrain" "Woe, woe! will be the cry …"

American libel laws are liberal and differ from state to state, and litigation is long. Even a successful action may not bring redress. Hardly any limit is in practice set to what may be said about a man singled out for defamation; the slanders are printed in the language that incites mob-passions and when broadcast are uttered in rabid accents that recalled to me the voices of primitive African tribespeople in moments of catalepsy. Among Mr.

Forrestal's effects was found a scrapbook full of these attacks, and towards the end he could not listen to the radio. The refuse of calumny was emptied on his head and at the end two broadcasters joined for the kill. One of them announced (January 9, 1949) that President Truman would "accept Forrestal's resignation within a week" (and followed this with some slander about shares in the German Dye Trust). On January 11 the second broadcaster told the millions that President Truman would by that time have accepted Mr. Forrestal's resignation, had not the first broadcaster anticipated the event (the jewel- robbery story was added to this). A few weeks earlier President Truman had told the Press that he had asked Mr. Forrestal *not* to resign; on March 1 he sent for Mr. Forrestal and demanded his immediate resignation, without explanation, to be effective from May 1. Mr. Forrestal committed suicide on May 21. At the funeral ceremony Mr. Truman described him as "a victim of the war"!

(In parentheses, at that time another man was being hounded to the same death, which he escaped, later in the same year, only by the failure of his suicide attempt. His persecution came from the same defamationist source, though his offence was in the other field, Communism. Mr. Whittaker Chambers sinned by his efforts to expose Communist infiltration of the American Government. I was in America at the time of his ordeal, which is described in his book; this contains the striking example, to which I earlier alluded, of the Talmudic practice of "cursing by an angry, fixed look" (the *Jewish Encyclopaedia*). Literal Talmudists would presumably see in Mr. Chambers's suicide attempt, and in the ill-health which subsequently afflicted him, a token of the literal efficacy of "the Law" in this respect).

After Mr. Forrestal's retreat into silence, at the warning of Mr . Baruch, the responsible men at the State Department continued their struggle, headed by General Marshall. (All this while, in England, Mr. Bevin was carrying on his lonely fight against the Conservative opposition and against the mass of his own party alike). At one point, for the first time since 1917, the responsible Cabinet officers and officials in both countries seemed to have won the day.

This was in March 1948. Violence in Palestine had so greatly increased after the United Nations' "recommendation" for the country' s bisection that the Security Council grew alarmed and beat a retreat. Even President Truman was shaken and his representative in the Security Council announced *the reversal of American policy*, proposing (March 19, 1948) that the partition proposal be *suspended*, that a truce be arranged, and that the end of the "Mandate" be followed by a "Trusteeship" (this was in effect the proposal of the State Department memorandum of January).

At the last moment the idea of "the Jewish state" thus seemed about to collapse. The post-war return to reason was beginning (that process which Mr. Lloyd George, thirty years before, had warningly called the "thaw") and if the coup now failed only a third world war could provide another opportunity. The "Trusteeship" would be the "Mandate" in a new form, but with the United States as the country chiefly involved, and in another ten or twenty years America, foreseeably, would find the "Trusteeship" as "unworkable," under Zionist pressure, as the British had found the "Mandate."

It was then or never, and the Zionists struck at once. They presented the "United Nations" with the accomplished fact by bisecting Palestine themselves. The terrorist deed by means of which this was accomplished was the result of the policy adopted at the World Zionist Congress of 1946, where "the demoralizing forces in the movement" (Dr. Weizmann's words) had recommended methods of "Resistance ... defence ... activism," and Dr. Weizmann, who knew what was meant, had been deposed for objecting to them.

Dr. Weizmann then had called "the terror in Palestine" the "old evil in a new and horrible guise." April 9, 1948 showed what he meant, and in particular why he called it the *old* evil. On that day the "activists," the terror-and-assassination group of Zionism, "utterly destroyed" an Arab village in exact and literal fulfilment of "the Law" laid down in *Deuteronomy* (which, the reader will recall, is the basic Judaic law but was itself an amendment of the original Mosaic law of the Israelites).

This was the most significant day in the entire story of Zionism. To the Arabs (who knew the Torah and "had known for two thousand years what you have fought two world wars to learn") it meant that the savage Law of Judah, devised by the Levites between 700 and 400 BC, was to be resurrected and imposed on them in full force and violence, with the support of the Christian West and of Communized Russia alike. The symbolic massacre, they knew, was intended to show what would happen to all of them if they stayed. Thereon almost the entire Arab population of Palestine fled into the neighbouring Arab states.

The massacre at Deir Yasin was briefly reported in the West, for instance *Time* magazine of New York said: "Jewish terrorists of the Stem Gang and Irgun Zvai Leumi stormed the village of Deir Yasin and butchered everyone in sight. The corpses of 250 Arabs, mostly women and small children, were later found tossed into wells."

At the Versailles Peace Conference in 1919 Dr. Weizmann had declared, "The Bible is our mandate," and the words sounded good to Western ears. This event showed what they meant, and the same words were repeated by the Zionist leaders in Palestine thirty years after Dr. Weizmann used them. The massacre at Deir Yasin was an act of "observance" of the ancient "statutes and commandments," including the relevant passage in *Deuteronomy*, "When the Lord thy God shall bring thee into the land whither thou goest to possess it, and shall cast out ... seven nations greater and mightier than thou ... then thou shalt *utterly destroy them;* thou shalt make no covenant with them, *nor show mercy unto them,*" and the related passage, "*thou shalt save alive nothing that breatheth, but thou shalt utterly destroy them.*" There are *seven* Arab states today, and each of them has its share of the fugitives of 1948, who for eight years now have been a living reminder to them of the common future fate with which Zionism threatens them under the ancient Law.

The passive condonation of this deed by Jewry as a whole showed more clearly than anything else the change which Zionism had wrought in the Jewish mind in a few years. Writing in 1933 (only fifteen years before Deir Yasin), Mr. Bernard J. Brown quoted the above passage from *Deuteronomy* as the reason for Arab fears, and added, "Of course, the uncultured Arabs do not understand that the modem Jew does not take his bible literally, and that he is a kind and charitable person and would not be so cruel to his fellow-man, but he suspects that if the Jews bottom their claim to Palestine on the strength of the historic rights to that land, *they can only do so on the authority of the Bible, and the Arab refuses to reject any part of it.*" The Arabs were right and Mr. Brown was wrong; this enlightened Western Jew could not conceive, in 1933, that Zionism meant a full return to the superstition of antiquity in its most barbaric form.

Probably Deir Yasin remained an isolated incident only because its meaning was so clear that the Arabs left the country. Mr. Arthur Koestler is definite about this cause-and-effect. He was in Palestine and says the Arab civilian population, after Deir Yasin, at once fled from Haifa, Tiberia, Jaffa and all other cities and then from the entire country, so that "by May 14 all had gone save for a few thousand." All impartial authorities agree about the intention and effect of Deir Yasin, and from April 9, 1948 no doubt remained about the governing force of the ancient Judaic Law on all future acts and ambitions of Zion. Deir Yasin explains the fear of the surviving Arab states today as fully as it explains the flight of the Palestinian Arabs.

THE ZIONIST STATE (2)

Deir Yasin, for a little while, solved the Zionists' problem. The partition of Palestine had been achieved, by force. At the same time the event revealed (to the Arabs, if not then to the West) the nature of Dr. Weizmann's "abyss into which terrorism leads." From April 9, 1948 the West itself stood on the brink of this abyss, dug by the acts of two generations of its politicians.

Thus the situation changed completely between March 19, 1948, when the American Government decided that partition was "unworkable" and reversed its policy, and April 9, 1948, when terrorism effected partition. Dr. Weizmann must still have been haunted by his fears, but now that the territory for the Jewish state had been cleared he would not or could not withdraw from "the abyss." The aim now was to achieve a second reversal of American policy, to gain an expression of approval for what had been done by terrorism, and to this end, once more, Dr. Weizmann bent all his efforts. At the first reversal of American policy he had been urgently summoned from London to Lake Success by letters, cables and telephone calls, and the day before it was announced he was again closeted with President Truman. As the days passed, and the news from Deir Yasin flickered briefly over the tapes, he laboured tirelessly at his supreme task: the winning of "recognition" for the Jewish State set up by the terrorists at Deir Yasin.

Dr. Weizmann's energy was extraordinary. He conducted a one-man siege of the entire "United Nations" (of course, he was everywhere received as the representative of a new kind of world-power). He was "in close contact," for instance, with the delegates of Uruguay and Guatemala, whom he calls "the ever gallant defenders" of Zionism, and with the Secretary General of the United Nations, at that time a Mr. Trygve Lie from Norway. In mid-April, with the tidings from Deir Yasin rising to its very nostrils, the General Assembly of the United Nations met. The American vote was clearly to be decisive, and Dr. Weizmann remarks that he "began to be preoccupied with the idea of American recognition of the Jewish state." In other words, American state policy, formed in the constitutional process of consultation between the Chief Executive and his responsible Cabinet officers, was once more to be reversed at the demand of Chaim Weizmann.

Dates are again significant. On *May 13,* 1948, Dr. Weizmann saw President Truman; the contest for the presidential nominations then lay immediately ahead and the presidential election a few months beyond, so that this was the ideal moment to apply "irresistible pressure." Dr. Weizmann informed President Truman that the British mandate would end on May 15 and a provisional government would then take over "the Jewish state." He urged that the United States "promptly" recognize it and the President acted with zealous alacrity.

On *May 14* (Palestine time) the Zionists in Tel Aviv proclaimed their new state. A few minutes later "unofficial news" reached Lake Success that President Truman had recognized it. The American delegates (who had not been informed) "were incredulous," but "after much confusion" they made contact with the White House and received from it Dr. Weizmann's instructions, transmitted through the President. Dr. Weizmann forthwith repaired to Washington as the President of the new state, and President Truman received his guest, thereafter announcing that the moment of recognition was "the proudest of my life."

Eight years later President Truman in his memoirs depicted the circumstances in which his "proudest moment" came about, and his account may appropriately be cited here. Describing the six-month period (from the "partition-vote" in November 1947 to "recognition" in April 1948), he says: "Dr. Chaim Weizmann ... called on me on November 19 and a few days later I received a letter from him." Mr. Truman then quotes this letter, dated *November* 27; in it Dr. Weizmann refers to "rumours" that "our people have exerted undue and excessive pressure on certain" (United Nations) "delegations" and, speaking for himself [Weizmann], says "there is no substance in this charge." Mr. Truman comments, "The facts were that not only were there pressure movements around the United Nations *unlike anything that had been seen there before, but that the White House, too, was subjected to a constant barrage. I do not think I ever had as much pressure and propaganda aimed at the White House as I had in this instance. The persistence of a few of the extreme Zionist leaders - actuated by political motives and engaging in political threats - disturbed me and annoyed me. Some were even suggesting that we pressure sovereign nations into favourable votes in the General Assembly."*

The "political threats" mentioned here obviously related to President Truman's approaching re-election campaign; this is the only reasonable interpretation of the words. Mr. Truman (according to Dr. Weizmann) promised, at the interview on November 19, "to communicate at once with the American delegation" and the United States vote was then given, on *November 29*, to the "recommendation" that Palestine be partitioned. Thus President Truman's anger (as recorded in his narrative of 1956) at the methods used in no wise delayed his capitulation to them in 1947 (if that were not made plain the reader of his *Memoirs* might gain a different impression).

Mr. Truman (in 1956) recorded the outcome of the "solution" (the partition recommendation) supported by him in November 1947: "every day now brought reports of *new violence* in the Holy Land." He also found that his capitulation of November and Dr. Weizmann's disclaimer of "undue pressure" had no effect at all in the months that followed: "*The Jewish pressure on the White House did not diminish in the days following the partition vote in the United Nations. Individuals and groups asked me, usually in rather quarrelsome and emotional ways, to stop the Arabs, to keep the British from supporting the Arabs, to furnish*

American soldiers, to do this, that and the other" (Disraeli's picture of "the world being governed by very different persons from what is imagined by those who are not behind the scenes"). The President sought refuge in retreat: "As the pressure *mounted*, I found it necessary to give instructions that I did not want to be approached by any more spokesmen for the extreme Zionist cause. *I was even so disturbed that I put off seeing Dr. Weizmann,* who had returned to the United States and had asked for an interview with me." Mr. Truman, in 1956, evidently still held the postponement of an interview with Dr. Weizmann to have been so drastic a measure as to deserve permanent record. He was then visited (March 13, 1948) by an old Jewish business associate "who was deeply moved by the sufferings of the Jewish people abroad" (this was less than a month before the massacre at Deir Yasin) and who implored him to receive Dr. Weizmann, which President Truman at once did (March 18).

This was the day before American support was withdrawn from the partition recommendation (March 19). Mr. Truman says that when Dr. Weizmann left him (on March 18) "I felt he had reached a full understanding of my policy and that I knew what it was he wanted." Mr. Truman then passes over the bloody weeks that followed without a word (he does not mention Deir Yasin), except for an incidental statement that "the Department of State's specialists on the Near East were, almost without exception, unfriendly to the idea of a Jewish state … I am sorry to say that there were some among them who were also inclined to be anti-Semitic." He resumes his narrative two months later (May 14, after Deir Yasin and the accompanying bloodshed) then saying, "Partition was not taking place in *exactly* the peaceful manner I had hoped, but the fact was that the Jews were controlling the area in which their people lived … Now that the Jews were ready to proclaim the State of Israel I decided to move at once and give American recognition to the new nation. About thirty minutes later, *exactly eleven minutes* after Israel had been proclaimed a state, Charlie Ross, my press secretary, handed the press the announcement of the *de facto* recognition by the United States of the provisional government of Israel. I was told that to some of the career men of the State Department this announcement came as a surprise."

Mr. Truman does not in his *Memoirs* recall his statement of 1948 that this was "the proudest moment of my life," or explain why he felt it to be so; after many months of such "pressure" and "political threats" at the beleaguered White House that at one moment he was led to deny himself, if only for a short time, even to Dr. Weizmann! For the purposes of this narrative he now virtually passes from the story, having served his turn. He was elected president six months after his proudest moment and at the date of this book looks fit to live another twenty years, a dapper, hearty man on whom the consequences of the acts with which his name is identified apparently had as little effect as the fury of the ocean cyclone has on the bobbing cork. (In 1956 he joined the company of those who have been awarded an honorary degree by the ancient University of Oxford, a woman don there raising a lonely and unheeded voice against its bestowal on the Chief Executive whose name is best known from its association with the order to atom-bomb Nagasaki and Hiroshima).

After President Truman's proud recognition of what had been done in Palestine between November 1947 and May 1948 the debate at the "United Nations" lost importance and Dr. Weizmann (who in his letter to President Truman of November 27, 1947 had warmly denied the use of "undue pressure") set to work to muster other recognitions, so that the issue should be put beyond doubt. He learned that Mr. Bevin, in London, "was bringing pressure to bear on the British Dominions ... to withhold recognition," and he at once showed who was the greater expert in applying "pressure."

Historically regarded, this was a moment of the first importance, because it showed for the first time that Zionism, which had so deeply divided Jewry, had divided the nations of the British Empire, or Commonwealth; what no warlike menace or danger had ever achieved, "irresistible pressure on international politics" smoothly accomplished. Suddenly Zion was shown to be supreme in capitals as far from the central scene as Ottawa, Canberra, Cape Town and Wellington.

This gave proof of superb staffwork and synchronization; miracles of secret organization must have been performed, in a few decades, to ensure the obedience, at the decisive moment, of the "top-line politicians" in Canada, Australia, South Africa and New Zealand. These countries were remote from Palestine; they had no interest in implanting the fuse of new world war in the Middle East; their Jewish populations were tiny. Yet submission was instantaneous. This was world power in operation.

The great significance of what transpired may need explaining to non-British readers. The bonds between the British island and the overseas nations sprung from it, though they were intangible and rested on no compulsion, had in emergency repeatedly shown a strength, mysterious to outsiders. An anecdote may illustrate:

The New Zealand Brigadier George Clifton relates that when he was captured in the Western Desert in 1941 he was brought before Field Marshal Rommel, who asked, "Why are you New Zealanders fighting? This is a European war, not yours! Are you here for the sport?"

Brigadier Clifton was perplexed to explain something which to him was as natural as life itself: "Realizing he was quite serious and really meant this, and never having previously tried to put into words the, to us, self-evident fact that if Britain fought then we fought too, I held up my hand with the fingers together and said, 'We stand together. If you attack England, you attack New Zealand and Australia and Canada too. The British Commonwealth fights together.'"

That was true, in respect of *people,* but it was no longer true in respect of "topline politicians." Through them, the conspiracy from Russia had found the chink in the armour. The "pressure" in Wellington (and the other capitals) was as powerful and effective as it was around the White House. In this particular case (New Zealand) a typical figure of that time and group of helots was a Mr. Peter Fraser, Prime Minister of New Zealand. None could have had less cause to hate, or even to know anything about Arabs, but he was their implacable enemy, because he had somehow become another captive of Zionism. This poor Scottish lad, who went to the other edge of the world and found fame and fortune there, apparently picked up the infection during impressionable youthful years in London (when it was spreading among ambitious young politicians there) and took it with him to the new country, so that decades later he applied all his energies and the power of his office to the destruction of harmless folk in Palestine! When he died in 1950 a Zionist newspaper wrote of him:

"He was a convinced Zionist ... He was busy leading the United Nations delegation of his country at the Paris Assembly, but gave much time and attention to the Palestine issue ... *sitting day after day at the Political Committee when Palestine was discussed. He never left the room for one moment;* no detail escaped his attention ... *He was the only Premier on the committee and left it as soon as Palestine was dealt with ... Time and again Peter Fraser found himself voting against the United Kingdom, but he did not care ... He remained a friend until his last day."*

A man with this alien ambition in his heart certainly thought quite differently from Brigadier Clifton and his kind, and had he known how his Prime Minister felt Brigadier Clifton might have been much more puzzled to know how to reply to Field Marshal Rommel. Being so much preoccupied with Zionism Mr. Fraser could not be expected to be wholehearted in his country's interest and New Zealand went into the Second War all unready, so that when he met New Zealand survivors from Greece and Crete at Port Said in 1941 they were "haggard, unshaven, battle-stained, many of them wounded, all badly worn both physically and mentally, all worried by the loss of so many good 'Cobbers'; Mr. Fraser was responsible, in part, for this" (Brigadier Clifton). With this man as prime minister, New Zealand's quick recognition of what had been done in Palestine was assured, little though the New Zealanders knew it. In South Africa, Dr. Weizmann, in his moves to discomfort Mr. Bevin, turned at once to General Smuts, whom the reader met long ago. By chance I was in South Africa at that moment. A well-known Zionist emissary came speeding from New York by air and when I read of his arrival I foresaw what would follow. (This man appeared before a Zionist audience and told it that "the Jews need not feel themselves bound by any frontiers which the United Nations might lay down"; the only remonstrance against this, seen by me, came from a Jewish objector, who said such words boded ill for future peace).

General Smuts received this airborne visitor and then announced "recognition" at once, being beaten in promptness only by President Truman and the Soviet dictator Stalin, (who in this one question were perfectly agreed). This was, I believe, General Smuts's last political act, for he was defeated at an election two days later. His son strongly warned him against recognition, holding that it would lose him votes. General Smuts brushed the advice aside (rightly, from the electioneering point of view, for his opponents no doubt were ready to bid for the Zionist vote and South Africa contained no Arab voters).

General Smuts's renown throughout the British Commonwealth (and his unpopularity with most of his fellow Boers) rested entirely on the popular belief that he was the architect of "Anglo-Boer reconciliation" and a champion of the great-family concept. In this one question he deserted the hard-pressed government in London with the unquestioning obedience of long-instilled discipline. I achieved an old ambition to meet him at that time. His days were ending and he too now disappears from this tale, but before he died he, like Dr. Weizmann, had seen "the abyss" which he had helped dig: "in the problem of Palestine" (he told his son later in the same year, 1948) "there is *tragedy at our doorstep* ... No wonder Britain is getting sick and tired of it all. Failure in Palestine will not only be a British failure. Other nations have also taken a hand, including America, and they have also failed. Palestine ... is one of the great problems of the world and can have a great effect on the future of the world ... We have thought to let the Arabs and Jews fight it out, *but we cannot do that. Power is on the move, and Palestine lies on the road.*"

So he spoke privately, but not publicly. Apparently politicians, like the clown in the opera, feel they must ever wear the mask in public. Like Mr. Truman, he did what Dr. Weizmann commanded without delay and even in 1949, for the benefit of a Zionist audience, said he was "happy to have been associated with at least *one thing in my life which has been successful.*"

The retreat from London became a rout. Dr. Weizmann records that the New Zealand representative, Sir Carl Berendsen, then "won support from Australia," and soon the "top-line politicians" in Canada followed suit. When the British Dominions followed Mr. Truman and Generalissimo Stalin the smaller states thronged to give "recognition"; they could not refuse to tread where these great ones had rushed in, and thus "the Jewish state" took shape "de facto," the fact being the massacre at Deir Yasin.

Although he became its president, this is in truth the point at which Dr. Chaim Weizmann passes from the narrative, after fifty years of an activity, essentially conspiratorial, in which he encompassed the capitulation of all political leaders of the West and left "tragedy," like a foundling, on its common doorstep. I would not know where to look for a more fascinating life and another writer might be able to depict it in heroic tones. To me it seems to have been given to a destructive purpose and Dr. Weizmann, whose years were nearly done when he reached his triumph, found triumph a bitter, perhaps a lethal cup.

So I judge, at all events, from his book, the last part of which is of absorbing interest. It was published in 1949, so that he could have brought his account to the point now reached by this one, at least. He did not. He closed it in 1947. Now, why did he do that?

I think the answer is obvious. In 1946 he had warned the World Zionist Organization against "terror" and depicted "the abyss" into which "the old evil" must lead, and had been deposed in consequence. Then he had become president of the new state set up by "terror." I think he wished to leave his warning to Jewry on record and could not bring himself to discuss the deeds of terror and assassination in which the new state was born, so that he pretended to have ended the manuscript *before* they occurred.

He put the date of completion as November 30, 1947, the day after his triumph at Lake Success (when President Truman, at his prompting, telephoned the American delegation to vote for partition). Evidently he wished the book to end on that note. The reversal of American policy, and the deeds against which he had uttered warning, soon followed, and as the book was not to appear until 1949 he had plenty of time to express his opinion of them. All he did was to add an epilogue in which he did not even mention the determining deed at Deir Yasin, the contemptuous answer to his warnings. Moreover, he again went out of his way to say that this epilogue was finished in *August* 1948; this saved him the need to make any reference to the next determining deed of terrorism, the assassination of Count Bernadotte, which occurred in *September* 1948. Obviously Dr. Weizmann quailed. He had identified himself with both massacre and murder by accepting and retaining the presidency of the new state.

For that reason his earlier warnings are of the greatest significance; he *could* have deleted them before publication. For instance, he charged "the terrorists" (into whose hands he delivered the future of Palestine, and of much more than Palestine) with trying to *"force the hand of God."* This, obviously was the heresy of Zionism, and of all those who supported it, whether Jew or Gentile, from the very start, and of Dr. Weizmann more than most others. He added, *"the terrorist groups in Palestine represented a grave danger to the whole future of the Jewish state; actually their behaviour has been next door to anarchy."* It *was* anarchy, not neighbour to anarchy, and Dr. Weizmann's life's effort was anarchic. Even in this argument he was not moved by moral recoil; his complaint was not against the destructive nature of anarchy itself, but merely that it was inexpedient, "because the Jews have hostages all over the world."

On the very day after his triumph at Lake Success he returned to his new theme: "There must not be one law for the Jew and another for the Arabs ... The Arabs must be given the feeling that the decision of the United Nations is final, and that the Jews will not trespass on any territory outside the boundaries assigned to them. There does exist such a fear in the hearts of many Arabs and this fear must be eliminated in every way … They must see from the outset that their brethren within the Jewish state are treated exactly like the Jewish citizens … We must not bend the knee to strange gods. The Prophets have always chastised the Jewish people with the utmost severity for this tendency, and whenever it slipped back into paganism, whenever it reverted, it was punished by the stern god of Israel … I am certain that the world will judge the Jewish state by what it will do with the Arabs."

Thou sayest! Here Dr. Weizmann put on the robes of an Israelite prophet, or perhaps the crown of Canute bidding the tide retreat. When these words were published the Arabs had already been driven from their native lands, the Jews *had* "trespassed" on territory outside the boundaries earlier "recommended"; the Arabs were not being treated "exactly like the Jewish citizens" but were homeless and destitute fugitives. Dr. Weizmann pretended not to know all that! He ignored all that had happened and said it must not happen. As an example of published hypocrisy this can hardly be excelled even in politics. The probable explanation is that he still could not bring himself to denounce what had been done but, as his death approached, felt he must point out its consequences; those consequences to which his life's work from the start was bound to lead, if it were successful. At the last he cried "Back!," and all in vain.

A greater man than he cried out in horror and linked the consequences to the *deeds,* which he did not fear to name. Dr. Judah Magnes was in the direct line of the Israelite remonstrants of old. Born in America in 1877, like Dr. Weizmann he had given his life to Zionism, but in a different spirit. He was a *religious* Zionist, not a political one, and did not presume "to force God's hand." From the start he had worked for the establishment of an Arab-Jewish binational state and had attacked Zionist chauvinism from its first appearance. He became Chancellor of the Hebrew University at Jerusalem in 1925 (having strongly objected to Dr. Weizmann's pompous foundation-stone ceremony in 1918), was its president from 1935, and in 1948 was in Jerusalem. He was appalled by the emergence of "the old evil in a new and horrible guise" and left a valedictory lament condemning the Zionists and the Western politicians alike:

"Refugees should never be made use of as a trump in the hands of politicians. It is deplorable, incredible even, after all that the Jews in Europe have gone through, that an Arab problem of displaced persons should be created in the Holy Land."

He died immediately after saying this and I have not been able to discover the circumstances of his death; references to it in Jewish literature are often cryptic and resemble those concerning the breakdown and sudden death of Dr. Herzl. For instance, one such allusion (in the foreword to Rabbi Elmer Berger's book of 1951) says he "died of a broken heart."

In Dr. Magnes another Jewish peacemaker joined the group of responsible men who for fifty years had vainly sought to keep the West (and the Jews) out of the grip of a Talmudic conspiracy from Russia. He founded and left an organization, the Ihud Association, which still speaks with his voice, and even from Jerusalem. Its organ there, NER, in December 1955 said, "Ultimately we shall have to come out with the truth openly: We have no right whatever, on principle, to prevent the return of the Arab refugees to their soil ... What should Ihud strive for? To transform the perennial powder keg (which is the State of Israel, according to Minister Pinhas Lavon) into a place of peaceful habitation. And what weapons is the Ihud to use? The weapons of truth ... We had no right to occupy an Arab house without first paying its price; and the same is true of the fields and groves, the stores and factories. We have had no right whatever to colonize and materialize Zionism at the expense of others. This is robbery; this is banditry ... We are once more among the very rich nations, but we are not ashamed to rob the property of the fellaheen."

This is a still small voice in Jewry at the present moment (incidentally, Dr. Albert Einstein spoke with the same voice: "My awareness of the essential nature of Judaism resists the idea of a Jewish state with borders, an army and a measure of temporal power, no matter how modest; I am afraid of the inner damage Judaism will sustain," 1950), but it is the only one which gives Jewry the hope of ultimate salvation from the Zionism of the Chazars. Today the probability, if not the certainty, is that this salvation can only come after the final tribulation in which the wanton adventure in Palestine must involve the multitudes of the West, the Jews among them.

One final point remains to be established about the creation, "*de facto*," of the Zionist state; namely, that it was the child of the revolution. The revolution enabled the Jews "to become a majority in Palestine," as the British authors of the Balfour Declaration of 1917 had desired, and this transformation in Palestine could not have been effected in any other way, for no large body of Jews anywhere else in the world could have been brought to go there. The mass-movement was only possible in the case of these Eastern Jews who for centuries had lived in close Talmudic regimentation, and the manner of their transportation to Palestine has been shown. In 1951 Israeli Government statistics showed that of the "majority" which had been achieved (about 1,400,000 Jews), 1,061,000 were foreign-born, and 577,000 of these came from the communized countries behind the Iron curtain, where non-Jews were not allowed to move even from one town to another without police and other permits. (Most of the remaining 484,000 were North African or Asiatic Jews who arrived after the establishment of the state and took no part in its violent acquisition).

The invaders, therefore, were the Eastern Jews of Tartar-Mongol stock, but force of numbers alone would not have ensured their success. They needed arms for that. During the war General Wavell had informed Mr. Churchill that the Jews, if allowed to, could "beat the Arabs," and he evidently based this judgment on the arms which, as he knew, the Zionists had then amassed. At that time these could only have been British or American arms, clandestinely obtained from the depots of the Allied armies operating in North Africa and the Middle East (a process at least winked at, if not officially approved, by the political leaders in London and Washington, as has been shown). General Wavell, though his opinion proved correct, may at the time have overestimated the Zionist strength or have underestimated Arab resistance, for the Zionists, after the event, did not attribute it to the Allied weapons obtained by them. On the contrary, they believed that they owed their victory in the six months of fighting (between the "partition" vote and Deir Yasin) to the arms they received from the revolution. The Iron Curtain, which had opened to let the invaders of Palestine leave, opened again to allow arms to reach them in decisive quantities.

This was the first major consequence of General Eisenhower's order, issued under President Roosevelt's direction, to halt the Allied armies west of the Berlin-Vienna line and allow Czechoslovakia to fall to the Soviet; the arms came from that captive country, where the great Skoda arsenal, as a result of his order, had merely passed from Nazi into Communist hands. A few weeks after President Truman's recognition of the Zionist state the *New York Herald-Tribune* published this report from Israel:

"Russian prestige has soared enormously among all political factions ... Through its consistent espousal of Israel's cause in the United Nations, the Soviet Union has established a goodwill reservoir with leftists, moderates and right wing elements. Perhaps of more importance to a new nation fighting for its existence has been a fact less generally known: that Russia provided practical help when practical help was needed ... Russia opened its military stores to Israel. From the Soviet satellite nation of Czechoslovakia, Jews made some of their most important and possibly their most sizable bulk purchases. Certain Czech arms shipments which reached Israel during critical junctures of the war played a vital role ... When Jewish troops marched in review down Tel Aviv's Allenby Street last week, new Czechoslovak rifles appeared on the shoulders of infantry soldiers" (August 5, 1948).

At that time the Zionist and Zionist-controlled press throughout the West began explicitly to identify "anti-Semitism," with "anti- Communism" (the attribution of Jewish origins and leadership to Communism had long been denounced as the mark of the "anti- Semite"). The Jewish *Sentinel* of Chicago, for instance, in June 1946 had already declared, "We recognize anti-Sovietism for what it really is ... Did you ever hear of any anti-Semites anywhere in the world who were not also anti-Soviet? ... We recognize our foes. Let us also recognize our friends, the Soviet people." In the schools of the new state itself the flag of the revolution was flown and its hymn sung on

May Day, an ostentatious acknowledgement of affinity if not of parenthood. In January 1950 the Tel Aviv correspondent of the London *Times* reported that Czechoslovakia was still the source of arms supply for the Zionist' state.

So much for the birth of "Israel" and the pains it caused to others. No offspring of political illegitimacy was ever ushered into the world by so many sponsors; the "recognitions" poured in and the peacemakers were everywhere discomfited. Mr. Bevin continued in office for a few years and then resigned, soon to die; General Marshall and Mr. Forrestal were dropped at the first opportunity, obviously for the discouragement of others who might take their responsible duty seriously.

Within a few weeks the new state took another step towards "the abyss" of "the old evil." The "United Nations," having accepted the accomplished bisection of Europe and recommended the bisection of Palestine, showed a tardy concern for "peace" and appealed to Count Folke Bernadotte of Sweden to go to Palestine and mediate between the parties. Count Bernadotte had always given himself to the mitigation of human suffering, particularly to the relief and rescue of Jewish victims during the Second War. He worked in the sign of the Cross (the red one) and was killed at the very place where the Cross first became a symbol of faith and hope. No deed can be more atrocious than the murder of an accepted peacemaker and mediator by one of the combatant parties, and within four months of its creation the Zionist state added this second symbolic act to its calendar.

Count Bernadotte (like Mr. Forrestal) kept a diary, published after his death. This records that, after accepting the mission of peace, he passed through London and was visited by Dr. Nahum Goldman, then vice-president of the Jewish Agency and the Zionist state's representative, who told him that: "the state of Israel *was now in a position to take full and complete responsibility for the acts committed by the Stern Gang and the members of Irgun.*"

These were the killer-groups whose deed at Deir Yasin effected the clearance of territory for the Zionists and was implicitly "recognized" by the West. They were the "activists" against whom Dr. Weizmann had uttered warning at the Zionist Congress of 1946. Deir Yasin had shown that they had the power, by calculated acts of terrorism, to change the whole course of world affairs, irrespective of anything said by Zionist leaders, by politicians in the West, or by the "United Nations."

They have this power in 1956, and will continue to have it. They can at any time precipitate the world into new war, for they have been placed in the most inflammable spot in the world, rightly described as "the powder keg" by an American Secretary of State, a British Foreign Secretary and the Zionist Premier himself. Up to the time when Dr. Nahum Goldman made the above-quoted statement to Count Bernadotte a pretence had been kept up that they were beyond the control of the "responsible" Zionist leaders, who deplored their acts. Dr. Goldman's assurance was presumably meant to convince

Count Bernadotte that his work of mediation would not be wantonly destroyed by any such act as that of Deir Yasin. The terrorists then murdered Count Bernadotte himself, and in the sequel (as will be shown) the Israeli government took responsibility for them and their deeds.

Count Bernadotte, after hearing these reassuring words, set out to pacify. In Egypt he saw the Prime Minister, Nokrashi Pasha, who said he "recognized the extent of Jewish economic power, *since it controlled the economic system of many countries, including the United States, England, France, Egypt itself and perhaps even Sweden*" (Count Bernadotte did not demur to the last statement). Nokrashi Pasha said the Arabs *did not expect to escape that domination.* However, for the Jews to achieve *economic* domination of the whole of Palestine was one thing; what the Arabs would not accept, and would resist, was the attempt *by force and terrorism,* and with the assistance of international Zionism, to set up a Zionist state based on coercion. After this King Farouk told Count Bernadotte that if the war continued (it has not yet ended) it would develop into a third world war; Count Bernadotte agreed and said he had for that reason accepted the task of Mediator.

He also mentioned that in the war he had had "the privilege of rescuing about 20,000 persons, many of them Jews; I myself had been in charge of this work." He evidently thought this would qualify him for Zionist respect, and was wrong. Within a few days he had persuaded the Arabs (on June 9, 1948) to agree unconditionally to a cease-fire, but then read a fanatical Zionist attack on himself for "having forced the truce on the Jews." "I began to realize what an exposed position I was in … the friendliness towards me would unquestionably turn to suspicion and ill will if, in my later activities as Mediator, *I failed to study primarily the interest of the Jewish party* but sought to find *an impartial and just solution* of the problem."

Irgun (for which the Zionist government through Dr. Goldman in London had claimed "full and complete responsibility") then broke the truce (June 18-30, 1948) by landing men and arms. Count Bernadotte and his observers "were unable to judge the number of Irgun men landed or the quantity of war material unloaded" because the Zionist government refused to allow them near the spot. In the first week of July "the Jewish press made very violent attacks on me." The defamationist method (used against Mr. Forrestal) was now employed and Count Bernadotte's efforts to rescue Jewish victims during the war were turned against him; the insinuation was made that his negotiations with the Nazi Gestapo chief, Heinrich Himmler, towards the war's end about the liberation of Jews had been of dubious character. "It was unjust to cast aspersions on me," (the innuendo was that Count Bernadotte was "a Nazi") "my work having been the means of saving the lives of about 10,000 Jews."

That meant as little to the Zionists as Alexander II's and Count Stolypin's efforts to "improve the lot of the Jews" forty years earlier; Count

Bernadotte's mortal offence was impartiality. Between July 19 and August 12 he had to tell Dr. Joseph, Zionist military governor of Jerusalem, that according to his observers' reports "the Jews were the most aggressive party in Jerusalem." On September 16, on the historic peacemaker's path "to Jerusalem" (the title of his book) Count Bernadotte in effect wrote his own death warrant; on that day he sent his "Progress Report" as Mediator from Rhodes to the United Nations, and within twenty-four hours he was murdered. The reason lay in his proposals. He accepted the "de facto" establishment of the Zionist state but, building on that basis, sought to reconcile and pacify by impartial proposals, as just to each party as the accomplished fact would allow. His chief concern was for the civilian Arab population, driven by the pogrom at Deir Yasin from its native villages and huddled beyond the frontiers. Nothing like this had ever been done under the wing of the West, and Count Bernadotte was fresh from efforts to rescue Jews from Hitler. Thus he proposed:

(l) that the boundaries of the Zionist state should be those envisaged in the "recommendation" of the United Nations on November 29, 1947, the Negev to remain Arab territory and the United Nations to ensure that these boundaries were "respected and maintained"; (2) that (as also "recommended") Jerusalem be internationalized under United Nations control; (3) that the United Nations should *"affirm and give effect to"* the right of the Arab fugitives to return to their homes.

Having despatched these proposals on September 16, 1948, Count Bernadotte, before they could reach New York, flew to Jerusalem (September 17). He and his party, unarmed and defenceless, drove towards Government House when their car was halted by a Zionist jeep pulled across the road. Their movements were clearly as well known as the contents of Count Bernadotte's report; three men jumped from the jeep, ran to his car, and with sten guns killed him and his Chief Observer in Jerusalem, the French Colonel Serot.

The survivors, in an appendix to his diary, describe the killing in detail. Their accounts show its efficient preparation and execution and plainly point to the identity of the chief organizer. The actual murderers escaped without hindrance, two in the jeep and one across country. None was arrested or charged (report, probably credible, says that a waiting aeroplane removed the murderers to communized Czechoslovakia). The subsequent Israeli enquiry stated that:

"The murder as it was actually carried out and all the preparations that went with it are predicated on the following points: (a) a clear decision to assassinate Count Bernadotte and the elaboration of a detailed plan for its carrying out; (b) a complex spy network capable of keeping track of the Count's movements during the time of his stay in Jerusalem so as to enable those responsible for the operation to fix its place and time; (c) men experienced in this kind of activities or who had received in good time training for it; (d) appropriate arms and methods of communication as well as safe refuge after the murder; (e) a commander well experienced and responsible for the actual perpetration."

For such men the new state had declared itself "fully responsible." Three days later a French news agency received a letter expressing regret that Colonel Serot, had been killed in mistake for the Mediator's Chief-of-Staff, the Swedish General Lundstrom, he being "an anti-Semite" (General Lundstrom was in another seat of the car). This letter was signed "Hazit Moledeth"; the Israeli police report stated that this was the name of the secret terrorist group within the Stern Gang.

General Lundstrom announced (September 18) that "These deliberate murders of two high international officials constitute a breach of the truce of the utmost gravity and a black page in Palestine's history *for which the United Nations will demand a full accounting.*" No such demand was to be expected from the United Nations which (as this account has shown) responds only to the strongest pressure exerted behind the scenes. It has (or then had; none can say what wondrous transformation the future might bring) no morality of its own; it was an oracle, worked by a hidden mechanism, and it did not trouble itself about the murder of its Mediator any more than the Washington and London governments had troubled about the persecution of Mr. Forrestal and the murder of Lord Moyne. It ignored the Mediator's proposals; the Zionists took and kept what territory they then wanted (*including* the Negev), refused to let the Arabs return, and proclaimed that they would not allow Jerusalem to be internationalized (they are implacable in these points today, eight years later). The world-newspapers brought out the editorial which they seemed to keep in standing-type for such occasions ("Incalculable harm has been done to the Zionist cause ...") and then resumed their daily denunciations of any who pleaded the Arab case as "anti-Semites." The *Times* of London even blamed Count Bernadotte for his own murder; it said the proposal to internationalize Jerusalem "undoubtedly *incited* certain Jews to kill Count Bernadotte," and in the common understanding the word "incite" imputes *blame.*

In Israel four months later two Stern Group leaders named Yellin and Shmuelevitz were sentenced to eight and five years imprisonment in this connection by a special court, the president of which, in reading the judgment, said there was "no proof that the order to kill Count Bernadotte had been given by the leadership." The two men (according to the Jewish Telegraph Agency) "scarcely paid heed to the proceedings in view of the fact that the State Council was expected to approve a general amnesty," and within a few hours of their sentencing they were released, then being escorted in triumph to a popular reception. The "Commander-in-Chief" of Irgun, a Mr. Menachem Begin, some years later made "a triumphal tour" of Western cities, being received in Montreal, for instance, by "a guard of honour of the Montreal police headed by Rabbis bearing Scrolls of the Law" (the South African *Jewish Herald*). Speaking at Tel Aviv during an election campaign in 1950 Mr. Begin claimed credit for the foundation of the Zionist state, through the deed at Deir Yasin. He said the Irgun had "occupied Jaffa," which the government party "had been ready to hand over to the Arabs," and added:

"The other part of the Irgun's contribution was Deir Yasin, which has caused the Arabs to leave the country and make room for the newcomers. Without Deir Yasin and the subsequent Arab rout, the present government could not absorb one-tenth of the immigrants." Throughout the ensuing years, to this day, Mr. Begin continued to make sanguinary threats against the neighbouring Arab states,[31] to whom the presence of the Palestinian Arabs within their borders was a constant reminder of Deir Yasin and of the dire meaning of his

menaces. For five years the public pretence was maintained that "the terrorists" had acted without authority at Deir Yasin and then, in April 1953, four Irgun men wounded at Deir Yasin claimed compensation. The Israeli government, through its Ministry of Security, denied the claim on the ground that the attack was "unauthorized," whereon the Irgun commander produced a letter from the official Zionist military headquarters in Jerusalem authorizing the action. By that time the signatory was Israeli Minister in Brazil.

In the city where the "United Nations" had their headquarters, a strong reason offered why no "accounting" for Count Bernadotte's murder should be demanded. When it happened the American presidential election was close at hand. The campaign was at full heat and *both* candidates (Mr. Truman and Mr. Thomas Dewey) held the Zionist vote to be indispensable to success. They were vying for it and Palestine was a long way from New York. Mr. Truman was the better-qualified aspirant, for he had recognized the new state and proclaimed the act "the proudest" of his life. On another occasion he said it was one guided by "the highest *humanitarian* purpose." A few weeks after the murder on the road to Jerusalem he was elected president; at the year's end he gave White House employees a bookmarker with the words, "I would rather have peace than be President."

By 1948 Colonel House's electoral strategy of 1910 had been developed into a high-precision instrument controlled by the Zionist international; the masterswitch being in New York State. The machine and

---

[31] Begin Calls For War: Jerusalem. Attack the Arabs smash one weak spot after another, crush one front after another until victory is assured... this was the essence of the speech which Mr. Menahem Begin, leader of the Herut Party made last week in Jerusalem. He was speaking from the balcony of a hotel overlooking Zion Square filled with a few thousand persons. 'Our losses in such an action will not be negligible but at any rate they will be much less than when we face the combined Arab armies in the field,' he said, '... today the Defence Forces are stronger than all the Arab armies combined . . Moses needed ten blows to take the Israelies out of Egypt; with one blow we can throw the Egyptians out of Israel,' he said, referring to the Gaza Strip. (Johannesburg *Zionist Record*, August 20, 1954).

company-flotation era added a new verb to the English language: "to rig," meaning to arrange or manipulate. Experts are able to "rig" machines. An example is the gambling, or "slot" machine in America. John Doe inserts his coin in the vague belief that the machine is operated by the laws of chance, and that if he is chance's favourite its entire contents will pour into his hands; in fact the machine is expertly adjusted so that a precisely-calculated proportion of its receipts (probably between eighty and ninety percent) go to the gambling syndicate and the residue goes in small windfalls to John Doe.

The "rigging" of the American electoral system is the determining factor in the events of the 20th Century. A mechanism originally designed to enable John Doe to express his opinion about policies and parties has been adjusted to such a point of nicety, almost precluding error, that he is left without voice in his national affairs; no matter what coin he inserts in which slot, the governing syndicate wins.

The electoral system itself might at the start have been designed to make easy the task of "a foreign group" bent on dictating the course of American state policy. An election *always* impends: a Congressional one every second, a presidential one every fourth year. No sooner is a Congress or President elected than the "pressure-groups" begin to work on the aspirants for the next election; the party- managers begin to worry about the next contest; and the would be Senators, Congressmen and Presidents start to feel, and respond to, "the pressure." There is no breathing-space in which prudence might prevail and the stranglehold be broken (in 1953, as will be seen, even the struggle for the mayoralty of New York City produced an abrupt, major reversal of American state policy, the issue being "support for Israel." The intensification of "pressure" at these recurrent moments, and the consequent warnings from the party- managers to incumbents in Congress or the White House, bring about these back-somersaults, which upset the whole edifice of policy laboriously erected by responsible ministers and competent permanent officials).

In these circumstances the new "state" set up in Palestine in 1948 was never, and never can be, a "state" in any meaning of the word formerly used in recorded history. It was the outpost of a world organization with special access to every government, parliament and foreign office in the Western world (and most especially to the government, parliament and foreign office of the United States, which in the 1950's was the most powerful country in the world), and its chief function was to exercise control over the American Republic, not to afford "a home" for the Jews of the world. The prospect opened by this state of affairs was that of increasing American involvement in an explosive situation in the Levant, artificially created and pregnant with the danger of world war.

When 1948 ended, thirty-one years after the first triumph of the dual conspiracy (the Balfour Declaration and the Bolshevik revolution) the Zionist state had been set up. Mr. Truman, the pacemaker in "recognition," had been advised by his responsible officers that the partition forcibly effected at Deir Yasin would lead to a third world war; all leading Western politicians had received the same counsel from their responsible advisers. None of the "top-line politicians" concerned can have been in doubt about the shape which their support of Zionism would give to the future, and their public utterances about it cannot have expressed their private knowledge or belief. The American politicians of the 1940's and 1950's, like Mr. Leopold Amery and Mr. Winston Churchill during the earlier decades, evidently were captive to the belief that, for some reason never disclosed, "policy" in this one matter could never "change." The captivity of the London and Washington governments, and the identity of the captors, even today (1956) is not realized by the American and British masses (though the now apparent danger of a new world war beginning in and spreading outward from Zionised Palestine is for the first time disquietening them). In the rest of the world it has long been understood. As long ago as the 1920's for instance, the Maharajah of Kashmir asked Sir Arthur Lothian (as that British diplomat relates), "why the British government was establishing a 'Yehudi ka Raj' (Rule of the Jews) in India. I demurred to this description, but he insisted that it was true, saying the Viceroy, Lord Reading, was a Jew, the Secretary of State, Mr. Edwin Montague, was a Jew, the High Commissioner, Sir William Meyer, was a Jew, and what more evidence did I want?" Thus a remote Indian Maharajah, thirty years ago, clearly saw the true shape of coming events in the Western world.

I quoted earlier the statement of the Egyptian Prime Minister to Count Bernadotte, that "Jewish economic power controlled the economic system of … the United States, England, France, Egypt itself …" In the seven years that have passed the leaders of all the Arab states have openly and repeatedly charged that the American government has become merely the instrument of Zionist ambitions and have pointed to their own experience as the proof.

Far on the other side of the world the effect of the "rigged" electoral machine in New York was felt in its other manifestation: support of the revolution. Chiang Kai-shek, the Chinese leader, was driven by similar shifts in American state policy from the Chinese mainland (where Communism with American support established itself) to the island of Formosa, where for the time being he again received some measure of American support. A well-known American broadcaster, Mr. Tex McCrary, visited him there and reported back to the listening millions of New York State: "I squirmed with embarrassment when I was told, 'We have learned never to trust America for more than eighteen months at a time, *between elections.*'"

This control of American state policy, through control of the election machine, led in 1952 to a culminating act of the Talmudic vengeance, wreaked this time on the half of Germany which had been left "free" by the bisection.

This half of Germany was forced to pay tribute to the Zionist state, set up three years after Germany's defeat in the Second War!

After the First War the Western victor powers tried to exact tribute ("reparations") but failed; what was received was merely by book-entry, for it was cancelled out by American and British loans. After the Second War the revolution exacted tribute from captive East Germany by simply helping itself. The Western victor powers made no demand for "reparations" on their *own* account, but extorted it for Zion.

As the years passed the alarm of responsible men in the Middle East again made itself felt in the State Department. It was constantly reminded by its advisers on the spot that the seven Arab States had never accepted the deed of 1948, that they held themselves still to be in a state of war with the interloping state, and held the United States to be paying for arms to be used against themselves.

Thus the idea was born, several years after the war's end, of making the "free" half of Germany pay "reparations" to a state which had not even existed during the Second War; the continued propping-up of the new state was to be ensured and the true source of its support obscured. The idea was long bruited behind the scenes and (like the judgment of Nuremberg) then was suddenly given symbolic realization on the eve of the Jewish High Holy days in 1952 (or, as *Time* magazine of New York put it, "In the last week of the Jewish year 5711"). It formed the dominant theme of the ensuing Judaic celebrations, one Jewish newspaper remarking that it was "The finest New Year present for Jewry we could think of."

The Chancellor of occupied West Germany, Dr. Adenauer ("waxy pale") informed the Bundestag at Bonn of "the obligation to make moral and material amends." His Minister for Justice, Dr. Dehler, spoke differently to an audience at Coburg: "The agreement with Israel was concluded *at the wish of the Americans, because the United States, in view of the feeling in the Arab countries, cannot continue to support the state of Israel in the same way as heretofore.*"

The American presidential election of 1952 was then immediately at hand. The West German government was constrained to pay, over a period of twelve to fourteen years, 822 million dollars to Israel, mostly in goods. The picture resulting from this transaction somewhat strikingly recalls Stehelin's summary of passages from the Cabala depicting the Messianic consummation: "But let us see a little after what manner the Jews are to live in their ancient country under the Administration of the Messiah. In the first place, the strange nations, which they shall suffer to live, shall build them houses and cities, till them ground and plant them vineyards; and all this, without so much as looking for any reward of their labour." This picture is not far different from that offered by the British, American and German taxpayers under the different forms of constraint (hidden in the first two cases, open in the third case) to which they have been subjected in the matter of tribute for Zionism.

The Western masses were not informed about the manner in which this payment of tribute was extorted; it was presented to them as an independent act of the West German government, prompted by high moral feeling. Jewish readers, on the other hand, were as well informed as Dr. Dehler's audience at Coburg. To quote two examples: the Jewish Telegraph Agency "revealed that the United States Government has played a very important role in pushing Western Germany to make a decent reparations offer to the Jews; the British government has also done its share, although to a smaller extent"; and the Johannesburg *Zionist Herald* said, 'The agreement with Germany could not have been possible without the active and very effective support of the United States government in Washington and of the United States High Commissioner's office in Germany." The entire Arab press reported similarly, and an American newspaperman who sought to make his way in to one of the Arab refugee camps was rebuffed with the words, "What is the use of talking with you? We Arabs know very well that in America no newspaper dares to tell the whole truth about the Palestine question." In England the official version was given to parliament by Lord Reading, Foreign Under Secretary and son of the Viceroy mentioned in the Maharajah of Kashmir's question to Sir Arthur Lothian thirty years earlier. Lord Reading's statement was prompted by the usual expedient of a "question," on this occasion from a Socialist peer, Lord Henderson, who began by saying that "over six million Jews were done to death." Lord Reading's answer is of permanent interest; he said that the West German payments to the new state would be: "in the nature of *some measure of reparation of moral*, even more than material value," and that they would be "based upon the calculated cost of resettlement in Israel of *Jews driven out of Europe by the Nazis.*"

This statement implicitly reasserts the principle that the *only* Nazi crime morally reparable was the treatment of Jews; none ever suggested that West Germany should pay the cost of resettling Poles, Czechs and all other victims. Its peculiar interest lies in the allusion to "reparation *of moral* value"; when it was made nearly a million Arabs had been "driven out" of Palestine by the Zionists and their claim to return to their homes had been repeatedly, even contemptuously rejected.

Probably the most characteristic passage in this typical statement is that which refers to "resettling Jews driven out of Europe by the Nazis." Israel is the one place in the world where the numbers of the Jewish population may with accuracy be learned. According to Israeli government statistics, it was about 1,400,000 in 1953, and among these were only 63,000 Jews (less *than five percent) from Germany and Austria.* These 63,000 were the *only* inhabitants of Israel who by any stretch of imagination might have been said to have been driven out of Europe and to resettle in Israel. The great mass came from Poland, Rumania, Hungary and Bulgaria some time *after* the war's end (and certainly were not "driven out" as they were protected in those countries by special laws and preference in state employment) or from North Africa.

No moral basis existed for the extortion of tribute from the West Germans for the Zionist state, and if any had ever existed, in respect of the 63,000, it had long been cancelled by the Zionists' "driving out" of nearly a million Arabs. The affair is unique in Western history and proves only the extent of the American and British government's submission to Zionism.

West Germany was compelled to bear a large part of the cost of the new state's armaments and development; therewith the likelihood of another great war was brought nearer and the outlook for the Arabs was made much worse. The Zionist state was at length propped up and the consequences at once began to flow. The exertion of "pressure" on the West German government in this matter was about the last major act of American state policy under President Truman, whose term was about to expire.[32]

---

[32] As a footnote to the West German affair, the Western Powers in Vienna, (on this occasion acting in perfect accord with the Soviet state) at the same bidding humbled little Austria (Hitler's first victim) by vetoing a law of amnesty and restitution which might have benefited some non-Jews. The Austrian government (at that time supposed to be "sovereign" again) protested in writing to the American High Commissioner, specifically accusing him of submitting to the orders of "emigrants from Austria" who were on his staff as "Jewish advisers." No intelligible account of this episode reached the British or American newspaper reader.

Chapter 44

THE WORLD INSTRUMENT

The Second War produced a third result, additional to the advance of the revolution into Europe and the establishment by force of the Zionist state: namely, the second attempt to set up the structure of a "world government," on the altar of which *Western* nationhood was to be sacrificed. This is the final consummation to which the parallel processes of Communism and Zionism are evidently intended to lead; the idea first emerged in the Weishaupt papers, began to take vigorous shape in the 19th Century, and was expounded in full detail in the Protocols of 1905. In the First War it was the master-idea of all the ideas which Mr. House and his associates "oozed into the mind" of President Wilson, and sought to make the president think were "his own." It then took shape, first as "The League to Enforce Peace" and at the war's end as "The League of Nations."

Thus it was given first and partial realization, like all the ideas auxiliary to it, during the confusion period of a great war, that is, the later period of the fighting and the early aftermath of it. It was never submitted before that war to the peoples who became embroiled, nor was any reasoned explanation of its nature and purpose given to them; during the "emergency" the "premier-dictators" took their assent for granted; the only expression of popular opinion ever given was the immediate refusal of the United States Congress, as the fog of the First War cleared, to have anything to do with it.

The twenty years between the two wars showed that "the League of Nations" was unable to enforce or preserve peace and that nations would not of their own will surrender their sovereignty to it. Nevertheless, as the Second War approached the men who were to conduct it again were busy with this idea of setting up what they called a "world authority" of some kind and the one common thing in all their thought about it was that "nations" should give up "sovereignty." Mr. Roosevelt (according to Mr. Baruch's biographer, Mr. Morris V. Rosenbloom) as far back as 1923, after his paralysis, devoted his sickbed time to drafting "a plan to preserve peace" which, as president, he revised in the White House, then giving his blueprint the title, "The United Nations."

Similarly in England, the champion of British nationhood, Mr. Winston Churchill, in 1936 became president of the British section of an international association called "The New Commonwealth Society" which advocated "a world police force to maintain peace" (the conjunction of the words "force" and "peace" occurs in all these programmes and pronouncements), and publicly declared (November 26, 1936) that it differed from "other peace societies" in the fact that it "advocated the use of *force* against an aggressor in support of *law*." Mr. Churchill did not say what law, or whose law, but he *did* offer "force" as the path to "peace."

Thus it was logical that at the meeting of President Roosevelt and Mr. Churchill in August 1941, when the sterile "Atlantic Charter" was produced, Mr. Churchill (as he records) should tell the president that "opinion in England would be disappointed at the absence of any intention to establish an international organization for keeping peace after the war." I was in England at that time and, for one, was disappointed at the inclusion of the reference which Mr. Churchill desired; as for "opinion in England" in general, there was none, for no informative basis for any opinion had been offered to the people. Mr. Churchill was pursuing the idea on his own authority, as was Mr. Roosevelt: "Roosevelt spoke and acted with complete freedom and authority in every sphere ... I represented Great Britain with almost equal latitude. Thus a very high degree of concert was obtained, and the saving in time *and the reduction in the number of people informed* were both invaluable" (Mr. Churchill, describing how "the chief business between our two countries was virtually conducted by personal interchanges" between himself and Mr. Roosevelt in "perfect understanding").

Consequently, in the concluding stages of the war and without any reference to the battling multitudes, "the questions of World Organization" (Mr. Churchill) dominated the private debate between these two, General Smuts in South Africa, and the premiers of the other British oversea countries. By that time (1944) Mr. Churchill was using the term "World Instrument" and (as in the earlier case of his allusion to "law") the obvious question arose, *whose* instrument? "The prevention of future aggression" was stock language in all these interchanges. The difficulty of determining *who* is the aggressor has been shown in the cases of Havana harbour in 1898 and Pearl Harbour in 1941, and for that matter the co-aggressor at the start of the Second War, the Soviet state, was to be the party most lavishly rewarded at its end, so that all this talk about stopping "aggression" cannot have been seriously intended. Clearly the idea was to set up a "world instrument" for the use of whoever might gain control of it. *Against* whom would it be used? The answer is given by all the propagandists for this idea; the one thing they *all* attack is "the sovereignty of nations." Ergo, it would be used to erase separate nationhood (in fact, only in the West). *By whom* would it be used? The results of the two great wars of this century supply the answer to that question.

Against that background the "United Nations Organization" was set up in 1945. Within two years (that is, while the confusion-period of the Second War still continued), the true nature of "world-government" and the "world instrument" was for an instant revealed. For the first time the peoples were shown what awaited them if this idea were ever fully realized. They did not understand what they were shown then and forgot it at once, but the disclosure is on record and is of permanent value to the student now and for as long as this idea of the super-national "authority," so clearly foretold in the Protocols of 1905, continues to be promoted by powerful men behind the scenes of international politics. At this point in the narrative the figure of Mr. Bernard Baruch first emerges from advisory shadows into full light, so that reasonable inferences may be drawn about his long part in the events of our century.

As has been shown, he made a decisive intervention in favour of the Zionist state in 1947 by "changing a great deal" from his earlier hostility to Zionism (Dr. Weizmann) and by advising a responsible Cabinet officer, Mr. James Forrestal, to discontinue *his* opposition. That is the first point at which Mr. Baruch's influence on state policy may be clearly traced, and it is a significant one, discouraging to those who hope for Jewish "involvement in Mankind," for up to that time he seemed to be (and presumably wished to appear) a fully integrated American, a paragon of Jewish emancipation, tall, handsome, venerable and greatly successful in his affairs.

If Mr. Baruch's "change" was as sudden as Dr. Weizmann's narrative suggests, another incident of that period makes it appear also to have been radical, even violent. One of the most extreme Zionist chauvinists in America then was a Mr. Ben Hecht, who once published the following dictum:

"One of the finest things ever done by *the mob* was the crucifixion of Christ. Intellectually it was a splendid gesture. But trust *the mob* to bungle. If I'd had charge of executing Christ I'd have handled it differently. You see, what I'd have done was had him shipped to Rome and fed to the lions. They never could have made a saviour out of mincemeat."

During the period of violence in Palestine which culminated in the pogrom of Arabs at Deir Yasin, this Mr. Hecht inserted a full-page advertisement in many of the leading newspapers throughout America. It was addressed "To the Terrorists of Palestine" and included this message:

"The Jews of America are for you. You are their champions ... Every time you blow up a British arsenal, or wreck a British railroad train sky high, or rob a British bank, or let go with your guns and bombs at the British betrayers and invaders of your homeland, the Jews of America make a little holiday in their hearts."

It was the author of this advertisement (according to his autobiography) whom Mr. Baruch chose to visit and inform of his affinity and support:

"One day the door of my room opened and a tall white-haired man entered. It was Bernard Baruch, my first Jewish social visitor. He sat down, observed me for a moment and then spoke. 'I am on your side,' said Baruch, 'the only way the Jews will ever get anything is by fighting for it. I'd like you to think of me as one of your Jewish fighters in the tall grass with a long gun. I've always done my best work that way, out of sight.'"

This revelatory passage (added to Mr. Baruch's intervention in the Forrestal affair) gives the student insight into the personality of Mr. Bernard Baruch. If *this* was the sense in which he had done his best work ("as a Jewish fighter in the tall grass with a long gun … out of sight") during his thirty-five years of "advising six Presidents," the shape of American policy and of world events during the 20th Century is explained. The reader is entitled to take the quoted words at full value and to consider Mr. Baruch's influence on American and world affairs in the light they shed. They are equally relevant to Mr. Baruch's *one* great *public* intervention in world affairs, which came about the same time. This was the "Baruch Plan" for a despotic world authority backed by annihilating force, and the words cited above justify the strongest misgivings about the purposes to which such a "world instrument" would be used. The "Baruch Plan" is of such importance to this narrative that a glance at Mr. Baruch's entire background and life is appropriate.

He was always generally assumed to be of the aristocratic Jewish type, that is to say, of Sephardic descent leading back, by way of the experience in Spain and Portugal, to a remote possibility of Palestinian origin. In fact, as he himself stated (February 7, 1947) his father was "a Polish Jew who came to this country a hundred years ago." That places Mr. Baruch among the Slavic Ashkenazi, the non-semitic "Eastern Jews," who are now said (by the Judaist statisticians) to comprize almost the whole of Jewry.

He was born in 1870 at Camden in South Carolina. His family *seemed* to have identified itself with the weal or woe of the new country, for his father served as a Confederate surgeon and Mr. Baruch himself was born during the evil days of "Reconstruction"; as a child he saw the Negroes, inflamed by carpetbagger oratory and scallawag liquor, surge through the sleepy streets of this plantation country town, and his elder brothers stand with shotguns and the upstairs porch; his father wore the hood and robe of the Ku Klux Klan. Thus in childhood he saw the destructive revolution at work (for it took charge during the final stages and aftermath of the Civil War and "Reconstruction" was recognizably its work) and later saw the enduring values of a free society. However, his family was not truly part of the South and soon the pull of New York drew it thither. There, before he was thirty, Bernard Baruch was a rich and rising man, and before he was forty he was already a power, though an unseen one, behind politics. He is probably the original of the master- financier, "Thor," in Mr. House's novel. Against much opposition Mr. House included him in the group around Mr. Wilson.

His life-story then was already full of great financial coups, "selling short," "cashing in on the crash," "driving the price down," and the like. Gold, rubber, copper, sulphur, everything turned into dollars at his touch. In 1917, during an investigation into stock-market movements prompted in 1916 by the dissemination of "peace reports," he informed the House Rules Committee of Congress that he had "made half a million dollars in one day by short selling." He stated that his support of President Wilson (to whose electoral campaigns he made lavish contributions) was first prompted by Professor Wilson's attack on exclusive "fraternities" at Princeton University (which in 1956 distinguished itself by allowing Mr. Alger Hiss to address one of its student clubs). The implication here is that he is of those who detest all "discrimination of race, class or creed"; however few men can have suffered less than Mr. Baruch from "discrimination."

His first appearance in Wall Street was much disliked by the great men there on the ground that he was "a gambler" (a reproach apparently first made by Mr. J. Pierpont Morgan). He survived all such criticisms and described himself as "a speculator." During the First World War President Wilson appointed Mr. Baruch head of the War Industries Board (Mr. Baruch having repeatedly urged President Wilson that the head of this dictatorial body should be "one man") and he later described himself as having been, in that capacity, the most powerful man in the world. When President Wilson returned, completely incapacitated, from the Versailles Peace Conference Mr. Baruch "became one of the group that made decisions during the President's illness ... called 'the Regency Council,'" and President Wilson rallied from his sickbed long enough to dismiss his Secretary of State, Mr. Robert Lansing, who had been calling Cabinet meetings in opposition to this "Regency Council."

Mr. Baruch's biographer states that he continued to be "adviser" to the three Republican Presidents of the 1920's, and Mrs Eleanor Roosevelt testifies to the fact that he was President Roosevelt's adviser both *before* and during the twelve-year Democratic regime that followed. By March 1939 Mr. Winston Churchill felt able to inform Mr. Baruch (then in residence at his Barony in South Carolina) that "War is coming very soon ... You will be running the show over there."

By that time Mr. Baruch had been "advising" Presidents for nearly thirty years and in spite of that the zealous student cannot definitely discover or state what Mr. Baruch's motives were, the nature of "advice" he gave, or what the effect of his counsel was on American policy and world events. This is natural, for he had worked always "in the long grass ... out of sight." He was never an elected or responsible officer of state so that his work was beyond audit. He was the first of the "advisers," the new type of potentate foreseen, at the century's start, only in the much-abused "Protocols" of 1905.

Deductions and inferences alone were possible in his case; fragments here and there might be pieced together to make the parts of a picture. First, his publicly recorded recommendations were always for measures of "control." In the First and the Second War alike this was his panacea: "control," "discipline" and the like. It amounted always to the demand for power over people, and for the centralization of authority in one man's hands, and the demand was raised again long after the Second War, once more in the plea that it would prevent a third: "*before the bullets have begun to fly* ... the country must accept *disciplines* such as rationing and price control" (May 28, 1952, before a Senate Committee).

Each time this recommendation was made it was presented as a means for defeating a dictator ("the Kaiser," "Hitler." "Stalin"). The controlled and disciplined world which Mr. Baruch envisaged was depicted by him in testimony before a Congressional Committee in 1935: "had the 1914-1918 war gone on another year our whole population would have emerged in cheap but serviceable uniforms ... types of shoes were to be reduced to two or three." This statement provoked strongrotests at the time; Americans, having helped defeat the "regimented" Germans, did not like to think that they would have presented a spectacle of drab regimentation, had the war but lasted "another year." At the time Mr. Baruch denied that he had intended "to goose-step the nation," but his biographer records that he "revived his proposal for similar drab clothing in World War II." In contemplating the picture thus conjured up the student cannot put out of his mind the similar picture, of a drab, enslaved mass inhabiting the former nation-states, which is given in the Protocols.

Other fragments showed that Mr. Baruch's thought culminated in a picture of a controlled and disciplined *world*. The *folie de grandeur*, the megalomania with which the Wilsons and Lloyd Georges, the Roosevelts and Winston Churchill reproached the Kaiser and Hitler, was in him. His biographer quotes: "of course we can fix the world, Baruch has said on many occasions." And then, during the Second War, "Baruch had agreed with President Roosevelt and other leaders that a world organization should be established *at the height of allied unity in the war.*"

The italicized words are the key ones: they relate to the confusion-period of a great war, when the "advisers" submit their plans, the "premier-dictators" initial them (and later cannot understand how they could have done so), and the great coups are brought off.

These are all fragments, significant but partial. Immediately after the Second War Mr. Baruch made his first great public appearance in world affairs as the author of a plan for world-dictatorship, and dictatorship (in my opinion) by terror. For the first time his mind and work lie open to audit, and it is in connection with this plan that (again in my opinion) his words to Mr. Ben Hecht are of such importance.

According to his biographer, Mr. Baruch was 74 "when he began to prepare himself for the undertaking he considered the most vital of his life ... to shape a workable plan for international control of atomic energy and, as United States representatives to the United Nations Atomic Energy Commission, to promote adoption of that plan by the Commission." That would have been in 1944, a year before the first atom bomb was dropped and the United Nations was even established."

If this is correct, Mr. Baruch knew what was to happen in the world about two years in advance of events; "the assignment" for which he was preparing himself in 1944 was first proposed by Secretary of State Byrnes (after a discussion with Mr. Baruch) to President Truman in *March 1946* (seven months after the first atom bombs). President Truman duly made the appointment, whereon Mr. Baruch at last appeared publicly in an official capacity. He set to work on the "Baruch Plan."

The law governing America's membership of the United Nations requires all American representatives in it to follow the policy determined by the President and transmitted through the Secretary of State. According to his biographer Mr. Baruch enquired what "the policy" was to be, possibly as a matter of form, because he was told to draft it himself. Therefore the "Baruch Plan" was literally Mr. Baruch's plan, if this account is correct (it was published with his approval). It was devised on a bench in Central Park in consultation with one Ferdinand Eberstadt, Mr. Baruch's assistant in 1919 at Versailles and "an active disciple" of Mr. Baruch's in the Second War. This might be described as the 20th Century method of formulating state policy, and apparently Mr. Baruch owes to it his popular title, "the park-bench statesman."

Mr. Baruch then presented his Plan to the United Nations Atomic Energy Commission at its opening session on June 14, 1946. He spoke with the voice of the Levites' Jehovah offering "blessings or cursings," alluded to the atom bomb as "the absolute weapon" (within a few years an even more pulverizing explosive was in competitive production), and used the familiar argument of false prophets, namely, that if his advice were followed "peace" would ensue and if it were ignored all would be "destroyed." The proposal he made seems to me to amount to a universal dictatorship supported by a reign of terror on the worldwide scale; the reader may judge for himself.

"We must elect *world peace* or *world destruction* ... We must provide the mechanism to assure that atomic energy is used for peaceful purposes and preclude its use in war. To that end, we must provide *immediate, swift and sure punishment* of those who violate the agreements that are reached by the nations. *Penalization is essential* if peace is to be more than a feverish interlude between wars. And, too, the United Nations can prescribe *individual responsibility and punishment on the principles applied at Nuremberg* by the Union of Soviet Socialist Republics, the United Kingdom, France and the United States – *a formula certain to benefit the world's future.* In this crisis, we represent *not only our governments,* but, in a larger way, *we represent the peoples of the world* ... The peoples of these democracies gathered here are not afraid of *an internationalism that protects*; they are unwilling to be fobbed off by *mouthings about narrow sovereignty,* which is today's phrase for yesterday's isolation."

Thus Mr. Baruch appeared, not as the representative of the United States, but as the spokesman of "the peoples of the world," and in that capacity recommended a permanent Nuremberg Tribunal as certain to benefit the world (presumably by judgments handed down on the Day of Atonement).

On the basis thus laid down, he proposed "managerial control or ownership" of all atomic-energy activities potentially dangerous to world security and power to control, inspect and license all other atomic activities. As to "violations of this order," he proposed that "penalties as immediate and certain in their execution as possible should be fixed for (1) illegal possession or use of an atomic bomb or atomic material or for wilful interference with the activities of the Authority." He then reiterated his proposal for "punishment": "... the matter of punishment lies at the very heart of our present security system ... The Charter permits penalization only by concurrence of each of the five great powers ... There must be *no veto* to protect those who violate their solemn agreements ... The bomb does not wait upon delay. To delay may be to die. The time between violation and preventive action or punishment would be all too short for extended discussion as to the course to be followed ... The solution will require apparent sacrifice in pride and in position, but better pain as the price of peace than death as the price of war."

The reader will see that Mr. Baruch contended that the world could only escape "destruction" by "precluding the use of atomic energy in war" and proposed that "an Authority" with a *monopoly* of atomic energy be set up, *which should be free from all check in its punitive use of atomic energy against any party deemed by it to be deserving of punishment.*

This is the proposal of which I earlier said that the world for the first time received a glimpse of what "world government" meant. Mr. Baruch's biographer says that President Truman "endorsed the plan" and then records Mr. Baruch's efforts to "round up" votes for it on the Commission. After six months (December 5, 1946) he was impatient and begged the Commission to remember "that to delay may be to die." The confusion-period was coming to an end and even a United Nations Commission could not be brought to swallow this plan. On December 31, 1946 Mr. Baruch resigned and the plan was shelved by reference to the United Nations Disarmament Commission.

In January 1947 Mr. Baruch announced that he was "retiring from *public* life" (in which he was only conspicuous on this one occasion), "Interested onlookers were not overly alarmed" (his biographer adds); "the betting odds were that Baruch would be back at the White House and on Capitol Hill before the month was over, and so he was." Later in 1947 he intervened "decisively" (though not publicly) with Mr. Forrestal and had his significant meeting with Mr. Ben Hecht. Six years later his biographer (who was evidently aware that Mr. Eisenhower was then to be elected) summarized the recommendations which the new President would receive from the permanent "adviser." These related entirely to preparatory mobilization for war, "controls," "global strategy" and the like.

By that time Mr. Baruch had specified what particular new "aggression" these proposals were designed to meet, having told a Senate Committee in 1952 that to forestall "Soviet aggression" the President "should be given all the power he needed to carry through an armament and mobilization programme, including price and priority controls." This was the programme, under "one-man" direction, urged by him during two world wars. However, his private view about the aggressor named apparently was not that of alarm and repugnance, depicted to the Senate Committee, for in 1956 he told an interviewer, "A few years ago I met Vyshinsky at a party and said to him, 'You're a fool and I'm a fool: You have the bomb and we have the bomb ... Let's control the thing while we can because while we are talking all nations will sooner or later get the bomb" *(Daily Telegraph* January 9, 1956). Nor did the Soviet regard Mr. Baruch with hostility; in 1948 (as he confirmed in 1951) he was invited to Moscow to confer with the dictators there and actually left America on that journey; only "a sudden illness in Paris" (he explained) caused him to break it off.

The disclosure in 1946 of his plan "to fix the world" gave that world a glimpse of what it might expect to be attempted in the later stages and aftermath of any third war; the "global plan" was fully revealed. In 1947 Mr. Baruch stated that his father "came to this country a hundred years ago." The case offers the most significant example of the effect on America, and through America on world affairs, of the "new immigration" of the 19th Century. After just that hundred years the son had already for nearly forty years been one of the most powerful men in the world, though he worked "in the long grass ... out of sight," and he was to continue this work for at least another ten years.

Chapter 45

THE JEWISH SOUL

The first fifty years of "the Jewish century" have had their natural effect on the Jewish soul, which once again is in violent unrest. They have made chauvinists of a mass of Jews who, a hundred and fifty years ago, seemed committed to involvement in mankind. They are once more in captivity (the recurrent "captivities" of the Jews were always captivity by the elders and their creed of exclusion, not by alien taskmasters). In the Zionist captivity, and under the pressure of the elders, they have been made into the most explosive force in recorded history. The story of this century, of its wars and revolutions and the denouement yet to come, is that of Talmudic chauvinism, which has its roots in *Deuteronomy*.

The very word, chauvinism, means an extravagant emotion; Nicolas Chauvin was the Napoleonic soldier whose bombastic and unbridled fervour for his Emperor brought patriotism into disrepute even at a period of patriotic ardour. Nevertheless, the word is inadequate to describe the effect of Talmudic Zionism on the Jewish soul; no word exists, other than "Talmudism," for this unique and boundless frenzy.

In 1933 Mr. Bernard J. Brown wrote, "Being consciously Jewish is the lowest kind of chauvinism, for it is the only chauvinism that is based on false premises." The premises are those of the Talmud-Torah; namely, that God promised a certain tribe supremacy over all enslaved others in this world, and exclusive inheritance of the next world in return for strict observance of a law based on blood sacrifice and the destruction or enslavement of the lesser breeds without this Law. Whether Talmudic chauvinism or Zionist chauvinism (I believe either term is more correct than Mr. Brown's "Jewish chauvinism") is or is not "the lowest kind" of chauvinism, these fifty years have shown that it is the most violent kind yet known to man.

Its effect on the Jewish soul is reflected in the changed tone of Jewish literature in our time. Before adducing examples of this, an illustration of its effect between one generation and the next may be given by briefly citing the cases of two Jews, father and son. Mr. Henry Morgenthau senior was a notable Jew of America who became an ambassador. He was the product of Jewish emancipation during the last century; he was what the Jews today might have been, but for Talmudic chauvinism. He said:

"Zionism is the most stupendous fallacy in Jewish history. I assert that it is wrong in principle and sterile in its spiritual ideas. Zionism is a betrayal, an *Eastern European* proposal, fathered in this country by American Jews ... which, if they were to succeed, would cost the Jews of America most of what they have gained of liberty, equality and fraternity. I refuse to allow myself to be called a Zionist. I am an American."

In the next generation the name of the son, Mr. Henry Morgenthau junior, became inseparably associated with the founding of the Zionist state (his father's "stupendous fallacy") and with the Talmudic vengeance in Europe. In the sequel the son might prove to be one of the men most responsible for bringing about the consequences which the father feared.

Dr. Weizmann records the great part played by the junior Mr. Morgenthau in the backstage drama in New York which culminated in the violent establishment of the Zionist state and an American president's "recognition" of the deed. In Europe he fathered (through the "Morgenthau Plan") the bisection of the continent and the advance of the revolution to its middle. Some passages in that plan (initialled by Messrs' Roosevelt and Churchill, who both repudiated it when the damage was done) are of especial significance, namely, those which propose that "all industrial plants and equipment *not destroyed* by military action" (in Germany) "shall be ... *completely destroyed ... and the mines wrecked*." The original source of this idea of "utter destruction" apparently can only be the Talmud-Torah, where it is part of the "Law of God." The Zionist state itself, as I have shown, was founded on a deed of "utter destruction," and thus of literal "observance" of this Law, at Deir Yasin.

But for Zionist chauvinism and the Western politicos who served it in the office of "administrators," the son might have been another such man as the father, and this particular illustration is valid for a great mass of Jews and the change which has been produced in the Jewish soul. When Jews of great name lent themselves to such undertakings, and proved able to command the support of American presidents and British prime ministers, the Jewish masses were bound to follow. This general trend is reflected in the growing literature of Talmudic chauvinism.

Up to the middle of the last century distinctively "Jewish" literature was small and was in the main produced for and read in the closed communities. In the general bookshops Jewish writers held a place roughly proportionate to their numbers in the population, which was the natural thing, and in their works did not in the rule write as "Jews" or dwell on the exclusively Jewish theme. They addressed themselves to the general audience and avoided the chauvinist appeal to Jews, as well as anything that non-Jews might regard as blasphemy, sedition, obscenity or slander.

The transformation that has come about in the last fifty years reflects equally the spread of Talmudic chauvinism and the enforced subordination of the non-Jewish masses to it. Today books by Jews and non-Jews about Jewish things, if they were counted, might be found to form the largest single body of Western literature, outside fiction, and the change in tone and standard is very great.

As it has come about gradually, and critical comment today is in practice virtually forbidden as "anti-semitic," the change has not been consciously remarked by the mass of people. Its extent may be measured by this comparison; a good deal of what is contained in the literature of Talmudic chauvinism today (a few examples follow) would not have been published at all fifty years ago, as offensive to the standards then generally accepted. Fear of critical and public anathema would have kept publishers from issuing many of these works, or at all events from including in them the most flagrant passages.

The starting-point of this process, which might be called one of degeneration in Jewry, was possibly the appearance in 1895 of Max Nordau's *Degeneration*, which struck the keynote for the chorus to come. This book was in effect an epistle to the Gentiles, informing them that they were degenerate, and it enjoyed great vogue with *fin de siècle* "Liberals," as the accumulating mass of kindred literature has enjoyed among their kind ever since. Jewish degeneracy was no part of its theme, and the author would have seen Jewish degeneracy only in opposition to Zionism, for he was Herzl's lieutenant, and the man who at the Zionist Congress after Herzl's death foretold the first World War and the part played in it by England in setting up the Zionist "homeland." *Degeneration* was significant both in time and theme; it appeared in the same year as Herzl's *The Jewish State* and this was also the year of the first revolutionary outbreak in Russia. The revolution and Zionism are both essential to the Deuteronomic Talmudic concept, and both movements, in my estimate, were developed under Talmudic direction.

After *Degeneration* followed the full tide and spate of Talmudic-chauvinist literature. An example from our time is a book published in New York in the year, 1941, when Hitler and Stalin fell out and America entered the Second War.

Germany Must Perish, by a Mr. Theodore N. Kaufmann, proposed the extermination of the German people in the literal sense of the Law of the Talmud-Torah. Mr. Kaufmann proposed that "German extinction" be achieved by sterilizing all Germans of procreation age (males under 60, females under 45) within a period of three years after the war's end, Germany to be sealed off during the process and its territory then to be shared among other people, so that it should disappear from the map together with its people. Mr. Kaufmann calculated that, with births stopped through sterilization, the normal death rate would extinguish the German race within fifty or sixty years.

I feel sure that public abhorrence would have deterred any publisher from issuing this work during the First War, and possibly at any previous time since printing was invented. In 1941 it appeared with the commendation of two leading American newspapers (both Jewish-owned or Jewish-controlled). The *New York Times* described the proposal as "a plan for permanent *peace* among *civilized* nations"; the *Washington Post* called it "a provocative theory, interestingly presented."

This proposal was more literally Talmudic than anything else I can find, but the spirit that prompted it breathed in many other books. The hatred evinced was not limited to Germans; it extended to Arabs and for a period to the British; as it had earlier been directed against Spaniards, Russians, Poles and others. It was not a personal thing; being the end-product of Talmudic teaching it ranged impartially over all things non-Judaist, taking first one symbolic enemy and then another from a world where, under the Levitical Law, all were enemies.

The growth and open expression of this violent feeling, no longer held in bounds by the earlier need to take account of generally- accepted standards in the West, explains the misgivings expressed by Mr. Brown in 1933, by the Rabbi Elmer Berger in the 1940's, and by Mr. Alfred Lilienthal in the present decade. Its reflection in the Jewish published word justified their anxiety. In one book after another Jewish writers with introspective writings examined "the Jewish soul" and at the end came up with expressions of contempt or hatred for somebody or other of non-Jews, couched in chauvinist terms.

Mr. Arthur Koestler, describing his scrutiny of Judaism, wrote, "Most bewildering of all was the discovery that the saga of the 'Chosen Race' seemed to be taken quite literally by traditionalist Jews. They protested against racial discrimination, and affirmed in the same breath their racial superiority based on Jacob's covenant with God." The effect of this "bewildering discovery" on this particular Jewish soul was that "the more I found out about Judaism the more distressed I became, *and the more fervently Zionist.*"

The presumable cause ("reason" cannot be used to describe so illogical a reaction) of this strange effect on Mr. Koestler is indicated by his two hundred pages of complaint about Jews being persecuted in and driven from Europe. He avoided this complaint of justice by his assumption that the Arabs, who were not to blame, should suffer, depicting an Arab family (persecuted in and driven from Palestine by the Zionists) in these words: "The old woman will walk ahead leading the donkey by the rein and the old man will ride on it ... *sunk in solemn meditation about the lost opportunity of raping his youngest grandchild.*" In this depictment the acts of persecution and driving-out are made to appear respectable, others than Jews being the sufferers, by the attribution of a revolting thought to the victim.

The change in the tone and standards of Jewish literature in our time is again shown by the writings of Mr. Ben Hecht, some of which were earlier quoted, including his complaint that if Jesus had only been made into mincemeat, instead of being dignified by crucifixion, Christianity would never have taken shape. I doubt whether newspapers or publishers at any previous period would have given currency to words which patently had only the purpose of offending others.

Mr. Hecht once wrote, "I lived forty years in my country" (America) "without encountering anti-semitism or concerning myself even remotely with its existence." Therefore Mr. Hecht logically intended to live nowhere else. Nevertheless, when the Zionist state was being set up, he wrote that every time a British soldier was killed in Palestine "the Jews of America make a little holiday in their hearts."

Deep, if not enlightening insight into the development of the Jewish soul during this century is given by the books of a Mr. Meyer Levine; these also contain things which, in my estimation, would not have found print in earlier times. Mr. Levine's *In Search* shows what Mr. Sylvain Lévi meant when, at the 1919 Peace Conference, he gave warning against the "explosive tendencies" of the Eastern Jews.

Mr. Levine, born in America of immigrant parents from Eastern Europe was reared to hatred of Russians and Poles. He seems to have found little to please him in "the new country" where he was born and when he grew to young manhood busied himself in agitation among the Chicago workers.

He tells of half a lifetime of tortured efforts to escape from Jewishness and to immerse himself in Jewishness, alternately. If some Jews believe themselves unchangeably distinct from all other mankind, Mr. Levine gives two glimpses which make the reader feel that this belief is the product of a strained, almost mystic perversity. He says he finds himself constantly asking himself "What am I?" and "What am I doing here?," and asserts that "Jews everywhere are asking the same questions." Subsequently he related some of the discoveries to which this self-scrutiny led him.

Describing the Leopold-Loeb murder in Chicago (when two young Jews, of wealthy parents, killed and mutilated a small boy, also a Jew, from motives of extreme morbidity) he says, "I believe that beneath the very real horror that the case inspired, the horror in realizing that human beings carried in them murderous motives beyond the simple motives of lust and greed and hatred, beneath all this was a suppressed sense of pride in the brilliance of these boys, a sympathy for them in being slaves of their intellectual curiosities; a pride that this particular new level of crime, even this should have been reached by Jews. In a confused and awed way, and in the momentary fashionableness of 'lust for experience,' I felt that I understood them, that I, particularly, being a young intellectual Jew, had a kinship with them."

On another occasion he describes his part (he calls it that of "a volunteer aid," but the-term "agitator" might be fairly applicable) in the Chicago steelworkers strike of 1937, when strikers and police came into conflict and shots were fired, several persons being killed. Mr. Levine, as "a volunteer aid," had "fallen in alongside" the strikers' procession and he "ran with the others" when the firing began. He was not a steelworker or striker. Subsequently he and others, apparently also volunteer aids, organized a mass meeting. At this he showed slides made from newspaper-pictures from which he had removed the descriptions. He accompanied these pictures with a recital of his own, in words chosen to give the pictures an inflammatory interpretation, different from that of the original captions. He says:

"So strange a roar arose that it seemed to me as though the vast auditorium was a cauldron of rage, overturning upon me ... I felt I could never control the crowd, that they would burst through the doors, rush out and burn the city hall – the impact of the pictures was so enraging ... In that instant I experienced the full sense of the danger of power, for I felt that a few words would have unleashed violence beyond what we had seen on Memorial Day ... If I had sometimes felt *unincluded* as a stranger, artist and Jew, I knew that *universal action exists* ... I felt that perhaps one of the reasons for the social reformism of the Jew is the need to melt himself into these movements that engulf his own problem."

Once again, the words recall Mr. Maurice Samuel's lament or menace, (whichever was intended) of 1924, "We Jews, the destroyers, will remain the destroyers forever." Only in the incitement of others, Mr. Levine appears to say, could he, the "stranger," feel himself "included," or "his problem" engulfed. The incitement of the unreasoning, stupid "mob" is the theme that runs through the "Protocols" of 1905. In the passage quoted Mr. Levine seemed to imply that he could only feel involvement in general mankind when so inciting a mob.

His later travels were made in the same spirit. In his youth Zionism was almost unknown and in 1925, when he was twenty, it was still "a question that had scarcely penetrated to Jews born in America ... It was something that occupied the bearded ones *from the old country* and if an American Jew happened to be dragged to a Zionist meeting he found that the speakers talked *with Russian accents,* or simply reverted to Yiddish. My own family, indeed, had no interest in the movement."

As in the case of the Morgenthaus, father and son, one generation saw the change. Mr. Levine's parents, migrants from a country of alleged "persecution," were content to have found another where they prospered. The son was not content. Soon he was in Palestine, and developed vengeful feelings towards the Arabs of whom he had never heard in his youth. He tells, as a good jest, of an incident in a Zionist settlement when an Arab, coming across the fields, humbly asked for a drink of water. Mr. Levine and his friends pointed to a barrel, at which the Arab thankfully drank while they laughed; it was the horse-water.

Ten years after that he was in Germany and played his part in the Talmudic vengeance there. He was an American newspaper correspondent and describes how he and another Jewish correspondent roamed about Germany as "*conquerors,*" armed (illicitly), in a jeep, looting and wrecking as they pleased. He then says that the passive submission of German women to the "conquerors" thwarted the furious desire to rape them and "sometimes *the hatred* in a man rose so high that he felt the absolute need of violence." In this mood, his companion and he swore that "the only thing to do was to throw them down, tear them apart," and they discussed "the ideal conditions for such a scene of violence; there would have to be a wooded stretch of road, little traffic, and a lone girl on foot or a bicycle." The pair then made "a tentative sally" in search of these "ideal conditions" and at length found a lonely girl and "the conditions, all fulfilled." (He says the terrified girl was spared at the last and wonders if the reason, in each man, was that the presence of the other embarrassed him).

Mr. Levine began his book of 1950, "This is a book about being a Jew." It and the many like it account for the anxiety expressed by the rare Jewish remonstrants about the development of the last fifty years, for they testify to the degeneration of the Jewish soul under the stress of Talmudic chauvinism. The only thing proved by the book is that at its end Mr. Levine knew as little as at the start of his quest about what "being a Jew" meant (presumably he would not wish the above-quoted passages to be taken as supplying the answer). Hundreds of others on this same elusive and unproductive theme have appeared; so might an electric eel devour its own tail in search of the source of its peculiar sensation, and come to no enlightening conclusion. A book by a Jew on being a human being among other human beings was by the mid-century rare.

The accumulating literature of incitement and hatred, of which a few examples have been given, and the virtual suppression of objection to it as "anti-semitism," give the 20th century its distinctive character; it is the age of Talmudic chauvinism and Talmudic imperialism. Our present situation was foretold nearly a hundred years ago by a German, Wilhelm Marr.

Marr was a revolutionary and conspirator who helped the Jewish-led "secret societies" (Disraeli) prepare the abortive outbreaks of 1848. His writings of that period are recognizably Talmudic (he was not a Jew); they are violently anti-Christian, atheist and anarchist. Later, like Bakunin (Marr was a similar man) he became aware of the true nature of the revolutionary hierarchy, and in 1879 he wrote: "The advent of Jewish imperialism, I am firmly convinced, is only a question of time ... The empire of the world belongs to the Jews

... Woe to the conquered! ... I am quite certain that before four generations have passed there will not be a single function in the State, the highest included, which will not be in the hands of the Jews ... At the present moment, alone among European states, Russia still holds out against the official recognition of the invading foreigners. Russia is the last rampart and against her the Jews have constructed their final trench. To judge by the course of events, the capitulation of Russia is only a question of time ... In that vast empire ... Judaism will find the fulcrum of Archimedes which will enable it to drag the whole of Western Europe off its hinges once for all. The Jewish spirit of intrigue will bring about a revolution in Russia such as the world has never yet seen ... The present situation of Judaism in Russia is such that it has still to fear expulsion. But when it has laid Russia prostrate it will no longer have any attacks to fear. When the Jews have got control of the Russian state ... they will set about the destruction of the social organization of Western Europe. This last hour of Europe will arrive at latest in a hundred or a hundred and fifty years."

The present state of Europe, as it has been left by the Second War, shows this forecast to have been largely fulfilled. Indeed, only the full denouement remains, for its complete fulfilment. As to that, Marr may have seen too darkly. The history of the world thus far knows no irrevocable decisions, decisive victories, permanent conquests or absolute weapons. The last word, so far, has always proved to lie with the New Testamentary dictum: "The end is not yet."

However, the last stage in Marr's forecast, the third act in the 20th Century drama, is evidently at hand, whatever its outcome and whatever its subsequent aftermath, and in preparation for it the Jewish soul has been made captive by Talmudic chauvinism once again. Mr. George Sokolsky, the notable Jewish diarist of New York, observed in January 1956 that, "There was considerable opposition" (to Zionism) "inside world Jewry, but over the years the opposition died down and where it still exists it is so unpopular as generally to be hidden away; in the United States opposition to Israel among Jews is negligible."

The few warning voices which are still being raised, like Jeremiah's of old, are nearly all those of Jews. The reason is not that non-Jewish writers are worse informed, shorter sighted or less courageous; it has long been the unwritten rule that Jewish objectors may within limits be heard, as they are of "ourselves," but that objection from non-Jews must not be tolerated.[33] In the

---

[33] A good example: during 1956, a presidential election year, criticism of Zionism or of "Israel" was an almost inconceivable thing in the United States, especially in the later months, as the actual vote approached. Israeli attacks on the neighbouring Arab countries were invariably reported in all leading newspapers as "reprisal" or "retaliation." The President, his Cabinet members and State Department officials remained silent as one attack followed another, each of them resulting in an act of merciless destruction on the pattern af Deir Yasin in 1948. Indeed, leading candidates of the opposing parties, as in 1952 and 1948, vied with each other in demanding arms for Israel and in competing by this means for the Zionist-controlled vote which was supposed to be decisive. At the same time (11 September 1956) over two thousand Orthodox *Jews* met in Union Square, New York, to protest against "the persecution of religion in the state of Israel." The name of the Israel Premier, Ben-Gurion, was jeered and several rabbis made violent attacks on him and his government. These in no way related to the case of the Arabs, who were not mentioned; the attack was solely on ground of religious orthodoxy, the Ben-Gurion government being assailed for its disregard of orthodox ritual in Sabbatarian and other questions. Nevertheless, the attack was public, whereas criticism on any ground whatever from non-Jewish quarters was in fact virtually forbidden at this time. At the same period (1 September 1956) recurrent Jewish riots in Israel itself culminated in an outbreak which was suppressed by police, one man being killed. The dead man belonged to a group which refused to recognize the Israel government, maintaining that "re-establishment of a Jewish state must await the divine will" (incidentally, this is one of the main theses of the present, non-

condition of the Western press today, in the third quarter of the 20th century, this rule is enforced almost without exception.

On this account the few warnings here quoted are Jewish ones. Mr. Frank Chodorov told the American Government *(Human Events,* March 10, 1956) that in the Middle East "in reality it is not dealing with the government of Israel but with American Jews ... It is a certainty that many good, loyal Americans of the Jewish faith would welcome a showdown, not only to register their loyalty to this country and against world Zionism, but also to loosen the grip the Zionists have on them."

Similarly, Mr. Alfred Lilienthal *(Human Events,* September 10, 1955) echoed the despairing plea of the late Mr. James Forrestal eight years before; as the shadow of the 1956 presidential election fell across America he, too, begged the two great political parties, when they joined conflict, "to take the Arab-Israeli issue out of domestic politics." Both these Jewish warnings appeared in a Washington newsletter of repute but small circulation; the mass-circulation newspapers were closed to them.

Other latterday Jewish remonstrants raised the ancient cry of a coming "catastrophe." In 1933 Mr. Bernard J. Brown had seen disaster coming: "Never in the history of the human race has there ever been a group of people who have enmeshed themselves into so many errors and persisted in refusing to see the truth, as our people have done during the last three hundred years" (the period which saw the emergence of the Talmudic "Eastern Jews" and the victorious Talmudist war against Jewish assimilation).

Fifteen years after that warning Jewish remonstrants were pronouncing the word which it only implied: "catastrophe." Rabbi Elmer Berger wrote in 1951, "Unless Americans of Jewish faith and a great many Americans of other faiths who have been misguided into supporting Zionism return to the fundamentals both of American life and of Judaism we are headed for *something of a catastrophe.*" The foreword to Rabbi Berger's book was written by a non-Jewish authority, Dr. Paul Hutchinson, editor of *The Christian Century.* He was more explicit: "This claim of the right of American Jews to refuse amalgamation is building towards a crisis which may have lamentable consequences. Already it is becoming clear that every time Israel gets in a jam (and many of its policies, especially with regard to economics and immigration, seem almost designed to produce jams) American Jews will be expected to high-pressure the United States government to step in and straighten matters out. Zionist leaders have not hesitated to carry this sort of thing to the extremes of political blackmail" (this was written many years before ex-President Truman in his memoirs confirmed the fact). "This can continue for a little while because of our peculiar electoral system ... but New

Jewish writer's book). The victim, on account of his belief, was described by New York newspapers as "a religious extremist."

York is not the United States, and if this sort of strong-arm intervention in behalf of a foreign state keeps up, *look out for an explosion.*"

These warnings, though clear to Jews, might produce in non-Jewish minds the false impression that "the Jews" are headed towards "a catastrophe" of their own making; that in that event Talmudic chauvinism will recoil on their own heads; and, *schliesslich*, that they will then only have themselves to thank. The smug and the rancorous, especially, might fall into this delusion.

Delusion it would be. That recurrent phenomenon of history-as-it-is-written, "the Jewish catastrophe," is invariably the small Jewish share in a general catastrophe, the proportion being, say, around one percent of the total woe. The monstrous prevarication of the Second War about the "six million Jews who perished" does not change that enduring truth. The catastrophe which has been brewed in these fifty years will be a general one, and the Jewish share of it will be fractional. It will be *depicted* as "a Jewish catastrophe," as the Second War was so depicted, but that is the false picture shown on the lighted screen to "the mob" in its dark room.

Jews often, and quite genuinely, cannot envisage a calamity involving Jews, and no matter how many more non-Jews, as anything but "a Jewish catastrophe." This is a mental attitude deriving from the original teaching of the Talmud-Torah, wherein the chosen people alone have true existence and the others are shadows or cattle. Mr. Karl Stern's book, *Pillar of Fire,* provides an illustration.

Mr. Stern (a Jew who grew up in Germany between the wars, went to Canada and there was converted to the Catholic faith) says that there was in the Jewish youth Movement in Germany in the 1920's "a general mood which seemed to point at events which later came to pass. Latent in the situation were sorrows, questions and doubts pointing towards *the great Jewish catastrophe* – or rather the great European catastrophe with which the fate of the Jews was interwoven in so mysterious a fashion."

In this passage the truth appears in an obvious, corrective afterthought, which would not occur to or be expressed by the run of Jewish writers. Mr. Stern's is an exceptional case, and when he had written the words "the great Jewish catastrophe" he saw their untruth and qualified them; nevertheless, even he left the original statement to stand. The influence of his heredity and upbringing were still strong enough in him, a Catholic in North America, to form his first thought in those terms: the ordeal of 350,000,000 souls in Europe, which has left nearly half of them enslaved, was "the great Jewish catastrophe."

In a different case Mr. Stern would be the first to object to such a presentation. Indeed, he relates that he was offended by reading in a Catholic paper the statement that so-many members of the crew of a sunken British submarine were "Catholics." He was affronted because one group of the victims was singled out in this way; "I do not understand why anyone would care for such statistics." And yet: "the great *Jewish* catastrophe ..."

The "catastrophe," involving all, which has been prepared in these fifty years, will not be distinctively Jewish in the predominance of Jewish suffering, but in its domination, once again, by "the Jewish question," by the effort to subordinate all the energy generated to aims represented to be Jewish, and in the use of the Jewish masses to help detonate it. The Jewish mass, or mob, is in one respect different from any other mob, or mass: it is more prone to surrender itself to chauvinist incitement, and more frenzied in this surrender. The *Jewish Encyclopaedia*, in a small section devoted to the subject of hysteria among Jews, affirms that their tendency towards it is higher than average. As a layman, I would hazard the guess that this is the result of the centuries of close confinement in the ghettoes and of Talmudic absolutism in them (for today we have to do almost exclusively with the "Eastern Jews" who but yesterday lived in those confines).

I have given some examples of this rising wave of chauvinist hysteria from literature accessible to the general reader. This shows the results, but not the root cause. To locate that the reader needs to do something more difficult; namely, attentively to follow the Yiddish and Hebrew press, in the original or in translation. Then he will receive the picture of an almost demoniac scourging of the Jewish soul so that it shall never find rest and he might conclude that nowhere outside Jewry is anything so anti-Jewish to be found as in some of these utterances, which show a scientific mastery of methods of implanting and fostering fear.

Before studying the examples which follow the reader might consider that the great mass of "explosive Eastern Jews" is now in America. This fact, more pregnant with possible consequences than any other of our day, seems scarcely to have entered the consciousness of the Western world, or even of America. The extracts which now follow show what is said in Hebrew and Yiddish (that is, outside the aural range of the non-Jew) among the Jewish masses, and the effect produced on them within the short space of five years.

Mr. William Zukerman, one of the most notable Jewish diarists of America and of our time, in May 1950 published an article called "Raising the Hair of the Jewish People" *(South African Jewish Times* of May 19, 1950; I imagine it also appeared in Jewish publications in many countries). He began by saying, "A great debate is on in the Zionist world. As yet it has not reached the non- Jewish, or even English-Jewish press; but it is raging in the Hebrew newspapers in Israel and in the Yiddish press in America and in Europe ... it reveals, as nothing else has done in recent years, a cross-section of Jewish thought and emotions in the period following the emergence of Israel." The debate, he explained, was "on the question of *Chalutziot*; organized and prepared emigration of Jews to Israel from all over the world – *but particularly from the United States.*"

At that time (1950) Mr. Zukerman wrote with only an undertone of foreboding. He quoted Mr. Sholem Niger, "dean of Yiddish literary critics and essayists," as attacking, not "the campaign for emigration of American Jews to Israel," but "the *manner* in which it is being presented to American Jews ..." This, said Mr. Niger, was entirely negative, being anti-all others rather than pro-Israel: "the nationalists conduct a campaign of negation, vilification and destruction of everything Jewish outside Israel. *Jewish life in the United States and everywhere else in the world is depicted as contemptible and hateful ... Everything Jewish outside Israel is declared to be slavish, undignified, suppressed and dishonourable. No Jew with any self-respect can live fully as a Jew in the United States or anywhere else except in Israel is the major contention of the nationalists in this debate.*"

Another favourite technique in selling *Chalutziot* to American Jews (the article continued) "is to undermine Jewish morale, faith and hope in their American home; *to keep Jews constantly on edge with the scare of anti-semitism*; not to let them forget the Hitler horrors *and to spread doubts, fear and despair about the future of Jews in America.* Every manifestation of anti-semitism is being seized upon and exaggerated to create an impression that *American Jews, like the Germans under Hitler, stand on the brink of a catastrophe,* and that sooner or later they, too, will have to run for safety."

Mr. Niger quoted as example from an article by "a leading Israeli Zionist, Jonah Kossoi, in a highly literary Jerusalem Hebrew journal, *Israel*":

"Upon us, Zionists, now lies *the old responsibility of constantly raising the hair of the Jewish people; not to let them rest; to keep them forever on the edge of a precipice and make them aware of the dangers facing them.* We must not wait until after the 'catastrophe' because if we do, where will we take the hundreds of thousands of Jews needed to build up our State? ... Not in the future, but right now is the time for Jews to save themselves ..."

The reader will see: the "catastrophe" is a political necessity, or an inevitability; and from these extracts he may begin to understand why the *Jewish Encyclopaedia* records a tendency towards hysteria among Jews. Mr. Zukerman said that this "extreme form of *Chalutziot* propaganda is the most prevalent one in Israel now." He quoted a "more moderate form of the theory" expounded by Mr. L. Jefroikin, editor of the Zionist *Kiyum* in Paris. Mr. Jefroikin, said Mr. Zukerman, "while he subscribes to the truth of every word of the nationalistic theory that no Jew can live a full and dignified life anywhere else but in Israel, and while he too says that 'American Jews live in a fool's paradise,' nevertheless admits that in their present state of mind American Jews will never agree that the U.S.A. is to be placed in the same category as Germany *and Poland* and that they would not consent to regard their home as a place of transit for Israel. He concludes, therefore, that American Jews should be *propagandized* to become only 'Lovers of Israel,' not actual Israelis in body and soul."

The effect of this "propaganda" carried by Zionist emissaries from Israel into the United States, may next be studied in some remarks printed eighteen months later (December 1951) in the *Intermountain Jewish News* of Denver, Colorado. Its editor, Mr. Robert Gamzey, was critical of the action of the Jewish Agency and the World Zionist Congress for allocating $2,800,000 to promote *Chalutziot* in the United States. He said he knew "from personal experience in Israel of the widespread erroneous attitude there that America has no future for the Jews and that anti-semitism dooms U.S. Jewry to the fate of German Jews." He added, "It is inconceivable therefore that the sending of Israel emissaries here to encourage American youth to settle in Israel would be conducted in any other way but to *deride and deprecate the future of American Judaism.*"

These forebodings of 1950 and 1951 were justified in the next five years, when "the campaign" and "the emissaries" from Israel succeeded in injecting "the nationalistic theory," as above expounded, into the minds of the Jewish masses in America. Thus in 1955, Mr. William Zukerman, who in 1950 had been but faintly alarmed, was greatly so. He wrote (*Jewish Newsletter*, November 1955, reprinted in *Time* Magazine of New York, November 28):

"There cannot be the slightest doubt that a state of mind *very much like that of Israel now prevails among American Jews*. There is a fanatical certainty abroad, that there is only one truth and that Israel is the sole custodian of it. No distinction is made between the Jews of the world and Israel, and not even between the Israeli government and Israel. Israeli statesmen and their policies are assumed to be inviolate and above criticism. There is a frightening intolerance of opinions differing from those of the majority, a complete disregard of reason, and a yielding to the *emotions of a stampeding herd*.

"There is only one important difference between the Israeli and the American Jews. In Israel, the outburst of emotionalism, as far as one can judge from outside, has a basis in reality. It wells from the hidden springs of a disillusioned people who were promised security and peace and find themselves in a war trap. *The American-Jewish brand of hysteria is entirely without roots in the realities of American-Jewish life. It is completely artificial, manufactured by the Zionist leaders, and foisted on a people who have no cause for hysteria by an army of paid propagandists as a means of advancing a policy of avowed political pressure and of stimulating fund raising. Never before has a propaganda campaign in behalf of a foreign government been planned and carried out more blatantly and cynically, in the blaze of limelight and to the fanfare of publicity, than the present wave of hysteria now being worked up among American Jews.*"

These two quotations, separated by five years, again portray the degeneration of the Jewish soul under the tutelage of Talmudic Zionism. They also bring this tale of three wars to the eve of the third one, if "eve" is the apt word. In fact the third war began when the fighting in the Second War ended and has been in unbroken progress, somewhere or other in the world, ever since. It needs only a puff from any bellows to ignite it into another general war.

The process could have been, and possibly still could be halted by two responsible statesmen, one on either side of the Atlantic, speaking in unison, for it is in essence the biggest bluff in history. Today such mortal salvation seems too much to hope for and the writer probably does not exaggerate in opining that only God, who has done much bigger things, could avert the third general war. Unless that happens the concluding decades of this century foreseeably will see either the fiasco or the transient triumph of Talmudic chauvinism. Either way, in failure or success, the accompanying "catastrophe" would be that of the non-Jewish masses and Jewish suffering would be a minute fraction of it.

Afterwards, as the world obviously will not accept the Talmud, the Jews would at last have to accept the world as it is.

Chapter 46

THE CLIMACTERIC

This book, first written between 1949 and 1952, was rewritten in the years 1953-1956, and its concluding chapter in October and November of 1956. This was a timely moment to sum up the impact of Talmudic Zionism on human affairs, for just fifty years, or one- half of "the Jewish century," then had passed from the day when it first broke the political surface, after submergence for some 1800 years.[34] (The British Uganda offer, in 1903, was the first public revelation that Western politicians were privily negotiating with "the

Jewish power" as an *entity*. Mr. Balfour's hotel-room reception of Dr. Weizmann in 1906, after the Zionist rejection of Uganda, now may be seen as the second step, and the first step on the fateful road of *full* involvement in Palestinian Zionism.)

In 1956, too, the revolution (which I hold to have been demonstrably Talmudic in our time) was also about fifty years old (from the revolutionary outbreaks following Japan's defeat of Russia in 1905) as a permanent factor in our daily lives (its roots, of course, go back through 1848 to the revolution in France and to Weishaupt, and to the one in England and Cromwell).

Finally, 1956 was the year of one more presidential election in America, and this, more openly than any previous one, was held under the paralyzing pressure *of* Zionism.

Therefore if I could so have planned when I began the book in 1949 (I was in no position to make any such timetable) I could not have chosen a better moment than the autumn of 1956 to review the process depicted, its consequences up to this date, and the apparent denouement now near at hand: the climax to which it was all bound to lead.

During the writing of the book I have had small expectation, for the reasons I have given, that it would be published when it was ready; at this stage of "the Jewish century" that seems unlikely. If it does not appear now, I believe it will still be valid in five, ten or more years, and I expect it to be published one day or another because I anticipate the collapse, sooner or later, of the virtual law of heresy which has prevented open discussion of "the Jewish question" during the past three decades. Some day the subject will be

---

[34] About 1952, a coelenterate fish, of a kind until then believed to have been extinct for millions of years, was brought to the surface of the Indian Ocean (seriously damaging the chain of the Darwinian theory by its appearance, as did the discovery, a little later, that the Piltdown skull was a fake). The emergence of Levitical Zionism, when it broke the political surface of the 20th Century, was a somewhat similar surprise from the deep.

freely debated again and something of what this book records will then be relevant.

Whatever the sequel in that respect, I end the book in October and November of 1956 and when I look around see that all is turning out just as was to be foreseen from the sequence of events related in it. The year has been full of rumours of war, louder and more insistent than any since the end of the Second War in 1945, and they come from the two places whence they were bound to come, given the arrangements made in 1945 by the "top-line politicians" of the West. They come from Palestine, where the Zionists from Russia were installed by the West, and from Eastern Europe, where the Talmudic revolution was installed by the West. These two movements (I recall again) are the ones which Dr. Weizmann showed taking shape, within the *same* Jewish households of Russia in the late 19th Century: revolutionary-Communism and revolutionary-Zionism.

At two moments during recent years the war-noises made by the politicians of the West were louder than at any others. On each occasion the immediate cause of the outburst was soon lost to sight in the outcry about the *particular* case of "the Jews," so that, even before general war began (in both instances it receded) it was presented to the public masses as war which, if it came, would be fought primarily for, on behalf of or in defence of "the Jews" (or "Israel").

I earlier opined that any third general war would be of that nature, because the events of 1917-1945 led inevitably to that conclusion, which has been greatly strengthened by the events of 1953 and 1956. The wars which in 1953 and 1956 seemed to threaten would evidently have been waged by the West in that understanding, this time much more explicitly avowed in advance than on the two previous occasions. By any time when this book may appear the short-memoried "public," if it has not again been afflicted by general war, may have forgotten the war-crises, or near-war-crises, of 1953 and 1956, so that I will briefly put them on record.

In 1953 some Jews appeared among the prisoners in one of the innumerable mock-trials announced (this one was never held) in Moscow. This caused violent uproar among the Western politicians, who again and with one voice cried that "the Jews" were being "exterminated" and "singled out" for "persecution." The outcry had reached the pitch of warlike menace when Stalin died, the trial was cancelled and the clamour abruptly ceased. To my mind the episode plainly indicated that if the war "against Communism" came about (which Western politicians and newspapers in these years spoke of as an accepted probability) it would be fought, and this time even avowedly, for "the Jews." The general multitude of enslaved humanity would be left unsuccoured, as in 1945.

In July 1956 threats of war again were uttered when Egypt nationalized the Suez Canal. For the first few days of this war-crisis the British Prime

Minister justified the menaces to the British people, by the argument that Egypt's action imperilled "the vital British lifeline." Very soon he switched to the argument (presumably held to be more effective) that "Egypt's *next* act, if this is allowed to succeed, *will be to attack Israel.*" The Zionist state then began to figure in the news as the worst sufferer from Egyptian control of the Suez Canal. Ergo, war in the Middle East too, if it came, was to be a war "for the Jews."

Thirdly, 1956 saw a presidential election held, for the seventh time under the direct, and for the third time under the *open* pressure of the Zionists in New York. The election campaign became a public contest for "the Jewish vote," with the rival parties outbidding each other in the promise of arms, money and guarantees to the Zionist state. Both parties, on the brink of war in that part of the world, publicly pledged themselves to the support of "Israel" in any circumstances whatever.

These results of the process which I have described from its start were to be expected. The conclusion to be drawn for the future seems inescapable: the millions of the West, through their politicians and their own indifference, are chained to a powder-keg with a sputtering, shortening fuse. The West approaches the climax of its relationship with Zion, publicly begun fifty years ago, and the climax is precisely what was to be foreseen when that servience started.

In our century each of the two great wars was followed by numerous books of revelation, in which the origins of the war were scrutinized and found to be different from what the mass, or mob, had been told, and the responsibility elsewhere located. These books have found general acceptance among those who read them, for a mood of enquiry always follows the credulity of wartime. However, they produce no lasting effect and the general mass may be expected to prove no less responsive to high-pressure incitement at the start of another war, for mass-resistance to mass-propaganda is negligible, and the power of propaganda is intoxicating as well as toxic.

Whether full public information about the causes of wars would avail against this continuing human instinct ("By a divine instinct, men's minds mistrust ensuing danger") if it were given *before* war's outbreak, I cannot surmise; I believe this has never been tried. One modest ambition of this book is to establish that the origins and nature of and responsibility for a war *can* be shown before it begins, not merely when it has run its course. I believe the body of the book has demonstrated this and that its argument has already been borne out by events.

I believe also that the particular events of the years 1953-1956 in the West greatly strengthen its argument and the conclusion drawn, and for that reason devote the remainder of its concluding chapter to a resume of the relevant events of those years; (1) in the area enslaved by the revolution; (2) in and around the Zionist state; and (3) in "the free world" of the West, respectively. They appear to me to add the last word to the tale thus told: Climax, near or at hand.

Author's interpolation: *The preceding part of this concluding chapter, up to the words, "Climax, near or at hand," was written on Friday, October 26, 1956. I then went away for the weekend, intending to resume and complete the chapter on Tuesday, October 30, 1956; it was already in rough draft. When I resumed it on that day Israel had invaded Egypt, on Monday, October 29, 1956. Therefore the rest of the chapter is written in the light of the events which followed; these made it much longer than I expected.*

The Revolution

In the area of the revolution, swollen to enslave half of Europe, the death of Stalin in 1953 was followed by a series of popular uprisings in 1953 and 1956.

Both events rejoiced the watching world, for they revived the almost forgotten hope that one day the destructive revolution would destroy itself and that men and nations would again be free. This clear meaning was then confused by the forced intrusion into each of "the Jewish question." In "the Jewish century" the public masses were prevented from receiving or considering tidings of any great event save in terms of what its effect would be "for the Jews."

Stalin's death (March 6,1953) startled the world because the life of this man, who probably caused the death and enslavement of more human beings than any other in history, had come to seem endless, like the uncoiling of the serpent.[35] The circumstances of his death remain unclear, but the timetable of the events attending it may be significant.

On *January 15, 1953* the Moscow newspapers announced that nine men were to be tried on charges of conspiring to assassinate seven high Communist notables. Either six or seven of these nine men were Jews (the accounts disagree). The other two or three might never have been born for all the world heard of them, for in the uproar which immediately arose in the West the affair was dubbed that of "the Jewish doctors."[36]

---

[35] His leading place was briefly taken by one Grigori Malenkov, who yielded it to duumvirs, Nikita Kruschev (partyleader) and Nikolai Bulganin (Premier). The world could not tell to what extent they inherited Stalin's personal power or were dominated by others. A survivor of all changes and purges, Mr. Lazar Kaganovich, a Jew, remained a First Deputy Premier throughout and on the Bolshevik anniversary in November 1955 was chosen to tell the world, "Revolutionary ideas know no frontiers." When the duumvirs visited India in that month the *New York Times*, asking who ruled the Soviet Union in their absence, answered "Lazar M. Kaganovich, veteran Commmunist leader." Mr. Kaganovich was among Stalin's oldest and closest intimates, but neither this nor any other relevant fact deterred the Western press from attacking Stalin, in his last months, as the new, anti-semitic "Hitler."

[36] This outcry in the West had begun ten weeks earlier, on the eve of the Presidential election in America, on the strength of a trial in Prague, when eleven of fourteen defendants were hanged, after the usual "confessions," on charges of *Zionist* conspiracy. Three of the victims were not Jews, but they too might not have been born or hanged for all the notice they received in the press of the West.

In February, while the clamour in the West continued, diplomats who saw Stalin remarked on his healthy look and good spirits.

On March 6 Stalin died. A month later the "Jewish doctors" were released. Six months later Stalin's terrorist chief, Lavrenti Beria, was shot for having arrested them and the charges were denounced as false. Of Stalin's death, a notable American correspondent in Moscow, Mr. Harrison Salisbury, wrote that after it Russia was ruled by a group or junta "more dangerous than Stalin," consisting of Messrs' Malenkov, Molotov, Bulganin and Kaganovich. To acquire power, he said, the junta might have murdered Stalin, everything pointed to it; "if Stalin just happened to be struck down by a ruptured artery in his brain on March 2, *it must be recorded as one of the most* fortuitous occurrences in history."

For the West these attendant circumstances and possibilities of Stalin's end had no interest. The entire period of some nine months, between the Prague trial (and presidential election) and the liquidation of Beria was filled with the uproar in the West about "anti-semitism in Russia." While the clamour continued (it ceased after "the Jewish doctors" were released and vindicated) things were said which seemed plainly to signify that any Western war against the Communist union would be waged, like the one against Germany, solely on behalf of "the Jews," or of those who claimed to represent the Jews. In 1953 Sovietized Russia was held up as the new anti-semitic monster, as Germany was held up in 1939 and Czarist Russia in 1914. This all-obscuring issue, to judge by the propagandist hubbub of that period, would again have befogged the battle and deceived the nations.

The timing of this campaign is significant and can no longer be explained by the theory of coincidence. In order to give maximum effect to the "pressure-machine" in America, the "Jewish question" has to become acute at the period of any presidential election there. Nowadays it always becomes acute at that precise period in one of its two forms: "anti-semitism" somewhere (this happened in 1912, 1932, 1936, 1940 and 1952) or a peril to "Israel" (this happened in 1948 and 1956). The prediction that, in one of the two forms, it will dominate the Presidential election of 1960 may be made without much risk.

Nothing changed in the situation of the Jews in Russia at that time.[37] Some Jews had been included among the defendants in a show- trial at Prague and in one announced, but never held, in Moscow. The thirty-five Communist years had seen innumerable show-trials; the world had become indifferent through familiarity with them. As the terrorist state was based on imprisonment without *any* trial, the show-trials obviously were only held in order to produce some effect, either on the Sovietized masses or on the outer

---

[37] Of whom, according to the current Jewish "estimates" there were some two millions, or about one percent of the total Soviet population, (stated by the Soviet Government's Statistical Manual of the Soviet Economy in June 1956 to be 200,000,000).

world. Even the charge of "Zionist conspiracy" was not new; it had been made in some trials of the 1920's, and Communism from the start (as Lenin and Stalin testify) *formally* outlawed Zionism, just as it provided the Zionists from Russia with the arms to establish "Israel" in 1948. If Stalin went further than was allowed in attacking "Zionism" on this occasion, his death quickly followed. To the end he was obviously not anti-*Jewish*. Mr. Kaganovich remained at his right hand. A few days before he died Stalin ordered one of the most pompous funerals ever seen in Soviet Moscow to be given to Lev Mechlis, one of the most feared and hated Jewish Commissars of the thirty-five years. Mechlis's coffin was carried by all the surviving grandees of the Bolshevik revolution, who also shared the watch at his lying in state, so that this was plainly a warning to the captive Russian masses, if any still were needed, that "the law against anti- semitism" was still in full force. Immediately after Mechlis's funeral (Jan. 27, 1953) the "Stalin Peace Prize" was with great public ostentation presented to the apostle of Talmudic vengeance, Mr. Ilya Ehrenburg, whose broadcasts to the Red Armies as they advanced into Europe incited them not to spare "even *unborn* Fascists." A few days before he died Stalin prompted the *Red Star* to state that the struggle against Zionism "had nothing to do with anti-semitism; Zionism is the enemy of the working people all over the world, of Jews no less than Gentiles."

The plight of the Jews, in their fractional minority in Russia, thus had not changed for the better or for worse. They still had "a higher degree of equality in the Soviet Union than any other part of the world" (to quote the derisive answer given, at this period, by a Jewish witness to a Republican Congressman, Mr. Kit Clardy, before a Congressional Committee, Mr. Clardy having asked "Do you not shrink in horror from what Soviet Russia is doing to the Jews?"). They remained a privileged class.

The uproar in the West therefore was artificial and had no factual basis, yet it reached a pitch just short of actual warlike threat and might have risen to that note had not Stalin died and "the Jewish doctors" been released (I was never able to discover whether the non- Jewish ones also were liberated). There could only be one reason for it: that *Zionism* had been attacked, and by 1952-3 opposition to Zionism was deemed by the frontal politicians of the West to be "Hitlerism" and provocation of war. The episode showed that this propaganda of incitement can be unleashed at the touch of a button and be "beamed" in any direction at changing need (not excluding America, in the long run). When this propaganda has been brought to white heat, it is used to extort the "commitments" which are later invoked.

The six month period, between nomination-and-election, election-and-inauguration is that in which American presidents now come under this pressure. President Eisenhower in 1952-3 was under the same pressure as President Woodrow Wilson in 1912-3, Mr. Roosevelt in 1938-9, and President Truman in 1947-8. The whole period of his canvass, nomination, election and inauguration was dominated by "the Jewish question" in its two forms, "anti-semitism" here, there or everywhere, and the adventure in Palestine. Immediately after nomination he told a Mr. Maxwell Abbell, President of the United Synagogue of America, "The Jewish people could not have a better friend than me ... I grew up believing that Jews was the chosen people and that they gave us the high ethical and moral principles of our civilization" (all Jewish newspapers, September 1952).[38]

This was the basic commitment, familiar in our century and always taken to mean much more than the givers comprehend. Immediately after it came the Prague trial and President Eisenhower, just elected, was evidently pressed for something more specific. In a message to a Jewish Labour Committee in Manhattan (Dec. 21, 1952) he said the Prague trial "was designed to unloose a campaign of rabid anti-semitism throughout Soviet Europe and the satellite nations of Eastern Europe. *I am honoured to take my stand with American Jewry* ... to show the world the indignation all America feels at the outrages perpetrated by the Soviets against the sacred principles of our civilization."

The "outrages" at that moment consisted in the hanging of eleven men, three of them Gentiles, among the millions done to death in the thirty-five Bolshevik years; their fate was not included in these "outrages." The new president could not have known what "campaign" the trial was "designed to unloose," and innumerable other trials had received no presidential denunciation. The words implicitly tarred the captives of Communism, too, with the "anti-semitic" brush, for they were termed "satellite nations" and the primary meaning of "satellite" is "An attendant attached to a prince or other powerful person; hence, an obsequious dependent or follower" (Webster's Dictionary). As the commander whose military order, issued in agreement with the Soviet dictator, had ensured their captivity, President Eisenhower's choice of word was strange. It reflected the attitude of those who were able to put "pressure" on all American presidents and governments. To them the enslavement of millions meant nothing; indeed, their power was used to perpetuate it.

This state of affairs was reflected, again, in two of the new President's first acts. In seeking election, he had appealed to the strong American aversion to the deed of 1945 by pledging to repudiate the Yalta agreements (the political charter of his own military order halting the Allied advance west of Berlin and thus abandoning Eastern Europe to Communism) in these explicit words:

"The Government of the United States, under Republican leadership, *will repudiate all commitments contained in secret understandings such as those of Yalta*

---

[38] Mr. Eisenhower "added that his mother had reared him and his brother, in teachings of the Old Testament." This somewhat cryptic allusion is to the Christian sect of Jehovah's Witnesses, in which Mr. Eisenhower and his brothers were brought up in their parental home.

which aid Communist enslavement." Elected, the new president sent to Congress (20 February 1953) a resolution merely proposing that Congress join him "in rejecting any interpretations or applications ... of secret agreements which have been perverted to bring about the subjugation of free people." By that time he had publicly referred to the enslaved peoples as "satellites." As the resolution neither "repudiated" nor even referred to "Yalta," it was disappointing to the party led by President Eisenhower and in the end it was dropped altogether.

In its place, the new President transmitted to Congress a resolution condemning "the vicious and inhuman campaigns against *the Jews*" in the Soviet area. Thus "the enslaved" were deleted altogether and "the Jews" put in their place, an amendment typical of our time. The perspiring State Department succeeded in having this resolution amended to include "other minorities." The present Jewish "estimates" are that there are in all "about 2,500,000 Jews behind the Iron Curtain," where the non-Jewish captives amount to between 300 and 350 millions; these masses, which included whole nations like the Poles, Hungarians, Bulgars and Ukrainians, to say nothing of the smaller ones or even of the Russians themselves, were lumped together in two words "other minorities." The Senate adopted *this* resolution (Feb. 27, 1953) by unanimous consent, but this was not deemed enough for proper discipline, so that every American Senator (like the Members of the British House of Commons, at Mr. Eden's behest, during the war) stood up to be counted. A few who were absent hurriedly asked in writing to have their names added to the roll-call.

Had the peoples behind "the Iron Curtain" understood the story of these two resolutions, or been allowed to learn of it, they would not have hoped (as they *did* hope) for any American succour in their national uprisings against the terror in 1956.

The President having spoken and acted thus, the uproar waxed. One of the most powerful Zionist leaders of that period (in the line of Justice Brandeis and Rabbi Stephen Wise) was Rabbi Hillel Silver, who during the election had defended Mr. Eisenhower against ex- President Truman's charge of "antisemitism" (now invariably used in presidential elections), and later was invited by the new president to pronounce the "prayer for grace and guidance" at his inauguration. Thus Rabbi Silver may be seen as a man speaking with authority when he announced that *if* Russia were *destroyed*, it would be on behalf of the Jews: he "warned Russia *that it will be destroyed if it makes a spiritual pact with Hitlerism*." This method of giving the "Hitler" label to any individual threatened with "destruction" later was generally adopted (President Nasser of Egypt being a case in point).

The menace was always implicitly the same: "Persecute men if you will, but you will be destroyed if you oppose the Jews." Mr. Thomas E. Dewey (twice a presidential aspirant and the architect of Mr. Eisenhower's nomination in 1952) outdid Rabbi Silver at the same meeting (Jan. 15, 1953): "Now all are beginning to see it" ("anti-semitism" in Russia) "as the newest and most terrible programme of genocide yet launched ... Zionism, as such, has now become a crime and merely being born a Jew is now cause for hanging. Stalin has swallowed the last drop of Hitler's poison, becoming the newest and most vituperative persecutor of Jewry ... It seems that Stalin is willing to admit to the whole world that he would like to accomplish for Hitler what Hitler could not do in life." The extravagance of this campaign astonishes even the experienced observer, in retrospect. For instance, the *Montreal Gazette,* which by chance I saw in the summer of 1953, editorially stated that "thousands of Jews are being murdered in East Germany"; the Johannesburg *Zionist Record* three years earlier (July 7, 1950) had stated that the entire Jewish population of Eastern Germany was 4,200 souls, most of whom enjoyed preference for government employ.

The new president's "commitments" became ever firmer, at all events in the minds of those to whom they were addressed. In March 1953, either just before or after Stalin's death, he sent a letter to the Jewish Labour Committee above-cited *pledging* (the word used in the *New York Times*; I have not the full text of his message) that America would be "*forever vigilant* against any resurgence of anti- semitism." When the recipient committee held its congress at Atlantic City the "Jewish doctors" had been released and the whole rumpus was dying down, so that it was no longer eager to make the letter public and returned it to the sender. The president was insistent on publication and sent it back "with a very tough note bitterly condemning Soviet anti-semitism."

In this world of propagandist fictions the masses of the West were led by their governors from disappointment to disappointment. Who knows whither they would have been led on this occasion, had Stalin not died, the "Jewish doctors" not been released, the finger not been removed from the button of mass-incitement?

Stalin died and the machine-made outcry (on both sides of the Atlantic) died with him. What if he had lived and "the Jewish doctors" been tried? When he died the propaganda had already reached eve-of-war pitch; the "new Hitler" had begun "the newest and most terrible programme of genocide yet launched"; "thousands of Jews" were being "murdered" in a place where only hundreds lived: soon these thousands would have become millions, one ... two ... six millions. The entire holocaust of Lenin's and Stalin's thirty-five years, with its myriads of unknown victims and graves, would have been transformed, by the witchcraft of this propaganda, into one more "anti-Jewish persecution"; indeed, this was done by the shelving of President Eisenhower's "repudiation of Yalta and Communist enslavement" pledge and the substitution for it of a resolution which singled out for "condemnation" the "vicious and inhuman treatment of the Jews" (who continued, behind the Iran Curtain, to wield the terror over those enslaved by Communism). In that cause alone, had war come, another generation of Western youth would have gone to war, thinking their mission was to "destroy Communism."

Stalin died. The West was spared war at that time and stumbled on, behind its Zionised leaders, towards the next disappointment, which was of a different kind. During the ten years that had passed since the ending of the Second War their leaders had made them accustomed to the thought that one day they would have to crush Communism and thus amend the deed of 1945. The sincerity of the Western leaders in this matter was again to be tested in the years 1953 and 1956.

In those years the enslaved people *themselves* began to destroy Communism and to strike, for that liberation which the American president, the military architect of their enslavement, promised them but counselled them not militantly to effect.[39] Stalin's death seemed to have the effect of a thaw on the rigid fear which gripped these peoples and it set this process of self-liberation in motion.

The writer of this book was confounded, in this case, in his expectations. I believed, from observation and experience, that any national uprising was impossible against tanks and automatic weapons, and against the day-to-day methods of the terror (arrest, imprisonment, deportation or death without charge or trial), which seemed to have been perfected during three centuries (that is, through the revolutions in England, France and Russia) to a point where, I thought, only outside succour could make any uprising possible. I had forgotten the infinite resources of the human spirit.

The first of these revolts occurred in Sovietized East Berlin on June 17, 1953, when unarmed men and youths attacked Soviet tanks with bands and stones.[40] This example produced an unprecedented result deep inside the Soviet Union itself: a rising at the Vorkuta slave camp in the Arctic Circle, where the prisoners chased the terrorist guards from the camp and held it for a week until secret police troops from Moscow arrived and broke them with machine-gun fire.

These two uprisings occurred while the clamour in the West about "anti-semitism behind the Iron Curtain" was still loud. No similar outcry was

---

[39] "While once again proclaiming the policy of liberation, Mr. Dulles, the Secretary of State, disclaimed any United States responsibility for the ill-fated uprising in Hungary. He said that beginning in 1952, he and the President consistently had declared that liberation must be achieved by peaceful, evolutionary means." Statement at Augusta, Georgia, Dec. 2, 1956.

[40] This was crushed and ruthless vengeance taken by "the dreaded Frau Hilde Benjamin" (The Times, July 17, 1953) who was promoted Minister of Justice for the purpose and became notorious for her death sentences (one on a boy in his teens who distributed anti-Communist leaflets) and for her especial persecution of the sect of Jehovah's Witnesses, in which President Eisenhower was brought up. In the popular thought and in New York newspaper descriptions she was described as "a Jewess." As far as my research can discover, though married to a Jew, she was not by birth Jewish.

raised on behalf of the legion of human beings, a hundred times as numerous, whose plight was once more revealed. No threats of war or "destruction" were uttered against the Soviet Union on their account. On the contrary, the politicians and the press of the West urged them to remain quiet and simply to hope for "the liberation" which, by some untold means, one day would come to them from America, which had abandoned them in 1945.

Nevertheless, the anguished longing for liberation continued to work in the souls of the peoples and in the sequence to the East Berlin and Vorkuta outbursts came the risings in Poland and Hungary in October, 1956, after I began this concluding chapter. The first was a spontaneous national uprising. The second, ignited by the first, became something which history can scarcely match: a national *war* of a whole, captive people against the captor's overwhelming might. I believe the passage of time will show this event either to have marked the rebirth of "the West" and the revival of Europe, or the end of Europe as it has been known to mankind for the past thousand years and therewith the end of anything the words, "the West," have stood for.

Whatever the future, one thing was achieved by the October uprisings, and more especially by the Hungarian uprisings. Never again could the revolution pretend to have even the passive acceptance of its captives. These showed that, under Karl Marx's Communism, they found they had nothing to lose but their chains and would face death rather than endure them.

The causes for which both nations rose were the same and were made completely clear. They wanted, in each case, the liberation of the nation through the withdrawal of the Red Army; the liberation of individual men from the terror through the abolition of the secret police and the punishment of the chief terrorists; the restoration of their faith through the release of the head of their church (who in both cases was imprisoned); the release of their political system from the one-party thrall through the return of contending parties and elections.

Thus the issue at stake was completely plain: through a little nation on its eastern borders "the West" rose against Asiatic despotism; here was God against godlessness, liberty against slavery, human dignity against human degradation. The issue at the moment turned, and the final decision will turn, on the measure of support which these outpost-nations of the West found in the remainder of the West, which professed kinship and fellowship with them but in the hour of need had abandoned them before.

In that quarter, vision of the clear issue at stake was obscured by the intrusion of the all-obscuring side-issue of our century: "the Jewish question." The tale of the October events in Poland and Hungary is as clear, in itself, as crystal, but was not allowed to become clear to the masses of America and England because of this one aspect, concerning which information has consistently been denied to them since the Bolshevik overthrow of the legitimate regime in Russia in 1917.

Three months before the Polish and Hungarian uprisings an article by Mr. C.L. Sulzberger published in the *New York Times* revived the cry of "Anti-semitism behind the Iron Curtain" which had been raised in 1953. As an instance of this "anti-semitism" the article cited the dismissal of Jakub Berman, "detested party theorist and a Jew," who was the chief Moscovite terrorist in Poland.

In this article lurked the secret of which the Western masses have never been allowed to become aware; Mr. Robert Wilton, who "lost the confidence" of *The Times* for trying to impart it to that newspaper's readers in 1917-1918, was the first of a long line of correspondents who tried, and failed, during the next thirty-nine years. The masses in Russia, and later in the other countries which were abandoned to Communism, could not rise against the terror without being accused of "anti-semitism," because the terror was always a *Jewish* and Talmudic terror, thus identifiable by its acts, and not a Russian, Communist or Soviet terror.

In this one thing the ruling power in Moscow, whatever it truly was and is, never departed from the original pattern, and that is the basic fact from which all research into the events of our century must start. The theory of coincidence might conceivably be applied to the 90 percent-Jewish governments which appeared in Russia, Hungary and Bavaria in 1917-1919; (Even at that time, as I have shown earlier, a Jewish writer described the national abhorrence of the Jewish Bolshevik government in Hungary as "anti-semitism," an epithet which could only have been escaped by submission to it). But when the Moscow Government installed Jewish governments in the countries abandoned to it in 1945 no doubt remained that this was set and calculated policy, with a considered purpose.

I repeat here information, from unchallengeable sources, about the composition of these governments at the very moment in 1952- 1953 when Stalin was being called "the new Hitler" and "Russia" was being threatened with "destruction" from New York and Washington if it permitted "any resurgence of anti-semitism": "In Czechoslovakia, as elsewhere in Central and South-Eastern Europe, both the party intellectuals *and the key men in the secret police* are largely Jewish in origin; the man in the street, therefore, has been inclined to equate the party cares with the Jews and to blame the 'Jewish Communists' for all his troubles" *(New Statesman, 1952)*; "... The strongly Jewish (90 percent in the top echelons) Government of Communist Hungary under Communist Premier Matyas Rakosi, who is himself a Jew" *(Time, New York, 1953)*. "Rumania, together with Hungary, probably has the greatest number of Jews in the administration" *(New York Herald-Tribune, 1953)*. All these, and many similar reports in my files, come from articles reprobating "anti-semitism" in "the satellite countries," and at this period, when these countries were known to be Jewish-ruled, President Eisenhower made his statement about "a wave of rabid anti-semitism in … the satellite countries of Eastern Europe."

What could these menaces from Washington mean to the captive peoples, other than a warning not to murmur against the wielders of the knout; yet at the same time they were promised "liberation," and "The Voice of America" and "Radio Free Europe" daily and nightly tormented them with descriptions of their own plight.

This was the confusing background to the Polish and Hungarian national uprisings of October 1956, the first sign of which, again, was given by the riots at Poznan, in Poland, in June 1956. Immediately after that Mr. Sulzberger's article about "Anti-semitism behind the Iron Curtain" appeared, complaining that Mr. Jakub Berman had been dismissed and that Marshal Rokossovsky, commander of the Polish army, had dismissed "several hundred Jewish officers." In August one of the two Deputy Premiers, Mr. Zenon Nowak (the other was a Jew, Mr. Hilary Mine) said the campaign for "democratization" or "liberalization" which was being conducted in the Polish press was being distorted by the introduction of, and the especial prominence given to the case of "the Jews," He said the nation believed there was "a disproportionate number of Jews in leading party and government positions" and in evidence read a list of their representation in the various ministries. A Professor Kotabinski, replying to and attacking Mr. Nowak, said the Jews "had become almost a majority in key positions, and preference for their own people in giving out jobs has not been avoided" *(New York Times,* Oct. 11, 1956).

By that time Poland had been for eleven years under *Soviet* rule and *Jewish* terror. Little had changed in the picture given by the American Ambassador, Mr. Arthur Bliss Lane, of the years 1945-1947: "Many an arrest by the Security Police was witnessed by members of the American Embassy … . terrifying methods, such as arrests in the middle of the night, and the person arrested generally was not permitted to communicate with the outside world, perhaps for months, perhaps for all time … Even our Jewish sources admitted … the great unpopularity of the Jews in key government positions. These men included Minc, Berman, Olczewski, Radkiewic and Spychalski … there was bitter feeling within the militia against the Jews because the Security police, controlled by Radkiewicz, dominated the militia and the army … Furthermore, both the Security Police and Internal Security Police had among their members many Jews of Russian origin."

Only after eleven years did this Jewish control of the terror begin to weaken. In May 1956 Mr. Jakub Berman ("thought to be Moscow's No. 1 man in the Polish Party," *New York Times,* Oct. 21, 1956) resigned as one deputy Premier and early in October 1956, Mr. Hilary Minc ("thought to be Moscow's No. 2 man") also resigned. (Mr. Nowak, one of the new Deputy Premiers, from the start was assailed as "anti-semitic").

This was the significant background to the national uprising of October 20. Poland, at its first experience of Communist rule, like Russia, Hungary and Bavaria in 1917-1919, had found the terror, on which that rule rested, to be *Jewish* and was already being attacked for "anti-semitism" in America and England because it tried to throw off the terror. Like all other countries, it was caught in the dilemma caused by "the Jewish question." The actual situation of such Jews as were not in high position in Poland appears to have been better than that of other sections of the population, to judge from various reports made at this period by visiting rabbis and journalists from America. Incidentally, the total number of Jews in Poland at that time ranges, in published Jewish "estimates," from "thirty thousand" *(New York Times,* July 13, 1956) to "about fifty thousand" *(New York Times,* Aug. 31, 1956), the total population of Poland being given, in current reference works as approximately 25,000,000. Their proportion, therefore, is a small fraction of one percent, and never before this century has a minority of this minuteness, anywhere, claimed to become "almost a majority in key positions" and in showing "preference for their own people in giving out jobs."

The case of Hungary was more significant, for this country after 1945 endured its *second* experience of Communist rule. It not only found the terror to be Jewish again, but it was wielded *by the same men.* This deliberate reinstalment of Jewish terrorists detested by a nation for their deeds of twenty-six years before (the details are given later in this chapter) is the strongest evidence yet provided of the existence in Moscow of a power, controlling the revolution, which deliberately gives its savageries the *Talmudic* signature, not the Soviet, Communist or Russian one.

Against this background, which was not comprehended in "the free world," the forces of national regeneration gradually worked to throw off the terror. In April 1956 Mr. Vladislav Gomulka (imprisoned from 1951 to 1956 under the Berman-Minc regime as a "deviationist") was released and became the symbol of the national hope at this instant, for although he was a Communist he was a Pole. He was restored to the Central Committee of the Polish Communist Party on October 19, 1956 and on October 20 did something which might have changed the whole shape of our century, but for the shadow which soon fell across the ensuing events (this time from the other centre of "the Jewish question," Palestine). He presented the Polish nation with a virtual declaration of independence, attacked "the misrule of the last twelve years," promised elections and declared that "the Polish people will defend themselves with all means so that we may not be pushed off the road to democratization."

He did this in face of a flying visit from the Moscovite chiefs themselves. Mr. Kruschev was accompanied by generals and threatened the use of the Red Army. He seems to have been utterly discomfited by the bold front offered to him by Mr. Gomulka and, in particular by Mr. Edward

Ochab (also an "anti-semite" in Mr. Sulzberger's article) who said, according to report, "If you do not halt your troops immediately, we will walk out of here and break off all contact." The Polish army was evidently ready to defend the national cause and Mr. Kruschev capitulated. Marshal Rokossovsky disappeared to Moscow[41] and, as the symbol of the nation's rebirth, Cardinal Wyszynski (deprived of his office under the Berman-Minc regime in 1953) was released.

Jubilation spread over Poland. The revolution [Communist] had suffered its first major defeat; the faith had been restored (this was the meaning of the Cardinal's liberation); the nation, abandoned by the outer world, had taken a great first step towards its self-liberation. At once the bush-fire spread to Hungary. The great event in Poland was forgotten in the excitement caused by a greater one. All the processes of human nature, time and providence seemed at last to be converging to a good end.

In Hungary on October 22, 1956, two days after the Polish declaration of independence, the people gathered in the streets to demand that Mr. Imre Nagy return to the premiership and the Soviet occupation troops be withdrawn. None of them realized at that moment that they were beginning a national uprising which was to turn into a national war of liberation.

The spark came from Poland and the background was the same, with the difference that Hungary was undergoing its *second* ordeal at the hands of Jewish commissars. The chief object of its fear and detestation at that instant was one Erno Geroe, head of the Hungarian Communist Party and the *third* of the Jewish terrorists of 1919 sent to Hungary by Moscow to wield the terror there. Thus in this event, not only the accumulated bitterness of the years 1945-1956 exploded, but also the memories of the terror in 1918-1919.

Mr. Imre Nagy, like Mr. Gomulka in Poland, became the symbol of the nation's hopes at that moment because he was a "national" Communist. That is to say, he was a Magyar, as Gomulka was a Pole, and not an alien. His part in the historical process, had he been allowed to fulfil it, would probably have been to take the first steps towards the restoration of Hungarian national sovereignty and individual liberty, after which he would have given way to an elected successor. His symbolic popularity at the moment of the national uprising was chiefly due to the fact that he had been forced out of the premiership in 1953, and expelled from the Communist party in 1955, by the hated Matyas Rakosi and Erno Geroe.

In Hungary, as in Poland, the nation wanted distinct things, all made clear by the words and deeds of the ensuing days: the restoration of the

---

[41] A good instance of the confusion introduced into this event by the "Jewish question." Rokossovsky, Polish-born and a Soviet marshal, halted the advancing troops at the gates of Warsaw in 1944 to give the SS. and Gestapo troops time and freedom to massacre the Polish resistance army. He was thus the most hated man in Poland. At the same time he was held to be "anti-semitic" by the New York newspapers. Which current of feeling counted most heavily against him, one cannot at this stage determine.

national faith (symbolized by the release of the Cardinal, imprisoned by the Jewish terrorists), the liberation of the nation (through the withdrawal of the Soviet troops), the abolition of the terrorist secret police and the punishment of the terrorist chiefs. The initial demand for these things, however, was expressed by peaceful demonstration, not by riot or uprising.[42] They became noisy after a violently abusive speech by Geroe, the party leader, who retained that post when the party's central committee installed Mr. Nagy as premier. Geroe then instructed the Soviet troops to enter Budapest and restore order. Encountering demonstrators in Parliament Square, who were gathered to demand Geroe's dismissal, the Soviet tanks and Geroe's terrorist police opened fire, leaving the streets littered with dead and dying men and women (Oct. 24, 1956). This was the start of the true uprising; the nation unitedly rose against the Soviet troops and the hated terrorist police and within a few days the Communist revolution suffered a defeat which made the one in Poland look like a mere rebuff.

The Cardinal was released, Mr. Nagy established himself as premier, the hated Geroe disappeared (to the Crimean Riviera, in company with Rakosi, said one report), the terrorist police were hunted down and their barracks wrecked. The statue of Stalin was thrown down and smashed to pieces; the Hungarian troops everywhere helped the uprising or remained passive; the Soviet troops (who at that moment were mainly *Russian*) often showed sympathy with the Hungarians and many of their tanks were destroyed. This was the most hopeful moment in Europe's story since 1917, but far away Zionism was moving to rescue the revolution from its discomfiture and in a few days, even hours, all that was gained was to be undone.

The background should be briefly sketched here, before the second stage of the Hungarian people's war is described, because the case of Hungary is probably the most significant of all. For some reason the Moscovite power was more determined in this case than any other to identify Jews with the terror, so that the Hungarian experience, more strongly than any, points to

---

[42] The best authentic account of the original event was given, for reasons of his own, by the Communist dictator of Yugoslavia, Tito, in a national broadcast on Nov. 15, 1956. He said, among much else, "When we were in Moscow we declared that Rakosi's regime and Rakosi himself did not have the necessary qualifications to lead the Hungarian state or to lead it to internal unity ... Unfortunately, the Soviet comrades did not believe us ... When Hungarian Communists themselves demanded that Rakosi should go, the Soviet leaders realized that it was impossible to continue in this way and agreed that he should be removed. But they committed a mistake by not also allowing the removal of Geroe and other Rakosi followers ... They agreed to the removal of Rakosi on the condition that Geroe would obligatorily remain ... He followed the same policy and was as guilty as Rakosi ... He called those hundreds of thousands of demonstrators, who were still demonstrators at the time, a mob" (a participant stated that Geroe's words were "filthy Fascist bandits and other words too dirty to repeat")."
... This was enough to ignite the barrel of gunpowder and cause it to explode ... Geroe called in the army. It was a fatal mistake to call in the Soviet Army at a time when the demonstrations were still going on ... This angered these people even more and thus a spontaneous revolt ensued ... Nagy called the people to arms against the Soviet Army and appealed to the Western countries to intervene ..."

continuing Jewish, or Talmudic, control of the revolution itself at its seat of power in Moscow.

The 1919 regime in Hungary, which the Magyars themselves threw out after a brief but merciless terror, was Jewish. The presence of one or two non-Jews in the regime did not qualify this, its essential nature. It was the terror of four chief Jewish leaders, supported by a mass of subordinate Jews, namely Bela Kun, Matyas Rakosi, Tibor Szamuely and Erno Geroe, none of whom could be called Hungarians and all of whom were trained for their task in Moscow.

After the Second War free elections, for some reason of political expediency, were permitted in Hungary (Nov. 1945). These produced the natural result: a huge majority for the Smallholders Party; the Communists, despite the presence of the Red Army, made a poor showing. Then Matyas Rakosi was sent again to Hungary (Szamuely had committed suicide in 1919; Bela Kun disappeared in some nameless Soviet purge of the 1930's, but in February 1956 his memory was pompously "rehabilitated" at the Twentieth Soviet Congress in Moscow, and this may now be seen as an intimation to the Hungarians of what they had to expect in October 1956).

With the help of the terrorist police and the Red Army Rakosi began to destroy other parties and opponents, five of whom (including the renowned Mr. Laszlo Rajk) he and Geroe had hanged in 1949 after the familiar "confessions" of conspiracy with "the imperialist powers" (an allegation which left the imperialist powers as unmoved as they were infuriated by the allegation of "*Zionist* conspiracy" in 1952). By 1948 Hungary, under Rakosi, was completely Sovietized and terrorized. The chief terrorist this time, under Rakosi himself, was Erno Geroe, also returned to Hungary from Moscow after twenty years; he staged the trial and ordered the incarceration

of Hungary's religious leader, Cardinal Mindszenty[43] (who before he disappeared into durance instructed the nation not to believe any confession imputed to him by his jailers). After that Hungary for several years lay under the terror of two of the men who had crucified it in 1919, and the entire government became "90 percent Jewish in the top echelons." To Hungarians also, then, the terror was Jewish and Talmudic, not Communist, Soviet or Russian, and it was most deliberately given that nature; the intent of the return of Rakosi and Geroe after the Second War is unmistakable, and their acts were equally unmistakable.

In July 1953 Rakosi resigned the premiership and *The Times* announced that "Mr. Geroe is the only Jew left in the Cabinet, which under Mr. Rakosi

---

[43] The invariable and deliberate anti-Christian trait appeared again in the treatment given to Cardinal Mindszenty, the details of which were published by him after his liberation. In summary, he said he was tortured by his captors for twenty-nine days and nights between his arrest and trial, being stripped nude, beaten for days on end with a rubber hose, kept in a cold, damp cell to irritate his weak lung, forced to watch obscene performances and questioned without sleep throughout the period (interview published in many newspapers and periodicals, December 1956).

was predominantly Jewish." As Rakosi remained party leader and Geroe was Deputy-Premier, nothing very much changed, and in July 1956, when Rakosi also resigned his party-leadership, he was succeeded in that post by Geroe, with the consequences which were seen in October.

Even Geroe seemed to have done his worst at that moment, for after the Hungarian people's victory the Red Army troops were withdrawn (Oct. 28) and two days later (Oct. 30) the Soviet Government broadcast to the world a statement admitting "violations and mistakes which infringed the principles of equality in relations between Socialist states," offering to discuss "measures … to remove any possibilities of violating the principle of national sovereignty," and undertaking "to examine the question of the Soviet troops stationed on the territory of Hungary, Rumania and Poland."

Was it a ruse, intended only to lull the peoples while the assassin took respite, or was it a true retreat and enforced admission of error, opening great vistas of conciliation and hope to the peoples?

If Israel had not attacked Egypt … *if* Britain and France had not joined in that attack … if these things had not happened the world would now know the answer to that question. Now it will never know, for the Zionist attack on Egypt, and the British and French participation in it, released the revolution from its dilemma; as if by magic, the eyes of the watching world turned from Hungary to the Middle East and Hungary was forgotten. Vainly did Mr. Nagy broadcast his appeal to the world the very next day, saying that 200,000 men with five thousand tanks were moving into Hungary.

Budapest was pulverized. On November 7 the voice of the last free Hungarian radio faded from the air (Radio Rakoczy at Dunapentele), as the voices of the Poles had faded in 1944 and of the Czechs in 1939, bequeathing their sorrows to "the West."

"This is our last broadcast. We are being inundated with Soviet tanks and planes." These words, the Vienna correspondent of the *New York Times* recorded, "were followed by a loud crashing sound. Then there was silence."

Mr. Nagy took refuge in the Yugoslav Legation, and on leaving it under Soviet safe-conduct was deported some-whither, none knows where. The Cardinal took refuge in the American Embassy. At the end of November the Cuban delegate to the United Nations, a well- informed authority, stated that 65,000 people had been killed in Hungary. More than 100,000 by that time had fled across the frontier into Austria, a small country which upheld the tattered standard of "the West" by taking in all who came, without question. A few thousand of these reached America, where they were received by the U.S. Secretary of the Army, a Mr. Wilbur M. Brucker, who ordered them "to applaud the American flag" and then "to applaud President Eisenhower."

These truly were ten days that shocked the world, and will shock it ever more if the true tale is ever told. They showed that the values which once were symbolized by the two words, "The West," now were embodied in the captive peoples of Eastern Europe, not in America or England or France.

Those countries had their backs turned to the scene in Hungary. They were intent on events in the Middle East. "The Jewish question" in the Middle East intervened to blot out the dawn of hope in Europe again. Once more revolutionary-Communism and revolutionary- Zionism worked as in perfect synchronization, as in October 1917; the acts of each directly benefited the other. The United Nations could not find time to discuss the Hungarian appeal for help before the new terror crushed the appellants and restored approved agents of the revolution to the delegates' places.

In Hungary itself the place of the vanished Geroe was taken by yet another commissar of 1919. Mr. Ference Munnich, who had taken prominent part in the Bela Kun regime then, also had returned to Hungary after the Second War with the Red Army. From 1946 to 1949, when Rakosi was clamping down the second terror, Mr. Munnich was Budapest chief of police. Now he became "Deputy Premier, Minister of National Defence and of Public Security" in the government of one Janos Kadar, set up by Moscow. Mr. Kadar also had a record of some independence, and therefore was not likely to be allowed to wield any power. Mr. Munnich, (said the *New York Times*) was "Moscow's ace in the hole, controlling Mr. Kadar."

In this way the night came down again on Hungary and it had to find what consolation it might in the President's words that his heart went out to it. The time bomb in the Middle East, originally planted there in the very week of the Bolshevik revolution's triumph in Moscow, blew up at the moment of the revolution's fiasco and defeat. This diversion changed the brightest situation for many years into the darkest one. The Soviet Union was left undisturbed in its work of massacre in Hungary while the great powers of the West began to dispute among themselves about Israel, Egypt and the Suez Canal; all the world turned to watch them, and the Soviet state, with the blood of a European nation on its hands, was able to join in the general anathema of Britain and France when they joined in the Israeli attack.

The creation of the Zionist state proved to be even more ill-omened than the other creation of the Talmudic Jews in Russia, the Communist revolution. The second section of this record of the years of climax therefore has to do with events in the Zionist state in the eight years between its creation by terror in 1948 and its attack on Egypt in October 1956.

The Zionist State

In those years the little state misnamed "Israel" proved to be something unique in history. It was governed, as it was devised, set up and largely peopled, by non-semitic Jews from Russia, of the Chazar breed. Founded on a tribal tradition of antiquity, with which these folk could have no conceivable tie of blood, it developed a savage chauvinism based on the literal application of the Law of the Levites in ancient Judah. Tiny, it had no true life of its own and from the start lived only by the wealth and weapons its powerful supporters in the great Western countries could extort from these. During these years it outdid the most bellicose warlords of history in warlike words and deeds. Ruled by men of the same stock as those who wielded the terror in Poland and Hungary, it daily threatened the seven neighbouring Semitic peoples with the destruction and enslavement prescribed for them in *Deuteronomy* of the Levites.

It did this in the open belief that its power in the Western capitals was sufficient to deter the governments there from ever gainsaying its will, and to command their support in any circumstances. It behaved as if America, in particular, was its colony, and that country's deeds conformed with that idea. Within its borders its laws against conversion and intermarriage were those of the much-cited Hitler; beyond its borders lay a destitute horde of Arabs, driven into the wilderness by it, whose numbers rose through childbirth to nearly a million as the eight years went by. These, and their involuntary hosts, were by repeated raid and massacre reminded that the fate of Deir Yasin yet hung over them too: "utterly destroy, man, woman and child, leave nothing alive that breatheth." The Western countries, its creators, murmured reproof while they sent it money and the wherewithal of the war which they claimed to fear; thus, like Frankenstein, they created the destructive agency which they could not control.

Based on fantasy, the little state had no real existence, only the power to spread unease throughout the world, which from the moment of its creation had no moment's true respite from fear. It began to fulfil the words of the ancient Promise: "This day will I begin to put the dread of thee and the fear of thee upon the nations that are under the whole heaven … who shall be in anguish because of thee." Left to its own resources, it would have collapsed, as the "Jewish Homeland" of the inter-war years would have collapsed. The urge to leave it once more began to master the urge to enter it, and this despite the power of chauvinism, which for a time will overcome almost any other impulse in those who yield to it. In 1951, already, departures would have out-numbered arrivals save that the "amazing crack" earlier mentioned *(New York Herald-Tribune*, April 1953) then opened "in the Iron Curtain" (where cracks do not occur unless they are intended; the Communist-revolutionary state evidently had a calculated purpose in replenishing the Zionist- revolutionary state with inhabitants at that time). Nevertheless, in 1952, 13,000 emigrants left and only 24,470 entered, and in 1953 (the last year for which I have figures) emigration exceeded immigration, according to the Jewish Agency. A Dr. Benjamin Avniel, speaking in Jerusalem, said in June that in the first five months 8,500 immigrants had arrived and 25,000 persons had departed.

This was the natural development, if "Israel" were left alone, for it had nothing to offer but chauvinism. The picture of conditions in the land is given by Jewish authorities. Mr. Moshe Smilanski (of sixty years' experience in Palestine) wrote in the *Jewish Review* of February, 1952:

"When the British mandate came to an end the country was well off. Food warehouses, private and governmental, were full and there were good stacks of raw materials. The country had thirty million pounds in the Bank of England, besides British and American securities to a large amount. The currency in circulation was about thirty million pounds, which had the same value as sterling ... The Mandatory Government left us a valuable legacy, the deep harbour in Haifa, two moles in Jaffa and Tel Aviv, railways, many good roads and government buildings, large equipped military and civil airfields, good army barracks and the Haifa refineries. The Arabs who fled left behind about five million dunams of cultivable land, containing orchards, orange graves, olives, grape vines and fruit trees, about 75,000 dwelling houses in the towns, some of them very elegant, about 75,000 shops and factories and much movable property, furniture, carpets, jewellery, etc. All this is wealth, and if we in Israel are sunk in poverty we blame the excessive bureaucratic centralization, the restriction of private enterprise and the promise of a Socialistic regime in our day."

In April 1953 Mr. Hurwitz of the Revisionist Party in Israel told a Jewish audience in Johannesburg of the "degeneration" of the Zionist state. He said he could not blind himself to the alarming position: "Economically the country is on the verge of bankruptcy. Immigration has diminished and in the past few months more people have left the country than have come in. In addition, there are 50,000 unemployed and thousands more working on short time."

These two quotations (I have many others of similar tenor) by Jewish residents may be compared with the picture of life in Israel which the Western masses received from their politicians. A Mr. Clement Davies (leader of that British Liberal Party which had 401 seats in the 1906 House of Commons and six, under his leadership, in that of 1956) before a Jewish audience in Tel Aviv "hailed the progress being made in the Jewish state, which to him seemed to be a miracle of progress along the road to restoring the country to a land flowing with milk and honey" (printed in the same Jewish newspaper as Mr. Hurwitz's remarks). At the same period, the younger Mr. Franklin D. Roosevelt, electioneering in New York (where "the Jewish vote" is held to be decisive) said, "Israel is a pocket of life and hope in the sea of seething Arab peoples. It 'sells freedom' for the free world more successfully than all the propaganda we could send out from the U.S.A."

Mr. Adlai Stevenson, campaigning for the presidency in 1952, told the Zionist audience that "Israel has welcomed into her midst with open arms and a warm heart all her people seeking refuge from tribulation ... America would do well to model her own immigration policies after the generosity of the nation of Israel and we must work to that end" (the only conceivable meaning of this is that the American people should be driven from the United States and the North American Indians be restored to their lands). Another presidential aspirant, a Mr. Stuart Symington, said "Israel is an example of how firmness, courage and constructive action can win through for democratic ideals, instead of abandoning the field to Soviet imperialism" (about that time Israeli state scholars were by governmental decree singing the Red Flag on May Day, while the politicians of Washington and London inveighed against "anti- semitism behind the Iron Curtain").

Against this sustained inversion of truth by the frontal politicians of all parties in America and England, only Jewish protests, as in the preceding decades, were heard (for the reason I previously gave, that non-Jewish writers were effectively prevented from publishing any). Mr. William Zukerman wrote:

"The generally accepted theory that the emergence of the state of Israel would serve to unify and cement the Jewish people has turned out to be wrong. On the contrary, the Congress" (the Zionist Congress in Jerusalem, 1951) "has dramatically demonstrated that the creation of a Jewish political state after two thousand years has introduced a new and potent distinction which Jews as a group have not known in centuries and that Israel is likely to separate rather than unite Jews in the future ... In some mystical manner Israel is supposed to have a unique jurisdiction over the ten to twelve million Jews who live in every country of the world outside it ... It must continue to grow by bringing in Jews from all over the world, no matter how happily they live in their present homes ... Jews who have lived there for generations and centuries, must according to this theory be 'redeemed' from 'exile' and brought to Israel through a process of mass immigration ... Israeli leaders of all parties, from the extreme Right to the extreme Left, including Premier Ben-Gurion, have begun to demand that American Jews, and particularly Zionists, redeem their pledges to the ancient homeland, leave their American 'exile,' and settle in Israel, or at least send their children there ... The Jerusalem Congress marked officially the end of the glory of American Zionism and the ushering in of a period of intense Middle Eastern nationalism ... fashioned after the pattern of the late Vladimir Jabotinsky, who dreamed of a big Jewish state on both sides of the Jordan to take in all the Jews and to become the largest military power in the Near East."

Mr. Lessing J. Rosenwald similarly protested: "We declare our unalterable opposition to all programmes designed to transform Jews into a nationalist bloc with special interests in the foreign state of Israel. The policy laid down by Mr. Ben-Gurion for American Zionism encourages Zionists to intensify their efforts to organize American Jews as a separate political pressure-block in the United States. This programme is designed to transform

American Jews into a spiritual and cultural dependency of a foreign state ... We believe that 'Jewish' nationalism is a distortion of our faith, reducing it from universal proportions to the dimensions of a nationalistic cult."

These Jewish protests, as was natural, were prompted by fear of the divisive effect of Zionism on *Jews*. That was but a fractional aspect of the matter: The real danger of Zionism lay in its power to divide the nations of the world against each other and to bring them into collision, in which catastrophe the great masses of mankind would be involved in the proportion of a hundred or a thousand to every Jew.

To depict this obvious possibility was heresy in the 1950's, and the non-Jewish protests remained unpublished while the Jewish ones were ineffective. In 1953 the New York Jewish journal, *Commentary*, thus was able to announce that the foreseeable catastrophe had been brought another step nearer in the following terms: "Israel's survival and strengthening have become a firm element of United States foreign policy and *no electoral result or change will affect this*."

Here, once more, is the cryptic reference to a power superior to all presidents, prime ministers and parties to which I earlier drew attention. It is what Mr. Leopold Amery, one of the British Ministers responsible for Palestine in the inter-war period, once said: The policy is *set* and *cannot change*. The inner secret of the whole affair is contained in these menacing statements, in which the note of authority and superior knowledge is clear. They are cryptic, but specific and categorical, and express *certainty* that the West cannot and will not withdraw its hand from the Zionist ambition in any circumstances. *Certainty* must rest on something firmer than threats, or even the ability, to sway "the Jewish vote" and the public press this way or that. The tone is that of taskmasters who *know* the galleyslaves must do their bidding because they are chained and cannot escape. The *New York Times*, which I judge to speak with authority for "the Jewish power" in the world, has often alluded to this secret compact, or capitulation, or whatever its nature is: for instance, "In essence, the political support the state of Israel has in the United States makes any settlement antagonistic to Israeli interests *impossible* for a United States administration to contemplate" (1956). If this merely alludes to control of the election-machine, it means that the process of parliamentary government through "free elections" has been completely falsified. In my opinion, that is the case in the West in this century.

This state of affairs in the West alone enabled the new state to survive. It was kept alive by infusions of money from America. *Commentary* (above quoted) stated that by June 1953 total United States Government assistance to Israel amounted to $293,000,000, with a further $200,000,000 in such forms as Export-Import bank loans. The Jerusalem representative of President Truman's "technical aid" programme stated (October, 1952) that Israel received the largest share of any country in the world, in proportion to its population, and more than all the other Middle East states together. The *New York Herald-Tribune* (March 12, 1953) said the total amount of United States money, including private gifts and loans, amounted to "more than $1,000,000,000 during the first five years of Israel's existence," which, it added, had thus been "ensured." On top of all this came the German tribute, extorted by the American Government, of 520,000,000 Israeli pounds annually. I have not been able to find official figures for the cumulative total up to 1956; the Syrian delegate to the United Nations, after one of the Zionist attacks during the year, said that "since 1948 a stream of

$1,500,000,000 has been flowing from the United States to Israel in the form of contributions, grants in aid, bonds and loans" (even this figure excluded the German payments and other forms of Western tribute).

Nothing like this was ever seen in the world before. A state so financed from abroad can well afford (in the monetary sense) to be belligerent, and the menacing behaviour of the new state was only made possible by this huge inflow of Western, chiefly American money. Assured of this unstinting monetary backing, and of a political support in Washington which *could not change*, the new state set out on its grandiose ambition: to restore to full force, in the 20th Century of our era, the "New Law" promulgated by the Levites in *Deuteronomy* in 621 B.C. All that was to come was to be "fulfilment" of it; the Mongolian Chazars were to see that Jehovah kept his compact, as the Levites had published it. And what ensued was in fact an instalment on account of this "fulfilment"; the vision of "the heathen" bringing the treasures of the earth to Jerusalem began to become reality in the form of American money, German tribute and the like.

With a purse thus filled, the little state began to pursue the fantasy of entire and literal "fulfilment," which in the miraculous end is to see all the great ones of the earth humbled, Zion all-powerful and all the Jews "gathered." It drew up the charter of this "gathering": the "nationality law," which made all Jewish residents in the Zionist state Israelis, and the "law of the return," which claimed all Jews anywhere in the world for Israel, in both cases whether they wished or not.[44]

These were the laws which, like ghosts from vanished ghettoes, alarmed Mr. Zukerman and Mr, Rosenwald. They express the greatest ambition ever proclaimed by any state in history, and the Premier, a Mr. Ben-Gurion from Russia, was explicit about it on many occasions, for instance in his message of June 16, 1951 to the Zionists of America: "A rare opportunity

---

[44] The Law of the Return, 1953, says among other things, "The ingathering of the exiles requires constant efforts from the Jewish *nation in dispersion* and the state of Israel therefore *expects the participation of all Jews*, either privately or in organizations, in the upbuilding of the state and in assisting mass immigration and sees the necessity of all Jewish communities uniting for this purpose." A permanent state of "anti-semitism" in the world is obviously the pre-requisite for the realization of this law, and as the largest single body of Jews in the world is now in America, an "anti-semitic" situation there would evidently have to be declared at some stage in the process.

has been given to your organization to pave a way for a unifying and united Zionist movement which will stand at the head of American Jewry in the great era opened to the Jewish people with the establishment of the state and *beginning of ingathering of exiles*." Rabbi Hillel Silver, President Eisenhower's close associate, expressed particular gratification that "Mr. Ben-Gurion now accepts the view that main tasks of the Zionist movement, as heretofore, include the *full and undiminished programme of Zionism*," In New York in June, 1952 Mr. Ben- Gurion was more explicit: "The Jewish state is *not* the fulfilment of Zionism … Zionism *embraces all Jews everywhere*." Israel's second president, Mr. Ben Zvi, at his inauguration in December 1952, said, "The ingathering of the exiles still remains our central task and we will not retreat … Our historic task will not be accomplished without the assistance of *the entire nation* in the West and East." The world would have raised a pandemonium of protest if a Kaiser or a Hitler had said such things. The ambition expressed by such words as "the full and undiminished programme of Zionism" is in fact boundless, for it is the political programme contained, in the guise of a compact with Jehovah, in the Torah; world dominion over "the heathen," wielded from an empire stretching from the Nile to the Euphrates. The support of Western governments gave reality to what otherwise would be the most absurd pretension in all history. That the politicians of the West comprehended this full meaning of what they did seemed impossible until 1953, when a statement was made that implied full understanding. In May, 1953, Mr. Winston Churchill, then British Prime Minister, was in dispute with the Egyptian premier about the Suez Canal and threatened him, not with British but with *Jewish* retribution. He spoke, in Parliament, of the Israeli army as "the best in the Levant" and said that "nothing we shall do in the supply of aircraft to this part of the world will be allowed to place Israel at a disadvantage." Then he added, in words closely akin to those of Mr. Ben-Gurion and Rabbi Hillel Silver, that he "looked forward to *the fulfilment of Zionist aspirations*."

Here, in an aside, is probably the largest commitment ever undertaken by a head of government on behalf of an unsuspecting nation. The Israeli parliament at once recorded its gratification at "Mr. Churchill's friendly attitude towards the Israeli government now and towards the Zionist movement throughout its existence." The public masses in England read the loaded words uncomprehendingly, if at all. They startled many Jews, among them even Mr. A. Abrahams, who as a veteran Revisionist might logically have been pleased (the Revisionists openly pursue the late Mr. Jabotinsky's ambition for "a big Jewish state on both sides of the Jordan to take in all the Jews and to become the largest military power in the Near East"; Mr. William Zukerman).

Mr. Abrahams asked wonderingly, with an undernote even of alarm, if Mr. Churchill's words could be genuinely intended, saying, "The Prime

Minister is an old student of the Bible; he knows very well that the Zionist aspirations remain unfulfilled until Israel is fully restored within the historic boundaries, the land of the Ten Tribes."

This "aspiration," of course, cannot be "fulfilled" without universal war, and that is evidently why Mr. Abrahams was taken aback, and made almost aghast. Mr. Churchill's words, if they were considered and deliberately intended, signified support for the grandiose ambition in all its literalness, and the final price of that could only be the extinction of "the West" as it has always been known.[45]

---

[45] An event of a month earlier, April 1953, had already shown that Mr. Churchill was prepared to go further, in his tributes to Zionism, than any would have thought possible who judged him by his public record and legend. In that month he ostentatiously associated himself with the Zionist canonization of an English officer called Orde Wingate, and in so doing humiliated the English people in general and in particular all those British officials, officers and soldiers who for thirty years loyally did their duty in Palestine. Wingate, an officer of the British intelligence in Palestine during the inter-war years, so far deviated from the honourable impartiality, between Arabs and Jews, which was the pride and duty of his comrades as to become, not simply an enemy of the Arabs but a renegade to his country and calling. His perfidy first became public knowledge on this occasion when Mr. Ben-Gurion, dedicating a children's village on Mount Carmel to Wingate's memory (he was killed during the Second War) said "He was ready to fight with the Jews against his own government" and at the time of the British White Paper in 1939 "he came to me with plans to combat the British policy." One proposal of Wingate's was to blow up a British oil pipeline. Mr. Churchill in his message read at the dedication ceremony described the village named after Wingate as "a monument to the friendship which should always unite Great Britain and Israel," and the British Minister was required to attend in official token of the British Government's approval. Thus the one Britisher so honoured in the Zionist state was a traitor to his duty and the British Prime Minister of the day joined in honouring him. The significant history of Wingate's army service is given in Dr. Chaim Weizmann's book. Dr. Weizmann, who speaks indulgently of Wingate's efforts to ingratiate himself with Zionist settlers by trying to speak Hebrew, says he was "a fanatical Zionist." In fact Wingate was a very similar man to the Prophet Monk in the preceding century, but in the circumstances of this one was able to do much more harm. He copied Monk in trying to look like a Judahite prophet by letting his beard grow, and significantly found his true calling in the land of Judas. He was either demented or hopelessly unstable and was adjudged by the British Army "too unbalanced to command men in a responsible capacity." He then turned to Dr. Weizmann, who asked a leading London physician (Lord Horder, an ardent Zionist sympathizer) to testify to the Army Medical Council "as to Wingate's reliability and sense of responsibility." As a result of this sponsorship Wingate "received an appointment as captain in the Palestine intelligence service," with the foreseeable result above recorded.

During the Second War this man, of all men, was singled out for especial honour by Mr. Churchill, being recalled to London at the time of the Quebec Conference to receive promotion to Major General. Dr. Weizmann says his "consuming desire" was to lead a British army into Berlin. The context of Dr. Weizmann's account suggests that this would have been headed by a Jewish brigade, led by Wingate, so that the event would have been given the visible nature of a Talmudic triumph, shorn of pretence of a "British victory." "The generals," Dr. Weizmann concludes, averted this humiliation; their refusal "was final and complete." The episode again throws into relief the uneven and enigmatic nature of Mr. Churchill, who preached honour, duty and loyalty more eloquently than any before him and bluntly asked a nation at bay to give its "blood and sweat, toil and tears" for those eternal principles. He had seen one of his own Ministers murdered and British sergeants symbolically hanged "on a tree" and yet gave especial patronage to this man, alive, and singled him out for honour when he was dead. Mr. Churchill, at an earlier period, once abandoned the task of writing the life of his great ancestor because of a letter which appeared to prove that John Churchill, Duke of Marlborough, betrayed an impending attack by the British fleet to its enemy of that day, the French. "The betrayal of the expedition against Brest," he then wrote, "was an obstacle I could not face"; and he refused from shame to write the biography, only reconsidering when he convinced himself that the letter was a forgery. Yet even in that book his conception of loyalty is not clear to follow, for in his preface he accepts as natural and even right Marlborough's first and proved act of treachery, when he rode out from London as King James's commander to meet the invading German and

The event of October 30, 1956 (though it was ordered by Sir Winston's political heir-designate) seems to show that Mr. Churchill's words of May, 1953, with all they boded for his country, *were* seriously meant. If the West, as these words implied, was secretly harnessed to the unqualified "fulfilment of Zionist aspirations," that could only mean a greater war than the West had yet endured, in which its armies would play the parts of pawns in a ruinous game, for the purpose of dividing the Christian peoples, crushing the Muslim ones, setting up the Zionist empire, and thereafter acting as its janissaries. In this great gamble, Jews everywhere in the world, on whatever side of the apparent fighting line, would be expected under the "law of the return" to act in the overriding interest of Zion. What that might mean may be seen from an article published in the Johannesburg *Jewish Herald* of Nov. 10, 1950, about a secret episode of the Second War. It stated that when the production of atomic weapons began "a proposal was put forward to Dr. Weizmann to bring together some of the most noted Jewish scientists in order to establish a team which would bargain with the allies in the interest of Jewry … I saw the project as originally outlined and submitted to Dr. Weizmann by a scientist who had himself achieved some renown in the sphere of military invention."

The threat is plain, in such words. As to "the fulfilment of Zionist aspirations," by these or other means, Dr. Nahum Goldman, leader of the World Zionist Organization, made a significant statement to a Jewish audience at Johannesburg in August, 1950. Describing an interview with Mr. Ernest Bevin, then British Foreign Minister, Dr Goldman said, "This tiny country (Israel) is a very unique country, it is in a unique geographical position. In the days when trying to get the Jewish state with the consent of the British Government, and at one of the private talks I had with Mr. Bevin, he said, 'Do you know what you are asking me to do? You are asking me to deliver the key to one of the most vital and strategic areas in the world.' And I said, 'It is not written in either the New or Old Testament that Great Britain must have this key.'"

Mr. Churchill, if his words were fully intended, apparently was ready to hand over the key, and after Mr. Bevin died all others in Washington and London seemed equally ready. The effects are already plain to see and foresee, and these effects can no longer be dismissed as chance. Here a great plan is plainly moving to its fulfilment or fiasco, with the great nations of the West acting as its armed escort and themselves assured of humiliation if it succeeds; they are like a man who takes employment under the condition that his wage shall fall as the firm prospers.

At all its ill-omened stages this adventure has been discussed among the initiates as a *plan*. I earlier quoted the words of Max Nordau at the sixth Zionist Congress in 1903: "Let me show you the rungs of a ladder leading

---

Dutch armies of William of Orange and went over to the enemy, so that the invasion of England succeeded without an English shot fired.

upward and upward … the future world war, the peace conference where, with the help of England, a free and Jewish Palestine will be erected."

Twenty-five years later a leading Zionist in England, Lord Melchett, spoke in the same tone of secret knowledge to Zionists in New York: "If I had stood here in 1913 and said to you 'Come to a conference to discuss the reconstruction of a national home in Palestine,' you would have looked upon me as an idle dreamer, even if I had told you in 1913 that the Austrian archduke would be killed and that out of all that followed would come the chance, the opportunity, the occasion for establishing a national home for the Jews in Palestine. Has it ever occurred to you how remarkable it is that out of the welter of world blood there has arisen this opportunity? Do you really believe that we have been led back to Israel by nothing but a fluke?" (*Jewish Chronicle*, Nov. 9, 1928).

Today the third world war, if it comes, will obviously not be a "fluke"; the sequence of cause leading to consequence, and the identity of the controlling power, has been made visible by the developing fluid of time. Thirty-one years after Lord Melchett's imperial pronouncement I was by chance (February, 1956) in South Carolina, and only by that chance, and the local newspaper, learned of a comment in similar vein, apparently inspired from a similar, Olympian source, about the *third* war. Mr. Randolph Churchill, Sir Winston's son, was at that time visiting his family's friend Mr. Bernard Baruch, whose residence is the Barony of Little Hobcaw in South Carolina. On emerging from his interview with this authority Mr. Randolph Churchill stated (Associated Press, Feb. 8, 1956) that "the tense Middle East situation could explode into armed conflict at any moment. But I don't think civilization is going to *stumble* into the next war … World War III, if it comes, will be *coldly calculated and planned* rather than accidental."

Against the background of "fulfilment" (the payment of tribute by the great nations of the world and the declaration that all Jews of the world were its subjects) the new state gave earnest of its intention to restore the "historic frontiers" by word and deed. No Western "warmonger" ever used such words. Mr. Ben-Gurion proclaimed (Johannesburg *Jewish Herald*, Dec. 24, 1952) that Israel "would not under any conditions permit the return of the Arab emigrants" (the native inhabitants). As to Jerusalem (partitioned between Zionists and Jordanians pending "internationalization" under United Nations administration), "for us that city's future is as settled as that of London, despite its ridiculous boundaries; this cannot be an issue for negotiations." The "exiles" abroad were to be "ingathered" at the rate of "four million immigrants in the next ten years" (the Foreign Minister, Mr. Moshe Sharett, June 1952) or "the next ten to fifteen years" (on another occasion).

Two world wars had been needed to set up the "homeland" and "state," successively, and to get some 1,500,000 Jews into it. These intimations meant another world war within fifteen years at the latest, for by no other means could so many Jews be extracted from the countries where they were. As to the cost of their transportation, Mr. Ben-Gurion said this would be between 7,000 and 8,000 million dollars (at present rates, equal to the entire national debt of Italy, and about five times the British national debt in 1914) and he "looked to American Jewry to provide this money." Obviously, even American Jewry could not find such sums; they could only be obtained from the taxpayers of the West.

Everything that was said was thus a plain threat of war to the neighbouring Arabs, and it had an especial meaning when it was said (which was often) by Mr. Menachem Beigin, chief of the "activist," or killer, group which had carried out the massacre at Deir Yasin. Formally disowned at that time, they had been honoured in the new state and formed a major political party, Herut, in its parliament. Therefore the Arabs knew exactly with what they were menaced when Mr. Beigin spoke to them.

I give a typical instance. In May 1953 he threatened the 18-year old King of Jordan, at the moment of his coronation, with death under the Law of *Deuteronomy* (which governed the deed of Deir Yasin). Speaking to a mass meeting in the Zionist part of Jerusalem, a stone's throw from the Jordan lines, Mr. Beigin said, "At this hour a coronation is taking place of a young Arab as King of Gilead, Bashan, Nablus, Jericho and Jerusalem. This is the proper time to declare in his and his masters' ears: 'We shall be back, and David's city shall be free.'"

The allusion, obscure to Western readers and explicit to any Arab or Jew, is to a verse in the third chapter of *Deuteronomy:* "The King of Bashan came out against us ... And the Lord said unto me, Fear him not: for I will deliver him, and all his people, and his land into thy hand ... So the Lord our God delivered into our hands Og also, the king of Bashan, and all his people and we smote him, until none was left to him remaining ... And we *utterly destroyed them ... utterly destroying the men, women and children.*"

These threats had a lethal meaning for the hordes of Arab fugitives huddled beyond the frontiers. According to the report of Mr. Henry R. Labouisse, Director of the UN Relief and Works Agency for Palestine, made in April 1956 there were of these more than 900,000: 499,000 in Jordan, 88,000 in Syria, 103,000 in Lebanon and 21,000 in Egypt (the Gaza area). Mr. Beigin's threats kept them in constant prospect of new flight, or attempted flight, into some deeper, even more inhospitable desert. Then the words were made real by deeds; a long series of symbolic local raids and massacres was perpetrated, to show them that the fate of Deir Yasin hung actually over them.

These began on October 14, 1953 when a strong force suddenly crossed the Jordan frontier, murdered every living soul found in Qibya and destroyed that village, sixty-six victims, most of them women and children, being found slaughtered. The 499,000 Arab refugees in Jordan drew the natural conclusion. The Archbishop of York said the civilized world was "horrified," that "the Jewish vote in New York had a paralyzing effect on the United Nations in dealing with Palestine," and that unless strong action were taken "the Middle East will be ablaze." The Board of Deputies of British Jews called this statement "provocative and one-sided"; the Mayor of New York (a Mr. Robert Wagner) said it "shocked" him, and "the good Archbishop is evidently unfamiliar with the American scene." The United Nations mildly censured Israel.

On February 28, 1955 a strong Israeli force drove into the Gaza area ("awarded" to the Arabs by the United Nations in 1949, and under Egyptian military occupation) where the 215,000 Arab refugees repined "in abject poverty along a narrow strip of barren coastline, two-thirds of it sand-dunes" (Sir Thomas Rapp, *The Listener*, March 6, 1955). Thirty-nine Egyptians were killed and an unspecified number of the Arab refugees, who then in hopeless protest against their lot burned five United Nations relief centres, and therewith their own meagre rations. The Mixed Armistice Commission condemned Israel for "brutal aggression" in "a prearranged and planned attack."[46]

The case then went to the United Nations Security Council itself, which by unanimous vote of eleven countries censured Israel. The United States delegate said this was the fourth similar case and "the most serious because of its obvious premeditation"; the French delegate said the resolution should serve as "a last warning" to Israel, (an admonition which received a footnote in the shape of French collusion in the Israeli attack on Egypt twenty months later).

On June 8, 1955 the U.N.M.A.C. censured Israel for another "flagrant armistice violation" when Israeli troops crossed into Gaza and killed some Egyptians. The only apparent effect of this censure was that the Israelis promptly arrested six United Nations military observers and three other members of the staff of the United Nations Truce Supervisor (Major General E.L.M. Burns, of Canada) before they again attacked into Gaza, killing 35 Egyptians *(Time*, September 1955). In this same month of September 1955 Mr. Ben- Gurion in an interview said that he would attack Egypt "within a

---

[46] These United Nations Mixed Armistice Commissions, which will henceforth be denoted by U.N.M.A.C. comprized in each case a representative of Israel and of the neighbour Arab state, and a United Nations representative whose finding and vote thus decided the Source of blame. The findings were invariably against Israel until, as in the case of the British administrators between 1917 and 1948, "pressure" began to be put on the home governments of the officials concerned to withdraw any who impartially upheld the Arab case. At least two American officials who found against Israel in such incidents were withdrawn. All these officials, of whatever nationality, of course worked with the memory of Count Bernadotte's fate, and that of many others, ever in their minds. In the general rule they, like the British administrators earlier, proved impossible to intimidate or suborn, and thus the striking contrast between the conduct of the men on the spot and the governments in the distant Western capitals was continued.

year" (the attack came in October, 1956) if the blockade of the Israeli port of Elath on the Gulf of Aqaba were not lifted.

The United Nations Security Council seemed nervous about "censuring" this new attack (the American presidential election campaign was beginning) and merely proposed that the Israelis and Egyptians withdraw 500 metres from each other, leaving a demilitarized zone, a proposal which the Egyptians had already vainly made. Then on October 23, 1955 General Burns "condemned Israel" for a "well planned attack" into Syria, when several Syrians were kidnapped and General Burns's observers were again prevented by detention from observing what happened. On October 27, 1955 Mr. Moshe Sharett, the Israeli Foreign Minister, told newspaper correspondents at Geneva that Israel would wage a "preventive war" against the Arabs if necessary. On November 28, 1955 the Zionist Organization of America announced in leading newspapers (by paid advertisement) that "Britain, too, has joined the camp of Israel's enemies"; Sir Anthony Eden, who within the year was to join in the Israeli attack, at that moment had some idea about minor frontier rectifications.

On December 11, 1955 the Israelis attacked into Syria in strength and killed 56 persons. This produced the strongest United Nations "censure," which is of some historic interest because the presidential-election year had opened and "censure" on any account at all soon became unfashionable. The Syrian delegate pointed out that repeated condemnations "have not deterred Israel from committing the criminal attack we are now considering." The Security Council (Jan. 12, 1956) recalled four earlier resolutions of censure and condemned the attack as "a flagrant violation of ... the terms of the general armistice agreement between Israel and Syria and of Israel's obligations under the Charter" and undertook "to consider what further measures" it should take if Israel continued so to behave.

The response to this was imperious Israeli demands for more arms. Mr. Ben-Gurion (at Tel Aviv, Mar. 18, 1956) said that only early delivery of arms could prevent "an Arab attack" and added that "the aggressors would be the Egyptian dictator, Nasser" (seven months earlier Mr. Ben-Gurion had undertaken to attack Egypt "within a year") "together with his allies, Syria and Saudi Arabia." On April 5, 1956, as the UN Security Council was about to send its Secretary General, Mr. Dag Hammarskjold, on a "peace mission" to the Middle East, Israeli artillery bombarded the Gaza area, killing 42 and wounding 103 Arab civilians, nearly half of them women and children.

On June 19 Mr. Ben-Gurion dismissed Mr. Sharett from the Foreign Ministry in favour of Mrs Golda Myerson (now Meier, and also from Russia) and the *New York Times* significantly reported that this might denote a change from "moderation" to "activism" (Mr. Sharett, like Dr. Weizmann and Dr. Herzl earlier, having incurred the reproach of moderation). The issue was that which led to Dr. Weizmann's discomfiture at the Zionist Congress of 1946, when "activism" won and Dr. Weizmann saw the resurgence of "the old evil, in a new and even more horrible guise." "Activism" was always, from the old days in Russia, a euphemism for violence in the forms of terror and assassination. From the moment when this word reappeared in the news the student of Zionism knew what to expect before the year's end.

On June 24, 1956 the Israelis opened fire across the Jordan border and the U.N.M.A.C. censured Israel. Thereon Israel pressed for the removal of the UN Member of the Commission, whose casting vote had decided the issue, and General Burns yielded, supplanting him (an American naval officer, Commander Terrill) by a Canadian officer. The UN observers were being put in the same position as the British administrators in the inter-war years; they could not count on support by their home governments. They had a constant reminder before their eyes (the Wingate Village in Israel) that preferment and promotion, in Palestine, were the rewards of treachery, not of duty. Two years earlier another American observer, Commander E.H. Hutchison, had voted against censure of Jordan and been removed when the Israelis then boycotted the Commission. Returned to America, he wrote a book about this period in the Middle East which is of permanent historical value. Like all good men before him, he reported that the only way out of the tangle was to establish the right of the expelled Arabs to return to their homes, to admit that the armistice lines of 1949 were only temporary (and not "frontiers"), and to internationalize the city of Jerusalem so that it might not become the scene of world battle.

On July 24, 1956 two U.N. military observers and a Jordanian officer of the M.A.C. were blown up by mines on Mount Scopus which, the Zionists blandly explained, were part of "an old Israeli minefield." Two Egyptian colonels, said by the Zionists to belong to the Egyptian intelligence service, were killed by "letter bombs" delivered to them through the post (this method was used a decade earlier against a British officer in England, Captain Roy Farran, who had served in intelligence in Palestine and incurred Zionist enmity; his brother, whose initial was also R., opened the package and was killed). On July 29, 1956 a U.N. truce observer, a Dane, was killed by a mine or bomb near the Gaza strip and two others were wounded by rifle fire. "Activism" was taking its toll by the method of assassination, as in earlier times.

On August 28, 1956 Israel was again censured by the M.A.C. for "a serious breach of the armistice." The censure was followed by another Israeli attack (Sept.12) when a strong military force drove into Jordan, killed some twenty Jordanians and blew up a police post at Rahaw. General Burns protested that such deeds "have been repeatedly condemned by the U.N. Security Council," whereon another strong force at once (Sept.14) attacked Jordan, killing between twenty and thirty Jordanians at Gharandai. The British Foreign Office (Britain had an alliance with Jordan) expressed "strong disapproval," whereon the Board of Deputies of British Jews attacked it for this "biased statement." On September 19 the M.A.C. again "condemned" Israel for "hostile and warlike acts" (these two attacks apparently were made with symbolic intent, the moment chosen for them being during the Jewish New Year period), and on September 26 the Commission "censured" Israel specifically for the September 12 attack.

The immediate answer to this particular censure was *an official announcement* in Jerusalem *on the same day* (Sept. 26) that the biggest attack up to that time had been made by the Israeli regular army, in strength, on a Jordanian post at Husan, when some 25 Jordanians were killed, among them a child of twelve. The M.A.C. responded (Oct. 4) with its severest "censure," for "planned and unprovoked aggression." The retort was another, larger attack (Oct. 10) with artillery, mortars, bazookas, Bangalore torpedoes and grenades. The U.N. observers afterwards found the bodies of 48 Arabs, including a woman and a child. An armoured battalion and ten jet aeroplanes appear to have taken part in this massacre, which produced a British statement that if Jordan, its ally, were attacked, Britain would fulfil its undertakings. The Israeli Government said it received this warning "with alarm and amazement."[47]

The September 26 attack was the last of the series which filled the years 1953-1956; the next one was to be full-scale *war*. I have summarized the list of raids and massacres to give the later reader the true picture of the Middle East in the autumn of 1956, when Mr. Ben-Gurion declared that Israel was "defenceless" and the politicians of Washington and London were competing with each other in the demand that Israel receive arms to ward off "Arab aggression." If the accumulated pile of resolutions which at that time lay on the United Nations table, "condemning" Israel's "unprovoked aggression," "flagrant violation" and the like, had meant anything at all, this last attack, openly announced while it occurred and flung contemptuously in the teeth of the latest "censure," must have produced some *action* against Israel by the United Nations, or the implicit admission that Israel was its master.

The matter was never tested because, before Jordan's appeal to the United Nations Security Council had even been considered the attack on Egypt came. It had been announced, to any who cared to heed, at the very

---

[47] From the start of the presidential-election year all leading American newspapers, and many British ones, reported these Israeli attacks as "reprisals" or "retaliations," so that the victims were by the propaganda-machine converted into the aggressors in each case. General Burns, in his report on the last attack, told the U.N. that Israel "paralyzed the investigating machinery" by boycotting the Mixed Armistice Commissions whenever these voted against it, and added: "At present the situation is that one of the parties to the general armistice agreement makes its own investigations, which are not subject to check or confirmation by any disinterested observers, publishes the results of such investigations, draws its own conclusions from them and undertakes actions by its military forces on that basis." The British and American press, by adopting the Israeli word "reprisal" in its reports, throughout this period gave the public masses in the two countries the false picture of what went on which was desired by the Zionists.

moment of the attack on Jordan, for Mr. Menachem Beigin at Tel Aviv "urged an immediate Israeli attack on Egypt" *(Daily Telegraph,* Sept. 26, 1956). Mr. Beigin was the voice of "activism" and from the moment he said that all who had watched the developing situation knew what would come next: a full-scale Zionist invasion of Egypt.

The story I have related shows that, at the moment of the Israeli invasion, no attentive observer could hope that the United Nations would do much more than reprobate it. The Zionists obviously had chosen a moment when, they calculated, the imminence of the vote in the American presidential election would paralyze all means of effective action against them. I believed I was prepared for Western submission to Zionism once again, in some form or other. What even I would not have believed, until it happened, was that my own country, Britain, would join in the attack. This, the latest and greatest of the series of errors into which the people of England were led by their rulers in the sequence to the original involvement in Zionism, in 1903, darkened the prospect for England and the West during the remainder of this century, just when it was brightening; it was like a sudden eclipse of the sun, confounding all the calculations of astronomers.

In this event, "irresistible pressure" of "international politics" in the capitals of the West produced a result, the full consequences of which will be calculable only when many years have passed. Therefore the last section of this chapter and book must survey again the workings of "irresistible pressure" behind the Western scene, this time in the phase of the approaching climacteric, the years 1952- 1956. At the end of this phase revolutionary-Communism and revolutionary-Zionism, the twin destructive forces released from the Talmudic areas of Russia in the last century, were in extremis. By the act of the West, in the autumn of 1956, both were reprieved for further destruction.

The Years of Climax

The years 1952-1956 brought the peoples of the West ever nearer to the reckoning for the support which their leaders, through two generations and two world wars, had given to the revolution and to Zionism. They were being drawn towards two wars which foreseeably would merge into one war serving one dominant purpose. On the one hand, they were committed by their politicians and parties to the preservation of the Zionist state, the declared policy of which was to enlarge its population by "three or four million people" in "ten to fifteen years"; that meant war. On the other hand, they were daily made accustomed to the idea that it was their destiny and duty to destroy Communism, which had overflowed into half of Europe when the West opened the sluice-gates; that meant war.

These two wars inevitably would become one war. The calculation is simple. The *territory* for the expansion of the Zionist state could only be taken from the neighbouring Arab peoples; the *people* for the expansion of the Zionist state could only be taken from the area occupied by the revolution, because "three or four million" Jews could not be found anywhere else save in the United States.[48]

For this purpose the West, in the phase that began in 1952, will have to be persuaded that "anti-semitism" is rife in the Soviet area, just as it was persuaded in the four following years that Zionist attacks on Arab countries were Arab attacks on Israel. Mr. Ben-Gurion (Dec. 8, 1951) officially informed the Soviet Government that "the return of the Jews to their historic homeland is *the pivotal mission* of the state of Israel … the Government of Israel appeals to the Soviet Union to enable those Jews in the Soviet Union who wish to emigrate to do so." The *New York Times* two years later, reporting declining immigration to Israel, said Mr. Ben-Gurion's aim "seems very remote" and added that "the present pattern of immigration" would only change radically if there were "an upsurge of anti- semitism" somewhere (at that period, June 26, 1953, the denunciation of "anti-semitism behind the Iron Curtain" had begun). The *New York Herald-Tribune* at the same period (Apr. 12, 1953) said "anti-semitism" had become virulent in the Soviet Union and "the most crucial rescue job" facing Israel in its sixth year was that of the "2,500,000 Jews sealed in Russia and the satellite countries."

Therefore it was clear, in the light of the two world wars and their outcome in each case, that any war undertaken by "the West" against "Communism" would in fact be fought for the primary purpose of supplying the Zionist state with new inhabitants from Russia; that any Middle East war in which the West engaged would be waged for the primary purpose of enlarging the territory of the Zionist state, to accommodate this larger population; and that the two wars would effectively merge into one, in the course of which this dominant purpose would remain hidden from the embroiled masses until it was achieved, and confirmed by some new "world instrument," at the fighting's end.

Such was the position of "the West, fifty years after Mr. Balfour's and Mr. Woodrow Wilson's first ensnarement by Zionism. I have a reason for

---

[48] The extraction of the Jews from the United States, although essential to the "ingathering of the exiles," obviously belongs to a later stage of the process and would depend on the success of the next phase, the "ingathering" of the Jews from the Soviet area and from the African Arab countries. After that, strange though the idea will seem to Americans and Britishers today, there would have to be a "Jewish persecution" in America and this would be produced by the propagandist method used in the past and applied impartially to one country after another, including Russia, Poland, Germany, France, Spain and Britain. Dr. Nahum Goldman, leader of the World Zionist Organization, in October 1952 told an Israeli audience that there was one problem Zionism must solve if it was to succeed: "How to get the Jews of the countries *where they are not persecuted to emigrate to Israel.*" He said this problem was "especially difficult in the United States because the United States is *less* a country of Jewish persecution or any prospect of Jewish persecution than any other" (Johannesburg *Zionist Record*, Oct. 24, 1952). The reader will note that there are *no* countries without "Jewish persecution"; there are only degrees of "Jewish persecution" in various countries.

enclosing the words, "The West," in quotation marks, namely, that they no longer mean what The West meant. Earlier the term signified the Christian area, from the eastern borders of Europe across the Atlantic to the western seaboard of America and including the outlying English-speaking countries in North America, Africa and the Antipodes. After the Second War, when half of Europe was abandoned to the Talmudic revolution, the two words received a more limited application. In the popular mind "the West" meant England and America, ranked against the new barbarism which one day it would extirpate in Europe and thrust back into its barbaric, Asiatic homeland. America and England, first and foremost, still represented "the free world" which one day would be restored throughout its former area and with it, as in earlier times, the hopes of men outside it who wanted to be free; so the mass mind understood.

Militarily, this was a proper assumption; the physical strength of "the West," supported by the longing of the captive peoples, was more than equal to the task. Actually the great countries to which the enslaved peoples looked were themselves captive of the power which had brought about this enslavement; and twice had shown that their arms, if used, would not be employed to liberate and redress, but to prolong the 20th Century's ordeal.

What moral and spiritual values were earlier contained in those two words, The West, were strongest in the countries abandoned to Communism, and those menaced by Zionism, where suffering and peril were rekindling them in the souls of men. In the once great citadels of the West, London and Washington, they were repressed and dormant.

For this reason America was not truly qualified to takeover from England the leading part in the world in the second half of the 20th Century and to perform the task of liberation which the public masses were led to expect from it. Materially, the Republic founded nearly two hundred years before was prodigious. The riches of the world had poured into it during two world wars; its population rapidly increased to two hundred millions; its navy and air force were the greatest in the world and, like its army, were built on that order of compulsion which its people long had held to be the curse of Europe. In industry and technical skill it was so formidable as to be a nightmare to itself. Its production was so vast that it could not be absorbed and the dread memory of the 1929 slump caused its leaders to devise many ways of distributing goods about the world in the form of gifts and paying the producer for them out of revenues, so that, for a while, manufacturer and workmen should be paid for an output for which, in peace, no natural market offered. Its military bases, on the territory of once sovereign peoples, were strewn over the globe, so that at any instant it could strike in overwhelming force … at what, and for what?

At "Communism," its people were told, and for the liberation of the enslaved, the relief of the world in thrall, the rectification of the deed of 1945.

If that was true, the end of the century's ordeal was at least in prospect, some day, for the hearts of men everywhere were in *that* cause. But every major act of the government in Washington in the years 1952-1956 belied these professions. It seemed more in thrall to "the Jewish power" than even the British governments of the preceding fifty years. It appeared to be unable to handle any leading question of American foreign or domestic affairs save in terms of its bearing on the lot of "the Jews," as the case of the Jews was presented to it by the imperious Zionists. No small, puppet government looked much more vassal in its acts than this, which the general masses held to be the most powerful government in the world: that of the United States under its chief executive, President Eisenhower, in the years 1953 to 1956.

Like that of a chancellor at a royal birth, the shadow of Zionism fell over the selection, nomination and election of General Eisenhower. His meteoric promotion during the 1939-1945 war, from the rank of a colonel, unversed in combat, to that of Supreme Commander of all the Allied armies invading Europe, seems to indicate that he was marked down for advancement long before, and research supports that inference. In the 1920's young Lieutenant Eisenhower attended the National War College in Washington, where a Mr. Bernard Baruch (who had played so important a part in the selection, nomination and election of President Woodrow Wilson in 1911-1912) gave instruction. Mr. Baruch at that early period decided that Lieutenant Eisenhower was a star pupil, and when General Eisenhower was elected president thirty years later he told American veterans that he had for a quarter-century "had the privilege of sitting at Bernard's feet and listening to his words." Early in his presidency Mr. Eisenhower intervened to resolve, in Mr. Baruch's favour, a small dispute at the National War College, where some opposed acceptance of a bust of Mr. Baruch, presented by admirers (no living civilian's bust was ever displayed there before).

The support of "the adviser to six Presidents" obviously may have helped bring about Lieutenant Eisenhower's rapid rise to the command of the greatest army in history. On public record is the support which Mr. Baruch gave when General Eisenhower (who had no party affiliations or history) in 1952 offered himself as *Republican* Party candidate for the presidency. Up to that time Mr. Baruch had been a staunch member of the Democratic Party, not just a regular Democrat, but a *passionate* approver of the party label and *an almost fanatical hater of the Republican label"* (his approved biography). In 1952 Mr. Baruch suddenly became a passionate approver of the Republican label, provided that Mr. Eisenhower wore it. Evidently strong reasons must have caused this sudden change in a lifetime's allegiance, and they are worth seeking.

In 1952 the Republican Party had been out of office for twenty years. Under the pendulum theory alone, therefore, it was due to return and thus to oust the Democratic Party, of which Mr. Baruch for fifty years had been "a passionate approver." Apart from the normal turn of the tide against a party overlong in office, which was to be anticipated, the American elector in 1952 had especial reasons to vote against the Democrats; the chief of these was the exposure of Communist infestation of government under the Roosevelt and Truman regimes and the public desire for a drastic cleansing of the stables.

In these circumstances it was reasonably clear, in 1952, that the Republican Party and its candidate would win the election and the presidency. The natural candidate was the party's leader, Senator Robert E. Taft, whose lifetime had been given to it. At that very moment, and after his own lifetime of "passionate" support of the Democratic Party (his cash contributions were very large, and Mr. Forrestal's diary records the part played by such contributions, in general, in determining the course of American elections and state policy) Mr. Baruch, the "fanatical hater" of the Republican label, produced an alternative candidate for the Republican nomination. That is to say, the officer so long admired by him suddenly appeared in the ring, and Mr. Baruch's warm commendation of him indicated the source of his strongest support.

The prospect which then opened was that if Mr. Eisenhower, instead of Senator Taft, could obtain the party's nomination, the Republican Party would through him be committed to pursue the Democratic policy of "internationalism" begun by Presidents Woodrow Wilson, Roosevelt and Truman. That, in turn, meant that if the party-leader could be ousted the American elector would be deprived of any genuine choice, for the only man who offered him an alternative, different policy was Senator Taft.

This had been made plain, to the initiated, more than a year before the election by the Republican leader next in importance to Senator Taft, Governor Thomas E. Dewey of New York State. Mr. Dewey (who had astonished himself and the country by losing the 1948 presidential election to Mr. Truman, a classic example of the foredoomed failure of the "me too" method) stated, "I am an internationalist. That's why I am for Eisenhower. Eisenhower is a Republican at heart, but more important than that, he is an internationalist" (*Look*, Sept. 11, 1951). Among initiates "internationalist" (like "activist" in Zionism) is a keyword, signifying many unavowed things; thus far in our century no avowed "internationalist" in a frontal post has genuinely opposed the advance of Communism, the advance of Zionism, and the world-government project towards which these two forces convergingly lead. Senator Taft, on the other hand, was violently attacked at this time as an "isolationist" (another key-word; it means only that the person attacked believes in national sovereignty and national interest, but it is made to sound bad in the ear of the masses).

Thus Mr. Eisenhower offered himself at the Republican Party convention at Chicago in 1952 in opposition to Senator Taft. I was an eye-witness, through television, and, although no novice, was astonished by the smoothness with which Senator Taft's defeat was achieved. This event showed, long before the actual election, that the nomination-mechanism had been so mastered that neither party could even *nominate* any but a candidate approved by powerful selectors behind the scene. The outcome of the presidential election itself is in these circumstances of relatively little account in America today, nor can the observer picture how the Republic might escape from this occult control. It is *not* possible for either party to nominate its party-leader, or any other man, unless he has been passed as acceptable to "the internationalists" beforehand.

The supplanting of the veteran party-leader, on the eve of his party's return to office, was achieved through control of the block votes of the "key states." Population-strength governs the number of votes cast by the state-delegations, and at least two of these preponderant states (New York and California) are those to which the Jewish immigration of the last seventy years had evidently been directed for this purpose.[49] In 1952, when I watched, the voting for the two men was running fairly even when Mr. Dewey smilingly delivered the large package-vote of New York State against his party's leader and for Mr. Eisenhower. Other "key states" followed suit and he received the nomination, which in the circumstances of that moment also meant the presidency.

It also meant, in effect, the end of any genuine two-party system in America for the present; the system of elected representatives which is known as "democracy" sinks to the level of the one-party system in non-democracies if the two parties do not offer a true choice of policy. The situation was so depicted to Jewish readers by the *Jerusalem Post* on the eve of the election (Nov. 5, 1952), which instructed them that there was "not much to choose between the two." (Mr. Eisenhower, Republican; Mr. Stevenson, Democrat) "from the point of view of the Jewish elector" and that Jewish interest should be concentrated on "the fate" of those Congressmen and Senators held to be "hostile to the Jewish cause."

Immediately after the new President's inauguration (January, 1953) the British Prime Minister, Sir Winston Churchill hastened to America to confer with him, though not to Washington, where Presidents reside; Mr. Eisenhower suggested that they meet "at Bernie's place," Mr. Baruch's Fifth Avenue mansion (Associated Press, Feb. 7, 1953). Mr. Baruch at that time had been urgently recommending the adoption of his "atom bomb plan" as

---

[49] This is essential to the electoral strategy laid down, though presumably not originally devised by Colonel House. The spanner-in-the-works problem posed by it is the subject of many allusions earlier quoted, i.e.: "Our failure to go along with the Zionists might lose the states of New York, Pennsylvania and California; I thought it was about time that somebody should pay some consideration to whether we might not lose the United States" (Mr. James J. Forrestal); "Niles had told the President that Dewey was about to come out with a statement favouring the Zionist position and unless the President anticipated this New York State would be lost to the Democrats" (Secretary of State James J. Byrnes); "The Democratic Party would not be willing to relinquish the advantages of the Jewish Vote" (Governor Thomas E. Dewey).

Douglas Reed

the only effective deterrent to "Soviet aggression" (his remarks to the Senate Committee were quoted in an earlier chapter). Apparently he was not so suspicious of or hostile to the Soviet as he then seemed, for some years later he disclosed that the notion of a joint American-Soviet atomic dictatorship of the world had also appealed to him: "A few years ago I met Vyshinsky at a party and said to him ... 'You have the bomb and we have the bomb ... Let's control the thing while we can because while we are talking all the nations will sooner or later get the bomb'" *(Daily Telegraph,* June 9, 1956).

General Eisenhower's election as the Republican candidate deprived America of its last means of dissociating itself, through electoral repudiation, from the Wilson-Roosevelt-Truman policy of "internationalism." Senator Taft was the only leading politician who, in the public mind, clearly stood for the clean break with that policy, and evidently for this reason the powers which have effectively governed America in the last forty years attached major importance to preventing his nomination. Some extracts from his book of 1952 have enduring historic value, if only as a picture of what might have been if the Republican voter had been allowed to vote for the Republican party leader:

"The result of the" (Roosevelt-Truman) "Administration policy has been to build up the strength of Soviet Russia so that it is, in fact, a threat to the security of the United States ... Russia is far more a threat to the security of the United States than Hitler in Germany ever was ... There is no question that we have the largest navy in the world, and certainly, while the British are our allies, complete control of the sea throughout the world ... We should be willing to assist with our own sea and air forces any island nations which desire our help. Among them are Japan, Formosa, the Philippines, Indonesia, Australia and New Zealand; on the Atlantic side, Great Britain of course ... I believe that an alliance with England and a defence of the British Isles are far more important than an alliance with any continental nation ... With the British there can be little doubt of our complete control of sea and air throughout the world ... *If we really mean our anti-Communist policy* ... we should definitely eliminate from the government all those who are directly or indirectly connected with the Communist organization ... Fundamentally I believe the ultimate purpose of our foreign policy must be to protect the liberty of the people of America ... I feel that the last two presidents have put all kinds of political and policy considerations ahead of their interest in liberty and peace ... It seems to me that the sending of troops without authorization of Congress to a country under attack, as was done in Korea, is clearly prohibited" (by the American Constitution) "... The European Army project, however, goes further ... It involves the sending of troops to an international army similar to that which was contemplated under the United Nations Charter ... I was never satisfied with the United Nations Charter ...it is not based on an underlying law and an administration of justice under that law ...

586

I see no choice except to develop our own military policy and our own policy of alliances, without substantial regard to the non-existent power of the United Nations to prevent aggression ... The other form of international organization which is being urged strenuously upon the people of the United States, namely, a world state with an international legislature to make the laws and an international executive to direct the army of the organization ... appears to me, at least in this century, to be fantastic, dangerous and impractical. Such a state, in my opinion, would fall to pieces in ten years ... The difficulties of holding together such a Tower of Babel under one direct government would be insuperable ... But above all, anyone who suggests such a plan is proposing an end to that liberty which has produced in this country the greatest happiness ... the world has ever seen. It would subject the American people to the government of a majority who do not understand what American principles are, and have little sympathy with them. Any international organization which is worth the paper it is written on must be based on retaining the sovereignty of all states. Peace must be sought, not by destroying and consolidating nations, but by developing a rule of law in the relations between nations ..."

These extracts show that Senator Taft saw through today's "deception of nations"; they explain also why his name was anathema to the powers which control "the vote of the key states" and why he was not allowed even to run for president.[50] The entire period of Mr. Eisenhower's canvass, nomination, election and early presidency was dominated by "the Jewish question"; he might have been elected president only of the Zionists, so constantly were his words and deeds directed towards the furtherance of their ambition.

Immediately after the nomination he told a Mr. Maxwell Abbell, president of the United Synagogue of America, "The Jewish people could not have a better friend than me" and added that he and his brothers had been reared by their mother in "the teachings of the Old Testament" (Mrs Eisenhower was a fervent adherent of the sect of Jehovah's Witnesses), and "I grew up believing that *Jews* were the chosen people and that they gave us

---

[50] Whether Senator Taft, had he become president would have found himself able to carry out the clear, alternative policy here outlined is a question now never to be answered. In the particular case of Zionism, which is an essential part of the entire proposition here denounced by him, he was as submissive as all other leading politicians and presumably did not discern the inseparable relationship between it and the "world state" ambition which he scarified. A leading Zionist of Philadelphia, a Mr. Jack Martin, was asked to become Senator Taft's "executive secretary" in 1945 and records that his first question to Mr. Taft was, "Senator, what can I tell you about the aspirations of Zionism?" Taft is quoted as answering, in Balfourean or Wilsonian vein, "What is there to explain? The Jews are being persecuted. They need a land, a government of their own. We have to help them to get Palestine. This will also contribute incidentally to world peace ..." The contrast between this, the typical talk of a vote-seeking ward politician, and the enlightened exposition given above is obvious. Mr. Martin, who is described in the article now quoted (*Jewish Sentinel*, June 10, 1954) as Senator Taft's "alter ego" and "heir," after Taft's death was invited by President Eisenhower to become *his* "assistant, advisor and liaison with Congress." Mr. Martin's comment: "President Eisenhower is ready to listen freely to your opinion and it is easy to advise him."

the high ethical and moral principles of our civilization" (many Jewish newspapers, September 1952).

This was followed by ardent professions of sympathy for "the Jews" and for "Israel" from both candidates on the occasion of the Jewish New Year (Sept. 1952); during this festival, also, American pressure on the "free" Germans in West Germany succeeded in extorting their signature to the agreement to pay "reparations" to Israel. In October came the Prague trial, with the charge of "Zionist conspiracy," and Mr. Eisenhower began to make his menacing statements about "anti-semitism in the Soviet Union and the satellite countries."

The charge of "anti-semitism" was deemed to be a vote-getter in the election itself and was brought by the outgoing president, Mr. Truman, against Mr. Eisenhower, who told an audience that he was overcome by the insinuation: "I just choke up and leave it to you." Rabbi Hillel Silver of Cleveland (who threatened the Soviet Union with war on the count of "anti-semitism") was called into conclave with Mr. Eisenhower and on emerging from it exonerated the aspirant from all anti-semitic taint (Rabbi Silver had offered a prayer at the Republican Convention which nominated Mr. Eisenhower; at the new President's inauguration, and at Mr. Eisenhower's request, he offered the prayer "for grace and guidance.") Among the rival campaigners the outgoing Vice-President, a Mr. Alben Barkley, excelled all others. Of a typical statement by Mr. Barkley ("I predict a glorious future for Israel as a model on which most of the Middle East might pattern itself") *Time* magazine said; "The star of the speech circuit is Vice President Alben Barkley, who for years has drawn up to $1 000 for each appearance. Barkley is a paid platform favourite for Israel bond-selling drives. Many Arabs think … that this fact has had an influence on United States policy in the Middle East; but not many Arabs vote in U.S. elections."

A few weeks after the inauguration the West German tribute agreement was ratified, a German Minister then announcing that the Bonn Government had yielded to pressure from America, which did not wish to appear openly as the financier of the Zionist state. In the same month (April 1953) Jewish newspapers, under the heading "Israel Shows Its Might," reported that "The whole diplomatic corps and the foreign military attaches who watched the Israel Army's biggest parade in Haifa, with the Navy drawn up offshore and units of the Air Force flying overhead, were duly impressed and the parade's aim, to demonstrate that Israel was ready to meet a decision in the field, was achieved."

In these circumstances, with various new "pledges" and undertakings given and noted for the future, with Stalin dead, Israel ready for "a decision in the field" and the "free" half of Germany toiling to pay tribute, one more presidential term began in 1953. A curious incident marked the great Inauguration Day parade in Washington. At the tail of the procession rode a mounted man in cowboy dress who reined in as he reached the presidential stand and asked if he might try his lariat. Obediently Mr. Eisenhower stood up and bowed his head; the noose fell around him and was pulled taut; the moving pictures showed a man, with bared head, at the end of a rope.

The new president many have thought to utter simple platitudes when he said, "The state of Israel is *democracy's outpost* in the Middle East and *every American who loves liberty must join* in an effort to make secure forever the future of this newest member of the family of nations." In fact, this was a commitment, or so held by those to whom it was addressed, like similar words of Mr. Roosevelt and Mr. Woodrow Wilson. Eight years after Hitler's death the new state, where Hitler's very laws held and whence the native people had been driven by massacre and terror, was "democracy's outpost" and all who "loved liberty" *must* (the imperative) join to preserve it.

If the new president thought he was free to form state policy, after he uttered such words, he was taught better within nine months of his inauguration. In October 1953 the commitment was called, and imperiously. An effort to act independently, and in the American national interest, in an issue affecting "the newest member of the family of nations" was crushed, and the American President made to perform public penance, in much the same way that "Rockland" (Woodrow Wilson) was brought to heel in Mr. House's novel in 1912. This humiliation of the head of what mankind saw as the most powerful government in the world is the most significant incident in the present story, which has recounted many episodes, similar in nature but less open to public audit. The series of Zionist attacks on the Arab neighbour-states (listed in the preceding section) began on Oct. 14, 1953, when every living soul in the Arab village of Qibya, in Jordan was massacred. This was a repetition of the Deir Yasin massacre of 1948, with the difference that it was done outside Palestine, and thus deliberately intimated to the entire body of Arab peoples that they all in time would suffer "utter destruction," again with the connivance of "the West."

The facts were reported to the United Nations by the Danish General Vagn Bennike, chief of the U.N. Truce Observation Organization (who received threats against his life) and his immediately-responsible subordinate, Commander E.D. Hutchison of the U.S. Navy, who described the attack as "cold blooded murder" (and was later removed). At the subsequent discussion before the U.N. Security Council, the French delegate said "the massacre" had aroused "horror and reprobation" in France and reproached Israel, the state founded on the claim of "persecution," with "wreaking vengeance on the innocent." The Greek delegate spoke of "the horrible massacre" and the British and American delegates joined in the chorus of "condemnation" (Nov. 9, 1953). In England the Archbishop of York denounced this "horrible act of terrorism" and a Conservative M.P., Major H.

Legge-Bourke, called it "the culminating atrocity in a long chain of incursions into non-Israeli territory, made as part of a concerted plan of vengeance."

When these expressions of horror were uttered Israel had, in effect, been awarded an American bonus of $60,000,000 for the deed and the American President had publicly submitted to the Zionist "pressure" in New York. This is the chronology of events:

Four days after the massacre (Oct. 18, 1953) the American Government "decided to administer a stern rebuke to its protégé" *(The Times,* Oct. 19). It announced that "the shocking reports which have reached the Department of State of the loss of lives and property involved in this incident convince us that those who are responsible should be *brought to account and effective measures be taken to prevent such incidents* in the future" (these words are worth comparing with what happened within a few days). *The Times* added that "behind this statement is a growing resentment at the high-handed way in which the Israel Government is inclined to treat the United States – presumably because it believes that it can always count on *domestic political pressure* in this country." It was even reported (added *The Times,* as if with bated breath) "that a grant of several million dollars to the Israel Government may be held up until some guarantee is given that there will be no more border incidents."

Two days later (Oct. 20) the State Department announced that the grant to Israel would be halted. If President Eisenhower calculated that, with the election a year behind and the next three years ahead, his administration was free to formulate American state policy, he was wrong. The weakness of America, and the strength of the master-key method, is that an election *always* impends, if not a presidential election, then a Congressional, mayoral, municipal or other one. At that instant three candidates (two Jews and a non-Jew) were contending for the mayoralty of New York, and the campaign was beginning for the 1954 Congressional elections, when all 435 members of the House of Representatives and one third of the Senators were to seek election. Against this background, the screw was applied to the White House.

The three rivals in New York began to outbid each other for the "Jewish vote." Five hundred Zionists gathered in New York (Oct. 25), announced that they were "shocked" by the cancellation of "aid to Israel," and demanded that the Government "reconsider and reverse its hasty and unfair action." The Republican candidate wired to Washington for an immediate interview with the Secretary of State; returning from it he assured the anxious electors that "full U.S. economic aid *will* be given to Israel" *(New York Times,* Oct. 26) and said this would amount in all to $63,000,000 (nevertheless, he was not elected).

Meanwhile the Republican party-managers clamoured at the President's door with warnings of what would happen in the 1954 election if he did not recant. On October 28 he capitulated, an official statement announcing that

Israel would receive the amount previously earmarked, and $26,000,000 of it in the first six months of the fiscal year, (out of a total of about $60,000,000).

The Republican candidate for the New York mayoralty welcomed this as "recognition of the fact that Israel is a staunch bastion of free world security in the Near East," and an act of "world statesmanship" typical of President Eisenhower. The true picture of what had produced the act was given by Mr. John O'Donnell in the *New York Daily News*, Oct. 28: "The professional politicians moved in on him with a vengeance. Ike didn't like it at all ... but the pressure was so violent that to keep peace in the family he had to reverse himself. And the about-face, politically and personally, was about the smartest and swiftest seen in this political capital of the world in many a month ... For a week the pressure of candidates, seeking the huge Jewish vote in New York City, has been terrific ... The political education of President Eisenhower has moved with dizzy speed in the last ten days." (Nevertheless, the Republican Party *did* lose control of Congress in the 1954 election, this being the familiar and invariable result of these capitulations; and after even greater capitulations it suffered a still greater setback in 1956, when its nominee, again Mr. Eisenhower, was re-elected president).

After this the American Government never again ventured to "rebuke its protegé" during the long series of equally "horrible acts" committed by it, and on the anniversary of Israel's creation (May 7, 1954) the Israeli Army proudly displayed the arms received by it from the United States and Great Britain; a massive display of American and British tanks, jet aircraft, bombers and fighters was then offered to the view. (The United States had reported Israel "eligible for arms aid" on August 12, 1952, and Great Britain authorized arms exports to Israel by private dealers on January 17, 1952).

Two years of relative quiet followed, but it was merely the hush of preparation; the next series of events was obviously being staged for the next presidential election year, 1956. In May 1955 (the month when Sir Anthony Eden succeeded Sir Winston Churchill as Prime Minister in England), the American Secretary of State, Mr. John Foster Dulles, like Mr. Balfour thirty years before, at last visited the country which was wrecking American foreign policy, as it had wrecked that of England. After his experience with the "rebuke," so swiftly swallowed, he must have realized that he was dealing with the most powerful force in the world, supreme in his country, of which "Israel" was but the instrument used to divide and rule others.

Like Mr. Balfour, he was received with Arab riots when he went outside Palestine. In Israel he was seen by few Israelis, being hurried in a closed car, between hedges of police, from the airport into Tel Aviv. The police operation for his escort and guard was called "Operation Kitavo," *Kitavo* being Hebrew for "Whence thou art come." The allusion is to Deuteronomy 26: "And it shall be, when thou art come into the land which the Lord thy God giveth thee for an inheritance ... and the Lord hath avouched thee this day to be his peculiar people, as he hath promised thee, and that thou shouldest keep all his commandments, and to make thee high above all nations which he hath made ... that thou mayest be an holy people unto the Lord thy God." Thus an American Secretary of State was seen in Zionist Israel merely as a minor character in the great drama of "fulfilling" the Levitical Law.

Mr. Dulles on his return said he had found that the Arabs feared Zionism more than Communism, a discovery of the obvious; the Arabs had read the Torah and seen its literal application to themselves at Deir Yasin and Qibya. He said in a television broadcast (according to the Associated Press, June 1, 1953), "the United States stands firmly behind the 1950 declaration made jointly with Britain and France; it pledges the three nations to action in the event *the present Israeli borders* are violated by any military action" (the famous "Tripartite Declaration"). I have not been able to discover if Mr. Dulles said this or was misquoted (the Declaration was supposedly impartial and guaranteed "Middle East frontiers and armistice lines *not* "Israeli borders" but this was the kind of news which always reached the Arabs and in fact the verbal lapse, or misquotation, came much nearer to the obvious truth of affairs.

Once more the generations were passing, but the lengthening shadow of Zionism fell more heavily on each new one. Sir Winston Churchill, his powers at last failing, relinquished his post to the man on whom he had already bestowed it in the manner of a potentate determining the succession: "I take no step in public life without consulting Mr. Eden; he will carry on the torch of Conservatism when other and older hands have let it fall." That being the case, Sir Anthony presumably inherited Sir Winston's unqualified support for "the fulfilment of the aspirations of Zionism" and might well have wished the torch in other hands, for it could only ruin, not illumine "Conservatism," and England. From the moment when he reached the office for which all his life had prepared him his administration of it was bedevilled by "the problem of the Middle East," so that his political end seemed likely to be as unhappy as that of Mr. Roosevelt and Mr. Woodrow Wilson.

And, the scribe might add, that of President Eisenhower. In September 1955 he was stricken down, and although he recovered the pictures of him began to show the traits which appeared in those of Messrs' Roosevelt and Woodrow Wilson towards the end of their terms. The "pressure" which these apparently powerful men have to endure in this, "the Jewish century," seems to have some effect which shows in a careworn physiognomy. They are surrounded by the praise-makers, but if they try to follow conscience and duty they are relentlessly brought to book. After his first experience the general expectation was that he would not run a second time.

He was not a Republican and during his first term felt uncomfortable as a "Republican" president. Indeed, soon after his inauguration his "vexation with the powerful right wing of the party" (in other words, with the traditional Republicans, who had wanted Senator Taft) "reached such extremes that for a time he gave prolonged thought to the idea of a new political party in America, a party to which persons of his own philosophy, regardless of their previous affiliations, might rally ... He began asking his most intimate associates whether he did not have to start thinking about a new party. As he conceived it, such a party would have been essentially *his* party. It would have represented those doctrines, international and domestic, which *he believed* were best for the United States *and indeed for the world.*"[51] He only gave up this idea when Senator Taft's death left the Republican Party without a natural leader and when the Senate, at the President's personal encouragement, censured Senator Joseph McCarthy of Wisconsin for the ardour of his attack on Communism-in-government. The public anger aroused by the exposure of Communist infestation of the administration under Presidents Roosevelt and Truman was one of the main causes for the swing of votes to the Republican Party (and its nominee, Mr. Eisenhower) in 1952.

Thus at the end of 1955 a presidential-election year again impended, in circumstances which the dominant power in America had always found ideal: an ailing president, party-politicians avid for "the Jewish vote," a war situation in the Middle East and another in Europe. In such a state of affairs "domestic political pressure" in the capital of the world's wealthiest and best-armed country might produce almost any result. The Republican party-managers, desperate to retain at least a nominal Republican in the White House if they could not gain a majority in Congress, gathered round a sick man and urged him to run.[52]

---

[51] This significant disclosure comes from a book, *Eisenhower. The Inside Story,* published in 1956 by a White House correspondent, Mr. Robert J. Donovan, evidently at Mr. Eisenhower's wish, for it is based on the minutes of Cabinet meetings and other documents which relate to highly confidential proceedings at the highest level. Nothing of the kind was ever published in America before and the author does not explain the reasons for the innovation. Things are recorded which the President's Cabinet officers probably would not have said, had they known that they would be published; for instance, a jocose suggestion that a Senator Bricker and his supporters (who were pressing a Constitutional amendment to limit the President's power to make treaties, and thus to subject him to great Congressional control) ought to be atom-bombed.

[52] The most significant domestic events of President Eisenhower's first term (in view of the fact that his election chiefly expressed the desire   of American voters, in 1952, to redress the proved Communist infestation of government and combat the menace of Communist aggression) were the censure of the most persistent investigator, Senator McCarthy, which received the President's personal encouragement and approval; and the ruling of the United States Supreme Court in 1955, which denied the right of the forty-eight individual States to take measures against sedition and reserved this to the Federal Government. This ruling, if given effect, will greatly reduce the power of the Republic to "contend with sedition" (the "Protocols"). The third major domestic event was the Supreme Court ruling against segregation of White and Negro pupils in the public schools, which in effect was directed against the South and, if pressed, might produce violently explosive results. These events draw attention to the peculiar position held in the United States by the Supreme Court, in view of the fact that appointments to it are political, not the reward of a lifetime's service in an independent judiciary. In these circumstances the Supreme Court, under President Eisenhower, showed signs of developing into a supreme political body (Supreme Politburo might not be too inapt a word), able to overrule Congress. The United States Solicitor General in 1956, Mr.

The real campaign began, as always, a full year before the election itself. In September 1955 the Egyptian Government of President Gamel Abdel Nasser contracted with the Soviet Union for the purchase of some arms. The American, British and French "Tripartite Declaration" of 1950 provided that Israel and the Arab states might buy arms from the West. President Nasser, in justification of his act, stated (Nov. 16, 1955) that he had been unable to obtain "one single piece of armament from the United States in three years of trying" and accused the American government of "a deliberate attempt to keep the Arabs perpetually at the mercy of Israel and her threats."

This Egyptian arms purchase from the Soviet produced an immediate uproar in Washington and London similar to that which was raised in 1952-3 about "the trial of the Jewish doctors." President Eisenhower appealed to the Soviet Union to withhold arms shipments to Egypt (the bulk of these came from the Skoda arms factory in Czechoslovakia, which fell into Soviet possession in consequence of the Yalta agreement of 1945 and which had supplied the arms enabling "Israel" to set up house in 1947-8 and to "hail the Soviets as deliverers"). In London on the same day (Nov. 9, 1955) Sir Anthony Eden accused the Soviet Union of creating war tensions in the Middle East; the British Foreign Secretary, Mr. Harold Macmillan, complained of the introduction of a "new and disturbing factor into this delicate situation." To the Arabs all these words from the West meant what they had always meant: that Israel would be given, and the Arabs would be denied, arms.

After this the propaganda campaign swelled day by day, in the same way as that of 1952-3, until, within a few weeks, the memory of the three years of Israeli attacks on the Arab countries and the United Nations' condemnations of these had been blotted out of the public mind. In its place, the general reader received the daily impression that unarmed Israel, through the fault of the West, was being left to the mercy of Egypt, armed to the teeth with "Red" weapons. At that early stage the truth of the matter was once published: the leading American military authority, Mr. Hanson W. Baldwin, speaking of the supply of American arms to Israel, said, "We are trying to maintain a very uneasy 'balance' between the Israelis and the Arabs. This is not now, nor is it likely to be soon, a true balance in the sense that the two sides possess equal military strength. Today, Israel is clearly superior to Egypt, in fact to the combined strength of Egypt, Jordan, Saudi Arabia, Lebanon, Syria and Iraq" (*New York Times*, Nov. 11, 1955).

Simon E. Sobeloff, stated, "In our system the Supreme Court is not merely the adjudicator of controversies, but in the process of adjudication it is in many ways *the final formulator of national policy*" (quoted in the *New York Times*, July 19, 1956).

This truth was not again allowed to reach the newspaper-reading masses in the eleven months that followed, at any rate in my observation.[53] They were kept bemused by the growing clamour about "Red Arms for the Arabs," which set the note for both election campaigns (for Congress and for the presidency) then beginning.[54] All the presidential aspirants on the Democratic side (Messrs' Estes Kefauver, Governor Harriman of New York State, Stuart Symington and Adlai Stevenson) made inflammatory statements in this sense.[55] At one point an American Zionist committee considered a "march on Denver" but refrained (the President was in hospital there after his stroke), and instead approached all candidates, of either party, with a demand that they sign a "policy declaration" against the grant of arms to any Arab state. 120 Congressional aspirants signed forthwith, and the number later increased to 102 Democrats and 51

Republicans (New York Times, Apr. 5, 1956). This excess of Democratic signatories accounts for the statement made at the World Zionist Congress in Jerusalem on April 26 by Mr. Yishak Gruenbaum, a leading Israeli politician and former Minister: "Israel will get no support from the United States so long as the Republican leadership is in control." This was a public demand, from Israel, that American Jews should vote Democratic, and the belief of the American party-managers in the power of "the Jewish vote" there was strengthened, on this occasion, by the Democratic success in the Congressional election, desired by Mr. Gruenbaum in Jerusalem.

Against this background of "pressure" on an ailing President through the party-managers and of one more campaign about "the persecution of the Jews" (symbolized, this time, by Israel) the year of the presidential election began. From the start, experienced observers saw that it had been chosen (like preceding presidential-election years) as a year of staged and rising crisis which might erupt in general war. The basis of all calculations was the "domestic political pressure" which could be exercized on the American government and its acts.

In the real world the year opened, typically, with one more unanimous "condemnation" (Jan. 19, 1956) of Israel for a "deliberate" and "flagrant" attack (the one on Syria on Dec. 11, 1955). This was the fourth major condemnation in two years and it came at a moment when the propaganda campaign about Israel's "defencelessness" and Arab "aggression" was already

---

[53] However, *fourteen* months later (Jan 4, 1957), after the attack on Egypt, Mr. Hanson Baldwin, writing from the Middle East, confirmed the continuance of "defenceless" Israel's military predominance: "Israel has been, since 1949, the strongest indigenous military force in the area. She is stronger today, as compared with the Arab states, than ever before."

[54] "The supply of arms by Soviet Czechoslovakia made Jews in Israel and elsewhere look to the Soviets as deliverers," Johannesburg *Jewish Times*, Dec. 24, 1952.

[55] "The state of Israel will be defended if necessary with overwhelming outside help," Governor Harriman, *New York Times*, March 23, 1955.

in full swing in the West. At the same period a "state of national emergency" was declared in Israel.

The Zionist attack then turned on the core of responsible officials in the American State Department who (like those in the British Colonial Office and Foreign Office in the earlier generation) tried to ward off the perilous "commitments" to Israel. In November 1955 the world's largest religious Zionist organization, the Mizrachi Organization of America, had declared at Atlantic City that "a clique" of "anti-Israel elements in the United States State Department" was "blocking effective United States aid to Israel" (this, word for word, is the complaint made by Dr. Chaim Weizmann against the British responsible officials over a period of three decades, 1914- 1947).

In the presidential-election year 1956 the man who had succeeded to the burden in America, was Mr. John Foster Dulles, the Secretary of State. Immediately after the U.N. Security Council's "condemnation" of Israel in January Mr. Dulles announced that he was trying to gain the agreement of leading Democratic politicians to keep the Israeli-Arab question "out of debate in the Presidential election campaign" (Jan. 24, 1956). The *New York Times* commented, "it is known that Mr. Dulles has complained that Israeli Embassy officials here have sought to persuade candidates for congress to take positions favourable to the Israeli cause ... The Secretary is eager that neither party should complicate the delicate negotiations for a Mid-East settlement by discussing the Israeli question for personal or party advantage in the election campaign ... Specifically, he is apprehensive lest anything be said in the Presidential campaign that would encourage Israelis to think that the United States could condone or co-operate with an Israeli invasion of Arab territory."

Thus Mr. Dulles was complaining of the "political pressure" recorded by President Truman in his memoirs,[56] and was attempting in 1956 what Mr. Forrestal in 1947 had attempted, at the price of dismissal, breakdown and suicide. He at once came under attack from the press (equally in America and England) in the same way as Mr. Ernest Bevin and Mr. Forrestal in the years 1947-8. He received a reproachful letter from "a group of Republican members of Congress," to whom he placatingly replied (Feb. 7, 1955) that "The foreign policy of the United States embraces the preservation of the state of Israel ... We do not exclude the possibility of arms sales to Israel." By this time he had further sinned, for the *Jerusalem Post*, which in 1956 was a sort of *Court Gazette* for the Western capitals, announced that he had committed "a

---

[56] In the intervening years another book had appeared. Mr. Chesly Manly's *The U.N. Record*, which said that four senior officials of the American Foreign Service, called from the Middle East to Washington during the congressional elections of 1946 for consultation on the Palestine question, had presented the Arab case and received from President Truman the answer, "Sorry, gentlemen, I have to answer hundreds of thousands who are anxious for the success of Zionism; I do not have hundreds of thousands of Arabs among my constituents." Mr. Truman's submissiveness to Zionist pressure, when in office, and his complaint about it, when in retirement, thus are both on record.

minor but unfriendly act ... he received for 45 minutes a delegation of the American Council for Judaism."[57]

The American Zionist Council immediately "protested' against Mr. Dulles's proposal that the Palestine issue "be kept out of debate during the presidential election; its chairman, a Rabbi Irving Miller, called this "the misguided view that any particular segment of foreign policy should be withdrawn from the arena of *free and untrammelled* public discussion." As to this freedom from trammel, the following rare allusions to the state of affairs prevailing appeared at that time in the American press: "Israel's quarrels with her neighbours have been transferred to every American platform, where merely to explain why the Arabs feel the way they do is to become a candidate for professional extinction" (Miss Dorothy Thompson); "A pro-Egypt policy will make no votes for Republicans in New Jersey, Connecticut or Massachusetts and when one talks to professional politicians he hears much on the subject" (Mr. George Sokolsky); "The political masterminds argue that to get the Jewish vote in such critical states as New York, Massachusetts, Illinois, New Jersey and Pennsylvania the United States should go down the line against the Arabs" (Mr. John O'Donnell).

The next development was an announcement in the *New York Times* (Feb. 21, 1956) that Mr. Dulles would have "to face an investigation on foreign policy" called by the Senate Foreign Relations Committee "to enquire into the twistings and turnings of the Administration's arms policy in the Mid-East." Mr. Dulles duly appeared before the Committee (Feb. 24, 1956) and this led to a significant incident. In the ordinary way the public masses, in America as in England, are debarred from expressing any adverse opinion about the adventure in Palestine, so costly to them; candidates for election cannot expect party-nomination unless they subscribe to the Zionist view, and the press in general will not print any other. On this occasion the responsible Cabinet officer had an audience comprizing as many Americans as could crowd into the space reserved for spectators and they gave him ovations when he entered, while he spoke, and when he left.

The reason for these ovations was plain, and the incident showed how the general masses of the West would all react if their political leaders ever appealed to them candidly in this question. Mr. Dulles said among other things, "one of the greatest difficulties facing the United States in its role of attempted mediation between Arabs and Israelis is the belief of the Arab

---

[57] This is an example, in the new generation, of the "outside interference, entirely from Jews" of which Dr. Weizmann bitterly complained in the earlier one. The Council feared and fought the involvement of the West in Zionist chauvinism. It was headed by Mr. Lessing Rosenwald, formerly head of the great mercantile house of Sears, Roebuck, and Rabbi Elmer Berger. Meeting in Chicago at this period, it resolved that President Truman's memoirs "confirm that Zionist pressures – labelled as those of American Jews – were excessive beyond all bounds of propriety" and "offered a spectacle of American citizens advancing the causes of a foreign nationalism" The reader, if he refers to earlier chapters, will see how precisely the situation in England in 1914-1917 had been reproduced in America in 1947-8 and 1955-6.

world that Washington's approach would be guided by *domestic political pressures*" There was danger that the Israelis might "precipitate what is called a preventive war." If that occurred the United States "will not be involved on the side of Israel" because it had commitments with its allies to oppose any nation that started "aggression" in the Middle East. He "suggested several times that *domestic political pressures* were being applied to attempt to force the Administration to take an unduly and unwisely pro-Israel course in the Middle East."

What was applauded, then, is clear, and this was the first official and public allusion, within hearing of a general audience, to the clutch that holds the West in thrall. The demonstration of public approval did not diminish the "pressures" of which Mr. Dulles complained. A few weeks later (Apr. 12, 1956) he was hailed before Congressional leaders to report on the Middle East and told them "I fear the time may have passed for a peaceful solution." He pointed out that the two "key factors" in United States policy there were "in conflict," namely, "Retention of the immense oil resources of the region for the military and economic use of Western Europe," (these resources are at present in the Arab countries) and "preservation of Israel as a nation." The Democratic House leader, Mr. John McCormack then asked peremptorily, "Which policy comes first, saving Israel, or keeping hold of the oil?" By his answer, "We are trying to do both," Mr. Dulles showed that the entire West was more deeply than ever imprisoned in the insoluble dilemma created by Britain's original involvement in Zionism.

In the vain effort to "do both" Mr. Dulles soon made the matter worse. Apparently he never had any hope that his original proposal would succeed; he "gave a bellow of sardonic laughter" when asked, at a press conference at this time, if he truly believed that he could get the Arab-Israeli issue taken out of election politics. Even as he spoke to the Senate Committee (would those spectators have applauded, had they known?) the method was being devised whereby America could officially announce that it would *not* supply "arms to the Middle East" at all, and at the same time *would* ensure that *Israel* receive such arms, enabling it to launch the "preventive war" which the Secretary of State "feared." The device was similar to that used in the case of West German "reparations," which were exacted under American pressure and ensured the flow of money or goods to Israel without this appearing in any American budget.

Immediately after Mr. Dulles's report to the Senate Committee, and apparently in reply to it, Israeli troops made "a pre-arranged and planned" attack on the Egyptians in the Gaza area, killing thirty-eight persons (Feb. 27, 1956), and was condemned for "brutal aggression" by the U.N.M.A.C. Within a few weeks the columnists then began to hint at the new method of supplying arms to Israel: "If the United States sold arms to Israel, it would reopen the Communist pipeline of arms to the Arab States … apparently it is felt that the same would not be true if Britain, France and Canada met Israeli requests for weapons ... It is assumed here that if the Allies sell Israel arms, the United States can maintain its own position of impartiality."

This was "doing both" in practice. Rabbi Hillel Silver (the Zionist leader who had uttered the prayer for "grace and guidance" at the President's inauguration) then stated in Israel that "the Eisenhower Administration has not yet said the last word on arms for Israel" (*New York Times*, Apr. 4, 1956). Returned to Washington, he had "a very frank and friendly discussion" with the President. Then it was revealed that the United States was "discreetly encouraging the French and Canadian governments to sell arms to Israel" (*New York Times*, April 1956). Next, these proved in truth to be American-supplied arms, for the French Government officially announced (May 12, 1956) that the American Government "had agreed to a delay in deliveries to allow France to make speedily a last delivery of twelve Mystere IV planes to Israel." These were some of the French aircraft used in the attack an Egypt five months later; that the French Air Force itself would take part was not in May disclosed.[58]

In explanation: the American Government was financing the purchase of arms for its allies in the North Atlantic Treaty Organization at that time, by placing orders with the foreign manufacturers. These American-financed deliveries were diverted to Israel at American "encouragement." Thus the North Atlantic Treaty, supposed at the start to be an alliance of the West against "Soviet aggression" and "Communism," also was turned to the purpose of Zionism. Signed in 1949, the ostensible, original purpose was that the members (America and Canada, England, France and ten other European countries, and Turkey) would regard any attack on one as an attack on all and aid the one attacked.

Therefore the American Government, while attacking the Soviet Union for supplying Egypt with arms and declaring that it would not itself promote "the arms race" in the Middle East by supplying them to Israel, was in fact procuring arms for Israel to maintain its superiority over all seven Arab countries. Here Mr. Dulles operated with a Machiavellian touch which had the effect of oil on fire. The act of procurement was not even kept secret; as the above quotations show, it was given publicity and used as a vote-getting vaunt in that election campaign, from which Mr. Dulles had appealed for the Israeli-Arab issue to be kept aloof.

---

[58] Six months later, on the eve of the presidential election and immediately before the Israeli attack on Egypt, the *New York Daily News* appealed to "the Jewish voter" by recounting the following Republican services: "The Eisenhower Administration has not seen its way clear to supplying Israel with heavy hardware, because of various touchy international situations. However, the Administration, last April and May, did help Israel get 24 Mystere jet planes from France, and last month Canada announced sale of 24 Sabre jets to Israel. Mr. Dulles was declared by Israeli officials to have actively used United States Government influence in promoting both the French and Canadian plane sales."

A strange side effect on these machinations in the West was that statements made, on this particular question, by the utterly unscrupulous rulers in Moscow gained a look of honest respectability. For instance, the Soviet Government, when the Western uproar about "arms for Egypt" began, sent a note to the American, British, Egyptian and Czechoslovak Governments stating, "The Soviet Government holds that each state has the legitimate right to look after its defence and to buy weapons for its defence requirements from other states on usual commercial terms, and that no foreign state has the right to intervene." That was an irreproachable statement of the legal, and even moral position, and it was echoed by Israel, for while the Western rumpus welled the Israeli Foreign Minister, then Mr. Moshe Sharett, stated in New York (Nov. 10, 1955) "If driven to a tight corner and our existence is at stake we will seek and accept arms from any source in the world" (in answer to a question whether the Soviet had *offered* Israel arms). Thus the whole burden of the outcry in the West was in fact that Soviet arms ought not to go to the *Arab* states, and for this no moral or legal argument whatever can be found.

Against this background, "defenceless Israel" (Mr. Ben-Gurion) on April 16, 1956 held its anniversary parade with great display of United States, British and French aircraft and tanks *(New York Times,* Apr. 17); the Soviet weapons were presumably withheld from the parade on that occasion in harmony with the propaganda of that moment in the West. On April 24, in Jerusalem, Mr. Ben-Gurion once more proclaimed the nationalist and expansionist aim: "The continued ingathering of exiles is the supreme goal of Israel and an essential precondition for realization of the messianic mission which has made us an eternal people."

The subterfuge by means of which the United States procured arms for Israel while officially refusing to supply them ("Nobody particularly welcomes our decision not to sell weapons to Israel but to encourage other allies to do so, and to relinquish earmarked equipment for this purpose," *New York Times,* May 19, 1956) brought no respite to the American President. *Open* submission is the invariable requirement, and the Zionist wrath began to turn against him. On the eve of his second breakdown in health (in the early summer he had to undergo an operation for hepatitis) the jeer began to be thrown at him that he was but "a part-time president." A leading woman Zionist, Mrs Agnes Meyer, launched it by telling a Jewish audience in New York that while "the bastion of democracy" (Israel) was in peril "the President is not at his post in Washington; he is playing golf in Augusta," and urging him to ask himself "whether this nation can afford a part-time president." His second illness, which followed almost at once, stopped this particular attack for the time, but President Eisenhower, like others before him, was not allowed to forget that the full resources of Zionist propaganda might at any moment be turned against him if he stepped out of his predecessors' line.

While he struggled in these toils, across the Atlantic another Prime Minister seemed likely to be broken on the Zionist wheel. Sir Anthony Eden, in any other century, would have become a major statesman; in this one, the "commitment" he inherited was from the start of his premiership a millstone round his neck.

No politician in the world was equal to him, when he took the chief office in 1955, in qualification and experience. He was of the First War generation, so that the memory of Flanders fields formed the background of all his adult life, which thereafter was spent entirely in politics. He came of old family with an inherited tradition of service, and was gifted and personable. He rose to ministerial rank at an early age and with brief intervals held one high post after another for over twenty years, during which he came to know personally every dictator and parliamentary politician in Europe and North America. He thus gained a unique experience for the testing years ahead; only Sir Winston Churchill, in the entire world, had a comparable range of acquaintanceship, negotiation and in general of training in what was once held to be the art of statesmanship.

He was still young, for the chief office, when Sir Winston yielded to the law of age and handed on "the torch" to the man he had described as embodying "the life hope of the British nation" (1938), Mr. Eden (as he was in 1938) gained the hope of men of his generation through his resignation from the British Government in protest against the placation of Hitler, which (he rightly judged) was the one sure road to war. The event of October 1956 was made harder for his contemporaries to endure by the fact that his name was given to it.

I knew Mr. Eden, as a foreign correspondent may know a politician, in the years that led to the Second War, and on the strength of our similar feelings at that darkling time was later able to write to him at moments when he seemed to be losing touch with the mind of his generation; and to receive pleasant reply, acknowledging earlier acquaintanceship and perusal of my books. I saw him, in 1935 emerge, with troubled mien, from a first encounter with Hitler, who in menacing tones had told him that the German air force (then officially non-existent) was greater than the English one. I accompanied him to Moscow and was able to confirm with him something I had heard of his first encounter with Stalin: that the Georgian bandit had pointed to the little point on the world's map that represented England and said how strange it was that so small a country should hold the key to the world's peace (a true statement at that time). Having these personal memories, I was probably more aghast than most men when I learned of the deed to which he was misled in October 1956.

From the start in May 1955 the professional observer saw that he was in truth, not so much Prime Minister, as Minister for the Jewish Question, in his generation represented by the Zionist state and its ambition. This meant that his whole term of office would fall under that shadow and that his political fate would be determined by his actions in regard to Zionism, not by his success or failure in matters of native interest. That was shown on the eve of his premiership, when he was still Foreign Secretary for a few weeks more. The British Government had concluded an arrangement with Iran and Turkey to ensure the defence of British interests in the Middle East, the oil resources of which were vital to England and the Antipodean Dominions. The debate in the House of Commons ignored this aspect and raged around the effect of the agreement "on Israel," so that two lonely members (among 625) protested: "This debate is not about Palestine and the Foreign Secretary must look after world interests and the interests of Britain, even though they cause annoyance and embarrassment to other states" (Mr Thomas Reid); "Judging by nearly every speech from hon. Members on both sides of the House, one might be forgiven for imagining that the debate was primarily concerned with the effect of a pact on Israel instead of the improvement of our worldwide defensive system against the threat of Russian imperialism" (Mr. F. W. Bennett).

To this a Jewish Socialist member replied, "Why not?" In effect, it was by that time almost impossible to debate any major issue save in terms of its effect for Israel, and this plainly prefigured the course of Sir Anthony's premiership.

During the remaining months of 1955, as Prime Minister, he continued to struggle with "the Middle East question," at one time suggesting that an international force be placed between Israel and the Arab states (the United States demurred) and at another, that Israel might agree to minor frontier rectifications, having seized in 1948 more territory than that "awarded" to it by the United Nations (this brought angry Zionist charges in the New York newspapers that "Britain has now joined the ranks of Israel's enemies"). Then the presidential-election year, and Sir Anthony's crisis, began. The Zionist machine went into top gear, playing Washington against London and London against Washington with the skill of forty years' experience. In March a significant thing occurred; unknown to the world, it made an early attack on Egypt seem a certainty to the diligent watcher of events.

On the eve of the Jewish Passover the mysterious "Voice of America" broadcast a commemoration, laden with explosive topical allusions, of "the escape of the Jews from *the Egyptian captivity*." Considered in its obvious relationship to the propaganda bombardment of Egypt which was then in progress in Washington and London, this plainly portended violent events before the next Passover. The American people in general know nothing of what "The Voice of America" says, or to whom it speaks. Even my research has not discovered what official department is supposed to supervise this "voice," which to listening peoples far away is taken to express the intentions of the American Government. I was able to learn that its funds, budgetary and other, are immense and that it is largely staffed by Eastern Jews. It appears to work in irresponsibility and secrecy.[59]

From this moment the whole weight of Western propaganda was turned against Egypt. The events which followed might be considered in the light of Secretary of War, Henry Stimson's diarial note in the period preceding Pearl Harbour, to the effect that the aim of President Roosevelt's administration was to manoeuvre Japan into "firing the first shot." Subsequent events had all the appearance of being designed to manoeuvre Egypt into firing the first shot. Egypt did not do this. Then the world found that the firing of a first shot was no longer necessary to qualify as an aggressor; the country in question could be dubbed the aggressor while it was being invaded, and even before that; so far had the resources of mass-propaganda developed in the 20th century. All the "condemnations" of Israel on the score of aggression had meant nothing.

This crisis-period began on March 7, 1956 (just before the "Voice of America's" Egyptian-captivity broadcast) when Sir Anthony Eden again faced the House of Commons on the eternal question. By that time his Socialist

---

[59] During the Hungarian uprising against the Soviet in October-November 1956, several American correspondents, returning from the shambles, and Hungarian fugitives attributed a large measure of responsibility for the tragedy to this "Voice." The Americans had found the Hungarian people confident of American intervention; the Hungarians complained that, although the word "revolt" was not used, the "Voice" in effect incited and instigated revolt and held out the prospect of American succour. At the same time President Eisenhower told the American people, "We have never counselled the captive peoples to rise against armed force." Similar criticisms were made against "Radio Free Europe," a private American organization which operated from Germany under West German Government license.

One of the first Hungarian refugees to reach America complained that the Voice of America and Radio Free Europe for years "picked at us" to revolt, but when the national uprising came no American help was given (*New York Times*, Nov. 23, 1956).

The West German Government ordered an investigation into Radio Free Europe's broadcasts during the Hungarian uprising (it operated from Munich) after widespread charges appeared in the West German press that it had, in effect, played a provocative part; as example, a script prepared on Nov. 5, 1956, while the uprising was in progress, told the Hungarian people that "Western military aid could not be expected before 2am tomorrow," an obvious intimation that it would come at some moment (*N.Y.T.*, Dec. 8, 1956) The gravest implication of a provocative purpose was contained in statements made by Mrs Anna Kethly, head of the Hungarian Social Democratic party, who escaped during the brief liberation of the country. She said that while she was in jail in 1952 Radio Free Europe in a broadcast to the captive countries said "that I was leading the underground liberation movement from my jail and quoted the names of several leaders of the alleged movement. I was taken out of the jail where I had been in complete seclusion since 1950 and confronted with hundreds of former militants of the Social Democratic party and the trade unions. All of them were tortured by the political police to confess their participation in the non-existent anti-Communist plot. There was absolutely no truth in the Radio Free Europe report; I had lived in complete seclusion since my arrest and had met nobody. Radio Free Europe has gravely sinned by making the Hungarian people believe that Western military aid was coming, when no such aid was planned" (*N.Y.T.*, Nov. 30, 1956).

Thus America spoke with two voices, those of the President addressing himself officially to the world, and of the "Voice" speaking in more dangerous terms over the head of the American people to the peoples of the world. At this period the *New York Times* described the *official* line: "High officials have made clear privately that the Administration wants to avoid being identified solely with Israel and thus surrendering the Arab countries to the influence of the Soviet Union." The Arab peoples, if they ever heard of these "private" intimations, could not be expected to believe them, in view of what they heard from "The Voice of America" about the liberation of the Jews from "the Egyptian captivity."

adversaries (despite the many "condemnations" of Israel) were furious in their demand for arms for Israel and "a new treaty of guarantees for Israel"; like the New York politicians, they saw the hope of office in new submissions to Zion. The Prime Minister "was subjected to a storm of vituperation and abuse beyond anything heard in the House of Commons since the last days of Neville Chamberlain's prime ministership" (the *New York Times*); "It was a scene which, for a time, seemed to shock even those who had caused it; the Speaker himself had to intervene to plead that the House should give the Prime Minister a hearing" (the *Daily Telegraph*). Sir Anthony vainly protested that he had thereto been heard with courtesy "for over thirty years" by the House. At that moment he might have hoped for American support, for on the same day President Eisenhower said it was "useless to try to maintain peace in the Middle East by arming Israel, with its 1,700,000 people, against 40,000,000 Arabs" (the American procurement of arms for Israel was then under way).

In England Sir Anthony found all hands against him. The *Daily Telegraph* (ostensibly of his own party) might in its news reports appear shocked by his treatment in the House, but editorially it said the case for giving Israel arms was "incontrovertible," a word which always spares the need for supporting argument. His opponents, the Socialists, cast off all restraint in their eagerness to overthrow him by way of Israel. The leading leftist journal, the *New Statesman,* in two successive issues said that England had no right or means to wage war in any circumstances whatever and should lay down all arms ("Effective defence is now beyond our means and disarmament is the only alternative to annihilation," March 10) and that England should arm Israel and pledge itself to go to war for Israel ("War is less likely if Israel is supplied with up to date arms and the Labour Party is correct in urging that Israel must now have them ... The problem is not so much the undesirability of guaranteeing a frontier which has not yet been formally established ... but the military problem of *assembling and delivering the necessary force* ... Is sufficient naval strength available in the Eastern Mediterranean? Does Mr Gaitskell (the Socialist leader) "even feel sure that the British public would back him in going to war, probably without the endorsement of the United Nations, in defence of Israel?" (March 17).

The endless effects of the original, apparently small commitment to Zion may be studied in such quotations. Sir Anthony Eden on this occasion appeared to be trying, in unison with the United States Government, to stem a lunatic tide, but he gave a "warning to Egypt" which was not then justified and was ominous, as events proved. At that moment both the British and American Governments were (officially) courting Egyptian friendship in the hope of helping to pacify the Middle East. To that joint end England, "under

American pressure" was preparing to withdraw its troops from the Suez Canal.[60]

Why Sir Anthony Eden yielded without security to "the pressure" to let go of what, immediately after, was proclaimed to be "the vital lifeline" of the British Commonwealth is of those questions which politicians never answer. "Pressure" from Washington in matters related to the Middle East has in the last four decades always been Zionist pressure, ultimately; and about this time an Egyptian journalist, Mr. Ibrahim Izzat, was cordially received by the Premier, Foreign Minister and Labour Minister of Israel who told him "Israel and Egypt had the identical aim of opposing British influence in the Middle East" *(Ros el Youssef,* May, 1956; *New York Times,* May 20, 1956).

The effect of this submission to pressure very soon became clear: it was to be war, involving England in a great humiliation and fiasco. The British withdrawal was supposed to be one-half of a larger, Anglo-American arrangement for "winning the friendship of the Arabs," and the American half had yet to be performed. This was to join with the British Government and the World Bank in providing $900,000,000 for the construction of a dam on the Nile at Aswan (the offer had been made to Egypt in December 1955).

The chronology of events again becomes important. The British troops withdrew from the Suez Canal in June 1956, as undertaken. On July 6, 1956 the State Department spokesman told the press that the Aswan Dam offer "still stood." A few days later the Egyptian Ambassador in Washington announced that Egypt had "definitely decided that she wanted Western help for the dam." On July 19 the Egyptian Ambassador called on Mr. Dulles to accept the offer. He was told that the United States government had changed its mind. In London the day before the Foreign Office spokesman had announced that the British share of the offer "still stood." On July 19 the spokesman informed *the press* (not the Egyptian Ambassador) that the British offer, too, was withdrawn. The spokesman declined to give reasons but admitted to "continuous consultation between Whitehall and Washington."

Therefore the "pressure" to infuriate the Egyptians by this contemptuous affront came from the same quarter as the "pressure" to mollify them by withdrawing from the Suez Canal. The British Government was left far out on a limb, in the American phrase; if the first submission was made in reliance on President Eisenhower's announcement of February (that he wanted "to stem the deterioration in relations between the Arab nations and the United States" and "restore the Arabs' confidence and trust" in America), the about-face in the Aswan Dam offer should have warned it, and it would then have saved much if it had resisted the "pressure" in the second

---

[60] The fact that this "'pressure" was used is authentic. It was everywhere recorded in terms of an American success by the American press, for instance, "Secretary of State Dulles was confident that he could win the friendship of the Arabs, as when he brought pressure on the British to get out of Egypt, while retaining that of the Israelis *(New York Times,* Oct. 21, 1956).

case. I cannot remember any more calculated or offensive provocation to a government with which "the West" was ostensibly seeking friendship. Such behaviour by the Washington and London governments has only become imaginable since they fell under the thrall of Zionism. American withdrawal of the offer, and the manner of withdrawal (its imitation by London is beyond comment) were clearly the true start of the war crisis of 1956, but the original source, the "pressure," was not "American." "Some Congressmen feared Zionist disapproval," discreetly remarked the *New York Times* of the withdrawn offer to Egypt; and this was election year.

Within the week President Nasser of Egypt nationalized the Suez Canal and at once the air was filled with war-talk, as in 1952-3 during the episode of "the Jewish doctors." From that moment President Nasser received the "wicked man" treatment; this is the sure sign of the imminence of war. I have seen many "wicked men" built up in my life, and have observed that this propaganda can be turned on and off as by a tap, and infused with toxic effect into the public mind:

Cursed juice of hebenon in a vial; And into mine ear did pour The leprous distilment ...[61]

My early childhood was clouded by the wickedness of The Mad Mullah (a Muslim leader now universally forgotten) and of a respectable old Boer called Paul Kruger. Of all the figures in this Chamber of Horrors, built around me as I went along, I now see that nearly all were no better or worse than those who called them wicked.

Even before the war-talk reached the "wicked man" stage, and long before the unprecedented provocation of July 19, (which still provoked no warlike act from Egypt), President Nasser had been declared the aggressor in a war yet to begin. In March Mr. Ben- Gurion stated at Tel Aviv that early delivery of arms to Israel alone could prevent "an *attack* by the Arab states within the next few months" and added that the aggressor "*would be* the Egyptian dictator Nasser." On April 13 Sir Winston Churchill emerged from a year's retirement to tell a Primrose League audience that "prudence and honour" demanded British aid for Israel *if it were attacked by Egypt*. Sir Winston expressed implicit, but clear approval of the Israeli attack *on* Egypt which the "activists" in Israel were then demanding: "If Israel is dissuaded from using the life force of their race to *ward off* the Egyptians until the Egyptians have learned to use the Russian weapons with which they have been supplied and the Egyptians then attack, it will become not only a matter of prudence but a measure of honour to make sure that they are not the losers by waiting." This was followed in May by an Israeli attack *on* Egyptian troops in the Gaza area in which about 150 men, women and children were killed or wounded.

[61] [Hamlet, 1, v.]

Nevertheless, the outcry about the "wicked man" and "Egyptian aggression" grew ever louder in the West.

The state of servitude into which England had fallen at this period was shown by two symbolic events. In June 1956 the "Anglo- Jewish Community" held a banquet at the Guildhall to commemorate "the three hundredth anniversary of the resettlement of the Jews in the British Isles"; the young Queen's consort, the Duke of Edinburgh, was required to appear in a Jewish skullcap. In September the "Cromwell Association" held a service at the statue of the regicide and butcher of Drogheda to celebrate this same fiction (that he "restored" the Jews to England three hundred years before). In his speech the president of this body, a Mr. Isaac Foot, recommended that the young Prince Charles, when he reached the throne, take the name of "Oliver II," because "We don't want Charles III."[62]

After President Nasser's seizure of the Suez Canal the war cries from the West rose to a high note. "Nationalization" in itself was not startling or shocking enough, in 1956, to account for it. America had accepted the seizure of foreign-owned oilfields, Mexico agreeing (as President Nasser agreed) to pay the going price for the property; domestically, America, through the Tennessee Valley Authority, was already treading this well-worn path to impoverishment; in England the Socialist Government had nationalized railways and coalmines. A valid legal or moral ground for violent denunciation was not easy to find, although shades of difference, admittedly existed between President Nasser's act and the many precedents and his action was obviously one of protest against provocation, not of rational policy.

In any case, the only effective answer, if his act was intolerable, was to reoccupy the Canal forthwith, and that was not done. Instead, all the oracles, as if reading from a long-prepared script, began to dub him "Hitler." Premier Ben-Gurion began with "dictator," which soon became "Fascist dictator," and the French Prime Minister (a M. Guy Mollet at that instant) changed this to "Hitler." Thereafter the campaign followed the lines of the one against Stalin in 1952-3. Dictator-Fascist Dictator-Hitler: the inference was plain; President Nasser was to be depicted, and punished if he were punished, as an enemy of *the Jews*.

When Sir Anthony Eden again rose in the House of Commons (Aug. 9, 1956) to grapple with that monster of his dreams, "the Middle East question," the Socialist leader, Mr. Hugh Gaitskell, said, "It is all terribly familiar … It is exactly the same as we encountered with Mussolini and *Hitler*

---

[62] The same shadow was with deliberate intent cast across the coronation of Queen Elizabeth in 1953. As part of the festival the newly- crowned queen reviewed at Spithead a great assembly of war vessels from every country that could send a ship. Among the many craft, between the lines of which the Queen's ship passed, was one alone, the crew of which did not cheer (a mistake, the later explanation asserted). This Soviet ship was the *Sverdlov*, named for Yankel Sverdlov, the assassin of the Romanoff family, in whose honour the town where they were butchered, Ekaterinburg, was renamed Sverdlovsk.

before the war." Another Socialist speaker, Mr. Paget Q.C., (events having altered K.C's[63]) baited him thus:

"This weekend technique is just what we got from *Hitler.* Are you aware of the consequences of not answering force with force until it is too late?"

The Socialists were deliberately prodding Sir Anthony to use force (they shouted "Murderer" at him when he used it) by these taunting allusions to his political past. He was the man who resigned in 1938 in protest against the placation of Hitler, and his resignation was immediately vindicated by Hitler's invasion of Austria. That *was* "force," long foreseen, and Mr. Eden of 1938 was right. In 1956 the case was different, and no comparison was possible. Egypt was not a great military power but a very weak one. Egypt had not been "appeased" after the British withdrawal, but subjected to provocation by public humiliation. Egypt was not a proven aggressor; it had been the victim of attack and Israel had declared that it would make war on Egypt.

Therefore the comparison with "Hitler" was absurd, unless it was intended solely to denote that the Zionists held Egypt for their enemy. Nevertheless Sir Anthony Eden yielded to this fiction (perhaps the memory of 1938 had too strong a hold on him) for he alluded to President Nasser as "a Fascist plunderer whose appetite grows with feeding," which was just the language he and Mr. Churchill had rightly used about Hitler eighteen years before. I must add that I do not find these exact words in the text of his speech but this is the form in which they reached "the mob" through the *New York Times* and that is what counts, as Prime Ministers should know. For the rest, Sir Anthony based his attack on President Nasser on the argument that the Suez Canal "is vital to other countries in all parts of the world ... a matter of life and death to us all ... the canal must be run efficiently and kept open, as it always has been in the past, as a free and secure international waterway *for the ships of all nations* ..."

But President Nasser had not *closed* the canal, only nationalized it. It *was* "open" to *the ships of all nations,* with one exception. In those five words lay the secret. The *only* country which was denied full freedom of passage was *Israel,* with which Egypt was still technically at war; Egypt had been stopping ships bound for Israel and examining them for arms. This was the *only* case of interference; ergo, Sir Anthony represented *only that case*; not any British one. However, he concluded: "My friends, we do not intend to seek a solution by force,"

In the following weeks, while "a solution" was sought at various conferences in London and Washington, the press informed the masses that "the Egyptians" would not be able to run the canal, where traffic would soon

---

[63] [Queen's Counsel / King's Counsel.]

break down. In fact, they proved able to operate it and shipping continued to pass without hindrance, with the one exception. By clear implication, therefore, the case of Israel was the sole one on which Sir Anthony's Government could rest its increasingly angry protest. This was soon made clear. On August 22, 1956 Mrs Rose Halprin, acting chairman of the Jewish Agency for Palestine, stated in the *New York Times* that "*the only legal case* which the Western powers have against Egypt in terms of the contravention of the 1888 convention is *Egypt's denial of the canal to Israel ships and the strictures on ships bound for Israel.*"

Mrs Halprin's statement of the legal position is correct. If the whole dispute rested on a point of *law*, then the *only* case which could be invoked was that of Israel; and that would open the whole question of the *legality* of the creation of Israel itself and of the unterminated state of war between Israel and Egypt. Therefore any government which joined in the uproar against President Nasser was in fact acting on behalf of Israel and Israel alone, and was prejudging all *legal* questions in favour of Israel.

By October Sir Anthony Eden had gone further in presuming Egyptian aggression. I have not the text of this speech but the version distributed by the Associated Press, and therefore reproduced in thousands of newspapers all over the world, says, "Prime Minister Eden predicted tonight that President Nasser *would* attack Israel next *if* he got away with seizure of the Suez Canal. Sir Anthony hinted that Britain *would go to Israel's rescue with arms* if necessary" (Sept. 13, 1956).

Thus the British Prime Minister was sliding on a slippery path. Within the space of six weeks the "vital lifeline" and "matter of life and death" theme had become subordinate and the world faced the menace of war based on something that the Egyptian president *would* do *if* something else happened. From this point on "the mob" was fed with news of an impending Egyptian attack on Israel (the "interference with international navigation" theme was dropped, as it could not be maintained) and in time this took on so definite a note that many casual readers, I fancy, must have thought that Egypt *had* already attacked Israel. I give one of many examples (from the London *Weekly Review*, September 1956, a few weeks before the Israeli attack on Egypt): "We can be *absolutely certain* that the Arabs, encouraged by Russia, *will attack Israel. This is now beyond all doubt and should form the basis of our calculations.*"

In writing this book I have been chiefly impelled by the hope of giving the later reader, in what I hope will be a more rational time, some idea of the astonishing condition of the public prints during the 1950's. He will certainly be unable to comprehend the things that happened unless he is aware of this regime of sustained mis-information and of the boundless lengths to which it was carried. The last statement quoted came after years of repeated Israeli attacks on the various Arab neighbours and of repeated United Nations condemnations of these acts.

In the way I have summarized above the ground was prepared, during the first nine months of the presidential-election year, for the climactic events of October. Arms continued to move into Israel from the West. After the seizure of the Suez Canal Sir Anthony Eden announced that "all arms shipments to Egypt had been stopped"; in the same month (July) two British destroyers were delivered to Israel. Throughout the spring and summer months France, under American "pressure," supplied jet fighters and other weapons to Israel. In September Canada, at the same prompting, agreed to send jet aircraft to Israel, the Ottawa Government announcing that it had "consulted with the United States before the decision was made" *(New York Times,* Sept. 22, 1956).

All this time the presidential-election campaign continued. The Democrats, eager to regain the White House, exceeded all past performances in their bids for "the Jewish vote" (the Mayor of New York demanded that Israel should receive arms "as a gift"); the Republican incumbents were slightly more reserved. However, when the rival nomination conventions were held (the Republican at San Francisco, the Democratic at Chicago, both in August) there was little to choose between the submissions which each party made (so that the *Jerusalem Post* might have repeated, and perhaps did repeat its dictum of 1952, that for the Jewish voter there was "little to choose" between the presidential aspirants).

The only passage of any vital meaning in the "foreign policy programmes" adopted by the two parties related, in each case, to Israel; the other foreign policy statements were platitudinous. The commitments to Israel were in both cases specific.

The Republican Party programme, on which President Eisenhower was unanimously elected candidate, said: "We regard the preservation of Israel as an important tenet of American foreign policy. We are determined that the integrity of an independent Jewish state shall be maintained. We shall support the independence of Israel against armed aggression."

The Democratic Party programme said: "The Democratic Party will act to redress the dangerous imbalance of arms in the area created by the shipment of Communist arms to Egypt, by selling or supplying defensive weapons to Israel, and will take such steps, including security guarantees, as may be required to deter aggression and war in the area." (The phrase, "dangerous imbalance of arms," reflected the propagandist fiction that Israel was "defenceless" and the Arab countries strong; the truth, a little earlier established by Mr Hanson Baldwin was that Israel was stronger in arms than all seven Arab countries together).

These two policy statements gave the picture of a world in the Zionist thrall, and complemented the statements then being made by the British Government. They had no relation to any native American interest but reflected simply Zionist control of the election-machine, or the unshakeable belief of the party-managers in that control. (On this occasion events appeared to justify that belief; the Democratic Party, the higher bidder, captured Congress, although the nominal "Republican" was re-elected President).

The only other event of importance in the two conventions was one which may appear to have little bearing on the theme of this book, but in the later sequel might prove to be of direct significance; the re-nomination of Mr. Richard Nixon as President Eisenhower's running-mate (and in effect as Vice-President). Mr Eisenhower's state of health made the Vice-Presidency more important than usual, and the possibility that Mr. Nixon might succeed to the Presidency between 1956 and 1960 was evidently regarded as a major danger by the powers that govern America today, so that a supreme effort was made to prevent his nomination. That was not remarkable, in this century; what was remarkable is that the attempt *failed*. At some time men will obviously emerge who will break the thrall that lies on American and British political life, and this failure was a portent of that coming liberation, so that the person of Mr. Richard Nixon gains a symbolic importance in our day, even though he, if he became President, might find himself unable to break the bonds.

The reason for this powerful enmity to Mr. Nixon is that he is not an "internationalist." Far from it, he played the decisive part in the unmasking and conviction of Mr. Alger Hiss, the Soviet agent in Mr. Roosevelt's administration. This is the true reason why he has ever since had a uniformly bad "press," not only in America but elsewhere in the Western world. Having that black mark against him, he is held to be a man who, in the chief office, might conceivably rebel against the constraints to which American Presidents and

British Prime Ministers, almost without exception, have submitted in the last fifty years and which Vice-President's automatically incur.[64]

Hence a campaign of great force and ingenuity was begun to prevent his nomination. A member of the President's own political household (and nominal party) was released from duty for some weeks to conduct a nationwide "Stop Nixon" offensive, with committee-rooms, placards and meetings. This had no effect on the general public, with whom Mr. Nixon appears to be popular. Then, for his particular discomfiture, new tactics were introduced at the convention of the rival, Democratic party. Instead of the elected nominee (Mr Adlai Stevenson) choosing his own vice-presidential "running mate" as on former occasions, the selection of a "running mate" was thrown open to vote and of various competitors Senator Estes Kefauver

---

[64] The inevitable twin-reproach, of "anti-semitism," was also raised against him during the election campaign. A rabbi who knew him well came forward to defend him against it.

(an exceptionally zealous Zionist) received the nomination as vice-presidential candidate.

The aim of the manoeuvre was to force the Republican Party's convention to follow this "democratic procedure" and also to submit the choice of the vice-presidential candidate to vote. It did so and Mr. Nixon, like Mr. Eisenhower, received a unanimous vote. This event, and his deportment during President Eisenhower's illnesses, made Mr. Nixon's prospects of becoming President in his own right one day much better than they had ever been deemed before. His story up to now makes him a hopeful figure (as Mr. Eden appeared to be in 1938), and in the chief office he might conceivably produce a sanative effect on American policy and foreign relations.

After the nominations America sat back with relief, for Mr. Eisenhower's re-election was held sure and he had been given a rousing build-up in the press as "the man who kept us out of war." The phrase was reminiscent of similar phrases used about Mr. Woodrow Wilson in 1916 and Mr. Roosevelt in 1940, but by 1956 a respite of three years was held to be a boon and he was given credit for this period of "peace," such as it was.

I was a witness of this election, as of the one in 1952, and realized that in fact war, localized or general, was near. I felt that a respite, at least, would be gained if election day (Nov. 6) passed without the eruption in the Middle East which for months obviously had been preparing (once the election is over the Zionist power to exert pressure diminishes, for a little while). I remember saying to an American friend on October 20 that if the next seventeen days could be got over without war the world might be spared it for another three or four years.[65]

On October 29, eight days before the election, war came, by obvious predetermination of the moment held most suitable to cause consternation in Washington and London. From that moment events swept along on a tide of elemental forces let loose and only much later will mankind be able to see what was destroyed and what survived. For Britain and the family of oversea nations offspring from it, this was nearly ruin, the foreseeable end of the involvement in Zionism.

---

[65] I had in mind what is known to American politicians as "the Farley law." Named after an exceptionally astute party-manager, Mr James A. Farley, who was held to have contrived the early electoral triumphs of Mr. Roosevelt, the essence of this "law" is that American voters have decided by mid-October for whom they will vote and only their candidate's death, war or some great scandal between then and November 6 can change their minds. The morning after the Israeli attack on Egypt Mr. John O'Donnell wrote, "Spokesmen in the worried State Department, Pentagon" (War Office) "and headquarters of both parties agree that the Israelis launched their attack on Egypt because they were convinced that the United States would take no action in an Israeli war so close to the Presidential elections ... Word came through to political headquarters that American Zionists had informed Tel Aviv that Israel would probably fare better under a Democratic administration of Stevenson and Kefauver than under a Republican regime of Eisenhower and Nixon" (*New York Daily News*).

On October 29, 1956 the Israeli Government announced that it had begun a full-scale invasion of Egypt and that its troops had "advanced 75 miles into Egypt's Sinai Peninsula."[66]

The news, coming after the long series of earlier attacks on the Arabs and their repeated "condemnation" by the United Nations, sent a shock of repugnance round the world. At that very moment the Hungarians were fighting and winning their people's war against the Communist revolution. The two destructive forces released from Russia in October 1917 stood self-condemned by acts equally brutal. They were destroying themselves; there was no need to destroy them. At this instant great counter-forces of universal reprobation were released which would have been too strong for them. Not even the "Zionist pressure" in New York could make this deed appear to be "Egyptian aggression" or induce the public multitudes to accept it. This was a gift from heaven, releasing "The West" from both its dilemmas. It only needed to stand aside and, for once, let "world opinion" do the work; for on *this* occasion there *was* world opinion, produced by deeds that could not be hidden, disguised or misrepresented by "the press."

Within twenty-four hours the golden opportunity was cast away, The British and French Governments announced that they would invade the Suez Canal zone "unless Israeli and Egyptian troops agree to stop fighting and withdraw ten miles from the canal within twelve hours," As this would have left the Israeli troops nearly a hundred miles inside Egyptian territory, the demand obviously was not meant to be accepted by Egypt. Thereon the British and French air forces began intensive bombing of Egyptian airfields

---

[66] At the very moment of the invasion of Egypt another massacre of Arabs was carried out *inside* Israel and at a point far removed from the Egyptian frontier, namely, the frontier with Jordan, on the other side of Israel. 48 Arabs, men, women and children, of the village of Kafr Kassem, were killed in cold blood. This new Deir Yasin could only be taken by the Arabs, inside or outside Israel, as a symbolic warning that the fate of "utter destruction ... man, woman and child ... save nothing that breatheth" hung over *all* of them, for these people were of the small Arab population that stayed in Israel after Deir Yasin and the creation of the new state. The deed was officially admitted, after it had become widely known and was the subject of an Arab protest en route to the United Nations (where it seems to have been ignored up to the date of adding this footnote), by the Israeli premier, Mr. Ben-Gurion six weeks later (Dec. 12). He then told the Israeli Parliament that the murderers "faced trial," but as the Arabs remembered that the murderers of Deir Yasin, after "facing trial" and being convicted, had been released at once and publicly feted, this was of small reassurance to them. Up to the time this footnote (Dec 20) I have not seen any allusion, among the millions of words that have been printed, to the fate of the 215,000 fugitive Arabs (U.N. Report, April 1956) who were huddled in the Gaza Strip when the Israelis attacked it and Egypt. The Israeli Government has announced that it will *not* give up this territory: earlier, it had announced that it would under no conditions permit the return of the Arab refugees to Israel. Therefore the lot of this quarter-million people, which at any earlier time would have received the indignant compassion of the world, has been entirely ignored. Presumably they are referred to in the only statement I have seen on the subject, the letter of eleven Arab states to the United Nations of Dec 14, stating that "Hundreds of men, women and children have been ruthlessly murdered in cold blood," but there seems small prospect of impartial investigation or corroboration, and the Arab letter itself says, "The whole story will never be told and the extent of the tragedy will never be known." However, in the particular case of Kafr Kassem the facts are on authentic record.

and other targets and by destroying Egypt's air weapon gave unchallenged victory to the invader.

The future reader will hardly be able to imagine the feelings of an Englishman of my kind, who heard the news in America. Shame is too small a word, but as it is the only word I use it to express something I felt more deeply than even at the time of Munich, when I resigned from *The Times* as the only protest (a stupid one, I now estimate) I could make. I shall always remember the fair-mindedness of Americans at this moment. Incredulous, shocked and bewildered, none that I met gave way to the glee over a British discomfiture which is instinctive, though irrational, in many Americans. Some of them realized that American policy, twisting and turning under "the pressure," had mainly caused this calamitous denouement and shared my sense of shame. These were the ones who understood that the shame was that of all "the West," in its servience, not particularly of England or America.

However, the blame, as distinct from the shame, at that moment was Britain's. The consequences of this act reach so far into the future that they cannot be estimated now, but one thing will always be clear: that the glorious opportunity offered by the simultaneous events in Sinai and Hungary was thrown away, apparently through a series of miscalculations unprecedented, I should think, in history.

I aim to show here that merely as a political gamble (surely it cannot be considered as an act of statesmanship) this was like the act of a man who might wager his entire fortune on a horse already withdrawn from a race. By no imaginable turn of events could it have benefited England or France.

Of the three parties concerned, Israel had nothing to lose and much to gain: the world's instant reprobation glanced off Israel when England and France dashed in to snatch the aggressor's cloak and win its war; it was left deep in Egyptian territory, cheering its "conquest." France had no more to lose, unhappily, than the lady in the soldiers' song who "lost her name again." France was left by its revolution the land of the recurrent fiasco, ever unable to rise out of the spiritual despondency where it lay. During 160 years it tried every form of government conceivable by man and found reinvigoration and new confidence in none. Its prime ministers changed so often that the public masses seldom knew their names; shadowy figures, they seemed indistinguishable even in appearance, and the French politician acquired a tradition of venality; the American comedian said he went to London to see the changing of the Guard and to Paris to see the changing of the Cabinet. A country rendered incapable, by a series of corrupted governments, of resistance to the German invader of its own soil in 1940, in 1956 invaded Egyptian soil in the service of Israel. But this was only an episode in the sad story of France since 1789 and could not much affect its future.

England was a different case, an example, a great name and a tradition of honourable dealing not less in hard times than in good ones. England had a soul to lose, in such company, and no world to gain. England had shown wisdom in applying the lessons of history. It had not tried to petrify an empire and to ward off the tides of change with bayonets. It had accepted the inevitability of change and successfully ridden those tides, successively transforming its Empire of colonies, first into a Commonwealth of independent oversea nations and colonies, and next, as more and more colonies attained to self-government, into a great family of peoples, held together by no compulsion at all, but by intangible bonds which, as the Coronation of the young Queen Elizabeth showed in 1953, were, if anything stronger than ever before, not weaker. The avoidance of any rigid organization based on force, and the ever-open door to new forms of relationship between these associated peoples, made the family of nations sprung from "England" and "the British Empire" a unique experiment in human history, in 1956, and one of boundless promise, if the same course were continued.[67] The outstanding result of the apparent *weakness* of this elastic process was the *strength* it produced under strain; it yielded, without collapsing, to stresses which would have snapped a rigid organization based on dogmatic rules, and became taut again when the strain was past.

Thus England had the whole achievement of British history to imperil, or lose, in 1956 by any act which, in fact or even in appearance, reversed the policy, or method, which had gained it so great a reputation and produced, on balance, good material results. In that light the British Government's action of October 30, 1956 has to be considered.

If the Suez Canal was "vital" to it, why had it ever withdrawn? If a friendly Egypt was vital after the withdrawal, why the calculated affront in July? If British ships were freely using the Canal, why the pretence that it was not "open" and that "the freedom and security of international shipping" were endangered? If any vital *British* interest was at stake, why did it wait until *Israel* attacked Egypt and only *then* attack Egypt?

The question may be turned and scrutinized from every angle, and always the same answer emerges. This cannot have been done for the sake of Britain or France; the moment chosen is incriminating. It would not have been done at all, had Israel not existed; ergo, the humiliation which England (and France, if the reader will) suffered was in that cause. The involvement begun by Mr. Balfour fifty years before produced its logical consequence, and

---

[67] This method is the exact opposite of that by which the world would be ruled under the "world-government" schemes propounded from New York by Mr. Bernard Baruch and his school of "internationalists." Their concept may in fact be called that of "super-Colonialism" and rests entirely on rigid organization, force and penalty. Speaking at the dedication of a memorial to President Woodrow Wilson in Washington Cathedral in December 1956, Mr. Baruch again raised his demand, in the following, startlingly contradictory terms: "After two world wars ... we still seek what Wilson sought ... a reign of law based *on the consent of the governed* ... that reign of law can exist only when there is *the force* to maintain it ... which is why we must continue to insist that any agreement on the control of atomic energy and disarmament be accompanied by ironclad provisions for inspection, control *and punishment of transgressors*."

by this act its continuance was ensured when release from it was at last at hand.

If any rational calculations of national interest prompted this foolhardiest of Jameson Raids, they will one day appear in the memoirs of men concerned; personally, I doubt if it can ever be justified. At this moment it can only be examined in the light of four weeks' developments, which have already seen the great fiasco.

The enterprise was evidently long prepared between two of the parties at least, Israel and France, evidence of that soon appeared.[68]

In England the Government (up to the time of concluding this book) has refused the demand for enquiry into the charge of collusion, which cannot be established in the British (as distinct from the French) case. There does seem a possibility that the British action was a sudden one, taken on the spur of a moment deemed to be favourable. In that case, it was a titanic miscalculation, for when the British and French "ultimatum" was launched the United States had already called an emergency meeting of the U.N. Security Council and presented a resolution censuring the Israeli attack and demanding that the Israelis withdraw from Egyptian territory (Oct. 29).

Thus the only effect of the British and French attack was to divert the reprobation of the world from Israel to themselves and by November 7 (after a second resolution calling on Israel to withdraw) an overwhelming majority of the General Assembly had duly transferred the weight of its censure to "Britain and France," Israel then appearing in the third place among the parties told to withdraw.[69]

A characteristic public comment of this period was made by Mrs Eleanor Roosevelt, who was generally accepted in America as the voice of her husband, the late President. She said at a news conference three days before the presidential election (she was campaigning for the Democratic nominee),

---

[68] Correspondents of *The Times, Reuters* and other newspapers and agencies subsequently reported that they had seen *French* aircraft and *French* air officers in uniform on Israeli fields during the invasion, and at the "victory party" given in Tel Aviv by the Israeli air force, when the Israeli commander, General Moshe Dayan, was present. These reports agreed in an important point: that the French Air Force was present to "cover" or provide "an air umbrella" for Tel Aviv if it were attacked by Egyptian aircraft. *Reuters* reported that same French air officers admitted attacking Egyptian tanks during the Sinai fighting. As far as the French were concerned, therefore, the pretence of a descent on the Suez Canal to "separate" the belligerents was shown to be false. French officers and aircraft having been seen *behind* the Israeli lines in Israel and Sinai during the fighting. *The Times* correspondent reported "an undertaking on the part of France to do her best, if war broke out between Israel and Egypt, to *prevent any action against Israel under the terms of the tripartite declaration of 1950 and to see that Israel had appropriate arms with which to fight.*" The 1950 declaration pledged France *impartially* "to oppose the use of force or threat of force in that area. The three governments, should they find *any of these states were preparing to violate frontiers or armistice lines, would ... immediately take action ... to prevent such violations.*"

[69] From that moment, following the example set by the American President, the weight of censure was by stages shifted from "Israel" to "Israel, Britain and France," then to "Britain and France," and in the last stage to "Britain" (thus recalling the transformation earlier effected in the case of Hitler's persecution of men, which began as "the persecution of political opponents," then became "the persecution of political opponents and Jews," then "Jews and political opponents" and, at the end, "of Jews").

"I do not consider that Israel is an aggressor; she acted in self-defence ... I believe Britain and France were technically guilty of aggression" *(New York Times,* Nov, 4, 1956).

By that time the military fiasco was as clear as the political one; English ears had had to listen for nearly five days to the reports of British bombing of Egyptians, the Suez Canal was blocked by sunken ships, President Nasser was more popular in the Arab world than he had ever been, and the British Government was gradually retreating from "no withdrawal" through "conditional withdrawal" to "unconditional withdrawal."

President Eisenhower and his administration, made the most of these events. What was coming was evidently known in Washington, (as the attack on Pearl Harbour had been foreknown). American residents had been told to leave the danger zone some days before the attack, and in the two days preceding it President Eisenhower twice admonished Mr Ben-Gurion, once in "urgent" and then in "grave" terms; the only answer he received was a radio message, delivered to him during an aeroplane trip from Florida to Virginia, telling him that Mr. Ben-Gurion had launched the attack.

However, the British government did not *officially* inform the President (or even the Dominion Governments) of its intention, and Mr. Eisenhower was able to present a face of patient suffering to his people when he appeared on the television screen with the words, "We believe it" (the attack) "to have been taken in error for we do not accept the use of force as a wise or proper instrument for the settlement of international disputes." This was an irreproachable statement, against a background of culpability (the American-prompted supply of French, British and Canadian arms to Israel all through the summer). If the British Government counted on "Zionist pressure" in Washington, it was deceived at that moment. There is always a margin of error in these things and Mr. Eisenhower was ensured of election; in any case, the opportunity to divert his wrath to Britain spared him the need to spend any more of it on Israel (which, for that matter, had got what it wanted). A harsh word to England, moreover, has been a popular thing in America since the Boston Tea Party; is it conceivable that a British government did not realize that?

The British action seems to be accountable only in the context of the entire Zionist delusion. If the thing was to be done at all, the only hope lay in a swift and massively efficient operation which would have gained possession of an intact canal and have confronted the world with something accomplished. The British undertaking was slow from the start and very soon showed all the signs of second thoughts. After the fiasco *The Times* (Nov. 16) reported from the British base at Cyprus, "The British Government's decision to intervene in Egypt was taken without the advice of nearly all its senior diplomatic representatives in the area. It was continued against the warnings of most of them about its probable effects on the future of British relations with the Arab nations ... When details of the British ultimatum to Cairo and the decision to intervene militarily against Egypt were first learned in British Embassies and Legations in the Arab countries the reactions in nearly all of them appear to have ranged from frank disbelief to talk of its being potentially a disaster ... Many were incredulous or aghast when the form of this direct action appeared to associate British policy with that of Israel and France" (this passage vividly recalled to me the feeling I found in "British Embassies and Legations" throughout Europe at the time of Munich).

So much for the political decision; next, the military execution of it. *The Times* (Nov. 17) reported that among the military commanders in Cyprus "There was a nearly unanimous feeling that if it were done it had best be done quickly. The failure to allow them to complete the job has produced a sense of frustration and confusion among many senior officers here, as well as among many of their subordinates." The eminent American military writer, Mr. Hanson Baldwin, later discussing "A Confused Invasion" which was "likely to become a famous case study in the world's military staff colleges," said that under the confused direction from London "the multiple political, psychological and military objectives became inextricably confused; the result was no clear-cut purpose, or at least no objective that military force could achieve, given the limitations imposed on it."

It soon became apparent that something was indeed delaying and deterring the British and French governments in carrying out the enterprise. To the French this mattered little, for the reasons previously given; for the British, reputation, honour, the hope of prosperity, the cohesion of the great British family were all at stake. Already, in the stress of those days, the Canadian Prime Minister had given warning that such actions might lead to the dissolution of the Commonwealth. In the United Nations Britain stood in the pillory with Israel and France, a sorry sight indeed. Against huge adverse votes, only Australia and New Zealand remained at its side, and that possibly from dogged fidelity more than conviction.

What caused the hazardous undertaking, so vaingloriously announced, to be delayed until it fizzled out? The "vigorous and emphatic protest" from President Eisenhower and the United Nations resolution presumably caused the first reconsideration in London. Then there was the agonizing coincidence of events. As soon as the British and French began to bomb Egyptians the Moscovites turned back into Hungary and began to massacre Hungarians. Then at the United Nations the spokesmen of East and West began to shout "You're another" at each other; while British and French aeroplanes bombed Port Said the British and French delegates accused the Soviet of inhuman savagery; while Soviet tanks murdered the Magyars the Soviet delegates accused the British and French of naked aggression. These exchanges began to show something of the professional mendacity of peddlers in a Levantine bazaar.

The picture then took on nightmare shapes. Sir Anthony Eden, the rising young man when he resigned in 1938, received the resignation of Mr. Anthony Nutting, the rising young man of 1956, who as Minister of State for Foreign Affairs "had most strongly advised against British intervention in Egypt," and of other colleagues. To restore his position he had recourse to Sir Winston Churchill, who proclaimed, "Israel, under the gravest provocation, erupted against Egypt … I do not doubt that we can shortly lead our course to a just and victorious conclusion. We intend to restore peace and order in the Middle East and I am convinced that we shall achieve our aim. World peace, the Middle East and our national interest will surely benefit in the long run from the Government's resolute action."

This, possibly one of the last of Sir Winston's pronouncements, remains for the future to audit. The British action has strongly Churchillian traits, and his successor was so closely associated with him that, at all events, it is unlikely to have been done without Sir Winston's approval. At that same moment the veteran published the second volume of his *History of the English-speaking Peoples*, and the *New York Times* said of it, "The author is proud of the fact that his small island, 'the little kingdom in the northern sea,' although possessing when this volume begins but three million inhabitants, should have civilized three continents and educated half the world." Only time can show whether the British attack on Egypt was in that civilizing and educating tradition, or will remain to the discredit of England.

Then came the biggest of the shocks resulting from the British Government's action. The Soviet Premier Bulganin, in notes to Sir Anthony Eden and the French Prime Minister, plainly threatened them with rocket and atomic attack if they did not "stop the aggression, stop the bloodshed" (the bloodshed, in Budapest continued and the stream of Hungarian fugitives across the hospitable Austrian frontier swelled towards a hundred thousand souls; in Budapest another Bela Kun man of 1919, Mr. Ferenc Munnich, became Moscow's "key man" in succession to Rakosi and Geroe, and began the new terror). More than that, Mr. Bulganin in a letter to President Eisenhower proposed a joint American-Soviet attack "within the next few hours" on Britain and France, a proposal which the White House in a press statement, merely termed "unthinkable."

Is anything "unthinkable" in our time? The Hitler-Stalin alliance of 1939 (an obvious development, which the present writer and others foretold) was portrayed to the masses as something "unthinkable" until it was made and the Second War begun. The *New York Times* at this period quoted "a senior United States diplomat with long experience in the Arab world" as implicitly approving the suggestion: "Our rejection of the Russian offer as 'unthinkable,' without offering to consider it within the framework of the United Nations, is interpreted here" (he was in Jordan) "as meaning that despite whatever we may say we will always side with the West and Israel when the chips are down."

No doubt the proposed joint American-Soviet atomic attack on England was unthinkable at that time, but in fact the two countries were acting together against England in different ways, which combined to produce a massive pressure from two sides. Sir Anthony Eden had embarked on torrential rapids in a frail canoe. There is in America a constant, latent matricidal instinct towards Europe in general and England in particular (it cannot be explained but must always be taken into account) which is most easily made active by the charge of "colonialism." The fact that America is the greatest *colonial* power in the world (for I see no valid difference between *oversea* and *overland* expansion)[70] does not alter this; it is an irrational impulse which has always to be taken into account in calculating the results of any contemplated action involving "American opinion."

However, "opinion" today is a manufactured product and can be produced in any form desired. What was much more important and should not have been overlooked, was that President Eisenhower, quite evidently, was selected, nominated and in effect elected by the "internationalist" group which dominated Presidents Wilson, Roosevelt and Truman, and that American state policy, under this direction, has always supported the revolution and taken on an anti-British nature at moments of peak-crisis. The ultimate "internationalist" ambition is the world-government project, to be achieved through the convergent, destructive forces of revolutionary-Communism and revolutionary-Zionism, and it is the essence of this ambition that the two great English-speaking countries on either side of the Atlantic be kept divided, for only through their division can empire be achieved. This ambition dominated the Second War.

President Eisenhower first emerged as the third figure in the Roosevelt-Marshall-Eisenhower group. The anti-British nature of General Marshall's proposals in the war years has been earlier shown; he was, in fact, Mr Churchill's great adversary and the man responsible for the fact that (as the official British history of the war recorded in 1956) despite Mr Churchill's worldwide renown and apparently formidable authority, he proved, in fact, unable to shape a single major strategic decision during that war; by the outcome of which the Roosevelt-Marshall-Eisenhower policy must be judged.

---

[70] The United States, of course, is the occupant, by conquest or by purchase, of British, Dutch, French and Spanish *colonies*, and of vast Mexican and Russian *territories*. Only the virtual extirpation, during the life of the American Republic, of the original inhabitants of this great area produces a present picture differing from that of today's British, Dutch, French and Spanish colonies, with their millions of "colonial peoples." American's *oversea* possessions, by conquest or purchase, are few. The Panama Canal Zone, which is under permanent United States sovereignty, is a separate case; if it proves anything, in relation to the Suez Canal and Britain, it proves only the advantages of good "title" and of military adjacency.

In the final palaver, at Yalta, Mr Roosevelt's dominant wish was to effect injury on Britain, as the Yalta papers show.[71]

General Eisenhower, as the commander in Europe, gave the military order resulting, in effect, in the cession of half Europe to the revolution.

Against this background, the support of President Eisenhower could not have been counted on by the British Government; the prehistory is too weighty. He was the executor of the Roosevelt-Marshall policy in the war, and seven years after its end was patently selected by powerful backers, in opposition to Senator Taft, as a man who would further pursue the "internationalist" policy. What was unexpected, and cannot be justified, is the length to which he went in publicly humiliating Britain at this time, by enforcing the "unconditional" withdrawal in the most abject circumstances, by virtually ostracizing the British Ambassador in Washington, and generally by displaying a rancour reminiscent of President Roosevelt at Yalta.

This display of repugnance (the reproachful mien was seen by the entire country on the television screen) was without moral basis. The "pressure" on Britain to withdraw from the Canal, and the ensuing "pressure" on Britain to join with America in the provocative insult to Egypt, which was the true start of the war-crisis of 1956, originated in the White House.

Moreover, this was done while the massacre in Hungary went on and apart from saying that his heart went out to the victims the American President and his administration remained passive in face of that, much graver affair. In this, again, he was consistent with his earlier acts: the dropping of the" repudiation of Yalta" pledge, after his election in 1952, and the order to halt the Allied armies east of Berlin in 1945. The effect of all these was to continue that "support of the revolution" which was the dominant tenet of American state policy during two wars.

One great lesson was learned through the events of October and November, 1956. They showed that, if sufficiently shocked, something like "world opinion" *can* express itself through the debating society known as the United Nations in New York. The demonstration of repugnance was overwhelming in *both* cases, those of the attack on Egypt and of the Soviet massacre in Hungary. They showed, further, that as an instrument for giving *effect* to any such moral censure the United Nations is utterly impotent. In the graver case, that of Hungary, it could do nothing whatever, because the Soviet was in possession and the United States was passive. In the other case, that of Egypt, an immediate result was produced *only* because both these countries

---

[71] "The President said he would tell the marshall" (Stalin) "something indiscreet, since he would not wish to say it in front of Prime Minister Churchill ... The British were a peculiar people and wished to have their cake and eat it too ... He suggested the 'internationalizing' of the British colony of Hong Kong and that Korea be placed under a trusteeship with the British excluded. Stalin indicated that he did not think this was a good idea and added that 'Churchill would kill us.' When post-war political questions came up, he often took positions that were anti- British." *(New York Times,* March 17, 1955).

joined against Britain; the one with "measures short of war" (the refusal of oil supplies) and the other with the direct threat of war.

In fact, the British withdrawal from Suez was effected by American-Soviet collaboration, and while "the internationalists" are able to control the American selection-and election-machine that will remain a great danger to the world. An Eisenhower-Bulganin pact is not inherently more "unthinkable," in the circumstances of this century, than was the Hitler-Stalin pact in 1939; at all events, the professed intention (to crush "Communism") is the same in both cases.

If the British Government put reliance on "Zionist pressure" in Washington (and this *had* effected the British withdrawal from Palestine and the establishment of Israel in 1947-8), this was another miscalculation at that particular moment. It left out of account the shock-effect of the Israeli attack and the greater shock-effect of the British and French one, which turned the eyes of the world chiefly on Britain and much strengthened President Eisenhower in adopting the moral attitude.

Thus the British Government found itself between threats of Soviet attack, on the one hand, and a hostility, apparently surprising to it, from the White House, on the other. The "vital lifeline" was blocked, and Britain's oil supplies were blocked with it. Apparently it looked confidently to the American Government to make these good and then learned that it could expect no American oil until it "got out"; by this time the entire brunt of the affair fell on Britain. British representatives in Washington were coldly received and found that no matter of substance would be discussed with them; they were left to understand that they might call again if they wished, in their quest for oil, when Britain had "got out." The American President in those days went much further in the public humiliation of the British Government than he needed to go, and the reason for this must be sought in the anti-British feeling which was shown in the recorded deeds and words of his patron, President Roosevelt. The whole history of American governmental machinations in the matter, during his presidency, deprived him of ground for the posture of honest indignation.

Unhappily, the British humiliations were earned. The attack on Egypt was disastrous in every major point: in its plain appearance of complicity with Israel, in its delivery at the very moment of Soviet defeat in Hungary, and in its indecision and ineffectiveness, once begun. Sir Anthony Eden, worn down by the strain and politically ruined, retired to Jamaica to recuperate. "Unconditional withdrawal" (of the British and French, not of the original aggressor, Israel) began. An "international force," hurriedly assembled by the United Nations, appeared on the Suez Canal and hung around, wondering what it was supposed to do. President Nasser's renown soared in the Arab world; the Canal remained blocked; Egypt declared that it would not give up an inch of Egyptian territory; Israel began to complain about "anti-semitism" in Egypt.

Three weeks after the attack the drunken Kruschev, the Soviet Communist leader, jeered at the British and French Ambassadors at a Polish Embassy reception in Moscow: "You say we want war, but you now have got yourselves in a position I would call idiotic ... You have given us a lesson in Egypt." Who could gainsay him?

A week later the *New York Times* summed up the balance: "Britain and France have gambled and appear to be losing disastrously ... Israel has so far emerged from the crisis in a somewhat better position" (Nov. 25).[72]

The same issue prominently reported the remarks of a member of the Israeli Parliament, a Mr. Michael Hazani: "Mr. Hazani expounded his theory that the failure of Britain and France to clinch their Suez Canal objective was a lucky thing for Israel ... The Israelis feel less isolated today than before their October 29 thrust into Sinai which alienated friends and raised the hackles of enemies around the world ... Israelis revelled in their newly developed friendship with France which supplied the tools which enabled their forces to whip the Egyptians ... A few weeks ago Israelis had a fright *when they feared they might have brought the world to the brink of a thermonuclear war.* The initial scare has worn off, the threats are regarded as tactics in a war of nerves ... Some Knesset members said that Israel too could play that game ... so they ask why Israel should not exploit her current nuisance value to induce the great powers to press Egypt and the other Arab states to negotiate peace."

These sentences may show the reader how little hope of respite the world has until the Zionist adventure is liquidated. Fiasco is the inevitable fate of all who associate themselves with it because its own inevitable end is fiasco, but the brunt of each disaster must and always will fall on these associates, not on the original authors of the mad ambition. Today it cuts across all rational relationships between nations, antagonizing those which have no reason for discord, misleading some to undertakings which cannot possibly bring them good, and prompting others to threats of world war.

In the case of England, which by this act was reinvolved in the morass from which Mr. Ernest Bevin had extricated it in 1947-8, the penalties on this occasion were so heavy that, if the entire process of involvement in Zionism be likened to thirteen steps to the gallows, this may be said to have been the twelfth step; the only worse thing that could befall England through it would be final calamity. Already, on this occasion, the warning about the disintegration of the Commonwealth was heard from the highest place outside the British island itself, and on no earlier occasion had that been even

---

[72] Two weeks later, after this chapter was finished, the same newspaper dismissed Britain as henceforth "a second class power."

a remote peril. It was put in the dock, beside Israel (and France) before the world and rebuked like a miscreant. It suddenly found alarming menaces arising on all sides. None of the aims announced were achieved, its fighting forces were not allowed to complete even a repugnant task, nothing but discredit remained. At the end higher taxation, deprivation and hardship fell on the land, as the price, and this was in truth further tribute to Zion.

In all this, one thing is clear: none of it could have happened but for the state set up in 1948. If general war had come, it would have been begun by Israel; if it should yet come out of this affair (and that is still an open possibility as this book is ended) it would have been begun by Israel.

Speaking for myself, if I could have persuaded myself that the British attack on Egypt was truly prompted by concern for any British interest, I would have accepted it in the belief that the British Government knew things, unknown to me, which somehow justified what seemed by all outer appearance indefensible and foredoomed. I cannot persuade myself of that. This was but the latest misstep in the tragedy of errors which began with the original British commitment to Zionism in 1903; I have traced them all in this book.

I think this is clearly implicit in what was said from the Government benches in the House of Commons at the fiasco's end. Sir Anthony Eden being in Jamaica, the task of the apologia fell to his colleagues and one of these, Mr Anthony Head, the Minister of Defence, rested the apologia, not on any British interest at all, but on the claim to have averted "a crippled Israel, a bombed Tel Aviv and a united Arab world" (again, I have not the text and quote from the *New York Times*; I hold that politicians must stand to what the world understands them to say).

Now, the corollary of the achievement claimed is a disunited Arab world, a bombed Port Said and a crippled Egypt (of these three things one was done, the bombing, and the others were not achieved). What British interest is served by disuniting the Arab world and crippling Egypt? What Englishman would have supported the act if it had been put to him in those terms before it was done? When was the case, for supporting "the fulfilment of Zionist aspirations," ever put to the British elector in those terms?

In some diseases modern medicine is able to identify the original source of infection, the primary sore. The primary source of all these troubles, as they culminated in the deeds of October 29 and 30, 1956 is demonstrably Zionism; they could not have happened in that way without it. In the logical sequence to its every act since it took shape as a political force in the ghettoes of Russia some eighty years ago, it led the world to the edge of universal war, and on that, brink none knew which of their friends of yesterday would be the foe of the morrow. Here was "the deception of nations" at the full, indeed.

Can time distil good of all this? Clearly it can and will; only for contemporaries is the needless turmoil in which we live infuriating. The first signs of the long-delayed turn for the better begin to show. The nations which lie in the chains of revolutionary-Communism are beginning to throw them off; the Eastern European peoples yet may save themselves by their exertions and the rest of the captive West by their example. I believe the Jews of the world are equally beginning to see the error of revolutionary-Zionism, the twin of the other destructive movement, and as this century ends will at last decide to seek involvement in common mankind.[73]

The events of October and November 1956 themselves supplied the apt concluding chapter for this book.[74] I believe they also added the conclusive evidence to its argument.

---

[73] A development which may have been foreshadowed by a report (if it was accurate) published in the *New York Times* on December 30, 1956, that "fewer than 900 of the 14,000 Jews who have fled from Hungary ... have decided to resettle in Israel," the "vast majority" preferring to go to America or Canada. On the other hand, if they follow the example of their predecessors they will swell the mass of "explosive" Eastern Jews there whose transplantation, during the last seventy years, has produced the present situation; the incitement of these against America was shown by quotation from Jewish authorities in the preceding chapter.

[74] As to the Suez affair, the apt footnote was supplied by President Eisenhower on January 5, 1957 when he asked Congress for standing authority to use the armed forces of the United States against "*overt* armed aggression from any nation *controlled* by international Communism" in the Middle East. He thus envisaged doing very much what he had censured the Eden Government for doing. An example of "overt" aggression is presumably the sinking of the *Maine* in Havana Harbour; the explosion was "overt" and it was *attributed to* Spain.

Before and after the attack on Egypt the international press began to accuse one Arab nation after another of being "controlled" by international Communism, and President Eisenhower's request to Congress again opens the prospect that the much-heralded extirpation of Communism might prove, in the event, to be an attack on the Arabs, not on Communism. The description, "controlled by Communism," is incapable of definition or proof, and simple to falsify through propaganda. For instance, the *New York Times* on Dec 2. 1956 published pictures of "Russian tanks captured by the Israelis" during the attack an Egypt. Readers' objections led it to admit that the tanks were in fact American. Whether they were captured from the Egyptians remains open to question; anyone can photograph a tank and write a caption.

Israel was originally set up with Soviet arms, but is not on that account said to be "controlled by international Communism."

The news of President Eisenhower's act was followed by a sharp rise in various Israel shares on the American Stock Exchange and by sermons of praise in several New York synagogues. A possible reason for this was the fact that the President undertook to act militarily in the Middle East only in response to request from "any nation or group of nations" attacked. As Egypt was widely declared to be "the aggressor" in the attack on itself in October 1956, this proviso again lies open to many interpretations, at need. If the words were earnestly meant, they imply that American forces would have been used, on Egyptian request, to repel the Israeli attack of October, 1956. That is difficult to imagine; to put it mildly, American military intervention in response to a request from any other Middle Eastern state than Israel is hard to picture; however, times change and all things are possible.

EPILOGUE

If this book has any sombre look, that is the native hue of the story it tells, not the reflection of my own cast of mind. I have written with feeling: the feeling of a contemporary, participant, eye-witness and of a journalist thwarted in his calling, which in my belief should serve truth without fear or favour, not special interests. I have seen more of the events of our century and of the secret perversions of national purposes than most, and have discovered through this experience that it was not all chance, but design. Therefore I have written a protest, but it is a protest against the suppression of truth, not against life.

It is a contemporary's tale of history in the making. After my time will come the historians, who from the fragments they disinter will assemble the story in all its elements. As well might one judge the impulses of a man from his skeleton. However, they may perceive things now hidden from me, and, above all, they will find that it was all necessary to the state of affairs in which they find themselves (and that, in the case of historians, is usually a comfortable one). Between the two depictments, somewhere lays the whole truth; my part of it is the living protest of the living participant.

No doubt all these things are essential to the ultimate purpose, and I have no doubt about the nature of that, but they were unnecessary when they happened, and that is the theme of my remonstrance. The ultimate good end could have been reached more quickly without them, I believe; however, I know that all these things are not for mortal man to comprehend and can imagine that in God's dispensation these recurrent ordeals are necessary to the ultimate self-liberation of the human soul. Under that same dispensation, the believer must protest against them as they occur.

Anyway, I leave the dispassionate analysis to the future scribe, whose flesh and heartbeat will not be involved; to him the microscope, to me the living spectacle. I *am* involved. "In history" (said Lord Macaulay) "only the interpretation according to doctrinal necessity ever seems to survive, as the inconvenient and contradictory facts are forgotten or ignored." On that count, this living scribe may be acquitted. I have not ignored anything known to me and I have presented what I know as truly as I am able. I have given the picture of our century as it appeared to a man involved, and as it was withheld from the public masses, who as they went along received only "the interpretation" according to what politicians held to be necessity.

In our time, I judge, a barbaric superstition born in antiquity and nurtured through the ages by a semi-secret priesthood, has returned to plague us in the form of a political movement supported by great wealth and power in all great capitals of the world. Through the two methods used, revolution from below and the corruption of governments from above, it has come far towards success in a fantastic ambition of achieving world dominion, using these two instruments to incite nations against each other.

I cannot presume to judge what is evil; thinking makes it so. I only know what I feel to be evil; perhaps I am wrong. Anyway, by my own sensations and standards I have felt, during the labour of preparing this book, that I lived with evil. The forces which have been projected into the 20th Century, as from some dinosauric cavern, are superstitious ones. I have had a constant sense of contact with the minds of men like Ezekiel, who in barbarous times had barbarous thoughts. I had a distinct feeling of re-encounter with such minds in our present time, though in a place recently redeemed from barbarism, when I read a book, *A Pattern of Islands*, by Sir Arthur Grimble.

His recounts the author's experiences, early in the 20thCentury, as a British colonial administrator in a remote group of Pacific islands, the Gilberts, where the people lived in a state of primeval superstition until 1892, when a British protectorate was proclaimed. I find an uncanny resemblance between the curses enumerated in *Deuteronomy*, which forms The Law of Zionist nationalism today, and the words of a curse on a cooking oven, used by these islands before the British came. The sorcerer, squatting naked in the dark before dawn over his enemy's fireplace and stabbing it with a stick, mutters:

"Spirit of madness, spirit of excrement, spirit of eating alive, spirit of rottenness! I stab the fire of his food, the fire of that man Naewa. Strike west of him, you! Strike east of him, you! Strike as I stab, strike death! Strangle him, madden him, shame him with rottenness! His liver heaves, it heaves, it is overturned and torn apart. His bowels heave, they heave, they are torn apart and gnawed. He is black mad, he is dead. It is finished: he is dead, dead, dead. He rots."

The comparison between this and many passages in *Deuteronomy* and *Ezekiel* is instructive in this time when the Talmud-Torah is literally invoked as The Law ordaining such deeds as that committed at Deir Yasin; the statement of the *Jewish Encyclopaedia*, that the Talmud teaches belief in the literal efficacy of cursing, is also relevant. Such passages always occur to me when politicians invoke "the Old Testament"; each time I wonder if they have read it, and if they comprehend the relationship between these superstitions of antiquity and current events, brought about with their help.

In my judgment we have to deal with a force, released on the world in the 20th Century, the leaders of which think in terms of such superstitions; to what else can Dr. Chaim Weizmann's belated, tormented words have alluded, "… the resurgence of the old evil in a new and more horrible guise."

Only this element of dark superstition, in my estimate, can account for the fear to which the Jewish masses yield, when they surrender to Zionist nationalism. They were almost liberated from it by the century of emancipation and in another fifty years would have been involved in mankind, but now have been drawn back into its clutch. Again, I felt as if I were reading a description of the ghettoized masses in the Talmudic areas when I came across this description of pre-protectorate days in the Gilbert Islands:

"A man with sixty generations of terror-struck belief whispering in his blood … was easy meat for the death magic … Generation on generation of sorcerers who willed evil, and of people who dreaded their power, had lived out their lives in these islands. The piled-up horror of their convictions had achieved, down the ages, a weight and shadow of its own, an immanence that brooded over everything. It was man's thoughts, more potent than ghosts, that haunted the habitation of men. One felt that practically anything could happen in that atmosphere."

"Men's thoughts, more potent than ghosts, haunted the habitations of men." The words seemed to me to apply to the condition of these masses, with more than sixty generations of such beliefs whispering to them, who towards the end of last century began to be wrested back from the daylight towards the tribal gloom. Again, the liberation so barely missed seemed to me to be described in these words of an old woman of the Gilbert Islands who remembered the earlier time:

"Listen to the voices of the people in their lodges. We work in peace, we talk in peace, for the days of anger are gone … How beautiful is life in our villages, now that there is no killing and war is no more"; and these words, again, most strongly recall Jeremiah's lament for the former happiness of Israel ("the kindness of thy youth, the love of thine espousals") in his rebuke to the heresy of "treacherous Judah."

The feeling I had, in tracing the story of this ancient superstition and its re-emergence as a political force in our century, was that of contact with a living, evil thing. The destructive revolution, in my view, is part of it and I could have written exactly what an American diplomat, Mr. Frank Rounds, junior, wrote in his diary on Christmas Day of 1951: "In Moscow, you feel that evil exists as a thing, as a presence; that is my thought this Christmas Day."

In this 20th Century process, which I feel as an accompanying, evil presence, all of us now alive, Jew and Gentile, are involved, and most of us will see the denouement. As to that, Mr. Bernard J. Brown in 1933 misgivingly wrote, "Of course we must be feared *and eventually hated* if we persist in absorbing everything America offers us and yet refuse to become Americans just as we have always refused to become Russians or Pales."

This statement applies to all countries of the West, not only to America, but Mr Brown was wrong. What he foresaw is one thing the Talmudists cannot achieve; hatred is their monopoly, and creed, and they cannot make Christians, or Gentiles, hate Jews. The hateful things done by the West in this century were done under Talmudic prompting; hatred and vengeance are not innate in Westerners, and their faith forbids these. The teaching of hatred, as part of a religion, still comes only from the literal Torah-Talmudists in the revolutionary area, in Palestine, and where they have nested in the Western capitals. No Westerner would speak as a Zionist leader spoke to a Jewish meeting at Johannesburg in May, 1953: "The beast that is called Germany must not be trusted. The Germans must never be forgiven and the Jews must never have any contact or dealings with the Germans."

The world cannot live like that, and for this reason the insensate plan must ultimately fail. This is the heresy which the teaching of Christ above all else repudiated; it is the one to which the political leaders of the West have lent themselves since Mr. Balfour, just fifty years ago, began to subordinate national policy to it. When the approaching climax has been overcome this heretic teaching, injected into the West from the Talmudic centre in Russia, will pass.

As a writer, I believe it will pass sooner and with less trouble for all involved, the more the general masses know about what has gone on in these fifty years.

For nothing is secret that shall not be made manifest; Neither anything hid, that shall not be known and come abroad.

– Luke 8:17.

Printed in April 2024
by Rotomail Italia S.p.A., Vignate (MI) - Italy